MANAGEMENT, WORK AND ORC

CW00549148

Series editors: **Gibson Burrell**, School of Management, Univer:
Mick Marchington, Manchester Business Schoc
Business School, University of Strathclyde, UK
Paul Thompson, Strathclyde Business School, University or Strathclyde, U.

This series of textbooks covers the areas of human resource management, employee relations, organisational behaviour and related business and management fields. Each text has been specially commissioned to be written by leading experts in a clear and accessible way. The books contain serious and challenging material, take an analytical rather than prescriptive approach and are particularly suitable for use by students with no prior specialist knowledge.

The series is relevant for many business and management courses, including MBA and post-experience courses, specialist masters and postgraduate diplomas, professional courses and final-year undergraduate courses. These texts have become essential reading at business and management schools worldwide.

Titles include:

Maurizio Atzeni
WORKERS AND LABOUR IN A GLOBALISED CAPITALISM

Stephen Bach and Ian Kessler
THE MODERNISATION OF THE PUBLIC SERVICES AND EMPLOYEE RELATIONS

Emma Bell
READING MANAGEMENT AND ORGANIZATION IN FILM

Paul Blyton and Peter Turnbull
THE DYNAMICS OF EMPLOYEE RELATIONS (*3rd edition*)

Paul Blyton, Edmund Heery and Peter Turnbull (*editors*)
REASSESSING THE EMPLOYMENT RELATIONSHIP

Sharon C. Bolton
EMOTION MANAGEMENT IN THE WORKPLACE

Sharon C. Bolton and Maeve Houlihan (*editors*)
SEARCHING FOR THE HUMAN IN HUMAN RESOURCE MANAGEMENT

Peter Boxall and John Purcell
STRATEGY AND HUMAN RESOURCE MANAGEMENT (*3rd edition*)

J. Martin Corbett
CRITICAL CASES IN ORGANISATIONAL BEHAVIOUR

Susan Corby, Steve Palmer and Esmond Lindop
RETHINKING REWARD

Ian Greener
PUBLIC MANAGEMENT (*2nd edition*)

David Farnham
THE CHANGING FACES OF EMPLOYMENT RELATIONS

Keith Grint
LEADERSHIP

Irena Grugulis
SKILLS, TRAINING AND HUMAN RESOURCE DEVELOPMENT

Geraldine Healy, Gill Kirton and Mike Noon (*editors*)
EQUALITY, INEQUALITIES AND DIVERSITY

Damian Hodgson and Svetlana Cicmil (*editors*)
MAKING PROJECTS CRITICAL

Marek Korczynski
HUMAN RESOURCE MANAGEMENT IN SERVICE WORK

Karen Legge
HUMAN RESOURCE MANAGEMENT: ANNIVERSARY EDITION

Patricia Lewis and Ruth Simpson (*editors*)
GENDERING EMOTIONS IN ORGANIZATIONS

Patricia Lewis and Ruth Simpson (*editors*)
VOICE, VISIBILITY AND THE GENDERING OF ORGANIZATIONS

Alison Pullen, Nic Beech and David Sims (*editors*)
EXPLORING IDENTITY

Jill Rubery and Damian Grimshaw
THE ORGANISATION OF EMPLOYMENT

Hugh Scullion and Margaret Linehan (*editors*)
INTERNATIONAL HUMAN RESOURCE MANAGEMENT

John Walton and Claire Valentin (*editors*)
HUMAN RESOURCE DEVELOPMENT

For more information on titles in the Series please go to **www.palgrave.com/business/mwo**

Also by David Farnham

COMPETENCY MANAGEMENT IN THE PUBLIC SECTOR (*with S. Horton and A. Hondeghem*)

EMPLOYEE RELATIONS

EMPLOYEE RELATIONS IN CONTEXT

HUMAN RESOURCE MANAGEMENT IN CONTEXT

HUMAN RESOURCES FLEXIBILITIES IN THE PUBLIC SERVICES (*with S. Horton*)

MANAGING ACADEMIC STAFF IN CHANGING UNIVERSITY SYSTEMS

MANAGING PEOPLE IN THE PUBLIC SERVICES (*with S. Horton, S. Corby, L. Giles, B. Hutchinson and G. White*)

MANAGING THE NEW PUBLIC SERVICES (*with S. Horton*)

NEW PUBLIC MANAGERS IN EUROPE (*with S. Horton, J. Barlow and A. Hondeghem*)

PERSONNEL IN CONTEXT

PUBLIC MANAGEMENT IN BRITAIN (*with S. Horton*)

STAFF PARTICIPATION AND PUBLIC MANAGEMENT REFORM (*with A. Hondeghem and S. Horton*)

UNDERSTANDING INDUSTRIAL RELATIONS (*with J. Pimlott*)

THE CHANGING FACES OF EMPLOYMENT RELATIONS

Global, Comparative and Theoretical Perspectives

David Farnham
University of Portsmouth, UK

 palgrave

First published 2015 by
PALGRAVE

Palgrave in the UK is an imprint of Macmillan Publishers Limited,
registered in England, company number 785998, of 4 Crinan Street,
London N1 9XW.

Palgrave Macmillan in the US is a division of St Martin's Press LLC,
175 Fifth Avenue, New York, NY 10010.

Palgrave is a global imprint of the above companies and is represented
throughout the world.

Palgrave® and Macmillan® are registered trademarks in the United States,
the United Kingdom, Europe and other countries.

ISBN 978–1–137–02712–2

This book is printed on paper suitable for recycling and made from fully
managed and sustained forest sources. Logging, pulping and manufacturing
processes are expected to conform to the environmental regulations of the
country of origin.

A catalogue record for this book is available from the British Library.

A catalog record for this book is available from the Library of Congress.

Library of Congress Cataloging-in-Publication Data
Farnham, David.
    The changing faces of employment relations: global, comparative and
    theoretical perspectives / David Farnham.
       pages   cm. — (Management, work and organisations)
    Includes bibliographical references and index.
    ISBN 978–1–137–02712–2
    1. Industrial relations.   2. Personnel management.   I. Title.
    HD6971.F27 2015
    658.3—dc23   2014028733

Printed in China

For Cora, Frances, Joe, Hilda and Felicity

CONTENTS

LIST OF FIGURES

LIST OF TABLES

SELECTED ABBREVIATIONS

ACAS	Advisory Conciliation and Arbitration Service
ASEAN	Association of South-East Asian Nations
BBC	British Broadcasting Corporation
BRIC	Brazil, Russia, India and China
CEEP	Centre européen des enterprises à participation publique (European Centre of Employers and Enterprises providing Public Services)
CIPD	Chartered Institute of Personnel and Development
EI	Employee Involvement
EIRO	European Industrial Relations Observatory
EIU	Economist Intelligence Unit
EPI	European Participation Index
ETUC	European Trade Union Confederation
EU	European Union
EUROFOUND	European Foundation for the Improvement of Living and Working Conditions
EWC	European Works Council
GDP	gross domestic product
GGFCE	General Government Final Consumption Expenditure
HPWS	high-performance work systems
HR	Human Resources
HRM	Human Resource Management
HSCs	Health and Safety Committees
ICT	information and communication technology
ILO	International Labour Organization
IMF	International Monetary Fund
ISSA	International Social Security Association
ITUC	International Trade Union Confederation

LO	Landsorganisationen i Sverige (Swedish Trade Union Confederation)
NAFTA	North American Free Trade Area
NLRA	National Labor Relations Act
NPM	new public management
OECD	Organisation for Economic Co-operation and Development
PAR	participative action research
PMR	public management reform
PRP	performance-related pay
PWC	Price Waterhouse Cranfield
RBVF	resource-based view of the firm
SACO	Sveriges Akademikers Central Organisation (Swedish Confederation of Professional Associations)
SE	*Societas Europaea* (European Company)
SHRM	Strategic HRM
SMEs	small and medium size enterprises
SNB	special negotiating body
TCO	Tjänstemännens Centralorganisation (Swedish Confederation of Professional Employees)
TNCs	trans-national corporations
UK	United Kingdom
UN	United Nations
UNCTAD	United Nations Conference on Trade and Development
US	United States
WERS	Workplace Employment Relations Survey/Study
WWW	World Wide Web

PREFACE

Targeted at postgraduate students, this book has an ambitious but realisable objective. It provides an introduction to the study of the many 'faces' and 'sides' of contemporary employment relations, drawing on global, comparative and theoretical perspectives. An 'employment relationship' is created when an employer recruits and selects an employee in the labour market and employment relations, as a subject, studies how these relationships are regulated. The parties or players involved in regulation of employment relationships are employers and managers, workers, trade unions, and government and the processes used include managerial regulation, collective bargaining and the law. Basically, there are two types of employment relationship in capitalist market economies: the (singular) *individual* employment relationship and (plural) *collective* employment relationships. The first is between an employer and individual employee or worker. Here the terms (wages) and conditions (other benefits, duties and obligations) of the relationship are normally determined by an individual or personal 'bargain' between employer and worker. In most cases, however, the manager representing the employer or owner simply 'tells' the employee what these terms and conditions are, rather than negotiating them. This individual relationship is a contractual one expressed in the contract of employment between them, whether it is written or unwritten. But in all jurisdictions around the world, the employee is legally subordinate to the employer, being under the ultimate direction and control of managers in the workplace and employing organisation. Thus the individual employment relationship is based on managerial power and the ideological assumptions upon which the right to manage is based. Individual employment relationships are also normally private between employer and employee, not subject to public scrutiny.

Collective employment relationships are between an employer and a group of workers, where the terms and conditions of employment are determined jointly by collective bargaining between managers, representing the employer, and the union representing the workers. The terms of the collective agreement between the employer and union are then incorporated into the individual contracts of employment of all employees in the bargaining group, whether or not they are union members. Further, the union normally has the right to represent individual union members in any differences, disputes or disciplinary issues with management through the relevant employment relations procedures. Collective employment relationships are unlike the individual employment relationship in at least three respects. First, collective employment relationships are based on compromises made between employer and union representatives, driven by managerial self-interest and worker solidarity. Second, unlike personal employment contracts, collective agreements are commonly transparent public documents, available for general scrutiny. Third, collective employment relations create a further relationship – that between the worker and the union. The field of employment relations is thus a broad one. It is the study and practice of *both* the individual employment relationship *and* collective employment relationships in modern societies, in their many manifestations, changing contexts and various contingencies over time. It is the tension and interaction between these two faces of employment relations, in practice and theory, which provide a recurring theme in this book.

For the first three-quarters of the twentieth century, the dominant paradigm or orthodoxy in employment relations, then described as 'industrial relations', was the collective approach. Since the last quarter of that century, and with the emergence of an open global economy, academic and practical interest has focused increasingly on the individual employment relationship, as the coverage of collective bargaining has steadily declined around the world. On the one hand, this has led some scholars and commentators to identify a 'crisis' in employment relations, suggesting the field is being excluded from the academic curriculum, falling off the research agenda, and is in terminal decline (Clarke *et al.* 2011). On the other hand, there has been a surge in interest in the study and practices of the individual employment relationship. This is epitomised by the rise of Human Resource Management (HRM) as a new orthodoxy in the English-speaking world. HRM is viewed as a distinctive approach to employment management, where firms seek competitive advantage in global markets, through the deployment of committed workforces, 'using an array of cultural, structural and personnel techniques' (Storey 2007: 7).

There have always been intellectual and ideological divisions between the study of the individual employment relationship and collective employment relationships. This was demonstrated graphically both academically and geographically at the London School of Economics and Political Science (LSE) in the 1970s. At that time, the Department of Personnel Management, led by Nancy Seear, provided a prestigious Diploma course from the fourth floor of the Houghton Building for aspiring 'personnel managers'. This Department was separated by not only title but also location from the Department of Industrial Relations. This Department, led by Ben Roberts, provided a Masters degree and a series of research programmes from the fifth floor of the building for aspiring teachers, researchers and practitioners in industrial relations. But the argument presented in this text is that HRM is not a separate field of study in its own right, any more than personnel management was at the LSE in the 1970s. It is, rather, an integral and most recent episode in the study of the individual employment relationship within the generic field of employment relations, but from a managerial perspective. Thus HRM and its various manifestations are a specific way of *managing* the employment relationship, commonly in its individualised form with a particular management style, and is thus part of the field of employment relations.

Within the definition of employment relations provided here, its subject matter is a dynamic one, with a number of contrasting and changing faces over time. These include the individual and collective faces of employment relationships; its disciplinary or academic faces; its theoretical and methodological faces; its national, cross-national, international and comparative faces; its global faces; its private and public sector faces; and its intellectual and ideological faces. Contemporary employment relations, as a field of study, is thus a wide-ranging and demanding subject. It is of great importance to employers, workers, unions and the state, as well as to students of management, business and social science. And, despite the observations of some commentators, it is in robust and vigorous health but now incorporates a wide variety of forms, structures, practices and insights, compared with the 'golden age of labour' in the mid-twentieth century. So a second theme recurring in this book is that there is no single trajectory of employment relations at the beginning of the twenty-first century, but a series of complex, contradictory ones, consisting of a multiplicity of faces, practical approaches and theoretical perspectives within its subject area.

A third recurring theme in this text is the worldwide phenomena, since the 1980s, of expanded international trade between nation states facilitated by technological changes and trans-national corporations (economic globalisation) and economic policies by national governments promoting the primacy of markets (neo-liberalism or economic liberalism) in human affairs (Sandel 2013). Neo-liberalism is a philosophy of political economy which promotes de-regulation of markets, 'free' markets, free trade, privatising public enterprises, cutting back the size of the state and the public sector, reducing government spending, regressive tax policies, and an increasing role for the private sector in national economic affairs. The dominance of neo-liberal orthodoxy has been further sustained by the advent of economic austerity in many states, following the financial crisis of 2007–08 (Blyth 2013).

Howsoever they are described, economic globalisation and neo-liberalism have had pervading impacts on employers, managers, employees, trade unions and employment relationships in recent years. To gain competitive advantage in product markets for their firms, employers and senior managers have had to re-design their business and employment relations strategies by improving business performance, not recognising trade unions (or de-recognising them) and promoting individual employment relationships in preference to collective ones. Employees and unions, in turn, have had to adapt to de-regulated, flexible labour markets and individualism in the workplace to retain jobs, employment and union voice. Economic globalisation and neo-liberalism have also altered the balance of power between capital and labour in nation states, because financial capital and those controlling it are significantly more mobile in an open international economy than is labour. Such developments generally favour corporate managements and owners of capital rather than labour. This often places labour at a relative disadvantage in the employment relationship. This is not to ignore the large increase in international labour migrations of recent years. But these demographic shifts are typified by the mobility of either young unskilled and unattached men or skilled, well-educated professional people from developing economies to advanced economies. International labour migration of this sort differs from patterns in the 1970s, because its composition has changed (World Bank 1995). Powerful trans-national corporations (TNCs) now employ labour in different countries at lower cost, in ways that destroy the employment of workers in the originating country where labour costs are higher, resulting in rising unemployment and income inequality around the world. But more of these issues later.

I owe intellectual and personal debts to many people at various stages in my professional life; far too many to acknowledge here. However, I'd like to thank all the individuals who helped bring this book to press, after it was commissioned in the Management, Work and Organisations series. These include the Series Editors, Gibson Burrell, Mick Marchington and Paul Thompson, for their support throughout this project; the Commissioning Editor, Ursula Gavin, and the production and professional staff at Palgrave Macmillan for their patience and guidance throughout the process of getting this book into shape and into print; and the external reviewers for their helpful comments to improve my draft manuscript. A number of colleagues read some draft chapters and also gave me useful suggestions for changes in the text. These were Alan Blackburn, Iona Byford, Chris Evans, Graham Hollinshead, Sylvia Horton, Alan Peacock, Pete Scott, Rob Thomas and Steve Williams. Chris Evans, Rob Thomas and Chris Turner also helped with some of the graphics. My thanks are due to all of them. Any remaining but unintended errors of fact or of judgement are mine alone.

1

UNRAVELLING THE EMPLOYMENT RELATIONSHIP

The purpose of this chapter is to provide the background to the study of employment relationships between employers and employees, by highlighting some key issues and debates in the field. A central theme running throughout this book is the wide variety of employment relationships that exist between employers, as buyers of labour, and workers, as suppliers of labour, in capitalist market economies around the world today. Drawing on empirical studies at international, national, sector, enterprise and workplace levels, this book sets out a series of mosaics and observations of the complex landscape, diverse contours and multi-layers of employment relationships within a variety of socio-institutional settings. These demonstrate that employment relations are not static. Neither is the behaviour of the players, nor are the structures of employment relations the same in every nation state or even within them. These are embedded in national social cultures, institutions, locations and time, where cultural, structural, spatial and historical insights are helpful and revealing. Within these settings, this text provides an introduction to the study of employment relations at the beginning of the twenty-first century, by examining the various faces and forms the subject takes and how it is changing. This is done by drawing on global, comparative and theoretical perspectives as frameworks of analysis and critical evaluation. Within these frameworks, the book seeks to enable readers to: understand the complex nature of employment relations; become familiar with the mainstream literature in the field; and build on these studies when conducting their own research. The topics covered include: the underlying principles of employment relations, their socio-economic contexts, how employment relations are structured, and the outcomes for the parties.

WHY EMPLOYMENT RELATIONS AS A FIELD OF STUDY MATTERS

In its early days, the subject was called 'industrial relations', since its focus was the heavy or 'smoke-stack' industries of the time and on the relations between large-scale employers (or 'masters') and organised labour (representing the firm's 'servants'). These bodies of workers were variously called 'trade unions' in Britain, 'labor unions' in North America, *Gewerkschaften* in Germany, *syndicats* in France, *syndicatos* in Spain, *sindicatos* in Portugal and Brazil and *gōng huì* in China. Despite the range of words in non-English languages to describe the phenomenon of organised labour, the preferred term used throughout this work is 'trade unions'. Also the broader term 'employment relations' is used to describe all aspects of relationships between employers and workers and the contexts within which they operate, rather than the narrower term 'industrial relations'. In contrast to 'industrial relations', employment relations covers a wider range of subject matter, such as non-union firms and sectors, services, TNCs, small and medium size enterprises (SMEs) and public services.

Origins and development

Employment relations practices have a long history, beginning during the industrial, commercial and technological revolutions in the United States and Britain over 200 years ago. However, the *study* of employment relations did not become a serious field of academic inquiry until the 1920s and 1930s (Kaufman 2004a). Indeed up till the 1960s, the study of the employment relationship was largely limited to the English-speaking countries of the United States, the United Kingdom and Canada. In the following 40 years, it spread to other Western industrialised countries such as the English-speaking ones of Australia, New Zealand and Ireland and non-English-speaking countries in West Europe, such as France, Germany and the Netherlands. It also incorporated the social democratic Scandinavian states of North Europe. By the end of that century, the study of employment relations had spread still further to parts of East Europe, Latin America and Asia, including Japan, South Korea, India and China, but with differing degrees of effectiveness. Thus the countries involved in the study of employment relations today are wider than at any other time in the past. For example, it was reported that building up labour unions was a key element in the struggle to promote democracy in Egypt and the Arab world during the 'Arab Spring' 2010–2011 (Laws 2011) but it was not the only or most important one of course.

By the second decade of the twenty-first century, the domain and subject matter of 'employment relations' is distinctly different from the golden age of 'industrial relations', rooted in trade unionism and collective bargaining from 1945 until the 1970s. This is because of the rise of the neo-classical school of labour economics and neo-conservative political regimes in Western countries since the 1980s. The former were academic economists promoting the virtues of 'free markets'; the latter politicians who supported free markets and wanted fundamental economic reforms within their countries (Gamble 1988). It is a major contextual, theoretical and policy shift that extended beyond the West in the following years. Because of its importance, the phenomenon of neo-liberalism is examined in several places throughout this text.

Employment relations between employers and workers, whatever forms they take, are reciprocal relationships, imply obligations on both parties, and are based on a 'wage–work' bargain between them. As a central feature of contemporary market economies, employment relationships and employment relations are extremely important to the parties involved – employers, employees and, where they are recognised by employers, trade unions. Employers need workers to work for them and women and men of working age, who are looking for employment, need jobs to earn wage incomes to support themselves and their dependants. In some cases, workers join unions to negotiate for them and protect them against unfair management practices in the workplace. This requires each union using the collective power of its members to represent them. However, employment relationships involve not only *market* relations but also *authority* relations between the parties, since employers have the legal right to decide how to deploy and utilise the labour power of workers in the workplace, provided these acts are not themselves unlawful.

Capitalist market economies are normally political democracies; they combine market economic systems with democratic politics. This is where the economic and political spheres of human activity – their political economy – constantly interact within the boundaries of the nation state. National economic factors help shape national political choices and national politics help shape national economic policies. Both affect employment relationships, whatever the types and sizes of employing organisations. Further, each national political economy is not an isolated phenomenon, since it is influenced, in turn, by what is happening in the international or global political economy. The global factors include patterns of international trade, the rules and regulations regarding movements of financial capital and labour, the policies of international organisations – such as the Organisation for Economic Co-operation and Development (OECD), World Bank and International Labour Organization (ILO) – and the interests and activities of powerful TNCs (Oatley 2012).

Contemporary employment relations, in short, do not take place in economic or political vacuums; they are played out within the frameworks of national economic policies, national political systems, regional economic and political systems where they exist, as in the European Union (EU), and the wider international political economy.

The importance of employment relations

In capitalist market economies, whatever the type of capitalism practised, business activities are driven by the imperative of markets, especially financial markets, where money is invested to make a profit and where capital resources (whether physical investment goods or financial assets) are owned predominantly by private individuals, families or private corporations (Strauss-Kahn 1977). Business enterprises select and employ workers to work for them, providing pay and other benefits in return for the work done by their workforces. The mega-millions of wage–work bargains and employment contracts agreed between employers and workers in contemporary labour markets globally, with an estimated working population of some of 3.5 billion people (Central Intelligence Agency 2012), demonstrate that employment relations are an integral part of the economic, political, legal and social fabrics of any developed or developing state.

So why study employment relations and employment relationships? Why are they important and to whom are they important? In essence, employment relationships matter because they are one of the fundamental pillars upon which modern market economies and capitalist societies are built. In these societies, some people (workers) are employed by organisations (employers) to work for them, under the control or command of enterprise agents (managers): this is the core of the employment relationship. A formal employment relationship is established whenever an employer hires a worker as an *employee* in the labour market. In supplying goods and services to the marketplace, employers not only invest in financial and physical resources but also hire employees (variously described as 'workers', 'staff', 'human resources', 'human capital' or 'working people') to provide labour inputs into the work process directed by managers. Those working as independent traders for themselves and their families are not normally employed workers but are market traders or 'dealers'. They do not normally come within the definition of an employee, or within the subject matter of employment relations, unless of course they themselves hire workers to work for them.

In the complex world of work today, however, things can be even more complicated than this. For example, workers can be formally 'self-employed' but they are, to all intents and purposes, employees working for organisations.

This is the case in India, for example, where nearly 90 per cent of workers work in the informal economy. This has led some scholars to use the term 'work and employment relationships' to convey the idea that workers might be working for employing organisations but not formally as employees. In a world of flexible working, legal definitions of what is an employment relationship become increasingly problematic.

Crucially, where labour is unemployed and not working, there is lost productive output to the firm, lost spending power by unemployed workers and households, lost tax revenues by government, lost capacity in the national economy, and, where these exist, higher public spending on social security or public benefits for the unemployed. Stable employment relationships, in short, are important for employers, individual workers, households, the state authorities, national economic well-being and the stability of the social order within modern nation states.

This book is largely about contemporary employment relations and it seeks to provide a critical review and evaluation of employment relations as a field of study in the early twenty-first century, with particular emphasis on the changing faces of the subject in terms of its scope, boundaries and theoretical perspectives. Employment relations is also about a set of professional practices, with implications for public policy. However, this text concentrates on the academic study and underpinning knowledge base of employment relationships, rather than on the practices of negotiating, interviewing, problem solving, grievance handling, managing discipline and conciliating. As a field of study, employment relations examines and critically assesses all aspects of the employment relationship between employers and workers. This includes how workers are recruited, selected and made redundant, how workers are rewarded, how work is organised and performed, and how labour is managed within organisations in market economies. As a specialist field of study, rather than a subject-based academic discipline, such as modern languages, philosophy or physics, employment relations is a multidisciplinary field of inquiry. Like the study of management and organisations, it draws upon a number of academic disciplines and theoretical perspectives. These include economics, the law, political theory, organisational theory, sociology and psychology (Ackers and Wilkinson 2003).

BASIC ISSUES IN EMPLOYMENT RELATIONS

A number of basic issues can be identified in the field of employment relations. For example, by the early twenty-first century, the crucial importance of the employment relationship in business, economic and social affairs is reflected in the fact that employment is the dominant form of organising and managing work in a variety of enterprises and countries around the globe (Marsden 1999). All employees, whether employed by organisations or individuals, come within the field of employment relations. These include nuclear physicists, university professors, senior public servants, managers, bus drivers, hairdressers, fast-food staff, office workers, designers, street cleaners and farm workers. They may be wage or salary earners; they may be high or low paid; they may have high professional status or low job status; and they may work in private businesses, public services or the 'third', not-for-profit sector. The wages or salaries earned by employees are spent on their economic needs, and those of their households, in the market for goods and services. Employees need homes to live in, food and beverages to eat and drink, clothes to wear, transport to use and so on. It is their wage incomes that enable employees to buy these goods and services in the marketplace, as long as they are employed.

Employment relationships in their variety of forms and contexts are central not only to the functions of management and how work is organised within modern enterprises but also to workers within them. Organisations need labour power as well as capital resources to produce the goods and services demanded by individual consumers or corporate clients in an interconnected global economy. Employees, in turn, need wages and the other benefits of employment to live rewarding and fruitful lives outside the workplace. For people, work and employment are the major sources of sustenance for them in capitalist market economies. They make people into workers, who spend more time working than doing anything else, apart from sleeping. Thus in terms of the power relations between the players in the labour market, the *capitalist* owners of private business enterprises employ *labour* to work for them through the agency of appointed *managers*, who themselves are employees. But employment relations between the owners of capital and the suppliers of labour (employers and workers) matter not only to those who hire and sell labour but also to those not earning wages, who are *dependants* of those working and are not themselves directly involved in any employment relationships.

Another basic issue is that employment relations is about *power* and how it is applied and mediated in human affairs. This is exercised within and outside organisations by those individuals and institutions with 'power resources' such as economic, knowledge-based and normative power (Hales 2001). Power has a variety of definitions but is basically 'the capacity to control patterns of social interaction' among people, groups and institutions (Bradley 1999: 31). Within organisations, for example, there is the power to manage, the power to employ, the power to reward, the power to promote, the power to discipline, the power to dismiss, the power to take and implement decisions affecting the daily working lives of the people working in them, and the power to challenge and resist these decisions. These 'facts' of organisational life demonstrate that 'organizations comprise different groups with different goals and hence politics and bargaining are inevitable' (Edwards and Wajcman 2005: 116). The sources of power, within organisations and outside them, may be economic (the capacity to provide or withhold income or wealth), political (the ability of the state to enact and enforce the laws of the realm), ideological (the control of resources providing esteem and privilege) and coercive (the use of physical force to apply power).

All these sources of power are found within employment relationships, with both employers and workers using their power resources to advance their material interests in these relationships. With employers using power to pursue their material interests, employees seek to redress any power imbalances with employers in pursuit of their material interests. In these interactions, each party or player draws upon its own ideologies to justify their positions and act out their respective roles (Bendix 1956). This makes study and practice in the field a contentious one, not only academically but also ideologically. Those who view the employment relationship as non-controversial, harmonious and based intuitively on co-operation and goodwill between the parties, rather than on conflict, consensus and compromise, deny the power basis of employment relations.

The subject matter in the field is typically analysed in terms of the players or parties to the employment relationship, the degrees of co-operation and conflict between them, the processes through which the relationship is governed, the outcomes of these processes, and the socio-economic and ideological contexts of the relationship. During the mid-twentieth century, the dominant paradigm of the subject in Western developed countries was the pluralist 'industrial relations' model, rooted in collective bargaining, trade unionism, the regulation of industrial conflict, commonly supported by the 'personnel management' paradigm of managing people (Torrington 1991). This was in conditions of full employment, driven by Keynesian demand management economic policies, underpinned by a post-war political consensus and welfare state regimes in Western democracies (Skidelsky and Bogdanor 1970). The 'industrial relations consensus' was a third pillar and an integral part of the post-Second World War settlement. This orthodoxy has been challenged to varying degrees in Anglo-Saxon, English-speaking economies over the past 30 years by the Human Resource Management (HRM) paradigm. This is defined as a recent, distinctive, proactive form of managing employment relationships and the range of 'agreements' between organisations and those employed by them. The new orthodoxy is driven by market, managerial, business, technological and political agendas. HRM in its various forms is a response to changes in organisational systems and structures, management practices and the economic environment of businesses and employment relationships, both nationally and globally over the last 30 years (Wilkinson *et al.* 2010).

It is clear that the intellectual domain and faces of employment relations have shifted significantly in recent years away from one focusing on national systems and collective processes to one incorporating a broader range of subject matter, cross-national comparisons, a wider spread of countries and practices, psychological insights into work and employment and renewed theory building in the field. These current developments are underpinned by the ascendancy of the market and financial capital in human transactions, the 'new' globalisation, the economic orthodoxy of neo-liberalism, and the emergence of new market economies beyond the Western world. It also reflects the demise of socialism and social democratic ideas in much of the political domain, where the worker as a consumer is now prioritised over the worker as an industrial and civic citizen (Gray 1996).

Employment relationships are not static; they encompass both continuity and change, and stability and innovation in relations between employers and workers. Change and innovation commonly happen in response to the volatile socio-economic contexts impacting on organisations, managers, workers and employment relationships over time at all levels – workplace and enterprise, industry or sector, nationally, regionally, and internationally. Today, 'fast capitalism', driven by extensive global patterns of trade and finance, multinational businesses and information and communication technologies (ICTs), begets fast and diverse patterns of employment relations around the world, within both developed political economies and developing ones (Offe and Keane 1985).

As argued more extensively below, employment relations are becoming increasingly internationalised, as economic development proceeds and new market economies and political democracies emerge. These include employment relationships in long-established market economies in Western countries and the emerging 'BRIC' economies of Brazil, Russia, India and China – although China remains a single-party state, governed by the Communist Party. The BRIC countries are regarded as the fastest growing and largest emerging market economies and make up about half of the world's population. Employment relations is thus no longer the exclusive domain of Western advanced market economies and established political democracies in Europe, North America and Australasia. Some of its institutions, practices

Structured employment relations systems
North America, West Europe, some parts of Asia-Pacific (e.g. Australia, Canada, Germany, Ireland, Japan, Netherlands, Scandinavia, Singapore, UK, US)
Developmental employment relations systems
Parts of Latin America, other Asia-Pacific, some Africa and some Middle-East (e.g. Argentina, Bahrain, Chile, Mexico, Taiwan, South Africa)
***Ad hoc* employment relations systems**
Central and East Europe, other Latin American, other Africa and other Middle-East (e.g. China, India, Nigeria, North Africa, Poland, Russia, Turkey, Uruguay)

Figure 1.1 The geographical contours of employment relations systems in the global political economy

and behaviours are now emerging and being adapted to parts of Asia, Latin America and Africa.

The geographic contours of employment relations systems in the global political economy are loosely outlined in Figure 1.1. Although a broad analysis, Figure 1.1 suggests that these contours are regionalised within nationally embedded employment relations systems. Using this framework, three main groups of employment relations systems can be observed in the global political economy. First, there are regions with *structured employment relations systems*. Generally, countries within these regions have developed (or advanced) economies, stable political systems, and sophisticated employment relations processes, although each system varies by country and each country has its own internal variants. Developed or advanced economies tend to have resource-rich economic bases, segmented labour markets, strong employment regulation, middle-to-high incomes per head, high levels of gender and ethnic equality, high-to-upper access to digital technology, and generally high standards of education. Their markets operate in established political democracies, with legitimate governments. Sophisticated employment relations processes, in turn, provide well-established and agreed means for making employment relations decisions, such as collective bargaining and balanced human resources management outcomes between organisations and workers. Structured employment relations systems are found mainly in North America, West Europe and some Asia-Pacific states.

Second, regions with *developmental employment relations systems* are made up of countries with transition economies with the aim of becoming advanced economies. In broad terms, they are either relatively 'new' democracies or authoritarian political regimes, with emergent employment relations processes; again with variations within them. Compared with developed economies, transitional economies tend to have weaker economic bases, fragmented labour markets, weak employment regulation, low levels of gender and ethnic equality, middle-to-low incomes per head and variable access to digital technology. Their standards of education are bi-modal, where a minority of its citizens is typically highly educated but the majority is not. Their markets operate within either newly established political democracies or authoritarian regimes. Their emergent employment relations processes are likely to have either low legitimacy or no legitimacy at all with workers. Developmental employment relations systems are commonly found in parts of Latin America, other parts of Asia, some parts of Africa, and some Middle-East states.

Third, regions with ad hoc *employment relations systems* are found in developing economies, which are likely to be weakly established political democracies or authoritarian political regimes. They tend to have a variety of employment relations processes, with much wider differences among them than in other systems. Compared with developed and transition economies, developing economies tend to have lower standards of living, underdeveloped industrial bases, poor standards of digital competence and a low Human Development Index in terms of life expectancy, education and income per head. Distinctions between developmental employment relations systems and ad hoc ones are permeable and less well defined than with structured employment relations systems; but this general analysis is justified. Ad hoc employment relations systems are typically found in Central and East Europe, other Latin American, other Asian, other African and other Middle-East states.

This text focuses principally on countries and regions with structured employment relations systems, where much of the 'classical' (Webb and Webb 1920a, 1920b, Commons 1909, 1919), modern mainstream and critical literature is found and where 'good' employment relations practices are commonly observed. But, in other cases, evidence from developmental and ad hoc employment relations systems is also considered.

THE DISTINCTIVE FEATURES OF THIS TEXT

Written for postgraduate and final year undergraduate students of business, management and social sciences often with little prior knowledge of the field, this book has a number of distinctive features, as indicated in Figure 1.2. One is that employment relations today has many faces or outward appearances. These include institutional, conceptual, methodological, theoretical, practical, ideological and disciplinary ones; there is no single, authoritative approach

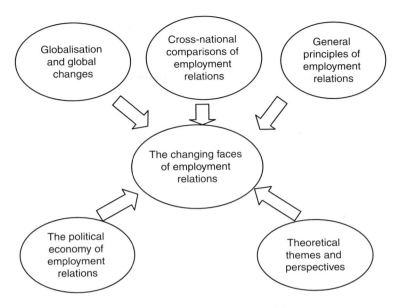

Figure 1.2 The distinctive features of this text

to the study of employment relations. As a field within the social sciences, employment relations consists of a complex set of institutions, processes, cultural influences, behaviours and academic disciplines (Kaufman 2004b). These make it a subject that is both intellectually demanding and socially contested, since employers, workers, unions and the state commonly have conflicting interests with one another and often conflicting views of the nature of the employment relationship. This text does not avoid these contentious issues or the subject's ambiguities. Effective arrangements for organising employment relationships, whatever forms they take, are critical to the economic and social well-being of employers, individual workers, their families and the state, wherever they take place. Here the nation state's role is critical, since how employment relationships are organised, and whether the state promotes balanced outcomes between employer and worker interests, are clear indicators of the importance that the state authorities attach to the concept of 'good employment relations', justice at work and the thinking or ideas behind these. The attitudes of the state authorities, expressed in terms of public policies in employment relations, range from relative indifference, abstention or bias, such as in some emerging free market societies in parts of the Middle East and Asia, to positive support for 'good', 'fair' or 'non-discriminatory' employment practices in social democratic societies, such as those in northern

Europe. These are provided through the law, collective bargaining and 'good' management and employment practices.

This text also takes account of the impact of globalisation and global changes on employment relationships at all levels. Employment relationships – at national, sector, enterprise and workplace levels – are no longer insulated from changes and developments in what is now a global, competitive and international marketplace. Today's global economy is a more integrated and international marketplace than it was a generation ago. In it, TNCs compete for customers and resources (including workers), small businesses seek networks and alliances with large business corporations and states try to promote economic growth, jobs and well-being for their increasingly consumer-driven populations. The end of national economic isolationism has promoted a global context of employment relations. Today national, relatively homogeneous, macro-systems of employment relations no longer persist; multiple, diverse patterns of employment relationships, processes and outcomes are the norm rather than the exception – both among countries and within them. This makes employment relations a subject where it is notoriously difficult to make definitive generalisations and draw universally applicable conclusions. This is demonstrated, among other things, by the wide range of theoretical positions in the field (Kaufman 2004b, Adams 1991).

Another feature of this text is it draws on cross-national comparisons at all levels of analysis around the world, rather than relying on solely non-comparative national and sub-national data as recognised country-based texts do (Dundon and Rollinson 2011, Williams and Adam-Smith 2010, Katz *et al.* 2007). This is of course very difficult to do in a book of this size. Indeed, certain cross-national issues and the geographic areas this writer has selected might be questioned by some observers, because there are no consistent comparisons of cross-national players, institutions, practices and processes or of national systems. This is deliberate and justified on practical grounds and student learning needs. The comparisons identified are selective 'polychromatic' or 'kaleidoscopic' ones, not generic ones. They incorporate changing subjects of comparisons and they draw upon a wide variety of employment relations data and sources. They include: paired comparisons of topics and countries; multi-comparisons of common topics drawn from more than two countries and sometimes regions; and comparisons at different levels of analysis, such as workplace, sector and nation state. The reasons for selecting particular comparators include the data available, their relevance to what is being discussed, and deliberately providing some variations in choices of comparators to readers. Critics of this approach might prefer a more systematic set of comparisons, but limitations of space and absence of complete data-sets preclude this.

The adoption of a comparative approach within this text reveals how employment relations phenomena, whether institutions, practices or ideas, are embedded within national systems over time. Each country, in short, has its own historical path dependency which affects employment relationships within it. The self-reinforcing persistence of historical structures and the institutions they encapsulate means that what has happened in the past affects what is happening in the present. Historical path dependency creates what may be described as an historical 'ratchet effect' that constrains the ability of human processes to be reversed once a specific series of actions has happened. 'History is still undervalued as a necessary contribution to social understanding . . . though far from entirely, we are the products of our history; a fact often forgotten or ignored by our masters' (Fox 1985: xii). This important historical dimension of employment relations is acknowledged throughout this text.

What this book lacks in *depth* of study of national employment relations systems is offset by the *breadth* of studies it draws upon for comparative purposes. Making comparisons is a difficult task anyway, given the varieties of frameworks, models, perspectives and cultures of employment relations within the field today. Indeed, as Hyman (2009: 18) argues, 'comparative analysis is essential but perhaps impossible'. Nevertheless, a main objective of comparative studies is to identify common patterns of employment relations, similarities and differences among and within different employment relations systems and some theoretical generalisations in the field (Bean 1994). Whatever the national system of employment relations in capitalist market economies, each one develops its own structures and processes for dealing with the 'basic principles' of work and employment relationships, as illustrated in Figure 1.3. An underlying theme running throughout this book is that 'civilised' employment relations reflect civilised nation states and civilised employment relations, in turn, promote civilised societies.

This text has strong theoretical themes and perspectives running through it too that seek to explain, analyse and critically review the range and scope of present-day employment relationships. It also identifies the ideas underpinning them and the forces driving them, as observed in different societies around the world with their varying degrees of sophistication and depth. However, as Hyman (2004: 289) perceptively warns, it is neither possible nor desirable to pursue a self-contained theory of employment relations: 'there will not be theories *of* industrial relations but applications of more encompassing theoretical insights'. So importantly in this work, no single trajectory of employment relations is identified but a series of complex, contradictory ones, incorporating a multiplicity of faces, practical approaches and theoretical perspectives within the field. Significantly, the text adopts a

Employment relations is concerned with:

- The central and indeterminate nature of the contract of employment
- How the economic, social and legal interests of managers, workers and the nation state in the employment relationship are structured and regularised
- How co-operation, resistance and conflict between managers and workers manifest themselves in work organisations
- How procedural justice and fairness for individuals, groups and among groups in the workplace and society are determined (or not determined)
- How and why conflicts at work and about work in society are regulated and controlled
- How ethical principles are (or are not) incorporated within work and employment relationships
- The role of the nation state in employment relations
- The impacts of culture, institutions, contexts and history on national employment relations systems
- The civilising impact of 'good' or structured employment relations on those living, working and consuming in nation states
- How international comparisons of these principles provide helpful insights into the similarities and differences amongst different employment relations systems, players and processes

Figure 1.3   Some basic principles of work and employment relationships in capitalist market economies

'post-industrial relations' analysis, by incorporating within it a number of competing insights or faces of the employment relationship in conditions of economic and social change. These include HRM, managerial, organisational, feminist, non-union, legal, public policy and international ones. This task is facilitated by drawing on recent empirical research and evidence-based data from a range of international sources.

Another feature of this text is the importance of the political economy of employment relationships. Employment relations are based on power, which involves all the actors and institutions in the economic and political systems with direct or indirect interests in the employment relationship. Employment relationships take place, that is, within the specific economic and political conditions in which they operate. They are not neutral, uncontested relationships and *objective* phenomena but contested and *subjective* ones within the contexts of their dominant national political economies and the increasingly global political economy, in which they take place (Ravenhill 2011). Every national employment relations system, in other words, is affected by the changing market and political factors impacting on employment relationships within it, where the dominant economic policy orthodoxy today is neo-liberalism.

Finally, as indicated in Figure 1.1, the geographic areas covered in this text are wider than in most other works. These include examples and comparisons taken from advanced political economies and some transitional and developing ones, drawing on the English-language literature in employment relations. Because the chapters in the text are on different players or processes in employment relations, with comparisons interwoven throughout, this also makes the book distinctive from some other books in the field. Further, the comparisons made are not only cross-national but also cross-disciplinary. This makes the book interesting to students from different employment relations cultures, by helping them understand the relevance of these comparisons in terms of the underlying principles of work and employment relationships outlined above.

THE GLOBAL DIMENSION AND NEO-LIBERAL SETTLEMENT

A major policy issue in international political economy in recent decades is globalisation. Loosely defined, globalisation is market capitalism based on international free trade. It is a controversial and contested phenomenon. Indeed, compared with the immediate post-Second World War period, which was an age of national economic protection with high levels of employment, tight employment regulation and job security in Western developed economies, the spread of a more open, global economy is a major factor impacting on businesses and employment relationships around the world today, with a variety of expected and unintended outcomes. At national level, the globalisation project is promoted and supported by neo-liberal economic policies implemented by governments, which is sometimes called the neo-liberal settlement.

The contested nature of globalisation

Globalisation is a complex phenomenon and, for some writers, it is seen largely as an economic issue. Petrella (1996), for example, argues that a new competitive era emerged from the 1970s, especially in relation to the globalisation or internationalisation of economic processes. By this view, international economic competition no longer describes a particular type of market configuration but has the status of a universal credo or ideology. Gray (2002), no supporter of globalisation, defines economic globalisation as the worldwide spread of industrial production promoted by the unrestricted mobility of capital (both financial and material capital goods) and greater freedom of trade. Economic globalisation is thus associated with the international trading of goods, services and finance, operating in relatively free, unregulated markets, reduced tariff barriers and the decline of protectionist national economic policies. It is underpinned by the belief of its supporters that 'Nothing must be allowed to inhibit the formation of markets' (Polanyi 1944: 69).

Conway and Heynen (2006) identify five factors promoting economic globalisation in recent decades. First, governments have promoted freer trade around the world by removing major tariff barriers on imports and exports. Thus China, in the early 1990s, removed many restrictions on its export markets. With its relatively low wages, a large, hard working labour force and absence of a social welfare system, China was able to flood the developed world with cheap manufactured goods. Second, many manufacturers based in the West have outsourced their production to low-wage countries in Asia and Central America. Third, new communication systems, such as ICTs and containerisation, have facilitated the rapid and cheap transfer of information and physical resources around the world. Fourth, with the demise of Communism in east and central Europe, international trade in these regions has been liberalised and Western trans-national firms have been able to identify new market opportunities there and satisfy them. Fifth, countries around the world have made strong efforts to harmonise property rights and intellectual property rights globally, with the result that international trade has been facilitated and grown in significance.

A key set of tenets underpinning the economic globalisation agenda are drawn from the ideas of the classical economists of nineteenth-century Britain. Thus Adam Smith (1977) and Ricardo (1973) viewed the free market as a self-regulating mechanism tending towards equilibrium in demand and supply. They considered any constraint on free trade and market competition would interfere with the natural efficiency of market mechanisms, leading to social stagnation, political corruption and the creation of unresponsive state bureaucracies. They advocated the elimination of tariffs on imports and other barriers to free trade and capital flows between nation states. Spencer (1969) added to this doctrine by arguing that free market economies constitute the most civilised form of human competition, enabling the fittest to survive thereby raising their economic performance to the highest levels. These 'old' classical economic ideas were first adopted and later revitalised by Western political leaders, such as Margaret Thatcher and Ronald Reagan and their supporters in the United Kingdom and the United States.

From the late 1970s, the leaders of other Western countries followed the trend. Known subsequently as neo-conservative or 'new right' politicians, these acolytes of the free market, who wanted fundamental economic reforms within their countries, embraced the ideology of traditional conservatism linking it with political individualism and strong state support for free markets (Gamble 1988). The concept that markets need to be 'free', however, is a disputed one. For observers, such as Chang (2010: 1), the free market does not exist. For him, every market has some rules and boundaries restricting freedom of choice. 'A market looks free only because we so unconditionally accept its underlying restrictions that we fail to see them.' How free a market is cannot be defined objectively. 'It is a political definition.'

After a generation of interventionist Keynesian economic policies post-1945 in advanced Western states, which aimed at maintaining high levels of employment within their relatively closed economies, new right governments challenged the post-war economic consensus by adopting a neo-liberal economic agenda and building a neo-liberal settlement. Underpinned by ideas supporting the efficiency of private enterprise, trade liberalisation and relatively open markets, neo-liberal economic policies opened up national economies to freer trade and international competition, thus promoting economic globalisation.

Neo-liberalism is an economic phenomenon but it is underpinned by contemporary political systems that have adjusted to support it, at their most radical in Anglophone states. On the one hand, elected governments and internationally mobile TNCs come in ever-closer contact together, since nation states need TNCs to employ people, invest, pay taxes and promote large cash flows in their countries. As a result, the state's role in economic provision declines, labour law is made employer friendly and the tax burden is shifted from corporations to individuals. On the other hand, citizen rights are less respected by the state, elections become unrepresentative and it is difficult to get balanced political debates. Crouch (2004) describes this political phenomenon as 'Post Democracy'. He argues that the decline in class politics and rise of global capitalism have resulted in the creation of a self-referential political class more concerned with forging links with wealthy business interests than with pursuing political programmes meeting the concerns of ordinary people. Indeed, in his view, politics at the beginning of the twenty-first century had returned to a pattern, established well before the beginning of the twentieth century, when it was a game played among social elites.

There are various brands of economic neo-liberalism, but with a dominant theme: 'that free markets in which individuals maximize their material interests provide the best means for satisfying human aspirations, and that markets are in particular to be preferred over states and politics, which are at best inefficient and at worst threats to freedom' (Crouch 2011: vii). Indeed, according to Crouch (2011: 17), the underpinning thinking of supporters of neo-liberalism is that optimal outcomes in markets are achieved, if the supply and demand for goods and services are allowed to adjust to each other through the price mechanism, 'without interference by government or other forces – *though subject to the pricing and marketing strategies of oligopolistic corporations*' (emphasis added).

The latest but revisited version of neo-liberalism is associated with the so-called 'austerity' economic programmes followed by many Western governments after the credit crisis in 2007–2008. In essence 'austerity' describes policies used by governments to reduce budget deficits during adverse economic conditions. These policies may include spending cuts, tax increases, or a mixture of the two. Austerity policies are aimed at demonstrating the liquidity of governments to their creditors and credit-rating agencies, by bringing fiscal incomes closer to expenditures. For example, recent austerity programmes in Europe – including Germany, Greece, Ireland, Italy, the Netherlands, Portugal, Romania, Spain and the United Kingdom – resulted in unemployment rising to record levels and rising debt-to-gross domestic product (GDP) ratios, despite reductions in budget deficits relative to GDP (Blyth 2013). Indeed, Eurostat (2013) reported that unemployment in the 17 Euro-area countries reached an all-time high of 12.1 per cent in March 2013.

Such economic policies let national labour markets find their 'natural' rate or level of unemployment, as determined by the supply side of their national economies. With economic growth, employment increases but when growth falls (or stagnates), unemployment rises until it finds its so-called natural level (Friedman 1968). This new economic orthodoxy took root in some Western states during the 1980s and was extended eastwards in the 1990s, following the collapse of communism in Soviet Russia and East Europe between 1989 and 1991. It went on to influence parts of Asia and the Far East subsequently. And as Crouch (2011: viii) comments: 'the issue today is not limited to a single country, as neoliberalism is an international, even global, phenomenon'. The principles underpinning neo-liberal and classical Keynesian economic policies are provided in Figure 1.4. This is an indicative analysis, not a definitive one, as elements of both supply-side and demand-side economic policy can be drawn upon by governments to varying degrees.

For writers such as Steger (2009), globalisation is more than an economic phenomenon. For him, one reason why globalisation remains a contested concept is because no scholarly consensus exists on what kinds of social processes make up its essence. He suggests that globalisation has five distinctive features. First, it is characterised by a global trend towards greater interdependence and integration of nations, economies and cultural values, particularly associated with the market. Second, it both creates new social networks and multiplies existing ones, which incrementally overcome traditional political,

	Neo-liberal economic policy (supply-side economics)	Orthodox Keynesian economic policy (demand-side economics)
Policy priority	Controlling inflation and promoting free markets	Maintaining high levels of employment and promoting economic growth
Fiscal policy	Cutting taxes	Varying taxes according to aggregate demand
Monetary policy	Using money supply to keep inflation in check	Using money supply to support fiscal policy
Incomes policy	Leaving market forces to determine incomes and income distribution	Intervening in income determination and income distribution, where appropriate
Size of the state and the public sector	Creating a smaller state by privatising public enterprises Downsizing government Reducing public spending Reforming public services	Developing a larger state Promoting a strategic public sector Increasing the role of government in the national economy Varying public spending
Role of government	Deregulating the national economy	Managing and steering the national economy
Trade and industry	Liberalising trade and industry	Protecting trade and industry and supporting them where necessary
International trade	Expanding international markets	Protecting domestic markets from international competition, while promoting exports
Capital markets	Removing controls on global financial flows	Maintaining controls over global financial flows
Government and organised labour	Weakening organised labour	Working with organised labour to control prices, promote employment, protect the balance of payments, promote growth

Figure 1.4 Neo-liberal and orthodox Keynesian economic policies

economic, cultural and geographic boundaries. Third, globalisation expands and stretches social relations, activities and interdependencies. For example, electronic trading takes place around the clock and international bodies, such as the UN, the EU and *Médecins Sans Frontières*, become more important social institutions in their own right. Fourth, there is intensification and acceleration of social exchanges and activities, with the World Wide Web (WWW) enabling instant communication around the world and satellites providing

Global category	Main features
Global manufacturing	Promoted largely by transnational corporations and technological innovations
Global tele-work	Includes call centres, data processing and software development facilities in countries with relative lower wage costs and a supply of well-qualified educated labour
Global tourism	Dominated by international airlines, hotel chains and travel companies but also including sex tourism
Global agriculture	Is due to capitalist production methods spreading to even small producers, which is resulting in agriculture being increasingly dominated by 'life science corporations' that cut across agri-business, biotechnology and the chemical and pharmaceutical industries
Global finance	Made possible by technological advances, powerful ICTs and financial market deregulation that facilitate the rapid transferral of large quantities of financial capital around the world

Figure 1.5   Main categories of globalisation
Source: Shiva (2000).

people with real-time pictures of remote events. Fifth, the creation, expansion and intensification of social interconnections and interdependencies do not occur merely at the objective material level. They also involve the subjective level of human consciousness, with people becoming increasingly aware of the receding importance of geographic boundaries in their lives.

By the 1970s, 'managed capitalism' in the Western world rooted in welfare states, corporatist relationships between governments and major interest groups such as employers and unions, extensive public ownership and Keynesian economic policies, was beginning to be challenged by neo-liberals and the neo-liberal agenda, especially in English-speaking countries. Increasing international competition was putting established industrial societies under pressure and newly industrialising states were beginning to emerge. The outcome was that markets for goods and services, capital and some labour services became increasingly global, rooted in the neo-liberal settlement (Steger 2010). As indicated in Figure 1.5, the new international economic order can be classified into five main global categories covering manufacturing, tele-work, tourism, agricultural and finance activities (Shiva 2000).

Promoters and critics of globalisation

Whether globalisation is a new phenomenon or not is open to debate. There is also the issue of how global is globalisation. Some scholars argue that globalisation has been around in one form or another since the discovery of the 'new world' in the sixteenth century and that it peaked in the years leading up the First World War (Hirst *et al.* 2009). Others argue that proto-globalism can be traced back to pre-history and that the chronology of globalisation can be traced through three further stages, culminating in its fifth and latest stage, the contemporary period since 1970 (McGrew and Held 2000). Those supporting the novelty of contemporary global markets, on the other hand, argue that the new globalisation has rendered the nation state irrelevant and that it is powerless countries and homeless large corporations that inhabit the global economy and the global marketplace today. For Ohmae (1996: 20), 'in a borderless economy, the nation-focused maps we typically use to make sense of economic activity are woefully misleading' and the 'old cartography no longer works. It has become no more than an illusion'.

The universality of global processes is challenged by those who argue that globalisation is not a single process but a set of processes that operate simultaneously and unevenly on several levels and in various dimensions (Steger 2009). Further, many small-scale businesses around the world remain local rather than global, as do most public and local services; the impact of globalisation on them is indirect rather than direct.

Other apologists for globalisation and the free market include the international financier and speculator, George Soros who argues that the collapse of the global marketplace would be a traumatic event with unimaginable consequences. He also claims that reform of global capitalism is a necessary condition for social peace (Soros 1995, 2000). Support for globalisation, and the transformation of social markets into free markets, is one of the overriding objectives of trans-national organisations such as the World Trade Organisation, the International Monetary Fund (IMF), OECD and World Bank. In promoting the 'globalisation project', these bodies are following the lead of the United States, where global economic progress, combined with the advancement of political democracy, are seen as optimistic steps towards a universal civilisation based on global free trade and a community of democratic states, sometimes called the 'Washington consensus'.

These views of individuals, organisations and political authorities are not without their critics. Gray (2002), for example, argues that the model of a single world-wide civilisation, supported by the 'Washington consensus', expects democratic capitalism to be accepted throughout the world in which a global free market becomes a final reality. He attributes this to the ascendancy of the neo-conservative lobby in the United States, where free markets are seen as not only the prime way of organising a market economy but also a prerequisite for human freedom everywhere – an ascendancy hardly challenged by the Obama administrations 2009–2017.

Critiques of the globalisation orthodoxy in international political economy arose out of a series of intellectual and political challenges to the neo-liberal ascendancy from the 1990s – an ascendancy sustained and supported by the leaders of large business corporations, wealthy holders of international capital and powerful political institutions such as the IMF, OECD and the World Bank (Stiglitz 2013). Anti-globalisation arguments and protests against globalisation emerged out of heightened public awareness that the profit-driven strategies of large TNCs were leading to widening disparities in personal wealth, distribution of household income and individual well-being in the global economy, as well as damaging the eco-environment, consuming the finite resources of the planet without regard to sustainability and conservation, and weakening human rights. Between 1999 and 2001, there were street confrontations in many cities around the world between the political authorities and anti-globalisation opposition groups, followed by further confrontations in 2011–2012, after the global financial crisis of 2007–2008, as in the 'Occupy' movement and Arab spring (Beaumont 2013).

These unprecedented changes in the global economy have been variously described by some critics as 'turbo capitalism' (Luttwak 1999), 'casino capitalism' (Strange 1986), 'market fundamentalism' (Soros 1998), 'the cancer-stage of capitalism' (McMurtry 1999) and 'McWorld' (Barber 1995). Organised opposition to the globalisation project, however, has not been homogeneous nor is it united. It has become concentrated into two ideological camps – 'particularist protectionists' and 'universalist protectionists'. Their political agenda and examples of some of their leading advocates are summarised in Figure 1.6. Tensions between these two groups (and of sub-groups within them) persist and organised opposition to globalisation continues to be fragmented and divided. Thus, with a split constituency, changing the globalisation agenda remains problematic and achieving the economic, political, social, ecological and ethical goals of anti-global reformers remain unresolved.

Whatever the ambiguities of present-day global capitalism, five generic observations can be made. First, globalisation is not a recent phenomenon but has deep historical roots. Second, in the current global economy, financial capital moves between a small group of rich countries; it does not circulate globally. Third, international market capitalism continues to be organised nationally not globally, since international differences are as important as

Particularist protectionists	Some leading advocates	Universalist protectionists	Some leading advocates
Blame globalisation for the ills of their countries	Patrick Buchanan (US)	Seek a more equitable relationship between the North and South of the world	Ralph Nader (US)
Are anti-free trade	Ross Perot (US)	Want a new international order based on a global re-distribution of power and wealth	Naomi Klein (Canada)
Oppose global investors	Jörg Haider (Austria)		International Forum on Globalisation (US)
Condemn neo-liberal transnational companies	J-M Le Pen (France)		Green Parties (Europe)
Believe Americanisation results in falling living standards and 'moral' decline	Hugo Chávez (Venezuela)	Guided by the ideals of equality and social justice for all, not just citizens in own countries	Anarchist groups (Europe)
Want protection from 'foreign' elements	Radical Islamists (Middle East)	Associated with some Non-Governmental Organisations and transnational networks	Zapatistas (Mexico)
Concerned with the well-being of their citizens, not a more equitable global order		Aim to protect the environment, fair trade, international labour issues, human rights, women's issues	
Adopt the rhetoric of economic nationalism		Seek to protect ordinary people from 'globalisation from above'	
Oppose immigration and imported labour			

Figure 1.6 The anti-globalisation agenda and some of their advocates

ever in global trade, where nation states maintain a key role in the activities of TNCs. Fourth, economic globalisation is underwritten by national neo-liberal economic and social policy, which has resulted in a shift of ownership and control of economic resources from the public to private domain. Fifth, despite the claim that global capitalism has an integrative function, it has created a more unequal world in terms of income and wealth distribution, concentrated the control of key economic resources and impacted in diverse ways on the regulation of employment and employment relationships around the world.

Globalisation and employment relations

Globalisation by definition is an international issue, which affects all economies and societies to varying degrees, even if some countries, such as the socialist states of Cuba and North Korea, attempt to isolate themselves from it. Historically, early examinations of employment relations 'systems' focused on national or country-wide studies (macro-level), sector or industry studies (meso-level) and corporate or workplace studies (micro-level) in developed economies (Clegg 1970, Craig and Solomon 1992, Dabscheck 1989). Industries such as engineering, manufacturing and financial services were largely protected from international economic competition by national economic policies that promoted protectionism by using tax barriers and tariffs on goods and services imported from overseas. Such policies strengthened trade unionism and collective pay bargaining within these sectors, while governments tried to counterbalance any excess bargaining power between the two parties in the national interest. The aim of national-level collective bargaining for both employers and unions was commonly to take wages out of competition in both the market and public sectors (Clay 1929, Richardson 1954, Clegg 1970, Ferner and Hyman 1994). All employers covered by a given collective agreement adopted the same terms and conditions for their workforces. Their employees, in turn, were protected from wage-cutting by the employers which had negotiated these agreements with the union. Non-federated firms also used national wage agreements as benchmarks.

Since the 1980s, economic protectionism has gradually broken down, giving rise to the new international economic order of globalisation, where national tariff barriers have been removed or reduced and international free trade has been promoted by national governments and some international bodies, supported by TNCs. Such patterns of international trade have resulted, in turn, in new forms of employment relations in some cases, such as team working, employee involvement and pay for performance in union-free, leading-edge companies. These HR policies seek to improve organisational performance, gain competitive advantage for firms, promote customer satisfaction and are common in TNCs engaged in international trade (Boxall and Purcell 2011). At another level, fierce competition in global product markets has resulted in wage-cutting, poor working conditions, long hours of work and exploitation of labour, such as child labour, in some developing countries. For example, ILO estimates that about 250 million children aged between five and 14 were engaged in low-paid economic activity at the end of the twentieth century (International Labour Office 2012). By 2012, the numbers of children, aged between 5 and 17, engaged in some kind of economic activity globally had increased to about 264 million, especially in Asia-Pacific and Africa, but also in Latin America, the Caribbean and parts of East and Central Europe following the dislocations caused by their transition to market economies. These were categorised as 'children in employment', 'child labour' and 'hazardous work' (Diallo *et al.* 2013).

The current era of economic globalisation in the late twentieth and early twenty-first centuries, however, differs from that of the late nineteenth and early twentieth centuries in at least two respects. First, in the earlier period, globalisation was characterised largely by the marked mobility of low-skill labour among developed and developing nations. Globalisation today is characterised by the movement of both unskilled labour and skilled labour from the less developed world into developed nations. Developed countries create immigration policies targeting skilled workers and business immigrants from the less developed world, while trying to restrict the international mobility of low-skill labour. However, as scholars such as McDowell *et al.* (2008) demonstrate, unskilled labour migration has been an important driver of globalisation. Second, immigration policies of developed countries work in parallel with other policies aimed at increasing foreign direct investment and decreasing restrictions on capital mobility. This is because TNCs in developed countries can move their capital and technological resources to those global locations where they can employ low paid, unskilled labour. This reduces the need to import unskilled workers into their home countries but it pits unskilled workers with unskilled labour in developing countries in a wage race 'to the bottom' (Juss 2006).

Although globalisation in the last 30 years has expanded employment and the demand for labour in developing nations, it has also altered the structure and operation of labour markets in developed countries. For example, there has been a decline in manufacturing employment within them. In the services sector, there has been faster relative growth in high-skill jobs rather than low-skill ones, reducing job opportunities for low-skill workers. These structural changes operate in tandem with the rise in atypical employment (particularly part-time) or flexible job arrangements, thus increasing the proportion of unskilled workers exposed to the threat of insecure employment and experience of unemployment. Globalisation also affects the market power of labour market institutions by creating a 'regulatory deficit'. National institutions which regulate the labour market, such as unions and collective bargaining, are either rendered less effective by the internationalisation of markets or abolished. Also across most developed nations during the past three decades, there has been to varying degrees a rolling back of the frontiers of the state, including privatisation, outsourcing and changes in social security payments to working people, their families and the unemployed. This reduces the price of labour, particularly unskilled labour, and removes a basic buttress against the financial strains of under-employment and unemployment in advanced market economies (OECD 2007). Not all scholars, however, accept that globalisation is responsible for driving these changes. Some argue, for example, the importance of domestic political choices in these areas (Doogan 2009).

COMPARATIVE EMPLOYMENT RELATIONS

The global dimension of much economic activity today has led to increasing interest in comparative employment relations. Yet there are disagreements, or even confusions, among scholars precisely what the term means and with other terms linked to comparative studies. It is necessary, for example, to distinguish between comparative and international employment relations and between comparative and global employment relations, as well as the links between them. As Barry and Wilkinson (2011: 3) conclude: 'the field of comparative employment relations is underdeveloped and lacks integration'. However, in their view, 'a range of different intellectual perspectives can be usefully employed to help us understand the field'. And for Frege and Kelly (2013: 9), 'One of the potential benefits of comparative research is that it can help to advance a more inter-disciplinary and theoretical understanding of employment relations.' For them, 'cross-national comparative methodology is in many ways the fundamental laboratory for employment relations'.

Historically, studies of comparative employment relations were relatively rare. Even today, Frege (2005: 179) argues that the bulk of employment relations research 'continues to be strongly embedded in nationally specific research traditions and cultures'. Early works on employment relations drew heavily upon the institutional tradition of the subject. These focused largely on macro-level, meso-level and micro-level studies in countries, sectors, companies or workplaces, where the case-study method was commonly used as the major research design (Hawkins 1972). At this time, the comparative approach was not common. Even today, the nation state remains an important unit of analysis in the field but comparative studies have had increasing academic attention in recent years, partly in response to the growing interdependence of national economies. And, as Dunlop (1958: vi) observes, the comparative method leads 'to questions regarding the reasons for the observed comparisons and contrasts'.

The boundaries of comparative employment relations are defined by six main factors. First, they have different starting points from national or sub-national studies. Comparative employment relations is based on research 'dealing with the same (or similar or related) phenomena in different countries', thus enabling international comparisons of these phenomena to be made. Examples include the determinants of union membership, management styles or industrial action (Sturmthal 1958). Slack (1980: 27) sees comparative studies as an attempt 'to provide analytical tools for cross-national comparisons' and to build theories to account for different patterns in the field. Similar observations are made by Bean (1994: 3, vii), who concludes that comparative employment relations is essentially 'a systematic method of investigation relating to two or more countries which has analytic rather than prescriptive implications'. The comparative study of employment relations phenomena, in other words, is organised around a 'number of central topics rather than in the form of a side-by-side treatment of a number of individual countries'. This is done by focusing on issues *across* national boundaries in an integrated way. For Whitfield and Strauss (1998: 175), comparative studies contribute to the understanding of not only national systems of employment relations but also 'the relative significance of factors, such as technology, economic fluctuations, laws, and culture' among countries. Clearly, comparative and international employment relations are linked, because comparative studies involve making comparisons between different national or sub-national systems and trying to explain the similarities and differences between them. Comparative studies, in short, are rooted in cross-national or international comparisons of employment relations phenomena in different nation states at all levels of analysis.

Second, an employment relations study is cross-national and comparative when individuals or research teams set out to examine particular issues or phenomena in two or more countries (or within them) with the purpose of comparing their manifestations in different socio-cultural settings, using the same research instruments to carry out secondary analysis of national data or conduct new empirical work. The aim is to seek explanations of similarities and differences in these employment relations phenomena, to generalise from them, or to gain a greater awareness and a deeper understanding of the reality of employment relationships in different national contexts. Using this definition of comparative work means comparative employment relations is not synonymous with international employment relations, which has two meanings. One interpretation of international studies is those focusing on macro-, meso- or micro-level research in single countries beyond the researcher's national domain. In other words, international employment relations of this sort examine employment systems in different countries on a case-by-case basis. These are described by Meyer (1967: 27) as 'foreign studies' or the 'case examination of phenomena in a foreign environment and . . . do not differ qualitatively from like case studies of the home environment'. Juxtaposing them shifts the analysis to comparative work.

Third, another interpretation of international studies is provided by Poole (1986: 6) who defines them as the 'substantive description and case analysis of supranational phenomena'. Thus trans-national or global employment relations deal with those institutions, processes or topics which are *above* national boundaries. They include employment relations in TNCs, international union organisations and bodies such as the ILO, which is the UN agency promoting social justice and international human and labour rights around the world. Analytically, then, it is useful to distinguish between international employment relations and global *level* institutions in the field. International employment relations studies institutions and practices in different nation states or regions; global institutions operate at international level and are commonly called 'international' bodies.

Fourth, comparative studies do not provide discrete summaries of employment relations in individual countries and then leave students to make their own international comparisons. Contemporary comparative employment relations examines the changing nature of employment practices and labour management processes cross-nationally in relation to the process of globalisation. It does this at one level by taking account of the international dimension of the field and engages with the literature and research covering, for example, comparative studies in collective bargaining, union organisation and methods of conflict resolution between managers and workers, by analysing and synthesising it. At another level, it compares contemporary developments in the field such as new management practices, employment relations in TNCs, HRM strategies and policies, employee engagement, non-union firms and non-union forms of employee voice; topics typically omitted in the industrial relations paradigm.

Fifth, comparative employment relations commonly takes an overview of developments and changes in the field, using a thematic, integrated approach to specific topics, examined by paired or multiple comparisons. These include comparisons of the role of law in employment relations, pay determination, pay systems, pay outcomes, HR practices and so on. As Kaufman (2004b) notes, the proper domain of comparative employment relations is the comparison of two or more employment relations systems (or phenomena) across (or within) two or more countries, with the intention of identifying the differences and similarities between them and generating new theoretical outcomes.

Sixth, and very importantly, comparative employment relations utilises a comparative method of analysis. Using the comparative *method* fosters distinctive insights into employment relations that non-comparative methods cannot do. It shows what may appear to be specific, distinguishing characteristics of employment relations within different systems, at national, sector, organisational or workplace levels, and then indicates their presence, modified presence or absence elsewhere; it also explains the reasons for this.

METHODOLOGICAL ISSUES AND THE BENEFITS OF COMPARATIVE STUDIES

There are a number of methodological problems in undertaking comparative studies of employment relations across national boundaries. Not least of these is language. How, for example, do employment relations terms translate into other languages or 'get lost' in translation? Even 'management', which has a number of meanings in the English language, has different meanings in others. Thus one translation of 'management' into German is *die Verwaltung*, which means literally the 'administration', as does the French, *la gestion*. So in practice, 'Denglisch' and 'Franglais' portmanteau words – '*der Manager*' and '*le manager*' – become incorporated into these languages in parallel with the mother-tongue words, each containing subtlety of differences in their meanings. This raises the question of the effect of translating the English-language lexicon of employment relations into other Western and non-Western languages and vice versa. Such basic linguistic issues need to be taken into account in doing comparative studies.

Comparative methodology

Whatever the type of comparative study, there are other problems in undertaking cross-national investigation in addition to linguistic and cultural factors. Differences in research traditions are one of them. Another is accessing comparable data. For example, national records may not exist; they may not go back far enough; or national statistics may not have been collected consistently and systematically over time. Also despite progress being made in developing large-scale harmonised international databases, some cross-national comparisons are rendered ineffectual by lack of a common understanding of the central concepts and societal contexts within which employment relations are conducted.

Different national employment relations systems commonly have their own cultural norms. Indeed, Ahiauzu (1982) argues that culture is an important contextual factor which needs to be taken into account in all cross-national studies of employment relations. Andersen's (1988) study of British and Norwegian workers and their unions on oil rigs, with identical workplaces and technology, demonstrates that variations in their institutional behaviours reflected the contrasting cultural traditions of the two countries. Indeed for Whitfield and Strauss (1998), national differences in culture, law and history play a large part in explaining variances in employment relations around the world. Research cultures are also embedded in broader national cultures. As Frege (2007: 49) observes, research in the field 'has developed differently in different countries and there is reason to suggest that this will continue for some time'.

The 'varieties of capitalism' approach (see Chapter 3), which developed out of political economy, provides a distinctive framework of analysis, with the potential for understanding and comparing patterns of employment relations in different countries (Hall and Soskice 2001, Coates 2005, Hancké 2009, Esping-Andersen 1990, Huber and Stephens 2001). Hall and Soskice (2001) challenge the view that there is any single way of organising business and employment relationships in capitalist market economies. In their analysis, institutional arrangements in market economies and capitalist societies play a key role in shaping how they function. These writers provide a firm-centric theory of comparative institutional advantage. For them, firms in market economies face a series of external and internal co-ordination problems. These are employment relations, vocational training and education, corporate governance, inter-firm relations, and relations with employees. Their text identifies two institutional solutions to co-ordinate these problems to produce superior economic outcomes. In liberal market economies, for example, such as in the Anglo-Saxon or English-speaking world, firms rely on markets and hierarchies to do this. Employment relations in these countries tend to be market-based, with relatively few long-term commitments by employers to their workers. In co-ordinated market economies, by contrast, such as in North Europe and at that time Japan, firms make greater use of non-market mechanisms to resolve these problems. In these regions, employment relations are more likely to be based on collective bargaining and managerial decisions that reflect a long-term commitment by employers to their employees than in market-based systems.

Other scholars have developed the varieties of capitalism framework further by including more varieties of market economy in their analyses. Thus Schmidt (2003) provides a framework to accommodate the statist tradition of

France. Thatcher *et al.* (2007) identify four varieties of capitalism by extending the framework to East European countries, while Marshall *et al.* (2008) identify an Asian market economy variety that captures some of the distinctive features in the organisation of the Chinese, South Korean and Japanese variants of capitalism. Other studies of Asia reveal that there is a wide range of institutional features, such as family-owned firms, employment relations systems and opportunities for education and training that produce an array of types and blends of capitalism in this diverse region (Carney 2008). Hence because of its adaptability, and the range of varieties of capitalism identified by scholars, this framework has become increasingly influential in analysing comparative employment relations. This is despite its 'determinism', or the view that societies cannot change their institutional pathways, and omission of international factors.

Another methodological problem in comparative employment relations is that studies need to be carefully designed and the cases being compared have to be judiciously selected. Within any grouping of countries, there is need to determine the number of states to be investigated and the levels at which comparisons are made. There are grounds for limiting the size of the comparative group, because it is not the number of countries, industries or workplaces which is important, but the range of variations that each provides (Walker 1967). Once countries to be compared have been selected, much analysis has traditionally focused on national-level macro-studies, with fewer investigations focusing on the workplace but with some notable exceptions (Burawoy 1983, Edwards 1979).

However, it has long been recognised that international comparisons targeted at national or macro-level may produce misleading results, because of the possible dominance of one or more industries within a country. Further, with the international spread of the neo-liberal economic agenda, and the shift to freer global markets for goods, services and financial transactions, the national approach to comparative employment relations has been challenged. Thus Locke (1992) among others claims that increasing market fragmentation and the opportunities provided by new technologies for firms to develop alternative business strategies has led to a proliferation of diverse employment relations patterns, both among nations and within them. He suggests the focus should turn to developments at micro-level to explain variations within countries, particularly the socio-economic conditions shaping managerial and union strategies in firms undergoing adjustments. Katz and Darbishire (2000), in turn, find increasing variation in the employment practices in the countries they studied, as well as many commonalities in the nature of the variations within them. The trends they note include a de-centralisation of collective

bargaining structures and a greater informality in labour-management interactions. Morley *et al.* (2006) conclude that many employment relations practices continue to be characterised by diversity across national borders and that
the nature and extent of these forces vary considerably.

A final methodological issue is the comparisons being made in such studies. Thus Strauss (1998) argues that an important distinction can be made
between 'splitters' and 'lumpers'. Splitters focus on explaining *differences*
among countries or research populations; lumpers are concerned with dis-
covering *similarities* or generalisations that apply universally. Thus a typical
splitting study of worker attitudes to union membership might examine differences in values such as individualism among countries. A lumping study,
in contrast, would use a variable such as union commitment to determine
whether it is validated across countries and, through testing, whether it
correlates between them.

The benefits of comparative studies

Whatever the difficulties and complexities inherent in studying employment
relations from a comparative perspective, the comparative approach has a
number of benefits for students and policy makers. For example, it fits in
with the internationalisation of the world economy. Globalisation impacts on
all national economies and their employment relations systems, albeit in different ways. Studying them comparatively contributes to understanding the
changes taking place within national systems and the effects of these changes
cross-nationally.

Comparative studies provide useful analyses and explanations of employment relations in different countries, including their similarities and differences. This is particularly useful for international students undertaking a
comparative unit within a university. They can see where their own countries
fit into the analysis and compare them with others. International comparisons
also enable international students to gain an 'overview' of the field rather than
concentrating on a single country, with its micro-details and subject matter
with which they may be unfamiliar and never need to understand. In any case,
national studies do not normally relate to the limited experiences students
have of work and employment relationships.

Comparative studies help identify the factors determining the structure,
processes and outcomes of specific employment relations systems at different analytical levels, and at various points in time. In this way, comparative
employment relations provides an academic lens for understanding or evaluating complex employment relations phenomena across countries over time.

Comparative studies enable, for example, typologies of cross-national phenomena to be developed and evaluated, such as trade union organisation or styles of management. They also contribute to an understanding of those elements of a national employment relations system that might usefully be replicated elsewhere. By undertaking comparative work, observers are obliged to venture outside their own immediate, national reference system and raise more questions than they would, had they had remained within a single national framework of analysis.

Examining employment relations comparatively requires students to define the principles of the comparability, which come in a variety of forms. This means constructing common conceptualisations of the topics or subject matter under review and providing a transverse, cross-cultural, cross-national system of analysis. This requires prior reflection on the components of the subject matter and conceptualisations likely to be the focus of comparison. Further, the comparative method avoids intellectual isolationism and seems the most suitable approach in the search for new angles on employment relations in an age of economic and social globalisation and the emergence of new intellectual challenges in the field.

Very importantly, as Strauss (1998) points out, comparative work contributes to new theoretical developments in the field and provides explanations and evaluations of the national and local developments studied. The comparative approach makes it possible to explain the development of changes in employment relations practices and processes. Comparative work, therefore, is an important development. But according to Poole (1986), scholars undertaking comparative analyses of employment relations phenomena need to follow four main principles to guide them. These are a focus upon the environmental influences emanating from societal structures and processes; a multidisciplinary perspective incorporating economic, political and socio-cultural factors; an emphasis upon explanatory variables rather than descriptive ones; and the importance of using an historical as well as a contemporary dimension. This book attempts to take all these factors into account.

SYSTEMS THEORY

As a text for postgraduate students, this book is organised thematically, as in the cases of Wilczynski (1983), Bean (1994) and Eaton (2000). But others in the field have used a mainly international approach, examining employment regulation in their national contexts with some comparative themes (Bamber *et al.* 2011, Frege and Kelly 2013), while Morley *et al.* (2006) examine comparative materials on regional or geographic bases. Another approach is to select a series of single issues such as comparative studies of trade unions or management (Fairbrother and Yates 2003, Frege 2007). The approach of Barry and Wilkinson (2011), in turn, is to focus on paired comparisons of national systems with similar embedded characteristics. Whatever comparative approach is used, however, in an introductory text like this one, a modified systems approach, drawing upon Dunlop's work (1958, 1993), provides a constructive and helpful framework for analysing comparative employment relations in the global economy.

Dunlop's systems model

Dunlop's (1958) seminal work, *Industrial Relations Systems*, is a useful heuristic model for classifying, analysing and comparing the parties, processes, contexts and outcomes of contemporary employment relations. His study has clarity of purpose and provides a robust focus of the field. Despite its critics (see below), Dunlop's systems perspective, or systems theory, is rooted in a rigorous and long-established framework and point of departure for studying what he calls 'industrial relations' but what in this text are described as employment relationships and employment relations, in their many faces and complexities. In essence, systems theory is a cross-sectional model of employment relations which has high utility as a framework of analysis and critical evaluation in this interdisciplinary field of study.

Dunlop (1958: v, xii, 7, 385) begins by arguing that any industrial state, regardless of its politics, has managers and workers. These societies, whether capitalist or socialist, create industrial relations, defined as the 'complex of interrelations among managers, workers, and agencies of government'. The central purposes of his work are to present a general theory of the subject, use the tools introduced to illuminate specific industrial relations experiences, and propose the collection of new facts and studies in the field. For Dunlop, an industrial relations system is not part of the economic or political systems but a separate and distinctive sub-system of its own, partially overlapping the economic and political domains or the political economy, with which it interacts. Industrial relations then becomes a specialist field of study in its own right. For him, the essence of an industrial relations system is that it comprises certain actors, contexts, an ideology, 'and a body of rules created to govern the actors at the work place and work community'. Industrial relations systems may be analysed at workplace, enterprise, sector or country-wide levels.

In Dunlop's analysis, an industrial relations system has three sets of inputs or *independent* variables: the actors, its contexts and an ideology. There are, in turn, three sets of actors and three environmental contexts. The three sets of actors are a hierarchy of managers and their representatives, a hierarchy of workers and their organisations and government or private agencies dealing with employment relations issues. The three environmental contexts of an industrial relations system are the technological characteristics of the workplace, the market or budgetary constraints impinging on the actors, and the locus or distribution of power in the wider society. The latter is important because the relative distribution of power in society tends to be reflected within the employment relations system. The distribution of power is likely to influence the state's specialist industrial relations agencies and helps explain differences between national systems in various countries. The third input to the system, its ideology, is the set of common ideas and beliefs held by the actors which binds the system together.

For Dunlop, the outputs or *dependent* variables of an industrial relations system are the network or web of rules created within it. These rules govern relations among the actors and their conduct at the workplace. Establishing this web of rules 'is the center of attention' in industrial relations. These rules take a variety of forms in different systems and include 'agreements, statutes, orders, decrees, regulations, awards, policies, and practices and customs'. For him, the central task of a theory of industrial relations is to explain why particular rules are established in specific systems 'and how and why they change in response to changes affecting the system'. The network of industrial relations rules consists of the procedures for establishing the rules, the substantive rules of employer–employee engagement and the procedures for deciding their application to particular situations. These rules may be custom and practice, oral or written. The processes or procedures used to make the rules, in turn, may be determined unilaterally by any of the actors, jointly between them, by law and by arbitrators or conciliators (Dunlop 1958: viii–ix, 13).

Dunlop's (1958: 380, 388–389) path-breaking work was an attempt to present a new way of thinking about 'systems' of industrial relations. He claimed to have developed a systematic body of ideas for arranging and interpreting the facts and interactions of managers, workers and governments in the regulation of employment relationships. He also claimed to have identified a set of concepts that required the collection of new facts, which could be presented in new categories by scholars working in the field. In his view, the concept of an 'industrial relations' system was most usefully applied when systems were viewed in their historical contexts and changes in these systems were analysed over time. He also argued that any national employment relations system emerges 'at a relatively early stage in economic development', because the power context is set very early on 'and is much influenced by the industrializing elite'.

Critiques of the systems model

Industrial Relations Systems was first published in 1958 and revised in 1993. By this time, its narrative was being challenged by both the emergence of new, strategic forms of HRM (Boxall and Purcell 2011) and, since the 1980s, by those supporting the neo-liberal model of political economy. It is not surprising that the systems model was subjected to a number of theoretical and conceptual critiques over this period. One critique is that within the model the rules of any employment relations system (the dependent variables) are explained by the five sets of independent variables in the schema. But, critics argue, this framework is simply a formal taxonomy or way of ordering the key elements and components to be taken into account in analysing and evaluating any employment relations system. Consequently, the systems model cannot claim to be a general theory in the field, because it is solely 'a general framework to organize a description of the interaction between the actors, environmental contexts and the ideologies' in each case (Meltz 1991: 14).

Another critique is that processes of conflict and change are absent in the Dunlop model. Dunlop regards unity and stability within the system as structural essentials and givens. For him, the actors producing the rules do so under a normative or ideological consensus. If they do not share a common ideology, their respective ideologies must at least be compatible. This is unlikely in practice, since managers and workers normally have different values and beliefs about the nature of work and the employment relationship. Further, little attention is paid by Dunlop to the conflicts and internal dynamics of the constituent parts of the system; they are treated as unitary elements within it (Hyman and Brough 1975, Fox 1966). Goldthorpe (1974), for example, stresses the anomic nature of employment relations and the absence of normative constraints on distributive conflict within advanced capitalist societies. Kochan *et al.* (1986), in turn, argue of the corrosive effect of American business ideology on work and employment relations. In their view, this has been a major force behind the transformation of employment relations in the United States, following Dunlop's and other studies in the 'golden age of labour' from the New Deal in the 1930s until the early 1980s (Kerr *et al.* 1962). Dunlop's model therefore does not take account of change within the system, since as a unitary static model it fails to include explanations or analysis of the impact of shifts of time in employment relationships. While he was willing to take history into account in his model, Dunlop did not incorporate the dynamics of the historical process within it.

Other critiques of Dunlop's model relate to its system actors, system boundaries and system outcomes. In terms of systems actors, critics argue that Dunlop's actors are too narrow, being focused on collective actors and state bureaucracies. Time has moved on, they claim. They challenge the relative exclusion, for example, of women's interests in formal employment relations. They say this demands a focus on women's workgroups and women in the field (Greene 2003). Other critics focus on absence of new institutional actors in the field, such as social movements representing workers' interests (Oysterman *et al.* 2001). Other sets of actors omitted by Dunlop include the clients or customers of organisations, since these help shape patterns of work and the employment relations systems underpinning them. In terms of systems boundaries, critics have extended these to incorporate the domestic sphere, family relationships and the political system, where successive state policies are recognised as important determinants of employment relations policies and practices (Wajcman 2000, Appelbaum and Leana 2011).

The system outcomes of Dunlop's model have attracted criticism from those claiming that the web of rules should not be perceived as defining outcomes but 'as independent or mediating variables' shaping outcomes and behaviours such as 'wage rates, strikes, work effort and union organizing success' (Kaufman 2004b: 48–49). Another development has been a focus on the business outcomes of employment relations such as productivity, financial performance and competitiveness at both firm and national levels (Freeman and Medoff 1984, Austin *et al.* 2012). In contrast, some scholars have assessed employment relations outcomes in terms of their impact on workers, such as worker well-being, quality of working life and ethical standards of employment (Brown *et al.* 2012, Budd 2004, 2005).

Another set of critics challenge Dunlop's explanation of employment relations phenomena in terms of technical change and market pressures. They reject the 'convergence' thesis of industrial societies claimed by Kerr and his colleagues (1962). The convergence thesis argues that as countries undergo common technological and market developments, they result in common forms of economic and social orders. In countering this set of arguments, Kochan *et al.* (1986) focus on the roles of 'strategic choice' and managerial ideology in shaping corporate responses to contextual pressures. In other words, employment relations systems vary under common technological, market and institutional features. Drawing upon new institutionalist literature, Godard (2004b), in turn, claims that the institutional structures of advanced capitalist societies provide more convincing explanations of the specific configurations and outcomes of different national employment relations systems, than do the conditioning effects of technology and the marketplace.

Finally, promoters of new right thinking challenge Dunlop's systems model. This is demonstrated by Hirschman's (1991) attack on conservative and reactionary thought, which he describes as 'the rhetoric of reaction'. He says three arguments are used to oppose progressive agendas: the 'perversity', 'futility' and 'jeopardy' theses. The perversity thesis posits that purposive action to improve any feature of the existing economic and social order only serves to exacerbate the condition to be remedied. The futility thesis posits that attempts at social transformation are pointless because they fail to achieve anything. And the jeopardy thesis posits that the cost of the proposed change or reform is too high, as it endangers previous valuable accomplishments. Applying these principles to the field of employment relations, and using collective wage bargaining, unions and minimum wage laws as examples, these are seen by people of a conservative or traditional persuasion as being: *perverse* because they are claimed to generate unemployment; *futile* because they are unable to challenge fundamental labour market pressures; and a *jeopardy* to individual liberty.

Renewing the systems model

In seeking to promote and revive employment relations as a field of study, Kaufman (2004b: 42–43, 49–50) accepts the limitations of Dunlop's systems theory but builds on its legacy to renew the tradition. For him, 'an integrative theory' is possible if the object of the study is defined, the outcomes and behaviours to be explained in the field are identified, and key explanatory components and processes are included in the theory.

In developing his modified systems model, Kaufman retains Dunlop's industrial relations system as the overall organising framework for his analysis but argues that specific features of this model need revising and developing further. He calls his model '*the employment relations system*', rather the industrial relations system, and he starts by identifying the object of study in the field as the employment relationship. In his view, this formal legal relationship is one way of operating the labour process, in contradistinction to slavery or indentured labour. He defines the employment relationship as the contractual relations created between an employer and employee. The employee agrees to be paid money by providing a labour service to an employer in the labour market for some period of time, while following the employer's orders and rules regarding job performance. For Kaufman, the employment relationship is the fundamental construct that underlies the field of study.

The outcomes and behaviours to be explained in the field, or the dependent variables, depend on the level of analysis. Broadly stated, 'the dependent variables in employment relations are all the endogenously determined institutions, structures, outcomes, practices and behaviors that emanate from or on impinge upon the employment relationship' (Kaufman 2004b: 69). At the highest level, the dependent variable is the existence and extent of the employment relationship. At the next level, the dependent variable is the institutional structure and configuration of the employment relationship. At the next level, the dependent variables are the form, operation and performance of individual institutions 'and functional areas in the employment relations system'. Finally, at the lowest level of analysis, there are the individual, personal and organisational outcomes and behaviours emanating from the employment relationship such as job satisfaction, productivity, and compensation and benefits.

Within any nation state, Kaufman (2004b: 56–57) identifies a number of key explanatory components and processes, or independent variables, in an employment relations system. For example, there is the profit-driven or revenue-driven firm or organisation that sells its outputs in the product market and buys its labour in the labour market, with its hierarchy of power, management and organisational structures. There are also a variety of institutions external to the firm that help shape and impact on employment relations within it, including employer, employee, governmental and non-governmental organisations – what Kaufman calls the 'Collective Actors'. Other influences and forces from the external environment impacting on employment relationships include culture, class, ethics, ideology and history, as well as the law covering property rights, labour rights and market structures. These are embodied in statutes, court decisions and other legal regulations enforced by the state authorities. Science and technology open up new processes and innovation in the world of work. Finally, political leaders of the nation state decide how an employment relation system is structured, organised and operated. All these forces create a complex array of formal and informal constraints, or a web of rules, that shape and guide individual and collective action. 'These rules may also be thought of as a *governance structure*' which defines 'the rights, duties, liberties, and resources of the parties in an employment relation' (Kaufman 2004b: 61).

Taking account of critiques and limitations of Dunlop's systems theory and Kaufman's thinking about 'employment relations systems', a modified systems model provides three main benefits in studying employment relations. It puts the network of rules, decisions, contexts and processes of employment relations at the centre of theoretical and practical analyses. It identifies and categorises the basic components which obtain within any employment relations system. It defines a set of analytical categories and provides a heuristic framework for studying national, international and comparative employment relations. A broad systems framework, in short, drawing on Kaufman's contribution to the debate, provides a constructive means, if not a universally agreed one, for structuring an introductory text on employment relations in their global, comparative and theoretical contexts.

CONCLUSION, IMPLICATIONS AND CONTENT OF THE BOOK

To summarise the debate so far, the central aim of this book is to enable its readers to understand and evaluate the changing faces of contemporary employment relations, taking account of their complexities, ambiguities and historical path-dependencies in different countries and geographical regions over time. It does this by drawing upon global, comparative and theoretical perspectives within a modified systems framework. For some, this would appear a cautious and unadventurous approach but it provides helpful points of reference for postgraduate students, new to the subject, seeking to explore similarities and differences in employment relations phenomena on a comparative basis. Using a modified systems framework, this text consists of this introductory chapter and 11 further chapters divided into four parts. Figure 1.7 demonstrates how these four parts are inter-related. Readers can either use the text in chronological order or proceed directly to Parts 2 and 3 of the book, if they do not wish to examine the theoretical and conceptual backgrounds to the subject.

The literature upon which this text is based is a wide one; some scholars will agree with its selection but others, with different frames of reference, might question some of it. This literature is described, analysed, synthesised and reviewed. It draws largely upon English-language books, articles and international and comparative data-sets in mainstream employment relations. The justification for the literature selected is that it incorporates the various academic faces of employment relations (such as economics, politics, sociology and law); its different theoretical faces (such as pluralist, managerial and political economy ones); its range of methodological faces (case studies, national and international surveys and ethnographic studies); its contrasting institutional and cultural faces; its contemporary and historical faces; and the subject's classical, orthodox and critical faces (such as institutionalism, HRM, labour process and radical perspectives). But certain themes persist

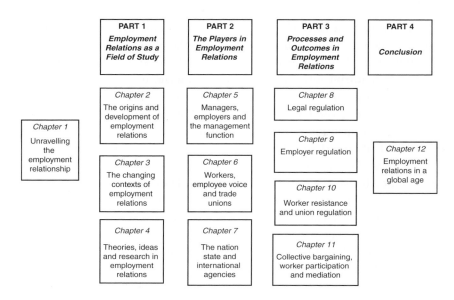

Figure 1.7 Structure of the book

throughout this book. These include: the central place of work and employment in the economics and politics of modern and modernising societies; the perennial problem of managers having to convert labour time into usable labour power and the resultant indeterminate nature of the employment relationship; the crucial importance of citizens finding means for 'earning a living' in capitalist market economies; the contested issue of how work and the employment relationship are controlled; the key role of the state in mediating the employment relationship; and ultimately the civilising impact of 'good' employment relations to those involved in them and the societies where they live.

All this makes the subject matter of employment relations a demanding one for students. This requires them to focus on the text attentively, reflect on it critically, and evaluate the subject matter as they 'unravel' the complexity of relations at work between employers and workers. This introductory chapter explores the nature of the employment relationship, defines employment relations and explains why work and employment relationships are an important field of study. It sets the scene for the rest of the book by examining and reviewing the impact of globalisation and economic liberalism (the neo-liberal settlement) on national economic policies and employment relations, and the rationale for adopting a comparative perspective of the field. It makes the case for using a modified systems theory as a heuristic device for studying the players, processes and outcomes of employment relations.

Part 1 consists of three chapters and considers employment relations as a field of academic inquiry. Chapter 2 examines the origins and development of the study of employment relations starting with the industrial revolutions in eighteenth-century United States and Britain. It debates the 'the social question', the 'labour problem' and maintaining social order in these emerging capitalist market economies, where capital (the financial and material assets or resources contributing to the production process) was owned by propertied individuals and shareholders in private businesses. A major problem was finding ways of improving capital–labour relations and facilitating industrial co-operation between 'masters' and 'men' [*sic*]. The chapter goes on to identify and explore seven core intellectual traditions or theoretical faces in employment relations, which are examined more extensively later in the book. These are the 'legal', 'managerial control', 'human resources management', 'union as a loyal opposition', 'institutional', 'class conflict and revolutionary' and 'labour process' traditions of employment relations.

Chapter 3 explores the major external contexts within which national employment relations systems operate. The chapter starts with an analysis and critical review of the varieties of capitalism debate, where the central question addressed is how different types of capitalism are linked to different employment relations institutions. Other issues include the crucial relationships between capital markets, product markets and employment relations, where it is argued the primacy of product markets largely determines the outcomes of pay decisions between employers and workers. The nature of labour markets and labour market institutions are also analysed and examined. The importance of state policy and its role in employment relations are then reviewed and the impacts of technology and broader social forces on employment relationships considered.

Chapter 4 focuses on theories, ideas and research in employment relations. Analyses and critical reviews are made of the main theories, disciplinary insights and ideas that seek to interpret and describe employment relations institutions, processes and outcomes. These include economic theories explaining labour market behaviour, wage determination and unemployment. Then, drawing on sociological and psychological studies, some theories of management and organisations and their implications for employment relations are discussed. These include scientific management, human relations theory, theories of post-bureaucracy and Japanese management theory. This leads into discussions on institutional theories of employment relations and theories of change. The chapter concludes by discussing ideology and frames of reference and how research in employment relations is conducted.

The three chapters in Part 2 identify and evaluate the key players or actors in employment relations. Chapter 5 reviews the roles of employers and managerial players in the employment relationship. This is followed by an examination of comparative theories of management. These theories draw on what are called 'universalistic' and 'particularistic' approaches to management, which show how both cultural and institutional influences affect management practices. This leads into a discussion of the contemporary human resources function in organisations, including a summary of regional differences in the dispersion of HRM practices in the United States, West Europe, Japan, and other parts of Asia. The chapter ends by outlining the nature of TNCs and how HRM is managed within them.

The focus in Chapter 6 is how workers participate with managers directly and indirectly in employment relations decisions and practices in workplaces. These include through employee voice, employee engagement, employee involvement and unions. The nature and purposes of voice, how voice is clustered, and the drivers and practices associated with employee engagement are all critically examined. The chapter then reviews various types of employee involvement, their aims and the forms they take. Some comparative data on union membership density are critically evaluated and the functions and external structures of national trade unions are analysed and reviewed. Three case studies of central trade union organisations in China, Sweden and the United States are discussed, as well as the role of the International Trade Union Confederation in union politics globally.

Chapter 7 examines the roles of nation states and international agencies in employment relations. This chapter shows the close relationship between the nation state and markets and the centrality of state influence on employment relations in capitalist market economies. Three 'ideal' types of state in terms of their economies and employment relations are considered: Anglo-Saxon laissez-faire states, West European social states, and developmental states in East Asia. After this, the responsibilities of the state as an employer of civil servants or public employees are discussed and reviewed. There is then an analysis of how the nation state shapes national economic and social protection or social security policies. This is followed by an examination of what some international and regional employers' associations do at supra-national level. The chapter concludes by reviewing the role of the ILO in advancing and promoting international labour standards and human rights in the workplace.

The focus of the four chapters in Part 3 is the processes and outcomes of employment relations. It begins with an examination and review of the legal regulation of employment relations in Chapter 8, which draws upon a social science and comparative labour law perspective. It discusses legal families, the origins of modern labour law, and different types of legal system. It goes on to examine the main features of national labour law, drawing examples from civil law and common law regimes. The focus then shifts to the subordinated place of labour within the employment relationship, as embodied in the contract of employment. It demonstrates how civil law and common law states took different pathways in the development of the employment relationship. It also shows that what is legally an employment relationship becomes more problematic, as developments in work organisation, the international division of labour and diversity of employment contracts grow. The chapter concludes by examining the scope of employment protection legislation in regulating the contract of employment and the role of the law in relation to trade unions and collective bargaining, especially the issue of 'freedom of association'.

In Chapter 9, the analysis returns to the managerial control and human resources management traditions of employment relations, rooted in unilateral employer regulation of the employment relationship. The chapter begins by examining continuity and change in work and organisations, building on the analysis provided in Chapter 5. It then moves on to discuss the nature and implications of psychological contracts between employers and employees. In market-driven organisations, managers attempt to regulate employment relationships by either 'hard' or 'soft' methods of job regulation. The hard approach is epitomised by non-union employer regulation; the soft approach draws upon the techniques and methods of contemporary HRM. Some cross-national comparisons are made of the respective roles of HR specialists, line managers and HR outsourcing. This is followed by an assessment of how workforces are managed with or without unions and management's role in employment relations. Debates about employers' associations, business performance and employment strategy and models of strategic HRM are also explored.

Chapter 10 explores and critically reviews the significance of worker resistance in organisations and the union as a loyal opposition in employment relations. Manifestations of what in managerial eyes are worker misbehaviour and dissent are explored and some theoretical perspectives on these phenomena discussed. The chapter then examines both the *external contexts* of trade union organisations and their *internal dynamics*. The former includes employer, economic, technological and legal forces; the latter union objectives, formation, strategy, internal structure and democracy, and bargaining power. Following this, some regional comparisons of trade unionism in Asia, Europe and the United States are summarised and reviewed. The chapter concludes by exploring organised industrial action by trade unions, particularly strikes and their causes. Some historical and contemporary comparisons of strike patterns are critically evaluated but no definitive explanations of the complexities of strike activity are identified.

Chapter 11 analyses and reviews the institutional tradition of employment relations. It starts by discussing collective bargaining as a method of joint regulation and some theories and concepts in this area, especially Chamberlain's and Kuhn's (1965) marketing, governmental and industrial relations concepts. The structure of collective bargaining is examined, where de-centralised collective bargaining at single-employer and/or enterprise levels is identified as the most common bargaining level in the world today. This is explained largely by product market and economic pressures on employers. Comparative analyses of collective bargaining coverage, extension mechanisms and co-ordination are provided, where large differences in collective bargaining indicators across OECD countries are observed. The chapter goes on to review worker representation at workplace level in Europe and concludes by examining the roles of conciliation, arbitration and workplace mediation in managing employment relations conflict.

In Part 4, there is a single chapter, which reflects on employment relations in a global and neo-liberal age. Chapter 12 examines some of the arguments set out in this text and considers major changes in the faces of employment relations in conditions of globalisation and neo-liberalism. Six key issues are discussed: why the contexts of employment relations matter; the increasing sophistication and diversity in HRM; the decline in scope and coverage of collective employment relationships; the resilience of institutions in some national systems of employment relations, paralleled by the growth of employee involvement and direct employee participation within workplaces; labour law, post-democracy and the democratic index; and change and continuity in the world of work and employment relationships. The book concludes by arguing that there is no single trajectory of contemporary employment relations globally, nationally or comparatively; only multiple, complex, contradictory ones.

EMPLOYMENT RELATIONS AS A FIELD OF STUDY

part 1

EMPLOYMENT RELATIONS AS A FIELD OF STUDY

2

THE ORIGINS AND DEVELOPMENT OF EMPLOYMENT RELATIONS

The purpose of this chapter is to explore why and how the study of employment relationships became a field of academic inquiry from the beginning of the twentieth century. It then goes on to identify and discuss seven core, intellectual traditions or major analytical faces within the field. The study of employment relations, called in its early days 'industrial relations', began in two English-speaking western countries, Britain and the United States. The scholars carrying out early empirical works in the field were Sidney and Beatrice Webb in Britain (1920a, 1920b) and John Commons in the United States (1919, 1921a, 1921b). The subject gestated as an area of study in the United States in the late 1910s but only really took off in the 1920s (Kaufman 2003). Employment relationships between employers and employees, or 'masters' and 'men', existed well before this time, with the growth of industrial market economies and the factory system in North America and parts of Europe in the nineteenth century. But they were not the subject of specific academic inquiry. The lives of the new working class during these times were generally dismal. Men, who made up the new industrial working class, were employed for long hours and low wages, worked in appalling conditions, had working lives commonly cut short by accidents or unsafe working arrangements, and lived with their families in crowded, poor-quality housing. Women commonly worked in domestic service, waiting on the growing middle class. Some workers, often skilled manual employees, formed and joined labour unions to negotiate wages, hours of work and conditions of employment with their employers, in an attempt to raise their incomes, job status and standards of living. These unions were often opposed by employers, so that strikes and industrial conflict were common features of working life at this time. Extensive periods of labour unemployment were also a normal feature of the new capitalist market economies (Casson 1983, Burnett 1994).

THE SOCIAL QUESTION, LABOUR PROBLEM AND SOCIAL ORDER

The origins of employment relations practices in capitalist enterprises lie in the rapid technological, economic, political and organisational revolutions that pervaded North America and Britain in the late-eighteenth century. These spread in the nineteenth century to other parts of West Europe, such as Belgium, France, Germany and Scandinavia. By the turn of the twentieth century, the capitalist market economies of the western world were based on large-scale manufacturing enterprises, sophisticated financial and banking systems, extensive national and international business transactions, and an interconnected global economy rooted in competing colonial or imperial systems (Di Vittorio 2006). The process of industrialisation, and the shift of people from country areas to towns, had resulted, like in Brazil, India and China today, in growing urban populations by migrations or natural increases, and in deepening class divisions between rich and poor. These cities commonly contained large numbers of poorly educated male workers and their families, who were employed in the new 'smoke stack' industries and firms created by the technological and capitalist revolutions. These included engineering, manufacturing, shipbuilding, coal mining, steel and iron, railways, printing and textiles. There was also a growing group of often single, young females working as domestic servants in the households of the rich and rising middle classes, while other women worked as clerks in the emerging civil services and new professions such as school teaching and nursing (Lockwood 1958, University of Chicago 1914, Abel-Smith 1960).

The employment relationship rooted in the law of contract underpinned these socio-economic-technical revolutions. Under feudalism in pre-industrial societies, there were no employment relations or employment relationships, just customary and commercial relations between landowners and peasants, merchants and households, traders and customers, and masters and domestic servants. There was also a variety of guilds or associations of merchants or craft workers in towns throughout Europe. These controlled the working practices of their members in trades or crafts and protected their common interests as merchandisers of goods and artisans (Weyrauch 1999). In the new capitalist, technologically driven economies, men and women worked for others, often in factories, under contracts of employment or contracts of 'service'. The capitalist, commercial and technological revolutions had resulted in an 'industrial relations' revolution that created modern labour markets and new labour market institutions such as trade unions and collective bargaining between employers and unions. The labour market had emerged in response to employer demand for labour and the willingness and need of workers to supply their labour market skills in return for wages and agreed conditions of employment from employers. The labour market mediated between demand for labour and its supply, by determining the 'wage price' of labour and how much would be employed by each employer following agreement of the 'wage–work' bargain with its workers. In the workplace, however, labour was subjected to the 'right to manage' and the authority of its owners. Employers justified this on the grounds not only of their ownership of the capital resources that financed the firms employing the workers but also of the risks associated with being capitalist entrepreneurs. Property rights, in short, had precedence over labour or social rights in the workplace.

A number of observers in the United States and Europe noted in mid-century the continuing economic and social tensions between the holders of capital (capitalists) and wage earners (labour). In 1848, Marx and Engels published the Communist manifesto, analysing the class struggle between capital and labour and the problems arising out of industrial capitalism (Marx and Engels 1970, 1973). A few years later in the United States, Greeley (1856), a journalist, wrote about the 'social problem' between the capitalist class and American wage earners. In England, Morrison (1854: 2), a wealthy businessman, wanted to help solve the 'great *social problem*' of relations between employers and 'the working majority of mankind [*sic*]'. In France, Germany and Japan, writers also commented on the 'social question' in discussions about the problems of labour, capital, wages and labour relations (Pilbeam 2013, Pankoke 1970). In English-speaking countries, the social question later evolved into the 'labour problem' or 'labour question'. In mainland Europe, however, the phrase 'social question' continued to be used well into the twentieth century. Indeed, Kaufman (2004b: 34) notes that this distinction between the labour problem in English-speaking countries and the social question in mainland Europe 'is of profound importance for understanding the divergent developments of the field of industrial relations' in these two regions. It helps explain, for example, the idea of 'labour movements', found predominantly in the English-speaking world, made up of organised labour and the groups supporting it, compared with the 'social partnership' approach to collaborative management–labour relations in mainland Europe.

The essential difference between these two approaches to the 'social problem' is that the social question was a much wider concept than the labour problem or labour question. In mainland West European countries at the end of the nineteenth and beginning of the twentieth centuries, the social question and labour problem were viewed as inescapably linked together. It was difficult to separate the two concepts. Indeed, the social question raised issues relating to the legitimacy and functionality of the existing social orders – economic, political and social. Within English-speaking countries, the labour problem or labour question was a much narrower concept, focusing solely on relations between employers and employees or capital and labour. This concept separated out the problems of relations between capital and labour from both wider social issues and the social order as a whole, by distinguishing labour policy reform from social policy reform. Labour policy and industrial relations were central to political debate in the English-speaking world during these years but only became part of mainland European debate following the end of the Second World War, when countries were reconstructing their social and political systems after Nazi occupation and military hostilities (James 2003). But, as the Royal Commission's final report on labour in Britain (1894: 5) states, it did not intend its review 'to survey what has been termed the "social question"'. Nor did it seek to 'undertake an examination of the fundamental causes of wealth and poverty'. Its intention, rather, was directed chiefly 'towards the amelioration of the relations of employers and employed'.

The key to understanding the nature of the labour problem, as perceived by the dominant political and social classes at the time, can be found in Morrison's (1854) pioneering work. Morrison was seeking to provide a policy framework for improving capital–labour relations and facilitating constructive co-operation between employers and workers. The issues raised by the labour problem contained four main elements: improving the welfare of workers; integrating labour into the political economy to ameliorate its exclusion; replacing conflict between capital and labour with trust and goodwill; and incorporating labour with capital in the social order, through improved co-operation and harmony between them (Kaufman 2004a). For Morrison (1854: 2), these multiple aims could be achieved by either reformist, constitutional methods, such as through trade union organisation and protective labour legislation, or by revolutionary methods aimed at replacing capitalism by socialism or communism. For him, 'numerous plans and theories of social improvement are put forth...from regulations for the management of a Trades Union to the extreme Communist doctrines'.

Between 1880 and 1914, when the First World War started in Europe, the labour problem did not recede from the politics agenda but was the main political issue threatening established social orders in North America and West Europe, especially in Britain, France and Germany. Episodic industrial conflict, increasing union membership, labour riots and social unrest in these countries, brought about by rising prices, unemployment, periodic economic recessions and poor working conditions, were continual challenges faced by governments and the political authorities. Social democratic, Labour and Communist political parties were formed in some countries and the traditional economic, social and political orders associated with laissez-faire capitalism were under increasing challenge by organised labour and its political supporters (Mommsen and Hirschfeld 1982). Immediately after the First World War, the labour problem came to a head; a problem inexorably linked with the growth of capitalism and the social injustices experienced by the working classes.

With revolution in Russia in 1917 and the need for post-war economic reconstruction, the War and its aftermath opened up opportunities for reforms of work and employment relationships in the Western world, especially in English-speaking countries. After more than 40 years of conflict, the labour problem was now recognised by governments and progressive employers as an important policy issue to be addressed and resolved by them. In retrospect, the formation of the International Labour Organization (ILO) on 11 April 1919, as an affiliated agency of the League of Nations, was an important event in the development of capital–labour relations round the world. It was an acceptance that the labour problem was to be superseded by recognition that universal and lasting peace could be accomplished, only if it was based on the principles of social justice and non-exploitation of labour in the industrialising countries of the time.

Given the diverse practical, academic and historical origins and faces of employment relations, as illustrated above, it is unsurprising that there are a number of intellectual traditions or analytical strands in the field. These are summarised in Figure 2.1 and each tradition, and its underpinning principles, is explored and reviewed in the remainder of this chapter. Five are 'mainstream' traditions. Those supporting them accept the nature of modern capitalism and the functions of employment relations within them, albeit from differing and competing viewpoints. These are the 'legal', 'managerial control', 'human resources management', 'union as a loyal opposition' and 'institutional' traditions. The 'revolutionary and class conflict' and 'labour process' traditions provide critical and contested perspectives of employment relationships.

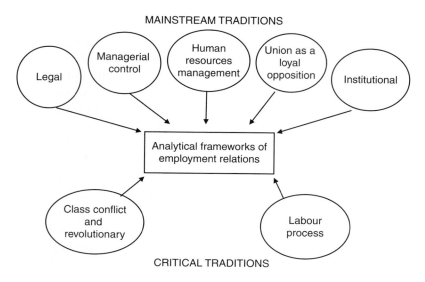

MAINSTREAM TRADITIONS

CRITICAL TRADITIONS

Figure 2.1 Intellectual traditions in employment relations

THE LEGAL TRADITION

The legal tradition of employment relations is concerned with how employment relationships, the parties to them, the institutions, and industrial conflict are regulated by law within nation states. The legal tradition of employment relations emerges early in the evolution of any national employment relations system and it underpins the behaviour of employers, workers, trade unions, government and third parties within it. The purpose of the law in employment relations in modern market economies is to establish an accepted, legitimate and known legal framework within which the parties to employment relations can operate and co-exist together. This enables them to know their legal rights, obligations and responsibilities, and the means for resolving any differences or conflicts between them. Historically, however, labour law or employment law has commonly been less supportive of the legal rights of workers in the workplace and of unions in the labour market, when organising their members, collective bargaining, and striking or imposing other forms of industrial action on employers, compared with property rights and the legal rights of employers (Wedderburn 1995, Harris 2007).

Even in some nation states and geographic regions today, and in the context of aggressive economic development programmes, the law is less supportive of worker and union rights, compared with those of employers and business corporations. In the Asia-Pacific region for example, such as in South Korea, there is an array of restrictions on worker's rights. Only one union is recognised in a company or industry; public servants and teachers cannot form their own unions; and strikes are prohibited in national or local government and designated defence industries. Other legal restrictions include: compulsory arbitration is invoked in labour disputes in public enterprises; government's labour agency is authorised to interfere in the internal affairs of trade unions; and political activities by trade unions are prohibited. Numerous workers have been arrested or dismissed because of these laws. The South Korean government continues to deploy the military services to control strikes. And industrial accidents affecting workers in South Korea are reportedly among some of the highest in the world (Byung-Sun 1997).

Labour laws in any society regulate individual market relations between employers and workers, collective relations between employers and unions and the welfare of workers in the workplace. This is a feature of all developed and developing market economies. As societies mature, governments at some point in their history have to establish a legal framework to regularise, develop and stabilise employment relationships within the boundaries of their states. However, as states develop in terms of complexity, size and levels of sophistication, so do their labour laws, whether in civil law or common law regimes. In civil law regimes, labour laws are set out in codified legislation covering all those aspects of employment relations that the state wishes to institutionalise and regulate. Examples of a basic, but hypothetical, set of codified legal rules, and areas typically covered, are provided in Figure 2.2 (Steiner 2010, Buckland 2010). These issues are also legally regulated in common law states but rarely codified. In common law regimes, labour laws develop incrementally through statute law, judge-made case law, and legal custom and practice.

In mainland Europe, the Roman law tradition is strongly rooted in legal practice and based on the legal system of ancient Rome. Under Roman law, the legal code was (and is) based on civil law or law enacted by governments. In Europe, civil law is particularly associated with France, Italy and Spain. In France, following the Revolution in 1789, the traditional but absolute authority of *le patron* over his workers, servants and apprentices was ended. After the French Revolution, the legal and social privileges of the aristocratic elite within the feudal social structure were removed forever. The ideals of the liberty, equality and autonomy of the individual were translated into the philosophy that freedom of contract was the only acceptable means of adjusting individual interests in a post-Feudal society, where equality of bargaining power underpinned all economic transactions, including the labour market. The new civil code envisaged workers and employees being linked with the *patronat* within a framework of contractual relations. By the late-twentieth

```
Preamble: The law on labour and labour relations

Chapter 1:  Definitions and general provisions
                    Employer
                    Worker
                    Firm
                    Employment contract
                    Work
                    Continuous service
                    Occupational injury
                    Labour Department
Chapter 2:  Employment of workers, including women and children
Chapter 3:  Employment contracts, records and wages
                    Individual employment contracts
                    Apprenticeship and vocational training contracts
                    Records and files
                    Wages including the minimum wage
Chapter 4:  Hours of work and holidays
                    Working hours
                    Statutory holidays
                    Statutory annual leave
                    Statutory sick leave
Chapter 5:  Workers' safety, health and protection
Chapter 6:  Disciplinary rules
Chapter 7:  Termination of employment and severance pay
Chapter 8:  Compensation for industrial injuries
Chapter 9:  Trade union recognition
Chapter 10: Trade union legal rights
Chapter 11: The legal rights of union members
Chapter 12: Collective labour disputes
Chapter 13: Labour inspections
Chapter 14: Penalties
Chapter 15: Concluding provisions
```

Figure 2.2 Examples of typical clauses in a basic civil code of labour law

century, however, the notion of the civil code was no longer tenable. Labour law in France was now focusing on the status of individuals in employment (Blanplan and Engels 1995).

In Germany, as in France, development of the law was strongly influenced by political ideas and national events, such as German unification in the late-nineteenth century. In Germany, legal scholars had argued at the time that the law for each country reflected its national 'spirit' and laws needed to be crafted to promote the national interest. German legal theory was used to develop a different legal regime from England's common law system in commercial and labour affairs. While English law was hostile to business cartels and ambivalent to union organisation and trade disputes, it nevertheless demonstrated over time willingness to provide some legal protections for unions as organisations, when engaged in strikes and other forms of industrial action against employers. This was done by providing unions with legal 'immunities', which prevented them from being sued by employers for damages, as a result of financial losses incurred during a trade dispute (Wedderburn 1986, Kahn-Freund 1977). In Germany, in contrast, the law was used to promote the 'national interest' by contributing to market stability and national industrial power. German law, therefore, was more lenient towards business cartels but even more repressive of trade unions than English law (Youngs 2007).

Common law traditions are typically found in the English-speaking world, as in North America, the United Kingdom, Ireland and Australasia. Common law is heavily based on custom, accepted practice and precedent. The latter is where a legal rule is established for the first time by a court for a particular type of case. The legal precedent is then used in deciding subsequent cases. The guiding principles of common law are rooted in property rights, freedom of contract and aversion to restraints of trade. For these reasons, common law has tended to reinforce individualism and economic laissez-faire. At the same time, common law states have traditionally challenged the legal rights of trade unions in the labour market and of workers in the workplace. So historically, laws protecting trade unions have often been overturned by the courts, on the grounds that unions acted in restraint of trade and were either criminal or civil conspiracies operating against the public interest. It is only in modern times that the protective common law duty of an employer to take care of employee health and safety, under the contract of employment, has been largely superseded by statutory protection. Other statutory rights give qualified employees some legal protections against 'bad' employers and 'unfair' employment or 'labor' practices, such as refusing to recognise trade unions for the purposes of collective bargaining or discriminating against union members in the employment relationship (Willey 2012, Buxton 1995).

Once established, national systems of employment law normally develop in ways rooted in their historical legacies and the limitations imposed on them by their historical path dependency, whether in common law, civil law or hybrid legal systems. Path dependency explains how institutions, social structures and patterns of behaviour in the present are influenced by what has happened in the past and continue to influence what happens in the present (Hathaway 2001). In most post-colonial states, for example, the legal systems inherited from their imperial rulers continued into their post-colonial periods, as in parts of Latin America, Asia and Africa (Mirow 2004). Thus where the Portuguese had been the imperial governing class, post-colonial states such as Brazil have adopted civil law systems based on Portuguese civil law. Similarly, in Chile, the legal system is based on civil law obtained from the former Spanish legal system. In earlier imperial colonies, such as India and other parts of the former British Empire, where the English were the governing class, the law is based mainly on English common law. In South Africa, where the English and Afrikaners competed for imperial hegemony, its system of law is based on a mixture of English common law, Dutch civil law and indigenous customary law (Chanock 2001). These legal systems impact differentially on the employment relations and labour laws in each of these countries, as they do in other states with similar legal histories and practices.

To understand fully the importance of the legal tradition of employment relations in most countries today, the fundamental legal principle underpinning labour law is the subordinate position 'labour' (or the employee) to that of 'capital' (or the employer) in the employment relationship. Thus a major feature of the employment relationship, in all legal jurisdictions around the world, each with its own legal tradition, is the hierarchical power of employers and their managerial agents over employees in the workplace and organisation. This hierarchical power has three inter-related elements. First, managers have the *directional* power to assign job tasks and give orders and directives to employees within their enterprises. Second, managers have the *control* power to monitor the performance of employees and their compliance with these orders and directives on behalf of the employer. Third, managers have the *disciplinary* power to sanction and respond the improper or negligent performance of these tasks and any disobedience to given orders and directives by employees, which can result ultimately in their dismissal (Casale 2011). As summarised by Kahn-Freund (1972: 9): 'there can be no employment relationship without a power to command and a duty to obey, that is without this element of subordination in which lawyers rightly see the hallmark of the "contract of employment"'.

THE MANAGERIAL CONTROL TRADITION

In the modern world, employers typically try to organise and control their workforces with a number of human resources (HR) objectives in mind. These include: to promote organisational efficiency, raise individual and corporate performance, increase labour productivity, maintain workforce discipline, engage workers in their jobs, protect workers from exploitation by bad employment practices, and minimise the possibilities of conflict within the workplace (Scullion and Morley 2004). There are a variety of means by which employers, through their managerial agents attempt to do this, although not always successfully. Normally it is much easier to manage a labour force in times of business expansion and economic growth than during periods of product market contraction and economic stagnation. And it is generally easier to manage small organisations rather than large ones. To achieve their business objectives, managers pursue three possible HR strategies. First, they can use their power and authority unilaterally to manage their employees. This is done in an authoritarian manner through 'hard' styles of management or a paternalist one using 'soft' styles of management. Second, they can gain the consent of their workforces by managing them through informal or formal consultation, negotiation and engagement, which may or may not involve trade unions in these processes. And third, they can use combinations of these approaches.

Origins of the managerial control tradition

In the managerial control tradition of employment relations, employees are managed directly, without intervention by trade unions. This can be traced back to the early days of emergent capitalism. In both the English-speaking world and beyond, this approach is underpinned by concepts such as the 'right to manage', 'managerial interests', 'managerial rights' or 'managerial prerogative'. As Hudson (1970: 9) comments in his study of railway workshop rules in the nineteenth-century England, armies and navies were always governed by strict rules, apprentices by indentures and domestic servants in large establishments by clearly laid-down patterns of instructions, all within a hierarchy of power and command. With the emergence of the capitalist factory system and industrialism, most works rules were imposed by employers unilaterally on their employees and discipline was commonly severe and administered harshly. The authoritarian approach to managing labour was typically dominant. Today with the growth in size of work units and organisations, as well as the necessity for states to prevent workers being exploited by powerful impersonal employers, 'good practice' employers not recognising unions for collective bargaining purposes continue to try controlling and managing their labour forces unilaterally. Management alone determines the terms, conditions and methods of working of employees in the workplace by asserting their right to manage, but normally taking account of what is humanly ethical, organisationally practicable and legally permissible. This management style is commonly paternalist and consensus building, but is informed by an underlying belief system based on the unilateral right to manage.

Managerial prerogative is the root concept in the managerial control tradition. It is particularly associated with managing employment relationships in the United States, the United Kingdom and other English-speaking countries, although it is not exclusively an Anglo-Saxon concept. A main reason why managerial prerogative and the right to manage are such central issues in the United States and the United Kingdom is because it is in these countries that the principles have been most seriously challenged by workers and trade unions, especially in the late-nineteenth century and first three-quarters of the twentieth century. In the Colorado Labor Wars in the United States in the 1900s, for example, the Colorado employers' movement actively defended the employers' right to manage their businesses without interference from organised labour, especially in mining, making managerial prerogative a key element in these disputes (Suggs 1991). Similarly, in the great employers' lock-out by British employers of members of the Amalgamated Society of Engineers in 1897, the immediate cause was the length of the working day. But 'the real issue was the limit of trade union interference with managerial decisions' (Clarke 1957: 128). Indeed, this dispute was considered at the time to be the 'the greatest struggle between Labour and Capital this country has ever seen'.

Managerial prerogative and the managerial control tradition relate to those areas of workplace and corporate decision-making which management considers its exclusive domain. These cover all decisions not subject to either collective bargaining with trade union representatives or legal regulation by the state. Such managerial 'rights' or 'interests' were traditionally taken to include the hiring and firing of employees, promotion, discipline, production control, allocation of overtime and other job-related issues. Marsh (1979: 186) argues that the notion of managerial prerogative 'carries with it the implication that there are actions or areas for action that are so essential to management that these must remain unilaterally the property of management if management itself is to continue to exist'. Marsh's list of possible managerial prerogatives is, of course, neither definitive nor exhaustive. It focuses only on labour management and does not include any strategic, financial or investment decisions which management takes. These fundamental functions of management are taken for granted as belonging to management alone within all market economies and capitalist free enterprise systems.

A robust defence of the managerial control tradition in the United States is provided by Torrence (1959: 1). For him, management prerogatives are about 'management's rights to decide what is to be done, when, where and by whom'. These include the right to move operations from one location to another, to determine hours of work and 'to take all other decisions which are normally and traditionally the sole responsibility of management'. Borrowing on ideas supporting the divine right of monarchy, another American company director wrote, in 1902, that the rights and interests of 'laboring men' will not be protected by labor union agitators 'but by the Christian men to whom God in his infinite wisdom has given control of the property interest of the country'. For him, it was the effective management of this property interest upon which 'so much depends' (Bakke *et al.* 1960: 187).

The managerial control tradition today

Although the scope and exercise of managerial prerogative and managerial control tradition varies widely across countries and within them, its supporters justify it, first, on grounds that the prerogative derives from the legal rights attached to the ownership of property within capitalist societies. It is managers as owners of property or agents of the owners, who must have control over these capital assets. Second, certainly in common law jurisdictions, the primary duty of company directors and managers is to prioritise the interests of shareholders over those of employees, customers and other stakeholders. In some civil law jurisdictions such as Germany, in contrast, laws relating to corporate governance put constraints on managerial freedoms but this is the exception rather than the rule (Mallin 2013). Third, the economic efficiency argument says managers should be left alone to carry out their professional tasks within enterprises, in the interests of all organisational stakeholders – shareholders, employees, consumers and society-at-large. This claim derives partly from management's technical expertise and specialist skills, including their education and training. As Storey (1983: 104) writes, 'A scalar chain of command is required to prevent separate departments sub-optimising at the expense of the whole.' Fourth, others support 'natural leaders' in organisations. Bendix (1956: 294) argues, in turn, all rulers 'develop some myth of their natural superiority'. Whatever their origins all arguments supporting managerial prerogative and the managerial control tradition arise out of the primacy of market rationality in capitalist business organisations.

Based on these observations, it is sometimes argued that the managerial control tradition is applied less assertively in mainland Europe, where the concept of partnership and joint decision-making in enterprises is more embedded than in Anglo-Saxon countries and other parts of the world. In Europe, it is claimed, there is only limited support for the idea that management can manage the employment relationship without sharing decision-making in some areas of human resources management and employment relations with workers and/or their unions. In practice, however, the principle of managerial prerogative is applied flexibly across these countries and within them. And it varies widely, except where it is specifically limited by collective agreement and national legislation. Thus in Finland, the legal right to issue instructions on the direction and supervision of work is vested in employers. It is the employer which, by giving orders to workers, is deemed to have authority to specify the content of the employment relationship and level of job performance. The employer's authority to regulate employment and performance is also linked with the duty of obedience. Thus the prerogative covers behaviours relating to the performance of work, such as what is done and how, where and when it is done. Provisions detailing the employer's right to determine how work is carried out, as well as the right to hire and fire, are laid down in Finnish collective agreements (Commission of the European Communities 1997a).

In Sweden, the employer's right to take unilateral decisions at work cannot be contested in the courts. The unilateral rights of employers belonging to the Association of Swedish Employers to hire and fire at will, and to direct and organise operations at work, as established by the 1906 December Compromise, are typical examples. They were subsequently upheld by the Labour Court as general principles of law and extended to all employers. However, the Employee Consultation and Participation in Working Life Act 1976 (the Co-determination Act) promotes employee participation in decision-making on employment and working conditions in the broadest sense in Swedish private and to a lesser degree public organisations. These rules, sanctioned by liability in damages, impose an obligation on the employer to take the initiative in negotiating with an established union before deciding on any major change to the business or to the employment and working conditions of union members (Commission of the European Communities 1997b).

THE HUMAN RESOURCES MANAGEMENT TRADITION

Following the industrial and technological revolutions of the eighteenth and nineteenth centuries, the management of labour in modern enterprises has been an endless managerial problem over time. Today this managerial activity, commonly involving to varying degrees both *line managers* and *HR specialists*, is described as 'personnel management', 'people management', 'human resources management' (in lower case and the plural), the 'management of human resources', 'the human resources management function' or the 'HR or personnel function of management'. Human Resource Management (HRM) – in upper case and the singular – has a specific meaning, as discussed below. In this text, the human resources management tradition of employment relations is used to encapsulate the wide variety of ways in which jobs and work are, and have been, organised by managers within enterprises around different technologies and production systems in different countries. This includes HRM as a particular type of human resources management. The human resources management tradition is how employers recruit, select, pay, reward, train, discipline, and protect the health and safety of employees and, where they exist, provide a range of 'employee voice' arrangements that enable workers to have some say in the ways in which their terms and conditions of employment are determined.

By middle of the twentieth century, each of the core economies of the United States, the United Kingdom, France, Germany and Japan exhibited distinctive systems of human resources management, particularly in large manufacturing firms and the public sectors. These reflected the market, technological, political, social and business contexts in which they operated, influenced strongly by their historical path dependencies where they had developed. But importantly there is no universal model of human resources management: 'employment systems differ noticeably between countries' and 'managing human resources has to vary from country to country' (Brewster *et al.* 2011: 12). Generally, less was or is known about SMEs and family firms, where HR practices vary widely (Landström 2010, Bannock 2005, Kapila and Mead 2002).

Today, as in the past, a firm's human resources can be managed unilaterally, drawing upon authoritarian or paternalist styles of management; in others, human resources management is more sophisticated and participative in its approach and uses HR specialists to lead a firm's labour force (Chandler and Hikino 1990, Gospel 2011, Noiriel 1990, Kochan 2009). Factors, other the organisation itself, such as sector and national culture, affect HR processes and how they are carried out in practice. These impact on the ways managers organise, conduct and manage work. Thus recruitment and selection, training and development, employment relations, reward, and performance appraisal are all affected by the cultural values of the country where they take place. Institutional differences among countries influence HR practices too. This means that HR policies and practices within nation states are both culturally sensitive and institutionally constrained, both now and historically. The HR function, then, is different from country to country and from organisation to organisation; there is no single way of defining or understanding its nature, scope and HR and organisational practices.

An historical perspective

Historically, a number of trends can be observed in the human resources management tradition. First, from the early-nineteenth century, industries such as textiles had both artisan and factory systems of management, whereas railways and heavy industry had more bureaucratic systems of 'personnel management' (see below), especially in the last years of the century. In the mid-twentieth century, union-based systems of human resources management existed in the large-firm sector. Indeed, this was the dominant HR paradigm or orthodoxy in many western countries. By the early-twenty-first century, however, growth of a more differentiated and flexible system of 'contemporary HRM' (see below) had emerged within both large manufacturing and service firms in many parts of the western world, especially in English-speaking countries. HRM had become a new academic and practitioner orthodoxy, based on experience of the HR function in the United States and had not been transmitted universally. Indeed, as Gospel (2009: 24–25) argues within this tradition, 'different stages have co-existed side-by-side and older industries have adapted to new developments. Overall, the tendency may be towards growing diversity [of human resources management] within firms and within countries'.

Second, shifts over time can be observed in human resources management practices. These changed from direct systems, to technical systems, to bureaucratic forms of working and employment. These changes involved movements from personal supervision, piecework payments and paternalism to scientific management, to internal labour markets and complex administrative hierarchies (Edwards 1979). More recently, there have been further reconfigurations of bureaucratic employment systems and internal labour markets, with backward and forward movements between direct control of work and more autonomy and responsibility on the job. In modern retailing and call centres, for example, direct supervision and computer control continue. Employee motivation based on mixes of coercive, remunerative and normative HR policies have always existed. But there 'is no linear movement in the management of human resources' (Gospel 2009: 25).

Third, in employment relations, historically most employers upheld their unilateral right to manage in authoritarian or paternalist ways. In the period after the Second World War, however, employers showed greater willingness to manage human resources collectively through collective agreements with trade unions, especially in manufacturing. But from the 1970s, the trend has been to substitute collective bargaining with new forms of joint consultation, employee voice and employee involvement such as teamwork and direct communication. These shifts have been greater in the United States, the United Kingdom and France, where union membership in the private sector is low, than in countries such as Germany (where union membership is also low but legal regulation of employment relations is robust) and Scandinavia in particular, where union membership remains high and much stronger (OECD 2012).

Fourth, firms can either internalise or externalise their production and HR decisions (Coase 1937). *Internalisation* means firms produce goods or services in-house, develop internal labour markets, provide job security and in-house training for their workers, fix wages and benefits by seniority, and promote employee voice by internal bargaining and consultative processes (Gospel 2011). *Externalisation* sub-contracts production, selection of workers from the external labour market, lay-offs when workers are not needed and the fixing of wages and benefits through outside bargaining with employers' associations, where unions are recognised. In practice, firms in different countries have followed mixes of internal and external strategies. In the nineteenth century, external strategies were common within a framework of paternalist employment policies. During the twentieth century, in contrast, the tendency was internalisation of work and employment relations, involving Fordist mass production techniques and internal labour markets in the United States, Canada and Japan. In Europe, however, considerable reliance was placed on externalising employment relations by sector-wide collective bargaining through employers' associations. By the early-twenty-first century, there has been some externalisation of production and labour services but greater internalisation of employment relations within firms (Hazama 1997, Jacoby 1997, Tolliday and Zeitlin 1986). Such changes in strategies were the results of the market and technological forces acting upon employers over time.

Human relations thinking

The human resources management tradition of employment relations like other traditions in the field originated in North America and West Europe. The tradition emerged out of a 'human relations' philosophy of managing employees, which some early historical case studies illustrate. Proto-examples of this are found in the beginning of the nineteenth century. Robert Owen, for example, a Welsh social reformer, transformed working life in the four textile factories he owned in New Lanark, a village in South Lanarkshire in Scotland. He drew upon progressive ideas about work and working which were at least 100 years ahead of their time. He abolished child labour and corporal punishment in his factories and local villagers were provided with decent homes, schools and evening classes, free health care, and affordable safe food. Owen deplored the bad working conditions of the factory system, arguing that improved working conditions and treating working people decently and humanely would pay for itself, through higher productivity and lower labour turnover (Morton 1962).

In France in the late nineteenth and early twentieth centuries, Léon Harmel, a French industrialist and reformer, promoted Catholic social teaching and Christian Democratic political movements by improving factory conditions and empowering workers in his model factory at *Val-des-Bois* in the Champagne-Ardenne region. His efforts at workplace reform demonstrated that mutual accord and respect were possible between management and labour and he turned his profitable spinning mill into a Christian corporation. His ethical business practices captured the attention of Pope Leo XIII and inspired the encyclical *Rerum Novarum*. The collaboration of Leo XIII and Léon Harmel laid the foundation of enterprises that became collectively known as the Movement of Christian Democracy. Harmel was a principled though by no means perfect advocate of social Catholicism but his ethical commitment to improving the lives of his workforce and other workers was unconditional and influential (Boileau 1998).

In another case, the wealthy John D. Rockefeller Jr., a principal stockholder of Standard Oil in the United States, hired William Lyon Mackenzie King, a Canadian politician and labour relations expert, to work for his philanthropic foundation as head of industrial research in 1914, where he remained for four years. Influenced by MacKenzie King, and following the violent strike and Ludlow massacre at a family-owned coal mine in Colorado, Rockefeller became a solid convert to and supporter of progressive labour management policies. Mackenzie King had argued that that capital and labour were natural allies, not implacable enemies, and that the community-at-large, represented by government, should be a third and decisive party in resolving industrial disputes (King 1918). Rockefeller concluded that managers needed to recognise the humanity of their workers who, in turn, needed to see that managers and investors were also human. In his view, this would help avoid bitterness between them. He had no sympathy for those who argued that the interests of capital and labour were separate and dissociated. With the world's wealth constantly being developed and distributed, he argued that both capital and labour were indispensible to creating wealth. If industrial production increases and conflict between capital and labour is removed, industrial co-operation between them enhances material progress and social well-being (Rockefeller 1923).

Personnel management

What was called 'personnel management' within the human resources management tradition derived out of human relations thinking. The first effective attempts by some businesses to manage labour professionally, systematically and with some enlightenment were during the First World War and immediately after, in both Britain and the United States. This was done using specialist techniques of labour management, which drew upon elementary social science knowledge. In Britain, the First World War 1914–1918 compelled British factory owners to make rapid and systematic progress in managing their workforces efficiently and effectively. Without this, there would have been labour shortages, low productivity, industrial conflict and lost output. There was an economic stimulus to modernise plants, standardise products and conform to product specifications in factories tied to government contracts. Such developments promoted more enlightened employment policies and supportive employment practices in workplaces. A small group of progressive-thinking managers moved on from the human relations phase of enlightened management practices to specialising in the 'personnel management function'. The personnel policies used by these firms included formalised recruitment and selection processes, incentive payment schemes, motivation techniques, and employee welfare provisions. Moxon (1946: 3) later described personnel management as 'the function of management primarily concerned with what is commonly called the human factor'. In the United Kingdom, the specialist workers employed for these purposes were initially known as 'welfare workers', subsequently called 'labour managers' and later still 'personnel managers'. In the United States, the United Kingdom, Ireland, Australia and New Zealand today, where the specialist personnel/HR function is deep-rooted, they are called 'HR professionals' and the term 'personnel management' has become largely redundant (Brewster and Mayrhofer 2012).

A parallel 'personnel management school' emerged in the United States, during the 1920s. This was only one of a number of disparate schools of American management thought at the time. The group of individuals supporting this approach was also relatively small in number, including Rockefeller, and who were seen as 'industrial liberals'. They were opposed by more conservative groups of employers and the labour unions, both of which wanted more control of work and work processes for themselves or for those whom they represented. The personnel management school of thought was that employer labour policy had to contribute to the firm's competitive advantage and profitability. If it did not, firms would be unable to survive long term. Known as the 'welfare capitalism' model, it incorporated four basic elements: personnel management, employee welfare benefits, human relations, and employee representation (Balderston 1935).

The personnel management school of thought in the United States metamorphosed into different professional configurations over the next six decades. By building up a body of theory, professional knowledge and good practices, promoters of welfare capitalism embraced a variety of personnel work and activities and developed successive waves of enlightened HR practices, with the aim of fostering higher output, reducing costs and protecting managerial autonomy from outside influences such as labour unions (Bernstein 1960). The overall strategy had a number of common elements, similar to those practised in the United Kingdom. They included scientific recruitment and selection, job evaluation, a range of employee welfare benefits (including pensions and employment security), employee voice, mechanisms for conflict resolution, support for human relations practices in the workplace, and specialised personnel staff responsible for supervising labour policy (Jacoby 1997).

The personnel management stream of the human resources management tradition reached its apogee in some western countries during the 1960s and 1970s. A vital function of the personnel theories and practices advanced at the time was to ensure the optimal efficiency of workers in business and public organisations, using proven personnel practices at minimal cost, implemented through accountability and delegation of authority to line managers (Osterman 1983). Yet the history of personnel management as a distinctive managerial science in the United States, the United Kingdom and elsewhere is not divorced from the political and social trends of the last century. Successive waves of 'model employer' personnel management practices in government, for example, heavily influenced ministries and departments and had implications for the private sector, which frequently followed these trends. This was particularly in the early days of personnel management and employee welfare programmes. The Great Depression, Roosevelt's New Deal in the United States, the Second World War and the post-war settlements in West Europe, in turn, all influenced development of the professional personnel management function over the following decades in the United States, parts of West Europe and some post-colonial regimes in Africa and Asia.

Contemporary HRM

Contemporary Human Resource Management – HRM in upper case and the singular – is the latest stage in the evolutionary journey of the human resources management tradition into new forms and trajectories of performance-based management in a global age. This is particularly the case in the Anglophone world but in other countries too. HRM, at its most sophisticated and in terms of its techniques and practices, is the most creative form of human resources management practised within the large corporate sector and is still evolving. HRM originated in the United States in the 1980s in response to product market competition and globalisation. It then spread to firms in some other nation states, especially through TNCs. As Gennard and Kelly (1997) observe, the scope and delivery of any organisation's HR's policies and practices, and the role of the personnel/HR function in developing and implementing them, have always been flexible. Indeed, the HR function, which involves both HR professionals *and* line managers delivering it, has adjusted its dominant values and practices historically and nationally, in responses to changes in the macro-environment.

What distinguishes the contemporary HRM paradigm from others is the argument it is a 'universalist' model of HR, rooted in shareholder capitalism, and is applicable everywhere. Indeed, one claim some people make for the universalist model is its applicability to all organisations, in all countries, in all circumstances. But scholars such as Brewster *et al.* (2011: 12, 74) contest this: 'Whereas, in many countries, some commentators look for universal issues [in HR], others are more concerned about understanding their local contingencies.' These commentators are more critical of contemporary HRM and argue that HR decision-makers have to take account of a number of organisational stakeholders, not just shareholders, whose interests do not always overlap. This is 'contextual HRM' or 'comparative HRM'. Contextual studies of HRM explore the importance of 'culture, ownership structures, labour markets, the role of the state and trade union organisation as aspects of the subject rather than as external influences on it'.

Torrington and his colleagues (2011) identify six main periods or themes in the history of personnel management and its transition into contemporary HRM in the United Kingdom. These are: 'social justice' (late nineteenth and early twentieth centuries); 'humane bureaucracy' (1920s till 1940s); 'negotiated consent' (1940s till 1960s); 'organisation' (1960s till 1970s); 'HRM' (1980s till 1990s); and 'a new HR' (since the 2000s). The 'new HR' is driven by employer demands for competitive advantage, characterised by a 'new trajectory' of HR in response to long-term trends in the business environment. These include global forces, market competition and multi-employer networks. This latest theme in the history of personnel management seems to reflect a shift away from the 'management of jobs' by organisations to the 'management of people' within them (Lepak and Snell 2007). Increasingly, in the modern world, the capabilities and knowledge incorporated in an organisation's human resources are deemed to be key to business performance. 'So on both the cost and benefit sides of the [human] equation, HRM is crucial to the survival, performance and success on the enterprise' (Brewster *et al.* 2011: 8).

In its ideal form, HRM is claimed to have three key features, but there is no single HRM model. Thus what are described and conceptualised as 'best-practice' HR, 'best-fit' HR and the 'resource-based view of the firm' are but only three of the main theories underpinning contemporary HRM strategies and practices (Farnham 2010a); see chapter 9 below). Reviews of the literature reveal that one feature of HRM is its strategic focus. Further, to be effective, it is argued that HR strategy needs to be aligned both *vertically* with an organisation's corporate strategy – however difficult to do in practice – and *horizontally* by integrating HR practices across an organisation. Senior HR people commonly play a role in strategy implementation, involving them working in partnership with top managers in developing, delivering and evaluating performance-driven business and HR strategies. Second, in employment relations, contemporary HRM typically supports coincidence of interests of all organisational stakeholders, including employees, de-emphasises conflict in the workplace, and adopts a unitary theory of the employment relationship (see chapter 4). Third, HRM is largely integrated into line management activities, in the belief that to be effective a partnership between line managers and HR professionals is both necessary and instrumental in delivering performance-driven HR practices (Boxall and Purcell 2011).

The modern HRM paradigm is not limited to the United States, the United Kingdom and other Anglophone countries. In a review of 17 studies on the external validity of strategic HRM theories, a number of regional clusters were noted. Six clusters were found: South Asia (India and Thailand), Confucian Asia (China, Hong Kong, South Korea, Singapore, Taiwan), Latin Europe (Spain, Belgium), Germanic Europe (the Netherlands), Eastern Europe (Russia) and the Anglo-Saxon cluster (New Zealand and Australia) (House *et al.* 2004). These commentators conclude that while the number of studies conducted in a single country is low, 'the empirical evidence that has accumulated on a regional cluster level is considerable; thus enabling generalizability inferences for strategic HRM models' (Colakoglu *et al.* 2010: 42) (Figure 2.3).

The essential distinctions between the 'new' HRM and 'old' traditional personnel management paradigms are summarised in Figure 2.3, where these are compared with the contextual HRM paradigm. In practice, of course, some organisations draw on elements of both traditional personnel management and contemporary HRM. In these cases, HRM activities are viewed as being strategic and linked with line management's HR roles, whereas personnel management is seen as being administrative and handled extensively by personnel specialists. The contextual HRM paradigm, in contrast, searches for an overall understanding of what is contextually unique in HRM and why, in each case.

The personnel management paradigm	The HRM paradigm	The contextual HRM paradigm
Driven by employer needs to treat people fairly in organisations	Driven by employer needs for competitive advantage in the market place at firm level	Driven by factors such as the role of the state, legislation, unions and patterns of corporate ownership that impact on HRM at national level
Operates in stable market conditions	Operates within competitive markets and a change agenda	Operates within regulated market conditions
A traditional approach to managing people, with a strong administrative purpose	A distinctive approach to managing people, with a strong strategic purpose	A comparative approach is used to understand the factors influencing HR decisions within firms
Short term, with an *ad hoc* perspective	Longer term, with a strategic perspective	A contingent perspective
Incorporates a pluralist frame of reference to organisations and people management	Incorporates a unitary frame of reference to organisations and people management	Incorporates a pluralist frame of reference to organisation and people management
Involves negotiation with trade unions where they are recognised	Involves managing employees individually rather than collectively	Involves managing employees contingently
Delivered, monitored and policed by personnel specialists	Delivered by HR professionals in collaboration with line managers	Delivered in line with national circumstances

Figure 2.3 The essential distinctions between the personnel management, HRM and contextual HRM paradigms

THE UNION AS A LOYAL OPPOSITION TRADITION

Trade unions independent of employers and the state are typically products of market capitalism; they do not exist in pre-industrial societies. But non-independent trade unions existed in the Soviet Union and exist in the People's Republic of China today (Ruble 1981, Pringle 2011). The union as a loyal opposition tradition in employment relations contrasts starkly with the managerial control tradition. If the latter is concerned with protecting the unilateral use of managerial power and authority within organisations, the former provides resistance, challenges and countervailing power to managerial hierarchies within workplaces in the interests of the members the union represents. But unions do not wish to replace the management function in organisations; hence the term 'loyal opposition'. Unions are able to assert their opposition to management decisions in three main ways: by market means (through collective bargaining and worker representation), by political means (through the law, lobbying and involvement in national and international politics), and by revolutionary means (through union militancy) usually at times of intense political conflict and instability. On May Day 2012, for example, it was reported that around the world millions of labour activists had held marches and rallies in protest against rising unemployment and economic austerity plans by their national governments (Devereaux 2012). What unions have in common is the underpinning functions they claim as essential to their operation as organisations representing the interests of workers, contrasted with the prerogatives or functions of management. Sometimes expressed as union 'rights', these include freedom of association, freedom to organise, the right to consultation and negotiation with employers, the right to strike, the right to work and the right to take action against employers resisting union rights (Goodrich 1920). These union functions are promoted by different types of unionism.

Business unionism

Job control unions are a prototypical model of trade unionism and a product of a business union philosophy. This was the dominant model of trade unionism in the United States immediately after the Second World War. It was also the dominant model in early-nineteenth-century Britain, where unions were created a generation before the formation of a British Labour Party that sought to advance working class interests through the ballot box. Business unions work within the framework of free enterprise systems, without challenging the existing economic and social orders, and try to keep the job interests of their members separate from their political ones. They are particularly associated with relatively skilled workers occupying a distinct labour market niche. For Hoxie (1917), business unions are market conscious rather than class-conscious and are economically not politically driven. Business unions aim to get 'more' for their members in the labour market such as higher wages, shorter hours of work, and better working conditions through union job control. They accept market capitalism, the wage system and property rights as inevitable. They are also committed to the binding force of contract in the employment relationship and regard the union primarily as a bargaining agent with management on behalf of its members, using the institutions of collective bargaining and grievance procedures to do this (Goldfield 1987). Hoxie believes that American business unions, with their focus on job-related issues, have displayed greater maturity and realism in their activities than their more politicised mainland European counterparts, where Labour or social democratic political parties were commonly formed before trade unions were created (Upchurch *et al.* 2009).

Worker empowerment unionism

The shift from national product markets to global ones results in different models of management–union and management–employee relations, with the result that traditional job control unionism is in decline today. Budd (2004: 138) describes empowerment unionism as an alternative to job control unionism, where the union, 'rather than negotiating restrictive job control provisions that determine outcomes', negotiates framework procedures in which workers are empowered to determine their own outcomes. Unlike job control unionism, worker empowerment unionism is an active organising model of business unionism in the workplace, rather than a passive servicing one, driven by union members rather than union officers. It rejects the bureaucratic tradition of industrial pluralism, replacing it with an empowered vision of workplace pluralism (Rubenstein and Kochan 2000). Within it, collective bargaining does not determine all works rules or employment outcomes, only some of them. Instead, it provides processes enabling individual workers to be empowered by having minimum standards of compensation and procedural safeguards against bad management practices.

Commonly found in the United States, two variants of this model exist: the *empowerment* variant and the *self-representation* variant (Budd 2004). In the first variant, individual employees are empowered to make employment decisions within a framework established by collective bargaining. Unions provide support and protection for employees who have substantial day-to-day discretion and autonomy at work, unlike in job control unionism. The second variant enables employees to represent themselves in negotiations or dispute resolution on terms and conditions, within a framework established by collective bargaining. Unions provide minimum standards and protection for employees, who are actively involved in their own representation. Both variants are compatible with flexible working, employee involvement, labour mobility and the declining attractiveness of the servicing model of union representation (Troy 1999).

Social unionism

Another alternative to business unionism is social unionism, which is commonly found in the United States and Europe. It replaces job-control collective bargaining with broader social and political agendas, involving active grassroots participation by union members in its processes. By concentrating on the social arena, social unionism is a form of worker representation with a wider focus than that of the workplace. It has two main variants: *social movement unionism* and *European social partnerships*. The first variant is an active organising model of trade unionism driven by union members. It embraces unions as part of a broader social movement of community, social and political activist groups that rely on active grassroots participation and mobilisation. Social movement unionism is a reaction against the passive servicing model of job control unionism, driven by union officers. Where it operates in the United States, social movement unionism is advocated as a means for increasing union organisation among excluded workers such as immigrant groups (Tillman and Cummings 1999).

The French labour movement is a prime example of social movement unionism. Strongly opposing business unionism, the multiplicity of French trade union federations, representing communist, socialist, catholic, anti-communist and anti-class based movements, has political or ideological agendas, in a country where workplace unionism is weak and fragmented (Daley 1999, Goetschy 1998). Rejection of job control unionism in favour of wider social and political interests is typical of many European unions and labour movements. These vary from social democratic models to radical oppositional unions seeking to reform or replace market capitalism with a new social order (Hyman 2001, Slomp 1998; see below). Hyman (2001: 55) defines social democratic unionism as 'a synthesis between pragmatic collective bargaining and a politics of state-directed social reform and economic management'. In the social movement union model, collective bargaining, organising, political action, and alliances with other advocacy groups are used in pursuit of social justice and a broadly defined 'social wage'. This commonly includes 'free' health care and education, child care and maternity allowances, family social benefits and state pensions, funded by taxation and social insurance payments as is the case in several west European states (Godard 2011).

The second variant is peak-level European social partnerships within nation states; but this is not to be conflated with European social partners *at EU level*. The European social partnership variant is typically a passive servicing model of trade unionism driven by union officers, although it is an elusive and slippery concept to define (Fernie and Metcalf 2005). Basically, social partnership is a 'bargained corporatist' arrangement where peak-level representatives of business, labour and government try to achieve a consensus on a national framework for determining economic and social developments nationally (Crouch 1979). Where social partnership agreements contain wage and pay guidelines, there are normally arrangements for centralised collective bargaining, as in Ireland in the 1980s and 1990s (Gunnigle *et al.* 1999).

Political unionism

Webb and Webb (1920b) identify a number of union 'regulations', such as the standard rate, normal day, sanitation and safety, and new processes and machinery, and three 'methods' for protecting their members' living standards and conditions of work. Such regulations are settled 'by some Common Rule' applicable to the bodies of workers covered by them. The three methods used by unions to enforce their regulations are mutual insurance, collective bargaining and legal enactment. Mutual insurance provides friendly and out of work benefits from the union; collective bargaining establishes joint agreements with employers on terms and conditions of employment; and legal enactment results in laws imposing regulations universally applicable to all firms in a sector. Each Act of Parliament corresponds 'to "a National [collective] Agreement made between a Trade Union including every man [*sic*] in a trade, and an Employers' Association from which no firm stands aloof"' (Farnham 2008: 541). The Webbs thought it inevitable that growing participation of wage earners in political life, and the rising influence of unions, would increase 'use of the Method of Legal Enactment' to enforce the common rules of the trade (Webb and Webb 1897: 256).

The political functions of trade unions vary widely. In parts of the world such as in Asia, the scope of the union political function is proscribed by law. In China, for example, the All-China Federation of Unions is the sole national trade union federation, with some 190 million members, and creation of competing unions is illegal (International Centre for Trade Union

Rights 2005). In North America, business unionism does not reject political action altogether but, when undertaking it, uses pressure-group politics on behalf of the 'labor' it represents. This is an interest-oriented approach to politics rather than one directed towards causes, as in some politicised unions in West Europe, North Europe and Australia, where there are close links between unions and social democratic labour parties. There is nothing stopping individual unions lobbying for their own political goals and interests, but there is greater strength in their unity and solidarity by acting together collectively.

The means used by free independent unions to achieve their economic and political goals, such as freedom to organise and bargain collectively, are influencing government, direct political action and various international activities, but only where the law permits this. However, across Latin America, for example, employers use a variety of activities to repress union activity. Thus workers in the informal sector face major obstacles to union rights, including lack of legal frameworks to organise. In Africa, the right to strike is commonly very restricted and strikes have been violently suppressed in Algeria, Mauritania, South Africa, Swaziland and Zambia. Trade union rights are also poorly respected in the Middle-East, where labour laws in Iran, Saudi Arabia and the United Arab Emirates prevent the establishment of genuinely independent trade unions. And in Asia-Pacific, organising unions remains difficult in many countries. In Myanmar and North Korea, for example, unions are not allowed to operate; in Fiji, unions have been repressed and their leaders intimidated or arrested; and in India, Japan and South Korea, public service workers have no right to strike (International Centre for Trade Union Rights 2012).

Thus where it is legal to do so, influencing government requires unions exerting strong pressure on national governments. This involves lobbying to enact legislation that strengthens collective bargaining or fill in gaps not covered by it. An example is initiating legislation providing a legal right to collective bargaining, as in the United States and the United Kingdom. Political action to promote labour interests is done either within national labour movements, such as in Scandinavia and the United Kingdom or in the EU by 'European social partnership' arrangements. European social partners are those organisations at EU level engaged in the European social dialogue set out in the Treaty on the Functioning of the European Union (European Commission 2008).

THE INSTITUTIONAL TRADITION

This tradition focuses on the social institutions created in societies involving 'patterns of human interaction and relationships that persist and reproduce themselves . . . independently of the identity of the biological individuals performing within them' (Crouch 2005: 10). The institutional tradition of employment relations was first analysed in studies of the trade union function in Britain and what the Webbs called 'Industrial Democracy' at the end of the nineteenth century (Webb and Webb 1897, 1920a, 1920b). Theirs was a detailed historical, empirical and theoretical evaluation of British trade unionism at that time. They provided a heterodox analysis of trade unions, which challenged the economic orthodoxy of classical and neo-classical economics. A few years later, in the United States, Commons (1919, 1921a, 1921b) wrote a series of books on 'industrial goodwill', trade unionism and labour problems, and industrial governance. These two sets of distinguished and distinctive works mark the beginning of the institutional tradition of employment relations.

The emergence of the institutional tradition of employment relations (or what by this time was called 'industrial relations') was a reaction to both the market liberal, laissez-faire approach of the English classical and neo-classical economists to the labour problem and the revolutionary pathway predicted by Marx (Hyman 1975, Marx and Engels 1973). The former argued that free markets, including labour markets, best served individual welfare by promoting personal freedoms and maximising production. The Marxian prescription was that the wider historical task of the working class was abolition of the capitalist economic system, and its exploitative employment relationships, replacing it with a new economic and social order based on socialist principles. For Marx, labour was not a commodity, labour power could not be separated from the persons supplying it, the employment relationship was inherently adversarial, only labour created economic value, and the wage system was inhumane and unjust. Those supporting the institutional tradition, in contrast, argued that labour markets are not perfectly competitive and that institutions have to be created to replace individual bargaining between employer and employee. In this way, labour would not be a commodity and employment relations would take place in democratic communities, organisations and the wider society, where workers have dignity and human rights.

Webb and Webb (1897) refuted critiques by classical economists of the trade union function in the market economy, by drawing upon the ideas of the German school of historical economists, and they managed to incorporate organised labour into the mainstream of economic and political thought for the first time. In reaction to the English classical school, who promoted individualism, acquisitiveness, commercialism and a limited state, the German historical economists were attracted to ideas of organisation, collectivism, romanticism and a strong state. They were sceptical of the classical model of 'economic man' and emphasised the role of institutions in determining economic relationships and the shaping of economic behaviour. They also saw social institutions as the basic frameworks within which individual behaviour developed (Herbst 1965). Refining these ideas, Webb and Webb put forward their major theoretical proposition of the agency model of trade unions, which in their view would play a major role in promoting an advanced system of industrial and political democracy in Britain. In their analysis, trade unions were not a form of labour monopoly but bargaining agencies whose role was to protect workers collectively in their individual relations with employers. By using union bargaining power to determine the wages of all the workers in a labour market, workers were able to offset their weak bargaining power with employers individually. Where there was no collective bargaining, protective labour laws were necessary to safeguard the interests of workers.

Towards the end of the First World War, the British government set up a Committee of Relations between Employers and Employed, commonly known as the 'Whitley Committee', to promote 'industrial reconstruction' which was a euphemism for industrial relations. Influenced by both what had happened in British employment relations at the time and the Webbs' analysis of trade unionism and collective bargaining, the Committee recommended that any improvement in relations between employers and employees should be founded upon more than a cash basis. It wanted workpeople to have greater opportunity of participating in the discussion about, and adjustment of, those parts of industry which most affected them (Ministry of Reconstruction 1918). The form of participation recommended was sector-wide collective bargaining, organised through joint industrial councils made up of equal numbers of employer and union representatives (Farnham 1978).

Commons (1919, 1921a, 1921b) expressed a number of normative propositions upon which ethical 'industrial relations' should be based. Underpinning his idea that a capitalist market economy should be preserved, and capital, labour and the public were all stakeholders in the economic system, was a series of moral principles. He believed that social justice should be an explicit goal of industrial relations policy. This meant that labour should not be treated like a commodity; workers should not be seen solely as a means towards an end but as an end in themselves; and, in the employment relationship, human rights should have precedence over property rights. Further, while the right of managers to manage and to direct the enterprise was legitimate, Commons believed that co-operation between capital and labour should be promoted and, as far as possible, the causes of industrial conflict could be removed or at least resolved. In a just system of industrial relations, workers should have the right to join or not to join a trade union and to collective representation in the workplace. This meant that workers should have opportunities for employee voice or representation and due process in the workplace, through trade union organisation and collective bargaining. Finally, government should set minimum standards for terms and conditions of employment, as well as providing security of person and the livelihood of workers. This included the right to work and freedom from arbitrary dismissal. Government's role was to establish fair 'rules of the game'. If the Webbs provided the intellectual case against individual wage bargaining, as defended by the English classical economists, and justifying the role of the unions in the process, Commons provided the elements of an institutional framework for studying industrial relations and the employment relationship, which he and other institutional writers would build upon (Kaufman 2004a).

As the study of employment relations institutions and practices has deepened in terms of subject matter and broadened in terms of geographical coverage, so new institutions have been created and new countries have come within its ambit. The concepts of 'works committees' and 'co-determination', for example, are now part of the institutional tradition of employment relations internationally. These not only have different functions from collective bargaining but also are commonly found in non-English speaking, civil law countries especially in Europe. Voluntary workplace committees in the United Kingdom, more usually described as 'works committees', are the exceptions. The patterns, functions and membership of works committees have varied enormously over time. Their powers and activities have partly reflected the strength of the unions, or lack of it, in the workplace at different historical junctures. Unlike works councils in Europe which are sometimes established by law, works committees are voluntary bodies with no legal basis at all. Although far less common today than in the 1960s and 1970s, works committees are a variety of bodies dealing with employment issues at workplace level. Some have union members only (such as shop steward committees); others are joint committees of workers and managers; and others consist of union representatives and managers. They are set up for a various purposes from welfare and social activities to collective bargaining, consultation, information and grievance handling (Beynon *et al.* 2002).

Co-determination is a structure of decision-making within enterprises, where employees and their representatives exert influence on management decisions, often at a senior level and at a relatively early stage in policy formulation. Co-determination may operate in parallel to, and complement, other employee representation mechanisms, such as collective bargaining. But it does not substitute them; they often operate in parallel. Co-determination is especially rooted in the employment relations traditions of a number of

EU member states. For example, in Germany there are two distinct levels of co-determination: at establishment level through the works council and at enterprise level on the supervisory board of some companies. In Denmark too, employees have the right to elect a third of members of the company board and, through this mechanism, to exercise a powerful voice in votes on matters that can have a major impact on the workforce (Marsden 1978).

A works council is a formal workplace committee consisting of elected employees representing all members of the workforce, except senior executives, in dealings with management on workplace issues. In Germany, works councils have a long history and were created immediately after the First World War to replace unofficial union structures, similar to shop steward committees in Britain, which were challenging official union policies and leaders at the time. National laws commonly support works councils, whatever their specific descriptions or functions, as in France, Germany, Spain and Sweden. Works councils are institutionalised systems of employee voice, sometimes linked with trade union organisation. In other cases, they are assisted by unions but are independent of them. Sometimes they are made up of non-union members. The list of countries operating works councils with employee representatives is extensive. But precise arrangements vary by country including their rights and responsibilities, membership and composition, and whether they are statutory or voluntary bodies. In Austria, Germany, Luxembourg and the Netherlands, for example, works councils are created by legislation and involve elections of representatives by all employees. In Belgium, France, Portugal and Spain, works councils operate in parallel with local union committees (Jenkins and Blyton 2008).

THE CLASS CONFLICT AND REVOLUTIONARY TRADITION

The 'class conflict' and 'revolutionary' tradition of employment relations emerged in late-nineteenth-century Europe and North America and is commonly linked with militant unionism. For example, the Independent Self-governing Labour Union 'Solidarity', led by the shipyard worker Lech Wałęsa, which undertook civil resistance against Communist governments in Warsaw during the 1980s, was a major player in the collapse of the Communist regime in Poland at this time (MacShane 1981). Paradoxically, Solidarity was a revolutionary union that brought about the collapse of a Communist state, not a capitalist one. But with the demise of Communism and expansion of powerful TNCs, the days of large-scale revolutionary unionism and the revolutionary impetus have weakened. However, in 2010–2012, mass union protests and some violence took place in Athens in response to the Euro-zone financial crisis and the effects it was having on the Greek economy and living standards of the Greek population (Thomson-Reuters 2011). A tradition of revolutionary trade unionism is also evident in parts of India and Latin America (Hensman 2011, Dunkerley 1984).

The class conflict or revolutionary tradition is particularly associated with periods of economic and political tension. It incorporates forms of union organisation as vehicles of collective protest and revolutionary opposition to hard market capitalism or political autocracy. A variety of groups and theorists has supported this tradition; all with the objective of promoting different models of the state, transformed by radical political change. From this, new forms of industrial organisation benefiting organised labour and the working class could be established. The ideas underpinning class conflict analyses are based on variations of social democracy, socialism, anarchism, syndicalism and communism. If there are any common themes in variants of this model, they are industrial militancy, worker solidarity, workers' control and workers' self-government of industry, an international perspective of the class struggle, and replacing an oppressive capitalist system by a more socially-just political economy organised in the interests of the working class. Hyman (2001: 2) summarises the position: 'The mission of trade unionism, in this configuration, was to advance class interests.'

Beyond these basic themes, there is wide diversity in the programmes and preferred courses of action by advocates of class conflict. Justification is based upon theories of Marxism, anarcho-syndicalism, workers' control, and radical socialism; each with strong opposition to the oppressive nature of the capitalist state. Opponents of market capitalism have always argued that any changes in the political economy of capitalism can only be brought about by a fundamental re-structuring of the state, re-formulated on socialist principles. Unsurprisingly, these revolutionary programmes for social change have been robustly opposed by the capitalist classes, political leaders representing them, some leading trade unionists and some social democrats who wanted reform, not revolution (Ridley 1970, Darlington 2008).

The origins of these debates can be traced to the controversies between the anarchist Bakunin and the 'scientific socialist' Marx in the second half of the nineteenth century about the means to achieve socialism, democratisation of the state and industrial democracy in the workplace (Duclos 1974). Both Bakunin and Marx provided analytical templates to promote socialist societies, which they believed would be free from class domination and human oppression. They thought that women and men would accept socialism, if means could be found to remove the barriers for attaining it. For Bakunin, any state was as much a barrier to socialism as was capitalism. He did not accept that the classless society could be achieved as long as the state existed. For him, destruction of the state was a necessary condition for establishing socialism. For Marx, the barrier to socialism was the class structure of society preserved by the state, which, in turn, was controlled by the capitalist ruling class. His prescription for creating a proletarian workers' state was to destroy it through revolution and prevent the return of the capitalists, until that danger was removed and the state withered away. His prescription and of fellow Marxists was creation of a political party, the Communist party, which would become the instrument for emancipating the working class. Unions had no role to play in this strategy for revolution and were not part of classical Marxist analyses (Miliband 1973).

The link between Bakunin's view and the doctrine of workers' control was the trade union. He and his supporters believed that the coercive capitalist state could be replaced by voluntary organisations, such as trade unions, which humankind was forming at that time. But it was not until the early-twentieth century, especially between 1910 and 1920, that ideas of revolutionary unionism spread rapidly, particularly in the United States and Europe, and as far afield as Australia and Norway. Hardly any industrialised country escaped its influence and powerful movements adopted this tradition in countries such as Spain, where industrialisation had not yet taken place (Shorter and Tilly 1974, Wigham 1982, Day *et al.* 2010, Haimson and Tilly 2002). The reasons were both economic and political. In the years immediately preceding the First World War, unemployment was high, wages were being squeezed by hard-pressed employers whose profits were falling, union militancy grew in intensity, and demands for further political reforms were being made by Labour and progressive political parties around the western world.

In the United States, the Industrial Workers of the World (IWW) or 'Wobblies' began to challenge the conservative policies of the American Federation of Labor, which represented skilled job-conscious trade unionists in the years before the First World War. Indeed, the IWW enjoyed a brief period of power before the end of the War (Foner 1997). In France, for some years prior to the War, its weak trade union movement was dominated by syndicalists. Their aim was to create a system of industrial government where workers organised in unions controlled the means of production. In Scotland, union shop stewards in engineering factories and shipyards challenged the official unions' wartime policy of co-operation with government (Ridley 1970). But revolutionary unionism was a libertarian movement, with no uniformity of ideas from country to country. In the Wobblies, union power was centralised; in French unions, power was concentrated in local units with wide autonomy, based on federal principles; and in Britain, shop stewards were organised locally, with variations in authority structures. What united these disparate groups of trade unionists was the conviction of the women and men in them that they could take over the industries where they were worked and run them for themselves by systems of self-government. In Clegg's words (1960: 50): 'They would be free, not slaves to their boss and their weekly wage.'

These drives for worker emancipation through revolutionary unionism did not long survive the aftermath of the First World War, with increasing unemployment, high inflation and economic depression. Economic depression in the United States during the early 1920s ended the Wobblies. In France, syndicalism never recovered from the decision of the French unions to support the government at the outbreak of war with Imperial Germany, the Austro-Hungarian Empire and Ottoman Empire in 1914. In the United Kingdom, the shop steward movement withered away. This was partly in response to post-war economic conditions and partly to actions by the political authorities which imprisoned some of the unofficial union leaders or deported them. Direct action by workers and direct workplace democracy had failed to achieve the objectives of those supporting workers' self-government at the time.

If the course of revolutionary unionism was running out of steam, new proposals for socialising certain industries came from a few mainstream unions and socialist intellectuals, such as Cole and his model of workers' control through Guild Socialism in Britain during the 1920s (Cole 1972). The British mineworkers wanted to nationalise the coal mines and the railway unions the railways. But the counter-argument was if the state and workers had stakes in industry, so too had consumers. Any compromises on the principles underlying the purposes of revolutionary unionism created difficulties for advocates of workers' control.

In the end, even Guild Socialism failed to take root in Britain, just as other schemes for workers' control had failed elsewhere. The reasons are complex. But briefly, many revolutionary union groups, including anarchists, socialists, syndicalists, shop stewards and others, were absorbed into the Communist parties in their own countries, following the Bolshevik Revolution in Imperial Russia in October 1917. Second, with rising unemployment, declining wages and falling prices, western countries after the First World War were unlikely to adopt radical political changes promoting union power or control. Conservative administrations became the norm in many states. In 1926, the General Strike in Britain collapsed and failed to achieve the objectives its leaders had set for it. Third, the rise of Fascism in Europe and civil war in Spain provoked political parties of the left and 'fellow travelling' union leaders to focus on international political events, rather than domestic issues.

Lastly, revolutionary unionism was not a single, united movement but a fragmented, disparate one. This enabled political leaders of the right to challenge it within their own countries and strongly oppose it by their policies and propaganda. Also many advocates of revolutionary unionism failed to see that working-class self-government and workers' control of industry were not possible in practice. Industrial self-government by the working class, in short, was not compatible with the structures of the large-scale modern industries of the time.

THE LABOUR PROCESS TRADITION

The labour process exists in all societies. In capitalist market economies, it is how labour resources are used in combination with raw materials, financial capital and physical capital to produce goods and services to be sold in the marketplace for profit. Labour is paid a wage for its contribution to the production process, with the owners of capital wanting to secure as much added-value as possible (surplus value) over and above what they are paying the factor inputs in the production process, including wages. Those owning capital (the capitalist class) or managing it (the managerial class) call it 'efficiency'; its critics (radical theorists) call it 'exploitation'. This is the starting point for understanding the labour process tradition and how it developed. The labour process tradition thus presents fundamental insights into the nature of the modern employment relationship from organisational and structural perspectives.

The labour and monopoly capital debate

The framework for the labour process tradition derives from Marx's and Engels's (1970) analysis of the capitalist production and labour process, later updated and revitalised by Braverman (1974), Edwards (1979), Burawoy (1979), Burrell and Morgan (1998) and others. Its starting point is that all societies have labour processes but, under capitalism, the labour process has specific characteristics. First, there is the centrality of the labour process and the way that labour is organised in the workplace. This provides a continuous source of contestation or struggle for control between capital and labour within organisations. Second, there is the 'de-skilling imperative', which results in the job skills deployed by workers being constantly changed and renewed by management, often with adverse consequences for the workers themselves. Third, there is the 'control imperative', where management typically seeks to secure and extend control over the labour process to its own advantage.

As Edwards (1979) notes, there are three elements in any system of managerial control: the specification of work tasks, assessing performance, and using rewards and discipline to gain worker co-operation and compliance. Fourth, relations between capital and labour within the workplace are typically characterised by the imperative of 'structured antagonism' between them. These structural interests do not determine the actions of the parties, since both sets of actors have some autonomy in their relationship. However, attempts at managerial control commonly generate conflict within the workforce, where a wide range of responses is possible. These include accommodation, compliance, consent and worker resistance (see chapter 10).

The key issue in the labour process tradition is what Marx and Engels (1970, 1974) describe as the transformation of labour power into 'labour'. It is only when the capital class employs or buys labour that labour has the potential or capacity to work. To maintain profitable enterprises, the capitalist class organises the conditions under which labour is employed. In response, workers seek higher pay, job security and more satisfying work through their countervailing power of informal job control, restriction of output and other devices of worker and workgroup control. For management, control of the work process is central to its business objectives. Because firms face tight competitive and market pressures, managers have to control the conditions under which work takes place. Control provides a means by which managements can transform the capacity to work into profitable production within the enterprise. As Berkeley Thomas (1993: 61) argues: 'In the capitalist system, the principal function of management is to exploit labour power to the maximum to secure profits for the owners of capital.'

Braverman (1974) reworks Marx's analysis of capitalist production in his book *Labor and Monopoly Capital*. This study provoked a series of radical critiques in organisational studies by Clegg and Dunkerley (1980), Salaman (1979), Storey (1983) and Burawoy (1979). Harry Braverman was an industrial worker for most of his working life in the United States, during the height of Fordist labour management and production techniques in manufacturing, inspired by Frederick Winslow Taylor in the early-twentieth century (Doray 1988). Braverman examines his own experiences through a Marxist perspective, drawing attention to the processes of work that were largely ignored by Marxists for much of the twentieth century. His studies coincided with 'autonomist' Marxist theory in Italy, which paid similar attention to the factory floor. Basically, labour process theory, as articulated by Braverman, examines how people work, who controls their work, their job skills, and how they are paid. Braverman's basic thesis is that under capitalism, management 'steals' the skills of workers, reduces the pleasurable nature of work, and removes the power that workers have of controlling their skills, while cutting their wages by reducing them to those of unskilled workers. Management also increases the amount of exertion required from workers to do their jobs.

The labour process perspective on the ordering of work suggests that managerial action is chiefly motivated by capital–labour relations and by employer strategies seeking to control and stabilise labour as the 'wild' element in the factors of production. Labour behaviour is indeterminate since, when a worker is hired, the employer only buys 'a capacity to work'. The persons hired must be managed effectively to optimise their economic contribution to the production process. Management must control or manage this capacity, since control is the rationale for management's existence. But management operates as a separate category of authority representing the global function of capital; otherwise it would just be another category of labour to be hired like any other skilled workers. Labour process analysis thus reinforces the inequality arising from market relations in the labour market to capital–labour relations in the workplace. It suggests the dynamic of this unequal social relationship limits, conditions and drives the structuring of work.

Following radical worker and student protests in the late 1960s and early 1970s, interest in Marxist studies developed, stimulated by Braverman's book. He was important because he used Marx's works to shift attention away from the regulation, crisis and collapse of capitalism at the systemic level towards more micro-patterns of structural conflict within the workplace itself. Thus Braverman led the way to more sustained theoretical examinations of Marx's discussion of the capitalist labour process, developed subsequently by French, British and United States economists, historians and sociologists.

Some general features of work and the organisation of work build on this analysis: the need for employers to exercise control over labour; the constant pressures on employers to lower labour costs; and how division of labour is structured around these objectives in terms of job design, labour specialisation and internal hierarchies. Thompson and McHugh (2009) set out five consequences of this for organisations. First, organisations can only be understood within a theory of capital accumulation and labour processes, taking account of the political economy of relationships to institutional environments at regional, national and international level. Second, organisations are structures of 'control' over productive activity seeking to maximise their 'surplus value'. Third, large-scale organisations are strategic units acting as mechanisms integrating economic, political, administrative and ideological structures. Fourth, organisational structures and processes, such as control systems, reward strategies and job design, involve political decisions and strategic choices. Fifth, organisations do not embody any single universality.

They comprise 'contested rationalities' arising from the partly antagonistic relations of capital to labour. Consequently, organisational change reflects the subsequent 'dialectic of control and resistance'.

Some critiques of Braverman

Braverman's message of 'work degradation' fits some societies better than others. Even in states with intrinsic craft apprenticeship systems, and an abundance of skilled labour, such as in German-speaking countries, there was confirmation in part of Braverman's thesis of 'skill polarisation'. Other studies reveal managers in firms committed to rationalising work through skill substitution and skill upgrading (Altmann *et al.* 1992). Nevertheless, lack of general fit between the degradation of work thesis and particular societies reveals an important limitation of Braverman's thesis – the linking of capitalism to a universal division of labour. This is more properly correlated with particular institutions such as a country's occupational and training systems. More generally, Braverman undervalues the way the labour process is embedded within specific socio-cultural contexts, since these incorporate different ways of institutionalising work and the employment relationship. However, he was writing at a time of the unquestioned hegemony of US capitalism. It is not surprising that Braverman fails to give sufficient attention to identifying and comparing the different ways that the labour process is managed cross-nationally.

Themes taken up in the post-Braverman debate on the labour process include the continuing variety among capitalist societies in their formal systems of skill acquisition. There is some questioning of Braverman's understanding of skill, such as underestimation of 'tacit' skills in skills development, which provide workers with power of resistance or non-compliance to counter-control the demands of management. Skills can also be tied to the gender of workers or in the form of 'emotional labour'. These are ways of looking, feeling or servicing capital in particular ways, which are not necessarily part of a formalised training structure. Hochschild (1983) develops labour process analysis indirectly, by focusing on the negative consequences for the mental health of workers and the sense of self in servicing employers in ways which compromise their identity as individuals. Braverman anticipates much of this development in his discussion of the shift towards mass service industries. Here household and other activities become subject to disciplinary and rationalising pressures of scientific management, involving the subjection of the identity of the worker to prescribed ways of acting and performing.

Another criticism relates to Braverman's treatment of scientific management and Taylorism, as if they were the final word in managerial theories of organisation. Debates on the nature of work since then begin with the rise of the Japanese economy on an international scale, together with powerful continental European economies, such as that of Germany. These deal in post-Taylorist concepts such as 'flexible specialisation', 'innovation mediated production' or 'lean production', where new skill structures are forged. Ideologically, these ideas suggest a break from 'deskilling', although empirical evidence of this remains less convincing (Thompson 1989). More recently the ideas of 'creative industries' or the 'knowledge economy' are suggested as a paradigmatic break from old organised capitalism (Thompson *et al.* 2000).

CONCLUSION AND IMPLICATIONS

This chapter demonstrates the importance of different historical and intellectual faces in employment relations. The intellectual foundations of industrial relations in the United States were established by Commons (1909, 1919) and Wisconsin School in the United Sates (Kaufman 2003). But in Britain, following the investigations of Sidney and Beatrice Webb (Webb and Webb 1920a, 1920b), and the country's economic difficulties after the Great War 1914–1918, further study of employment relations was delayed until the 1930s (Mowat 1955). This was when the first endowed professorial chairs in industrial relations were established at the Universities of Cambridge and Leeds and University College Cardiff in 1930. But by the early-twenty-first century, the study of what is now described as employment relations had spread well beyond the boundaries of western states and around the world into most market economies.

This chapter also traces the main ideas underpinning the nature of the employment relationship and shows its centrality in the economics and politics of contemporary capitalist market economies. These long-established historical roots of the field can be traced back to late-eighteenth and early-nineteenth-century North America and West Europe and now extend far beyond these narrow geographical boundaries around the world. These roots illustrate the commonly controversial and contested nature of the employment relationship and employment relations over time. Conflict occurs where goodwill between employers and unions or managers and workers break down over labour market, managerial or wider political decisions. In the history of employment relations, the balance of power between the major parties to employment relations constantly changes. At times, sustained and bitter industrial action by trade unionists against employers or the political authorities has appeared to threaten the established social order in different parts of the world, such as in early- and mid-twentieth-century North America and Europe (Cole 1913, Dunlop and Galenson 1978, Haimson and Tilly 1989, Day *et al.* 2010). Similar militancy took place in various regions in 2011–2012, where many hard-fought disputes were recorded in North America, Europe, Australia, Latin America, Africa, Asia and the Middle East – but on a fragmented basis. These were largely in response to the profound economic, political and social changes affecting working people in various countries at the time, following the credit crisis post-2007 and political unrest in the Middle East (Brookings Institution 2014).

The implication is that employment relations often take on a strong political dimension, when militant trade unions or workers collectively challenge the economic or political status quo. This normally happens where the jobs, employment interests or legal rights of union members and working people are threatened. However, what often seem to some employers, the mass media and opponents of the trade union function to be 'political' strikes by trade unionists are, in practice, economic strikes by workers against perceived socio-economic injustices between employers and employees in the workplace and wider society. Nevertheless, there is often a fine line to be drawn between the so-called economic and political dimensions of employment relations. Both the micro- and macro-political aspects of employment relations demonstrate their often contested nature. Indeed, areas of potential conflict are often near the surface in many day-to-day employer–worker relationships, and between unions and the political authorities, and need careful handling by the players involved.

This chapter also shows that the employment relationship is a complex politico-economic phenomenon, with contested views of its function, how it should be organised and what balance of power needs to be achieved among the players within modern political economies. From classical economic and traditional business perspectives, employment relations are a private matter between employer and employee in the labour market. As such, they are perceived to be unproblematic. This position is underpinned by the dominant belief that the prime purpose of private businesses in the Anglo-Saxon world at least is to make profits, through sales of their goods or services to customers or clients willing to buy them. In return for wages, hired labour contributes to the production function of organisations but is subject to the employer's legal and managerial authority within the workplace.

In other parts of the world – mainland Europe, Central and East Europe, Asia-Pacific, Africa, India and Brazil – patterns of corporate governance and accountability diverge from the Anglo-Saxon model. South Africa, for example, has nominally the most comprehensive corporate governance code in the world. This pays significant attention 'to integrated sustainability reporting, including stakeholder relations, ethical practices, and social and transformation issues'. Of particular importance is whether a company operates within a 'shareholder framework' focusing on shareholder value, or 'whether it takes a broader stakeholder approach, emphasizing the interests of diverse groups such as employees, providers of credit, suppliers, customers, and the local community' (Mallin 2006: 260, 11).

As noted, a number of intellectual traditions or faces of employment relations have been explored in this chapter. The legal tradition of employment relations, for example, interprets the employment relationship strictly in terms of the legal obligations and duties of the parties under the contract of employment, where labour has a subordinate position. However, from a managerial perspective, the wage–work bargain between employer and employee can be managed unilaterally. This is typical of the management control tradition of employment relations, where employers simply exert their managerial authority and legitimacy in the workplace over workers, because of their legal and property rights to do so.

Employers adopting the human resources management tradition use pre-personnel management methods, classical personnel management techniques or more sophisticated contemporary HRM thinking in dealings with their workers. But some revert to unilateral managerial control where they can. The aim of the human resources management tradition is to manage employees in enlightened, effective, and efficient ways to avoid conflict in the workplace. However, both the traditional personnel management and contemporary HRM approaches to managing people can be used to resist or bypass union involvement in managing the employment relationship. But within both paradigms some employers recognise labour unions through either recognition or partnership agreements (Walton 1985). Contextual HRM challenges the 'one-best' way approach to people management and analyses HR practices in terms of their institutional and cultural settings.

Where an employer recognises a union for collective bargaining purposes, the nature of the employment relationship fundamentally changes, because management has to share some HR decision-making authority with labour representatives. The institutional tradition of employment relations explicitly accepts the legitimacy of the trade union function in managing the employment relationship. It also recognises that employment is not only an *economic and market* relationship but also a *social and political* one. By sharing power with the union, management hopes to retain some control of decisions affecting the employment relationship; by negotiating with management, the union recognises management's right to manage but has some influence on those decisions most affecting their members' employment interests and daily working lives. The state also gains by the stability engendered in the employment relationship and reduction in potential conflicts between the parties through the institutional mechanisms of collective bargaining or other forms of worker representation.

The union as a loyal tradition of employment relations is subsumed within the trade union function. By acting as a 'loyal opposition' to management, unions behave solely in terms of what it is possible to achieve for their members. As bargaining agents, unions continually find ways to challenge the right to manage and protect the labour market and job interests of their members, without actually replacing management. The external focus of unions is typically the labour market, how they can regulate it to their members' advantage, and how they can influence those other decisions most affecting their members' working lives. Job-conscious business unionism alone is not enough to do this. If unions are to promote their members' job interests, collective bargaining is a necessary condition for achieving this but not a sufficient one. Political action by each union, or by national unions acting collectively, or even internationally, is also required. Through political action, unions are able to extend their control of terms and conditions in the workplace, as well as achieving those workplace benefits and job protections that collective bargaining alone cannot provide. Political action also extends non-wage benefits outside the workplace to union and non-union members. These are not determined within the job control arena but outside it. These include payments by the state when workers are unemployed, sick or retired. Thus in democratic countries, unions *have* to move into the political arena to achieve these benefits; this again makes the union function a contentious one to its industrial and political opponents.

The heydays of class conflict and revolutionary trade unionism in employment relations, through international trade union militancy, appear to be long-passed. The reasons are complicated. First, global business corporations are much more powerful than working people or their unions in the contemporary world. Global capital is inherently mobile and is moved to those locations which least threaten the highest financial returns on it. Unions find it very difficult to respond to these trends effectively and are weakly organised to do so internationally. Second, governments are stronger, more organised and have greater power resources than trade unions today. Any large-scale industrial action with political objectives is generally violently and strongly resisted by the political authorities in most countries. France and some European Mediterranean states are possible exceptions to this, where the 'right to protest' is strongly entrenched in their political cultures.

Third, with the demise of Marxism and Marxist ideology, there is no unifying set of ideas among union leaders and their members that might guide a revolutionary role or pathway for trade unions in global politics. Nor are union leaders likely to want to follow this road to perdition; they are themselves professional workers commonly with a job-conscious orientation to trade unionism, not a radical one. Fourth, labour globally is fissiparous, divided and typically organised by occupation, sector or industry within nation states. Fifth, unions globally are struggling to retain and recruit members and retain collective bargaining arrangements with employers and other representative systems, where these exist. Revolutionary trade unionism is not part of this agenda. But fierce academic and political debates about the nature of work within the labour process tradition continue.

3

THE CHANGING CONTEXTS OF EMPLOYMENT RELATIONS

The purpose of this chapter is to outline and critically review the main contextual faces of employment relations and their implications for the players, processes and outcomes in the field. Employment relationships are most commonly created and regulated at the level of the firm between individual employers and their employees, within the boundaries of the nation states where they operate. This is the case in TNCs, such as Toyota Industries (Japan), Bayer Pharmaceuticals (Germany) and PepsiCo (United States) and the thousands of other TNCs, which organise employment locally in the countries where they are located. TNCs do this in accordance with their global HR policies, national laws and the social customs of each country where they operate (Edwards and Rees 2011). Employment and terms and conditions are determined in a similar manner at organisational level or sometimes sub-organisation level in many large national firms, small and medium size enterprises (SMEs), and in the voluntary or third sector. In public services, these decisions are more likely to be determined at national or sector level (Peters and Pierre 2008). All organisations operate within the distinctive institutional and cultural frameworks of the countries where they are based, such as their market, political and social environments. Dunlop (1958) describes these as the 'contexts' of an 'industrial relations system'. For Kaufman (2004b), these are 'independent variables' that impact on national employment relations systems.

VARIETIES OF CAPITALISM

The importance of the varieties of capitalism debate for employment relations is there is no single model of capitalism but different types of capitalist political economy and that each one is linked to distinctive patterns of employment relationships. The debate started when scholars began examining the effects of international forces, such as globalisation, European integration and regional free trade areas like the North American Free Trade Agreement (NAFTA) or the Association of South-Asian Nations (ASEAN), and shifting macro-economic policies on the socio-economic structures of advanced political economies in the 1990s. One set of arguments is these trends have led capitalist economies to become more alike in their institutional make-ups and are converging, so that they can compete successfully in the global marketplace. It is also claimed that the de-regulating neo-liberal model of political economy is replacing the more co-ordinated and socially oriented economic development models in mainland West Europe and parts of South East Asia (Piore and Sabel 1984, Oliver and Wilkinson 1992, Dore *et al.* 1999). Whatever the state of this debate, there are two main streams to the varieties of capitalism debate: institutional-actor approaches and welfare-state approaches.

Institutional-actor approaches

Institutional-actor approaches examine national economic systems by taking the complex interactions between the institutions and major actors within them as a starting point for their analyses (Ebbinghaus and Manow 2001). The best-known and most prominent institutional-actor approach is provided by Hall and Soskice (2001), who make a robust challenge to the convergence orthodoxy. Using a comparative political economy methodology, their central argument is that advanced capitalist economies are not converging on a single neo-liberal trajectory. Indeed, far from causing convergence, globalisation pushes advanced political economies further apart from one another. This is a result of the comparative institutional advantages associated with different national socio-economic models of contemporary capitalism. Hall's and Soskice's approach to the varieties of capitalism debate has become one of the central theories in comparative political economy, with implications for employment relations (Coates 2005, Hancké 2009).

The aim of their work is to elaborate a 'new framework' for understanding the institutional similarities and differences among developed political economies and provide answers to questions at national economic policy level, such as policies most likely to improve national economic performance and the state's role in promoting this. Other questions are firm related, such as how firms in different nation states display systematic differences in their strategies and structures, especially in relation to innovation, and what drives these differences. A main purpose of their work is 'to bring firms back into the center of the analysis of comparative capitalism and, without neglecting trade unions, highlight the role that business associations and other types of relationships among firms play in the political economy' (Hall and Soskice 2001: 4). Their approach to the political economy of capitalism is sophisticated and actor-centred. They see the political economy as a terrain populated by multiple actors, with each one wanting to advance their own interests in a rational way by strategic interaction with the others (Scharf 1997). The actors include individuals, firms, unions and governments. These writers adopt a 'relational' view of the firm. For them, firms exploit core competencies and capacities for developing, producing, and distributing goods and services profitably. Critical to these is the quality of the relationships that the firm is able to establish *internally* with its own employees and *externally* with its suppliers, clients, stakeholders, trade unions, business associations and governments. Because of the range and complexities of these relationships, firms encounter a number of co-ordination problems, so a firm's 'success depends substantially on its ability to coordinate effectively with a wide range of actors' (Hall and Soskice 2001: 6).

According to Hall and Soskice, firms have five spheres for developing relationships to resolve the co-ordination problems central to their core competencies. First, there are employment relationships, where each company faces problems of co-ordinating bargaining over wages and conditions with their labour force, the unions and other employers. Second, in vocational education and training, firms need to secure and retain a skilled workforce, while workers have to decide how much they themselves should invest in developing those skills. Third, issues of co-ordination arise in the sphere of corporate governance, when firms access financial capital and where investors want assurances of returns on their investments. Fourth, in inter-firm relations, companies want to secure a stable demand for their products, appropriate supplies of inputs and access to current technology. Here co-ordination problems stem from the sharing of proprietary information and the risk of exploitation in joint ventures. Finally, firms face co-ordination problems in relation to their own employees. The central problem here 'is to ensure that employees have the requisite competencies and cooperate well with others to advance the objectives of the firm' (Hall and Soskice 2001: 7).

It follows that national political economies can be compared by referring to the ways in which firms resolve the co-ordination of these five 'spheres'. In this study, the authors identify six 'liberal market economies': Australia, Canada, Ireland, New Zealand, the United Kingdom and the United States.

Here firms co-ordinate their activities primarily by hierarchies and competitive market arrangements. These market relationships are characterised by the arm's length exchange of goods or services in competition with other firms in the marketplace and formal contracting between sellers and buyers of goods and services. In many respects, market institutions provide a highly effective means for co-ordinating the endeavours of the economic actors.

They also identify ten 'co-ordinated market economies': Austria, Belgium, Denmark, Germany, Finland, Japan, the Netherlands, Norway, Sweden and Switzerland. In these economies, firms depend more heavily on non-market relationships to co-ordinate their endeavours with other actors and to construct their core competencies. These non-market modes of co-ordination 'generally entail more extensive relational or incomplete contracting, network monitoring based on the exchange of private information inside networks, and more reliance on collaborative, as opposed to competitive, relationships to build the competencies of the firm'. The equilibrium outcomes which firms co-ordinate in these economies are commonly the result of strategic interaction among firms and other actors. In any national economy, firms gravitate 'toward the mode of coordination for which there is institutional support' (Hall and Soskice 2001: 8–9).

Hall and Soskice also briefly discuss a possible third variant of co-ordination, the Mediterranean economies. This variant, associated with France, Greece, Italy, Portugal, Spain and Turkey, is typified by large agrarian sectors and recent histories of extensive state intervention. These have tended to leave them with specific non-market co-ordination needs in corporate finance but more liberal arrangements in employment relations. These writers concentrate on the 'liberal market' and 'coordinated market' models, however, not the Mediterranean variant. But as the French economy has become more liberalised, thus weakening the traditional *dirigiste* or strong 'directive' role of the state since the 1980s, there has been extensive de-centralisation and flexible working arrangements in employment relations. But there have also been continual tensions between the traditional social movement role of the French unions and their recent institutionalised regulatory role. There are several reasons for this but basically these are claimed to arise out 'of the traditions, ideologies and strategies of unions, employers and the state', resulting in hostile interactions among the employment relations actors (Parsons 2013: 203). For Goetschy and Jobert (2011: 193), until the roles and responsibilities of the state and social partners are more clearly defined, 'it will be difficult to develop an autonomous and strong social dialogue in French employment relations'.

More recently, drawing upon Visser's (2013) analysis, Appelbaum and Schmitt (2013: 113) refine Hall's and Soskice's framework by distinguishing between: 'social-democratic' political regimes (Denmark, Finland, Norway and Sweden); continental market regimes (Austria, Belgium, France, Germany, Italy, the Netherlands and Switzerland); liberal market regimes (Australia, Canada, Ireland, Japan, New Zealand, the United Kingdom and the United States); and 'ex-dictatorships' (Greece, Portugal and Spain). These studies suggest that Japan has shifted towards a liberal market economy where, since the 1970s, there have been 'macro-economic changes in the Japanese economy as well as in employment relations' (Suzuki and Kubo 2011: 275). Thus for some observers, Japanese employment relations 'is now situated somewhere between the organizational pole of the "classic model" and the "market pole" of . . . the USA' (Whittaker 2013: 259).

A key concept in the varieties of capitalism analysis is 'institutional complementarities'. These reinforce the differences between liberal market economies and co-ordinated market economies. Hall and Soskice (2001: 18–19) go on to suggest that 'nations with a particular type of coordination in one sphere of the economy should tend to develop complementary practices in other spheres as well', since various types of institutional practices are not distributed randomly across nation states. They hypothesise that countries with a highly developed stock market indicate greater reliance on market modes of co-ordination in the financial sphere. But countries with high levels of employment protection reflect higher levels of non-market co-ordination in the sphere of employment relations. They demonstrate that liberal market economies tend to rely on markets to co-ordinate both the financial and employment relations systems, while co-ordinated market economies have 'institutions in both spheres that reflect higher levels of *non-market* co-ordination' (emphasis added).

Thelen (2001) takes the discussion further by arguing that distinctions between liberal market economies (LMEs) and co-ordinated market economies (CMEs) shed some light on the fragility of traditional 'labor institutions' in the former and sources of their resilience in the latter. In LMEs, as in English-speaking countries, employer strategies at firm level have brought them into conflict with traditional union structures and union strategies at both industry and plant levels. Here employers have seized on permissive political and economic environments to either sharply reduce union influence or eliminate it altogether. Alternatively, they have forced a reconfiguration of employment relations along lines that move them even further away from CMEs. In CMEs by contrast, as in Germany, Italy and Sweden, where union representatives at plant level enjoy extensive participatory rights, and are linked closely to strongly overarching unions, employers' dependence on stability and co-operation at firm level has helped shore up co-ordination at higher levels. She argues that despite 'important changes in some CMEs', especially in Sweden and Denmark, 'wage bargaining has re-equilibrated at a rather centralized level . . . Whilst significant, these changes do not amount to a wholesale deregulation, or to the return of widespread employer unilateralism, as in LMEs' (Thelen 2001: 102).

The varieties of capitalism debate in relation to Asia countries is less conclusive. But Hessels and Terjesen (2010) find some support for the varieties of capitalism thesis. They conclude that high quality vocational education and flexible systems of employment relations relate positively to export performance. The best regional performers – Australia (LME) and Japan which has shifted from being a CME to a LME resulting from macro-economic changes within the country – support the thesis. Similarly, Dodgson (2009) finds in Taiwan and South Korea that the shift from technology imitation to innovation is a function of cultural and institutional drivers and inhibitors. Taiwan's network-based innovation strategy resembles the LME model. But Korean firms are committed to large business-group capital formation methods that may retard leading-edge entrepreneurship. After its economic crisis in 1997, South Korea has moved towards a market-driven economy, 'exemplified by the proliferation of the non-regular workforce' (Lee 2011: 302). In Singapore, a competent economic bureaucracy establishes a complementary blend of LME and CME institutions that supports accumulation of high quality technical skills. However, Tipton's (2009) study of South-East Asia concludes that the post-colonial heritage is an obstacle to establishing the bureaucratic capacity to implement state-led industrialisation. And, as Andriesse and Van Westen (2012) conclude, in the peripheral regional economies of Malaysia and Thailand, development of tight complementary institutions generates little indigenous entrepreneurial activity.

In Latin America, in turn, Anner and Veiga (2013: 280, 282) argue that Brazil, with its tumultuous political history, is exceptional in terms of the varieties of capitalism debate, because it does not easily fit into the literature. It is neither a clear-cut case of a liberal market economy or a co-ordinated market economy. State intervention since the 1930s has been too intrusive to be incorporated in the LME typology, while 'the role of market forces and the relative weakness of the social actors preclude a CME conceptualization'. As a result, Brazil has a hybrid employment relations system 'influenced by social movement dynamics that is likely to continue to defy expectations for years to come'.

The varieties of capitalism approach, however, has it critics. First, they contest its focus on the firm as its centre of analysis. This arguably excludes organised labour and governments as political actors, not simply as resolvers of co-ordination problems. Yet some labour movements have played critical roles in shaping institutional conditions in their economies, such as in Scandinavian states. Second, as Howells (2003) argues, varieties of capitalism analyses assume that the interests of governments are perfectly aligned with those of business, since government's role in economic policy is to resolve co-ordination problems. But governments driven by ideology, such as those in the United Kingdom in the 1980s and 1990s, might try to change institutional arrangements in an economy and shift it from one type market system to another. Third, the co-ordinated market economy appears to be heavily reliant on the German example. But it is argued that Germany has been subject to a series of economic policy reforms in the 1990s and 2000s. Thus, Howells (2003: 109) questions the extent to which 'Germany can remain the poster child for an alternative to deregulated liberal market economies'.

Welfare-state approaches

Welfare-state approaches to the varieties of capitalism debate primarily address the types, origins and scope of welfare state regimes. These approaches are important because they are linked with specific employment relations issues in each type of regime. Esping-Andersen (1990), for example, identifies three types of welfare state: the social democratic, liberal and conservative models. He suggests these are the result of working class mobilisation and cross-class alliances. Social democratic welfare states emphasise universal provision of social benefits and de-commodify social rights by creating them as personal entitlements, as in Scandinavia. The liberal model provides means-tested welfare measures, with only modest degrees of universality, as in the United Kingdom, the United States, Canada and Australia. The conservative type of welfare state is found in corporatist countries, such as Austria, France and Germany, where powerful employer and labour interest groups are absorbed with the machinery of the state, which provides most of the welfare benefits but has weak redistributive policies.

Another study by Huber and Stephens (2001) examines the growth and crisis of the welfare state, whose development they see as being linked closely with the balance of power between different social groups and political institutions in societies. Combining quantitative studies with historical qualitative research, the authors look closely at nine countries that have achieved high degrees of social protection through different types of welfare state regime. They classify them as the social democratic, liberal, Christian democratic (or what Esping-Andersen describes as the conservative welfare state) and wage-earner welfare states of Australia and New Zealand. Huber and Stephens identify political parties as the motors of welfare state development, where party ideology is instrumental in shaping these regimes. They demonstrate that prolonged periods of government by different political parties result in markedly different welfare states, which display strong variations in levels of poverty and inequality within them. These authors emphasise the distribution of influence between political parties and labour movements, as well as the underestimated importance of gender, as the main bases for political mobilisation. They found that where welfare retrenchment was limited, there were clear 'veto' points that resisted change, such as in Switzerland and Germany with their federal political constitutions. But where the veto points were limited, as in the United Kingdom, welfare retrenchment was more rapidly achieved.

Importantly, types of welfare state regime correspond broadly to patterns of employment relations. Thus Huber and Stephens (2001) demonstrate that social democratic welfare states (as in Scandinavia) have high levels of union density and wide coverage of collective bargaining, while Christian democratic welfare states (such as Belgium, Germany and the Netherlands) have generally lower union density but wide bargaining coverage. Degrees of corporatism, where co-ordinated wage bargaining takes place at central level, also vary across different types of welfare state regime. Social democratic and Christian democratic welfare states have relatively high scores on the corporatism index, while liberal welfare states (such as the United Kingdom and Ireland) have lower scores. Liberal welfare states also have lower skills levels in the labour market, while social democratic welfare states have the highest skill levels. Wage dispersion is highest in liberal welfare states but is much less in other welfare state models and social democratic states show higher levels of active labour market policies by governments than other welfare state regimes. Finally, types of welfare state regime and varieties of capitalism overlap. For example, liberal welfare states lack co-ordination and broadly correspond to LMEs. According to Hamann and Kelly (2008: 132) in this varieties of capitalism approach, employment relations plays a central part, 'as the strength, organization, and representation of the working class forms a core component of the explanation for the emergence of welfare and industrial relations institutions'.

CAPITAL MARKETS, PRODUCT MARKETS AND EMPLOYMENT RELATIONS

In capitalist political economies, financial capital and product markets have great importance for employment relationships and employment relations. Financial markets, such as national stock exchanges around the world provide facilities for the buying and selling of company stocks and shares for listed private companies, while product markets are the conduits where firms sell their goods or services to their corporate or personal customers. Successful firms may need to raise new sources of financial capital to expand their businesses, which normally results in the creation of more jobs and employment opportunities within them. Also increased demand for a firm's products or services creates increased demand for labour by the firm and possibly increased demand for additional financial capital. Similarly, where investment of financial capital in firms declines, or where demand for a firm's products or services falls, this results in job losses for workers, reduced promotion opportunities in firms, and rising unemployment in the labour market. Clearly, what happens in financial markets and a firm's product markets are important determinants of what happens in employment relations.

In a global age, the situation is even more complex, as both financial markets and product markets have become increasingly internationalised. Financial markets have become global, the production of goods and services is widely distributed around the world, and both financial and product markets have been subject to periodic, destabilising fluctuations such as the global credit crisis and economic downturn of 2007–2009. But labour as an economic resource remains largely but not exclusively immobile. And the bargaining power of labour and labour unions with employers is generally weakened when, under competitive market pressures, firms seek lower labour costs, higher productivity per head, and increased profits for shareholders (O'Brien and Williams 2010).

Financial markets

Powerful global financial markets have been made possible by technological innovation, widening patterns of world trade, and market deregulation or re-regulation promoting freer movements of capital. The overarching role of global financial markets is to promote capital flows and economic growth internationally. With a few strokes on a computer key board, vast quantities of financial capital can be instantly transferred around the world between the buyers and sellers of a variety of money-based instruments. The power and scale of contemporary global financial markets are paralleled by their complexity, inter-connectedness and fragmentation. One element within them is stock markets. These include common and preferred stock (or equity capital) issued by businesses to finance their operations, fund permanent investments and ensure their balance-sheet leverage remains reasonable; they do this by magnifying profits and losses by using debt. All market economies feature companies that are capitalised by equity instruments, making the overall stock market both deep and broad. Examples of stock markets include those in Bombay, Frankfurt, London, Oslo, Paris, Rio de Janeiro, Shenzhen, Sydney, Tokyo, and New York, which collectively have the greatest depth and breadth of both securities and participants (Levich 2001).

Money markets consist of short-term liabilities issued by banks (such as certificates of deposits and bankers' acceptances), companies (such as commercial paper or unsecured discount instruments issued by the best companies) and sovereigns (such as treasury bills issued by governments). In the private sector, these instruments are used for liquidity management; in the sovereign sector (funds managed by governmental authorities at national level) they are used for both liquidity management and monetary policy management by governments. Virtually all advanced political economies and emerging nation states feature some type of money market. Debt markets, which include medium-term and long-term bonds and loans, constitute the largest single element of global financial markets. These bonds and loans are used for capital investment, acquisitions and expansion and may be renewed on a regular basis, making the financial capital appear semi-permanent. The largest debt markets are in advanced political economies (Cable 2009).

Another market for financial capital is the foreign exchange market. This sector represents the most singly actively traded element of financial markets. Intermediaries and end-users deal in very large amounts of 'spot' (current market) and 'forward' transactions every day, making the global foreign exchange market a 24-hour business. Market activity is centred on both major and emerging exchange rates.

Two other important financial markets are derivative markets and commodity markets. Derivative markets include financial contracts linked to specific asset classes. They include interest rates, equities, foreign exchange, credits and commodities. These markets are used by hedge funds (which are flexible investment conduits that can absorb greater risk than the average individual) and speculators to achieve specific goals; they inject liquidity into the process. Derivatives can serve as substitutes for, or complements to, other financial instruments. Commodity markets are broad and deep and feature a significant amount of spot and forward dealing. Hedge funds, such as commodity producers and commodity users, and speculators or any institution seeking a profit, are active in this market. Key traded commodities include precious metals (such as gold, silver, platinum and palladium), industrial metals (such as iron, copper, aluminium and zinc), energy (such as oil and oil products, natural gas, and electricity), agricultural products (such as corn, wheat and soybeans) and 'softs' (such as cocoa, coffee and sugar) (Ferguson 2009).

This brief summary of the key sectors of the global financial system indicates its complexity and dynamism in the early twenty-first century. Most importantly, changes in one financial market impacts on other financial markets, resulting sometimes in financial crises. These can involve banking, credit, currency or debt crises, which can be very difficult to resolve and can have major impacts on businesses, workers, consumers, citizens and levels of employment in national economies (Cable 2009). The dynamism, flexibility and innovative nature of the global financial system have come about primarily because of market de-regulation, the mobility of financial capital, market volatility, and advanced ICTs. The volatility caused by these forces has changed the face of financial capital over the past few decades. These developments impact on employment relationships, labour organisations collectively and employees individually. There is little to suggest that these markets are likely to slow down in coming years. The effects of the ascendancy of the 'markets' and their impacts outside their direct spheres of business are widespread. These include greater competition, more innovation, greater transparency, increased efficiencies, deeper global penetration and, worryingly, the possibility of more frequent and deeper financial crises in the future (Lanchester 2010).

De-regulation and the race for new business in international financial markets have intensified competition among traditional intermediaries (such as banks and insurers) as well as 'new' intermediaries (such as non-bank financial institutions), private equity funds and hedge funds. Since financial markets have long provided participants with innovative ways of solving financial problems, intermediaries are likely to develop increasingly innovative solutions, as technological advances permit more precise pricing of risks. Hence the risk-taking abilities of intermediaries continue to expand and competitive pressures threaten profits (Banks 2009). But, as the major accounting procedures of the world begin to harmonise, and investors demand more information as part of the governance process, financial transparency is likely to continue improving. Enterprise value is enhanced through improved efficiencies, while companies able to reduce their expenses and manage their working capital and risks more efficiently can boost value, although this may be at the expense of substituting technological inputs for labour. With deeper global penetration of financial capital and product markets, TNCs become increasingly powerful organisations. Large national firms can expand their geographic presence globally, by creating new businesses, acquiring operations in other countries or partnering with overseas organisations. De-regulation, the mobility of financial capital and efficient forms of technological, cross-national communications facilitate this. Tax avoidance or tax evasion by powerful TNCs are also important issues facing national governments in the global economy (Arun and Turner 2009).

However, the complex relationships within the global financial sector, the speed of communications within it, and the flexible and mobile features of financial capital instruments are likely to continue to promote further financial crises similar to those that have appeared in recent years; perhaps with greater frequency and severity. The contagion of a crisis from one market to another and then to others is more likely to occur where information and decision-making take place in real time (Lanchester 2010). Despite the efforts of regulators to try and contain these financial crises, past evidence indicates that they may be overwhelmed by the speed and ferocity of such market dislocations, with deleterious implications for employment, employment relationships and working lives (Franklin and Gale 2007).

Product markets

It has been long been recognised that product markets are important determinants of employment relations processes and outcomes. As Brown (1973: 175) argues in his classic study of piecework bargaining in the British engineering industry, 'the principal pressures influencing management control systems [in factories] are those of the product market, and different product markets can vary considerably in both the degree and character of their competitiveness'. In his analysis at that time, he argues that 'under relatively full employment and trade union organization, it is the product market rather than the labour market which has the major economic impact upon piecework wage determination'. A similar point is made more recently in Calmfors *et al.* (2001: 296): 'what unions do depends on what they *can* do, and this depends on the extent of product market competition'. Brown (2008: 125) reinforces this where he argues that 'product markets form the foundation upon which industrial relations institutions are built'. Union power is partly a function of labour market factors, such as levels of employment or unemployment. 'But it is pre-existing imperfections in the product market that permit collective bargaining to deliver benefits to workers.'

Firms without unions determine the terms and conditions of their workforces unilaterally, taking account of the product market and labour market factors facing them, without challenge. But where workers have a union to represent them in wage negotiations and to protect jobs, employers recognising the union for collective bargaining purposes determine wages differently. The union's function is to negotiate improvements in the terms and conditions of employment of their members and protect workers in the workplace against unfair or illegitimate managerial practices. They try to do this by either controlling the supply of labour to the firm or organising industrial action against the employer. If union negotiators are successful in doing this, market conditions are hard, and labour productivity does not increase, the firm's unit wage costs rise, thus jeopardising its success in the product market. This is one reason why some employers refuse to negotiate with unions.

Commons (1909: 65, 68) recognises this in his early historical study of the shoe industry in Philadelphia in the United States, where he distinguishes between the 'wage bargain' between employer and worker and the 'price bargain' between retailer and consumer. 'We have to do with two classes of bargains, the wage-bargain and the price-bargain. Each is affected by *the increasing distance of the ultimate purchaser*, the actual consumer, *from the worker*, the manual producer' (emphasis added). For him, it is the ever-widening product market for goods and services that steadily detaches workers from that market and diverts attention to the firm's price rather than to quality. This shifts the advantage in the series of bargains from the worker to consumers and their intermediaries. For Commons, the 'competitive menace' is the 'marginal producer' in a sector. This is 'the one with the lowest standards of living and cost and quality of work', 'whose competition tends to drag down the level of others toward his [*sic*] own'. The extension of the market for the sale of goods is accompanied by an extension of the field for producing them. This brings new competitors into the competitive arena; they are essentially a series of lower marginal producers.

Commons (1909: 78, 79) goes on to argue that in the course of industrial development, from craft work to mass production, the part played by the 'merchant' or producer stands out as the determining factor. The key is always the 'price-bargain'. It is the producer which controls both capital and labour and, if the producer has a market, it can secure financial capital to build the business. He writes: 'The "conflict of capital and labor" is a conflict of market and labor, of merchant and wage-earner, of prices and wages.' This is because capital follows the merchant and 'the manufacturers' protective organization is an organization to protect prices'. The manufacturers' association, in other words, is primarily price-regarding. Extension of the market provokes the conflict of prices and wages. This commonly results in wage-earners resorting to protective policies such as joining trade unions or using the law to defend themselves. The manufacturer or producer then turns from the market to face the worker through an employers' association. The employers' association 'is wholly different in method, object, or and social significance, and usually in personnel from [the] "manufacturers' association" '.

Commons notes that the effects of the expansion of product markets for shoes outside Philadelphia, due to improved transportation, were for local labour unions to make sure that wages continued to be taken out of competition by expanding the spread of collective bargaining to correspond with the relevant product market. The shoes coming from outside Philadelphia were made by non-union labour and were being sold at a lower price. Thus it was important for the shoemaker unions of Philadelphia to organise shoemakers from the surrounding cities and areas and to cover all of them under the same collective wage agreements, so as to equalise the price of labour. This case study shows that power in employment relations closely follows the shapes of the product markets for goods and services, not just those of the labour market.

Martin (1992: 29) claims that four features of the product market affect the outcomes of the 'negotiated order' between management and unions in firms. These are: the overall level of economic demand and other macro-economic factors; the level of demand and degree of competition within the specific product market; the company's ability to pay, linked closely to profitability; and the time sensitivity of the product itself. Three product market factors are directly relevant to understanding the union's position: 'the degree of "discretionary pricing power" available to management, the elasticity of demand for a firm's products, and the elasticity of substitution'. Union power is greatest when management has maximum discretionary bargaining power, since management is able to pass on any increases in costs to its customers (Mishel and Voos 2006). However, high elasticity of demand reduces management power, since increases in costs are likely to result in reduced sales. Similarly, high substitutability of product reduces management power, since consumers are able to switch demand to new products if prices rise.

With globalisation, however, collective bargaining structures tend to be devolved to enterprise level or, more commonly, disappear all together. This is underpinned by the predisposition of firms to concentrate, whether in competition or by collusion, on the product market where their goods or services are traded. Collective bargaining is based on the assumption that unions can organise all the workers in the sector producing the product, using national or sector-wide collective agreements. These apply to all the firms and workers within it. In the mid-twentieth century, these agreements took wages out of competition among the firms covered by them. In Europe, but not Japan or the United States, governments in the early-twentieth century had promoted industry-wide collective bargaining as a matter of policy. This type of collective bargaining began breaking down in the United Kingdom, for example, under labour market pressures and shop steward activity locally in the 1960s (Clegg 1970). But as Brown (2008: 118) argues since then unions globally have faced increasing challenges: 'Product markets have, in recent years, become substantially more exposed to international competitive pressures... because the world economy has become steadily more open to trade.' Competition through the globalisation of product markets, accompanied by the internationalisation of company ownership through TNCs, has gravely weakened national union power bases everywhere.

Collective wage bargaining softened labour markets when product markets were predominantly national. The globalisation of product markets has thrown these systems into disarray. This reflects Common's observation, based on the experience of the Philadelphia shoemakers some 200 years ago, that increasing distance from consumer to producer provokes the conflict between market prices and market wages. In a global age, this makes it much more difficult for unions to organise internationally to protect the wages and jobs of their members locally.

LABOUR MARKETS AND LABOUR MARKET INSTITUTIONS

Labour is all those persons working or seeking work in a given labour market, whether local, national or global. A labour market, in turn, is a conduit of the employment relationship and an economic concept used to describe and analyse the mechanisms and conditions under which labour is demanded and supplied within both firms (their *internal* labour markets) and the local, national or international economies (*external* labour markets) where employers and workers interact. It is the interactions between employers, which demand labour, and workers, who supply their knowledge, skills and experience in the labour market to firms, which determine the 'wage-price' of labour. Labour markets have conventionally been regarded as principally external to the firm and subject to the theory that changes in the distribution of labour occur when the balance of net advantages to workers can be improved by moving jobs, a view derived ultimately from Adam Smith (1977).

Labour markets

Labour markets were subsequently regarded as a special case of the general economic theory of value (Hicks 1932). Such a theory has long been regarded as inadequate, both as an explanation of wage determination and behaviour in labour markets. This is because some labour markets are subject to collective bargaining and all of them are subject to a complex set of institutional and social forces affecting behaviour within them. These forces include labour turnover, labour mobility, recruitment and selection, personal and social incentives, and the force of custom (Smith 2003). In 2009, the Central Intelligence Agency of the United States estimated that out of a total world population of some seven billion, the global labour force was about 3.5 billion, of which some 9 per cent were understood to be unemployed (Central Intelligence Agency 2012).

Internal labour markets incorporate formal sets of rules and procedural guidelines that constrain the employment relationship *within* firms. The ideal type of internal labour market is characterised by limited ports of entry for recruitment, regulated job ladders for each group of workers, ground rules for promotion, internal training and rules on-job security (Doeringer and Piore 1971). There is evidence, however, that many of the traditional pillars of the internal labour market have been dismantled in recent years. New corporate policies covering recruitment, career progression, training and job security have been introduced into business organisations in response to pressures and opportunities for change, both internal and external to them (Rubery 1999, Grimshaw *et al.* 1999).

External labour markets, whether local, national or international, can be analysed in terms of geography, occupation, industry, size and social characteristics. But labour markets are not static; they are dynamic. This is demonstrated by the shifts and changes that constantly occur in jobs, firms, occupations, industries, areas and countries, indicating that a measure of labour mobility takes place in response to the dynamics of product and labour market changes. In terms of labour *demand*, the prime forces at work include the general level of economic activity (whether the economy is growing or in recession and levels of employment and unemployment), the introduction of new products or services by firms, changes in technology, altered patterns of household consumption, and the size and scope of the public sector. In terms of labour *supply*, the main factors include the location of the labour force, its size and geographical distribution, its age and gender distribution, its levels of education and training (what some economists call investment in human capital), and its willingness to be geographically mobile. But labour supply is fixed in the short term, so any increase in labour supply needs time to take place.

The wages for labour are determined within the boundaries of these complex markets. The standard level of labour market analysis is at local and national levels. Firms and governments recruit and select their workforces predominantly in local and national labour markets, unions operate nationally and locally, and governments determine their labour market policies nationally. Wages, the price for labour or the use of human effort in the production process, tend to respond not promptly but over time to the forces affecting the demand and supply of particular categories or grades of labour. However, labour markets at all levels are not like markets for commodities and the behaviour of wages does not closely resemble that of most other 'prices'. Wages, in other words, whether by job, occupation, sector or geography, cannot be explained solely by market forces. This is because labour markets have unique social properties reflecting the human characteristics of the labour force and the relationships that develop between employers and workers in the workplace and organisations.

Labour markets are also dynamic and subject to constant change. Thus scholars such as Reich (1991) and Castells (2010) argue that the changing nature of business activities in information, knowledge-based economies results in two main types of employment and labour market structures within them. One is the *service economy* model, epitomised by the United States, the United Kingdom and Canada. This is characterised by a rapid phasing out of manufacturing, elimination of almost all agricultural employment, with differentiation of service activities becoming a key element in structuring work. This model emphasises 'capital management' services over 'producer services', while expanding employment in the social services and education sectors. The second model is an *advanced manufacturing* one, epitomised by the German and Japanese economies. This retains manufacturing at a relatively high level, allows for its restructuring by drawing upon socio-technical systems, and has producer services which are more important than financial services. The bulk of service sector growth is in services to companies and social services. A country such as France veers towards a service economy, while maintaining a strong manufacturing base.

Unions and collective bargaining

Because the employment relationship involves constant interaction between employer and worker, some workers, especially in large organisations, join unions. The function of a business enterprise is to produce the goods or services that consumers want to purchase at prices that cover their costs and provide profit to its owners. Managerial decisions must be directed at this aim, otherwise in the long run the firm will cease to exist (Coase 1937, Penrose 1980). These decisions involve a range of matters directly affecting the labour force of the enterprise. These include wages, hours of work, recruitment and selection, technological innovation, promotion and procedures for laying-off workers. The effective administration of these matters is enormously important to employee well-being and their capacity for work (Danna and Griffin 1999).

The basic function of the union is to provide a vehicle or institution by which decisions affecting wages, benefits, employee welfare and the status of workers in the enterprise are made jointly with management through collective bargaining, not by management alone. The collective agreements resulting from this process provide a framework of jointly determined rules in the 'bargaining unit' covering the unionised workers, where a wide variety of the day-to-day decisions affecting the workforce is made. The main factors binding workers to the union are they have participated indirectly in the decisions affecting their wages and working conditions. They also know that they have representation in those day-to-day decisions affecting them in the workplace, such as grievance handling and disciplinary issues.

There is a strong link between size of enterprise and union membership, with larger firms tending to be more willing to negotiate with unions than smaller ones (Barrett 1999). This is because links between top management and the workforce in large firms are remote and the diffusion of managerial responsibility in works rules and their administration often leads to questions of equity. In these situations, workers are more likely to want collective means for determining their terms and conditions, rather than through individual persuasion by management or by managerial power. In this way, the unionised workforce is able to achieve some degree of fairness in agreeing wages, works rules and their application. As Flanders notes (1968: 26): 'the value of a union to its members lies less in its economic achievements than in its capacity to protect their dignity'.

Government intervention

In addition to collective bargaining as an institutional constraint on the operation of naked market forces in the determination of wages, many governments intervene in wage-setting by legislating minimum wage standards in private industry for economic and social purposes. In the United States, a minimum wage was first provided in the Fair Labor Standards Act 1938, in the United Kingdom by the National Minimum Wage Act 1998, and in other parts of West and East Europe minimum wage arrangements are commonplace. In the EU, 18 out of its 27 member states currently have national minimum wages. Other countries, such as Sweden, Finland, Denmark, Switzerland, Germany, Austria and Italy have no minimum wage laws but rely on employer groups and trade unions setting minimum earnings through collective bargaining. In China, the Ministry of Human Resources and Social Security established the first minimum wage law in 2004. China's Regulations on Enterprises Minimum Wage, which vary by region, enforce the basic needs of workers and their families, help improve workers' performance and promote fair competition between enterprises (China Briefing 2012).

The setting of legally binding minimum wage standards for private industry represents a comparatively limited form of intervention by government in wage determination. It anchors national wage structures to minimum standards and significantly affects the market impact on wages in industries and areas. It also demonstrates that governments are committed to provide basic wage rights for employees and protect them from 'wage race to the bottom' policies of unscrupulous employers. In other cases, governments set wages for their own employees, which act as 'models' or examples for the private sector to follow (Bach and Kessler 2012).

Historically, governments have also intervened to control general wage and price movements in the 1940s, 1950s and 1960s, during the period of demand-side economics and Keynesian orthodoxy. These prices and incomes policies aimed to find ways of reconciling high levels of employment with reasonable levels of price stability. For example, Australia implemented an incomes policy, called the Prices and Incomes Accord during the 1980s. This was an agreement between the trade unions and Labor government, to which the employers were not a party. The unions agreed to restrict wage demands and government pledged to minimise inflation and price rises. Government was also to act on improving the 'social wage', including increasing public spending on education and welfare. Inflation declined during the period of the Accord, which was renegotiated several times. However, many of the key elements of the Accord were weakened over time, as unions sought a shift from central to enterprise bargaining. The Accord ceased to play a major role after the recession of 1989–1992 and was abandoned after the Labor government was defeated in 1996 (Lansbury and Wailes 2011).

The force of custom

In the determination of wages and conditions of employment, notions of fairness and equity play a key role in the labour-pricing process, especially when the pay of one job is linked with that of another through 'custom' (Hyman and Brough 1975). Brown (1962: 131–133) writes that custom is a powerful and distinct influence on rates of pay. 'The force of custom may show itself in [some] circularity of reasoning ... the job that once achieves high pay continues to stand high in esteem because the pay is proof that it deserves to. Equally, what costs little may be thought worth little.' Thus long-established wage differentials may be difficult to alter if they involve perceptions of fairness or status, even where an existing difference between them no longer conforms to underlying conditions of labour market demand and supply. Also the well-known downward rigidity in the level of money wages, even when the labour market is loose and the level of other prices is falling, is related to the instinctive human resistance to reductions in accustomed or customary levels of compensation and reward (Drobny 1988).

Another factor conditioning pay determination is that relations between employers and workers are quite different from those between buyers and sellers in commodity markets. Buying and selling in the markets for most goods and services usually involve little in the way of personal or interpersonal relationships between the parties and where, in many cases, there is no bargaining between them. Most employment relationships, on the other hand, tend to be of some duration. They create conditions of mutual dependence and, in many instances, of loyalty between the parties. In the employment relationship, the worker becomes used to the atmosphere, HR policies, working conditions and other workers of the firm. These ties are strengthened by the holiday pay, sick pay, pensions and other financial and non-financial benefits provided by the firm, geared to length of service (Perkins and White 2011). For the employer, in turn, competent workers familiar with the procedures of the enterprise, especially if they have acquired skills specific to their jobs, have a substantial value over a new recruit who may need a lot of training and additional supervision in the workplace (Garibaldi 2006).

Labour effort in the workplace is embodied in individuals, which tends to impede but not entirely eliminate labour mobility; this facilitates adjustments to changes in demand and supply conditions in labour markets. Workers tend to develop strong attachments and emotional ties to particular places, firms, occupations, industries or sectors. This is how they acquire identify and status at work (Lundberg and Cooper 2011). If changing jobs means leaving familiar surroundings, learning new skills, or adjusting to new working environments, some workers resist this. Labour mobility is often more attractive to young single people, or those with advanced professional qualifications, than to individuals doing routine work. This results in a measure of stability to working life within business undertakings. Much would be lost by an employer where each employee is looking for a small wage advantage from moving to a new employer. The same is true if employers constantly seek to secure small reductions in wage costs through the replacement of current workers with cheaper ones. Normally, only a limited proportion of the workforce needs to be mobile and informed of alternative job opportunities to bring about needed labour market adjustments within firms (Salt 1997).

Wage determination in practice

All the above factors impinge on the operation of labour markets. But some characteristics help distinguish the labour market from other markets. One is that workers, even within particular occupations or firms, are rarely perfect substitutes for one another. For example, not all medical practitioners or qualified economists have the same levels of professional proficiency. Worker selection processes and wage payment systems seek in part to take these variations into account. They also help explain the dispersion of wage rates that typically exists for given jobs within occupational labour markets. Second, there is also the problem of labour market information. Workers do not have complete or full information on alternative employment opportunities. Similarly, employers lack complete information about labour supply or the exact margin to which it is profitable to increase or reduce employment resulting from changes in product markets, wages or other costs. There are also transaction costs to workers doing job searches and for employers hiring and training new employees, although these problems are partly mitigated by the increased use of e-recruitment and sophisticated selection systems in recent years (Shah 2007).

There is a tendency in the labour economics literature to emphasise imperfections in labour markets, stemming from obstacles to labour mobility and other factors (Sassen 1988, Turmann 2004). However, although there are institutional and social elements conditioning wage determination, somehow wages do secure, reasonably effectively, allocations of labour among different occupations, industries and firms in ways that approximate to patterns of demand for output in product markets. If rates of pay did not tend towards balancing supply and demand for particular types of labour, then labour surpluses and shortages would continually persist. In short, although they sometimes require unpleasant and harsh decisions for individuals and firms and create economic difficulties for communities, market forces in capitalist market economies do serve prima facie to reconcile the freedom to spend, within the limits of a person's income, and the freedom to work at the kind of job individuals choose and prefer. This is, of course, within the limits of the availability of jobs which people are qualified to do and their mobility between employers. It is also conditioned very powerfully by the aggregate level of labour demand in national economies and, increasingly, globally. Recent international labour market indicators demonstrate that despite some signs of economic recovery from the global recession post 2008, labour market conditions continued to deteriorate in many countries in subsequent years under pressures of economic austerity (ILO 2012). In the United Kingdom, for example, it was reported in the WERS 2011 the 'widespread impact of the recession resulted in the majority of workplaces taking actions that directly affected employment and employees' terms and conditions of employment' (van Wanrooy *et al.* 2013).

THE NATION STATE AND EMPLOYMENT RELATIONS

The nation state and its agencies are major players in employment relations and the power of the nation state helps shape and condition employment relationships within it. At one level, the state sets the ground rules for employment relations in terms of the legal framework within which employment relationships are conducted and determined, such as the contract of employment, workers' rights, collective bargaining and industrial action. This legal framework provides the basis on which workers enter and exit the labour market, the processes for determining wages and conditions, and means for resolving industrial disputes within each country (see chapter 8). At another level, the state acts as an employer by employing civil servants or public employees to carry out their duties on behalf of the political authorities. Here the state has a direct role in organising and managing the employment relationships of its own workforce (Kaufmann 2007). At a further level, the modern state commonly creates a regime of welfare provision such as unemployment and other benefits, which facilitate transitions by workers out of and back into the labour market.

The state and the labour market are where the politics and economics of employment relations or its political economy interact. As Lindblom (1977: 8) writes: 'in all political systems of the world, much of politics is economics and most of economics is also politics'. This is reinforced by Crouch (1993: 299) who argues against Hayek's (1944) model of state–society relations where the 'natural state of affairs' is for economic relations to be governed by market forces alone. For Crouch, 'it is engagement by collectivity [in economic affairs], whether in the shape of the state or interest organizations, that needs special explanation'. However, the structures, practices and conventions of labour markets vary by place and time. State policy in employment relations helps explain these variations. The creation of conditions under which 'labour power is sold has historically been one of the basic unchanging functions of the capitalist state'. But how this function is carried out is neither uniform nor constant (Coates 2000: 225).

All modern nation states are embedded within the economic dynamics of contemporary capitalism, nationally and internationally, so their political leaders are unable to abstain from intervening in employment relationships in the national or public interest. In times of national emergencies, for example, the institutions of employment relations are often suspended, strikes are outlawed and wages controlled by government (Judt 2010). Yet the function of the state in employment relations is a problematic and contradictory one. Offe (1984) identifies three areas where state activity impinges on employment relationships. First, the contemporary state adopts economic policies to improve economic performance, increase productivity and promote market competitiveness. Offe (1984: 16) contends that while the modern state seeks to maintain the dominance of capital in its boundaries, it compensates 'for its disruptive and disorganizing consequences'. This is the 'capitalist accumulation' or 'economic efficiency' function of the state, with labour individually and labour organisations collectively expecting their shares of this capital accumulation. Second, democratic states want to maintain popular consent by pursuing some degree of social equity within them, by fostering citizenship and supporting employee voice at the workplace. This is the 'legitimation' or 'equity' function of the state, with its obvious implications for employment relations. Third, the state seeks to maintain the social order and defuse or suppress industrial conflict within it. As Offe (1984: 257) writes: the 'welfare-capitalist state assumes responsibilities for the maintenance of the entire social order'. This is the 'pacification' or 'stability' function of the state. Clearly, there are always trade-offs among these three functions and different types of capitalist state deal with them in their own ways.

Various classifications of national systems of employment relations and the role of the state within them have been proposed. Thus in the European literature, a three-fold classification is typically provided, according to the extent and depth of state engagement with employers and unions. Regini (1986), for example, distinguishes between the 'concertation', 'political isolation' and 'pluralistic fragmentation' models. In the concertation model, unions are closely involved in economic policy-making and regulation is generally centralised. In the political isolation model, governments exclude unions from the policy process. And the pluralistic fragmentation model is where politics and employment relations are institutionally separated, so that unions have to depend solely on their market power to protect their members. Crouch (1993), in turn, distinguishes between 'contestation', 'pluralism' and 'corporatism' and van Waarden (1995) between 'liberal pluralism', 'corporatism' and 'statism'. Liberal pluralism incorporates a passive state which upholds the principle of non-intervention in employment relations; corporatism involves active state interference in consultation with the social partners on employment relations issues; and statism provides direct state interference with terms and conditions of employment.

The literature in the English-speaking world typically takes 'pluralistic industrialism' as the norm but, in large parts of the world, the entire employment relations system is dominated, directly or indirectly, by government (Sturmthal 1973), so there is wide cross-national diversity in state regulation of employment relations. Further, the variety of capitalism approach reveals wide national differences in employment relations arrangements and employment regulation in nation states, indicating little 'convergence' in the state's role within them. In other cases, such as in most of Africa, Asia and Latin America, as well as in France and Italy, highly politicised employment relations systems persist. Also the 'pluralist industrialism' outcome, typically involving 'post-war settlements' between national employers, organised labour and government, was only sustained by increasingly overt state action at that time. But by the late twentieth and early twenty-first centuries, under pressures of globalisation and neo-liberal economic policies, these institutional compromises between employers, organised labour and the state were largely unravelling.

China is a special case in terms of the role of the state in employment relations, since it has experienced some 40 years of economic reforms, driven by the Communist party in a single-party state. During this period, China has been transformed from a planned economy to a mixed economy, with elements of both market forces and central planning within it. Here the state plays a pivotal role in economic co-ordination; a role strengthened since the global financial crisis 2007–2008. Further, the market-driven economic reforms have changed China's employment structure and employment relations (Liu 2013), where the role of the state 'continues to be crucial in shaping employment relations in the foreseeable future' (Cooke 2011b: 325). In the planned economy, Chinese employment relations were characterised by the 'iron rice bowl' mentality, supported by the state. This incorporated life-time employment, stable wages, and welfare for urban workers. Within workplaces, workers had high dependence on their enterprises and labour–management relations were vertically organised. With economic and labour market reforms initiated by the state, life-time employment has been replaced by contract labour; wages are contingent and variable; and 'cradle-to-the-grave' welfare has been replaced by contributory social insurance schemes. Workplace relations have changed, in turn, 'from organized dependence to disorganized despotism' (Liu 2013: 344, Lee 1999).

THE TECHNOLOGICAL AND SCIENTIFIC CONTEXT

In today's advanced market economies, modern technology is the application of scientific knowledge, through tools, techniques, systems and methods, to produce goods and services for sale in the marketplace. Technology is not merely applied science, because it sometimes runs ahead of science, but most technology today is increasingly science based and readily communicable to those qualified to use it. Grübler (1998: 117) summarises the technological changes in the world since the first industrial revolution and claims that these have been driven by a series of 'technology clusters'. A technology cluster is a 'set of interrelated technological and organizational innovations whose persuasive adoption drives a particular period of economic growth, productivity increases, industrialization, trade, and associated structural changes'. As the dominant technology structure expands, other technological innovations are developed through subsequent scientific discoveries, experimentation and small-scale applications. Grübler identifies four historical technological clusters and an emerging one, each with important implications for economic growth and development. Each cluster is characterised by dominant organisational styles and distinctive economic and social institutions. Beginning with 1750, he classifies these clusters into five overlapping periods: 1750–1820, 1800–1870, 1920–c2000, and post 1980. By the mid-twentieth century, for example, economy and society in the developed world were commonly linked with Keynesian economic policies, the welfare state and open societies. Since 1980, however, economy and society globally have been linked with economic de-regulation, environmental regulation and networks of actors. These developments have implications for labour markets and employment relationships.

Technological innovation and scientific developments

Whatever its form, continuous technological innovation is, and always has been, a driving force in the development and growth of successful enterprises and capitalist market economies. Schumpeter (1976) believes that the lifeblood of capitalism is the 'creative destruction' of technological innovation, where companies rise and fall and unleash innovation, which in the end makes an economy stronger. For him, the industrial process 'incessantly revolutionizes the economic structure *from within*, incessantly destroying the old one, incessantly creating a new one' (Schumpeter 1976: 82–83). This 'creative destruction' continues today, probably at an ever-increasing pace of change. It has important implications for the demand and supply of labour, employment relationships and the individuals affected by technological change. Technology and technological and scientific change, in short, are an important context of employment relations.

This fact is noted by Dunlop (1958: 61), who argues that the 'technical context' of an employment relations system 'defines the type of work place and the operations and functions of workers and managers and to some degree influences the role of specialized governmental agencies'. Dunlop distinguishes seven characteristics of the technical context – four characterise workers and managers and types of workplace; three are differentiated by the operations or functions that the actors perform in the workplace. The four types of workplace are: a fixed or variable one, the workplace's relation to the workers' residence, a stable or variable workforce and work operations, and the size of the workgroup. The nature of the services performed by workers and managers within the workplace are affected by: job content, the workers' relation to technology or customers, and scheduled hours of work and shifts. For Dunlop, the technical context is decisive both to the substantive rules established for the workplace 'and to the organizational configuration and the interaction of the actors'.

Kaufman (2004b: 60) builds upon this analysis. For him, science and technology subsume both scientific knowledge and its embodiment in machines, products and processes. In his observations, science and technology affect employment relations through several channels. First, inside firms, technology heavily influences the operation and structure of the production process and the work experience of employees. Second, technology influences organisational and market structures. Thus economies of scale favour large organisations and oligopolistic product markets, while computer technology, the WWW and telecommunications promote organisational decentralisation, rapid change and increased competition in markets. Finally, advances in the general state of scientific knowledge open up new ideas and processes in the world of work, 'such as new management methods (e.g. high-performance work systems) and ways of organizing and controlling work (e.g. telecommuting, electronic monitoring of employees)'.

Ever since Marx and Engels (1970, 1974), there have been divisive debates about the role of technological change in shaping employment relationships. Marx saw technology as a key explanatory variable in his theory of relations between capitalists and workers and between the capitalist class and working class. For Marx, it was the changing mode of production under early capitalism embodied in the factory system, which separated owners of the means of production from their workers. This separation created the class consciousness of the workers and, in Marx's analysis, influenced the course of history. For Marx and Engels (1973: 8), 'Society as a whole is more and more splitting up into two great hostile camps, into two great classes directly facing each other: Bourgeoisie and Proletariat.' Non-Marxist observers, in the North American liberal tradition, argue, in turn, that modern technology produces some uniformity in the rules governing employment relations in different societies. For them, it is industrialisation and technological changes that provide the dynamic causing changes in relations between employers and workers (Kerr *et al.* 1962).

Selective case studies indicate some of the effects of technology on relations between employers and workers. In the United Kingdom, for example, an early study by Woodward (1980) found the characteristics of employer–employee relations varied between small batch, large mass production and continuous process technologies. She found greater pressures on supervisors and employees, and ultimately greater conflict in the workplace, in mass production technologies than in the other two. Blauner (1964) argues that worker attitudes in terms of job satisfaction and alienation are influenced by the nature of technology. The focus is on the effects of mass production technologies and the side-effects of routine, repetitive and boring jobs on workers. Other researchers argue that technology not only affects the nature of the work setting but also impacts on the amount of interaction employees have on their jobs and on workgroup cohesion (Rousseau 1977). Kuhn (1961) shows that the nature of the technology influences the strategic position of employees in the production process and is an important source of bargaining power for workgroups. Sayles (1958), in turn, suggests that there are four types of workgroups in terms of management-union relations, each with differences deriving from the technology of the jobs they perform. The four workgroups – apathetic, erratic, strategic and conservative – give rise to different frequencies of grievances, spontaneous protest actions, degrees of internal unity, participation in union activities, and management evaluation of the organisational contribution of workgroups.

A more recent and in-depth case study in a trans-national engineering company in the south of England provides a detailed analysis of a strategic innovation and change programme over a nine-year period. Between January 1984 and December 1992, Pirelli General closed down its Southampton plant and opened a 'hi-tech' one in Aberdare, South Wales, 250 km away. At its opening in 1988, Pirelli Cables new plant was described as Britain's best example to-date of total automation and multi-skill employment. This study describes and explains how the idea of an automated factory emerged and how it was translated into reality. As its author discusses, what became clear as the project progressed was that the major innovation in the new organisation – *technology* – proved to have important implications for virtually all other aspects of the exercise. For example, high levels of computer integrated production at the Aberdare site would not have been possible without other incremental innovations having been made, such as in site location, building design and factory layout. Further innovations, some of them planned and others introduced incrementally, such as changes in organisation culture, organisation design and HRM (where a single union recognition agreement replaced a multi-union one), were also important. According to Clark (1995: 238), 'One of the important "lessons" of the Aberdare story is the extent to which technical, production, distribution, human resource, financial and commercial activities are interrelated.' Ensuring theoretical and practical fit was a 'highly complex and never-ending task, crucial to the realization of wider corporate, business and operational strategies'.

New technology, jobs and employment

Since the 1980s, a series of radical information-based technological advances has taken place globally, giving rise to the so-called digital age and the 'information based economy'. ICTs are the core of these developments. ICTs is the generic term given to the integration of the latest computer technology and networks with telecommunications systems, including telephone lines, mobile telephony, wireless signals, video conferencing, data sharing, interactive white boards, voicemail, email, text messaging, video-conferencing, faxing, the WWW, intranets, the social media (such as Facebook, Twitter and LinkedIn) and others. These developments promote e-business activities including e-commerce, procurement, knowledge management and customer relationships and have major implications for what work is done in organisations within national economies, who does it and how it is organised.

Two main conclusions can be drawn from these developments. First, the impact of ICTs is not uniform. They are potentially more revolutionary in some sectors or industries than in others. As communications-based technologies, ICTs have the ability to effect most change in communication-centred fields such as financial services, education, entertainment, direct sales retailing, health care and public information. They have a more limited role in manufacturing supply chains, travel and the energy sector. But they have a fundamental impact on any activity that relies heavily on communication and information flows, in both the marketplace and an organisation's systems for producing and delivering goods or services to its customers. ICTs also facilitate interdependence between organisations. As Child (2005: 33) concludes, the option of co-ordinating a range of complementary activities among network members through the use of ICTs 'has opened up a whole new area of choice about how to organize provision to customers and what to retain within the direct purview of a particular management team'.

A second conclusion is that the rate at which ICTs are introduced is affected by the regulatory barriers in fields such as financial services, government and institutional resistance in professional areas such as education and health care. However, ICTs are part of a wider trend in which technological innovation has come to play an increasingly important role in competitive strategy. The high economic return from innovation, when the first mover establishes new technical standards in the workplace, promotes technological development as a competitive strategy. The introduction of a new technology can generate that gust of 'creative destruction', identified by Schumpeter (1976) as a characteristic of business cycles, which can in extreme cases herald the demise of an entire industry, such as the impact that electronic technology had on the mechanical-based Swiss watch industry. Thus technological developments affect both the nature of what is produced and how it is produced. In manufacturing, new technologies such as biotechnology, genetic engineering and electronic publishing have had fundamental impacts. In banking, education, publishing, share dealing and telecommunications, the impact has been even more evident, where ICTs are facilitating new competitors and alliances across traditional industry boundaries (Ploetner 2012).

Given the intensity of these global technological changes, the impact of these new technologies on work, the distribution of work and how it is organised has been an issue of intense debate for some three decades. As Rifkin (2004: 290–292) argues, concern in western industrial countries about the transition to 'the third' industrial revolution 'over the jobs issue has led to growing ideological battles between warring groups'. He divides them into four sets of protagonists. First, there are the 'free-marketers' who accuse trade unionists of obstructing the process of globalisation and inciting the public with xenophobic appeals to protectionism. Second, 'the labor movement' counters with the claim that TNCs are pushing wages down by forcing their workers to compete with cheap labour from the developing world. Third, the 'technological optimists' accuse critics of advanced technology of trying to hold back progress and harbouring naïve neo-Luddite fantasies about the world of work. Fourth, the 'technological critics' charge technophiles with caring more about profits than people and, in pursuit of quick productivity gains, 'they are unmindful of the terrible toll that automation takes on the lives of millions of workers'. Interestingly, Rifkin's American solution to the 'end of work' debate is equally contentious and idealistic. His proposal is to find ways of transferring the productivity gains of the third industrial revolution 'from the market sector to the third sector, to keep pace with the increasing burden that will be placed on the social economy'.

Other writers, such as Gill (1985: 168–169), have, in retrospect, provided interesting and relatively accurate observations how ICTs, which were both labour saving and capital saving at the same time, could affect patterns of work and relations between employers and workers. His main predictions included, first, fewer people would be involved in full-time employment, which could not be guaranteed. Second, manufacturing would employ fewer people but operate at higher levels of productivity. Third, demand for higher qualified technically qualified workers would increase. Fourth, there would be more part-time and home working, short-term contracts and self-employment, with less guaranteed life-time employment. Fifth, there would be fewer manual jobs and more self-servicing in the home and community. Sixth, the trade union movement would be weakened. Presciently, he concluded, jobs 'will become increasingly difficult to find: an increasing number of economists are claiming that full employment will never return to Western societies'. All these factors have implications for how the employment relationship is organised and managed.

SOCIAL FORCES AND EMPLOYMENT RELATIONS

Employment relationships are also affected by wider social forces, in societies and internationally. 'Social forces' is a very broad term and includes virtually everything from population trends, crime and justice, the environment, and education and training to health, households and families, housing, transport, life styles and social policy. But these are not the categories of social forces discussed here. Drawing upon Kaufman (2004b: 58), the above broad categories of social forces can be narrowed down to more manageable and relevant ones to employment relations. Kaufman identifies five main social forces with 'an important influence' on employment relations. First, there is 'culture'. This influences behaviour 'operating through social norms, shared ideals and widely accepted customs and conventions'. Culture at national, organisational and workplace levels is important in employment relations, because it helps structure people's goals, values and preferences in terms of money and income, work and attitudes to work, the role of women and men in the workplace, and the value of individual versus collective action in employment relationships. Culture 'also defines rules for social behavior in the [employment] relations arena, such as standards for work effort and punctuality, acceptable forms of competition among workers, and the degree of acceptance of authority'.

The idea that national and organisational cultures have an impact on employment relationships is also taken up by Lewis *et al.* (2003: 93), where they suggest that strongly held 'beliefs and values will affect the nature of the employee relations policies and practices that are established within an organisation'. Such organisational cultures are likely to be differentiated, with a range of sub-cultures within them. The attributes of national cultures also affect aspects of the contract of employment and employment relationships, 'although this is likely to occur in a way that is taken for granted by those within a particular culture'. Unions typically owe their existence to lack of common interests between organisations and their employees. They have their own *separate* cultural histories, unique to each union and industry. There are therefore potential conflicts in values between, say, an employer's 'corporate' culture and the 'organising' culture of the union (Guglielmo 2011).

Second, social class is another primary force in the external environment of organisations and societies that affect employment relations. There are many definitions of social class but basically social classes 'are broad, relatively well-identified strata in society that determine one's position in the economic and social hierarchy' (Kaufman 2004b: 58–59). The impact of social class on employment relations is to separate employers from employees, or occupational and social groups within the workforce, into distinctive factions with divergent and conflicting interests and outlooks. Thus countries with rigid and well-defined class systems are more likely to feature highly developed forms of collective action, extensive union membership and corporate forms of economic organisation, as in parts of West Europe. Other countries, with less antagonistic social class structures, such as in North America, are more likely to have business unions and pragmatic market approaches to labour–management relations. Further, the language of class struggle, rooted in Marxist or socialist analyses of employment relations, sometimes permeates the rhetoric of union leaders with this social thinking (Hyman 1975, Kelly 1998). Thus in some countries, there are union leaders with political roots in Marxist thought, with little time for the notion of 'partnership' with employers. Indeed, writers such as Poole (1981: 135) argue that the 'structuration' of class 'is functionally integrated into the market structure of capitalism'. Goldthorpe and McKnight (2004: 1) claim, in turn, that class positions 'are seen as deriving social relations in economic life or, more specifically, from *employment* relations'. It seems likely that the varied tasks and operations of the contemporary capitalist function within enterprises have been absorbed by specialist agencies within them. This has resulted in a more complex class structure than in earlier periods of history, where some workers (such as managers) now perform both capitalist and labour functions at work (Crompton 1998).

A third social force is ethics. This represents the influence of moral principles and ethical values on the employment relationship. This relationship is ultimately 'about people and quality of life', thus warranting ethical analysis (Budd 2004: 66). For Budd, the normative aspects of work and employment, whether employment actions are thought of as 'right' or 'wrong', and the incorporation of business ethics into HRM and employment relations, provide 'the needed framework of evaluating existing employment [relations] practices'. In his view, business ethics can analyse these alternative ethical standards, as well as making HR and employment relations practitioners 'more comfortable facing moral complexity', thus enabling them to become better professionals (Solomon 1992: 4). Such an approach demands an explicit ethical element being incorporated into debates on employment, using known ethical theories for this analysis. These are generally divided into two categories: the first focusing on *outcomes* (teleological ethics), the second on *actions* (deontological ethics). Utilitarianism is a main example of the former and Kantian moral philosophy of the latter. But Budd (2004: 67) goes beyond this by providing six additional ethical frameworks for analysing the employment relationship: 'the ethics of utility, the ethics of duty, the ethics of liberty, the ethics of fairness, the ethics of virtue, and the ethics of care'.

A fourth social force is ideology in employment relations. For Dunlop (1958: 16–17), an employment relations ideology is the 'set of ideas and beliefs commonly held by the actors that helps to bind or to integrate the system together as an entity'. Ideology is the body of common ideas that defines the role and place of each actor 'and defines the ideas which each actor holds toward the place and function of the others in the system'. The problem with this definition of ideology is there is commonly more than one ideology in any employment relations system. In other words, an ideology is less likely 'to bind or integrate the system together' where one employment relations ideology competes with others. In this case, rather than binding 'the system together', such ideologies are not integrative at all but are in conflict with one another. If an ideology is a theory 'used to advocate and justify behaviors', there could be both an employer's ideology and, where a union is present, a union one, which may not be compatible with each other (Budd and Bhave 2008: 94). In this case, employer ideology may support the belief that employment relations decisions should be determined unilaterally by management, whereas the union ideology is likely to support the belief that employment relations decisions should be determined jointly between employer and union. This means an integrative ideology can only emerge where the organisation's managers decide to change their ideology by accepting the union function, thus binding the system and players together.

Fifth, history is another social force in employment relations. This arises because history reflects the influence of past events on current and future employment relationships. Further, employment relations systems at all levels are built incrementally on what has preceded them. This is what is meant by historical path dependency. Thus nation states with histories of class consciousness, militant trade unionism and frequent strike activity, and others with individualist cultures, individual bargaining and low strike frequency reflect these histories in their current employment relations systems. Early studies of 'industrial democracy' and 'labor relations' in the United States commonly embedded the historical method in their analyses and evaluations. In Britain, the works of Sidney and Beatrice Webb (1920a, 1920b) on British trade unions and the trade union function were rooted solidly in the tradition of English and German historical economics. According to Koot (1987: 178–179), these joint historical and economic works of the Webbs bore the trademarks of 'a vigorous opposition to the method and many of the conclusions of orthodox economics, a pessimistic interpretation of the social effects of the Industrial Revolution [and] an embrace of a state-regulated economy of trusts and labor union'. They also called 'for a measure of national social reform that they termed evolutionary socialism'.

Institutional labour economists in the United States, such as Commons, also specialised in historical labour research. This is exemplified in Commons' studies of the American shoemakers (1909) and his multi-volume history of labour in the United States (1918). These approaches to institutional economics and employment relations demonstrate their evolutionary and historical components, the path dependency of institutions leading to economic development, and how social, legal and technical relations, which market exchanges rest upon, are continually changing over time.

Some major historical studies in the field are found in the United Kingdom. These include: Turner's (1962) comparative history of the cotton workers' unions in the north of England; Fox's (1985) in-depth study of the historical and social origins of the United Kingdom's system of employment relations; Clegg's three volume history of British trade unionism (Clegg *et al.* 1964, Clegg 1985, 1994); and Gennard and his colleagues studies of British print worker unions (1990, 1995, 2008). Generally, limited use is made of history in the study of employment relations around the world today. Lyddon (2003: 102, 111, 108) argues that most current students of employment relations neglect the study of history in their subject, partly because of its dominant problem-solving approach. The reason is the problem-solving tradition in the field has 'generally elevated its practical over its theoretical content, making historians suspicious of its usefulness'. Historians, in turn, have reciprocated by 'ignoring industrial relations theory and concepts'. In Lyddon's view, this is reinforced by the tendency of many current employment relations specialists to abandon their own theoretical and conceptual heritages. If employment relations specialists cannot use the theoretical concepts common to their own field of study in their publications, 'then it is not surprising that historians take little notice of their work'.

CONCLUSION AND IMPLICATIONS

The varieties of capitalism debate is a good starting point in analysing the importance of the external contexts of employment relations. It contributes to explaining divergent patterns of employment relationships within different types of market economy. The basis of the varieties of capitalism approach is that employment relations between employers and workers are strongly influenced by the institutional structures within which they operate. Central to the varieties of capitalism debate is the idea of institutional complementarities. Institutions are said to be complementary to the extent that one enhances the effectiveness of another. Importantly, the varieties of capitalism approach argues it is not possible to understand employment relations phenomena in isolation and that comparative analysis needs to place changes in employment relations in these broader contexts.

Despite its apparent weaknesses, however, the variety of capitalism analysis is a helpful one, since it indicates that some forms of employment relations (such as sector-wide collective bargaining, or absence of collective bargaining, or corporatist arrangements at central level) are more widely adopted in some countries than in others. In liberal market economies, employers are driven by considerations of shareholder value, employees as an economic resource and short time-frames of decision-making that reduce the scope for partnerships between employers and employees. Business strategies are finance-driven, employee commitment is sought through financial incentives, and there are weak ties between firms. These are reflected in plant-level collective bargaining or absence of collective bargaining altogether. The reverse pattern is observed in co-ordinated market economies, which are characterised by longer-term decision-making, with less emphasis on financial controls. This type of market economy provides the basis for a less adversarial and more investment orientation to the labour force. Labour market institutions are more likely to be deeply embedded in co-ordinated market economies than in liberal market ones.

Gallie (2007) and his colleagues, in turn, compare quality of working life in Britain, France, Germany, Spain and Sweden. They focus particularly on skills and skill development, opportunities for training, scope for initiative in work, how to combine work and family life, and security of employment. Drawing on a range of national representative surveys, this study shows striking differences in quality of work in different European countries. It also provides comparative evidence on the experiences of different types of employee and an assessment of whether there has been a trend towards greater polarisation between a core workforce of secure employees and a peripheral one with cumulative disadvantages. Three theoretical perspectives are drawn upon: the common dynamics of capitalist societies, differences in production regimes between capitalist societies, and differences in institutional systems of employment regulation. It concludes that an 'employment regime' perspective (whether market, dualist, or inclusive) provides the most convincing account of the factors affecting quality of work in capitalist market societies.

In the global economy, the prime drivers of economic change and growth are international capital and product markets. Capital is relatively mobile and can be easily transferred between countries and between different segments of international money markets. The relationships between these segmented financial markets are complex and dynamic. Changes in one market impact on capital flows into or out of other markets. These market relationships may be relatively stable in normal economic conditions, but they are more volatile during periods of market stress (Cassidy 2010). This questions previously held notions of what 'normal market behaviour' is. Interest rates, inflation and economic growth rates, all affect the performance of different asset classes. However, national fiscal and monetary policies are not always sufficient to manage the dynamic aspects of international financial markets and national economies. It is now widely recognised that international financial crises could recur in the current financial system in the forms of credit, currency or debt dislocations. Any of these are likely to have adverse effects on business confidence, employment prospects and labour market outcomes when they happen, as they did in the global credit crisis 2007–2009 (Cable 2009).

There is powerful evidence that product market competition plays a critical role in determining union influence on wages and working practices. With slack product market competition, union influence is strong; but with tight product market competition, union influence is weak. As Metcalf (2005: 157) writes, 'more intense product market competition implies a corrosion of the impact of union recognition in the workplace which suggests that in the longer term unions may need to find a different role if they are to prosper'. This is confirmed by detailed quantitative studies of recent labour market performance in the United States and Europe. These demonstrate that current declines in union memberships might be a direct consequence of the product market reforms of the 1980s (Ebell and Haefke 2006). Also as product markets become more internationally exposed, employers cannot exercise control over wages by being members of employers' associations. 'If employers' associations do break up, the ending of the industrial collective agreements associated with them has severe implications for trade unions' (Brown 2008: 123). This means that the scope of private sector unions in industries exposed to global competition becomes increasingly weakened.

The labour market has to be looked at as a phenomenon affected by a range of conditions that are not ordinarily applicable to commodity or services markets and to which it is tied through the production process. It is a market through which wages are formed and labour is allocated among alternative uses. Adjustments within the labour market and its sub-markets are affected by impediments to labour mobility among occupations, industries and geographical areas. These are also related to the time required for substitutions of factors of production to take place, indicated by changes in the relative prices of labour and capital. The real dislocations associated with modern labour markets are in periods of low growth, rising unemployment and increasing industrial conflict over terms, conditions and the allocation of jobs in response to economic uncertainties.

The functions of labour market institutions, such as trade unions, are critical in terms of balance of bargaining power and issues of fairness between employers and unions, since union power declines in loose labour market conditions and increases in tight labour markets. However, during the period post-2008, the unshackling and freeing of financial markets particularly, supported by neo-classical economic policies, led many national economies from boom to bust and to recession. This created rising unemployment, weaker labour market institutions and declining union membership. It was only a return to government-led expansion in some states that moderated the global slump and vindicated a partial neo-Keynesian revival. In these circumstances, it was recognised that *both* macro-economic fiscal and monetary policies to adjust aggregate demand *and* micro-economic policies to free up trade were necessary instruments of economic management by national governments (Cassidy 2010).

State policy is an important influence on the contexts of labour markets and employment relations. States can promote collective bargaining or resist it; they can establish legally binding minimum wages or leave this to market forces and/or collective bargaining; they can create legal protections for workers against 'unfair' or unethical employment policies by managements or leave ethical policy decisions to employers alone; they can pursue Keynesian full employment labour market policies or rely on supply-side measures; or they can adopt mixes of these economic policy instruments. Whether the state intervenes in these employment policy decisions depends on how public policy is developed and implemented. It also depends on whether the state's role in employment and labour market issues is an active, passive or neutral one. Differences in economic policy goals, institutional arrangements and labour market factors are the key influences.

The technological revolution that contemporary societies are experiencing also impacts on employment relations, labour markets and the organisation of work. The pervasiveness of these technologies, and their impact on production costs, together with the rapid pace of their introduction, highlight the importance of finding ways to deal with their consequences for the future of work. It is Scandinavian countries that have taken the most positive steps to ensure that technological innovation is used to benefit society as a whole, instead of being limited by the 'laws' of the free market, thereby benefiting only the most powerful groups in society. In Scandinavia, the control and application of new technology is a political issue, not just an economic one. The threats and opportunities it offers are deemed to be too important to be left to market forces alone. New technology has implications for the future of not only work but also societies themselves. Technology and science are not neutral; the direction they take and the uses to which they are put reflect the interests of dominant groups in society (Graverson and Lansbury 1988).

This chapter shows that important social forces impact on employment relations too such as culture, social class, ethics, ideology and history. These forces demonstrate the inter-disciplinary nature of employment relations and the employment relationship. Thus scholars need to draw on concepts of sociology, philosophy and the history of ideas to contribute to their understanding of the complexity of the subject and the topics it covers, as well as economics, politics and law. Further, these social forces are constructs that affect people's perceptions of the employment relationship, its character and the values underpinning how the parties behave towards one another, including the role of the state. What unites the range of scholars studying the employment relationship is putting it at the centre of what modern market capitalism is about. As Stanworth and Giddens (1974) and others argue, what distinguishes capitalism as an economic system is that labour power becomes a commodity, where labour is bought and sold in the market. In capitalist market economies, with the partial exception of the European social model, treating labour as commodity is a universal human condition; this is the critical foundation upon which employment relations are created and organised.

4

THEORIES, IDEAS AND RESEARCH IN EMPLOYMENT RELATIONS

The purpose of this chapter is to discuss the specialist subjects which contribute to employment relations theory-building. These are the academic faces of the field. It also explores some of the ideas and values underpinning the field and outlines how scholars research empirical studies in employment relationships. Employment relations is an inter-disciplinary area of academic work, so there is no academic consensus about the theoretical frameworks used in categorising, analysing and evaluating issues in work and employment relationships. For Adams and Meltz (1993: 2), theory in employment relations, 'its nature, its content and its bounds are problematic. There is little consensus about what the term means or about the empirical phenomena to which it is intended to refer'. Indeed, many scholars hold there is no such thing as employment relations theory (Adams 1988). A similar point is made by Voos (1993: 19) who claims theory in employment relations 'is often the theory of its contributing social science and management disciplines, applied to the employment relationship'. Consequently, there is 'not one theoretical paradigm, but many'. Theories in the field are drawn from a series of academic disciplines such as economics, sociology, politics, law, psychology, geography and history, each with its own disciplinary perspective and distinctive analysis of the employment relationship (Ackers and Wilkinson 2003). Subjects having links with employment relations include management, organisational theory and gender studies. Employment relations also draws upon a range of concepts and ideas that are open to interpretation and academic debate. Examples include 'individualism', 'collectivism', 'unitarism', 'pluralism', 'fairness', 'ethical behaviour', 'the right to manage', 'institutional economics', 'managerialism', 'distributive justice', 'Marxism', 'psychological contracts', 'Catholic social teaching' and many others. These concepts are drawn from economics, social theory, political theory, ethics, and psychology. As an empirical social science, employment relations also uses a range of research methods.

ECONOMIC THEORY

Economics is an academic discipline, whose impact on the study of employment relations has been a major one since its early days. Economists have always been interested in the employment relationship, especially in the United States and United Kingdom, where economic perspectives have focused particularly on the labour market, wage determination and the effects of union intervention in the wage determination process. Interest has also been shown by economists in relative wage distribution, the occupational distribution of wages and the changing share of wages in national income (Ehrenberg and Smith 2006). Further, it is common for professors of 'industrial relations' in both American and British universities to be economists first and specialists in the employment relationship second (Clay 1929, Bakke *et al.* 1960, Richardson 1954, Metcalf 1999). However, the economics profession is sometimes criticised for its narrow and limited approach to employment relationships, because it is slow to recognise the role of institutions and power relations in shaping work and employment.

Economic concepts in employment relations

Compared with non-economists, there are distinctive methodological and conceptual differences in the ways in which economists study the employment relationship and labour market issues. As Grimshaw and Rubbery (2003: 44) write: 'Economics vacillates between attempting to explain all economic and social phenomena within its own framework of methodological individualism, thereby negating the need for other disciplinary approaches.' Some economists also selectively adopt 'the descriptive parts of other disciplinary approaches to "explain" why its universal models fail to hold in the empirical world'. The assertion by Hicks (1932: 1) that the 'theory of the determination of wages in a free market is simply a special case of the general theory of value', where wages are the price of labour and, 'in the absence of control, they are determined, like all prices, by supply and demand', has subsequently been discredited. Thus an economic analysis of the labour market without reference to trade unions makes little empirical sense. But for economists, the central role of market forces in studying wages and employment issues persists, where 'earnings are not determined in one market alone' but 'are a result of a multimarket equilibrium within all factor markets' (Polachek and Siebert 1993: 5).

When economists analyse labour markets and employment relationships, they draw upon two distinguishing features of economics methodology. First, they assume that *economic rationality* underpins the organisation of labour markets. Second, they use *methodological individualism* to explain behaviour and structures in labour markets and the role of incentives in motivating workers (Pfeffer 1997). Traditionally, economists have treated labour markets as purely economic constructs but, more recently, some have incorporated new variables and other relationships in their analyses. Thus Heilbroner and Milberg (2012) challenge the 'crisis of vision' in modern economic thought and Solow (1990: 21–22) argues that wage rates and jobs 'are not exactly like other prices and quantities'. For him, people's pay reflects the way they see themselves, including their social status and 'whether they are getting a fair shake out of society'. Further, buyers and sellers of labour might not accede to perceived injustice 'merely because of a little excess supply and demand'.

Figure 4.1 shows the three markets in which firms operate in capitalist market economies: the capital market, product market and labour market. Capital and product markets were considered in Chapter 3. Here the labour market is examined. In the labour market, employers demand labour; workers supply labour; and the major labour market outcomes between the parties are the *terms* of employment (such as wages, conditions, and other benefits) and *levels* of employment for different occupations and skills. Some elementary economic analysis is necessary to understand how demand and supply affect labour markets and wage determination, with and without unions. This is done by using professional engineers as an example.

Labour demand

In economic theory, a firm combines various economic factors of production, mainly labour and capital, to produce the goods or services it sells to customers. A firm's total output and the ways in which it combines capital and labour resources depend on product market demand, the amount of capital and labour it can buy at current prices, and the choice of technologies available to it (Garibaldi 2006). Firm demand for a particular type of labour, say professional engineers, and the number of professional engineers employed, depends on changes in wages and other forces affecting labour market demand – such as demand for its products or services, the supply of capital

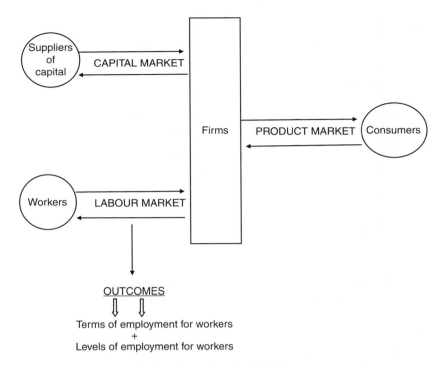

Figure 4.1 The markets in which firms operate

and existing technology. But basically, other things being equal, the higher the wages paid, the fewer the number of professional engineers are employed by the firm; the lower the wages paid, the greater the number of professional engineers are demanded. The underpinning issue is the firm employs professional engineers to increase profits; thus if wages rise, then engineers generate less profit, so the firm employs fewer of them, as indicated in Figure 4.2. The demand for professional engineers can be analysed not only at firm level, as in this example, but also at sector level and within the entire labour market.

What happens when one of the other forces affecting a firm's demand for professional engineers changes? First, where the demand for a firm's products increases, this is an *output* effect. This creates an increase in the number of professional engineers demanded at each possible wage rate. Second, a fall in the price of capital results in a fall in production costs, which increases the demand for capital, which stimulates production. The output effect in this case tends to increase the demand for professional engineers at each wage rate. However, it is also possible that a fall in capital prices might result in a *substitution* effect. This is where the firm adopts more capital-intensive technologies in response

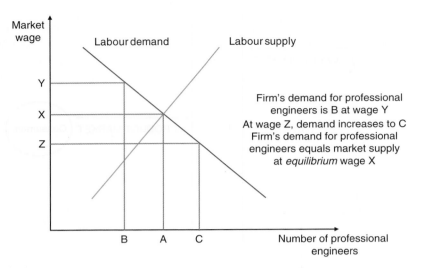

Figure 4.2 A firm's demand for professional engineers in relation to supply at different wage rates, assuming all other factors remain constant

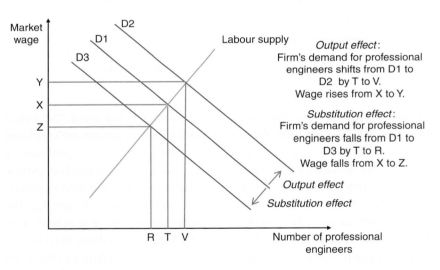

Figure 4.3 Possible effects on a firm's demand for professional engineers, arising from increased demand for a firm's products or a firm's capital

to cheaper capital. By substituting capital for labour, the firm demands less professional engineers at each wage rate, as shown in Figure 4.3. When a price of a substitute changes, therefore, the effect on demand for labour by a firm is unpredictable, because the output and substitution effects can work in opposite directions (Das 2007).

Economic theory also distinguishes between the firm's short-term demand for professional engineers and its long-term demand. Over very short time periods, an employer finds it difficult to substitute capital for labour (and vice versa) and customers may not change their demand for the firm's products in response to price increases. It takes time for a firm to adjust fully to changes in consumption and production behaviour. Over longer periods of time, responses to changes in wages or other forces affecting the demand for labour are larger.

Labour supply

In attracting a supply of professional engineers to work for it, a firm is unwise to pay the engineers it employs less than the 'going' or market wage rate, because at that wage it is not able to attract sufficient numbers of engineers of the right quality to work for it. Similarly, no firm will pay more than it needs to, if it is to recruit a suitable number of quality professional engineers, because it will have to pay more than the market wage rate. Thus in the short term, the supply of professional engineers to a firm is perfectly 'inelastic'. This means that market supply is fixed by the number of engineers who are available at that time. By paying the going wage rate, a firm is able to recruit all the professional engineers it needs. If it pays less, supply shrinks to zero, because engineers will prefer to work for firms paying the market rate. The assumption is that the individual firm is normally a 'wage taker'. Hence if a firm faces competition for the services of professional engineers in the labour market, the wages it pays must be fairly close to the going wage rate (Mulhearn and Vane 2012).

Examining the *market* supply of professional engineers raises the question: how does market supply respond to changes in the wages that these engineers might receive? If the wages of related occupations are held constant and those of professional engineers rise, this is likely to result in more individuals wanting to become engineers. Thus supply of labour to a particular market is related positively to the wage rate in that sector, holding other wages constant. And, if the wages of professional engineers rise, then more people will want to become engineers, because of their relative improvement in compensation. Similarly, if the wages of comparable workers rise, then the supply of professional engineers falls, since fewer people will want to become engineers. In other words, increases in the wages of comparable workers result in a decrease in the market supply of professional engineers. Conversely, decreases in the wages of comparable workers can result in an increase in market supply of engineers.

Another way of looking at labour market supply is to view professional engineers as sources of 'human capital'. This measures an engineer's or any other worker's professional competencies, knowledge, social attributes, health attributes, and personality including creativity which enable engineers to work and thus produce something of economic value in the marketplace. 'Thus, it can be recognized that human capital means one of production elements which can generate added-values through inputting it' (Kwon 2009: 1). Basically, it takes time to train engineers, so when demand for engineers increases, all firms can do initially is poach from one another or go overseas to recruit. In the longer term, individuals train to become engineers, because the higher wage results in an increase in the supply of professional engineers nationally.

Determination of the wage

Economic analysis demonstrates that the wage in a particular labour market is heavily influenced by demand and supply. Using the example of professional engineers again, the market demand indicates how many engineers employers want to employ at each wage rate, holding capital and consumer incomes constant. The market supply of professional engineers indicates, in turn, how many will enter the labour market at each wage rate, holding the wages of other occupations constant. The wage rate at which market demand for professional engineers equals the market supply is the *market-clearing* or *equilibrium* wage (Borjas 2013). At this wage, employers can fill all the jobs they have and all professional engineers wanting jobs can find them. At the market-clearing rate, there is no shortage or surplus of professional engineers. All parties are satisfied and no forces exist to alter the market wage rate. This means the market is in equilibrium and the wage remains at this level, until conditions change, assuming perfect competition in the firm's product and labour markets. When the labour market clears, all those willing to work at that wage can get jobs; but some professional engineers wanting jobs are not willing to take them at the market clearing rate.

Once market equilibrium for professional engineers is achieved, changes can occur in either the demand for or supply of them. Thus if opportunities for employment in comparable occupations rise, fewer individuals will want to be professional engineers. There is now a shortage, because market demand exceeds supply. The *new* equilibrium wage is higher than the original, with the result that improved job opportunities elsewhere result in increases in the market wage of professional engineers. Similarly, if there is an increase in market demand for professional engineers, the old equilibrium wage rate no longer equates demand with supply, since there will be a shortage of engineers in the labour market. This labour shortage induces employers to improve their wage offers to professional engineers, eventually driving up the wage rate from the original equilibrium to a higher level. In both cases, the decrease in market supply of engineers and the increase in market demand create market shortages, leading to increases in the market wage rate. Thus a shift in the market supply and demand for professional engineers results in increases in market wage rates. But whereas the supply shift leads to a fall in the equilibrium level of employment, the demand shift results in an increase.

Although this rarely happens, the equilibrium wage for professional engineers can also fall. This occurs when there is an increase in market supply, as more people enter the labour market and the equilibrium level of employment increases. The causes of an increased supply of professional engineers at each wage rate are due to either a greater desire of people to become engineers or reductions in the wages of comparable occupations. A decrease in the market demand for engineers, in turn, causes a decrease in the equilibrium wage, accompanied by a fall in the equilibrium level of employment. It is possible, of course, for the market wage for professional engineers to be affected by changes in both their market demand and supply at the same time. These simultaneous market changes might either reinforce or work against each other (Borjas 2013).

Unions and wage determination

In any elementary economic analysis of the effect of unions on the wages of professional engineers, unions representing them are assumed to be able to affect market supply in two ways. First, unions operate through collective agreements negotiated with firms, covering wages and conditions of employment. As indicated in Figure 4.4, with industry-wide or sector bargaining, the union is able to raise the 'mark-up' wage above the market-clearing or equilibrium rate from X to Y through collective bargaining and the threat of possible industrial action against employers, if they fail to agree to the union's wage demands. With a collectively negotiated wage rate above equilibrium level, *employment levels* are below those if the market wage was lower. In economic analysis, because the wage cannot fall, there is a surplus of unemployed professional engineers who cannot get jobs with unionised employers. The second way in which unions can affect the supply of professional engineers is by controlling entry to the labour market. Unions use 'closed shop' or 'union shop' agreements to do this, where engineers have to be union members to get a job. With union-only labour agreements, firms are required to hire *all* professional engineers through the union. In other words, the union controls which

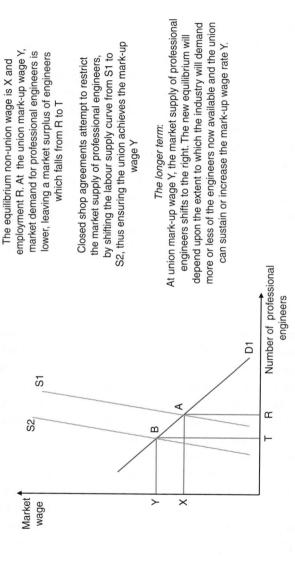

The short term:

The equilibrium non-union wage is X and employment R. At the union mark-up wage Y, market demand for professional engineers is lower, leaving a market surplus of engineers which falls from R to T

Closed shop agreements attempt to restrict the market supply of professional engineers, by shifting the labour supply curve from S1 to S2, thus ensuring the union achieves the mark-up wage Y

The longer term:

At union mark-up wage Y, the market supply of professional engineers shifts to the right. The new equilibrium will depend upon the extent to which the industry will demand more or less of the engineers now available and the union can sustain or increase the mark-up wage rate Y.

Figure 4.4 The wages and employment of professional engineers under industry-wide collective bargaining and closed shop agreements

and how many engineers it recruits into membership. The dual power of the union to restrict its membership and require firms to hire only union members to work for them allows it to control the supply of professional engineers to the labour market (Booth 1995).

INSTITUTIONAL THEORY

There is no single, integrated theory of employment relations that plays a central role in the subject. Compared with mainstream economics, theory in employment relations 'has a lower status and a much greater range of ideas' (Voos 1993: 19). But if there *is* a common body of widely accepted thinking underpinning the study of employment relations over time, it is the institutional approach. Rooted in institutional economics and the works of Commons and his colleagues of the Wisconsin school of industrial relations in the early twentieth century, institutional theorists insist that any theory of employment relations should be grounded in the *facts* of real life. Institutional theory was developed to counteract neo-classical orthodoxy and observes the historical, social and political contexts in which economic activity takes place.

Institutional economics

According to Kaufman (1988: 190), the institutional approach attempts to build an economic theory built around humankind congruent with the principles of social psychology, 'a model of markets that is grounded in the economics of imperfect competition, and a conception of the market process that gives considerable weight to the role of institutions (broadly defined)'. Studies of collective bargaining and trade unionism in Britain by Sidney and Beatrice Webb (1920a, 1920b) pioneered some key aspects of the institutional tradition. As Farnham (2008: 547) concludes, the theoretical legacy of the Webbs was to provide 'the intellectual foundations of the pluralist-institutional model of industrial relations in Britain'. The Webbs, in short, 'discovered' trade unions. Before them, 'neither governments, nor civil servants, nor politicians, nor trade unions themselves [knew] what the form of the trade union movement was, what it had achieved, and what its functions had been and might be' (Woolf 1949: 254).

It was Commons and his colleagues in the University of Wisconsin who were pivotal in developing and establishing institutional employment relations. Commons gave all actors in employment relations – management, employees, unions, and government – both legitimacy and functionality. He also formulated the essential logic of employment relations. His analytical starting point is the special nature of labour as a human commodity and he builds his analytical system upon this. For him, labour's 'soul' and humans with 'wills of their own' do not bend easily to management's drive for cost effectiveness and the engineer's theory of labour as machinery (Commons 1950: 155). As the Webbs had argued before him, the worker as a 'propertyless seller of himself [*sic*]' lacks the bargaining power of the 'propertied buyer' of labour and the worker alone is unable to bargain equally with the employer (Commons and Andrews 1936: 1). For Commons, this inequality of bargaining power is not resolved by eliminating market capitalism but by reforming it. This is done by building collective bargaining institutions between employers and unions within nation states and by enlightened employers acting in their own self-interest within pluralist political democracies. Collective bargaining is responsive to labour's needs by giving it 'voice' and how labour is employed. Thus the 'new equity' of Commons (1959: 307) protects the job, 'as the older equity protected the business'. Labour's 'goodwill' can improve efficiency and the intangible 'goodwill of labor may be as profitable as the scientific management of labor' (Commons 1919: 18).

Much of Commons' framework was developed by his students at Wisconsin. Perlman (1928) spells out the Wisconsin model of job-conscious unionism. Like Commons, Perlman rejects socialism as the necessary historical mission of the working class and union movement. For him, workers care more about getting the best wage bargain from employers than who owns the means of production (Perlman 1922: 267). Slichter (1928: 287) more incisively than anyone else formulates the major premise of employment relations: the labour problem exists because humankind 'is not only the end but also the means of production', causing 'a clash between life and work'. He views collective bargaining as a system 'of industrial jurisprudence' promoting 'civil rights in industry', where management is 'by rule rather than by arbitrary decision' (Slichter 1941: 2). Further, in the 'laboristic state', there is the gradual shift from a capitalistic community 'to a community in which employees rather than businessmen [*sic*] are the strongest single influence' (Slichter 1961: 255).

Many employment relations scholars subsequently adopted the institutional approach. They explained and analysed employment relations and were instrumental in building collective bargaining frameworks and public policy decisions in their countries. This was especially the case in the United States, Britain and Australasia, even if some of these scholars would have abjured the 'institutional' label (Dunlop 1958, Roberts 1968, Clegg 1970, Kochan *et al.* 2007, Dabscheck 1995).

Pluralism

A major element in institutional theory is pluralism. A noted apologist for pluralism is Clegg (1975: 309). He argues that pluralism emerged as a critique of the doctrine of political sovereignty, whose central feature is that in any independent political system there must be an ultimate, definitive authority whose decisions are final. 'Not so, said the pluralist, within a political system there are groups with their own interests and beliefs.' Governments depend on their consent and co-operation to govern effectively. Within pluralist political systems, there 'are no definitive decisions by final authorities: only continuous compromises'. A plural society, in other words, is a relatively stable but not a static one. Such societies have to accommodate different pressure groups to enable political, economic and social changes to be made and executed constitutionally. This is done through negotiation, concession and compromise between government and these bodies.

Translating political pluralism into employment relations pluralism is based on the argument that just as democratic societies are made up of a series of interest groups, held together in some sort of loose equilibrium by the agency of the state, so modern organisations are made up of a number of stakeholders held together in equilibrium by the agency of management. The pluralist concepts of political sovereignty and managerial prerogative have much in common. Pluralist thinking views trade unions or works councils, for example, as the legitimate representatives of employee interests, with the rights to challenge the right to manage or provide means for transmitting employee views to management. There are also similarities between the processes of political exchanges, concession and compromise and collective bargaining, joint consultation and participative styles of management. Above all, pluralists argue that 'greater stability and adaptability is given to industrial relations by collective bargaining than by shackling and outlawing trade unions' (Clegg 1975: 311).

Pluralist analyses of parliamentary democracy and collective bargaining as conflict-resolving and rule-making processes were the dominant academic orthodoxy in these fields during the 1950s, 1960s and 1970s. Pluralist scholars emphasise the 'mixed-motive' nature of the employment relationship. They see conflict between employers and employees as inevitable but as a product of their roles and functions, not because of unremitting class conflict between capital and labour. For the Webbs (1897, 1920a, 1920b), the issue turns on whether employers are willing to forego 'dictatorship' inside their own workshops and submit conditions of employment to an effective system of joint control by collective bargaining or other means. Commons and Andrews (1936) and Perlman (1928) also address this core issue. With both employers and employees having 'mixed motives' in the employment relationship, pluralists focus on both the conflicts between the parties and their capacity, through collective bargaining, to identify common ground between them. Pluralist analyses of collective bargaining highlight unions as independent worker institutions acting as agents between employers and employees, not as militant bodies within the critical tradition of employment relations.

Conflict theory

Institutional analyses of employment relations are underpinned not only by pluralist perceptions of employer–employee relations. They also incorporate acceptance of basic conflicts of interest between employer and employee in the employment relationship. Thus if an employer pays more wages to workers, its profits are likely to fall, unless there is an increase in worker productivity. Similarly, when employees take strike action against their employer, the firm loses revenues and incurs financial losses. In institutional analyses, a central feature of employment relationships is acceptance of possible conflicts between employer and employee, and between managers and managed, over terms, conditions or procedural issues. The ultimate expression of this conflict is strike action by workers or a lock-out by employers. Thus conflict theory accepts the rationale and nature of trade unionism, giving it both a representative function and an important role in regulating conflicts of 'interest' (about new issues) or conflicts of 'rights' (about existing issues) between the players. Unions are not viewed as *causing* these conflicts. Collective bargaining is recognised as the institutional means by which any differences between employers and employees over the wage–work bargain are adapted, regularised and resolved. Conflict at work is accepted by pluralists as being inevitable in the wage–work bargain. But conflict also needs to be contained within the institutional mechanisms of joint negotiation, conciliation, arbitration or the law.

Marx supports this assumption of workplace conflict throughout history but extends his analysis into the political sphere. Once this assumption is accepted, logic points towards worker ownership and control of the means of production to ameliorate conflict. For him, this is the only means for overcoming the exploitation of labour and alleviating its alienation from the production process. Thus early writings by Marx and Engels (1970), Lenin (1947), Luxemburg (1971) and Gramsci (1957) provide powerful challenges to the pluralist 'mixed motive' perspective, by arguing that non-Marxist analyses of workplace conflict are incomplete and justify the existing social order.

Coser (1956) devises a non-Marxist theory of social conflict by exploring the ideas of Simmel (1964) in his classical study of conflict and group affiliations. Coser analyses conflict in terms of its interactive processes and depicts it as a form of socialisation. No group can be entirely harmonious, since it would lack both process and structure. Group formation is a result of association and dissociation, so that both conflict and co-operation serve social functions within groups. For Coser some degree of conflict is an essential element in group formation and interactions between groups. He concludes that conflict tends to be dysfunctional only where it is either insufficiently tolerated or not institutionalised. According to Coser, highly intense conflicts threaten to tear societies apart and arise only within rigid social structures, as in the dictatorial political regimes of the Middle East in the Arab Spring after 2010 (Dabashi 2012). What threatens established social structures is not conflict but the rigid character of existing structures and the inflexibility of the key players within them. Transferred to employment relations, conflict between employers and employees, and employers and unions, is positively functional for the parties, provided these are regularised through appropriate institutional mechanisms.

Another non-Marxist observer, Dahrendorf (1959), claims that the social structures of advanced societies have undergone significant changes since Marx's time. These have resulted in a transformed capitalism – what he calls 'industrial society' – where power is vested in 'imperatively coordinated institutions' and professional experts. The structural changes incorporated within industrial society have produced a world fundamentally different from the capitalism of the past. For Dahrendorf (1959: 257), conflict is situated mainly in large bureaucratic institutions. Typical conflicts in industrial society are those which develop between experts and lay people and between groups of experts competing for influence. He argues that industrial conflict has both changed its forms and decreased in intensity. What mitigates conflict at work includes: organised groups of competing interests; negotiating bodies between employers and workers; institutions of mediation and arbitration; labour representation in enterprises; and 'tendencies towards institutionalization of workers' participation in industrial management'. Dahrendorf's vision of industrial societies is that they are 'open societies', where political, economic and social power is increasingly dispersed. And regulation of industrial and political conflict is dissociated and employment relationships are formally structured.

MANAGEMENT THEORIES AND EMPLOYMENT RELATIONS

In capitalist market economies, managerial ideology is the ways in which managers *think* about what management is and what it means in practice. Combined with ideology, theories of management and organisation in western countries are powerful sources of legitimacy for managers (Hales 2001); and many of these theories and ideas have been imported, through managerial practices in TNCs and international management education programmes, into other parts of the world,. Managers are able to draw upon these ideas to cope with and manage not only the *technical* complexities of organisation and management, especially in large enterprises, but also the *social* consequences of employment relationships and personnel management issues (Clegg *et al.* 2011, Legge 2005). The employer–employee relationship is a command one. Workers seeking jobs have freedom in principle to negotiate a wage contract with an employer. However, once selected and employed by an organisation, workers become employees subject to the legal authority of management for the jobs they do. Much management theory is directed at legitimising managerial rule in organisations. Such theories tend to argue that managers play an integrative function within organisations, especially regarding the workers employed by them, to enable these organisations achieve their business and economic purposes.

Bureaucracy

The sociologist Max Weber was a 'founding father' of the study of organisations and the role of power within them. He was an academic polymath writing in German on a wide range of sociological topics in the late-nineteenth century and early-twentieth century. His study of bureaucracy (*der Bürokratismus*) was only one field in which he worked (Mommsen 1974). Weber believed that what held societies and organisations together was a sense of authority. In his analysis, authority could be enforced by power or coercion, held together by the charisma of its leaders, or derived from 'tradition'. According to Weber, these forms of authority were being superseded by a new form of 'rational-legal' authority. Here, obedience to authority is secured through formal reasoning. This rational-legal authority takes the form of rules, procedures and duties. Thus the authority vested in a modern chief executive officer, for example, comes from the job itself, not the person. Chief executives are obeyed because of the job they hold, not because of their coercive power, charisma or the role of tradition. When a new person takes on that role, authority transfers to that individual. This is rule by 'office', not rule by power, personality or ascription. The kind of organisation emerging from the application of the rational-legal principle – a bureaucracy – is one defined by rules and a series of hierarchical relationships.

As an 'ideal type', bureaucracy incorporates rationality in decision-making, impersonality in social relations, standardisation of tasks, and centralisation of authority. Weber identifies five essential characteristics of bureaucracy. First, the activities supporting the bureaucratic structure are officially defined and supported by a consistent set of rules. Only those suitably qualified are employed and they are governed by these rules. Second, all bureaucratic structures have different levels of authority within a graded hierarchy, which regulate the relationships of their component parts. Third, uniformity of operation is ensured by managerial procedures based on written documents. Fourth, the nature of contacts among officials and between officials and members of the public are also governed by rules relating to office and hierarchy. Contacts are impersonal and the distance between hierarchical levels is maintained. Fifth, holding office is more than a job; it is a vocation. Formal training and qualifications are essential for entry to office and the working life of officials is bound up with a complex system of obligations and associated rewards.

Whatever the dysfunctions of bureaucracy, such as groups of managers with the same backgrounds, gender and education (Kanter 1996) or when bureaucrats indulge their own prejudices and preferences in their conduct (Crozier 1964), the implications for HR and employment relations are obvious. Bureaucratic organisations produce bureaucratic HR systems and employment relations structures, policies and rules. These normally cover recruitment and selection, dismissal and retirement, and negotiating procedures, mirroring the general bureaucratic order. But bureaucratic HR or employment relations systems and rules, in turn, can generate their own dysfunctions.

Scientific management

Scientific management or Taylorism is originally associated with Frederick Winslow Taylor. An American mechanical engineer, he worked in the iron and steel-making sector during the rapid industrialisation of the United States in the late nineteenth and early twentieth centuries. This was an industry where it was normal for workers to organise their own work. Gangs hired their own crews, worked at their own pace, used their own tools and knew more about their work than their supervisors. However, Taylor (1947) believed that workers were naturally lazy, would slack off when they wanted to (he called this 'soldiering'), and would deliberately restrict output and maximise staff levels to retain jobs. He argued that the solution was applying the principles of 'Scientific Management' to work processes within factories. It was a management theory based on his observations of analysing and synthesising workflows, with the objective of improving efficiency, raising labour productivity and changing methods of working. He identified five basic principles of scientific management: a 'science' of each element of work; scientific selection and training of workers; payment by piecework; a division of labour between workers and managers; and cooperation between managers and workers. He did not support trade unionism in the workplace.

Under scientific management, workers were regarded as no more than components in an efficiency-driven organisational machine. But Taylor believed his system of working embodied 'a fair day's work for a fair day's pay' and would make workplaces safer. Taylor's influence on management methods in the heydays of industrial capitalism was both global and revolutionary. The principles of scientific management, despite their weaknesses, spread throughout the United States, Britain, France, Nazi Germany, Canada, Switzerland and later in the Soviet Union and East Germany after the Second World War (Merkle 1980). This was despite Taylorism failing to take account that individuals are different from one another and the most efficient way of working for one person may be inefficient for another. Further, he did not recognise that the economic interests of workers and management are rarely identical. Thus both the measurement processes and the retraining required by Taylor's methods were frequently resented and sometimes sabotaged by workers and their workgroups.

Hostility to scientific management was enormous, especially by the workers affected by it. The outcome was an intense power struggle between management and their workforces and with unions for control of the work process. Shenhav (1999) shows how scientific management was part of the 'standardisation movement'. It was bitterly contested, with critics arguing it was inimical to American individualism, creative innovation and entrepreneurial initiatives. Indeed, Taylorism resulted in a massive transfer of power from workers to managers, reduced worker autonomy, eroded working conditions, and threatened unemployment. Later Braverman (1974) and other labour process scholars claimed that Taylorism was both radical and disruptive. It implemented a 'near complete separation between conception and execution' or 'planning and decision-making, on the one hand, and carrying out orders on the other' (Grey 2009: 40). Despite this hostility to Taylorism, it continues to survive in many organisations today.

Taylorism was later introduced in an even more intensive way to the Ford Motor Company and elsewhere by the moving assembly line (Beynon 1975). Fordism, as it became known, had three main effects. First, managers gained even greater control of the work rate by simply speeding up the conveyor belt. Second, industrial sabotage, high levels of absenteeism and staff turnover characterised the company. Third, management–union relations were inevitably adversarial and confrontational. As one union shop steward in Ford's Halewood plant in England was graphically reported as saying: 'I don't know what I am, or what I want to do. I hate Ford's. I'd give up a wage increase to have Henry Ford on this section and give him a good kick up the arse' (Beynon 1975: 131).

The human factor in management

Human relations theory has its roots in the so-called Hawthorne Studies conducted in the Hawthorne works of the Western Electric Company, near Chicago in the United States, in the 1920s and 1930s. A leading player in the Human Relations School' was an Australian, Elton Mayo, who had migrated to the United States in the 1920s. The major contribution that Mayo and his colleagues made to the study of management and theory in the field was the importance of the 'human factor' in organisations. Despite later criticisms of the Hawthorne data, based on the 'illumination' and 'bank wiring room' experiments, these studies argue that workers are not simply motivated by economic considerations but that the 'informal' side of organisation is just as important as the 'formal' side (Roethlisberger and Dickson 1939, Mayo 1933). The main themes running through the work of Mayo and his colleagues are, first, work is a group rather than an individual activity, where people find a sense of belonging and need for recognition. It is small groups that have an important influence on the disposition and well-being of individual workers. Second, when workers complain, this indicates underlying psychological issues. Third, management can foster collaboration with informal groups by creating greater cohesion and unity between them, with benefits to organisations. Thus human relations theory was offered as a remedy for the failures of Taylorism but there was no role for unions or employee voice in providing solutions to the dysfunctional characteristics of Taylorism.

Discovery of the human factor in organisations was not of course new. This had been present in the works of Robert Owen and other philanthropic factory owners in nineteenth-century Britain, such as in the Quakers businesses at Port Sunlight and Bourneville (Owen 1970). Critics of the human relations school also argue that whereas Taylor had sought to remove the informal side of organisation, early proponents of human relations theory wanted to find ways of aligning the informal with the formal organisation. In this way, managers would retain organisational control. Hence human relations theory in practice was an extension of scientific management, not a replacement for it, and, like Taylorism, was rooted in instrumental rationality at work.

There was renewed interest in the non-unionised human factor in organisations in the United States during the 1960s and 1970s. This followed the emergence of social movements there during the 1960s. These included the youth counter-culture on the West coast, the new feminist movement, and student protests in the universities (Boltanski and Chiapello 2005). The 'neo-human relations' school was made up of a disparate group of US scholars, who drew largely upon psychological and 'behavioral science' approaches to organisations and their managerial problems. These studies include: Argyris's (1970) concern with integrating individual and organisational needs in enterprises; McGregor's (1960) 'theory X' and 'theory Y' styles of management; Herzberg's *et al.* (1959) 'motivation-hygiene' model of worker behaviour; and Bennis's (1969) theories of 'organisational development'. Such writers were not hostile to trade unionism; they simply believed them unnecessary where the human factor was managed effectively.

By the 1970s and 1980s, however, the ideas generated by successive generations of human relations theorists were running out of steam. The next 'big idea' to be developed in 'person-centred management theory' in the United States was 'culture management'. The reasons for this were, first, American big business was beginning to be challenged by Japanese and other Asian competitors. As Pascale and Athos (1982) observe, whereas American management theory and practice had been preoccupied with rational and systemic aspects of management, the Japanese had adopted a more holistic approach to managerial issues, focusing on people skills and shared values in the enterprise. Further, Japanese corporations were successful. Second, the United States was recovering from the social and political scars resulting from its failures in the Vietnam and Cambodian wars and the economic effects of oil price rises in the 1970s. Third, there appeared to be an imminent collapse of the mystique of American management. For some observers, the positive effects of the long-term Puritan legacy on American management from the seventeenth century to the late 1970s had by this time effectively evaporated (Hopper and Hopper 2007, Locke, 1996).

Corporate culture, post-bureaucracy and change management

One outcome of this was widespread adoption of 'culture management' as the new nostrum in managerial thinking, in not only the United States but also other parts of the world. Just as human relations theory had presaged a fresh managerial initiative in managing people, culture management became the new orthodoxy for managers within some firms. In the search for 'shared values' in organisations, *workers* not work became the main focus of managerial attention. This affected recruitment and selection, rewards and compensation, and the measuring and evaluation of worker performance. From a management perspective, and in its ideal form, culture management 'aspires to intervene and regulate being, so that there is no distance between individuals' purposes and those of the organization for which they work' (Grey 2009: 69). Culture management, in short, aims to promote self-managing, self-disciplined individuals in organisations, where unions have no role in facilitating this.

Post-bureaucratic theories of management are a counter-response to bureaucracy in enterprises. Ideas of 'post-bureaucracy' began to emerge from the late 1970s, with the claim by some observers that Fordist conditions in organisations were no longer tenable. The basic argument was that Fordism was giving way to a post-Fordist era, where employees had to be more flexible and innovative in the ways in which they worked. It was also argued that advanced market economies were shifting away from manufacturing, based on standardisation and mass-production methods, to niche markets and short production runs in conditions of change (Farnham 2010a). The proposed outcome was that businesses had to adopt different forms of organisation. This required them to move from bureaucratic structures to what Hatch and Cunliffe (2012) and others call post-bureaucratic, post-modern or networked ones.

Donnellon *et al.* (1984) provide an ideal type of post-bureaucratic organisation in contrast to Weber's ideal type bureaucracy. First, rules are replaced by consensus and dialogue, based on personal influence rather than status. Within such organisations, people are trusted to act through shared values rather than through rigid rules. Second, responsibilities within post-bureaucracy are based on allocation by competence for tasks not by hierarchy, with people being treated as individuals rather than impersonally. Third, organisations are perceived as having 'open boundaries'. This requires people entering and exiting organisations flexibly rather than on a full-time, long-term basis. The result is increased use of part-time contracts, temporary contracts or consultancy arrangements. Work is no longer done in fixed numbers of hours or at designated locations but according to demand for it.

The extreme example of this is 'zero-hours contracts'. These create an on-call contract between employer and employee, where the employer does not provide regular work for the employee and the employee agrees to be available for work when the employer requires it. No particular hours or times of work are specified in the contract. And employees are paid the national minimum hourly rate. The CIPD estimates that in 2013 about one million workers were employed on zero-hours contracts in the United Kingdom, or 4 per cent of the country's workforce (CIPD 2013). In Australia too, over two millions employees were casualised in 2013, without 'access to sick pay or holiday pay, could be dismissed without notice and are not guaranteed fixed hours of work' (Teicher *et al.* 2013: 274).

Thompson and Alvesson and Thompson (2005) and other writers challenge these assumptions, through a series of case studies. They argue, in the world of practice, that bureaucracy never went away, though in crucial respects it has changed its form and content. They demonstrate that job structures and work experiences have been remarkably unaltered by a post-bureaucratic model of organisation. What has happened is the growth in some countries of service-based economies, resulting in increases in low-skill standardised work in catering, call centres and telesales, not in advanced technological work. Similarly, Delbridge (1998: 192) argues in his ethnographic studies of two British factories, a Japanese-owned electronics plant and a European-owned automotive component manufacturer, that there is considerable similarity between traditional and new forms of working. Contemporary manufacturing is hardly post-Fordist, he concludes. Neither is the shop floor 'a hotbed of worker autonomy and knowledge creation'.

A second narrative linked with post-bureaucracy and culture management is the ubiquity and pervasiveness of a 'change' agenda and its possible adverse effects on organisations if not managed effectively. Carnall (1995: 1) claims that in a changing world the only constant is change. For him, 'the stability which seemed to characterise the corporate world in the 1950s and 1960s has given way to increased and global competition, technological innovation and change, limited resources, deregulation, privatisation of public sector organisations and change in much more besides'. As a result, and following assertions about the constant threat of 'change' to organisations, another mantra proclaimed to and by managements is rediscovery of change and the need to respond to it to protect the integrity of organisations and the competitive pressures facing them (Lewin 2008). But for scholars such as Grey (2009: 107), this is exaggerated. Clearly change is an incremental process over time but for him: 'All these claims about post-bureaucracy and change are really an exercise of [managerial] power.'

Japanese management theory

Japanese management ideas or Japanisation became a focus of much management attention in some western states from the late 1970s and early 1980s. This arose partly from the large inward investment of Japanese companies in automobile manufacturing and the electronics sectors in North America and West Europe at this time. It was also the result of increasing competitive pressures in international markets. Early debates about Japanisation concentrated on the feasibility of transferring certain group-oriented employment relations and HR processes to the individualistic Western hemisphere, such as 'single-union deals' for collective bargaining, team working and managing quality at work (Wickens 1987). Later debates focused on what western managers could learn from the economic success of Japanese management methods in terms of production and labour control. The methods used included quality management, customer orientation, partnership agreements between employers and unions, no-strike agreements, and non-recognition of unions on 'greenfield' sites (Ackroyd and Procter 1998).

Stewart *et al.* (1990) identify three approaches to understanding Japanisation. First, the *structural* approach shows how Japanisation impacts on indigenous firms, ranging from direct impact, to mediated impact, to full Japanisation. Direct impact includes controlling suppliers; mediated impact is where indigenous firms imitate some aspects of Japanese management methods; and complete Japanisation is where firms seek to transplant the full range of Japanese management methods into their businesses. Second, the *process* approach is where Japanisation provides concentration of production. This is designed to secure managerial control over the firm's business and social environments. It includes involvement in local communities, close contacts with suppliers, and marginalising or eliminating trade unions from the business. The driver is increased global competition and is observed in its most extreme forms in the automobile sector.

Third, there is the *supermarket* approach. This is the extent to which an indigenous firm or industry adopts clusters of Japanese management techniques, which focus on labour flexibility and lean production (Wickens 1995, Deming 1986, Dale 2003). These techniques include *kaizen* (continuous improvement), *kanban* (just-in-time production), *ringsei* (team building), total quality management, and statistical process control. Some of these quality control techniques were developed by Edward Deming (2000) an American mathematician, statistician and engineer. In the 1950s, he had tried to introduce them into some American companies. But his efforts were rejected by American managements, on the grounds that his emphasis on statistical control techniques was fading into disuse at this time. This was in the face of large overseas demand for American mass-produced products during these years. However, he introduced these management methods in Japan from the 1950s, with great success for himself, Japanese companies and the Japanese economy.

EMPLOYMENT RELATIONS AND THEORIES OF CHANGE

Theorising in employment relations is dominated by static cross-sectional models, including systems theory. Despite attempts to build in a dynamic change element into the systems model, such as by Blain and Gennard (1970), this has never been done convincingly or effectively. However, adopting an historical approach to the study of employment relations enables its change dimensions to be built into the theorising process, since all history is ultimately the study of change in its various manifestations (Farnham 1974). As Lyddon (2003: 112) writes, specialists in employment relations can only benefit from engagement with history 'whether they want to change the world, to fix it, or just interpret it'. Heery (2008) accepts this premise and attempts to map various models of historical change used by employment relations scholars in their empirical work. He identifies six models of change and applies them to theories of union revitalisation. These models are based on changes driven by forces that are either external or internal to employment relations; the former are described as *exogenous* factors and the later as *endogenous* ones. Change is also observed as being *cyclical, incremental* or *catastrophic*. Adapting Heery's classification, six possible theories of historical change and employment relations are summarised below.

Exogenous cyclical change

Exogenous cyclical change is driven from outside employment relations and occurs in periodic, repetitive or iterative patterns of change over time. The economic business cycle or trade cycle is an example of exogenous cyclical change. This is reflected in the oscillations taking place in levels of business activity within an economy over time. It is based on the observation that economies pass through a sequence of expansionary growth, falling growth or recession, and depression or reduced growth, where this is not compensated by counter-cyclical interventions by government. When the economy begins to recover, the economic business cycle is renewed. There is no consensus about the causes of economic cycles. Within them, there are variations in the demand for goods and services in the economy, levels of employment and prices. Most explanations of the trade cycle are based on the determinants of business investment through the multiplier effect on levels of national income (O'Connor and Faille 2000). Nor is there agreement about the length of each phase within economic cycles. Some observers claim the cycle is about five years, with others arguing it lasts seven years. Kuznets (1966) argues there is a longer economic cycle of about 20 years, while Kondratiev's (1935) 'waves' of economic activity are said to last some 15 or 20 years. He claims that economic movements consist of 'long waves' of 'boom' and 'recession' averaging about half a century long. These are driven by major technological and industrial advances, such as by ICTs since 1980s.

Using this model, changes in employment relations are claimed to take place in response to changing cycles of decline and renewal in the external economic, political and social contexts. In the economic sphere, for example, the business cycle is identified by Bain and Elsheikh (1976) as the key factor explaining the aggregate growth and decline of union membership in Australia, Sweden, the United Kingdom and the United States, based on historical time series data. In politics, Ludlam and Taylor (2003) argue that government–union relations between the British Labour party and its affiliated unions follow a cyclical pattern when Labour is in government. These shift from tension to accommodation as the general election approaches, with the unions seeking the re-election of a sympathetic Labour government to office and the Party seeking union funding to help get a new majority in the UK House of Commons. In the United States, Cornfield (2006) shows that periodic crises within the American labour movement are explained by waves of mass immigration which impose tensions on established union structures.

Exogenous incremental change

Exogenous incremental change is driven from outside employment relations through gradual, cumulative changes over time. Change models of this type have been an enduring feature of employment relations since the foundation works of Commons and the Webbs. Thus Commons (1909) argues that growth of national trade unions and national systems of collective bargaining within the United States were responses to the growing scale of product markets. Similarly, in a study of labour in five countries – the United States, Great Britain, West Germany, France and Japan during the first three-quarters of the twentieth century – the authors conclude that 'the twentieth century is likely to be known as the century of the *worker* or of the *employee* in advanced democratic societies' (Dunlop and Galenson 1978: 1–2). Evidence was provided by the unprecedented improvements in the living standards, social status, economic security, political power and influence of industrial workers that had occurred and accumulated in that century. Further, the comparative method of reviewing the position of labour in these five countries helps highlight both the common elements and the distinctive features of each country 'during this remarkable period for the worker and the employee'.

Another example of exogenous incremental change in employment relations is provided by Kerr *et al.* (1962) in their classical study of industrialism and 'Industrial Man' [*sic*] and the problems of labour and management in economic growth. Their central argument is industrialism, not capitalism, was the great event of their times. The ghost haunting the world was not communist rebellion but the industrial revolution. For them, all economic roads lead inevitably to industrialism, not socialism. One of the most significant traits of industrialism was the separation of workforces into managers and managed. The result was growth of a complex web of rules governing employment relationships between the two parties. However, despite their common features, industrial societies were claimed to have some special features too. These derived from their resource endowment, history, culture and the particular road to industrialism pursued by their industrialising elites.

Each type of elite represents a different strategy of industrialisation: the dynastic elite (Japan), the middle-class elite (the United States and the United Kingdom), the revolutionary intellectual elite (in former Communist regimes), colonial administrators, and national leaders operating in former colonised countries such as India and parts of Africa. Dunlop and his colleagues argue that the colonial elite was heading for extinction and that the dynastic, national and revolutionary elites would become incorporated into the middle-class elite. Out these dynamics, a more uniform industrial society would emerge, with ideology receding, educational levels rising, and professional managers in the ascendancy. Class conflict would be replaced by bureaucratic conflicts among organised interest groups in pluralist societies. This theory of exogenous incremental change, in short, creates mature industrial societies and stable employment relations, through their functional adaptation to the processes of industrialisation over time.

Exogenous catastrophic change

Theories of catastrophic change emphasise discontinuity in the historical process, with episodes of change interspersed by periods of stability, with change triggered by forces exogenous to employment relations. Thus Sisson (1987) argues national systems of employment relations emerge out of general political and economic crises. These create an accommodation between capital and labour at particular times, such as in Sweden in the mid-1930s, where there had been intense industrial and class conflict between the employing and working classes. Such discontinuities result in historic compromises between capital and labour. 'Developments subsequent to this episode of institution-building are then channelled along established paths by the force of path dependency; that is until a new crisis disrupts the system' (Heery 2008: 80).

Another example is at the end of the Second World War, when new institutions were generated in the United States and West Germany 'to help mobilize the working populations in the victorious states and the transplant of institutions to defeated states'. Similar sets of events occurred in east Europe after the collapse of Soviet Russia in 1991. In this case, there was a search for new employment relations institutions across previously subordinate states (Frege 1999a, 1999b). In this model of change, 'short bursts of institution building, prompted by crises, are followed by long periods of inertia, followed by incremental change' (Heery 2008: 80).

Endogenous cyclical change

Cyclical change, driven through factors endogenous to employment relations, shows how employment relationships embody contradictory elements. For example, it is commonly claimed that the employment relationship is both adversarial and co-operative (Barbash 1984). This reflects the opposing interests of the parties and their mutual inter-dependence. Management attempts to obtain employee commitment to managerial goals may be undermined by its requirement to control labour costs or restructure the business. Similarly, adversarial strategies of labour control may be subverted by workers having tacit skills and discretion in how they carry out their job tasks. As Hyman (1987: 30) writes: employer strategy is 'the programmatic choice between alternatives none of which can prove satisfactory'. Or, as Heery (2008: 82) concludes, management strategy can follow 'a cyclical or oscillating pattern, prioritizing control or cooperation at one point but switching direction when the limits of each approach become apparent'.

Endogenous incremental change

This model focuses on incremental change driven by forces within employment relations. Maturation of employment relations institutions, as they become embedded through the practices and behaviours of the parties, results in them developing more complex differentiated goals as time goes by. Michels (1962) argues that that rule by an elite or 'oligarchy' is inevitable within any social organisation. This 'iron law of oligarchy' forms part of the tactical and technical necessities of organisational processes. His theory tries to explain why unions and socialist parties retreat from revolutionary to reformist politics over time. In his analysis, it is union bureaucracy that leads to goal displacement, as their leaders develop interests separate from those of their members as time passes. Thus union leaders use their leadership positions to advance their own organisational interests at the expense of those of their members. Similarly, in studies of union revitalisation, the organising model of trade unionism emphasises incremental change within unions through deliberate learning. This prioritises organising, developing capacity among workers and promoting an organisational discourse, focusing on dignity and respect at work. National union confederations sponsor the organising model and encourage its diffusion, by establishing training programmes for union organisers (Foester 2001, Heery *et al.* 2002).

Endogenous catastrophic change

Catastrophic change processes originate endogenously in the employment relationship itself. Such discontinuities in employment relations emerge out of changes in the policy choices made by the principal actors in the system, changes in the personalities involved, or changes in the employment relations contexts, resulting in new employment relations outcomes. An example is where employers develop new managerial policies, such as union de-recognition, substituting this with individual employment relationships. This happened in Qinetiq, a privatised United Kingdom defence technology company in 2012, when it ended collective bargaining with three unions and replaced it with an elected consultative body for the whole workforce – the Qinetiq Employee Engagement Group (Groom 2012). Second, the presence of HR managers and a strong HR function are identified as key factors shaping management policy and practices in the area of equality (Hoque and Noon 2004). A third example is studies of union strategy, where issues such as gender, intergenerational change and ideology help shape union strategic choices and shifts in union policy (Heery 2003). Here changes in union behaviour stem from replacing one set of union office-holders and activists with those of different viewpoints. Fourth, radical changes in labour law can have similar catastrophic impacts on the parties to employment relations and their outcomes, as happened in the United Kingdom during the 1980s and 1990s.

IDEOLOGY, FRAMES OF REFERENCE AND THEORY-BUILDING IN EMPLOYMENT RELATIONS

Social sciences study and explain social phenomena in human societies. They seek to produce systematic theories and explanations of human behaviour within particular academic disciplines, such as economics, sociology, psychology, politics or law. Employment relations is no exception. A central objective in the multidisciplinary field of the employment relationship is to develop theories and explanations of institutions, processes and behaviours. But theory-building is a complex task, since there are a multiplicity of concepts, ideas and intellectual perspectives or faces of the employment relationship that need to be taken into account in describing, analysing and explaining the world of work and employment relations.

Studying the employment relationship

A major problem studying and theory-building in employment relations, as in any social science, is that scholars work within sets of ideas, variously described as values, ideologies and frames of reference, which have subjective meanings to them as individuals. These are not necessarily identical with those of other scholars, actors or policy-makers in the field (Braybrooke 1987, Hollis 1994). In this sense, the study of the employment relationship is no different from the study of any social science. The key question is the extent to which the study of the subject is objective and value-free by those observing and evaluating it (Winch 1990). This is the traditional distinction between 'positive' and 'normative' social science; the first involves examining 'how things are'; the second is concerned with 'what ought to be' (Flyvbjerg 2001).

In employment relations, the positive and normative aspects of the field continually interact and are examined from the specific perspectives of each of the main actors – employers, workers, unions and the state. For example, 'good' employment relations for managers normally means having predictable labour costs, high productivity per worker, co-operative employees and absence of industrial conflict in the workplace. 'Good' employment relations for employees means fair terms and conditions of employment, decent management practices and freedom to join a union if they choose. Trade unionists, in turn, see 'good' employment relations as being represented by the union in wage determination and procedural issues at the workplace; union leaders see 'good' employment relations as professional, stable relationships with the employers with which they negotiate. For the state, 'good' employment relations means industrial peace between employers and unions, maintenance of law and order, and non-inflationary wage settlements between employer and union negotiators. Thus the underpinning ideas, values, ideologies and frames of reference that managers, employees, union leaders and agents of the state bring to the employment relationship are complicated, contestable and, in some cases, incompatible.

There are, first, a series of *ideas* or concepts in employment relations, made up of an array of social phenomena, such as 'collective bargaining', the 'closed shop', 'fair employment standards', 'the HR function' and many others. These define the field of study and its subject matter and give meaning to it. Second, *values* are the cognitive and expressive ideals learned and internalised by people, which they use to interpret and judge the situations they experience or conceptualise in employment relationships. These values include how employees are or ought to be treated by their employer, how employees behave or should behave towards an employer's property, or the grounds upon which an employer can discipline or dismiss an employee. These values vary widely among individuals and groups. Third, *ideology* has many meanings (Eagleton 1994) but its main use in employment relations is as a way of thinking that expresses the interests and outlook of a particular social group – whether employers, employees, unions or the state – which is conditioned and influenced by the socio-economic position of that group. This means that 'the right to manage' is not only a managerial activity or management function but also a managerial ideology, justifying what managers do in organisations. Similarly, 'the right to strike' is a both a union practice and a union ideology. A 'fair day's work for a fair day's pay' is both the standard by which the wage–work bargain can be judged or evaluated by managers and employees and an ideology associated with the idea of equity or balance in the employment relationship (Hyman and Brough 1975). Where the state seeks to be a 'model employer', this too is both a statement of 'good' management practice and one with an ideological basis or bias.

Fourth, a *frame of reference* in employment relations, as identified by Hyman and Brough (1975: 1), includes 'appeals to the idea of *fairness*', which provides 'an inescapable frame of reference in judging the exercise of managerial control, the imposition of dismissals and other disciplinary sanctions, the allocation of tasks and benefits among employees'. Fox (1966: 2), in turn, drawing on Thelen and Withall (1949), writes that a person's attitudes towards anything depend on their 'frame of reference'. Each person perceives and interprets events through 'a conceptual structure of generalisations or contexts, postulates about what is essential, assumptions as to what is valuable, attitudes about what is possible' and 'ideas about what will work effectively'. This is the frame of reference of that individual. It embodies 'the main selective influences at work as the perceiver supplements, omits and structures what he [*sic*] notices'. Frames of reference determine an individual's judgement and subsequent behaviour. Thus 'motivated behaviour in response to objects is determined by the frames of reference in which they are perceived'. For Budd and Bhave (2008: 94), *ideology* is how one *wants* to see the world and a *frame of reference* is 'how one sees the world'.

Theories of employment relations

Theories of employment relations are the intellectual products of the ideas, values, ideologies and frames of reference that scholars and actors bring to the field of study. These concepts and intellectual constructs attempt to make sense of the institutions, practices and processes of employment relationships, as well as behaviour by the players in work and employment situations. However, since values, ideologies and frames of reference are contested constructs, there is more than one theory of employment relations, with each one underpinned by a distinctive value system. Adapting the work of Budd and Bhave (2008), four main theoretical clusters can be identified. The four theories, the values underpinning them, and their links with the main intellectual traditions in the field are outlined in Figure 4.5. Each theory is an intellectual construct for understanding employment relationships; but it can also be an ideology and a frame of reference for those identifying with it.

Market theory

The market theory of employment relations, or what Budd and Bhave (2008) describe as the 'egotist' employment relationship, is aligned with the managerial control, human resources management and individualist legal traditions of employment relations. It is rooted in the pursuit of individual self-interest in the labour market by employers and workers, each of whom aims to achieve optimal market outcomes for themselves through free market transactions in determining the wage–work bargain. Firms seek to maximise profits; workers are a commodity seeking the best wages possible in the competitive labour market; and the state protects property rights and enforces employment contracts. Advocates of market theory see unions as distorting free market transactions between employers and workers. They view unions

Employment relations theory	Underpinning purpose of employment relations	Intellectual traditions in the field
Market	To promote economic efficiency and individual self-interest in the employment relationship, through competitive market forces	Managerial control, human resources management, legal
Unitary	To integrate employer and employee interests in the workplace and organisation, under managerial direction and control	Managerial control, human resources management, legal
Pluralist	To promote a balance of power in the employment relationship between employer and employees, through joint regulation between employers and unions, where the state upholds the public interest	Union as a loyal opposition, institutional, legal
Critical	To highlight the struggles for power and control in the employment relationship between different interest groups in society	Class conflict and revolutionary, labour process

Figure 4.5   Theories and intellectual traditions of employment relations
Source: Budd and Bhave (2007).

as institutions that distort the free market, by adversely affecting employment levels in the labour market and output in the macro-economy. Economics is the major disciplinary influence in the market theory of employment relations.

Unitary theory

The unitary theory of employment relations is also aligned with the managerial control, human resources management and individualist legal traditions of the field. Its underlying assumption is that HR policies need to integrate the interests of employers and workers in organisations to the mutual benefit of both parties. This is the ideology and frame of reference that underpins many contemporary HRM policies and practices. Those supporting it see it as promoting both profit maximisation for employers and fulfilling the needs of workers in their employment and job tasks (Pfeffer 1998, Ulrich and Brockbank 2005). In this theoretical model, as in the market theory, the role of the state is a limited one. Further, as Fox (1966: 3, 5) argues, within organisations driven by unitary theory, team spirit 'and undivided managerial authority co-exist to the benefit of all'. This doctrine of common purpose and harmony of interests between employers and workers means its advocates deny conflict in the employment relationship and, where it happens, it is dysfunctional and irrational. Most importantly, as an ideology, unitary theory 'is at once a method of self-reassurance, an instrument of persuasion, and a technique of seeking legitimation of authority'. Psychology is the major disciplinary influence in this theory of the employment relationship. And, arguably, its constructs can be used and applied by managements to achieve organisational economic ends.

Pluralist theory

Pluralist theory is aligned with the institutional, union as a loyal opposition and collectivist legal traditions of employment relations. Its fundamental tenets are that wage bargaining between employers and workers takes place in imperfect labour markets, conflict is endemic to the employment relationship, and labour is not a commodity but needs to be nurtured and treated with dignity in the workplace (Kaufman 2005). Building on the works of the Webbs (1920a, 1920b) and Commons (1909), supporters of pluralist theory believe that labour is entitled to equity and voice in the enterprise. By bargaining collectively with employers over terms and conditions of employment for the workers it represents, the union offsets the inequality of bargaining power of individual employees in labour markets. Bargaining also brings non-wage issues to the negotiating table. The state's role is to promote wage bargaining, provide third-party interventions in trade disputes, and administer social insurance or social security schemes which support workers when they are unemployed, sick and retired. As a frame of reference, pluralist theory legitimises and justifies the union's protective function in labour markets. It also rests 'on social values which recognise the right of interest groups to combine and have an effective voice in their own destiny' (Fox 1966: 7). Sociology and politics are the major academic influences on the pluralist frame of reference.

Critical theory

Critical theory in employment relations is rooted in the power and control interests of employers and workers. Its advocates view the employment relationship as a struggle for power and control in the workplace and wider society (Budd and Bhave 2008, Hyman 1975, Gall 2003b). Critical theory is also linked with the labour process tradition in employment relations. Critical theory has three streams of analysis: the political economy, feminist and ethnic versions.

The political economy version argues that labour interests are dominated by capitalist interests in the employment relationship and beyond it. Kelly (1998) links conflict in employment relations with wider conflict between competing social groups in society. Further, the employment relationship is not a voluntary but contested one (Bowles and Gintis 1990). Militant unions are seen as advocates of worker interests in the employment and political arenas. In feminist critical theory, male concerns are viewed as overriding those of females. For Greene (2003: 308), a change in direction in the subject is necessary if women's issues are to be addressed. Despite legislation and equal opportunities initiatives, 'labour markets around the world remain horizontally and vertically segregated by sex, with women predominantly holding the lowest paid and lowest status positions' (Hakim 1996). In the ethnic version of critical theory, the concerns of dominant ethnic groups, such as white people, are seen as being more important than those of non-white groups. The major academic disciplines used in critical theory are politics, sociology and economics.

RESEARCH IN EMPLOYMENT RELATIONS

Researching employment relationships is about observing and theorising how work is organised, how relations between employers and employees are conducted, the outcomes of these relationships, and the contexts within which they take place. Research in the field goes back to the late nineteenth and early twentieth centuries, beginning with the institutional research methodology used by Sidney and Beatrice Webb (1920a, 1920b) and Commons (1909). Since then, employment relations research has evolved from a strong historical inductive approach into a multidisciplinary, multi-topic, multi-layered, multi-method and multi-country area of study, reflecting the changing faces of employment relations in the early twenty-first century (Barry and Wilkinson 2011). Employment relations is not only multidisciplinary but also a contested academic domain. This means that research in the field draws upon a range of analytical tools, varying according to the ideologies, frames of reference and theoretical perspectives adopted by the researchers – whether market, unitary, pluralist or critical.

Research strategies

Research strategies in employment relations are determined by the purpose of the research, its methodological approach and the attention given to the validation of constructs, models and findings within it. Hakim (1992) suggests the nature of the research has a major impact on the research strategy adopted. She distinguishes between *policy-based* research and *theoretical* research. Policy-based research is likely to be multidisciplinary and conducted at a number of levels, based on representative samples and involving complex causal processes. Theoretical research is likely to involve hypothesis-testing and identifying causal relationships. There is also what Whyte (1991) calls *participatory action research*. This aims to incorporate researchers into the policy-making process by integrating their research with the implementation stages; it is closely related to consultancy in the field.

Research strategy can be *inductive* or *deductive*. The inductive approach collects empirical facts of particular cases and derives theories from them. The research methods used in the inductive approach are largely qualitative and the outcomes are helpful in determining policy advice and middle-range theory. 'Middle-range' research is the term used by Merton (1968) to link high-level social theory with empirically observable patterns of social action; this distinguishes it from 'grand theory' or highly abstract theorising. Much social and employment relations research in the United Kingdom, Australia and Canada, as well as in Europe and other parts of the world, is based on the inductive approach and middle-range theory. The deductive approach research seeks to discover general 'laws' that apply universally. It starts with hypotheses to be tested against empirical facts and uses largely quantitative research methods. It is a common research methodology used in disciplines such as economics and psychology, when linked to employment relations issues. In the United States, the deductive approach is most fully demonstrated in neo-classical labour economics and organisational behaviour. A possible weakness of the deductive approach is, depending on the subjectivity and validity of the data collected, the research may result in a self-fulfilling prophecy which is inaccurate.

In maximising the validity of social and employment relations research, a distinction is made between *construct*, *internal* and *external* validity. Construct validity concerns the degree to which the proxy variables accurately reflect the factors making up the underlying model; internal validity concerns the degree to which the empirical model is consistent in its own terms; external validity concerns the degree to which the results can be generalised to the populations to which they relate. Attainment of high degrees of validity is rare in any research and each has to be traded off against the others to complete the research. But in outline, construct validity is important for researchers in psychology but not in economics. Internal validity is particularly important for economists and external validity is important for policy-based research in employment relations. Laboratory experiments are strong on internal validity but weak on external validity, whereas field experiments are strong on external validity but weak on internal validity. The research *methods* used also affect degrees of validity. As Strauss and Whitfield (1998: 14) conclude: 'qualitative analyses and inductively oriented projects have high construct validity, whereas quantitative deductively oriented projects have high external validity, although there are many variations on this theme'.

Punch (2005) provides a simplified model of research: framing the research questions; determining the data to answer those questions; designing the research; collecting the data; analysing it; and using the data to answer the research questions posed. The inductive and deductive approaches differ slightly in their sequence. In inductive research, the pre-empirical stage includes a review of the literature and identification of the research questions. The empirical stage goes on to design the research, collect the data, analyse it and answer the research questions. In deductive research, following the literature review and identification of the research questions, the pre-empirical stage establishes the hypotheses to be tested. The empirical stage is identical with that of the inductive model, except the final task is to test the research hypotheses.

Qualitative research methods

The main qualitative research methods used in employment relations are the case study, interviews, ethnography, participative action research (PAR), and historical studies. Case studies are the gold-plated foundation of much employment relations research. Because of their flexibility, case studies are sometimes also described as a research strategy. They involve detailed investigation of a small number of research objects, such as groups, organisations, sectors, or firms in their social and institutional settings. A number of research techniques is combined in case-study research such as observation, interviews, questionnaires and documentary sources. Examples of the case study method include Flanders's (1964) analysis of the Fawley productivity agreements in England, Purcell's and Ahlstrand's (1994) study of human resources management in multi-divisional companies, and Kochan's (2009) examination of labour-management reforms in Kaiser Permanente in the US health care sector.

Face-to-face interviews between actors and researchers are the primary means of accessing the experiences and subjective views of managers, HR specialists, trade union officers, workers and public officials. In-depth semi-structured interviews, drawing upon appropriate interview schedules, are common ways of gathering qualitative data from individual respondents. Interviews need to be carefully prepared and administered. Where face-to-face interviews are not possible, data may be obtained through telephone interviews, email conversations, and diary entries. These types of data collection enable individuals to reflect on their feelings and experiences of the participants but lack the one-to-one interaction of face-to-face interviews. As Hakim (1992: 27) argues, the great strength of qualitative data is the validity of the data obtained: 'individuals are interviewed in sufficient detail for the results to be taken as true, correct, complete and believable reports of their views and experiences'.

Ethnography involves the direct observation by researchers of employment relations phenomena in their situational and work contexts. The objective is 'to describe what happens in the setting, how the people involved see their own actions and those of others, and the contexts in which the action takes place' (Hammersley and Atkinson 1995: 6). This requires periods of observation, prolonged face-to-face contacts with members of these groups, and direct participation by researchers in group activities. Thus Roy (1954) took a job in the company where he was observing inter-group relations in a piecework machine shop. He reveals how workgroups controlled the pace of the work through collective action. Twenty-five years later, Burawoy (1979) observed the same workshop. Based on his experience as a labourer in a piece-rate machine shop, Burawoy concludes that management controls workers by giving them the 'illusion of choice' in a highly restrictive environment. Worker participation in this process creates consent and minimises the potential of class consciousness and labour-management conflict but maximises productivity for the employer.

PAR is where one or more members of the group or organisation being studied participate in the research and the actions coming out of it (Whyte 1991). In PAR, members of the organisation being studied are committed to acting on the practical implications of the research, thus yielding 'creative surprises'. An example is Emery's and Thorsrud's (1976) study of industrial democracy in the Norwegian maritime industry. This was a collaborative project by behavioural scientists and practitioners involving government officials, managers, ships' officers and crew members. The aim was to improve the international competitive position of Norwegian ships, quality of working life aboard ships, and relations between engine room staff and deck crews. The programme led to the construction of a new type of ship, created to minimise the status differences between the ship's personnel. The outcomes of the study resulted in major changes in the global maritime industry and the development of working teams.

Historical studies in employment relations have traditionally focused on documentary evidence to produce histories of individual trade unions and union movements in Europe, the United States, Australia, and Japan (Ebbinghaus and Visser 2000, Bramble 2008, Dolan and Worden 1994). Today the horizons of historians are broader and they use new methods of data collection, such as oral history, visual history and observation of the material cultures of societies (Douglas *et al.* 1988). The benefits of the historical method in employment relations research are, first, to enable theories of employment relations to be developed and tested over time. Second, history provides a long-term view of employment relationships which take account of the changing economic, political and social contexts of the field. Third, history records and interprets the past but also helps explain the present and explores the impact of historical path dependency on employment relationships today. Zeitlin's (1987) rejection of 'history from below', or 'rank and file' history, is a critical one for research in the field. He concludes that labour history should be replaced by 'industrial relations history', defined as the historical study of the changing relationships between employers, employers' associations, unions, workers and the state over time.

Quantitative research methods

Quantitative research in employment relations is characterised in its ideal form by a series of linear steps, moving from theory to conclusions. This template of quantitative research consists of 10 steps or sequential actions: theory, hypothesis, research design, measuring concepts, research location, research instruments and data collection, data processing, data analysis, data presentation, and writing up. It is characterised by measurement, causality, generalisation, replication and establishing the reliability and validity of the measures used to assess their quality (Bryman and Bell 2011).

Whitfield (1998: 67) argues that quantitative analysis, largely using surveys and experimental methods, is concerned with explaining variations in a given variable (the *dependent* variable) by variations in other variables (*independent* variables). In most quantitative research, the aim is to explain the relationship between the dependent variable and a key independent or *explanatory* variable. The other independent variables allow for the remaining factors being held constant. For Whitfield, most quantitative analyses involve four elements: a quantitative data-set for measuring the key factors under investigation; a set of statistical techniques for estimating the numerical relationships between variables; a statistical model reflecting the processes generating variations in the data; and 'a functional form for each equation', reflecting 'the key properties of the relationship between the dependent and independent variables'. Functional form is the manner in which the independent variables are entered into an equation.

An example is Mulvey's (1986) study of the union wage differential (or the union 'mark-up') in Australia. Mulvey's data-set was an Australian Bureau of Statistics Survey of 30,000 households. The statistical technique used was least squares analysis. The statistical model estimated equations in which earnings were the dependent variable and union membership the explanatory variable. The personal and job characteristics of respondents, such as job titles and union membership, were independent variables. Separate equations were estimated for males and females to allow for differences between the dependent and independent variables for each group. Finally, the set of variables allowing for factors affecting earnings, other than union membership, was comprehensive. These included 'terms allowing for a non-linear relationship between the dependent and independent variables' (Whitfield 1998: 68). In this study, based on 1982 data, the union mark-up was estimated to be between seven and 17 per cent, with differences between male and female respondents.

Examples of large-scale national employment relations surveys are provided by the British Workplace Employment Relations Surveys/Studies (WERS) from 1980 to 2011 and the Australian Workplace Industrial Relations Surveys (AWIRS) in 1989–1990 and 1995 (Department of Industrial Relations 1997, Millward *et al.* 2000, Kersley *et al.* 2006, Brown *et al.* 2009, van Wanrooy *et al.* 2013). Successive WERS in Britain map employment relations in workplaces across the country, based on responses from large representative samples of managers, employee representatives and, since 1998, employees. These surveys inform policy development and provide a comprehensive and reliable data-set of workplace employment relations in Britain over this period. The cross-section surveys involve face-to-face interviews with managers and employee representatives, self-completion questionnaires for managers on workforce composition and financial performance, and self-completion questionnaires for employees. There have also been panel surveys of managers in post-1998 surveys. High response rates to these surveys demonstrate high levels of confidence by respondents in the integrity and robustness of these studies (Brown *et al.* 2009). In response to the 2011 survey, Freeman (2012) is reported as saying that WERS is the 'gold standard survey of personnel and labour relations. If only the United States was smart enough to imitate this masterful study!'.

Another quantitative research method is employee attitude surveys. These have a long history and are widely used in psychological and organisational research (Terrick and Baring 1995) and increasingly in mainstream employment relations (Edwards and Whitston 1993, Kochan 1979). Rossi and Freeman (1982: 90) define a survey as 'a systematic collection of information from large study groups, usually by means of interviews or questionnaires administered to samples of units in the population'. Employee attitude surveys also collect information 'to describe, compare, or explain knowledge, attitudes and behavior' (Fink 1995: 1). Attitude surveys explore a variety of psychological phenomena such as knowledge, beliefs, attributions, opinions, values, expectations, perceptions, satisfaction, behavioural intentions and reported behaviours. These phenomena are categorised as thoughts or perceptions, affections or feelings, and behaviours or behavioural intentions. French and Bell (1990) distinguish between informational surveys, which gather information about employees, and feedback surveys that provide employees with feedback. The instruments adopted in such surveys include self-completed questionnaires using fixed questions (commonly with Likert scales), while focus groups get responses from groups of respondents gathered together for the research exercise.

Experiments in employment relations examine issues relating to individuals or small groups covering job satisfaction, labour turnover, job performance, group decision-making and collective bargaining. There are two types of experiment: laboratory and field. Laboratory experiments are carried out under standardised or controlled circumstances, such as Lawler's *et al.* (1988) study of bargaining behaviour. This shows union members make more tentative and definitive statements than managers when negotiating. Field experiments are carried out in the specific setting where the subject being investigated takes place. An example is the relay assembly test room in the Hawthorne studies. This reveals how the effects of a new incentive scheme, rest breaks and a shorter working day increased productivity dramatically (Roethlisberger and Dickson 1939). Another example is Coch's and French's (1948) study about overcoming resistance to change in a pyjama-making factory in Virginia in the United States. These results show how degrees of worker participation in job design affected work performance and the learning of new job skills within the firm.

CONCLUSION AND IMPLICATIONS

Economics has been and remains a major intellectual influence on the study of employment relations in capitalist market economies. However, Grimshaw and Rubbery (2003: 48, 65) claim the record of economists taking employment relations seriously 'is by no means impressive'. Equally, employment relations scholarship 'has not distinguished itself as a discipline [*sic*] able and willing to encompass economic issues into its analytical frameworks'. They believe that economists and employment relations specialists provide different models 'about the dynamic relationship between the economic and social organization of the firm, its capacity to compete and survive in a changing external environment, and the implications for the nature of work and employment'. These writers advocate a bi-disciplinary approach, if these two 'divided perspectives' of employment relations are to be effective.

A crucial economic factor is the consequences of unemployment on employment relations. High levels of employment provide labour market advantages for workers and unions; high levels of unemployment in contrast give advantages to employers and managers. As the International Labour Office (2011) reports, following the global financial crisis in 2008, labour markets had not fully recovered by 2011. Indeed, there was still a deficit or short fall of an estimated 50 million jobs in the global labour market compared with the pre-crisis situation. Unemployment matters, since it determines the balance of bargaining power between employers and employees in labour markets and has implications for employers, workers, unions, governments and households. Unemployment can be broadly categorised into classical, frictional, structural, demand-deficient, seasonal, and 'disguised' variants, as indicated in Figure 4.6. Each type requires different policy responses to deal with it within nation states (International Labour Office 2011).

The purpose of management theories historically has been to justify the right to manage, find means for pacifying workers and enable managers incorporate workers into stable organisational systems. All management theory supports optimum use of organisational resources and legitimises management's leadership role in organisations, whether through evidence-based practice, persuasion or coercion. However, some observers claim that nothing has changed in the ideas underpinning management theory, since Taylor's initiatives in the late nineteenth and early twentieth centuries. Indeed, the thinking underpinning modern management theory and methods remains remarkably unchanged over time. The primary driver is 'instrumental rationality', where the search for improved organisational performance and control of work processes is the root of the managerial function. The managerial control and human resources traditions of employment relations are the instruments for doing this; management theories provide their intellectual justifications.

One implication is that managers drawing upon traditional theories of management see the employment relationship as non-problematic. For them, unions generally have no role to play in regulating it. There are not two 'sides' to employment – managers and employees – but two parties on the same side and members of the same team, working to a common purpose. Effective leadership in organisations is the key to good employment relations or 'good human relations'. This unitary theory of the employment relationship assumes that every organisation is an integrated and harmonious whole, where owners, agents of financial capital and those working for the organisation are joint

Type of unemployment	Main characteristics	Policy options to reduce unemployment
Classical	Created when wages are above the equilibrium level of market demand and supply of labour	Reduce wage levels and promote wage flexibility
Frictional	Is the minimum level of unemployment in a dynamic economy	Difficult to eradicate, except by providing appropriate labour market information to employers and workers
Structural	Arises from the mismatch of skills and job opportunities, as patterns of labour demand and supply change	Provide training opportunities for unemployed workers
Demand-deficient	Occurs when aggregate output in an economy is below full capacity	Stimulate the macro-economy, using interventionist fiscal and monetary policies
Seasonal	Is due to the seasonal nature of economic activity in some sectors or occupations such as hotels and catering	No policy clear options
Disguised	Is a potential addition to the labour force, which does not reveal itself unless opportunities for employment are available, such as students willing to take up jobs to suit their patterns of study, the early retired and those not qualified for state unemployment support	Identify and publicise the employment opportunities available

Figure 4.6 Main types of unemployment

'partners' or common 'stakeholders' in the business enterprise. Their common aims of efficiency, high profits and fair pay make everyone a stakeholder. The organisation's 'team' needs strong leadership from the top to ensure everyone's commitment to their tasks and the firm's managers. Critics of 'strong leadership' argue, however, that the effectiveness of this approach is undermined by imbalances in the priorities, power and influence of the key stakeholders in the business enterprise.

Unitary theory of employment relations and its links with market theory is the antithesis of pluralism and emerges from a fundamental belief that organisations are like professional football teams, where team spirit 'and undivided management authority co-exist to the benefit of all' (Fox 1966: 2). Organisations are viewed as unitary in their structures and purposes, with a single source of authority and a cohesive set of participants motivated by common goals. Employment relations are thus assumed to be based on mutual co-operation and harmony of interest between managers and subordinates. Any factionalism within the workplace is seen as a pathological social condition. Employees are not expected to challenge managerial decisions and unions are viewed as illegitimate intrusions into a unified workplace, which compete with management for the loyalty of workers. As Fox (1966: 12) writes, any conflicts between the parties are due to 'frictional' factors such as incompatible personalities, 'faulty communications', 'stupidity in the form of failure to grasp the communality of interest' or 'the work of agitators inciting the supine majority who would otherwise be content'.

A new form of unitary theory, neo-unitary theory, emerged in some nonunion organisations in the 1980s. It builds upon classical unitary concepts but is more sophisticated how it is articulated and applied within firms. Variants of best-practice HR epitomise it (Pfeffer 1998). The aim of neo-unitary theory is to integrate employees as individuals in organisations, through a market-centred, managerial and individual approach to employment relationships. Neo-unitary theory supports employee commitment to quality, customer needs and job flexibility.

The pluralist-institutional approach to employment relations was the dominant analytical framework for studying and practice in the field over many decades, when Keynesian economic policies and welfare-state regimes were in the ascendant. However, although institutional theory is very important within employment relations, 'it has never achieved the hegemonic position that neoclassical thought has within the discipline of economics' (Voos 1993: 21). The institutional approach focuses on documenting the history, origins and development of unions, employer organisations and governmental labour agencies (Kochan 1980), where any potential conflicts between the parties is accepted by researchers. Pluralist theory argues that employers and employees bring different expectations to their work roles, which are shaped by societal values, cultural heritage and experience. Workers accept the legitimacy of management's right to organise and direct the workforce but they reserve the right to challenge this authority through the trade union function or the law where their interests are affected adversely.

Pluralist-institutionalism in employment relations is challenged by both Marxist and non-Marxist critics. The latter argue that those working within this framework implicitly accept the institutions, principles and assumptions of the social and political status quo. Fox (1974: 219), for example, writes that supporters of pluralist institutionalism add their professional status and influential involvement in public policy to the forces which continue to view the status quo 'as unchangeable, "only to be expected", subject only to changes at the margin'. Goldthorpe (1974: 419f) also challenges the liberal pluralist consensus. For him, the changes it promotes are ones 'designed to bring about the more effective integration of labour into the existing structure of economic relations, in industry and the wider society, rather than ones intended to produce any basic alteration to this structure'.

The impact of change on employment relationships is hardly addressed in the traditional literature of the field. Further, the erosion and displacement of collective agreements by individual contracts and HRM practices means that optimistic theories of change in employment relations are no longer tenable (Kerr *et al.* 1962, Dunlop and Galenson 1978). The search for industrial democracy has been superseded in many instances by the search for continuous improvement and high performance organisations, often with little place for unions in this process. So models of historical change involving cyclical, incremental and catastrophic processes, prompted by forces external or internal to employment relations, are helpful in explaining different forms of change. These models or parts of them may be combined with each other, recognising that change can occur at variable speeds within different historical periods – such as the distinction made by Braudel (1995) between the history of events, conjunctures and the *longue durée* (Wickham 2005).

Another theory of change is the Marxist one, where all conflict is defined as class conflict. At the heart of Marx's dialectical materialist interpretation of history lies the assumption that there is fundamental class conflict between those who own capital and those who sell their labour power to the employer. Marxism examines 'the construction and mobilization of consent, compliance, cooperation, consensus, and conflict, providing a bulwark against managerialism and the status quo' (Gall 2003: 317). The application of Marxian analysis to employment relations derives largely from later Marxist scholars, not directly from Marx himself (Hyman 1975, Coates and Topham 1980, Beynon 1975). Further, Marxism is not a theory of employment relations per se. Marxist analysis provides a theory of social change in societies, where its present stage, capitalism, which derives out of feudalism, is only one stage leading to a working-class revolution, socialism and eventually the classless society. Under capitalism, it is the contradictions inherent between those owning capital and those selling their labour power in the marketplace that result in class conflict between them.

In Marxian theory, unions can be agents promoting the class interests of workers, 'schools of socialism' or strategists in the class struggle. For Allen (1971: 40), trade unions challenge 'all the prerogatives which go with the ownership of production, not simply the exercise of control over labour power in industry'. It is collective bargaining and militant trade unionism that temporarily accommodate the contradictions inherent within the capitalist mode of production and its social relationships (Allen 1966).

Theories in employment relations incorporate contradictory ideas, ideologies and frames of reference. Ideas provide meanings and structure to employment relations phenomena; ideologies are ways of thinking and how individuals want to view the employment relationship; and frames of reference are how actors and scholars perceive and interpret the 'world' of employment relations. As new ideas emerge in the field, old ones are displaced. Further, an individual's frame of reference informs that person's choice of research topics, research strategy and research methods. Complexity in the field is leading to changing research approaches and methods, with increasing use of quantitative research techniques and multi-methods of research. As Whitfield and Strauss (1998: 294) conclude: the 'need to triangulate and sharpen research tools by calibration and the use of a mixture of methods should be emphasized'.

part **2**

THE PLAYERS IN EMPLOYMENT RELATIONS

5

EMPLOYERS, MANAGERS AND THE MANAGEMENT FUNCTION

The purpose of this chapter is to analyse the changing faces of the employer and management roles in employment relations, using comparative and theoretical insights to review these defining functions in organisations. The chapter also links these faces to human resources management and what is today often called the HR function of management. In employment relations, the terms 'employer' and 'manager' are commonly used interchangeably. But technically, it is employers that employee people and managers who recruit, select, organise, reward, motivate, discipline, dismiss and negotiate with them. Employers are normally organisations but, in some cases, individuals. Managers, who are themselves commonly but not exclusively employees, are the individuals and group of people who are collectively responsible for ensuring that the organisation they work for operates efficiently and effectively and achieves its corporate objectives. Thus managers organise and execute its financial, operational, marketing, quality and HR activities, so that the organisation satisfies the expectations of its owners and customers or, in public services, its legal obligations to the state and its citizens. Increasingly, managers also have to ensure that their organisations fulfil their moral or ethical obligations to the wider communities where they operate (Porrini *et al.* 2009, Visser 2011b). Managers are hierarchically organised, headed in the English-speaking world by chief executive officers (CEOs) or managing directors. In other countries, the job titles of top managers differ widely. In Europe, the equivalent of the CEO is a *président-directeur general* (France), *Vorsizender* (Germany), *presidente* (Spain and Portugal), *verkstallande direktor* (Sweden) and *konzernchef* (Finland). The Chinese equivalent is *Shouxi Zhíxíngguān* and the Japanese title

177

is *Saikō keiei sekinin-sha*. Professional managers may be generalists, specialists or technical experts and they operate at various organisational levels.

THE EMPLOYER FUNCTION

In capitalist market economies, many employers tend to be big businesses, some of which operate globally, and are owned by financial stockholders who may be corporations or individuals. Small-scale employers are private businesses often owned by the individuals or sometimes the family members who run them. All these types of businesses are found around the world. In German-speaking countries, medium-size private firms, known as the *Mittelstand*, have an international reputation for innovative, high-value manufactured products, made in companies using modern management practices. They are financially cautious, research-oriented and work closely with their skilled workforces (Venohr and Meyer 2007). But the most important employers are large organisations. These include privately owned firms, public-sector organisations in central or local government, and third-sector voluntary bodies such as trade unions, professional bodies, charities and social enterprises of various sorts. Another group of employers is TNCs. These are privately owned businesses operating internationally (Rugman 2009). Clearly, employment is widely distributed in the organisational world, where employers of different sizes, sectors and locations are key players in managing employment relationships.

Private businesses or business corporations, owned by stockholders, are commonplace in countries around the world and their underlying purpose is to make profits. The stocks and shares of these companies are bought and sold in international stock exchanges, such as in North and South America, Europe, Asia and Africa. Individuals and businesses invest in these stocks and expect dividends or returns on their investments, as well as building up the value of their capital holdings (Valdez and Molyneux 2010). Small businesses may or may not be companies. In the not-for-profit sector, public service organisations include national and local civil services, public enterprises (such as the German Federal Print Office, the Irish Anglo-Irish Bank and the Belgian-Dutch Bank, Fortis, in Europe), state agencies and municipal authorities. Public organisations generally have welfare and community-based goals, as well as being publicly owned (Pollitt and Bouckaert 2004).

The phenomenon of TNCs is ascribed to the uneven geographical distribution of the factors of production around the world and the inability of some markets to match demand with supply and avoid waste or hardship (Dunning and Lundan 2008). Because of their national origins, some firms have superior assets to those in other countries, giving them competitive market advantage. Moreover, a substantial proportion of these firms know that they can successively exploit these assets, by transferring them across national boundaries *within* their own enterprises, rather than by selling the right to use to them to foreign-based firms. The nationally endowed assets of TNCs are supplemented by acquiring, developing and integrating strategically important assets, such as raw materials and human capital, located in other countries. Globally, it is estimated that TNCs generate about half of the world's output and about two-thirds of its trade (World Trade Organisation 2012).

Apart from small businesses, typical employers today are public corporations (whose stock is owned by members of the 'public') or private corporations (whose stock is owned by private individuals). The legal principle of incorporation means the employer has a distinct corporate identity in law. In most legal systems, the 'employer' has an artificial 'personality' or existence in law that acts as the legal party, or principal, which employs the people working for it. This legal entity – the corporate employer – means that the employer has a separate, distinct legal personality from anyone else who happens to be a member of the organisation at the time. As legal bodies, business firms, public bodies and not-for-profit enterprises are able to own corporate property, enter into commercial contracts and employ people. The contract of employment between an employer and an employee is drawn up by the managerial agents of the business, acting on behalf of the principal or legal entity which they represent. Corporate employers, in short, are not human persons but legal entities with defined legal rights and responsibilities (Portmann 2013).

COMPARATIVE THEORIES OF THE MANAGEMENT FUNCTION

The term 'management' is a surprisingly difficult term to define. It has become conflated with what managers do, how they do it and as a catch-all phrase for the managerial functions and processes within organisations. Lawrence and Edwards (2000: 14) distinguish between management as an activity, management as an idea, and management as a subject. There are many ways of conceptualising management or managerial work, such as Mintzberg's (1980) categorisation of managerial status and authority in terms of three sets of 'interpersonal skills' and seven 'roles', as shown in Figure 5.1. Analytically, it is useful to distinguish between the overall *management function*, the *classical functions of management* and the *functional activities* of managerial roles. The management function is what managers do collectively. Their overall purpose

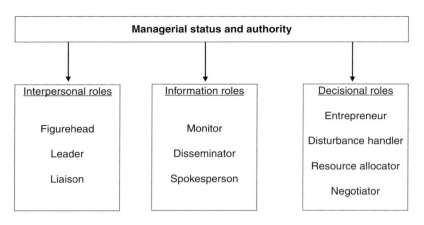

Figure 5.1 Managerial status and authority
Source: Mintzberg (1980).

is to organise and run the organisations (whether profit-making or non-profit-making) efficiently and effectively and ensure they meet the goals and objectives set for them. The classical functions of management are normally described as planning, organising, controlling and directing organisational resources such as labour, capital, technology and physical resources (Daft *et al.* 2010). How managers execute their authority is through a series of specialist functional activities or roles, which typically include strategy, finance, marketing, quality, operations, research and development, and HR including employment relations.

Hales's (2001) conceptualisation of management is a helpful starting point. For him, 'management' has become a complex differentiated process of planning, allocating, motivating, co-ordinating and controlling work. He distinguishes three key themes in the literature on management. First, the process of managing work has become separated from the execution of work. Second, the function of management has been extended by amalgamation with functions flowing from ownership of the inputs to and outputs of work. Third, as a combined function, management has become dispersed through different managerial specialists and levels of management. Most usefully, Hales views 'management' and 'organisation' as interdependent symbiotic concepts and sets up a 'management through organisation' model of the function. For him, this approach contains four elements: the management of operational work, management of professional and administrative work, problem of employee commitment, and problem of continuous change. A central focus for Hales in the management of work is it is carried out largely through the institutional mechanisms of organisation.

For the purposes of this text, 'managers' and 'management' are defined broadly as those individuals and groups of people who run organisations. Thus management incorporates both the classical functions of management and the functional activities of managers adopting particular managerial practices, as indicated in Figure 5.2. What is presented here is an analytical framework; it is not a justification of the classical position, since many observers challenge the 'rational' approach to management anyway (Lawrence and Elliott 1985). Indeed, writers such as Pedler *et al.* (2007) turn the issue on its head by arguing that what managers do is more a reflection of what they are like themselves as human beings, and how they manage themselves, than a working out of some higher administrative dynamic.

There is also a group of scholars associated with 'critical management studies'. These writers challenge prevailing conventional wisdoms and orthodoxies of management and organisations. They question and review established relations of power, control, domination and ideology in organisations, as well as exploring the relations of management and organisations with people and society. Although they challenge managerial orthodoxies, critical management theorists do not work in a unified theoretical framework but draw

Classical functions of management	Typical functional activities of managers
Planning: the process of setting objectives and choosing from among alternative ways to achieve them	Strategy formulation and implementation, financial management, marketing management, quality management, risk management, HRM, general management
Organising: the integration and co-ordination of resources and effort attending to organisation structure and flow of information and authority	Job design, organisational design, performance management, HRM, information technology
Controlling: the process of measuring and correcting performance and comparing results with objectives and adjusting actions or plans as necessary	Operations management, performance management, information technology
Directing: the influencing and guiding of human resources and provision of leadership, communication and motivation	HR strategy, HRM, employment relations
Staffing: the identification, selection recruitment, evaluation, and development of non-managerial employees and managers	HRM, employment relations

Figure 5.2   The classical functions of management and typical functional activities of managers

upon a range of analytical perspectives. These include anarchism, critical theory, feminism, Marxism, post-Marxism, post-structuralism, post-modernism, post-colonialism and psychoanalysis. These writers thus represent a pluralistic, multidisciplinary movement, which is continually evolving, and one that challenges the traditional curricula of mainstream business schools (Alvesson and Willmott 2003, Parker 2002, Grey and Willmott 2005).

If comparative employment relations is to be understood, including how the employment relationship is managed, it is important to explore the concept of comparative management. The central question in the research literature is whether theories of management are 'universalistic' or 'particularistic'. In his study of comparative international management, Koen (2005) argues universalistic theories of management claim management and organisation are subject to the same laws everywhere and, over time, cross-national differences are likely to disappear. Particularistic theories, in contrast, predict that cross-national differences in management and organisation persist, because they reflect cross-national differences among countries. Further, particularistic theories imply that history matters, because national systems of management and organisation are path-dependent phenomena. The debate is an important one, with implications for employment relations, since management theories and practices reflect managerial attitudes and behaviours and these affect how employment relationships are organised and managed.

Universalistic theories of management

Systems theory is an example of a universalistic management theory. Any management 'system' is said to consist of constituent 'parts' and elements or 'sub-systems', each of which affects the functioning of the whole, but none of which has an independent effect (Ackhoff and Rivett 1963). Another universalistic theory is contingency theory developed by the Aston School in the United Kingdom from the 1960s (Hickson *et al.* 1974). Contingency theory posits that given similar circumstances, the structure of an organisation, or its basic patterns of control, co-ordination and communication, can be expected to be much the same everywhere. If organisations are to be successful, they need to be structured in response to a series of contingencies posed by their scale of operations in terms of size, technology, and the external environment facing them. Its advocates argue that there needs to be an efficient 'fit' between these contingency factors. Thus large, mass-production, stable environments are deemed to promote mechanistic, rigid structures of management, whereas smaller, single product, turbulent environments are deemed to promote organic, flexible structures (Burns and Stalker 1961). The cultural

Dimension/Forms	Mechanistic	Organic
Job tasks	Narrow, specialised	Broad, enriched
Type of work	Precise, procedural	Indicative, results-oriented
Decision-making	Centralised, detailed, slow	De-centralised, indicative, fast
Hierarchy	Steep, many layered	Flat, with few layers

Figure 5.3 Mechanistic and organic forms of management and organisation
Source: Burns and Stalker (1961).

and societal conditions within which management is practised are considered to be negligible factors. Examples of mechanistic and organic organisational forms of management and organisation are shown in Figure 5.3.

The strengths of contingency theory include its straightforwardness and its methodology though complex is standardised. But it has weaknesses. First, although it is able to show consistency between organisational variables such as size or technology and the structural features of organisations, it has never provided adequate explanations of them. Second, the theoretical status of contingencies remains uncertain (Child and Tayeb 1983). Third, the contingency approach only considers the properties of formal structures and neglects informal structures (Lane 1989). Fourth, contingency approaches have evolved from western traditions of the rational design of organisations in mostly Anglo-American settings. Fifth, cultural and societal specifics are perceived to be negligible. Thus the contingency perspective claims that any variance in organisational structure is due primarily to the contingencies faced, not to its cultural or societal locations.

Particularistic theories of management

There are two approaches within particularistic theories of management and organisation: the cultural and institutional. Researchers recognise that both approaches are complementary and choice of approach depends on whether it is an exploratory or hypothesis-testing study. For some observers, the case for integrating the two is their complementarities. 'Moreover, the two kinds of explanation could complement each other in contributing to rich accounts of culture' (Koen 2005: 11).

The cultural approach

The cultural approach to understanding management and organisation has been promoted partly by the spread of globalisation and international markets. It is also in response to the universalistic focus on macro-level variables and structural relationships on organisations than on the behaviour of people within them (Child 1981). Cross-cultural studies take place at both individual and cultural levels. At individual level, studies explore the similarities and differences in the attitudes of managers in different cultures, where culture is considered to be an explanatory variable. Studies focusing on culture, rather than the individual, enable researchers to carry out comparative observations of management and examine the relationship between culture, management and organisational structure in different settings. Ethnographers such as Rohlen (1974) use an *inside* perspective to describe behaviour as seen from the viewpoints of cultural insiders, by drawing upon their understandings of the phenomena and describing the cultural system as a whole. Comparative cultural studies, such those by Hofstede *et al.* (2010), draw upon surveys; they use an *outside* perspective to describe behaviour from outside the culture in ways applying to other cultures. They also describe the ways in which cultural variables fit into general causal models of behaviour.

Figure 5.4 is based on four of Hofstede's (1993: 88–89) five dimensions of culture. It has implications for work and work relations and shows where these cultural values are commonly found. In Hofstede's view, there is something called 'management' in all nation states but its meaning differs from country to country. In his analysis, the meaning of management requires 'considerable historical and cultural insight into local conditions to understand its processes, philosophies and problems'. Further, management is 'not a phenomenon that can be isolated from other processes taking place in society'. Figure 5.5 illustrates another conceptual framework of culture, drawn from Hall (1959, 1976). He distinguishes between 'high-context' and 'low-context' cultures. These are based on patterns in personal communications, social relationships, and attitudes towards time.

Inglehart and Welzel (2005) analyse contemporary global cultural values in terms of two major dimensions, each with contrasting orientations. These comprise, on the one hand, *secular-rational values*, which tolerate divorce, abortion and suicide, contrasted with *traditional values*, which emphasise parent-children ties, family values and deference to authority. On the other hand, there are *self-expression values*, prioritised in knowledge-based societies, and *survival values*, prioritised in pre-industrial and industrial societies. Seven broad clusters of values can be identified: (1) Protestant Northern Europe which tends generally to be strongly supportive of both secular-rational and self-expression values; (2) Catholic South mid-Europe which tends to be moderately supportive of secular-rational and quite supportive of self-expression values; (3) North America, the United Kingdom and Ireland which tend to be

High power distance between individuals	Low power distance between individuals
Decisions are centralised	Decisions are de-centralised
Concentration of authority	Less concentration of authority
Tall structures	Flat structures
Subordinates expected to be told	Subordinates expect to be consulted
Managers are autocratic/paternalistic	Managers seek legitimacy
Found in South Europe, Latin America, Africa, Asia	*Found in North Europe and North America*
High individualism	**Low individualism**
Family relationships disadvantageous in selection decisions	Family relationships preferred in selection decisions
Poor performance reason for dismissal	Poor performance reason for other tasks
Business relationships more important than personal relationships	Personal relationships predominate in business
Direct appraisal improves performance	Direct appraisal is a threat to harmony
Found in English-speaking countries, especially the United States	*Found in mainland Europe, Latin America, the post-communist states, countries in transition*
High uncertainty avoidance	**Low uncertainty avoidance**
Strong loyalty to employer	Weak loyalty to employer
Innovators constrained by rules	Innovators feel independent of rules
Belief in specialists and expertise	Belief in generalists and 'common sense'
Power of superiors depends on controlling uncertainties	Power of superiors depends on position and relationships
Found in Germany, France, Italy, Japan, Latin America, Mediterranean countries	*Found in the United Kingdom, Sweden*
High masculinity	**Low masculinity**
Live to work	Work to live
Stress on equity, competition, performance	Stress on equality and quality of working life
Fewer women in management	More women in management
Conflict resolution through denial or overt conflict	Conflict resolution by problem-solving, compromise, negotiation
Found in Japan, Austria, Latin countries	*Found in Scandinavian countries, Netherlands*

Figure 5.4 Some implications of Hofstede's dimensions of culture for organisations and where found

Source: Hofstede (2010).

	High-context cultures	Low-context cultures
Personal communications	Implicit, indirect, full message to be deduced from indirect, contextual communications	Explicit, direct
Social relationships	Less formal, more personalised, importance of interpersonal rapport and trust, less reliant on formal agreements	More impersonal and formal
Attitudes to time	Time is viewed as flexible and polychromic	Time is more structured, measured and monochromic; punctuality is valued
Geographic locations	Arabic, Greek, Latin European, Latin America, Chinese, Korean, Japanese, Indian cultures	North European (Nordic, Germanic), Anglo-Saxon (United States, United Kingdom, Canada, Australian, New Zealand) cultures

Figure 5.5   High-context and low-context cultures
Source: Hall (1959, 1976).

weaker on secular-rational and moderate on self-expression values; (4) Former Communist East Europe which tends to be moderate on both secular-rational and survival values; (5) Latin America and Africa which tend to be strong on traditional and weak on self-expression values; (6) the Confucian world (China, Japan, South Korea, Taiwan) which tends to be moderately supportive of both secular rational and self-expression values; and (7) South Asia which tends to be moderately supportive of both traditional and survival values.

The institutional approach

The institutional approach to management focuses on comparisons highlighting differences that cannot be attributed to the different goals, contexts, environments, or strategies of enterprises. Cultural approaches focus on the minds of the individuals where differences occur, whereas institutional approaches focus on the wider norms and standards supported or enforced by institutional machineries or the social networks interacting with organisations (Sorge 2003). Institutional studies thus focus on differences between organisations that cannot be attributed to explanatory variables such as technology, firm size, products, innovation, ownership, and so on. Institutional theories, however, are similar to cultural analyses of management, because they do not develop a central set of standard variables. Institutional theory moves 'towards an increasingly explicit insistence upon the maintained diversity and qualitative specificity of social forms' in advanced societies (Rose

1985: 66). Similar to cultural approaches, varieties of institutional theory differ in the levels at which they are applied, by considering the societal, sectoral, organisational and departmental levels of analysis (Scott 2001).

Clearly, varying versions of institutional analysis identify different typologies of management, organisation and business relationships based on linkages among social institutions (Soskice 1996, Streeck 1992, Whitley 1999, Amable 2000). One example is the varieties of capitalism approach described and analysed in Chapter 3 (Hall and Soskice 2001). Another is Whitley's (1999) study of 'divergent capitalisms' and the social structuring of business systems. Drawing upon Whitley's study, Figure 5.6 summarises the claimed connections between dominant institutions and business systems. Whitley's research into organisations and their institutional contexts helps scholars understand how different institutional arrangements shape different forms of economic organisation and business system, such as South Korean *Chaebol* corporate groups and Japanese *Kieretsu* groups. Whitley (1999: 44) argues that differences in societal institutions encourage particular kinds of economic organisations and discourage others. This is done 'through structuring the ways that collective actors are constituted, cooperate, and compete for resources and legitimacy, including the standards used to evaluate their performance and behaviour'. He identifies six clusters of countries: Anglo-Saxon states; Germany and Scandinavia; France and Korea; Italy; Japan; and Hong Kong – each with its own differing business and management systems.

VARIATIONS IN NATIONAL MANAGEMENT SYSTEMS

The dominant management system described in the literature is the American (US) model, which is closely linked with that of the United Kingdom and other English-speaking countries. Its main values include: a commitment to market principles in business; a stress on short-termism in market relations; profit maximisation; the protection of management prerogatives in decision-making, especially in relation to employment and HR issues; a focus on shareholder value; a stress on individualism in workplace relations; entrepreneurialism; and differentiating individuals by their achievements and performance in the workplace (Lawrence 1996). An interesting example of the compatibility and cross-fertilisation between the US and UK management systems is the recruitment of Mark Thompson, as CEO and President of the New York Times, following his retirement, aged 55, from being Director-General of the British Broadcasting Corporation, an

Features of business system	Compartmentalised *Anglo-Saxon countries*	Collaborative *Germany, Scandinavia*	State organised *France, South Korea*	Co-ordinated industrial district *Italy*	Highly co-ordinated *Japan*	Fragmented *Hong Kong*
Ownership co-ordination						
Owner control	market	alliance	direct	direct	alliance	direct
Ownership integration of production chains	high	high	high	low	some	low
Ownership integration of sectors	high	limited	some-to-high	low	limited	low
Non-ownership co-ordination						
Alliance co-ordination of production chains	low	limited	low	limited	high	low
Collaboration between competitors	low	high	low	some	high	low
Alliance co-ordination of sectors	low	low	low	low	some	low
Employment relations						
Employer-employee inter-dependence	low	some	low	some	high	low
Delegation to employees	low	high	low	some	considerable	low

Figure 5.6 Business systems and dominant institutions for six countries

Source: Whitley (1999).

internationally recognised public-service media organisation (Thomson-Reuters 2012). However, the characteristics of management systems vary widely by country and, in some cases, even within them. These differences can be attributed to the specific histories and geographies of these countries, their dominant national cultures, and the political, economic, social and business institutions impacting on management systems at national level.

Differences in management practices and ideas between countries are typically connected with the economic roles played by managers in businesses, the historical roots of these systems, wider social values by country, and national institutions. For Lawrence and Edwards (2000: 220), there are regional similarities in management among the Scandinavian countries, for example, and a convergence in management attitudes between UK and US managers, but differences persist between management systems in most West European states. Differences are common 'in the soft areas of values, perceptions, priorities, style, deportment and the reflection in management behaviours of the wider cultural values of the national society concerned'. Three sets of examples are given below.

The Chinese Diaspora

The Chinese Diaspora, in mainland China, Taiwan, Hong Kong and member states of ASEAN, share a common cultural and religious heritage – Confucianism. This instils a belief in hierarchy and order in society, as well as harmonious interpersonal relations. Chinese people need to know their place in society and how to interact with others in appropriate ways. *Guanxi, renqing* and 'face' are important components in regulating interpersonal relationships, business relations and how organisations are managed in Chinese communities. *Guanxi* is the key to understanding the dynamics of interpersonal relations among the Chinese. The term refers to the special relationships two persons have with each other, which can best be translated as 'friendship' with implications of a continual exchange of favours between them (Pye 1992). *Guanxi* binds people together through exchange of favours rather than expressions of sympathy and friendship, with the relationship tending to be more utilitarian than emotional. In the Chinese art of relationship management, *renqing* plays an important role in the cultivation and development of *guanxi*. It covers 'not only sentiment but also its social expressions such as the offering of congratulations or condolences and the making of gifts on appropriate occasions' (Yang 1957: 292). As Chen (1995: 55) argues, if 'one fails to follow the rule of equity in exchange of *renqing*, one loses one's face, hurts the feelings of one's friends and looks morally bad, and one's *guanxiwang* (connection network) is in danger'. *Renqing* is related to the Confucian concept of behavioural propriety. This stresses the social responsibility of individuals to act according to certain prescribed rules of behaviour.

The central goal of Confucianism is to achieve social harmony between people. This depends on not only maintaining correct relationships among individuals but also protecting an individual's 'face' or one's dignity, self-respect and prestige. Social interactions in Chinese societies need to be conducted so nobody loses face. Thus aspects of the management process continue to be influenced by these cultural traditions throughout the Chinese world. In the foreseeable future, the didactic style of leadership is likely to remain the dominant mode in mainland China and other Chinese communities.

East Europe

In East Europe, diversity of management systems is widely recognised, following the breakdown of Communism in the late 1980s and early 1990s. This diversity is the result of the linguistic, national and historical origins of these states (Judt 2010). Except in the cases of East Germany and the Czech Republic, prior to 1945 the countries of the region were largely agricultural. Their industrial base was weak and a managerial class was little more than an embryonic one. Second, the industrialisation of these countries under Communist leadership followed the Soviet model of management 'which promoted bureaucratic rather than managerial-entrepreneurial modes of behaviour'. Hence 'the content and meaning of the work carried out by individuals in managerial positions consequently differed in significant ways' (Edwards and Lawrence 2000: 141–142). Third, the subsequent collapse of the Communist regimes made it necessary to completely overhaul management practices and management education in these countries. This overhaul was strongly influenced by American practices and the Anglo-Saxon model, although the Romance models (France, Spain and Italy) and Nordic ones also had their impacts, partly through the influence of collaboration among universities in Europe. 'The current situation is thus often a patchwork of former Soviet, pre-communist and imported practices.' Fourth, even within the frameworks of individual models, East European countries, as in West Europe, have developed distinctive managerial cadres and systems of management. 'The management cadres of individual countries derive from the general experience of economic and industrial development' and from the particular system of education in each country.

South Korea

In South Korea, the business environment has also experienced recent rapid change. South Korean businesses are influenced heavily by the country's national culture. Because of the strong influence of family traditions, Korean corporate leaders tend to manage using principles that govern the family or clan system. One legacy of this is a strong authoritarian style of management. A top-down decision-making style is fairly typical in South Korean firms. Corporate leadership is also heavily influenced by the key value of *inwha*, defined as harmony, where the emphasis is on harmony between persons who are unequal in rank, power and prestige (Alston 1989). Another aspect of *inwha* is that each party has responsibility to support the other. The harmony-oriented nature of South Korean business leadership is demonstrated in the decision patterns of Korean managers, who try to maintain good relationships with their subordinates.

Managers tend to take decisions by consulting subordinates, while maintaining informal interactions with them to achieve harmony-based leadership (Song 1990). The key Confucian values of diligence and harmony have also contributed to a relatively high work ethic among South Korean workers, who have been haunted by instability and poverty in the country's history. Thus high wages and job security tend to be important motivational factors. A main feature of organisational communication in Korean companies is that formal communication is mainly through vertical hierarchies, with superiors expected to give general directives to subordinates, rather than detailed ones. Subordinates, in turn, are expected to understand and implement these directives. Korean workers also usually attach greater importance to upward formal communication on hierarchical lines than communication on horizontal, inter-departmental lines. Like other Asian states, and with the internationalisation of South Korean businesses, management has become more professionalised. Korean management continues to maintain its uniqueness based on the country's cultural and social environments (Rowley and Yongsun 2009).

Convergence or divergence in management practices?

Despite the above analysis, some convergence on Anglo-Saxon capitalism could be partially counterbalancing diversity in national management systems, both in Europe and beyond it. This is due partly to the influence of US business practices and partly to management education programmes exemplified by the Master in Business Administration degree. Since the 1980s, 'managerialism' and its strong identification with shareholder value have resulted in renewed interest in the processes of management, wealth creation and entrepreneurship. Forces of convergence include national government fiscal retrenchments in the past 30 years, the rolling back of the frontiers of the state, globalisation, creation of a dominant managerial ethos in many countries, and the managerial movement in both the private and public sectors. These forces possibly interact together to reduce differences in national management practices among regions, at least in terms of business culture, resulting in some synergy among them (Farnham *et al.* 1996, Pollitt 1990, Van Thiel *et al.* 2007). But this is happening only slowly; no one really believes that Chinese management practices will ever converge fully towards the American model.

Figure 5.7 summarises some selected management characteristics in a number of countries and some of the cultural and institutional factors influencing

Region	Cultural-institutional contexts	Impact on management practices
United States and North America (structured employment relations systems)	• Business-government relations neutral • Low government ownership of enterprises • Competitive, free market economy • High individualism, equal opportunity, low context culture, direct communications • Formality in business agreements • Union political-economic power weak • Moderate, secular self-expression values	• CEOs low on international experience • Formalised long-term planning activities • Reliance on numeric performance indicators • Tendency to decentralise organisations • Strong pressures on financial performance • Leadership, communication, motivation non-authoritarian • Personal challenge strong motivator, not loyalty
West Europe (structured employment relations systems)	• Wide diversity of cultures: Anglo-Irishi,[1] Germanic, Scandinavian, Low Countries, Latin, Greek • Preference for social market economies • Welfare state tradition • Government intervention in labour relations	• Managers less mobile than in North America • Less performance related pay for managers • Managers tend to have international experience • Professionally rather than managerially qualified • Have long-term planning horizon

Figure 5.7 Some cultural and institutional contexts influencing management practices within selected regions in the global economy

[1] The United Kingdom and Ireland have many characteristics of the United States and North America contexts of management (and of managerial practices) than those of the rest of West Europe.

Sources: Daft *et al.* (2010), Edwards and Lawrence (2000), Faria and Guedes (2010), Hopper and Hopper (2007), Lawrence and Edwards (2000), Morikawa (2001), Rosefielde (2005), Rowley and Abdul-Rahman (2008), Rowley and Cooke (2010).

	• Strong tradition of political democracy • Employee involvement in works councils and company boards (North Europe) • Range of secular, self-expression values	• Less stockholder-oriented • Conservative but able to deal with diversity • Cultural differences between North and South
Japan (structured employment relations system)	• Confucian heritage, emphasis on hierarchy, groups, harmony, deference to authority • Reverence for education • Powers of prime minister and government weak • Free enterprise system, guided by the state • System favours larger companies • Less fixation on profits • Strong secular, survival values	• CEOs older than their Western counterparts • Managers homogenous in age, education • Managers generalists, not specialists • Long-range planning less formal than in West • Firms less diversified than in the West • Noted for production and quality control systems • Strong management hierarchies, central control • Enterprise unions • Conflict-avoiding management styles
Latin America (developmental employment relations systems)	• Cultural, linguistic, demographic ties with Iberian Europe • High context cultures • Relationships and personal connections important • Mixes of state and private enterprises • Markets for human, physical and financial resources constrained • Political democracies sometimes fragile	• CEOs well educated • Few female business leaders • Managerial mobility between firms limited • Formal corporate planning problematic • Prominent businesses remain family controlled • Stock markets weak instruments of corporate control • Leadership authoritarian, personal, paternalistic • Centralised authority, limited delegation
East Europe (*ad hoc* employment relations systems)	• Post-communist and agrarian legacies • Wide diversity in language, religion and ethnicity • New emerging political democracies • Re-nascent nationalisms • Some influence of West European ideas • Strong traditional, survival values	• Organisations sources of power for the few • Tendency towards authoritarian management • Preferment given to personal/family networks • Weak in strategic management • HR a low priority • Rapid marketisation and privatisation • Weak trade unions
The Russian Federation (*ad hoc* employment relations system)	• Widespread transfer of state assets to private hands • Many owner-managers	• Power of senior managers absolute • Different types of managers: post-socialist, pragmatic, predatory, socially responsible

Figure 5.7 (Continued)

	• Close links between politicians and business leaders; political legitimacy questioned • Strong traditional and survival values • Renaissance of religious belief	• Networks important in Russian management • Desire to create monopolies • Autocratic, paternalist management styles • Weak trade unions
The East Asia Diaspora (developmental employment relations systems)	• The region's cultural heritage predominantly Confucian • Includes mainland China, Hong Kong, Taiwan, South Korea, Singapore • Tendency for hierarchy, deference to authority, *guanxi*, social bonds • Predominantly capitalist, except China, with state-guided forms of capitalism • Taiwan, South Korea, Singapore dominant party democracies; China single-party state • Generally strong secular and survival values in these states	• Family the bedrock of social order • Private-sector managers patriarchal • High proportions of small-medium size firms • Nepotism and favouritism common in staffing • Private-sector planning informal • Stock markets have less control than in West • Older, benevolent, paternalist, authoritarian leaders than in West • Strong influence of the state on managers of public enterprises in China • State-controlled unions in China; free but constrained unions in other parts of East Asia

Figure 5.7   (Continued)

the management function within them. Modern management practices result from the complex interplay of cultural and institutional forces within nation states, as well as the history, geography and languages of these countries; each has implications for managing employment relationships.

THE HUMAN RESOURCES MANAGEMENT FUNCTION

Chapter 2 discusses the origins of the human resources management tradition in employment relations and the essential conceptual differences between the 'personnel management', 'contemporary HRM' and 'contextual' paradigms for managing people. However, elements of these first two paradigms coincide in some organisations, resulting in a hybrid form of HR function. A main feature of the human resources management function is that it is contingent on effective organisational HR policies, procedures and practices, taking account of the external contexts within which it operates. Thus in large enterprises, senior managers are likely to plan, organise and evaluate the HR function and draw on the knowledge and skills of HR professionals. This is less likely in smaller enterprises, because HR may simply be an administrative function carried out by either line managers or routine clerical staff. Thus what the HR function does, how it is structured, and the ways in which it is delivered differ by organisation and the contingencies facing it. But there is no universal model of HRM, as is commonly argued in the Anglo-American literature (Pfeffer 1994). Indeed, drawing upon institutional theory, Rosenzweig and Nohria (1994) suggest that of all the management functions HR tends to adhere most closely to local practices. These are often affected by local regulations and shaped by local conventions. They identify six key HR practices most clearly affected by local circumstances: benefits, gender composition, training, executive bonuses, time-off and employee participation. There are normally well-defined local norms for HR practices.

The HR function is also affected by national and regional cultural and institutional influences acting on it (Hall and Wailes 2009). As Hollinshead (2010: 226) concludes: 'the process of globalization is likely to spawn various "hydridized" models of HRM as universalized concepts and policies, particularly channelled through [TNCs] and other conduits, merge with indigenous customs and practices'. As Gueutal and Stone (2005) argue HR professionals are constantly challenged to meet three aims: make HR more cost-effective through reducing the costs of services; improve services to meet the increasing demands of line managers; and address the strategic objectives of their organisations. These are the operational, relational and transformational drivers of HRM respectively.

Ambiguities and contradictions in the HR function

There are and always have been tensions and ambiguities in the human resources management function. First, 'HR' as it is commonly called today is seen to be the concern of not only line managers in dealings with subordinates but also, with the increasing complexity of modern organisations, managerial specialists in the employment function known generically as HR managers or HR professionals. There is therefore always some degree of ambiguity and tension between which aspects of HRM belong to line managers and those belonging to HR specialists. As Legge (1978: 26) writes: 'ambiguities in definition generate confusion at the operational level about the nature and locus of [HR] responsibilities'. This can promote lack of coherence in allocation of HR tasks and activities between line managers and HR professionals, which sometimes gives rise to critical assessments of the HR role by managers. Second, since the essence of management's HR activities is to get the best out of people, implementing policies effectively to achieve corporate objectives is an important task. But the HR function also provides opportunities for individuals and groups to receive equitable rewards for their efforts and some degree of fulfilment at work. A potential conflict arises therefore between the *efficiency* objective of human resources management and the *social* objective of providing justice, fairness and consistency to individual workers in the workplace.

A third ambiguity is establishing whether corporate success is the direct result of effective HR policies and practices or other factors. HR outputs are often unquantifiable and difficult to relate to business outputs. Where organisations are successful, HR specialists may not get the credit; where they are not, the HR department may take the blame. Other observers are entirely hostile to the specialist HR function of management. Drucker (1968: 332) sees HRM as a 'hodgepodge' of unimportant activities. For him, it 'is largely a collection of incidental techniques without much cohesion . . . it is partly a file clerk's job, partly a social worker's job and partly fire-fighting to head off union trouble or to settle it'. He sees HR as having a fairly limited range of relatively important administrative tasks, without any advisory or executive ones.

A useful, early typology of the specialist HR function is provided by Tyson and Fell (1992), based on observations in the United Kingdom, but with cross-national implications. They tease out three HR roles, which partially dissipate some of these tensions. These writers distinguish between the 'clerk of works', 'contracts manager', and 'architect' roles of HR. In the clerk of works role, the specialist HR function is an *administrative support activity*, with no business planning involvement. Indeed this role may be carried out by people who are not HR specialists. HR authority is vested in line managers and the principal activities of HR staff are recruitment, welfare and record keeping. The contracts manager approach to HR is a *system model*, which is part of a policy framework acting on behalf of line managers to promote consistency in policy and effective policy implementation. Here HR specialists are valued for their capacity to make agreements with trade unions to maintain internal harmony within organisations. The architect model is a *strategic role* which aims to build the organisation as a whole. This is a creative view of HR which seeks to achieve corporate success 'with an integrated system of controls between [HR] and line managers'. In this model, it is people who provide the source of creative energy in organisations, by behaving in ways that take their organisations in the direction they are expected to go. The significance of the architect model is it changes the role of 'personnel' from one of a controlled supplier of labour and industrial peace in organisations to a strategic 'HRM' role, which acts as an 'overall human resource planning, development and utilization agency' (Tyson and Fell 1992: 526). Within the architect model, in short, the HR function seeks a symbiosis between the organisation and the effective use of the human resources it needs to achieve its immediate and long-term goals.

Contemporary HRM

Textbooks typically prescribe and describe *what* HRM is, its philosophy, its sub-functions, *how* it is organised, the *skills and techniques* required to carry it out, and some of the *contemporary issues* in the field. But the activities of managers in their HR roles as specialists and line managers, and *why* they do them, are inter-dependent and take place within specific organisational, societal and institutional contexts (Farnham 2010a). Many independent variables are important. These include: the sector(s) where the firm operates; its strategic purposes; product markets; sources of finance; organisational size; organisational structure; dominant culture; corporate ownership; management styles; location(s); make-up its workforce; the technology involved; its history; patterns of historical-path dependency; and the external constraints imposed by the political system(s) within which it operates (Legge2005). In this respect, labour law, public policy and international policy conventions are especially important sources shaping HR strategies and practices. The main HR issues to be decided in each organisation include identifying the objectives (explicit or implicit) of the HR function, how formal HR strategy (if there is one) relates to formal corporate strategy (if there is one), and how authority and responsibility for the function is allocated between line managers and HR professionals (if there are any). Figure 5.8 provides examples of typical HR activities in large organisations.

There are many definitions of contemporary HRM. A major UK text, Torrington *et al.* (2011: 6), for example, say the term 'HRM' is used in two ways. They distinguish between 'HRM mark 1' and 'HRM mark 2'. HRM mark 1 is a generic term that describes the body of management activities traditionally labelled 'personnel management'. Generic HRM seeks to achieve four key objectives: staffing, performance, change management, and administration, and is delivered primarily by personnel specialists or personnel generalists. It is still practised in some organisations, where the 'personnel function' is largely an administrative one, managed by HR professionals. HRM mark 2 is a distinctive approach to HRM and suggests a specific philosophy towards carrying out 'people-oriented organisational activities'. This distinctive approach to managing people delivers organisational objectives by

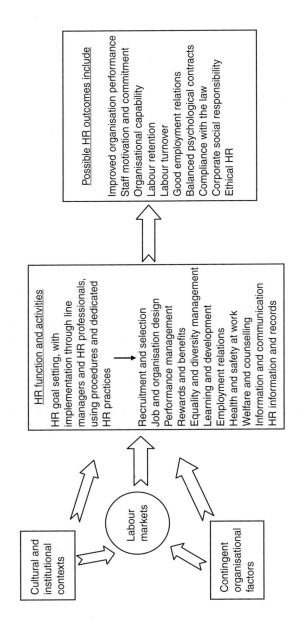

Figure 5.8 Typical HR activities in large organisations

HR professionals in collaboration with line managers. For Guest (1987), HRM mark 2 is not only integrated with line management. It also has a strategic perspective, a unitary, individualistic and union-free approach to managing employment relations, more organic, devolved, flexible organisational structures, and aims to maximise utilisation of human resources. As Goss (1997: 1–3) writes: 'HRM claims to be a novel approach to the management of people that reflects a concern with the flexibility and adaptability of labour and the integration of human resource issues with an organization's wider goals and objectives.'

It needs to be repeated that the concept of HRM (mark 2) builds on a particular view of HR and the business world originating in the United States and adopted particularly in Anglophone countries. Other countries, with different legal systems and political economies, are more resistant to the notion of HRM. They have either taken up the concept much later in their histories or stayed with the 'personnel management' label in organising their activities. For example, the European Association of Personnel Management, which operates under Swiss law and has a wide membership base of constituent national HR associations, retains 'personnel management' in its title. Similarly, the world body representing associations of HR professionals globally is called the World Federation of People Management Associations. Thus some HR observers and professional bodies seek to identify and resolve *universal* issues in human resources management, hence the appeal of HRM mark 2; others are more concerned with understanding their *local contingencies* and are more likely to identify with the personnel management, contextual or hybrid paradigms.

Researchers and practitioners in the United States typically assume that the focus of HRM mark 2 is on the well-being and performance of the organisation, whereas in other countries, with different HR traditions and institutional frameworks, there is a resistance to this. In West Europe, for example, observers are more critical of the contemporary HRM model and a number of stakeholders are taken into account in the employment relationship. In other words, they are less committed to the idea that shareholder interests are always paramount in organisational and economic affairs (Edwards *et al.* 2013). As a concept, therefore, contemporary 'HRM' is a particular version of the human resources management tradition, originating in the United States. As Pieper (1990: 82) points out, the major difference between HRM in the United States and West Europe is the extent to which HRM is influenced by state regulation, with European companies having 'a narrower scope in regard to personnel management than in the USA'.

Drivers of HRM

The drivers of contemporary HRM are both external and internal to organisations. First, globalisation has shrunk the time-frames of the world and opened up the world's product markets, financial capital markets, and some labour markets to global economic forces. One effect is to expose companies in advanced capitalist economies to sophisticated competition in manufactured goods and services from companies (often TNCs) in developing and transition economies around the world. Another effect has been that international competitiveness and quality of products and services have become issues of major concern to many business leaders. Firms have to respond to these pressures by cost-competitive innovation, corporate restructuring and continually re-inventing themselves to compete and stay in business. 'As these tensions work themselves out there will be few areas of employment that remain completely untouched, presenting a major challenge for HRM at all levels of the organization' (Goss 1997: 4).

Second, ICTs are having a profound effect on work and employment. Ideas, information and data can be transferred and accessed in seconds from global sources. This has resulted in changes in the skills sets and competencies required by employers and labour forces around the world. All advanced capitalist market economies in the western world have seen a decline in skilled manual employment and a marked shift from manufacturing to the services sector (Castells 2010). Most workers in the corporate, public and third sectors need some level of computer literacy to do their jobs effectively. Some of these technological changes typically require workers to manipulate large quantities of data in increasingly sophisticated ways. They also change the processes of work. Working either in corporate workplaces or at home, employees can be closely monitored by managements using intrusive systems of control and surveillance (Labour Research Department 2012). Such information systems deal with all aspects of an employee's personal details and performance over time (Burroughs *et al.* 2008).

Third, organisational downsizing, de-layering and decentralising have reduced the numbers employed in many organisations, stripped out layers of administration, and made organisations more effective by devolving responsibility to quasi-autonomous units (Sisson and Storey 2000). The outcome has been 'fit and lean' organisations, with different HR needs than those of traditional bureaucracies. Globalisation, loss of manufacturing and public sector employment, new technologies and organisational changes have all weakened trade union organisation and strengthened management's right to manage globally, albeit in different socio-economic and political economy contexts. HRM policies and practices are now more likely to reflect an individualist approach to work and employment than a collective one, with rewards being linked to performance, selective recruitment and selection, and opportunities for learning and development linked to business need (Storey 2007). HR strategy shifts since the 1980s are reinforced by the rise in individualism and consumerism around the world. Organisations expect their workforces to be customer-centred externally, while training employees to become sophisticated consumers internally. Everything is a commodity and becomes subordinated to the logic of the market in what Bauman (1998) calls a 'consumer culture'.

HRM IN PRACTICE

HRM is a *universal* model of HR, originating in US research and various case studies, but there is no single *theory* of HRM mark 2. The only consistent factor within the HRM paradigm is the almost manic search for improved performance within organisations. HRM, in short, is performance-driven. Torrington *et al.* (2011: 799) claim that everyone wants effective performance. Managers want individuals to be productive; customers want a good product or service at the right price; government wants efficient businesses within a growing economy; and employees want the satisfaction of achievement and results. For Torrington *et al.* (2011), achieving performance is a complicated matter and effective performance 'varies according to the work done'. But for senior managers, the achievement of improved performance is typically targeted at greater cost-effectiveness, profitability, shareholder value, customer satisfaction and productivity within organisations; all in the contexts of market competition and globalisation. In competitive product markets, improved performance is the key to organisational efficiency, effectiveness and survival. In this universalist version of HRM, managing human resources in ways to achieve these goals is a fundamental policy objective of top managers. Some go farther and argue this can be measured and cannot be ignored (Burchholder 2007).

Hard and soft versions of HRM

One stream of HRM in the literature is the 'hard' version. Hard HRM views employees as a cost to be minimised and tends to focus on flexibility techniques and limited investment in learning and development. Fombrun's *et al.* (1984) approach, for example, stresses the links between business and HR strategies and the importance of 'tight fit' between them. Human resources are seen as similar to other resources used by organisations, such as land and capital. Hard HRM also concentrates on the 'resource' aspect of labour, which has a commodity status: it is treated well when in short supply, less well with labour surpluses. People are managed according to the principles of profit maximisation and cost minimisation. As Boxall (1992: 68) argues, this model of 'HRM appears to be something that is "done to" passive human resources rather than something that is "done with" active human being'. Hard HRM allows for a range of different HR styles of management but its priorities are flexibility and cost-effectiveness.

The 'soft' version of HRM emphasises the 'human' aspects of human resources. Soft HRM recognises that employees are a resource worth investing in and tends to focus on high-commitment, high-involvement HR practices which seek high performance outcomes for firms (Murray 2002). The generic term commonly used to describe this approach to HRM is 'high-performance work systems' (HPWS). In essence, HPWS is the term used since the 1990s to link selected bundles of HR practices with increased employee commitment and increased organisational performance. These are claimed to enhance a firm's sustained competitive advantage, efficiency and profitability. The aim of HPWS, in short, is for organisations to encompass holistic arrangements for achieving sustained competitive advantage; the most notable being high commitment and high involvement approaches to managing employees (Appelbaum and Batt 1994). This HRM model assumes that employees are valued assets and a source of competitive advantage for firms through their qualifications, skills, abilities and experience. Within this conception of HRM, there is normally one 'best way' of managing people. Its objective is to get the commitment and loyalty of employees to the organisation and achieve high levels of performance. Storey (2002: 6) sees this variety of HRM as a 'distinctive approach to employment management which seeks to achieve competitive advantage through the strategic deployment of a highly committed and capable workforce using an array of cultural, structural and personnel techniques'. Soft HRM 'can be viewed as a particular style of managing that is capable of being measured and defined, as well as compared against the template of an ideal model' (Marchington and Wilkinson 2005: 7).

Goss (1997: 13) argues, however, that recognition of variations in definitions of HRM lead to sterile and irresolvable disagreements over basic terms. He thinks that a concern with 'process' and 'method' in HRM are more helpful than debates about general definitions of the field. He conceptualises HRM as a particular approach to the investigation of situations and development of policies, not the achievement of prescribed outcomes to match 'some *a priori* master-definition' of HRM. He addresses three dimensions for managing human resources in contemporary organisations. These are 'the setting of human resource objectives and the integration of these with other organizational strategies', 'the determination of specific policy designs that meet these objectives' and 'evaluation of the implications of these designs in terms of organisational politics and ethics'.

HR strategy and integration

A major feature of the universalist HRM mark 2 paradigm is the importance placed on HR strategy in the effective managing of people and its business focus. Tyson (1995: 3) defines HR strategy as 'a set of ideas, policies and practices which management adopt in order to achieve a people-management objective'. Thus HR strategy is the intentions of the firm towards its employees. Its aim is to influence key HR practices that promote improved organisational performance and competitive advantage by firms, taking account of organisational politics and what is practicable in each case. A number of HR strategy models is examined in Chapter 9 but each is underpinned by the idea that HR policies and practices need to be *vertically* integrated with and supportive of the goals of the business, if they are to be effective. It is argued, in other words, that HR strategies need to have 'external fit' with the organisation's business strategies and be vertically integrated with them (Fombrun *et al.* 1984, Guest 1987, Schuler and Jackson 2007, Pfeffer 1998). Vertical integration provides links between business strategy, the external contexts of the firm, and its HR policies and practices. Writers such as Legge (1995), however, question the claimed links between HRM and its strategic integration with business strategy. This is on the grounds that these can produce internal inflexibilities between them, because of too close a match between HR and business strategies.

In addition to 'external fit', it is also argued there needs to be 'internal fit' between different elements of the HR strategy so they are *horizontally* integrated. Horizontal integration of elements within the HR strategy requires high levels of compatibility and consistency among them. Any policy conflicts within the HR strategy need to be avoided. A number of studies indicate that organisations accrue clear benefits from having an appropriate mix of internally consistent HR practices, integrated and supportive of one another (Huselid *et al.* 2005). In the managerial literature on HR strategy, it is generally argued that the greater the degree of vertical and horizontal integration within an organisation, the more effective HR strategy is likely to be; however difficult it is to do in practice (Farnham 2010a). The nature and feasibility of possible links between business strategy and HR strategy, and the internal consistencies of HR strategy, are consistent themes in the strategy literature (Boxall and Purcell 2000).

Line manager involvement

Other studies in the literature on contemporary HRM stress the importance of line manager involvement in HR; this means working in partnership with HR professionals in delivering HR outcomes. This is highlighted by the UK research of Hutchinson and Purcell (2003: ix). They argue that behaviour of first-line managers is the most important factor explaining variations in job satisfaction and job discretion among employees. For these writers: 'It is one of the most important factors in developing organisational commitment.' They note that strengthening the relationship between line managers and subordinates results in positive attitudes to employee performance and motivation. Such studies indicate that line managers can make real differences in employee attitudes and behaviour, as well as demonstrating the critical role they play in implementing HR policies (Purcell 2009, Renwick 2003). However, to undertake their HR roles successfully, such as managing absence, performance appraisal, team briefing and staff development, it is commonly recognised that line managers need to work closely with HR practitioners to maintain consistency and effectiveness in carrying out their HR responsibilities. This is particularly important in areas such as induction, training and discipline, where line managers and HR professionals typically share responsibility for these activities (Armstrong 2009). Other studies show that line managers are typically involved in recruitment and selection, learning and development and employee relations. In general, successive surveys highlight the increasing HR responsibilities being devolved to line managers in organisations, in conjunction with HR professionals as 'business partners'.

THE GEOGRAPHIC DISPERSION OF HRM PRACTICES

Contemporary HRM first emerged in the late 1980s in the United States. This was followed by its dispersion, through HR practices such as performance pay and performance appraisal, into the United Kingdom, other Anglophone countries and countries and regions with different cultural and institutional traditions. The main geographic areas summarised here for illustrative purposes are Japan and other parts of Asia, the United States, West Europe. According to Trompenaars (1993), there are a number of factors why the United States is a special case, making it quite atypical of the world as a whole. This incursion into comparative HRM is explored more fully in Chapter 9 but the basic purpose of research in comparative HR studies is to examine how people are managed in different countries and the factors influencing this. As Brewster *et al.* (2011: 13) argue, the comparative approach considers 'the nature and impact of institutional differences between countries', 'which HRM practices are more or less culturally sensitive', and patterns of convergence or divergence 'in HRM practices across national borders'.

Japan and other parts of Asia

Japanese employers have always stressed the importance of human resources management. Culturally, Japan is a relatively homogenous society, with a common language, suspicion of other cultures, and a strong tradition of group identity. This results in distinctive forms of HRM, compared with those in other countries and geographic areas. A key aspect of the Japanese approach to HRM is internal labour markets, where one company effectively means one labour market (Ariga *et al.* 2000). New graduates are hired by employers from different levels of schools and universities, which lead to internal promotional ladders, which are typically gender-based. Traditionally, pay has been both seniority and age-based and welfare support is provided to Japanese workers by their employers – hence the phrase 'Welfare Capitalism'.

Japan's employment system played a central role in its strong economic growth in the second half of the twentieth century. The system was supported by three HR pillars: lifetime employment, seniority-based wages, and enterprise-based unionism. To these, a fourth pillar was added later: community consciousness within the company. This structure was based on vertical hierarchical relationships, reciprocal obligations between managers and workers, and consensus decision-making. Japanese companies have generally recruited workers immediately after graduation from school or university, without requiring them to have job-specific skills. This was due to mass production systems taking rapid hold in Japanese companies after the Second World War. To train employees, companies offer hands-on experience to them. Alternatively, firms invest in education and in-house professional training for new employees. This means that several years elapse before new employees become efficient workers. In exchange for this security and investment in human resources, employees have been expected to remain with the same employer until they reach mandatory retirement age (Kawasaki and Hart 1999).

When business is depressed in Japan, regular employees are dismissed only as a last resort. Wage increases and promotions are primarily governed by the employee's age and length of service in the company. This tradition of seniority-based wages, which was devised as a means of guaranteeing the stability of corporate employment to employees throughout their careers, is closely connected to lifetime employment as a distinguishing characteristic of Japanese-style management. Japanese companies typically provide fringe benefits that enable employees to enjoy recreation and leisure activities, such as sports competitions, employee excursions, and so on.

The traditional Japanese employment system was well suited to the building of a modern industrial society. It provided a stable and skilled resource base for manufacturers, as they expanded production during the decades of strong economic growth prior to 1990. However, two key elements of the system – lifetime employment and seniority-based pay – work best in a growing economy and have proven difficult to sustain in the prolonged recession following the collapse of the so-called bubble economy at the start of the 1990s. The need to cut costs and increase efficiency is now having a severe impact on employment in Japan. Companies are reducing the hiring of new graduates, providing voluntary early retirement schemes for older workers, transferring people to lower-paid positions, and resorting to layoffs as part of restructuring. More companies are replacing seniority-based wages with performance-based pay systems (Haak and Pudelko 2005).

Despite rising interest in HRM in Asia, its analysis is problematic, because HR practices are diverse across this geographic region and within particular economies. Thus traditional HR practices such as life-time employment, seniority pay and enterprise unionism in Japan and South Korea is noted by some observers, but such practices are not always consistently used or as widespread as some studies argue. Indeed they are under stress and change, resulting from lower economic performance and global competitive pressures. Similarly, the concept of the 'iron rice bowl' in China – that is jobs with security, steady incomes and other benefits – is also under stress and change. Other Asian economies, such as Thailand and Malaysia, have very different HR practices from other countries and between types of enterprise internally. These intra-Asian differences stem from several factors. These include their specific pathways to political and socio-economic development, as well as cultural and institutional factors. Although some common forces may be evident, such as economic liberalism and re-regulation, the HR landscapes across Asia remain diverse, so that they impact on patterns of HRM differentially. Thus despite their spatial closeness and some superficial cultural similarities in Asia, HRM within the region is variable, diverse and not always predictable (Rowley and Benson 2004).

HRM in Asia, in summary, as in other regions around the world, is responding to the demands of changing economic circumstances and declining certainty and predictability in business and finance. Importing some Western HR practices to meet these demands has led to reduced use of seniority systems for promotion, greater use of flexible labour, and a widening gap in practices between large and small companies. Many individual workers and small firms, for example, have been hit by HR outsourcing to other countries. Further, Benson and Debroux (2004) observe that the disillusionment felt by employees in many Japanese, South Korean and Taiwan organisations is likely to lead to issues around quality of output, workplace stress and declining trust in established powers and order in these societies.

United States

The dominant theme in HR literature in the United States is that competitive advantage stems from the quality of labour inputs and the ways in which labour is organised and managed. This relatively new orthodoxy argues that innovative technologies and systems of work organisation allow firms to achieve significant improvements in labour productivity, where managers obtain high levels of employee co-operation and commitment. HRM consists of a combination of strategies and practices to achieve these aims. Its key elements include team-working, job enrichment, wider forms of employee involvement including team briefing, problem-solving groups, investment in learning and development, employment security, and opportunities for internal promotion. Since the 1990s, some US firms have adopted these new forms of work organisation including quality improvement, self-managed teams, and facilitating roles by managers. These changes have also been linked to corporate downsizing and lean production, leading in some cases to employment security being compromised and internal promotion opportunities curtailed. Subsequently, these firms have reduced staff numbers and made greater use of contingent labour, resulting in losses of full-time jobs and higher levels of unemployment (Appelbaum and Batt 1994, Pfeffer 1998).

HRM has been promoted as a 'win-win' situation in managing the employment relationship but some proponents argue that owners and managers benefit to a greater degree than employees, because managers gain higher labour productivity on market share. The claim that employees benefit from more interesting work, better pay, improved job security and better opportunities for training is not always borne out by the evidence. Workers appear to value opportunities to exercise autonomy and responsibility in their job tasks but management does not always share productivity gains with them. Further, firms that introduce new forms of work organisation are more likely to shed jobs but no more likely to increase employee wages than other firms (Osterman 1999). This raises the question how high levels of employee co-operation required by these systems are maintained. Possible explanations for this are the benefits to employees from increased autonomy and involvement, fear of job losses from restructuring, and reduced expectations of job security (Cappelli 1999).

West Europe

In West Europe, penetration of the HRM orthodoxy is greatest in the Anglo-Saxon states of the United Kingdom and Ireland and countries like the Netherlands, where English is the second language. The reason is there is greater convergence in economic policy, political ideology, corporate governance, business practices, and social values between these countries and the United States than between other West European countries and the United States (Scholz and Boehm 2008). In the United Kingdom and Ireland, for example, the term 'HRM' rather than 'personnel management' is now virtually ubiquitous, whereas in other parts of Europe the terms personnel administration and personnel management persist. Numerical flexibility is also more likely to be used in the United Kingdom and Ireland, as it is in the United States, than in other parts of Europe, where it is easier to dismiss employees than in countries such as Germany, France and Sweden because labour market regulation is tighter. Thus given the wide cultural and institutional diversity of West European states and West Europe's varied geographic regions – classified in terms of their Anglo-Irish, Germanic, Scandinavian, Low Countries, Latin and Greek roots – adoption of HRM within these parts of continental Europe has been a relatively slow and piecemeal process. Further, absorption varies from one national and regional context to another. It is variations in national institutions, business systems, and local cultures, in short, which have influenced the style and scope of HRM policies and practices across West Europe to different degrees and depths (Sparrow and Hiltrop 1994, Brewster and Mayrhofer 2012).

Research in over 20 European countries within and outside the EU through the Price Waterhouse Cranfield (PWC) surveys indicates some increases in HR practices over time. Nearly all countries in these studies show a rise in the use of flexible working practices. Flexibility is increasing in both its newer functional and contractual forms and its older patterns involving overtime and part-time working. The growth of flexible working practices is not homogeneous across Europe, however, indicating the strong institutional and ideological factors influencing these. The institutional factors include the history and development of employment customs and practices nationally, as embodied in national and European laws. Thus numerical flexibility is less likely to be used in those central and north European countries, where downsizing practices are highly regulated. On the other hand, functional flexibility in mainland Europe is more efficiently practised, as in Germany for example, supported by its dual systems of national vocational educational and training. The evidence indicates high productivity levels compared with Anglo-Saxon states. Flexibility also reflects ideological concerns about regulated and deregulated labour markets. However, although UK governments have promoted the adoption of the American orthodox model since the 1980s, there continues to be resistance to it by other member states of the EU, which have other policies to solve long-term unemployment (Gold 2010).

There have also been increases in learning and development in West Europe, as managers see the need for more skilled and educated workforces, prompted by shortages of workers with appropriate skills in key areas. This has been supported by a series of European policy directives and a variety of national initiatives (European Commission 2010). The PWC data also identify notable increases in organisational communications associated with HRM, including employee involvement schemes. These are used to incorporate employee needs into the goals and values of organisations, by encouraging high levels of commitment within them and to weaken other forms of employee communication such as trade union structures. This trend is countered by EU and national policies on works councils in mainland Europe (Brewster *et al.* 2011, Brewster 2007).

TRANSNATIONAL CORPORATIONS

Present-day globalisation has been promoted by a number of factors. One is the liberalisation of cross-national trade through the reduction or removal of tariff barriers over the past 30 years. Second, there has been the sometimes forcible removal of obstacles to cross-national investment and financial flows across national borders, which combined with advances in ICTs and telecommunications, render transactions in shares and currencies continuous and instantaneous. A third factor influencing the spread of globalisation is the cross-national integration of production, distribution and exchange within and between TNCs – sometimes called multinational corporations (MNCs) or multinational enterprises (MNEs). Some commentators argue that a growing number of firms have been involved in multi-national activities since the early twentieth century but the process accelerated after the Second World War. Indeed, by the end of the last century, it is estimated that just over half of the 100 largest economic entities in the world were TNCs, not nation states (Gospel 2009, Hertz 2001).

What TNCs do

The term, TNC, is commonly used by bodies such as the United Nations Conference on Trade and Development (UNCTAD) in preference to MNCs or MNEs. This is because it best represents one of the main characteristics of this type of organisation – its ability to operate *across* countries, nation states and geographical regions, not just in some of them, independently and autonomously. As Ietto-Gillies (2005: 11) argues, TNCs are corporations that operate direct business activities in at least two countries and have the 'ability to manage, control and develop strategies across and above national frontiers that distinguishes them from other actors in the economic system'. To operate trans-nationally, a company must operate directly in an overseas or foreign country by setting up affiliates there and through the ownership of assets abroad. More generally, most large companies operate trans-nationally and there is increasing participation by smaller companies within the ambits of TNCs through networking and inter-corporate co-operation. Most TNCs originate in developed countries, although an increasing number is emerging in the developing world and transition economies.

TNCs typically comprise 'parent enterprises' and 'foreign affiliates'. Parent enterprises control assets of entities in other countries other than their home country, by owning a certain amount of their equity capital, where 10 per cent or more is considered a threshold. Foreign affiliates are enterprises in which an investor, resident in another state, owns a stake that permits an interest in the management of that company, again where 10 per cent of equity is considered to be the threshold holding. UNCTAD categorises affiliates as 'subsidiaries', 'associates' or 'branches'. A subsidiary is a corporation in the host country in which another entity directly owns more than half of shareholder voting power and has the right to appoint or remove a majority of the members of the management or supervisory board. An associate is a corporation in the host country in which the investor owns at least 10 per cent, but not more than half, of shareholder voting power. A branch is a wholly or jointly owned non-corporate enterprise in the host country. Branches include the permanent office of the financial investor, a joint venture between the foreign direct investor and one of more third parties or other forms of resource ownership such as mobile equipment for gas or oil rigs, land and objects owned by a foreign resident (UNCTAD 2012).

Type of business activity	Main features
International trade	Involves the exchange of goods or services by TNCs across national frontiers, including intra-firm trade and intra-industry trade.
International investment	Takes the forms of international portfolio investment (IPI) and foreign direct investment (FDI). IPI is investment undertaken purely for financial reasons, often on a short-term basis, but includes long-term bonds and corporate equities other than those included in direct investment and reserves. It enables investors to have an effective voice in the management of the enterprise.
Foreign Direct Investment	Is a long-term investment relationship and reflects a lasting interest and control by a resident entity in an enterprise resident in one economy or in an enterprise resident in an economy other than that of the foreign direct investor. FDI implies that the investor exerts a significant degree of influence on the management of the enterprise resident in the other economy and involves subsequent transactions between the two entities and among foreign affiliates.
Non-equity investment	Includes subcontracting, management contracts, turn-key arrangements where projects are delivered in a completed state, and product sharing.
Inter-firm collaborative agreements	Is made up of (a) licensing agreements, (b) franchising which allows the franchisee to undertake business activities in a certain domain in relation to a product/service and/or a geographical territory, (c) alliances and joint ventures which involve either creating a new business entity or equity ownership, and (d) subcontracting where a firm places an order with another firm for the manufacture of parts, sub-assemblies or assemblies, which are incorporated into the contracting party's product.

Figure 5.9   Types of TNC international business activity and their main features
Source: International Monetary Fund (2013).

A wide variety of business activities takes place across national frontiers. In either *direct* or *indirect* ways, the activities of TNCs result in movements of goods and/or services and/or labour, finance capital and physical capital between nation states. Five types of business and commercial activities of TNCs are identified by UNCTAD and summarised in Figure 5.9.

HRM in TNCs

TNCs and the international business they generate also result in large movements of people across frontiers. Such movements include tourism, international transport, expatriate workers and traditional migration in the forms of unskilled and skilled labour around the world. From an HRM perspective, companies become involved in the exchange of labour services between businesses located in different units in different countries. Expatriate employees are sent on international assignments to other parts of the company, which either employs them or places them in an independent company which has collaborative arrangements with the TNC. These movements may be either long or short term. But the evidence points to movements of skilled labour, for either long-term or short-term assignments, having increased in recent decades (Salt 1997). This is in line with increased cross-border business activities originating in TNCs. Further, the migration of unskilled labour to the advanced economies has increased, with migrant workers often remitting part of their wages to their families and relatives in their own countries.

The human resources management function across borders within TNCs is described as international HRM (IHRM). Taylor *et al.* (1996: 960) define IHRM as: 'The set of distinctive activities, functions and processes that are directed at attracting, developing and maintaining a [TNC's] human resources. It is thus the aggregate of the various HRM systems used to manage people in the [TNC] both at home and overseas.' The essential feature distinguishing IHRM from HRM in domestic companies is that it deals with the management of people across countries – in terms of policy, HR planning, recruitment and selection, rewards, learning and development, managing performance, employment relations and employee welfare – where there are different systems for organising business in general and HR in particular. There is also a strong overlap between IHRM and comparative HRM, since comparative studies are largely concerned with questions about why and to what extent there are differences in HR practices between countries (Clark *et al.* 1999). The key issue is the relationship between TNCs and their HR systems which transcend national borders. Operating across national borders would not matter, if national systems were highly convergent due to globalisation. Yet significant differences remain in how countries organise business activity and, more specifically, how they manage employees (Brewster *et al.* 2005).

Another key issue is how IHRM is conceptualised, taking account of cross-national differences. Like the study of management in general, IHRM can be examined in terms of either cultural values, drawing upon the works of Hofstede (1993) and others, or institutional forces, drawing upon the varieties of capitalism and forms of organisation and business system debates (Hall and Soskice 2001, Crouch 2005). The cultural perspective suggests that persistent differences in cross-national behaviours derive out of fundamental national cultural values. Thus Ferner (2009: 542) sees the problem as: 'how can "multicultural" organisations be managed, and to what extent are modifications necessary to parent country culture in a [TNC's] operations abroad?' The institutional approach when used to understand cross-national differences of IHRM, in contrast, seeks explanations for differences in behaviour in the ways in which economic activity is structured around national business systems, and the contexts within which they operate, as discussed in this chapter and Chapter 3.

A third issue in IHRM is the extent to which there are cross-national transfers of HR policies and practices within TNCs. Czarniawska and Joerges (1996) describe this phenomenon as the 'travel of ideas'. Travel of ideas is examined in terms of 'motive' and 'opportunity'. In reviewing the resource-based view of the firm (see Chapter 9), Taylor *et al.* (1996) perceive motive in terms of attaining competitive advantage through deploying resources that are rare, valuable, and difficult to imitate. For them, firms with an 'exportive' HR orientation seek to transfer parent-country HR practices to foreign affiliates. Firms with an 'adaptive' HR orientation let local adaptations adjust to their environment. Firms with an 'integrative' HR orientation take what they think are the 'best' approaches to managing people, whatever their sources, and use them to create integrated worldwide systems. Thus business leaders in firms with exported and integrated HR strategies use the dissemination of cross-national HR practices as sources of competitive advantage. Firms with standardised HR operations, in turn, use these as sources of competitive advantage (Edwards and Rees 2011). However, TNCs with an internationally segmented division of labour may gain little competitive advantage in disseminating standardised HR practices (Dedoussis 1995).

In considering opportunity for transferring HR practices, Taylor *et al.* (1996) use the concept 'context generalisability'. This is the degree to which HR practices are capable of being transferred out of their original context. The factors include the role of the subsidiary within the TNC, the employee group in question, and whether the transfer is to a either a greenfield or a brownfield site. Greenfield sites tend to be more conducive to transferral, because there is no structure capable of resisting these practices; brownfield locations may be more resistant for the opposite reason.

In any analysis of context generalisability, national institutional arrangements are deemed to play an important role in either promoting or hindering them. Thus, first, TNCs are likely to gain competitive advantage from not only corporate-specific factors but also supportive institutions of the parent-country's business system (Porter 1998). North American TNCs, for example, tend to transfer their HR practices into subsidiaries abroad more than companies from other countries (Edwards *et al.* 2007). Also the dominance effect of HR practices in a leading economy like that of the United States promotes images of the efficacy of these practices universally (Smith and Meiksins 1995).

Second, context generalisability is also affected by the extent to which national innovations, such as skills systems, can be detached from their domestic context. Third, transferability also depends on the host country's receptivity or hostility towards HR and employment regulation. Fourth, in some cases, however, there are distinct obstacles to the transfer of HR practices between countries, such as the *guanxi* relationships that permeate Chinese business communities (Tung and Worm 2001).

Fifth, as Ferner (2009: 549) highlights, subsidiary actors are able to use power resources from their knowledge of how embedded local HR practices are within their local institutional culture. 'Actors may influence whether "imported" policies are adopted wholesale, paid lip service to, adapted, hybridised, or even resisted and rejected by the subsidiary.' The concept of embedded HR means that certain HR practices originate and become established in given legal, institutional, political and cultural contexts. To some extent, they are dependent on these contexts and cannot operate outside them. As argued in Edwards and Rees (2011: 121): 'The extent of this dependence varies from one area of HRM to another; in other words, the "diffusability" of some practices is higher than that of others.'

CONCLUSION AND IMPLICATIONS

Employers are the main source of paid work for all types of labour and occupations, while managers are one of the fastest growing occupational groups in the global labour market, as organisations – whether for profit or non-profit ones – become larger, more complex, more technological and more penetrating in the world economy (Edfelt 2009, Nedopil *et al.* 2011). As this chapter demonstrates, contemporary management practices vary widely among nation states, within them, regionally and around the world. Some difficulties arise in defining 'management', since within any single country, it is at one and the same time a decision-making activity, a system of authority and an elite group with particular social attributes (Harbison and Myers 1959). But if management is regarded primarily as a decision-making process undertaken by an elite group called 'managers' through which the aims of the enterprise and methods of achieving them are decided, then emphasising the functions of management, rather than its role as a social class or an occupational group, is a useful route towards analysing managerial approaches to employment relations and HR issues globally and comparatively. What is clear from the foregoing review is that the management function is heavily influenced by the cultural factors acting on it, the national institutional and business systems within which it operates, and the contingencies of the organisations where it is located. Critical management theorists, however, explore alternative interpretations of management and organisations and typically challenge these orthodox explanations and models.

National cultural values differ widely among nation states, as do each country's institutional arrangements for regulating business and employment issues. Each has differential impacts on managerial practices and systems in different countries, including their HR implications. The characteristics of employment relations actors and institutions vary considerably across international regions too. The factors here include 'variations in trade union membership, structures and objectives, in the significance and functions of employers' associations, and in systems of collective bargaining and pay determination'. Employment relations and HRM practices internationally, in short, vary widely (Hollinshead 2010: 221).

The preceding analysis also demonstrates that the managerial role in employment relations and HR is problematic, wherever it is located. First, management is constrained by the employment relations 'rules' imposed on it – whatever their sources. Thus the law regulates managerial conduct and, when freed from these influences, managements that recognise unions are further constrained by the collective agreements drawn up jointly with them. These agreements seek to regulate the relationship between the parties and avoid mutual damage between them. Thus managers trying to avoid such agreements may not be necessarily acting logically. Further, worker subordination to the authority of management carries with it ethical implications for relations between managers and employees. As Anthony (1986: 138) writes: 'The way in which authority is exercised and the way in which it is resisted by organised workers entail problems with justice and equity for society as a whole, problems which are partly the concern of law and social administration'.

Second, determining an organisation's employment relations policy objectives is a sensitive and difficult process, since it can weaken management's right to manage, requires internal management agreement, and its outcomes may not always work out as planned, thus creating uncertainty. Employment relations policy anyway has a lower priority than other policies, because it appears to derive out of the organisation's business policy as a 'third order' issue involving policy implementation rather than policy formulation (Purcell and Ahlstrand 1994). Third, time spent by management on employment relations issues is commonly seen by line managers as time *not* spent on doing management's 'real' jobs of meeting production targets, containing costs and improving business performance. Further, where they exist, HR professionals are commonly criticised by line managers for promulgating policies which are seen as fine in theory but hard to put into effect or inappropriate for the workplace (Marchington and Wilkinson 2005).

There are always ambiguities and tensions in the HR function of management. This is partially because human resources management is part of every manager's job and all managerial work. However, in larger organisations, particular aspects of HR work are the special concern of HR professionals working in HR departments. This means it must be decided how HR activities are allocated between line managers and HR specialists. It must also be determined whether the work of HR professionals has staff or line authority. Then there is the problem of co-ordinating HR activities across an organisation. Thus HR professionals have to demonstrate their specific contributions to organisational efficiency and effectiveness. They also have to address the hostility and indifference of some line managers to the HR department and try and increase its power and authority within the organisation.

Legge (1978) argues very persuasively that in their search for professional credibility and functional authority in organisations, HR professionals have to adapt to the contexts and situations facing them. From her analysis, when seeking power and influence in organisations, HR professionals derive authority from three possible pathways: 'conformist innovation', 'deviant innovation' and as HR 'problem solver'. Conformist innovation is illustrated by attempts of HR practitioners to demonstrate a close relationship between their professional activities and enterprise success. This means adopting the dominant utilitarian values and bureaucratic structures of their organisations and demonstrating the importance of their specialist activities to the organisation, where part of HR's role is to anticipate and prevent organisational malfunctions. The conformist innovation approach is commonly based on the assumption that HR's contribution appears more tangible if presented in financial or numeric terms. Thus conformist innovators are likely to do cost-benefit analyses of HR work in terms of reduced labour turnover, the added value of learning and development, and the benefits of new HR practices in an organisation. Such an approach is located firmly in the HRM mark 2 model of the function.

In the role of deviant innovator, which is more closely linked with the HRM mark 1 model or the personnel management paradigm, the HR specialist seeks to gain acceptance of HR policies and procedures, based on altruistic as well as utilitarian values in the enterprise. Here HR specialists define the needs of line managers and decide how these can be met. For example, they may give advice to managers on courses of action in HR's role as legal experts. The HR professional also acts as an interpreter and advocate of societal norms to the enterprise, showing its dominant norms and values are not necessarily the same as those held in society generally – such as corporate social responsibility. HR specialists using the deviant innovation strategy base their activities and authority more on a third-party consultancy role than on an exclusively managerial one. Deviant innovators expect their clients, in turn, to accept HR's definition of the activities to be provided, rather than asserting their own right to do so. In practice, few HR professionals are able to change dominant organisational values so fundamentally, since these are normally derived from the commercial needs of the enterprise.

In practice, neither of these roles to gain professional authority is fully viable; so HR specialists tend to oscillate between the two. For Legge (1978: 115), it is the role of HR as 'problem-solver' that provides HR's most effective approach to HR policy and practice. This is a contingency approach to HR problem-solving, bringing with it the combined advantages of flexibility and 'sensitivity to the political dimensions of organizational life'.

More recently, Ulrich and Brockbank (2005), building on Ulrich's (1997) earlier formulation of the 'business partner' role of HR, identify five key roles in the universalist model of the HR function advocated in US practice. The first is the role of 'employee advocate'. Here HR professionals focus on the needs of employees through listening, understanding and empathising with them. Second, the role of 'human capital developer' focuses on preparing employees to be successful in the future. Third, the 'functional expert' role is concerned with HR practices that are central to creating HR value, based on the body of knowledge that HR practitioners bring to the organisation. Some are delivered through administrative efficiency, such as by using technology or process design, and others through specific policies and practitioner interventions. These include 'foundation' HR practices, such as recruitment, learning and development, and rewards; 'emerging' ones include communication, work processes, organisation design, and executive leadership development.

Fourth, there is the complex role of 'strategic partner'. This consists of the HR professional being a business expert, change agent, strategic HR planner, knowledge manager and internal consultant. By combining these activities, this role aligns HR systems and helps accomplish the vision and mission of the organisation. In this role, HR professionals help line managers get things done and disseminate learning throughout the organisation. Fifth, HR has responsibility for 'leading the HR function'. This involves collaborating with other management functions, providing leadership to them, setting and enhancing the standards for strategic thinking, and ensuring effective corporate governance. Clearly, this broad set of roles identified by Ulrich and Brockbank aims to demonstrate HR's central contribution to achieving the business goals of the enterprise and is aligned with HRM mark 2.

However, in the contexts of globalisation, increased market competition, corporate acquisitions and the continual search for improved organisational performance, ambiguities in the HR function remain. In terms of Tyson's and Fell's typology and with the reduced role of unions in the labour market, for example, Armstrong (1989: 155) argues that the contracts manager model in the United Kingdom has been 'dying out'. For him, it is being replaced by 'a polarized profession consisting of a mass of "clerk of works", performing routine administrative work for a newly self-confident line management', while 'a few elite "architects" of strategic human resource policy continue to operate at corporate headquarters'. Further, in divisionalised companies, many activities which might make up the architect role for HR professionals are being either performed by managers in other functions or devalued by the managerialist cultures within organisations operate (Scullion and Sisson 1985). Also, with the growth of accounting controls in UK companies and the decentralisation of company structures, the tendency is for corporate headquarters to concentrate on company finance, investment and acquisition policies and for HR and employment relations issues to be decentralised to operating subsidiaries (Hall and Pickering 1986). But in those organisations where HR has adopted the conformist innovation strategy advocated by Legge (1978), 'seeking to justify [HR] work in accounting terms may cede too much to the dominant accounting culture and may also, in the end, achieve little security for the [HR] function' (Armstrong 1989: 160).

An important conclusion is that an unmodified architect model of HR in the United Kingdom, for example, cannot be easily transplanted into typically diversified companies. 'In these companies, projected futures for the [HR] function which ignore the centrality of financial control systems or which seek to locate them in some grandiose vision of company-level human resource policy making are simply unrealistic.' Moreover, in those organisations with a managerial culture increasingly dominated by the language and structures of management accountancy, the key role for the HR function lies 'in a more modest and practical version of "deviant innovation"'. This recognises the enduring fact of accounting controls but it 'also seeks to exploit their problematic aspects as a means of promoting intervention by the [HR] profession' (Armstrong 1989: 165). In the multi-divisional companies reported by Purcell and Gray (1986), the employment relations function of corporate HR departments is reduced to making sure that the bargaining activities of divisional HR personnel are compatible with pre-determined budgets. In these instances, HR input degenerates into an imitation of devolved collective bargaining. Where centralised financial controls operate unobstructed, these dictate employment relations outcomes.

Ultimately, however, context matters, so it is difficult to extrapolate the above analysis and generalise how HR specialists organisationally, nationally, regionally and globally are adapting to the imperatives of market competition, economic globalisation and corporate contingencies on a comparative basis. The influences of national cultural and institutional environments on HR departments within organisations cross-nationally are strong, varied and diverse. But it is 'the embeddedness of firms in a particular national business system' that 'will continue to shape the behaviour of managers and firms, even when firms expand beyond particular national boundaries' (Hall and Wailes 2009: 117).

6

WORKERS, EMPLOYEE VOICE AND TRADE UNIONS

The purpose of this chapter is to outline and analyse the changing faces of employee voice and trade unionism in the world of work and employment relationships in recent years. This is done by examining the methods that enable workers to participate with managers (or challenge them) indirectly and directly in the management of the employment relationship at workplace, industry, national and international levels. Workers as employees are central players in the employment relationship, where employer bargaining power in the labour market is normally greater than that of an individual employee. The employment relationship is thus a power relationship. The main exceptions to employer dominance in labour markets are special cases, such as top-level international sports players or global performers in the arts and music, where the supply of labour relative to demand is relatively inelastic in the short term. Similarly, employer decision-making power and management's authority relations with workers in the workplace are much greater than those of individual workers and are contractually legitimised. Thus managerial discretion is often the dominant orthodoxy within many organisations in terms of labour resourcing. This includes recruitment and selection, allocation and deployment, rewards, learning and development promotion, discipline and redundancy. This is how work is typically paid for, allocated and organised in capitalist market economies, especially in the contexts of economic austerity and the after-effects of the global financial crisis 2007–2008.

EMPLOYEE VOICE

Given these imbalances and inequities in the employment relationship, worker resistance and collective representation against unilateral managerial power is a common theme in the literature of employment relations; from the early days of industrial relations up to the present time (Thompson and McHugh 2009). Thus for Commons and Andrews (1916: 1), the worker as a 'property-less seller of himself [sic]', who is unable to bargain equally with the agents of capital, lacks the organisational power of the 'propertied buyer' of labour – the employer. Collective bargaining through the union is labour's traditional form of 'voice' to determine how it is employed and what it is paid when working for the employer. It is the 'new equity' through collective bargaining which protects 'the job as the older equity protected the business' (Common's 1959: 307). The Webbs (1913: 173) note too that 'if a group of workmen [sic] concert together on behalf of the whole body, the position of [individual workers] is at once changed'.

Context

Trade unions and their power bases are generally in decline in the early twenty-first century, so that contemporary analyses of trade unionism, labour relations and human resources management need to take this contextual factor into account. Early trade unionism was the product of the industrial revolution, while the successful development of organised labour internationally was a reaction to the inequities inherent within capitalist labour markets. Writing in the late 1970s, Dunlop and Galenson (1978: 4–5) in their comparative study of labour and labour unions in the United States, the United Kingdom, Germany, France and Japan assert that in the twentieth century, labour unions had established a secure base in the economies and societies of these five countries, despite wartime repressions in three of them. These five countries had, at this time, an aggregate population of almost 500 million, with a combined labour force of approximately 220 million, 'one-fourth of whom were reported to be members of labor unions'.

Over 30 years later, Gall *et al.* (2011: 6) note the impact of national neo-liberal economic policies around the world and the adverse effects they have had on labour, labour organisations and equitable labour management. The outcome has been 'greater exposure of workers to the vagaries of the market and to the ability of employers to intensify the wage-effort bargain in their own favour'. Responses to these developments by both workers and managers in Western countries have led to new initiatives in managing the employment contract and managerial attempts at 'empowering' employees in the workplace. These include growing interest in employee voice and employee involvement practices, which seek to gain the commitment and co-operation of employees in employing organisations. Economic recession, however, after the financial crisis of 2007–2008, impacted adversely on how the interests of employees 'are heard' within organisations cross-nationally.

Thus in Australia, for example, Teicher and Bryan (2013: 21) characterise recent change in the labour market 'as a shift in the organising principles of employment from criteria of "fairness" to "flexibility" in the name of international competitiveness'. Further, 'the emphasis was on individualistic rather than collectivist approaches to employment relations, in which industrial tribunals played a diminished role and unions were increasingly marginalised' (Lansbury and Wailes 2011: 135). In the United Kingdom, in turn, the most common action taken by managers in response to economic recession 'was to freeze or cut wages, which occurred in 41 per cent of workplaces' surveyed in WERS 2011. Indeed, the 'most immediate and palpable effect of the recession on management practice was through the direct actions taken in response to the recession'. These included not only wage freezes but also hiring embargos and changes to work organisation (van Wanrooy *et al.* 2013: 19, 194).

For Budd (2004: 13, 23, 24, 28), the starting point for analysing the employment relationship is to consider its objectives for employers, employees and society. He identifies three objectives: efficiency, equity and voice. Efficiency – which is 'the effective use of scarce resources that provides the means for consumption and investment' – is the primary objective of the employer. The objectives of labour, in contrast, are equity and voice. Equity is an instrumental standard of treatment, such as fair wages, non-discrimination in employment, and social or private insurance against uncertainties in the world of work. In Budd's analysis, voice 'is an *intrinsic* standard of participation – participation in decision-making is an end in itself for rational human beings in a democratic society'. For him, it does not matter whether voice improves economic performance or the distribution of economic rewards but has two elements: 'industrial democracy rooted in political theories of self-determination, and employee decision making that stems from the importance of autonomy for human dignity'. Budd adds that the principle of employee voice as one of the three objectives of the employment relationship stems 'from political, moral, religious, psychological, and even property rights foundations'. The industrial democracy dimension of voice suggests that a *collective* component is necessary but 'the self-determination dimension implies that *individual* voice mechanisms are also important' (original emphasis). Exploration of the concept of employee voice reveals a variety of different forms, practices and purposes. Boxall and Purcell (2011) summarise the debate by saying that employee voice incorporates a whole variety of processes and structures which enable, and at times empower, employees, directly and indirectly, to contribute to decision-making in the firm.

Forms and purposes

Figure 6.1 provides a systematic framework for analysing employee voice in terms of *forms* and *levels* of voice, *scope* of voice, and *depth* of voice. Where practised, voice mechanisms are found within both private-sector and public-sector organisations (Farnham *et al.* 2005). Forms of voice and levels of voice are closely linked, starting with low levels of voice ascending vertically upwards to higher levels. Five forms of voice are identified: information, communication, consultation, co-determination, and control. Voice as *Information* is a low-level activity, where management tells employees of managerial decisions already made. *Communication* is the next level of voice and explains managerial decisions, or changes that have already been made within an organisation or workplace, to employees. *Consultation* is an intermediate level of voice, where management and employees (or their representatives) talk jointly about decisions that may or may not have been made. *Co-determination* is high-level voice, involving negotiation or consultation between management and employee or union representatives, prior to certain decisions being taken. *Control* is the highest level of voice, involving either

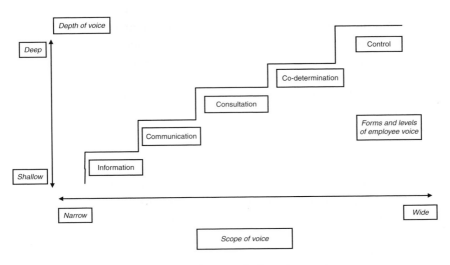

Figure 6.1 The framework of employee voice
Source: Marchington *et al.* (2012).

joint decision-making with management or full worker control, as in worker co-operatives. The most extensive of these is the Mondragon federation of co-operatives in the Basque region of Spain (Flecha and Santa Cruz 2011).

Figure 6.1 also illustrates the scope and depth of voice. Scope is a horizontal dimension of voice and ranges from narrow to wide. Thus information provision is narrow in scope, while co-determination is wide in scope. Depth, in turn, provides a vertical dimension of voice and ranges from being shallow in the case of information and communication, but deeper in the cases of consultation, co-determination or control. Further, voice is typically *direct* or *indirect*. Direct voice is between individuals or small groups of employees and their managers, whereas indirect voice takes place between managers and employee or union representatives. Using this distinction, information and individual communication are direct voice, and collective communication, consultation and control are indirect voice. The linkage between level and voice is important, because low-level direct voice is generally supported by managers and takes place at lower levels in organisations, whereas indirect voice takes place at higher levels in organisations and is favoured by unions and their representatives.

According to Dundon *et al.* (2004), different voice practices serve different employment relations purposes. Grievance procedures, for example, are used to convey individual dissatisfactions with management, with the purpose of rectifying problems or preventing deterioration in employment relations. The purpose of upward problem-solving and staff surveys, in contrast, are to contribute to organisational efficiency and seek improvements in organisation, quality and productivity. The purpose of collective representation is to provide a countervailing source to managerial power, through union recognition, collective bargaining and using or threatening an employer with industrial action. Partnership agreements between employer and union seek to achieve long-term viability of the firm by joint agreements, collective consultation or works councils (Dietz 2004).

Clusters of voice

Voice mechanisms are typically clustered into three groupings. First, *communications voice* provides opportunities for information giving or information exchange between management and its workforce, as embodied in direct voice. As Dundon and Rollinson (2011: 283) explain, 'there is a very real sense in which the communication of information can be thought of as the life blood of a firm and an essential component of the psychological contract'. Communication is normally analysed in terms of 'one-way' downwards communication from management to employees and 'two-way' upwards and downwards communications between management and employees, where information is exchanged between them. Typical information communicated to employees by managers includes: contractual terms and conditions of employment; jobs and job performance; organisational performance; business progress and prospects; and changes to any of these.

A variety of communications methods is used by management, both verbally and in writing. These include face-to-face meetings, company handbooks, video conferencing, electronic media, email and social media. Which methods are used depend mainly on the size and structure of the organisation. Employees also have concerns and points they might wish to raise about their jobs and the organisation, so there is commonly provision for communicating this information up the line. The dividing line between consultation and communications is not always clear-cut and the terms are often used interchangeably. However, there is a fundamental difference. Communications is concerned with the interchange of information and ideas within an organisation. Consultation goes beyond this, by managers actively seeking and then taking account of the views of employees before making a decision.

A second cluster is *upward problem-solving groups* or joint-working parties of managers and employees. These are usually set up to consider and suggest ways of resolving specific issues affecting an organisation (Wilkinson *et al.* 2004). This includes high rates of employee turnover or problems with the pay system. The emphasis in problem-solving groups and working parties is managers and employee representatives working together to understand issues and overcome common problems in a non-confrontational way. Once recommendations have been made, such groups are normally disbanded and further work is left to other forms of voice such as consultative bodies. The advantages of the joint-working approach to consultation are its format. This promotes joint problem-solving in a non-negotiating forum, which helps ensure eventual solutions are acceptable to those concerned, as well as a prospect that any proposals may be later accepted in a negotiating forum. Further, it allows the parties to concentrate on a specific issue and establishes the commitment of both parties through joint involvement.

A third cluster of voice is *representative voice*, through either union representation or non-union representation. Union representative voice is where union members in the workplace (or organisation) speak to management on issues of common concern to their constituents. Representatives are employees, elected or appointed in accordance with union rules, to represent their members in a company or a group of companies. The methods used include partnership schemes between employer and employee representatives seeking mutual gains, employee forums consisting of union and non-union members, and, in member states in the EU, European Works Councils which bring together senior managers and employee representatives from a numbers of sites within a single company across Europe. Union representatives vary considerably between types of workplaces and sectors and between different types of representatives. In the United Kingdom, for example, the Advisory Arbitration and Conciliation Service (2009) identifies up to nine different types of *union* workplace representative, in a country where this role is deeply entrenched. These deal with: collective bargaining; learning; the environment; equality; health and safety; individual grievances and disciplinary matters; consultation with employees; consultation and negotiation over collective redundancies and pensions; and matters covering multiple concerns.

In their collective bargaining role, union workplace representatives deal with a range of issues. These include: terms and conditions of employment; physical conditions of work; engagement, non-engagement, termination or suspension of employment; allocation of work; and the duties of employed workers or groups of workers. Other issues cover discipline, membership or non-membership of a union, facilities for union representatives, and machinery for negotiation or consultation. In other cases, grievance procedures, union recognition procedures or the right of a union to represent workers in negotiation or consultation are covered too.

With non-union representative voice, four main roles are identified: consultations with the employer; consultation on collective redundancy and pensions; employee safety; and individual grievances and discipline. These forms of voice are less penetrating than union voice in workplaces. Indeed, Gollan (2003) shows that non-union consultative forums frequently lack opportunity to challenge managerial decisions. Also Dundon and Rollinson (2004) indicate that the scope of non-union works councils is often very narrow. Other research by Gall (2003b) and Kaufman and Taras (2000) demonstrates that employers often try to circumvent what they see as potentially intrusive types of employee representation, by substituting demands for union voice through customised company councils.

EMPLOYEE ENGAGEMENT

Employee engagement is a contested phenomenon, with a variety of meanings. A debate about what it is and its importance, for both organisations and the people employed in them, has been ongoing for a decade or so. Starting in North America, this debate has now extended into Europe and other parts of the world (Amabile and Kramer 2011). But incorporated and embedded in the employee engagement model is, by definition, the central role of that employees play in promoting the efficiency and effectiveness of the organisations they work for. In this sense, employee engagement is considered by some observers to be a vehicle for extending employee voice. Its central tenet is that an 'engaged' workforce, or one whose potential is unlocked at work, is more productive and efficient than an unengaged one, although a unanimous definition of 'engagement' is never given. Not surprisingly, a report commissioned by the UK government in 2008 concludes that providing a conclusive definition of employee engagement is problematic. But it goes on to argue that the most helpful thing is 'to see employee engagement as a workplace approach designed to ensure that employees are committed to their organisation's goals and values, motivated to contribute to organisational success, and are able at the same time to enhance their own sense of well-being'. In particular, engagement is seen as a two-way process: organisations must work to engage the employee, who in turn has choice about the level of engagement to offer the employer, where each 'reinforces the other' (MacLeod and Clarke 2009: 9). Defined this way, employee engagement coincides with Budd's self-determination dimension of employee voice.

Dimensions of employee engagement

Shortly after the global financial crisis beginning in 2007–2008, Towers Perrin (2009), at that time a US professional services firm operating internationally, and specialising in human resources and financial services, documented the impact that employee engagement was claimed to have had on financial performance in 50 multinational companies over a 12-month period. Companies with high levels of employee engagement were said to have outperformed those with less engaged employees in three key financial measures: operating income, net income growth and earnings per share. Towers Perrin claimed that its research and client experience had repeatedly shown the business benefits of employee engagement. In its view, engaged employees were people who put additional discretionary effort into their work, beyond what is considered to be 'enough'. These employees had the desire and commitment to do their 'best' and made a measurable contribution to organisational performance. It was also claimed that engaged employees were less likely to actively look for employment opportunities elsewhere, compared with non-engaged employees.

Tower Perrin's employee engagement model is shown in Figure 6.2. Other studies present similar findings (Truss *et al.* 2006, ACAS 2010, Gatenby *et al.*

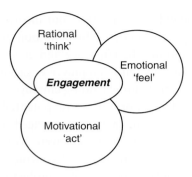

Figure 6.2 The dimensions of employee engagement
Source: Towers Perrin (2009).

2010). The Tower Perrin's model has three elements: a 'Rational' or 'Think' sector; an 'Emotional' or 'Feel' sector; and a 'Motivational' or 'Act' sector. The model's proposition is that to be fully engaged employees must, first, have a rational or cognitive understanding of the organisation's strategic goals, values, and their 'fit' within it. Second, employees must also have an emotional or affective attachment to these strategic goals, values, and their 'fit' within it. Third, employees must have the motivation or willingness to do more than the minimum effort in their jobs; they must, that is, be willing to put discretionary effort into their job tasks for benefit of the organisation.

Subsequently, Towers Perrin (2010) reported the results of a workforce study of over 86,000 workers in 16 countries on four continents: Asia, North America, Latin America, and Europe. Conflating these studies, Towers Perrin argues that highly engaged employees offer improved business performance and, through lower staff turnover, the means to sustain it. To address the issue, however, understanding levels of engagement was not enough. The factors that appear to build or destroy employee engagement were identified as driven by the unique situation in each organisation, region and country. A combination of the actions needed to boost engagement, therefore, was likely to be equally individualised. Reported levels of employee engagement, by country, are summarised in Table 6.1. Based on this limited but unevaluated evidence, it appears that levels of employee engagement were highest in Mexico and Brazil, lowest (or highly disengaged) in Asia in general, and variable across West Europe.

The European countries in this study were Belgium, France, Germany, Ireland, Italy, the Netherlands, Spain and the United Kingdom. Reporting on its European findings, Towers Perrin (2010: 1) argues that the starting point of this study was the importance of 'The Employee Voice' in organisations. The

Table 6.1 Reported levels of employee engagement by country 2010

Global	Country	Highly engaged (per cent)	Moderately engaged (per cent)	Disengaged (per cent)
Global	*All*	*14*	*62*	*24*
Asia	India	7	37	56
	Japan	2	57	41
	China	8	67	25
	Korea	9	71	20
Europe	*All Europe*	*11*	*67*	*22*
	Italy	7	64	29
	Spain	11	64	25
	France	9	68	23
	UK	12	65	23
	The Netherlands	8	73	19
	Belgium	18	67	15
	Ireland	15	70	15
	Germany	15	70	15
North America	Canada	17	66	17
	US	21	63	16
Latin America	Mexico	40	51	9
	Brazil	31	62	7

Source: Towers Perrin (2010).

essence of the argument presented is that employees understood it was the value of their individual contributions that brought job security, not seniority or tenure. Within this group, the number planning to move was relatively small, although many of them were open to job offers. This meant that 'self-determination is important since employees do not think that senior leaders have their best interests at heart. So employees want the chance to build their skills and their employability'. If they were generally negative about their employment deal, especially about lack of fairness and transparency of remuneration, 'highly-engaged employees' in this study were positive that they could help control costs, build customer satisfaction and boost turnover. 'The ultimate prize awaiting the organisation that harnesses employee engagement is significantly better business performance'.

Four rational factors and five emotional factors described what an engaged employee was. The four rational factors were: 'I understand how my unit/department contributes to the success of my organisation'; 'I am personally motivated to help my organisation be successful'; 'I am willing to put in a great deal of effort beyond what is normally expected to help my organisation succeed'; and 'I understand how my role in my organisation is related to my organisation's overall goals, objectives and direction'. The five emotional ones were: 'I really care about the future of my organisation'; 'I am proud to tell others I work for my organisation'; 'My job provides me with a sense of personal accomplishment'; 'I would recommend my organisation to a friend as a good place to work'; and 'My organisation inspires me to do my best work' (Tower Perrins 2010: 6).

The idea of employee engagement, however, is not unproblematic. As a number of studies note, employee engagement is a multi-level or multi-tiered concept (Redman and Snape 2005). For example, people have multiple loyalties in organisations and it is well known that employee commitment to a supervisor has a stronger link with performance than commitment to the organisation. It is not surprising to find that people have multiple loyalties. In some circumstances an employee, who is a professional worker, for example, may be ambivalent towards the employer but passionate about the job, co-workers, team leader, client, customer or patients. But as Rees *et al.* (2009) argue, employee engagement is multi-faceted, leading them to distinguish between intellectual engagement, affective engagement and social engagement. Other research by Attridge (2009) indicates that engagement at work is improved by adopting certain workplace behavioural health practices that address supervisory communication, job design, resource support, working conditions, corporate culture, and leadership style. This study also features several case studies from employers who measure and use employee engagement data to improve their work culture, retain employees, and increase business financial success.

Claimed drivers of employee engagement

The research literature identifies some key drivers of employee engagement. The MacLeod report (MacLeod and Clarke 2009: 75, 76, 81, 104) claims there are four broad enablers or drivers of engagement. First, there is leadership. Here it is argued that a strong narrative providing a clear, shared vision for the organisation is at the heart of employee engagement. 'Employees need to understand not only the purpose of the organisation they work for but also how their individual role contributes to that vision.' Second, engaging managers are important because they offer clarity for what is expected from individual members of staff. By treating their people as individuals, with fairness, respect and concern for employee well-being, they 'have a very important role in ensuring that work is designed efficiently and effectively'. Third, there is integrity. This means that most organisations have espoused values and all have behavioural norms. But where there is a gap between the two, the size of the gap is reflected in the degree of distrust within the organisation. If the gap is closed, high levels of trust usually result. Further: 'If an employee sees the stated values of the organisation being lived by the leadership and colleagues, a sense of trust in the organisation is more likely to be developed and this constitutes a powerful enabler of engagement'.

Finally, there is the issue of what effective and empowered employee voice is, in terms of employee views being sought, listened to, and making their opinions count. This enables employees to 'speak out and challenge when appropriate. A strong sense of listening and of responsiveness permeates the organisation, enabled by effective communication'. Other research by the CIPD (Gatenby *et al.* 2010) indicates that 'collective representation' can be as an effective driver for engagement as employee involvement and direct participation, since it includes joint consultation and partnerships with trade unions.

EMPLOYEE INVOLVEMENT

By the third quarter of the twentieth century, *indirect* power-based systems of employee participation, through the institutions of collective bargaining, works councils and employee representation on company boards, were to varying degrees being supported by governments in many western countries, with the aims of humanising work and promoting industrial democracy in parallel to political democracy in these societies (Ramsay 1977, Poole 1986). Since the 1980s, however, the climate of employee participation has changed, especially in liberal market economies. It is managements who have taken the initiative, by introducing new types of employee involvement and *direct* task-based employee participation in organisations. The concept and practices associated with employee involvement clearly overlap with those of employee voice and are commonly based on classifications such as that of Marchington *et al.* (2012). They focus on the *types* of participation by individual employees in processes initiated by managements. These have the aim of improving the economic performance of their organisations and gaining employee commitment to the goals of the enterprises in which they work (Becker and Gerhart 1996, Gill and Krieger 1999, Suzuki and Kubo 2011). Indirect participation was based on collectivist, unionised principles, whereas employee involvement (EI) and direct participation are founded on individualist, non-unionised principles. Figure 6.3 categorises the different types of EI used by employers today, which tend to be at the shallow and narrow ends of the employee voice spectrum. Examples from five countries are discussed below.

Type of employee involvement	Aims	Main forms
Downward communication	To inform and educate employees about management plans and to improve customer service	Team briefing, informal communications from management, reports for employees, in-house journals, videos, intranet
Upward problem-solving	To tap into the tacit knowledge of individual employees or small groups and to increase the stock of ideas in organisations	Quality circles, suggestion schemes, attitude surveys, staff surveys, continuous improvement groups, *kaizen*
Task participation and team-working	To extend the range and types of task in the workplace	Horizontal job design, job enrichment, team working, autonomous work groups, self-managing teams, T-groups
Financial involvement	To link individual reward with the success of the business and gain employee commitment to the enterprise	Employee share ownership, profit sharing
Employee voice and social partnership	To allow employees to influence events at work, without union involvement but through employee representatives	Staff forums, social partnership councils, joint management-staff committees, joint working parties

Figure 6.3 Types of employee involvement

Australia

Australian historical experience of employee participation has been predominantly of the indirect type, as through the Accord between the Australian Council of Trade Unions and the Labor Government from the mid-1980s till the mid-1990s (Lansbury and Wailes 2004). This provided for union involvement in macro-economic and social policy decision-making, with tripartite bodies being set up at national and sector levels. Since the mid-1990s, however, there has been a series of employment relations reforms, such as the Work Choices Act 2006, which have re-regulated labour markets and weakened union bargaining power. There have been reductions in union membership density, while individual wage agreements between employers and employees have been promoted at the expense of collective agreements.

Evidence from the last Australian Industrial Relations Survey of 1995 (Department of Industrial Relations 1997) shows that EI focuses on employee tasks and is designed to improve the performance of individuals and groups within workplaces. The most common form of EI was team-building (47 per cent of workplaces), followed by autonomous workgroups (43 per cent) and total quality management (37 per cent). In this survey, the majority of managers believed these schemes led to improved performance, the management of change, and improved product or service quality. Most employee respondents claimed that such schemes gave them increased influence in the workplace but, when managers were asked whether they had consulted staff about changes at work, 29 per cent responded positively and only 18 per cent said employees had any significant inputs into decision-making. Harley (1999) confirms these tendencies by showing that EI has had little effect in increasing employee autonomy or reducing the significance of organisational hierarchies. Further, as in other Anglo-Saxon states, research reveals that Australia has experienced high levels of precarious employment and significantly higher levels of earnings inequality over the last two decades. This has been accompanied by a collapse of union coverage 'and an attempt by many employers to replace collective values by a unitary commitment to the values of the organisation' (Teicher *et al.* 2013: 16).

Financial involvement has not increased significantly in Australia in recent years, as it has in other countries. In 1990, 16 per cent of workplaces offered share ownership arrangements to their employees, whereas by 1995 this had increased to 22 per cent. But only 28 per cent of workplaces with share ownership schemes had more than half their employees as shareholders. A report by a House of Representative's Standing Committee (2000) reported that employee share ownership schemes had been far less widely embraced in Australia than in the United States, despite the support of both major political parties.

Germany

Germany is characterised by a dual system of employment relations. This consists of sector-wide or industry collective bargaining between national trade unions and national employers' associations and co-determination at enterprise level, through works councils and other methods of employee representation (Mueller-Jentsch 2003). However, since German re-unification in 1990, this dual system has been under increasing strain from organisational change, rising unemployment and waning union influence (Frege 1999a). New forms of production and work organisation have created problems for both unions and works councils. In some enterprises and industries, such as car assembly, managements have attempted both centralisation and decentralisation of decision-making. Indeed, according to Behrens (2013: 222), employment relations in Germany by 2012 increasingly resembled 'the Italian political economy of the 1980s and 1990s'. This is what Locke (1995: 20) describes as a 'heterogeneous composite of diverse subnational patterns that coexist within the same national territory'.

Some strategic decisions have been centralised, such as location of production facilities but decisions about working arrangements have been decentralised. Thus the roles of regional union representatives have been weakened, since these decisions have been relocated to company headquarters, while new forms of work rationalisation set up by management have created problems for works councillors. With managements using team working and quality circles to enable employees to participate directly in organisational decision-making, many works councils are being effectively bypassed (Roth 1997). New production systems have also affected direct participation. For example, where lean production systems have been introduced, these remove inflexible working practices and reduce staffing in some plants (Auer 1996). Many German employers now involve employees directly rather than through representative bodies. In response, the unions have requested that employers introduce semi-autonomous workgroups, based on Swedish experience, rather than team-working as in the United States and Japan (Wever 1995).

Japan

Employee participation in quality circles, total quality management and consultative committees, as well as enterprise unions and high performance working, have long been associated with management practices and employment relations in Japan (Rebick 2005). More recently, attention has focused on bonus payment systems and profit sharing, where a number of studies show that there is a modest productivity gain from bonus systems (Jones and Kato 1995). Japanese experience of EI confirms its embeddedness in Japan's political economy and enterprise culture. The characteristics promoting direct participation in Japanese companies include 'relatively vague and wide job descriptions, flexibility of workforce allocation, lack of rigid work rules compared with those found in similar economies, long-term merit ratings for managers and employees and widespread use of annual bonus payments' (Lansbury and Wailes 2008: 443). More recently, however, and following continued economic reforms, there has been an erosion of long-term career employment within Japanese companies, absence of 'the collective dimension', and weakening of employee voice, which is becoming 'hardly audible' (Suzuki and Kubo 2011: 277).

United Kingdom

Much debate about EI in the United Kingdom focuses on what Marchington *et al.* (2012) describe as the 'ladder' or 'escalator' of direct participation. They identify five stages in the development and implementation of management-owned initiatives, with gradually increasing levels of influence: *information* provision to employees, *communication* structures, *consultation* processes, *co-determination* through upward problem-solving, and *control* such as through self-managing teams. What each stage has in common with the others is its departure from the traditional Taylorist view that division of labour is the key to organisational efficiency and effectiveness. Instead of being 'machine minders' carrying out repetitive and fragmented job tasks, workers are encouraged under EI to provide solutions to problems and be informed of changes likely to affect them (Wilkinson 1998).

This change in the context of employment relationships is couched in the language of a new 'knowledge economy', where firms have to use their 'intellectual capital' to remain competitive. EI complements the idea that people or human resources are the chief source of competitive advantage. Hyman and Mason (1995: 60) argue that EI 'is an essential component of any move towards [universalistic] HRM'. However, the claim that workers have a greater degree of direct involvement or participation through such schemes does not necessarily ensure greater employee autonomy, self-management or genuine power, particularly where the underlying managerial objective is to get rid of unions in the workplace. What determines the success or failure of such schemes depends on the perspective of the observer – management, worker, or union – and the extent to which they fulfil the needs of the players involved. Scholars such as Sinclair (1992) and Barker (1993) criticise the 'tyranny of teams' or team working on the grounds that these represent a more insidious, stronger form of control than the traditional division of labour does.

Retrospectively, the period between the WERS surveys in 1998 and 2004 saw some stability in arrangements for representative voice in British workplaces, following years of decline. In the period between the 2004 and 2011 WERS surveys, however, there was considerable change in British workplaces. But there was 'no substantial change in the prevalence of arrangements that were available for employee involvement in managerial decision-making'. Nor were there any major changes in the ways that managers approached consultation in workplaces. Further, it was clear from this research 'there remained a minority of workplaces with neither type of formal arrangement for employee voice – signifying the persistence of what [is] termed a "participation gap" in some British workplaces' (van Wanrooy *et al.* 2013).

United States

In the United States, the concept of employee participation is different from that of other countries. According to Derber (1980: 171) by the late 1970s, 'the predominant view is that industrial democracy has been widely achieved through collective bargaining. Only a small minority of labor activists call for new routes to industrial democracy'. However, as coverage of collective bargaining and union membership density have shrunk in recent years, experimentation with new forms of EI has increased. One category of EI is HPWS, noted by Appelbaum and Batt (1994), Appelbaum *et al.* (2000), and Kochan and Osterman (1994). These work systems incorporate forms of EI, including new and innovative approaches to work organisation providing greater flexibility, more co-operation between managers and workers, and employee participation in the decisions and financial well-being of firms. Many US businesses have adopted some of these workplace innovations, but only small numbers have adopted a fully integrated set of them (Ichniowski *et al.* 1996).

A second stream of EI is associated with job re-design activities that change the nature of work organisation and enable workers or workgroups to exercise greater discretion in the ways they conduct their work activities. In New United Manufacturing Industry, for example, a joint venture between General Motors and Toyota located in Fremont, California, there were problems with quality, productivity and employment relations. A new work system was developed in which the United Auto Workers was involved. This hired new workers to operate in teams, which were responsible for planning and organising work, as well as engaging in continuous improvement activities (*kaizen*). Team leaders were chosen by recommendations of a joint union-management committee. However, although teams could organise work assignments and rotate jobs, the fundamental assembly line technology of repeated short cycles was retained (Kochan and Rubenstein 2001). Some observers describe these processes as 'humanised Taylorism'. But these developments are deemed to be a more participative and effective work system than traditional mass production (Adler and Cole 1993, Adler *et al.* 1997).

A third stream of EI in the United States is employee stock ownership. Support for Employee Stock Ownership Plans (ESOPs) grew in the 1980s in the expectation that giving employees stock in their company would increase their sense of ownership and commitment to corporate performance. ESOPs are benefit programmes through which employees receive company stock in place of some wage and benefit increases or in addition to them. According to Lansbury and Wailes (2008: 439), the evidence 'suggests that ownership and other forms of direct participation together do more to raise productivity than ownership does by itself'. However, unions argue that stock ownership gives workers the illusion of ownership without any real control at work; they see it as a managerial device for weakening union organisation and reducing wages (Strauss 1996). Indeed, moving into the twenty-first century, Friedman (2013: 165) notes that American business has shifted 'towards a footloose capital without commitments to place or to people'.

NATIONAL TRADE UNIONS

Although some international trade union organisations exist, the most effective unions tend to be national organisations, because unions are largely embedded within and shaped by their own 'national cultures, institutions, and legal systems' (Fiorito and Jarley 2008: 189). Early local trade unions were formed in the United States and Britain during the late eighteenth and early nineteenth centuries, in response to industrialisation. Their most important institutional feature was they were voluntary organisations, with inverted hierarchies, formed, administered and democratically controlled by their members. The Webbs (1913: 8) describe this as a system of 'Primitive Democracy', where the general meeting sought 'to transact all the business, and grudgingly delegated any of its functions either to officers or to committees'. As these organisations grew in size and geographic coverage, local primitive democracy gave way to representative forms of union-wide democracy within them.

Over time, national trade unions and national union movements were created around the world, starting in western countries and spreading outwards (Dunlop and Galenson 1978). The classic definition of a trade union is provided by the Webbs (1920a: 1) where they state: 'A Trade Union, as we understand the term, is a continuous association of wage-earners for the purpose of maintaining or improving the conditions of their working lives.' The methods typically used by unions to fulfil this central purpose are further explained by the Webbs (1913: 150) in their study of industrial democracy, where they examine the methods of 'Mutual Insurance', 'Collective Bargaining', and 'Legal Enactment'. In the United States and Britain, labour unions first appeared historically among occupations with the highest degrees of social cohesion and democratic informal organisations, such as skilled craft trades. The early creation of unions in the United States and Britain was thus an expression of already existing structures of worker solidarity and occupational identity, which subsequently expanded into less skilled employment, mass production industries and the professions.

Comparative union membership density

Trade union membership density measures the percentage of workers who are union members out of all employees or workers eligible for membership. It can be measured at local, employer, industry and national levels. Union density is also an indicator of union power, since the higher the density of union membership, the stronger the union is in its relations with employers. High membership density enables unions to use their bargaining power against employers, since they can threaten industrial action where employers refuse to bargain with them in good faith.

Table 6.2 compares national union membership density over five decades in OECD countries where data are available. There were 20 OECD member states in 1970, rising to 33 in 2012. A number of trends is observable from this data-set. First, there has been a steady decline in the un-weighted OECD average union density since 1970; from 42 per cent in 1970 to 28 per cent in 2012, although the average increased to 47 per cent in 1980. Only four countries for which full data are available increased union membership density after 1970: Belgium, Denmark, Finland and Sweden. Another Nordic country where union density increased between 1980 and 2012 was Iceland. Union density increased in Spain during the same period, but it stayed at relatively low levels in comparison these countries. Second, there were three countries – Austria, Ireland and New Zealand – where union density was relatively high in 1970 but had dropped substantially to 28 per cent, 34 per cent and 21 per cent respectively by 2012. Third, out of 20 countries for which data are available from 1970, union density fell in 16 of them. In seven countries, union density fell by at least 50 per cent. In addition to Austria and New Zealand, these countries were Australia, France, Japan, the Netherlands, and the United States. Fourth, between 1980 and 2012, union density fell by 48 percentage points in New Zealand, 40 points in Portugal, 30 points in Australia, 29 points in Austria, and 23 points in Ireland. In most countries where union density fell, membership levels fell too, despite expanding employment opportunities in the 1990s and early 2000s. Fifth, the data presented in Table 6.2 'allow the generalisation that density rates in European countries are, as a rule, above those in North America, Oceania and Asia'. In the former socialist countries of Central and East Europe, where union membership had been virtually compulsory after the Second World War, union density is relatively low (OECD 2004a: 146, Lawrence and Ishikawa 2005).

Table 6.3 takes the analysis of comparative trade union membership density further, linking it with collective bargaining coverage detailed in chapter 11, drawing upon different sources and other countries in the early twenty-first

Table 6.2 Union membership density in OECD countries 1970, 1980, 1990, 2000, 2012

Country	1970		1980		1990		2000		2012	
	Per cent	Rank	Per cent	Rank	Per cent	Rank	Per cent	Rank	Per cent	Rank
Australia	44	10	48	14	40	15	25	18	18	20
Austria	63	2	57	9	47	12	37	8	28	10
Belgium	41	11	54	10	54	8	56	5	52	6
Canada	32	16	35	18	33	18	28	14	27	11
Chile	..	..	..	..	..	..	..	..	14	28
Czech Rep	..	..	..	..	46	13	27	15	17	22
Denmark	60	3	79	2	75	3	74	4	69	3
Estonia	..	..	..	..	..	..	..	..	8	31
Finland	51	7	69	4	72	4	76	3	70	2
France	22	19	18	22	10	30	10	30	8	32
Germany	32	15	35	17	31	22	25	17	19	18
Greece	..	..	39	15	32	20	27	16	24	14
Hungary	..	..	..	..	63	5	20	23	17	24
Iceland	..	..	75	3	88	1	84	1	79	1
Ireland	53	6	57	8	51	9	38	7	34	9
Italy	37	12	50	13	39	17	35	10	35	8
Japan	35	14	31	19	25	25	22	22	18	19
Korea	13	20	15	23	17	27	11	29	10	30
Luxembourg	47	8	52	11	50	11	34	11	37	7
Mexico	..	..	..	..	43	14	18	24	14	27
Netherlands	37	13	35	16	25	24	23	20	19	16
New Zealand	56	5	69	5	51	10	23	21	21	15
Norway	57	4	58	7	59	6	54	6	54	5

239

Table 6.2 (Continued)

Country	1970		1980		1990		2000		2012	
	Per cent	Rank	Per cent	Rank	Per cent	Rank	Per cent	Rank	Per cent	Rank
Poland	...	...	...	...	33	19	15	27	15	26
Portugal	...	...	61	6	32	21	24	19	19	17
Slovak Rep	...	...	...	...	57	7	36	9	17	23
Slovenia	...	...	...	...	...	...	...	...	27	13
Spain	...	...	7	24	11	29	15	26	16	25
Sweden	68	1	80	1	80	2	79	2	68	4
Switzerland	29	17	31	20	24	26	18	25	18	21
Turkey	...	...	...	...	27	23	33	12	6	33
UK	45	9	51	12	39	16	31	13	27	12
US	27	18	22	21	15	28	13	28	11	29
Un-weighted average	**42**		**47**		**42**		**34**		**28**	

... not available.
Source: Organisation for Economic Co-operation and Development (2004a), Organisation for Economic Co-operation and Development (2012).

century. Clearly, complete and definitive data in this field are difficult to collect and rely upon, but the data in Table 6.3 provide indicative comparisons of union density across selected geographic regions and countries at this time. The main findings from this data-set confirm, first, union density is much more robust in North Europe, especially in countries such as Sweden, Finland and Norway where collective bargaining coverage is more strongly rooted, than in other parts of the world where collective bargaining coverage is weak. Second, even in some European countries such as Ireland, the United Kingdom and the Netherlands, where union density is not extensive, it is generally higher than in most other geographic regions. Third, with a few exceptions, union density in the Americas, Asia, Oceania, and central and East Europe, is generally low and rarely exceeds 25 per cent of their working populations. Fourth, out of 21 countries listed in Table 6.3 where data are available, male union density exceeds female density in all these cases except in Sweden, Spain and Mexico. Fifth, in five cases, Canada, Singapore, New Zealand, Ireland, and the United Kingdom, union density for males and females is relatively equal, even although collective bargaining coverage is relatively low in comparison with the Nordic states.

A number of other inferences may be made from these data-sets. First, trade union membership density and collective bargaining coverage are generally falling around the world. But the incidence of union density and collective bargaining coverage are heavily influenced by the regulatory features of each state. Thus union density has fallen significantly in those liberal market economies, such as the United Kingdom, New Zealand and Australia, where legislation supporting the union 'closed shop' or compulsory union membership has been withdrawn since the 1980s; something that happened in the United States and Ireland earlier (Cramford *et al.* 1996, Galenson 1994, Visser 2002). In mainland Europe, in contrast, union shops have never been a major employment relations issue. However, they have remained more prevalent in Mexico, while in South Korea, almost half of union members are covered by union shop arrangements, where employees are required to become union members after being hired by firms (OECD 2004). Union density is also affected by the decline of manufacturing in some Western countries and the shift towards service economies within them. Another important institutional determinant of union membership density is the so-called Ghent system. This is where unemployment benefits are administered by union-affiliated institutions such as in Belgium, Denmark, Finland and Sweden.

Second, the evolution of union density and collective bargaining coverage rates has differed historically. In 2000, for example, these two indicators were at similar levels in only half-a-dozen OECD member states, mainly in those

Table 6.3 Estimated trade union density by gender and geographic region in the early twenty-first century

Country/Year	Total union density (%)	Male density (%)	Female density (%)
Africa			
Egypt 2003	42.8	45.2	32.5
Mauritius 2002	38.0	44.5	26.6
Americas			
Nicaragua 2003	36.1	. . .	. . .
Canada 2003	30.3	30.5	30.0
Brazil 2001	27.9	30.0	25.1
Mexico 2002	16.5	14.8	19.8
US 2000	12.3	14.0	10.6
Asia and Oceania			
Sri Lanka 2003	45.0	. . .	. . .
Australia 2000	24.7	26.3	22.9
Singapore 2003	23.3	23.7	22.9
Japan 2002	19.6	23.8	13.4
New Zealand 2004	17.9	18.2	17.7
India 2000	11.8	. . .	. . .
Korea 2001	11.5	15.7	5.4
Philippines 2003	3.2	3.6	2.7
Europe			
Sweden 2002	81.4	79.3	83.4
Norway 2003	71.9	. . .	. . .
Finland 2004	70.8	. . .	. . .
Ireland 2004	37.6	39.0	36.0
UK 2000	27.8	29.6	26.7
Netherlands 2001	27.7	27.1	15.8
Turkey 2001	25.7	27.1	19.9
Switzerland 2003	25.4	. . .	. . .
Spain 2000	23.0	. . .	. . .
Latvia 2003	20.0	16.7	23.3
Hungary 2004	19.7	. . .	. . .
France 2002	12.4	15.5	9.0
Poland 2002	9.1	10.3	7.7
Estonia 2004	9.0	8.1	9.9

. . . not available.

Source: Lawrence and Ishiskawa (2005).

countries where collective bargaining is de-centralised at company or enterprise levels. Often the collective bargaining rate exceeded the union density rate by a factor of 3-to-1 or even up to 9-to-1. This was the case in France in 2000, where union density was 10 per cent, compared with a collective bargaining coverage rate of more than 90 per cent. Japan was the only country where union density was below the coverage rate, since Japanese unions have members outside established bargaining units (Tachibanaki and Noda 2000).

Third, union density rates provide some indicators of collective bargaining coverage but other factors are also important. Thus effective and widespread collective bargaining structures are found in countries with strong social partners interacting with one another, and well-developed and socially embedded institutional and organisational settings, as in member states of the EU (Traxler *et al.* 2001). An important factor influencing union density and strength of collective bargaining coverage is whether significant collective bargaining takes place between social partners at sector level and whether extension mechanisms exist to spread collective agreements to the whole of an industry or sector. Further, within Western advanced economies of the western world, both union density and collective bargaining coverage are weakest in the liberal market economies of the United Kingdom, the United States, Canada, Australia and New Zealand (Visser 2013), with their de-centralised, fragmented and socially less-embedded employment relations systems.

Fourth, trade union density and collective bargaining coverage are generally higher in institutionally mature countries, with structured employment relations systems, and weaker in countries with developing and ad hoc employment systems. Thus union membership density and collective bargaining coverage are highest in West and North Europe, which have co-ordinated market economies. This is due to the presence of strong social partners, institutionally embedded in the European social model, the predominance of sector-wide bargaining, and bargaining extension mechanisms (Visser 2002). The patterns for South Europe, South America and East Asia are mixed, with the situation in specific countries, such as Malaysia and Singapore, being strongly dependent on the role played by the state in employment relations. In the Americas and Asia, union density and collective bargaining coverage are much lower than in West Europe. Again these regions have de-centralised and socially less embedded employment relations systems (Kuruvilla *et al.* 2002).

Fifth, in transition economies, such as East Europe, Latin America, South Asia and South-East Asia, both union density and collective bargaining coverage are generally low. In many countries in these regions, institutional structures in terms of social partnership are weak; union and employer organisations are commonly fragmented; and the parties are sometimes locked in adversarial relations. Additionally, a large share of employment in these regions takes place in the informal economy, where the structures of trade unionism and collective bargaining hardly exist at all. Thus in Brazil, for example, following the return to political democracy, almost 2,000 new unions were formed between 1991 and 2000. However, growth of union membership has not kept pace with increases in the size of the workforce and union density fell from about 25 per cent of the national workforce in the 1990s to about 18 per cent in 2007 (Anner and Viega 2013).

External union structure

The structure of national unions can be analysed *externally* or horizontally and *internally* or vertically. This section concentrates on external union structure; the internal structure of unions is analysed in chapter 10. The main features of a union's external structure are its membership base, criteria for membership and membership boundaries, and the policies that distinguish one union from another. But there is no consensus about what actually determines a union's external structure. Some observers, such as Strauss (1994) and Ebbinghaus and Visser (1999), for example, claim that structure is a function of a number of idiosyncratic forces including the union's path-dependent history, the personalities of its leadership, and random social, economic and political circumstances. Other factors include legislation on union organisation, union recognition and industrial action, workforce composition, a country's economic structure, state economic policy, and the institutional framework of employment relations. Another theme in the literature is that union organisational forms are a product of a complex historical process of interaction between unions, their environment and union origins (Poole 1981).

Craft, industrial and general unionism

Traditionally, discussions of the external structure of trade unions analyses them in terms of three typologies that developed historically: craft, industrial and general unions. This classification has been typically used in English-speaking countries, where trade unions were and are largely collective bargaining agents and their political roles are more muted, except when union rights or freedoms are threatened by the state. Craft unions are customarily based on the principle of the horizontal recruiting of members across sectors, drawing upon a distinct skilled trade or occupation. Former craft unions included those recruiting carpenters and joiners, electricians, plumbers, ship builders and engineering workers. Many of these unions first emerged at local level and in local labour markets, only becoming national bodies as they matured (Kochan 1980). The typical objective of old craft unions was to recruit new members entering their trade through an apprenticeship. Unions organised on this principle would enrol workers (normally men) possessing this set of skills, regardless of which industry their members might be employed in. Carpenters, for instance, would belong to the union for carpenters, irrespective of whether they worked in the shipbuilding or the house building sectors. By controlling the number of members admitted to the trade, and by regulating the length and nature of craft apprenticeships, craft unions could control the supply of labour into the labour market and place themselves in a strong position to negotiate wages for their members. Also, possessing a valuable skill with strong labour market demand ensures a high degree of labour mobility among craft workers. These skilled men were often supported by out-of-work benefits paid by the union, when looking for work (Clegg, Fox and Thompson 1964, Dray 2010). But the value of particular skills varies. Hence in a dynamic market economy with constantly developing technology, the craft is continuously challenged by technical change. Printing, for example, which is a repository of specialist job skills, is constantly being reduced to new sets of processes, by digitalisation and computerisation, which challenge established printing trade skills and traditional male monopoly of them (Perlman 1928).

Traditional craft unions therefore have two options. They can seek to preserve their pure forms and face up to relentless declines in their membership numbers to the extent they might even cease to be viable organisations. Alternatively, they can change their rules to admit other categories of members and skills. Hence craft unionism, with a few exceptions today, such as medical practitioners, musicians and narrow groups of professional workers like sports players or airline pilots, is in decline but is important because of its residual influence on trade union structure. Such unions, by definition, are strictly sectional, since they refuse membership to workers not meeting the strict rules and training required for membership.

Industrial unions, prima facie, are organisations of workers that recruit all their members vertically within a given industry or sector, regardless of their occupations. They were formerly most typically found in post-War Germany. Thus all employees in the railway sector potentially qualify for membership of a railway workers union. The advantages include, first, all railway employees, irrespective of their jobs, can potentially belong to a single, inclusive union for railway workers, which gives them strong bargaining power with their employer(s) and provides legitimacy for them with management representatives. Second, such a union is larger than a cluster of purely occupational unions, thus representing the united strength of all the workers in an industry and overcoming some of the sectionalism of craft or occupational groupings. Third, where multi-unionism exists, industrial unions eliminate any problems with this, as well as simplifying issues of membership demarcation and competing representative constituencies. Industrial unionism also raises possibilities of bringing demarcation disputes into the confines of a single union, making it possible to resolve such matters through internal union processes.

In Germany, there have been a number of major union mergers since the 1990s, which have fundamentally changed the industrial union structure, so that the German Confederation of Trade Unions is now dominated by three major union groupings rather than 16 industrial unions. First, the metal workers, with over two million members in 2012, merged with the textile union in 1997 and the wood and plastics union in 1999. It also has members in the information and communications sectors. Second, Verdi was created in 2001 from a merger of five unions, covering transport, a range of public services, retail and finance, post and telecommunications, and the graphical and media sector, together with a non-manual confederation. It had just over two million members in 2012. The third largest union, the chemical and energy workers union, had over 600,000 members in 2012 (European Trade Union Institute 2012).

One disadvantage of the industrial union is that craft, sectional and occupational unions can establish themselves *across* industrial boundaries, or *within* an industry, resulting in inter-union competition and conflict between them. Further, drawing boundaries to demarcate one industry from another is commonly a difficult and arbitrary process. Indeed, the possibility of promoting pure industrial unionism has often been pre-empted by existing labour unions, organised along craft or general union lines (Hughes and Pollins 1973).

The third traditional category of trade unionism, general unions with large membership bases, appears to suffer few of the basic disadvantages associated with craft and industrial unionism. By definition, general unions recruit across horizontal occupational boundaries and vertical industrial ones. In theory, general unions recognise no restrictions on their potential membership. In practice, of course, because of historical origins in particular sectors of national economies, their memberships are weighted around core workers in specific occupations and sectors. Yet general unions have shown themselves flexible enough to incorporate new occupations, skills and industries within them, as a result of economic and technological changes. When skills are diversified, the most obvious advantage of the general union is its appeal is not confined to unskilled workers. The ability of general unions to adapt their organisations and recruit members in line with shifting occupational and industrial patterns gives them a strong capacity to survive and grow, compared with other types of union. Further, by virtue of their size, general unions provide more extensive services to their members than smaller organisations. This has a strong influence on the union's potential for retaining its membership, as well as an insurance policy against any tendency for minority groups to form breakaway organisations.

Large general unions are typical of the United Kingdom. The largest UK union is Unite, a general union, formed through the merger of Amicus and the Transport and General Workers Union in 2007. In 2012, it had about 1.5 million members, who worked in almost every sector of the economy, including motor manufacturing, printing, finance, road transport, and the health service. Although stronger in the private than public sector, Unite has at least 200,000 members in the health service. UNISON is the second largest UK union, with 1.3 million members in 2012. It organises primarily in public services but, following privatisation and outsourcing schemes, it has substantial membership in private firms too. The third largest UK union is GMB, with 600,000 members in 2012. Like Unite, GMB has members across a number of industries, who are mainly manual workers (Fulton 2013).

However, the disadvantages of large general unions are the dangers attached to size. There is the problem that they become too bureaucratic and remote in their policy-making, thus undermining internal union democracy. Further, large general unions rarely use their full economic bargaining power, typically because there are large groups of low-paid workers within their ranks for whom only major industrial action by the whole union would advance their wage and employment interests. General unions rarely contemplate the deployment of such power, partly because of the political implications and partly because their well-paid members might not respond to a call for action on behalf of less well-off members.

Open and closed unionism

The traditional classification of unions applies, in their pure forms, to only a minority of organisations today so an alternative analytical framework for understanding union structure is to categorise unions into those with 'open' membership recruitment policies and those with 'closed' policies. Open membership policies are associated with large general unions which seek membership growth regardless of their members' jobs or the industries in which their members work. Open unions organise their membership structures to cope with diverse membership needs by recruiting members both vertically within and horizontally across sectors. Closed unions, in contrast, usually restrict or 'close' membership to those women and men working in definable trades, occupations or professions, normally involving an extended period of training for their members. Unions of this type operate closed recruitment policies, in line with their purpose of representing the interests of their members to the exclusion of all others. Their tendency is to recruit members horizontally across sectors; others recruit exclusively upwards and downwards vertically within a sector.

Union growth patterns and membership trends over time suggest that unions with open membership policies are more likely to prosper than unions with closed policies, even in conditions where union growth is limited, such as in the 1990s and 2000s with the ascendancy of neo-liberal economic policies internationally (Gall *et al.* 2011). Indeed, unions with closed policies are more likely to decline in size as the structure of an economy changes or disappear altogether. Thus the distinction between open and closed unionism is most significant when unions are viewed dynamically in relation to growth and decline. For Hughes (1976: 1), 'The main growth pattern in evidence is thus one of "open" unions, with boundaries that are increasingly difficult to define.' Closed unions, in contrast, find it more difficult to grow and even survive.

Sectarian and ideological unionism

Sectarian unions are a special case of trade unionism, typically found in parts of West Europe, such as in France and Italy, and in countries such as India, where sectarianism is deeply rooted and union membership is often low. Thus in India, for example, following the economic reforms since the 1990s, the trade union movement is weak and fragmented, which means that union 'influence on state policy and employer practices seems limited' (Badigannavar 2013: 320). Sectarian unionism is present in countries where a complex range of workers' organisations is structured along political or ideological affiliations, often in line with a country's historic and deep-rooted political divisions. Here issues of vertical and horizontal organisation are not relevant. Thus France has five main union confederations, Italy three and Portugal four, each based on sectarian and political divisions in these labour movements. These union structures reflect and underpin the often intense political contexts of employment relations in these countries within which wages, conditions and workers' pensions are determined (Ebbinghaus and Visser 2000).

Workers join French unions, for example, primarily because they align with them politically and because the state recognises some of them as negotiating partners. French unions are organised into five main confederations, comprising the negotiating partners, and six other specialist or independent groupings including magistrates and journalists. The largest organisation, with over 800,000 members, is the *Confédération Française Démocratique du Travail* (CFDT). Formerly aligned with the French socialist party, CFDT has adopted a more moderate political stance in recent years, aligning itself with reformist factions in the party. The *Confédération Générale du Travail* is the second largest union, with over 700,000 members. It cut its links with the French communist party in the 1990s and now adopts social democratic positions on most economic and social issues. *Force Ouvrière* is the next largest union organisation, with over 300,000 members, and has supported various political ideologies historically including the French Communist Party and anarcho-syndicalism. The *Confédération Française des Travailleurs Chrétians* belongs to the social-Christian tradition and has over 150,000 members. Finally, the *Confédération Française de l'Encadrement-Confédération Générale des Cadres*, with 140,000 members, represents the interests of professional employees, who have higher education qualifications and managerial expertise (International Centre for Trade Union Rights 2005).

CENTRAL ORGANISATIONS OF TRADE UNIONS: THREE CASE STUDIES

In most countries, trade unions are organised not only into national bodies by sector, occupation or skill, where they represent members in dealings with their employers. They are also organised at central level in 'umbrella' organisations, where they represent groups of unions collectively, in their dealings with the political authorities and confederations of employers. These central organisations are in effect the unions' unions, since they consist of constituent independent labour organisations within the country concerned. National trade union centres are structured in different ways. In some countries, as in the United States, Germany, the United Kingdom and China, for example, there is a *single* national union centre; in other cases, such as in Sweden, there are *multiple* union centres covering different groups of employees; and in others, as in India, there is literally an *array* of national union centres, organised on various political, religious and sectarian lines. The reasons for these diverse structures of central trade union organisations are largely historical, ideological and contextual, where the history and political economy of the country are important factors.

Some central trade union centres are powerful and influential bodies, as in North European states; others are weak and ineffective, as in transition economies with *ad hoc* employment relations systems, and in liberal market economies where collective bargaining today is either de-centralised or absent. From the thousands of central union organisations globally, the case studies below examine three central union organisations: one in a socialist market economy; the second in a liberal market economy; and the third in a co-ordinated market economy.

All-China Federation of Trade Unions

China provides an example of a single central trade union organisation in a large socialist market economy, where union density is more than 90 per cent. The All-China Federation of Trade Unions (*Zhǒnghuá Zǒnggōng Huì* ACFTU) is the sole body recognised by government as an organ for union representation in the country. The ACFTU was founded in 1925, 'when grassroots union organisations served as the [Communist] Party membership recruitment bases and provided vital support to the Communist Party by mobilising workers' (Cooke 2011a: 314). Because of the sheer geographic size of China, its complex and evolving industrial and economic structures, and its mass workforce of almost a billion workers, the ACFTU has a complex structure organised along both vertical and horizontal lines. At the end of 2006, it is estimated that the ACFTU was made up of 31 provincial trade union federations, 10 national industrial unions and 1.3 million grassroots trade union organisations in more than 2.7 million enterprises and institutions affiliated to it. Its claimed membership was 'over 1.3 million grassroots union organisations and nearly 170 million union members' and it had over 500,000 full-time trade union cadres and more than 4.5 million part-time cadres (All-China Federation of Trade Unions 2013, Cooke 2011a).

For Chinese unions, the country's Constitution provides some fundamental criteria for their activities and they exercise their rights and undertake their obligations according to the laws of the state. Under the Trade Union Law (1950, 1992, 2001), the Labour Law (1995) and the Labour Contract Law (2008), protecting the legitimate rights and interests of workers is the basic duty of Chinese unions, while at the same time upholding the rights of the state. The supreme organs of power in Chinese trade unions are the national congress of the trade unions and the executive committee of the ACFTU, which it elects. The leading bodies of the trade unions at lower levels are local trade union congresses and the trade union committees of trade union federations that they elect (Chinese Government 2013).

The underlying purpose of the Chinese trade union movement under the leadership of the ACFTU is an ideological one. Its main task is to engage trade unions in the Chinese 'road to socialism', while protecting the interests of workers according to the law across the country's diverse range of enterprises and workplaces. This means promoting economic and social development, defending workers' rights, and mobilising workers to contribute to the country's economic and social development, with the ultimate goal of building a prosperous, harmonious, socialist society. Under the Trade Union Law and the Constitution, Chinese unions led by the ACFTU assume an important role in the political, economic and social life of the state, by contributing to the shift from a planned economy to a socialist market system.

However, the specific priorities of unions within the umbrella of the ACFTU are difficult to determine with precision. What the stated or reported situations in Chinese enterprises are may not conform to what actually happens and the extents to which ACFTU's activities are sublimated to the demands of the state are questioned by independent observers. Thus the ACFTU has pressed for collective contracts to be determined for Chinese workers with wide coverage, such as by industry-wide or regional agreements through 'collective consultation'. But in practice, this does not provide an effective independent framework for regulating employment relations, since the majority of collective contracts are 'model' agreements between employer and union. These do not involve workers directly in the negotiating process or represent a system of free autonomous collective bargaining (Ma 2011).

Formally, unions in China have a number of claimed functions. First, they help establish a modern enterprise system in both state-owned and non-state-owned enterprises. Unions also participate in wage and housing issues, as well as insurance reforms covering retirement, unemployment, health care, industrial injury and maternity. Further, unions try to protect workers' interests in the country's drive for economic change. Second, in recent years, the ACFTU has participated directly in formulating and revising laws and regulations covering trade union work, workplace safety, and prevention of occupational diseases and industrial injuries. Third, Chinese trade unions actively promote tripartite consultation at various levels. In 2001, for example, a tripartite system of labour relations was established at national level, composed of the ACFTU, the Ministry of Labour and Social Security, and the Chinese Enterprise Directors Association. Tripartite consultation has also been set up in 31 provinces, autonomous regions and municipalities directly under the control of central government. By 2006, it is estimated that some 3,000 unions above grassroots level had introduced tripartite mechanisms, with practices varying widely across sectors and geographical regions (All-China Federation of Trade Unions 2013).

Fourth, Chinese unions have actively sought to build sound mediation and arbitration systems at all levels and to participate in resolving labour disputes. Union representatives participate in mediation committees at enterprise level and play an important role as members of tripartite arbitration committees at all levels. Fifth, trade unions also try to co-ordinate labour–management relations, so that they are standardised, equitable, mutually beneficial to employers and workers, and harmonious. Further, unions want all enterprises to improve arrangements for effective consultation, equal opportunities and collective contracts. Unions at all levels have also established legal services for members involved in labour disputes and lawsuits (Cooke 2011b).

Sixth, trade unions are especially interested in the problems associated with large-scale lay-offs during economic restructuring and they help laid-off workers find new jobs. In 2006–2008, for example, the ACFTU sought jobs for a million laid-off workers, helped 100,000 laid-off workers launch their own businesses by providing them with financial assistance, and provided one billion Renminbi (160 million USD) in loans for small business set-ups. Finally, Chinese unions carry out important welfare functions, such as trying to lift workers out of poverty (All-China Federation of Trade Unions 2013).

In summary, the functions of Chinese trade unions within the ACFTU are complex and contradictory, involving economic, social and welfare dimensions. Of these, the welfare and integrative function of Chinese trade unions, as outlined above, should not be dismissed as perfunctory, since in this respect they are acting as 'transmission belts' of ideas and policies from Party to workers, which is typical of earlier Communist regimes (Ashwin and Clarke 2002). Promoting welfare through trade unionism reflects not only the government's ideology of building harmonious employment relations but also traditional Chinese culture's association with Confucianism.

American Federation of Labor-Congress of Industrial Organisations (AFL-CIO)

The AFL-CIO was founded in 1955 by merger between the AFL and CIO. This organisation has been selected, because it is a single national centre, which is common in liberal market economies such as in the United Kingdom, Australia and New Zealand, where union membership density in recent years is typically low. The AFL originated as the Federation of Organised Trades and Labor Unions, formed in 1881 to fill the vacuum filled by the decline of the Knights of Labor at this time. Bloom and Northrup (1973: 49) describe the Knights as 'an interesting cross between a union and an uplift society'. It attempted to weld together all elements of the working classes and to do so 'it permitted craft unions to affiliate directly with its "general assembly" ', as well as organising 'mixed assemblies' of unskilled workers. The latter were local organisations of workers recruited on an industrial or heterogeneous basis. Led by Samuel Gompers, its president for almost 40 years, the AFL became the umbrella union representing skilled trades in the United States, whose main policy was promoting union organisation and collective bargaining for craft unions. Importantly, the constitution of the AFL maintained national unions as autonomous bodies, each with exclusive jurisdictional rights in its job territory. As a counterpart to American capitalism, the AFL opposed government intervention in union organisation, labour disputes and government social security, which, it believed, would weaken democracy by making US citizens too dependent upon the state (Fletcher and Gaspasin 2008).

In the 1930s, after Gompers' death, the AFL was in decline and was only revived by the economic and legislative reforms of the Roosevelt administrations following the stock market crash in 1929 (Galbraith 1975). Further, failure by the Federation to promote the interests of non-craft, industrial unions for less skilled workers, coupled with employer hostility to such unions, resulted in developments within the AFL for unionising mass production industries. Led by John L. Lewis, president of the coal miners union, these groups wanted to expand union membership on an industrial rather than a craft basis. But jealous of their power and the threat to craft union status, leaders of craft unions in the AFL did not accept industrial unionism for the unorganised mass production industries such as mining, the clothing industry, iron and steel, and meat packing. In 1935, key leaders of industrial unions met and formed the Committee for Industrial Organisation, with the avowed purpose of bringing unorganised workers into the AFL; something viewed with suspicion by existing union leaders. In 1938, the Committee for Industrial Organisation, which spoke for non-craft unions, was formally expelled from the AFL and the Congress of Industrial Organisations was formed. The CIO became the federation organising industrial workers in the United States and Canada from 1938 until 1955, when the AFL-CIO was created. Two umbrella union organisations had existed in the United States then, when total union membership grew steadily.

Since then, the AFL-CIO has been the sole umbrella union in the United States and Canada. In 2013, it had 57 national and international unions (which recruit Canadian workers) representing some 12 million workers, compared with over 17 million members in the early 1960s (Carrter and Marshall 1972). It has a wide membership constituency with open membership boundaries, including teachers, miners, fire-fighters, farm workers, bakers, engineers, pilots, public employees, doctors, nurses, painters, plumbers and others. The AFL-CIO also speaks for non-union members, as well as having partnerships with groups of people whose work is not protected by labour laws and are often mistreated in their work. These include taxi-drivers, car-wash workers, guest workers, nannies and in-home caretakers. Today, the AFL-CIO helps people who want to join together in unions so they can bargain collectively with their employers for better working conditions and how their jobs are done. It also campaigns to ensure all working people are treated fairly, with decent pay and benefits, safe jobs, respect and equal opportunities. To help working people acquire job skills for twenty-first-century work, the AFL-CIO operates one of the largest training networks in the United States (American Federation of Labor-Congress of Industrial Organisations 2013). ALO-CIO's power and influence is much reduced today, compared with the past.

Sweden

Examples of central union organisations in Sweden have been selected, because workers in Sweden enjoy some of the best employment benefits in the world in terms of paid holidays, health care, employer-paid continuing education, and job protection. This is due to the co-operative relationships established between the unions and employers since the 1930s. It is estimated about 70 per cent of Swedish workers belong to trade unions, making Sweden one of the most highly unionised countries in the world. For millions of their members, Swedish unions provide special insurance policies, training, representation for contract negotiations, and legal support. From seeking employment to becoming unemployed, workers draw upon their unions to strengthen their negotiating positions throughout their working lives, using union bargaining power and legal expertise. The Swedish labour market is built upon a long legacy of negotiations between businesses, trade unions and government, where all parties generally agree basic pay and conditions of employment. This enables employers to offer good working conditions to their workers and gain competitive advantage in product markets; employees are protected against exploitation by their employers; and the state has social peace.

Three union confederations exist in Sweden, which is a co-ordinated market economy, for manual, non-manual and professional workers. About 1.7 million blue-collar workers belong to the Swedish Trade Union Confederation

(*Landsorganisationen i Sverige* [LO] 2013). This is an umbrella organisation for 14 Swedish trade unions in both the public and private sectors, founded in 1898 by national trade unions for union policy co-ordination. As the union movement grew in power, increasing numbers of workers became organised and the number of national unions increased. During the 1940s, however, as unions merged to become stronger, the number of unions started to decline. During the second half of the twentieth century, and although industrialisation was relatively late in Sweden, Swedish unions had become among the strongest union movements in the world, with one of the highest membership densities. Further, compared with other central union organisations, LO has always had a strict membership strategy where, in principle, all organised blue-collar workers at a workplace belong to the same union, with very few exceptions.

LO affiliates have independent status and the LO is primarily an organisation for co-ordination, research, negotiating labour market insurance schemes and influencing public opinion at central and regional levels. Wage bargaining, international activities, trade union education, children's and young people's education, equality of the sexes, and social security are some of the main areas where the LO has co-ordinating responsibilities, although individual affiliates have sector responsibility within their particular industries at national, regional and local levels. They are also responsible for administering unemployment insurance funds.

An important task for the LO is to protect union interests in Parliament and with employers' organisations. The LO is a body that proposes legislation affecting society as a whole, has representatives on the governing bodies of various governmental authorities, is involved in Swedish labour market issues, and influences public policy. Through its districts and sections, the LO effectively co-ordinates trade union activities and shapes public opinion locally. Contacts with the Social Democratic Party are frequent and the LO has a representative on the Party's executive committee, elected by the Party Congress. But the LO and the Social Democratic Party are both independent organisations, which, although having common goals and common viewpoints on most questions, sometimes hold different opinions on the best way of achieving them (Swedish Trade Union Confederation 2000).

A second umbrella organisation is the Swedish Confederation of Professional Employees (*Tjänstemännens Centralorganisation* [TCO] 2013). A majority of its members is white-collar workers and it operates at national and international levels on issues such as job satisfaction, learning and development, and other labour-related matters. All members of TCO unions are professionally-qualified employees and the TCO is made up of 15 affiliated trade unions, with 1.2 million members. Members have major responsibilities for important functions in society in a variety of occupations and work in all parts of the labour market. These include schools, health care, trade, the media, the police, industry, IT and telecommunications. Over 60 per cent of TCO members are women, with approximately half working in the private sector and half in the public sector. It is the common interests and conditions of work of professional employees, expressed through their affiliated unions, which form the basis of TCO's operations. Unlike the LO, the TCO is independent of party politics and it undertakes a series of basic tasks on behalf of its affiliated unions. These include: organising and recruiting professionally qualified people; promoting and defending the needs and interests of its members in social debates and the political decision-making process; safeguarding trade union rights and freedoms; and representing affiliated unions in international trade union work.

The Swedish Confederation of Professional Associations (*Sveriges Akademikers Central Organisation* [SACO] 2013) is the third central organisation of trade unions, with approximately 600,000 union members. The SACO, a confederation of 22 affiliated organisations, represents about two dozen independent professional groups. These include economists, lawyers, engineers, physiotherapists, architects, doctors, teachers and other professions requiring a college or university degree. It assists affiliated associations by analysing, debating and forming public opinion on matters affecting the associations and their members. The hallmarks of the SACO are its high quality policy analysis, research reports, specialist seminars, opportunities for internships, and influence on public policy. Like the TCO, the SACO is politically independent. Its central policy objective is to promote a society with high economic growth and knowledge-based prosperity, where education and research are regarded as important investments for society and individuals within it.

The SACO does this by: supporting economic growth and raising the general level of prosperity; making it possible and profitable for everyone to invest in an education; improving educational quality; encouraging greater commitment to research; introducing clear simple rules for taxation and social insurance; strengthening the position of the individual in working life; and preventing discrimination at the workplace. The main areas where the SACO seeks to influence public policy are the labour market, labour law, social integration, international co-operation, equality between women and men, wages and collective agreements, economics, taxation, social insurance, education, and research and development. Its activities are seminal and broad-based.

INTERNATIONAL TRADE UNIONISM

Trade unions have a long history of international organisation. Gumbrell-McCormick (2008) classifies these by structure, regional coverage and ideology. Structurally, international unions are distinguished by sector and by national centres. Thus early international unions were industry-based, became known as international trade union secretariats, renamed recently as global union federations. These international federations are wide-ranging and include the International Transport Workers' Federation, the International Textile, Garment and Leather Workers Federation, Education International, Public Services International and the long-established International Metal Workers' Federation. Geographically, international unions can be distinguished by region and they are organised most effectively in the EU and globally (Croucher and Cotton 2009). From the 1960s, for example, the process of European integration led to the establishment of formal regional union structures in Europe, such as the European Trade Union Confederation (ETUC) founded in 1973.

Ideologically, international unions have been very segmented historically by politics and religion. Thus the International Federation of Trade Unions (IFTU), created from an earlier cross-sector body in 1913, encompassed both European social-democratic trade unionism and British and American business unionism. But it had international rivals in the mainly catholic International Federation of Christian Trade Unions (IFCTU) and the communist International of Labour Unions. In 1945, the World Federation of Trade Unions (WFTU), mainly supportive of Communist parties, was established but excluded the IFCTU. Four years later, most of the non-communist affiliates broke away to form the International Confederation of Free Trade Unions (ICFTU). In 1968, the IFCTU became secularised as the World Confederation of Labour (WCL). Meanwhile, the WFTU began losing members, following the rise of Euro-communism in west Europe during the 1970s and 1980s. Also the WFTU detached itself from the Communist Party of the Soviet Union, after the fall of the Berlin Wall in 1989 (Carew *et al.* 2000).

Today, the main body acting for trade unions globally is the International Trade Union Confederation (ITUC), with headquarters in Brussels. Its mission is to represent the interests of working people around the world and was founded at its inaugural Congress in Vienna in November 2006. The ITUC brings together former affiliates of the ICFTU, which was largely western-based, and the World Confederation of Labour (WCL) whose union members were drawn from former socialist and Marxist states (Carew *et al.* 2000). The ICFTU and the WCL were dissolved on 31 October 2006, and together with trade union organisations with no global affiliation, paved the way for the creation of the ITUC. Today, the ITUC claims to represent some 175 million workers through its 311 affiliated organisations, drawn from 155 countries and territories.

The ITUC is primarily a campaigning organisation for trade unions internationally. Its mission is to promote and defend workers' rights and interests globally. It does this through international co-operation between unions, global campaigning, and advocacy within major global institutions, using publicity, research, networking and social media. At its inaugural Congress in November 2006, the ITUC set out the Confederation's overall policy framework in its *Programme Document*. Its main areas of work include: trade union and human rights; economy, society and the workplace; equality and non-discrimination; and international solidarity (International Trade Union Confederation 2006). The ITUC adheres to trade union democratic principles and independence and is governed by four-yearly world congresses, a General Council and Executive Bureau.

The ITUC is involved in a wide network of regional organisations such as the Asia-Pacific Regional Organisation, African Regional Organisation, and American Regional Organisation. The ITUC also co-operates closely with the ETUC and has close relations with global union federations and the Trade Union Advisory Committee to the OECD, working together through the Global Unions Council. In addition, the ITUC works closely with the ILO and maintains institutional contacts with several other UN specialist agencies.

Eight policy areas drive the Confederation's global leadership role. First, it wants to change globalisation fundamentally, so it works for employed women and men, the unemployed, and the poor. In its view, the policies of free market neo-liberalism, and the manifest failings and incoherence of globalisation, must give way to new patterns of global governance. These include: promoting sustainable development, defending universal workers' rights, providing decent work for all, ending mass poverty, reducing inequality in and between nations, and supporting growth with equitable income distribution. Second, effective and democratic governance of the global economy requires fundamental reform of international organisations such as the IMF, World Bank, and the World Trade Organisation, which have traditionally promoted globalisation. In the ITUC's view, there must be greater transparency and democracy in the decision-making processes of each of these bodies and greater coherence in their collective policy positions.

Third, there is the challenge of TNCs. The Confederation recognises that the changing structures of international business pose particular challenges to defending workers' rights, since the effective exercise of the right to organise and bargain collectively is becoming increasingly difficult. This is because trans-national firms commonly threaten to relocate their operations, use their power to dictate the conditions under which work is undertaken, and evade their responsibilities to workers, communities, societies and environments where they are located. Fourth, defending and promoting trade union rights are a core objective within the ITUC's purposes, since trade union rights are seen as a key part of human rights at work. Universal respect of union rights constitutes a key objective of the ITUC, with globalisation adding to the urgency of this. The Confederation is concerned that violation of trade union rights is still widespread and a source of unfair competition in the global economy, which needs to be prevented on economic and human rights grounds (International Centre for Trade Union Rights 2005).

Fifth, the ITUC contests all forms of discrimination and wants equality in all workplaces. It campaigns to end discrimination in all forms, where millions of women and men are denied jobs, confined to certain occupations, denied advancement at work, and offered lower pay. Others are subject to intimidation and harassment because of their gender, religion, colour, nationality, ethnicity, sexual orientation, gender identity, political opinions, social origins, age, and disability. As a humanitarian organisation, the ITUC wants all workers to be able to live and work in conditions of equality, dignity and justice. Sixth, ending child labour is a priority; the Confederation wants every child to go to school and rejects arguments that child labour is inevitable, economically beneficial, socially acceptable, or to the advantage of the children concerned and their families. The ITUC supports campaigns against child labour in all its manifestations, its causes, and its ramifications in both the informal and formal economies.

Seventh, the Confederation wants a decent future for young workers. This means promoting the concerns and expectations of young working women and men, as well as integrating them in trade unions. This is crucial to the strengthening, revitalisation, creativity and future of the trade union movement everywhere. The ITUC campaigns for decent work, quality education, and relevant training for young people, as well as wanting to improve the recruitment and representation of young women and men in trade unions.

Eighth, making workplaces healthy and safe is another important policy goal. This means strengthening occupational health and safety for all workers and putting an end to the loss of over two million lives each year as a result of occupational accidents and work-related diseases. The ITUC wants access to safe and healthy work to be accepted as an undeniable right of all workers, recognising that involvement of workers and their representatives reduces injuries and illness in workplaces. To these ends, the ITUC promotes national and international initiatives and co-operation with employers and governments to promote health and safety at work.

CONCLUSION AND IMPLICATIONS

Employee voice, wherever and however practised, indicates how two-way communications between employers and employees are conducted and how this contributes to stable employment relations. In essence, voice is the process whereby employers communicate to employees and receive and listen to what employees have to say to them, and has implications for how employment relations are conducted. Employee voice has therefore something in common with employee communication. But the concept of employee voice focuses more on the opportunities provided by employers for employees to be involved in decisions collectively, whether through trade unions or other means, than on direct communications.

Voice appeals to those employers seeking greater business efficiency and those supporting employee involvement and dignity in the workplace; even if in the last two decades, many organisations have increasingly focused on initiatives that involve employees directly rather than through representative processes. But systematic employee voice claims to provide benefits to both employers and employees. For employers, greater voice for employees means: the skills and knowledge of employees can be better used, leading to higher productivity; employees feel more valued, so they are more likely to stay and to contribute to the organisation; the organisation gains a positive reputation, making it easier to recruit good employees; and conflict is reduced, with co-operation between employer and employee enhancing interdependence between them. Employees, in turn, benefit from: greater influence over their work; higher job satisfaction; more opportunity to develop their skills; and more job security, where their employer is more successful as a result of 'voice initiatives'.

Employee engagement is part of employee voice. Where employment engagement is practised, employers ideally want employees who do their best for the organisation and its customers; employees ideally want jobs that are worthwhile and inspire them. In these types of organisation, employers want an 'engaged' workforce. This provides a combination of employee commitment to the goals of the organisation and its values and willingness to work with others for common ends. Employee engagement thus goes beyond job satisfaction and is not simply about employee motivation. Engagement is something employees offer the employer, which cannot be demanded as part of the employment contract. When implementing strategies to increase employee engagement, many employers focus their attention only on exchanging information directly between managers and employees. But various studies suggest collective forms of employee voice also support employee engagement. For example, management messages are more credible and demonstrate that management cares for its workforce. Collective consultation is considered to be particularly appropriate for handling organisational change, but also has a role in protecting and developing long-term relationships with employees by promoting engagement with them (Alfes *et al.* 2010).

EI is management-driven but appeals to both some managers and some workers, because it contributes to organisational effectiveness, satisfies basic human needs at work, makes good use of employee skills, and reduces 'political inequalities' in organisations (Strauss 2006: 801). However, the overwhelming judgement of the literature is that a multitude of factors determine success or failure in this area. However, Strauss (2006: 778) concludes that his 'perspective on participation has always been somewhat ambivalent and sometimes cynical'. For him, the central objective of participation is to attempt to satisfy worker needs, while achieving organisational objectives. In his analysis, 'workers' participation can "work" (by a variety of measures) but making it work is very difficult'.

In response to complex external and internal factors, the structure of trade unions continually changes within national economies. External factors include occupational and industrial change, the business cycle, legislation, and economic policy – especially the impacts of neo-liberal policy instruments in recent years. Internal factors shaping union structure include the effectiveness of collective bargaining, quality of union leadership, union ideology, policy, financial considerations, merger-search policy, and economies of scale. But in terms of comparative union density and collective bargaining coverage, these indicators are declining around the world, especially across sections of the private sector, even though union density and bargaining coverage remain highest in manufacturing and construction. In Britain, for example, union density fell from 13 per cent to 9 per cent in private manufacturing between 2004 and 2011; from 13 per cent to 12 per cent in private services; but increased from 90 per cent to 92 per cent in the public sector (van Wanrooy 2013). In this process of institutional decline, government support or lack of it plays an important function in promoting or opposing trade unionism and collective bargaining. The liberalisation of trade, globalisation, deregulation of labour markets, and unemployment underlie these trends. Fragmentation of worker representation and de-centralisation of wage bargaining structures also result in falling collective bargaining coverage. In the case of Australia, union density fell from 43 per cent of the workforce in 1992 to 18 per cent in 2011 (Teicher *et al.* 2013). Such trends are observable around many other parts of the developed world.

Central organisations of trade unions are an important feature within national trade union movements. The more stable and established the trade union function at national level, the more important is the role of national trade union centres, even where there is more than one in a country. In small Nordic social democratic states, parallel trade union centres co-exist; in Anglo-Saxon states, a single centre is the norm; and in Communist China, a single national centre predominates. China is a special case where, as Cooke (2011b: 326) argues, 'Benevolent paternalism, collectivism and harmony are some of the key characteristics of the Chinese culture, which feature prominently in workplace relationships.' Indeed, the Chinese workplace plays an important role in social bonding by nurturing, developing and maintaining harmonious relationships among employees and between managers and workforces. Provision of employee welfare and support is a traditional means for improving employee morale and commitment within Chinese enterprises. Unions play an important role in this, in a country where the HR function remains underdeveloped.

Since its formation, the ITUC has sought to work in a spirit of solidarity, democracy, and equality to make the Confederation an effective instrument for renewing trade union internationalism in the post-Communist global age. It opposes rampant globalisation and is particularly concerned with combating poverty, exploitation, oppression, inequality and promoting universal human rights. It does this by supporting representation of working women and men worldwide, while recognising that to succeed international trade unionism has to adapt to the challenges and opportunities presented by globalisation. This means trying to make international union action an integral part of the work of national trade union organisations and by mobilising worldwide involvement in support of the movement's objectives. The ITUC, despite its obvious weaknesses as a campaigning organisation and its limited resources, is a body committed to promoting trade unions internationally. It wants to be instrumental in creating a 'new' form of trade union internationalism for the benefit of all working people. The ITUC also wants its affiliates to unite together and put their solidarity and influence to work for a better future in a more just world. Within the ITUC, however, ideological divisions remain; thus the challenges facing it, both externally and internally, are substantial.

7

THE NATION STATE AND INTERNATIONAL AGENCIES

The purpose of this chapter is to critically assess the multiple faces of the nation state and government in employment relations on a comparative basis. It also examines the roles of international non-governmental organisations, such as the ILO, that try to influence employment relationships and employment relations by doing research and campaigning on sensitive employment issues. These include combating human trafficking and fighting for union rights. The modern state is defined as any organised political system under democratic or authoritarian governments. It is the institutions of government, such as their legislatures, executives and judiciaries, made up of elected representatives and staffed by public servants, in turn, that provide the means by which any democratic state or political community is governed. The modern state is also normally synonymous with the geographic boundaries of a nation state, where the concept of a nation is characterised by its common history, a national identity or core culture, its language(s) and a plural variety of social strata, groups and ethnicities within its boundaries. Western states are typically political democracies, whereas other states such as present-day China, Cuba and North Korea, and past states such as Nazi Germany, are examples of authoritarian or non-democratic political regimes. In 2014 the United Nations had 193 member states, of which 185 were members of the ILO (2014). The modern nation state is found in a variety of forms around the world. These range from open, stable democracies to closed, corrupt dictatorships or autarchies.

THE NATION STATE AND EMPLOYMENT RELATIONS

Dunlop (1958) identifies government and its agencies representing the nation state as the third actor or player in industrial or employment relations systems. Yet in fact, both democratic politics and government play relatively minor roles in Dunlop's analytical framework, since it is collective bargaining that provides the central feature of his model. Further, in a later work, Dunlop and his co-authors argue that diversity in national employment relations systems is accounted for by the priorities of their industrialising elites, who act as drivers of economic modernisation. Kerr *et al.* (1962) go on to suggest that these systems were converging towards the Anglo-American model of 'pluralistic industrialism', where the role of the state in employment relationships is peripheral. Subsequent studies remedied this omission, where the state and politics in democratic societies were increasingly recognised as having major influences on both individual employment relationships and collective employment relations (Hyman 1975, Farnham and Pimlott 1979, Farnham 1993, Hall and Soskice 2001, Williams 2014). In short, politics and employment relations are not separate but overlapping institutional systems.

The idea of the state is a debated one. As Held (1983: 1) argues, 'there is nothing more central to political and social theory than the nature of the state, and nothing more contested'. Whatever its forms and the institutions involved, the modern nation state and the political power it subsumes shape and condition employment relationships within it, more especially in those agencies of the state that employ people to carry out the state's legislative, executive, administrative, judicial and military functions. However, perceptions of the state are ambivalent and ambiguous. On the one hand, the democratic state appears to be rooted in political legitimacy and popular consent; but, on the other hand, the state is also perceived as a coercive controlling constituent of the social order and as representing dominant class interests within it (Skocpol 1979). Yet in fact, the state is continually changing its forms and features, with no permanency or entirely enduring characteristics. The state, in other words, is 'constantly being recreated, in new forms, by the groups and structures active in society' (Stråth 1996: 218).

Whatever the forms and ambiguities of the nation state, the power and impact of governmental authorities on employment relationships are enormous. Governments control resources, raise and spend taxes, create laws, employ people and try to influence the micro and macro economic performance of their countries. This is because the state and markets, including the labour market, are not opposites or contradictory phenomena, as free market fundamentalists argue (Friedman 1962, Hayek 1960), they are interdependent and interacting institutions (Iversen 2005). For Crouch (1993: 299–300), the view that 'markets' are 'natural' and state involvement in them is 'unnatural' distorts reality. 'To view the subject historically is to see it the other way round; states and organizations are enmeshed in the economy from the outset; it is how they were often driven out that needs explanation.' And, as Hall (1986: 283) puts it, markets are themselves institutions and are 'ultimately artifacts of political action'.

Hyman (2008) provides a helpful classification of the economy, the role of the state and employment relations. Drawing on the literature by Howell (2005), Crouch and Streeck (1997), and Weiss (1998), he outlines a three-fold 'ideal type' classification of the interconnections between states and their systems of employment relations. Hyman calls these regimes: the laissez-faire state; the social state; and the developmental state.

The laissez-faire state

Laissez-faire states encompass employment relations systems that are commonly found in the liberal market economies discussed in the varieties of capitalism literature, such as those of the United Kingdom, the United States and other Anglo-phone states. Market individualism is embedded within this model, with its emphasis on individual contracts, common law and the legal doctrine that the state should *not* generally interfere with the processes of economic life including employment relations. In these states, there is also a preference by business leaders for de-regulated markets and corporate accountability to shareholders alone. But, as Hyman (2008: 271) argues, the idea of non-intervention by government in the market is illogical and bizarre, since every state defines what property is, what may and may not be sold, and adjudicates complaints of breach of contract between any parties in dispute. For Hyman, 'this might be described as "non-intervention in favour of capital" '. In the case of the United States, Skocpol (1985: 12) writes that state power is 'everywhere permeated by societal interests'. Also the funds of large business corporations in the United States increasingly dwarf those of trade unions (Masters and Delaney 2005). To some extent, the same trends can be observed in the United Kingdom, where the growing political power of employers 'virtually guarantees that in the contemporary *laissez-faire* state, the processes of industrial relations will be unfavorable to labor' (Hyman 2008: 272).

Kahn-Freund (1954: 44) develops a theory of legal abstention or collective laissez-faire in English labour law, arguing that there was 'no major country in the world in which the law has played a less significant role in the shaping of [employment] relations than in Great Britain'. He argues that in mid-twentieth-century Britain there was no legal protection for unions or their members from anti-union actions by employers, no legislation requiring employers to recognise unions for the purposes of collective bargaining, no legislation regulating the closed shop, no legislation regulating the circumstances in which industrial action could take place, and no legal regulation governing the legal status of collective agreements. The British system embodied, in other words, a set of trade union 'freedoms', which the law did not normally challenge, not a set of union legal rights supporting union interests. What promoted the theory of collective laissez-faire among its supporters was full employment, the strong bargaining power of the unions, and high union membership density in some UK unions at that time.

However, Ewing (1998) contests the conventional wisdom of collective laissez-faire and he questions whether collective laissez-faire really reflected the British system described by Kahn-Freund. What was unique was not the absence of state regulation but its form. State power, for example, was used to construct and direct the development of employment relations procedures, through the then-Ministry of Labour. This was a power grounded in law and constitutional principle, which, he claims, required nothing less (Laski 1935). In Ewing's view, this constitutional principle and the principle of collective laissez-faire would be seriously compromised today. The implication is that the primacy of free collective bargaining was a triumph of form over substance. In any case, subsequent changes in UK public policy and de-regulation of labour markets (or *re-regulation* in favour of employers) effectively undermined the ideology of collective laissez-faire. It eventually became superseded by neo-liberal ideas, with renewed state support for market principles in all areas of economic policy-making including labour markets and employment relations.

The social state

On mainland West Europe, in contrast, Hyman (2008) argues that the social state predominates. One feature of this model is it seeks to de-commodify employment relations and is commonly referred to as the 'European social model'. Although it is a contested concept (Hyman 2005), the European Social model is where nation states have distinctive national traditions and institutional arrangements for conducting employment relations, but with certain features common to many of them (European Trade Union Confederation 2013). For example, labour is not viewed as primarily as an economic commodity and the idea of work as largely or exclusively a market transaction is rejected. This emanates from the socialist and Catholic traditions of work and society embedded in mainland Europe, which have informed the ideas of the dominant political parties of both the left and the right since the end of the Second World War (Booth 2007). As Judt (2010: 80) writes, in post-War Europe after 1945 'Christian Democracy avoided class-based appeals and emphasized instead social and moral reforms'.

The main components of the European social model are outlined in the white paper on social policy by the Commission of the European Communities (1994). This model incorporates the values of 'democracy and individual rights, free collective bargaining, the market economy, equality of opportunity for all and social welfare and solidarity'. Its main features include, first, the dominant level of collective bargaining is at inter-sectoral level (as in Belgium, Finland, Ireland and Slovenia) and at sector level (as in Austria, Germany, Greece, Italy, the Netherlands, Portugal, Slovakia, Spain and Sweden). Thus the degree of centralisation of collective bargaining in most of the early member states of the EU is 'in striking contrast to the USA where, like the UK and France, the individual company level is predominant'. But company-level bargaining is prevalent in newer member states (such as Cyprus, Czech Republic, Estonia, Hungary, Lithuania, Latvia, Malta and Poland).

Second, rather than organisation decisions being taken unilaterally by management, mandatory systems of worker participation have developed in EU member states, where, as indicated by the European Foundation for the Improvement of Living and Working Conditions: 'Workers are involved in such decisions through representative structures of works councils, enterprise committees, trade union bodies and similar forms' (Eurofound 2005: 4–6). Third, in some countries collective agreements are extended through legal mechanisms, resulting in wide coverage of collective bargaining, even where union density is low, such as in France. Fourth, most of these countries have extensive, publicly funded welfare state or social security systems, in which the social partners made up of unions, employers and public enterprises commonly have a key role in their administration. Fifth, government frequently rests on coalition politics, resulting in compromises and stability in their political systems, which create obstacles to radical institutional changes within them.

Whether expansion of the EU eastwards, with its inferior employment conditions, weaker institutional foundations for collective employment relations and expanding globalisation pose a threat to this model is as yet indeterminate. Linked with this is the effects of the global financial crisis, and fiscal austerity, and how this has changed EU policy on labour market and employment issues.

The developmental state

In nation states that have developed modern market economies more recently, relations between the state and the market have followed different lines. The concept of the developmental state is explored by Johnson (1982) with special reference to Japan. It has since been applied to the newly industrialising countries of East Asia. The logic of the developmental state is that late industrialism takes place in a global economy dominated by wealthy developed nations and this requires overt and systematic direction by the state to make it happen. As Hyman (2008: 273) puts it: 'The developmental state has typically involved an elite state bureaucracy with control over the financial system and a symbiotic relationship with private capital, able to give priority to the accumulation function and to determine the strategic priorities for growth.' In providing explanations of patterns of employment relations within developmental states, the focus is on the political context and different modes of industrial development, whereas in the developed world the focus has been on the importance of industrialising elites in the process (Kerr *et al.* 1962).

One factor in the processes of modernisation in developmental states is the role of organised labour in contributing to the struggle for national independence within them. In these cases, unions were not easily excluded from the post-colonial settlements in politics and employment relations. In other post-colonial regimes, under the control of dictators or autarchies, exclusion of the unions from any political influence or power facilitated the suppression of possible sources of opposition to the new governing elites. In East Asian industrialising states, such as Singapore, anti-communist sentiments helped legitimise a sense of 'national unity' and 'national solidarity'. This opposed militant trade unionism and promoted 'harmonious' employment relations between employers and unions. This resulted in the state promoting co-operative labour–management relations in these countries (Öniş 1991).

A second element in the evolution of employments relations institutions in developmental states derives from Kuravilla's (1995) distinction between 'import substitution' and 'export-oriented' economic development processes. Import substitution uses high tariffs to enable the domestic production of industrial goods. This happened in parts of Latin America, where authoritarian regimes developed domestic industries, sometimes accompanied by collaboration between the state and corporatist trade unions, as in Argentina during the presidencies of Juan Domingo Perón (Cook 1998). In the case of export-oriented industrialisation, this takes place under external pressure for reducing or removing tariff barriers, sometimes in two phases. The first involves a price competitive strategy by exploiting the comparative advantage of low wage regimes, suppression of militant unions and creation of 'free enterprise zones' with even weaker worker protections than in other parts of the economy, such as in Hong Kong. A second phase in some East Asian states pursues an added-value export-oriented policy. This offers scope for incorporating unions at company level, such as in Japan, or adopting a non-union HRM approach to managing employees as in Malaysia (Frenkel and Peetz 1998, Ramasamy 2004).

For Hyman (2008: 274), a 'distinctive model of the developmental state is found in China'. This incorporates a rapid shift from a command to a market economy, directed by the state, which initially removed security of employment in the workplace, with no supportive welfare provisions. Under the Labour Contract Law 2007, however, which is targeted at domestic firms, employees of at least ten years standing are protected from being dismissed without due cause. This law also requires employers to contribute to employee social security accounts and set wage standards for employees on probation (Wei *et al.* 2013). China has a trade union movement controlled by the Communist Party, similar to the 'transmission belt' trade unionism found in Soviet Russia prior to the collapse of the soviet regime in 1991 (Davis 2001). Howell (2006) suggests, however, that democratic reform in the ACFTU at local level has invigorated some local union branches.

THE STATE AS EMPLOYER

The state as an employer is typically an important player in a country's national economic and employment relations systems. Where the state's role in the national economy is wide-ranging as in Scandinavia's social state regimes of Denmark, Sweden and Norway, and in the United Kingdom's laissez-faire state too, its employment function is extensive. But where the state's role is smaller, as in laissez-faire and 'developmental' states in Turkey, Mexico and the Far East, the state's employer function is scaled down (LABORSTA 2013). What determines the precise role of the state as an employer is partly a result of the wider economic, political, legal, social demographic and technological contexts within which laissez-faire, social and developmental state regimes operate. But, as Lane (1995) and Lane and Bachmann (1998) argue, much also depends on the state's system of governance. Factors here include the defined functions of the state, the organisations through which the state operates, and its preferred management system(s). The state's role in the national economy, for example, affects its employment structure (Bordogna and Cella 1999). Another factor is whether workers are employed directly by the state (such as civil servants or public employees) or indirectly by outsourcing or contracting out services and labour to private enterprises (Farnham 2010b). How the state manages its workforce is also important, since this involves governmental choices about what management system to adopt. The choices, which are not mutually exclusive, include classical bureaucracy and public administration, new public management (NPM), public management reform (PMR) or collective bargaining (Farnham *et al.* 2005). The role of the modern state and its employment relations systems, in short, continuously evolve in response to their changing contexts, successive waves of modernisation and governmental reforms, and the global transmission of new ideas, fads and fashions in management systems and practices. These are 'popular' changes imposed on workers, as received wisdoms in managerial circles (Furnham 2011).

The size and functions of government

The state's role as an employer in national economies is affected inter alia by the size of government, the functions or services it provides, and number of workers employed in public organisations. These include administrative and welfare services provided by central, regional and local government, as well as goods or services provided by public enterprises. Collectively these are commonly called 'public services'. A helpful indicator of the size of government is general government final consumption expenditure (GGFCE) expressed as a percentage of Gross Domestic Product (GDP). Formerly categorised as general government consumption, GGFCE is made up of all government current expenditure on purchases of goods and services in the national economy, including the pay of state employees, and most defence spending. Government military spending, however, which is part of government capital formation, is excluded. Freeman (2002) contends that governmental institutional arrangements seeking to protect labour do not actually hinder economic performance. He argues once a country has a strong set of basic market freedoms, 'it has considerable leeway in the precise way it structures institutions'. Gwatney *et al.* (1998), on the other hand, contend that national economic growth is adversely affected where government services go beyond its two core functions. These are legal and physical infrastructures for operating the market economy efficiently and a limited set of public goods. They argue that going beyond these functions creates disincentives due to higher taxation.

Despite these debates and controversies, the size of government has tended to grow within many national economies since the 1960s, although general policy in recent years has been to try reducing the size and roles of governments in advanced capitalist economies. This is mainly through privatisation and outsourcing, as advocated by international non-governmental organisations such as the OECD, World Bank and World Trade Organisation (Diehl 2001, Milner and Moravcsik 2009). Table 7.1 shows GGFCE as a

Table 7.1 General government final expenditure as a percentage of GDP for selected countries 2001–2011

Country	2001	2002	2003	2004	2005	2006	2007	2008	2009	2010	2011
Australia	18	17	18	17	17	17	17	17	18	18	18
Austria	19	18	19	18	18	18	18	19	20	19	19
Belgium	22	23	23	23	23	22	22	23	25	24	24
Brazil	20	21	19	19	20	20	20	20	21	21	21
Canada	19	20	19	19	19	19	19	20	22	22	21
China	16	16	15	14	14	14	14	13	13	13	13
Cuba	31	34	34	36	34	32	35	40	39	38	n/a
Denmark	26	26	27	27	21	21	26	27	30	29	28
Finland	21	21	22	22	23	22	21	23	25	25	24
France	23	24	24	24	24	24	23	23	25	25	25
Germany	19	19	19	19	19	18	18	18	20	20	19
Greece	18	19	18	18	18	17	18	18	21	18	17
Hong Kong	10	11	11	10	9	9	8	9	9	9	9
Hungary	21	22	24	22	23	23	22	22	23	22	10
Iceland	24	25	26	25	25	24	24	25	27	26	25
India	12	12	11	11	11	10	101	10	11	11	12
Ireland	16	16	16	16	16	16	17	19	21	19	19
Israel	27	29	28	27	26	25	25	25	24	24	24
Italy	19	19	20	20	20	20	20	20	21	21	21
Japan	18	18	18	18	18	18	18	19	20	20	21
Netherlands	23	24	24	24	24	25	25	26	29	28	28
Mexico	12	12	17	18	18	19	19	11	12	12	12
NZ	17	17	17	18	18	19	19	20	20	20	20
Norway	21	22	22	21	20	19	19	19	23	22	22
Poland	18	18	18	18	18	18	18	19	18	19	n/a
S Korea	13	13	13	13	14	15	15	15	16	15	15
Spain	17	17	17	18	18	18	18	20	21	21	21
Sweden	26	27	27	27	26	26	26	26	28	27	26
Turkey	12	13	12	12	12	12	13	13	15	14	14
UAE	9	9	9	8	7	6	6	6	9	8	n/a
UK	19	20	21	21	21	21	21	22	23	23	22
US	14	15	16	16	16	16	16	17	18	18	17

Note: n/a = not available.
Source: www.data,worldbank.org/data.

percentage of GDP for 32 selected countries between 2001 and 2011. These data indicate, first, that within the countries listed, five consistently had GGFCE of more than 25 per cent. Among these, GGFCE tended to rise in Cuba, Iceland and the Netherlands; remained stable in Sweden; and fell in Israel over the same period. Second, 10 countries had GGFCE of between 20 and 24 per cent. Within these states, it tended to rise in Belgium, Canada, Denmark, Finland, France, Italy and the United Kingdom and be stable in Brazil, Hungary and Norway. Third, 11 countries had GGFCE between 15 and 19 per cent. Within this group, it tended to rise in Germany, the United States, Ireland, Japan, New Zealand and Spain but was stable in Australia, Austria, Greece, Mexico and Poland. Fourth, six countries had GGFCE of less that 15 per cent. In these cases, GGFCE tended to rise in South Korea and Turkey; remain stable in India; and fall in China, Hong Kong and the United Arab Emirates.

In general, these data indicate that CGFCE falls into four loose groupings. It tends to be *highest* in some co-ordinated market economies and social state regimes (such as Sweden and the Netherlands), as well as in liberal-market Israel and socialist Cuba; to be *next highest* in other co-ordinated market economies and social state regimes (such as Belgium, Norway and France – although Schmidt (2003) describes France as a 'statist' market economy), in some liberal market economies and laissez-faire states (such as the United Kingdom and Canada), and in Brazil's liberal market economy and developmental state; and to be *lowest* in transition market economies and developmental states (such as India, China and Turkey). GGFCE tends to be *next lowest* in the remaining nation states. This last group is very mixed. It includes: co-ordinated market economies and social state regimes (such as Germany and Austria); liberal market economies and laissez-faire states (such as the United States, Ireland and Mexico); and other emerging market economies and 'new' democracies (such as Greece and Poland).

The OECD (2009a) defines the core functions of the state as law enforcement, citizen protection, justice and conflict resolution, raising and expanding revenues, provision of basic public services, and facilitating economic development. Figure 7.1 shows the core government functions in selected OECD countries. In all the countries listed, defence is provided centrally or at federal level. But provision of other core functions, such as education, health care, police, and social services, varies by country and are delivered at central, regional and local levels. Any changes in the functions of government clearly affect its size and responsibilities, such as when large-scale privatisations take place. Privatisation involves the transfer of public assets into the private sector through ownership, finance, control and management. This

Sector	Central or federal administration	Regional administration	Local administration
Defence	France Finland Greece Hungary Italy Luxembourg Netherlands Spain United States		
Education	France Hungary Italy Netherlands Luxembourg	Australia Germany Ireland Spain United States	Finland Greece Hungary Mexico United States
Health care	France Hungary Spain United States	Australia France Germany Ireland Japan Spain United States	Finland Germany Greece Hungary Mexico United States
Police	Finland Hungary Luxembourg Netherlands Spain	Ireland Japan	France Greece
Social services	Hungary Spain	Australia France Germany Ireland Japan United States	Finland France Germany Greece United States

Figure 7.1 Core functions of government in selected OECD countries
Source: OECD (2009a).

273

is done by selling state or government assets, contracting out former state services, using internal markets, and adopting private-public partnerships. It is estimated that between 1995 and 2000 alone over $650 billion worth of state-owned enterprises were transferred to the private sector in OECD countries (LABORSTA 2013). Sectors typically privatised included banking, oil, gas, telecommunications, transport, state enterprises and public utilities. According to early and revealing research by OECD, EU countries seeking to meet the conditions of the Treaty of Maastricht, which came into force in 1993, including Austria, France, Italy, Spain and Portugal, were responsible for nearly 60 per cent of privatisation revenues at that time (OECD 1999).

Figure 7.2 provides some indicative measures of the percent employment in general government in 26 OECD member states in 1995 and 2005. These varied quite widely from just over 5 per cent of all employment (in Japan) to almost 30 per cent (Norway and Sweden). These data show that public employment fell in only five states between these years – Sweden, Canada, Ireland, Germany and Austria. It increased marginally in eight states – France, Finland, Belgium, Italy, Portugal, Czech Republic, Spain and Slovak Republic – and stayed relatively stable in the remaining 13 countries. Eight states in Figure 7.2 had public-sector employment densities of 15 per cent (the average) or more and the remaining 18 states less than 15 per cent. The first group was predominantly West European social state regimes, the laissez-faire state regimes of the United Kingdom and Canada, and the emergent democracy of Hungary. The second group contained a diverse set of states including: West European social states, such as the Netherlands, Germany and Austria; developmental states such as Mexico and Turkey; some relatively 'new' East

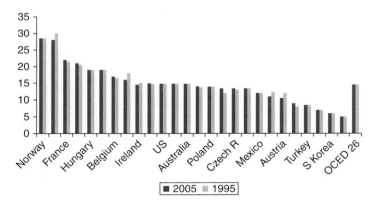

Figure 7.2 Percent employment in general government in OECD countries 1995 and 2005
Source: OECD (2009b).

European market economies and emergent democracies such as the Slovak and Czech Republics; and, in Asia, South Korea and Japan, with their Asian variants of capitalism.

Human resources management in public services

The public sector typically covers central government, such as the civil service and national agencies, and local government. In federal states such as Australia, Canada, Germany and the United States, there is an intermediate stratum of government at regional, provincial or 'state' level. Collectively these levels of government provide a variety of public services to their citizens funded by taxation. These include education, health care, national security and, in some cases, social security. In other cases, public services are supplied by non-governmental, not-for-profit, 'welfare' agencies funded partly by taxpayers and partly from voluntary sources. Normally, public services employ a wide range of occupational groups. Depending on the country in question, and in professional occupations alone, these include managers at all levels, whether specialists or generalists, ICT specialists, school teachers, university teachers, medical practitioners, dentists, other medical professionals, engineers, architects, surveyors and many other well qualified occupations. Public services need to recruit such people, manage them competently and retain them. Traditionally public servants were managed by tightly defined bureaucratic rules and systems, using personnel administration systems; today, there is more flexibility and greater contractual variations in employment and employment relationships across public services (Farnham and Horton 2000).

In response to the neo-liberal agenda of recent years, a major trend in public services is changes to how they are managed (Farnham *et al.* 1996). Various national studies confirm the largest, fastest expanding occupational group in public services over the past 20 years is 'managers'. In the United Kingdom alone, the senior civil service increased by some 35 per cent between 2000 and 2009, and by 15 per cent in the second-most senior grade in 2007–2008 (Senior Salaries Review Body 2009). An earlier study of reforms of the senior civil services of 12 OECD countries, covering Belgium, Canada, Finland, France, Italy, South Korea, Mexico, Netherlands, New Zealand, Spain, the United Kingdom and the United States, reveals that all were developing their management capacities. Starting initially with performance management, this was supplemented by programmes on leadership, change management and human resources management. In nine countries, appointment to posts with important management responsibilities determined whether somebody was a senior executive rather than their original grade, salary, length of service, or qualifications. The only exceptions at this time were France, South Korea and Mexico (OECD 2003).

Public service unions continue to play important roles in determining the pay, working conditions and introduction of new public service systems, although they play relatively minor roles in staff performance, recruitment and determination of numbers of employees. OECD countries with strong participation by unions in pay include Austria, Belgium, Denmark, the Nordic states and the United Kingdom. OECD countries with weak union participation in pay include Hungary, Poland, the Slovak Republic and Switzerland (Farnham *et al.* 2005, Farnham 2010b). Although it varies by country, union membership density is always higher in national public services than in the private sector. It is commonly more than 60 per cent in Austria, Belgium, Canada, Norway, Switzerland and the United Kingdom but lower in France, Italy, the Netherlands, Spain and the United States (Visser 2006).

Employment systems

The state employs public servants to provide public services; in law, these are either 'civil servants' or 'public employees' depending on the country where they work. As a general rule, civil law states tend to employ civil servants and common law states public employees, although some countries, such as Germany, have civil servants (*Beamte*), employees (*Angestellte*) and workers (*Arbeite*). In liberal-democratic states, activities of government are seen by some commentators as pursuing the 'common good' or the 'public good' on behalf of its citizens. The role of the market, in contrast, is to provide the goods and services bought by customers from firms or individuals in an increasingly global economy; the role of the state and its administrative system is to provide 'free' public goods and services to its citizens or at 'prices' subsidised by taxpayers. As states develop and mature, the scope of public services grows, increasing with the complexity of modern life. However, as the costs of public services rise, and shifts in political and economic ideas and inter-generational changes take place, the boundaries and shape of public services are constantly reconfigured and re-engineered, through what is variously described as public sector modernisation, NPM or PMR. Throughout the contemporary world, the boundaries and shapes of public services have been radically transformed in the past four decades. Successive waves of reforms have changed public services in a number of critical respects (Pollitt and Bouckaert 2004, van Thiel *et al.* 2007). Reform has affected *who* provides these services, *how* they are provided and *the ways* in which people work and perceive work within them.

	Career-based employment	Department-based employment	Position-based employment
Countries	France, Greece, Hungary, Ireland, Japan, South Korea, Luxembourg, Spain	Austria, Belgium, Germany, Italy, Mexico, Netherlands, Poland, Portugal	Australia, New Zealand, Norway, United Kingdom, United States
Employment status	Regulated by civil service employment laws	Regulated by both civil service and public or national employment laws	Regulated by public or national employment laws
Senior civil service, with differential managerial rules	Yes	No	Yes and no
Recruitment and selection	Competitive examination Mix of individual and pool recruitment, early in career Few lateral entries	No competitive examination Mix of individual and pool recruitment, early in career Few lateral entries	No competitive examination Individual recruitment Open recruitment to lateral entries
Fixed-term contracts	No	No	Yes
Training: entry training v life-long	At entry	Mixed	Life-long training
Career development	Emphasis on performance incentives/sanctions Few pay incentives	Emphasis on promotion as incentives/sanctions Some pay incentives	Emphasis on pay and promotion as incentives/sanctions
Pay	Centralised Little individualisation of pay	Partial pay delegation Little individualisation of pay	Partial/extensive pay delegation Extensive individualisation of pay
Central HRM body	Limited autonomy of ministries *vis-à-vis* central HRM body	Some autonomy of ministries or absence of central HRM body	Large autonomy of ministries or absence of central HRM body

Figure 7.3 Main characteristics of civil service employment systems
Source: OECD (2005).

Figure 7.3 summarises the main characteristics of civil service or public employment in 21 selected social and laissez-faire state regimes that are members of OECD. As can be seen in Figure 7.3, there are three models or types of public employment cross-nationally: career-based systems, department-based systems and position-based systems. Typically, career-based systems and department-based systems are more likely to be found in co-ordinated market economies and social states, although exceptions include Ireland, Japan, Mexico and Poland. Position-based systems, in contrast, are more likely found in liberal market economies and laissez-faire state regimes, where Norway is the exception. In outline, the main features of career-based systems include: employment status is regulated by specific civil service laws; recruitment and selection are by competitive examination, with few lateral entries; performance is emphasised in career development; and training takes place on entering the service. In department-based systems, employment status is regulated by public or national employment laws; recruitment and selection are by individual and pool recruitment in early career; the incentive in career development is promotion; and training is at both entry and through life-long learning. In position-based systems, employment status is regulated by public or national employment laws; recruitment and selection are by individual recruitment and open recruitment using lateral entry; the incentives in career development are pay and promotion; and training is based on life-long learning.

The employment systems within which public servants work have implications for HR management. As indicated in Figure 7.3, career-based systems provide limited autonomy for ministries *vis-à-vis* any central HR body. In department-based systems, in contrast, ministries have some autonomy in HR decisions, whereas in position-based systems, ministries have large autonomy in HR. Figure 7.4 takes the analysis further by examining HR individualisation (such as pay) and HR delegation (in terms of decision-making). This shows that 11 of these OECD countries have

	high/high (position-based systems)	high/low
HR individualisation/HR delegation	A Australia, Canada, Denmark, Finland, Iceland, New Zealand, Norway, Sweden, Switzerland, United Kingdom, United States	Not applicable
HR individualisation/HR delegation	B France, Greece, Ireland, Hungary, Japan, South Korea, Luxembourg, Slovak Republic, Spain	C Austria, Belgium, Czech Republic, Germany, Italy, Mexico, Netherlands, Poland, Portugal
	low/low (career-based systems)	low/high (department-based systems)

Figure 7.4 HR practices in central government: Degrees of HR individualisation and HR delegation in selected OECD countries
Source: OECD (2004b).

position-based systems, which tend to be *high* on both individualisation and delegation, as shown in quadrant A. Nine countries have predominantly career-based systems which tend to be *low* on both individualisation and delegation, as shown in quadrant B. Nine countries with predominantly department-based systems tend to be *low* on individualisation and *high* on delegation, as shown in quadrant C. Obviously, differences within national public service systems and their HR arrangements, and those between countries, are complex and diverse. They arise, in part at least, from the historical path-dependencies in each case (Thelen and Steinmo 1992).

Recruitment, selection and promotion

In addition to privatisation and outsourcing where HR is externalised, another trend in HR management in public services is that in most countries there have been contractual changes in the employment of public servants. In Denmark, Sweden and Switzerland, for example, rules governing life-time employment have been abolished and civil servants and public officials are now employed under general labour laws. In other countries, such as Belgium, Finland and the United Kingdom, life-time employment in central government remains but fixed-term contracts for positions are used to increase individual responsibility for delivering services. Civil servants remain in public service but in positions no longer guaranteed for life. In other countries, civil and public servants are on short-term or fixed-term contracts, with no guarantee of further employment on completion of the contract. Some countries also increasingly use flexible contractual arrangements for public employees in positions that could be filled by full-time staff (OECD 2004a). These changes and revisions of employment status in public services reflect the drive for staff flexibility to promote more efficient and effective public organisations in OECD countries and elsewhere (Farnham and Horton 2000).

In some countries, public servants at all levels have traditionally been managed through specific rules and management processes different from general labour laws. These rules applied to all public servants within their group or sector. In most countries, civil service rules used to be detailed and left little room for senior staff to manage public servants individually. This has changed in many countries, where there has been a significant trend towards individualised HR practices in recruitment and selection, terms of appointment, performance management, pay and rewards, and termination of employment. In general, some HR practices are more individualised and staff are increasingly being treated differentially, depending on the changing needs of organisations and individual performance. This individualisation of HR practices is aimed at increasing the responsiveness of public services to customer and client needs, but with adverse effects on the collective values and ethical behaviour of public servants (Ghere and Frederickson 2005).

In career-based systems, public officials are normally hired at the beginning of their careers and are expected to remain in public service throughout their working lives. Initial entry is based on academic qualifications and/or a national examination. Most posts are not open to non-civil servants, except for contract posts. The United States, which is a regarded as a position-based system, is an interesting special case, because most positions are open to anybody but senior executive positions are open only to staff belonging to the Senior Executive Service group. Such appointments normally take place solely after a long career in public service. This type of entry to public service ensures fairness by competitive examination and professional qualifications. The collective values of the service are ensured, since similar pre-entry training is adopted for different categories of public servant.

In position-based systems, by contrast, the best candidates are selected for each position, where the emphasis in recruitment, whether externally or by internal promotion, is by competition for posts and professional experience. These systems allow open access to positions, which are advertised both inside the service and outside it, and where lateral entry is relatively common. They tend to promote weaker cross-governmental values at the point of entry, while creating stronger links across hierarchical levels and status. A further strength of this type of entry to public service is that fairness is promoted by open and competitive processes for each position. Fairness in promotion is also ensured by having effective individual performance assessments (Derlien and Peters 2008). Position-based systems also tend to give enhanced roles to central HR bodies and have more centralised systems of management for senior managers (OECD 2003).

Promotion in career-based systems is based on a grading system attached to an individual rather than a specific position. Since these systems are characterised by limited possibilities of entering public service in mid-career, there is strong emphasis on career development. Career-based systems tend to promote values at the time of entry in specific sub-groups, such as 'corps' in France, but cross-hierarchical and cross corps values are relatively weaker. The strength of the promotion system in this case is the limited possibilities of unfair management practices, through separating the grade, acquired with time, and the specific post. Career-based systems also tend to increase the number of posts open to competition and they delegate HR practices to line ministries and lower hierarchical levels (OECD 2003).

Performance management and performance pay

All OECD countries, with very few exceptions, now have performance management and performance appraisal systems in place, whether career-based, department-based or position-based. The emphasis globally now is measuring, monitoring, assessing and rewarding improved performance across the public sector (Van Thiel *et al.* 2007). Incentives for promoting good performance and the measures taken in cases of poor performance vary. But evidence indicates that differential pay awards according to performance are increasingly an important HR practice throughout public services. Although the individualisation of pay at entry remains limited, many public employers have chosen pay for performance as a means of enhancing the individualisation of HR practices (OECD 2005). By the turn of the millennium, a significant number of civil servants and public employees in most OECD countries were covered by performance pay schemes of one kind or another, particularly among senior public managers, but increasingly for non-managerial staff too. There are multiple reasons for this. Performance pay schemes originated because of the economic and public budgetary problems facing OECD countries at particular times. However, they are also used because of the drive to improve individual motivation and accountability of public servants and as means for improving organisation performance. Performance pay also indicates to citizens that the performance of public workers is regularly assessed by public managers (Derlien and Peters 2008).

The first wave of performance-related pay (PRP) schemes took place in the 1980s, with the governments of Canada, Denmark, the Netherlands, New Zealand, Spain, Sweden and the United Kingdom being the first to adopt them. A second round in the early 1990s took place in Australia, Finland, Ireland and Italy. More recently, countries such as Germany, South Korea and Switzerland, as well as east European states such as the Czech Republic, Hungary, Poland and Slovak Republic, have put PRP mechanisms in place. By the early twenty-first century, France was experimenting with implementing performance pay for top civil servants. It is mostly countries with position-based systems and the highest delegation of HR and devolved budgets which have developed the strongest links between performance appraisals and pay as incentives. With few exceptions, emphasis on monetary incentives for good performance is relatively stronger in position-based systems than in career-based or department-based ones.

In career-based and department-based systems, such as Austria, France and Poland, emphasis is on career development or promotion rather than monetary incentives. In career-based systems also, the management of staff is more collectivised than individualised implying, if monetary incentives are used, that collective pay rewards are more appropriate than individual ones. In most OECD countries, salary policy for public officials and civil servants now consists of three components: base pay, remuneration linked to the nature or duties of a post and performance pay (Farnham and White 2011). A key issue is whether performance payments are given as a permanent addition to basic pay (merit increments) or one-off payments (bonuses), which have to be re-earned during each appraisal period. In recent years, use of bonuses has increased compared with merit payments, because bonuses are managed with greater flexibility and do not increase fixed payroll costs (OECD 2005).

Performance appraisal is normally incorporated within an annual cycle, where line managers identify key objectives for the year with their subordinates and, at the end of the year, review individual performances. Performance ratings rely more on assessing pre-identified objectives and discussions with line managers than strictly quantifiable indicators or standard criteria for a job. In other cases, more complex assessment systems are used. These are aimed at establishing a dialogue on objectives and results between managers and subordinates. In the case of senior public servants, most OECD countries have tried to formalise the link between assessing the total remuneration of senior managers and promotion. In most countries also, one part of total remuneration for senior staff is variable pay linked to the achievement of personal objectives. But there are variations related to the type of senior public service in which they work. Countries with position-based systems have implemented performance pay fully. Most career-based systems appear to have implemented variable pay systems for senior managers; but not all appear to be clearly linked with performance assessment (OECD 2003).

Training, learning and development

The purposes of performance appraisal and appraisal for staff development are related but normally the two processes are separated; but not in every case. However, staff development, work-based learning and continuing professional development for public servants are crucial management tools for responding to the increasing need for knowledge acquisition and up-to-date practices by public servants in knowledge-based economies. In some individualised position-based systems, learning and development are also used as a ways of developing a common culture and an opportunity to discuss professional issues across a service.

Countries with position-based systems, in particular British Commonwealth and Nordic countries, tend to provide more training to their staff than countries with career-based or department-based systems. In most career-based systems, entry into the service requires passing competitive examinations and/or taking pre-entry training provided by government training institutes, such as the *L'Ecole nationale d'administration* in Strasbourg, France. Promotion to a higher grade in these systems depends upon public officials acquiring further qualifications, often through new academic degrees or competitive examinations. This pre-entry training provides an environment where participants build a common managerial language and culture, in addition to gaining qualifications. At the same time, it is not clear whether it provides the necessary opportunities to develop the knowledge and skills needed in a knowledge economy (Farnham 2010b).

In many OECD countries, training policy is designed in central HR bodies, while implementation is left to departments or lower level units of management. Some position-based countries use private companies and universities more than other countries do; but most use a specific training institute for public servants. However, it is not clear whether life-long learning is a reality in most OECD countries. A few countries, including Germany, Iceland, Japan, Mexico, Sweden and the United States, appear to have developed coherent life-long learning strategies. But in the most cases, life-long learning has been developed within either performance management systems, as in Australia, or as part of business plans and reflections on required competencies or skills, as in Sweden (OECD 2004a).

THE STATE AS REGULATOR

Governments have multiple roles as actors and regulators in employment relations (Amable 2003). Hyman (2008: 270), while accepting his classification is arbitrary, lists and identifies seven possible key areas where the state intervenes and helps shape national employment relations systems. In addition to being an employer and providing procedural regulation defining the legal status, rights and obligations of the players or actors in the system, the state determines individual employment rights for employees through national legislation; macro-economic policies that structure national labour markets; supply-side economic policies promoting employability for workers; institutional state support for workers who are sick, unemployed or post-retirement age, as well as through social services or welfare services such as education and health care funded by taxation; and the 'construction of "industrial citizenship"'. This is what Marshall and Bottomore (1992) describe as a second form of citizenship, which takes place in the workplace through trade union organisation. For them, it is a system of industrial citizenship, parallel with and supplementary to political citizenship. How states carry out these activities depends on the interaction between their national economic and employment relations systems. In other words, there are marked differences between liberal market and co-ordinated market economies and between employment relations systems in laissez-faire, social state and developmental states. The legal aspects of the state's role in employment relations are considered in the next chapter and the state's role as an employer was examined in the previous section. This section concentrates on government regulation of the economy and of social protection.

The economy

Dahl and Lindblom (1976: xlv) argue that in all developed nations 'economics is married, if only at common law, to politics'. This results in the continuing influence that nation states have on economic activity within and beyond their domestic boundaries, even in an age of globalisation. A government's economic policy is a cardinal one, because so many other policies depend on there being a sustainable set of *economic* policy goals and outcomes in the first place. Even so, in those states labelled as liberal market economies with laissez-faire approaches to economic policy-making, governments and their bureaucracies play essential roles in funding, controlling, organising and informing economic activity, in spite globalisation. Among capitalist market economies, however, there is considerable divergence in economic policies, even if there is convergence in some policy areas. Whatever the preferred economic policy goals in society as supported at the ballot box, 'these goals are not all positively related' (Keech 1980: 345).

Traditional approaches to economic policy analysis rely predominantly on discussions of specific macro-economic, fiscal and industrial policy instruments and their impacts on economic performance. But comparing economic policies cross-nationally can also be done by considering the different policy drivers used by governments. These include: how government uses its financial resources, through raising taxes and public spending; how political authority is used to prescribe and regulate certain economic activities rather than others; and how the economy is organised by government, such as through planning or creation of economic policy institutions. In other cases, governments provide economic information and advice to the public, as well as indicators assessing the impacts of policy on performance, welfare and, more recently, 'happiness' (Hirata 2011).

But the changing contexts of economic policy development are important too. Historically, control of the public purse was the dominant economic orthodoxy in democratic states up till the 1930s, where spending was 'regarded simply as a means of paying for the government's own operations, not of regulating overall economic activity' (Heidenheimer *et al.* 1990: 135). Then, in the face of mounting unemployment and economic dislocation, Keynesian counter-cyclical demand management policies became the overriding orthodoxy for the next 50 years. It was Keynes in the 1930s and 1940s, and his followers, who advocated an active role for governments in smoothing out the capitalist business cycle, especially to promote 'full employment'. This meant raising taxes and reducing public spending in periods of economic growth (to contain inflation) and reducing taxes and raising public spending in periods of recession (Davidson 2009). However, in response to rising oil prices in the 1970s and rising inflation in the 1980s, policy-makers shifted their priorities from combating unemployment to containing inflation. This change in policy direction was supported by increasing acceptance of 'monetarism' among the economics profession and some politicians, such as Ronald Reagan in the United States and Margaret Thatcher in the United Kingdom. The monetarist revolution of the late 1970s and 1980s meant that governments now focused on influencing the supply-side of the economy rather than the demand-side, in an attempt to control inflation which was seen to be harmful to economic growth (Hall 1993).

There are a number of influences on policy determination by governments in democratic societies. For example, politicians can promote policies likely to get them re-elected, such as expanding the economy and increasing public spending as an election approaches, although there is no systematic evidence that this is normally the case (Heidenheimer *et al.* 1990). But producer groups, such as private businesses and trade unions, also attempt to influence economic policy. Some firms do this is on an ad hoc basis, by promoting their interests with government through lobbying and media campaigns. Olson's (1982) analysis of divergences in economic performance among nation states hinges on his 'theory of collective action'. He explains this in terms of the responses by politicians to organised pressure groups. His central claim is that in certain countries, some interest groups seek to extract exclusive benefits from government for themselves alone, without concern for increasing the size of the economic 'cake' and re-distributing it among a wider constituency. He maintains that where these interest groups are large and encompassing, and their interests are in line with those of the wider society, societies benefit. Thus at his time of writing, Germany, France and Japan appeared to have had some success in their economic policy outcomes, with numbers of relatively small interest groups being involved in the policy process during a period of social and political stability. In other economies, by contrast, such as those as the United Kingdom and the United States, special interest groups had largely been swept away and these countries were subject to radical policy changes. Later studies challenge these assumptions but they were probably correct at the time.

Another structural influence on policy-making by producer interests is through 'corporatism'. Schmitter (1974: 93–94) defines corporatism as a system of interest group representation 'in which the constituent units are organised into a number of singular, compulsory, noncompetitive, hierarchically ordered and functionally differentiated categories' recognised by the state, which are given representational authority within their respective constituencies. This is 'in exchange for observing certain controls on their selection of leaders and articulation of demands and supports'. The two interest groups normally involved in this process of concertation are businesses and trade unions, not consumer interest groups and single-issue lobbies. Nation states commonly falling into the corporatist tradition include Germany, Switzerland, Denmark, Sweden and Japan – although Japan is described as corporatism 'without labour' (Wilensky and Turner 1987). Corporatist arrangements are typically found in smaller trade-exposed states (with Germany the major exception), where it is relatively easy for the social partners to build up professional relationships and where a distinctive national interest is identified (Katzenstein 1985).

A third structural influence by producer interests on policy-making is the extent to which workers' interests are reflected in governing parties or governing coalitions in national politics. This is a 'power resources' perspective. It suggests that parties of the left adopt distinctive approaches to economic policy-making, rooted in links with trade unions or within the trade union movement. Parties of the right, in contrast, favour the interests of business and capital, especially investment capital. Esping-Andersen (1990) links patterns of welfare state development, for example, with the influence of trade unions and social democratic parties in politics. Those supporting power resources theories argue there is a trade-off between equality and efficiency in the policy process (Okun 1975). Thus in coalition political regimes, sustained economic growth promoting employment opportunities is most likely to be observed where governments made up of parties of the left have strong links with trade union movements. Without this link, these parties are not as successful in pursuing such objectives (Lange and Garrett 1987). However, with trade union membership in decline in most countries, the main power resource for parties of the left is declining too.

In targeting their economic policy goals, governments use financial resources to provide tax-funded services, change tax rates and provide tax breaks to key economic players. These are tools for achieving government's preferred macro-economic and micro-economic policy choices. Provision of tax-funded services varies among countries, although government spending in general is relatively stable over time. One area where countries differ, however, is industrial policy. In France, for example, public investment in nuclear power since the 1970s enabled it to become more sufficient in energy production (Hecht 2009). Some observers suggest that countries are distinguished according to the extent their governments play active roles in economic policy, such as providing subsidies for particular firms and industries (Shonfield 1965, Schmidt 2003). Thus France and Japan, whose governments have used their financial resources to support particular industries such as nuclear power, can be contrasted with those of the United Kingdom and the United States, with more laissez-faire approaches to policy, which do not. Some governments also try to provide conditions for economic growth by supporting training or active labour market policies. Examples of this are Sweden and Iceland, where extensive interventions in labour market policy by Social Democratic governments over the years have been an alternative state strategy to public ownership. Indeed, prior to the financial crisis of 2007, Iceland had very high levels of employment precisely because of this policy (Deacon 2008).

Governments also use their political authority to prescribe certain types of economic activities, regulate other activities, restrict pay, shape employment decisions, and control the flow of goods and services across national borders. According to Strange (1994: 175), governments always lay down 'rules for the conduct of trade, rules that put certain social and political objectives and certain political values above the freedom of the market'. Thus governments may try to influence prices, control who can engage in particular types of economic activity, and regulate the size and activities of different companies. In France, Germany and Italy, for example, product market restrictions have traditionally imposed high entry costs for foreign firms wishing to penetrate particular industries, although many restrictions have broken down as markets have become freer and more internationalised (OECD 2011a). Governments have also tried to constrain the size of firms through anti-trust policy, as in the United States under the Sherman Act 1890. Anti-trust actions became less frequent during and after the 1980s as scholars in the Chicago school of economics argued that market concentration was less economically harmful than price-fixing (Eisner and Meier 1990).

Another policy area is when governments try to control wage increases by incomes policies to reduce wage-cost inflation, as in Sweden and the United Kingdom in the 1960s (Grant 2002, Shonfield 1965). Others impose a legally enforceable minimum wage in their countries to help low paid and badly organised workers, as in Australia, France, Japan, the United Kingdom and United States. However, since the 1990s, increases in minimum wages are decided by committees of pay experts and representatives of business and labour, rather than by government officials (OECD 2011a). In addition to minimum wages, many governments try to provide some degree of employment protection for workers in labour markets. These include legal procedures in hiring and dismissing workers, holidays, time-off for child care, and preventing discrimination in employment. Figure 7.5 shows an index of employment protection laws for workers in selected countries in 2003 and 2008, ranging from 0 (the lowest) to six (the highest). Relatively high levels of job protection for permanent workers are found in Sweden, France, Japan and Italy, whereas they are much lower in Anglo-phone states such as Australia, the United Kingdom and especially the United States. Protections for non-permanent workers in Anglo-phone states, in turn, are significantly weaker than for permanent ones. The main factor accounting for this is the weaker controls exerted over non-permanent employment in the dual labour

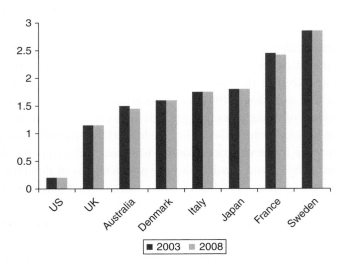

Figure 7.5 Index of employment protection laws in selected countries 2003 and 2008
Source: OECD (2011a).

markets in these countries. This involves a two-tier labour market of 'primary' permanent employment and a 'secondary' non-permanent one, with different working conditions (Barron and Norris 1976).

Until the 1970s, one of the key differences among governments using their organisational powers was the extent to which they adopted indicative economic planning methods, as in France. In Italy, the state actively supported a number of protected firms, such as Fiat, Pirelli and Olivetti, until they achieved near monopolies in their domestic markets. It was the same in Japan (Shonfield 1965). But with globalisation, national economic planning is less feasible. Public ownership is less common today too, although in some countries, such as the United Kingdom, ownership and financial structures are neither private nor public but consist of a complicated 'balance in the allocation of equity risk and incentives' (Helm and Tindall 2009: 412). In other countries, governments have ceded control over monetary policy to independent or quasi-independent bodies such as in the United Kingdom (Thatcher and Stone Sweet 2002).

Social protection

Article 22 of the UN's Universal Declaration of Human Rights states that all members of a society have a right to social security where they live. Support for social security means that all individuals have the right to develop themselves and make the most of the opportunities offered them in their country in relation to work, culture and social welfare. Further, they are helped by the state to do this (United Nations 2012). This is based on Western liberal ideas, linked to universal concepts of human dignity, the free development of people's personalities and satisfying people's life chances where they live. How these principles are applied or not applied in practice vary widely in different states around the world. The discussion here concentrates on how states regulate what is variously described in the literature as 'social welfare', 'social security' or 'social protection'.

For some writers the wider term 'welfare policy' is used rather than social security and for others the preferred term is 'social wage'. Like human rights, both welfare policy and the social wage are intrinsically Western concepts, with their roots in Christian democratic and social democratic thought and politics (Kaiser and Gehler 2004). Welfare policy is commonly defined as all the activities which governments engage in to promote the well-being of their populations in terms of income maintenance, health care, education, housing, nutrition and family policy (Wilensky 1975). The situation is complicated because for some observers welfare provision includes not only the 'public' activities of government but also the 'private' provision of welfare in the home. The social wage, in turn, is the term used to denote all those social benefits provided by the state to its citizens, funded wholly or partly through taxation, which are received 'free' or at subsidised cost to individuals and families as legal rights. The social wage, so defined, includes free education, health care, social housing and social security. Social security is thus a narrower concept than those of welfare or the social wage. It normally refers to any national schemes or programmes, established in law, that insure working people against interruption or loss of earnings. This may be due to unemployment, ill-health, retirement and certain special expenditures arising from marriage, birth and death. It also includes allowances paid to families for child support. A more descriptive term for these social functions of the state is 'social protection', which is used interchangeably in this section with social security.

From the Second World War up till the beginning of 1980s, the share of social expenditure within gross domestic product (GDP), as least in areas such as unemployment insurance, tended to rise over time across Western democracies. However, rather than nations catching up with each other, new patterns were forming as welfare states developed and matured (Alber 1981). Rather than relating growth in social expenditure to economic modernisation, some observers linked it with economic openness and freer international trade (Katzenstein 1985). In this case, the argument was that international economic co-operation pushes governments, especially in smaller more open nation states, to protect their domestic populations more actively by expanding their public sectors. More recently, economic liberalisation together with the forces promoting globalisation have led to reductions in social spending, based on the argument that high levels of taxation and regulation make national economies less competitive. Mishra (1999), for example, claims that international organisations, such as the IMF and World Bank, have been very effective in promoting the view that increasing social and welfare expenditure crowds out economic growth in nation states.

While there are some common trends in public spending retrenchments across developed nations recently, the ways in which these changes have been implemented varies significantly by country (Daly 1997). Sometimes, this has reflected changes in macro-economic conditions, such as reductions in unemployment, rather than anything else. In fact, a more differentiated and more confusing picture of the impact of growing social expenditure on national economic performance has emerged (Dodds 2012).

Social security spending in nation states is financed through a combination of general taxation and social insurance payments, with total and proportional contributions varying widely in relation to national income by country.

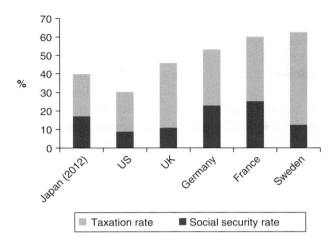

Figure 7.6 Ratios of taxation and social security expenditure to national income by country 2009

Source: Japanese Institute for Labour Policy and Training (2013).

Figure 7.6 indicates the ratios of taxation and social security expenditure to national income in six major national economies in 2009 (in the case of Japan 2013). This indicates, first, that the highest percentage of national expenditure on social security at this time was in the social market economies of Germany and France at around a fifth to a quarter. It was lowest in the liberal market economies of the United Kingdom and the United States at about 10 per cent. Japan was in an intermediate position, where social security spending was just under a fifth of national income. Social security spending was also surprisingly low as a proportion of national income in Sweden at just over 10 per cent but this was offset by the larger proportion of taxation going to social expenditure. Second, the proportion of taxes in national income contributing to social spending was about 50 per cent in Sweden, compared with about a third each in France, the United Kingdom and Germany, and about a fifth in Japan and the United States. Third, the total contributions of social security and taxation payments towards social expenditure at this time were about 60 per cent in France and Sweden, 50 per cent in Germany, and about 46 per cent, 40 per cent and 30 per cent in the United Kingdom, the United States and Japan. Whether taxes are progressive or regressive and whether social security contributions are flat-rate or according to income are important determinants how social security is financed and distributed within nation states.

In general, social protection for insured persons and their dependants is delivered through cash payments normally by the state to replace at least a proportion of lost incomes as a result of changes in an individual's economic and personal circumstances. The main five payments are: old age, disability or death; sickness and maternity (by cash benefits for both or by cash benefits plus medical care); injury at work; unemployment; and family allowances. Measures providing cash benefits to individuals are commonly referred to as 'income maintenance' schemes, while those providing direct services are 'benefits in kind'. Under income maintenance schemes, for example, there are three broad approaches when giving cash benefits to recipients: employment-related, universal and means-tested. Under both employment-related and universal approaches, the insured, dependants and survivors claim benefits as rights. Under means-testing, cash benefits are based on comparing a person's income or personal and family resources against a standard measure. Some countries provide other types of coverage too, as demonstrated by the International Social Security Association (ISSA 2012a).

Employment-related schemes are often referred to as social insurance programmes. These generally base eligibility for pensions and other cash payments on length of employment or self-employment. In the cases of family allowances and injury at work, eligibility is usually based on the existence of an employment relationship, with the amount of benefits normally related to level of earnings. Social insurance schemes are funded largely from contributions made by employers, workers or both and are compulsory for defined categories of employers and workers. Universal schemes provide flat-rate cash benefits to residents or citizens, typically financed from general taxation. Many of these incorporate a second-tier earnings-related scheme. Universal schemes are funded by contributions from employers and workers, with some support from income taxes. Means-tested schemes establish eligibility for benefits by taking account of individual or family circumstances, with benefits being limited to those satisfying these tests. The specific character of means, needs or income testing, taking account of family resources, varies considerably by country. According to the ISSA, these 'equalisation payments' are normally funded from general tax revenues and are determined by administrative decisions within the law (ISSA 2012a).

Europe

Research by the ISSA (2012a: 18) shows that out of the 45 states or principalities examined throughout Europe, 44 provide cash benefits covering old age, disability and survivors, sickness and maternity, injury at work, unemployment and family allowances. Turkey provides all these benefits, except family allowances, but is recorded as having 'no program' in this area or 'information is not available'. In Bulgaria, Estonia, Jersey, San Marino and the Ukraine, family allowances are provided under 'other programs' or through 'social assistance'. Jersey is a British crown dependency and self-governing parliamentary democracy and San Marino an independent republic. Both are small but high-income per head countries, with strong financial services and ad hoc employment relations systems.

Table 7.2 illustrates some demographic characteristics, GDP per capita and the percentage social security contributions made by insurers and employers in the top 10 and bottom 10 European countries in 2012 (ranked by GDP per capita). From this data-set, it is clear that the higher the GDP per capita, the higher is the dependency ratio in these countries. Countries with a *high* dependency ratio have more people not of working age and fewer working and paying taxes. Thus the higher the dependency ratio, the greater the proportion of people being supported by the workforce. In Europe, the dependency ratio is higher in the top 10 countries than the bottom 10. Countries with a *low* dependency ratio have fewer people who are not of working age and more who are working and paying taxes. Thus the lower the dependency ratio, the fewer the proportion of people being supported by the workforce. In this case, it is in the bottom 10 European countries.

In both the top 10 and the bottom 10 countries, employer contributions to social protection schemes are higher than those of employees, with the exceptions of the Netherlands, Croatia and Poland. In the top 10 countries too, both employer and employee contributions are lower than those in the bottom 10. However, the percentage contributions to all social protection schemes by both insurers and employers is generally lower in the top 10 countries, with higher GDPs per head, than in the bottom 10 (ISSA 2012a).

The Americas

There are 36 nation states or principalities in this group of countries. Of these, compared with Europe, only eight have the full range of old age, disability and survivors, sickness and maternity, injury at work, unemployment and family allowance benefits. These are Argentina, Bolivia, Brazil, Canada, Chile, Colombia, Mexico and the United States. These tend to have larger populations than others in the group, with middling to high GDPs per head, except in Columbia which has a low GDP per head.

Of the remaining smaller countries, 26 have at least one area where either there is 'no program' or information is 'not available'. Ten of these, in turn, have three areas where no social protection schemes are recorded or information is not available. These are Antigua and Bermuda, British

Table 7.2 Demographic statistics and social security contributions in Europe 2012: Top 10 and bottom 10 countries by GDP per capita

Country	Population (millions)	GDP per capita (US$)	Dependency ratio*	Insurer per cent contribution to all social security programmes	Employer per cent contribution to all social security programmes	Total per cent contributions to all social security programmes
Top 10 countries						
Norway	4.9	56,214	50.2	7.8	14.1	21.9
Ireland	4.5	40,697	49.0	4.0	4.3	8.3
Netherlands	16.6	40,676	49.3	23.2	19.1	42.3
Austria	8.4	38,818	47.8	17.2	25.2	42.4
Denmark	5.6	37,720	52.6	8.0	8.0	16.0
Sweden	9.4	37,377	53.3	7.0	20.9	27.9
Iceland	0.3	36,795	48.8	4.0	15.8	19.8
Germany	82.3	36,338	51.2	20.4	20.9	41.3
Belgium	10.7	36,313	52.2	13.1	24.8	37.9
Finland	5.4	35,265	51.0	8.0	22.4	30.4
Bottom 10 countries						
Croatia	4.4	19,986	47.5	20.0	17.2	37.2
Russia	143.0	18,932	38.6	0.0	30.2	30.2
Poland	38.3	18,905	39.7	22.7	17.4	40.1
Lithuania	3.3	17,308	44.8	9.0	31.0	40.0
Latvia	2.3	16,437	46.3	11.0	24.1	35.1
Romania	21.5	14,278	43.1	16.5	38.9	55.4
Bulgaria	7.5	13,870	45.4	12.9	17.8	30.7
Turkey	72.8	13,668	47.8	15.0	21.5	36.5
Belarus	9.6	13,040	40.0	1.0	34.3	35.3
Serbia	9.9	11,893	47.0	17.9	17.9	35.8

Note: *The dependency ratio is the percentage of the population aged 14 and over, plus those aged over 65, divided by the population aged 15–64.
Source: ISSA: Europe 2012 (2012a).

Virgin Isles, Dominica, Grenada, Guyana, Haiti, Saint Kitts and Nevis, Saint Lucia, Saint Vincent and the Grenadines, and Trinidad and Tobago. Apart from Haiti and Trinidad and Tobago, these tend to be modest-sized territories with small populations and generally low GDPs per capita. The exceptions are the British Virgin Isles (US$38,000), Trinidad and Tobago (US$25,572), and Antigua and Barbuda (US$18,778). In Uruguay, sickness and maternity benefits are covered by 'other programs' and Venezuela provides recipients with maternity benefits only; there are no family allowances (ISSA 2012b).

Table 7.3 shows that the dependency ratio in the Americas, in contrast to Europe, is generally higher in the bottom 10 than the top 10 countries. Also employee contributions in both the top 10 and bottom 10 countries are lower than employer contributions in each case. But employee contributions are higher in the top 10 countries than the bottom 10, though considerably lower than in Europe. Compared with Europe, the total percentage of contributions by both insurers and employers also tends to be much lower in both the top 10 and bottom 10 countries.

Asia-Pacific

The ISSA (2013) examines social security in 49 countries in the Asia-Pacific region. Of these, only 13 states provide a full range of five sets of benefits. These are Armenia, Australia, Azerbaijan, China, Hong Kong, Iran, Israel, Japan, Kazakhstan, Kyrgyzstan, New Zealand, Thailand and Uzbekistan. These countries have varying levels of income per head but, with the exception of Armenia, larger populations than some other countries. Of the remaining 36 states, 21 have at least three maintenance benefits where there is either no programme or 'information is not available'. Further, out of these 21 countries, six – Kiribati, Kuwait, Marshall Islands, Oman, Saudi Arabia and Yemen – have more than four benefits where there is 'no program' or information available. Micronesia, Palau, Qatar and Vanuatu have more than five. This sub-group of 10 countries is almost evenly split between high-income per head oil-rich countries and low-income per head poor ones (ISSA 2013).

Table 7.4 shows that the bottom 10 countries in Asia-Pacific have a higher dependency ratio than the top 10 countries, as in the Americas. It also shows employee contributions to all social security schemes to be similar to those in the Americas in both groups of countries, with employer contributions tending to be generally higher in each case. The total percentage contributions to all social security schemes by both employees and employers are similar to both

Table 7.3 Demographic statistics and social security contributions in the Americas 2011: Top 10 and bottom 10 countries by GDP per capita

Country	Population (millions)	GDP per capita (US$)	Dependency ratio	Insurer per cent contribution to all social security programmes	Employer per cent contribution to all social security programmes	Total per cent contributions to all social security programmes
Top 10 countries						
Bermuda	0.069	69,900	49.3	5.0	5.0	10.0
US	310	45,989	49.6	5.7	9.7	15.4
British Virgin Isles	0.025	38,500	35.0	4.0	4.5	8.5
Canada	34.0	37,808	44.0	6.7	7.4	14.1
Bahamas	0.343	28,700	41.3	4.4	6.4	10.8
Trinidad & Tobago	1.3	25,572	38.0	3.6	7.2	10.8
Argentina	40.4	14,538	54.9	14.0	21.5	35.5
Chile	17.1	14,311	45.7	17.6	3.4	21.0
Mexico	113.4	14,258	54.9	2.0	8.6	10.6
Uruguay	3.4	13,189	54.0	18.0	12.5	30.5
Bottom 10 countries						
Jamaica	2.7	7,633	58.4	2.5	2.5	5.0
El Salvador	6.2	6,629	63.8	9.3	11.6	20.9
Belize	0.312	6,628	63.7	*	*	*
Guatemala	14.4	4,720	84.5	4.8	6.7	11.5
Paraguay	6.5	4,523	63.0	9.0	14.0	23.0
Bolivia	9.9	4,419	68.8	11.7	10.0	21.7
Honduras	7.6	3,842	69.7	3.5	7.0	10.5
Guyana	0.75	3,240	60.8	5.2	7.8	13.0
Nicaragua	5.8	2,641	64.2	6.3	14.5	20.8
Haiti	10.0	1,151	67.6	6.0	8.0	14.0

Note: *a flat rate weekly contribution to finance all benefits is paid according to eight earnings classes.
Source: ISSA: the Americas 2011 (2012b).

Table 7.4 Demographic statistics and social security contributions in Asia–Pacific 2012: Top 10 and bottom 10 countries by GDP per capita

Country	Population (millions)	GDP per capita (US$)	Dependency ratio	Insurer per cent contribution to all social security programmes	Employer per cent contribution to all social security programmes	Total per cent contributions to all social security programmes
Top 10 countries						
Qatar	1.8	91,379	17.0	5.0	10.0	15.0
Singapore	5.1	50,633	35.9	20.0	16.0	36.0
Brunei	0.40	49,500	42.1	8.5	8.5	17.0
Hong Kong	7.1	43,229	32.0	5.0	5.0	10.0
Kuwait	2.7	41,700	41.3	5.0	10.0	15.0
Australia	22.3	39,539	48.0	0.0	9.0	9.0
Taiwan	23.2	37,700	35.2	7.5	17.4	24.9
Japan	126.5	32,418	56.4	13.8	14.6	28.4
New Zealand	4.4	28,993	50.4	*	*	*
Bahrain	1.3	27,700	28.4	7.0	13.0	20.0
Bottom 10 countries						
Vietnam	87.8	2,953	42.1	9.5	21.0	29.5
Pakistan	173.6	2,609	65.8	1.0	11.0	11.1
Yemen	24.1	2,470	88.3	6.0	13.0	19.0
Kyrgyzstan	5.3	2,283	52.6	10.0	17.3	27.3
Papua New Guinea	6.9	2,281	71.9	6.0	8.4	14.4
Laos	6.2	2,255	62.3	4.5	5.0	9.5
Tajikistan	6.8	1,972	68.0	1.0	25.0	26.0
Bangladesh	148.7	1,416	56.0	8.5	8.5	17.0
Myanmar	48.0	1,300	44.4	1.5	3.5	5.0
Nepal	30.0	1,155	67.7	10.0	10.0	20.0

Note: *Government pays the total cost of most programmes from general revenues and employers pay the costs of injury at work.
Source: ISSA: Asia–Pacific 2012 (2013).

Europe and the Americas, with contributions within the bottom 10 countries tending to be higher than in the top 10. Total contributions, in descending order, are highest in Europe, lower in the Asia-Pacific region, and lowest in the Americas (ISSA 2013).

Africa

There are 44 countries in ISSA studies of all Africa. Compared with Europe, the Americas and Asia-Pacific, Africa is a relatively poor and undeveloped continent economically and politically. In 2011, the highest GDP per capita was in Equatorial Guinea (US$34,680) and the lowest was Zimbabwe (US$187), with wide variations across the continent. Further, many of these countries have large, young, dependent populations, such as Nigeria with a population of over 158 million, Ethiopia over 83 million, and Egypt over 81 million. The social security systems within African countries are emergent ones and are poorly financed, less stable and under-resourced, compared with other regions. Unambiguous patterns of organisation and provision in Africa are very difficult to discern with clarity. For example, only two North African states, Algeria and Tunisia, former French colonies with relatively low GDPs per head, provide a full range of benefits covering all five main categories identified by ISSA (2011).

Patterns of social security in Africa are therefore very diverse. First, all 44 countries have injury at work programmes, which are commonly funded by employers. Second, 40 countries have old age, disability and survivors benefits, with the exceptions of Botswana (with old age and orphans' benefits only), Senegal and South Africa (with old age and survivor benefits only), and Malawi's statutory system which is not yet implemented. Third, only 21 countries have sickness and maternity schemes, comprising cash benefits for both or cash benefits plus medical care. But these provisions are uneven and vary widely among countries. Indeed, sickness and maternity benefits in the remaining 23 countries have lots of exclusions and conditions. These include maternity benefits only, medical benefits only, coverage through social assistance, and maternity benefits financed under family allowance programmes. Fourth, 24 countries of various population size and GDPs per head have family allowances, with the rest having either no programmes or no information is available. Fifth, notably only five countries – Algeria, Egypt, Mauritius, South Africa and Tunisia – have unemployment benefits. Apart from Egypt and South Africa, three were former French colonies (ISSA 2011).

Table 7.5 shows dependency ratios in Africa tend to be much higher compared with those in Europe, the Americas and Asia-Pacific, especially in the

Table 7.5 Demographic statistics and social security contributions in Africa 2011: Top 10 and bottom 10 countries by GDP per capita

Country	Population (millions)	GDP per capita (US$)	Dependency ratio	Insurer per cent contribution to all social security programmes	Employer per cent contribution to all social security programmes	Total per cent contributions to all social security programmes
Top 10 countries						
Equatorial Guinea	0.7	34,680	72.8	4.5	21.5	26.0
Seychelles	0.1	20,828	40.9	2.5	20.0	22.5
Libya	6.4	16,999	53.2	5.3	12.9	18.2
Gabon	1.5	14,984	66.1	2.5	20.1	22.6
Botswana	2.0	13,462	57.6	0.0	0.0	0.0*
Mauritius	1.3	13,101	40.4	4.0	6.0	10.0
South Africa	50.1	10,140	53.3	1.0	1.0	2.0
Algeria	35.5	8,477	46.3	9.0	25.0	34.0
Tunisia	10.5	8,509	43.7	8.4	14.4	22.8
Egypt	81.1	5,840	72.8	14.0	26.0	40.0
Bottom 10 countries						
Madagascar	20.7	958	86.0	1.0	13.0	14.0
Malawi	14.9	902	95.7	0.0	0.0**	0.0
Togo	6.0	846	75.6	4.0	16.5	20.5
Sierra Leone	5.9	825	81.4	5.0	10.0	15.0
Central African Republic	4.4	766	79.7	3.0	19.0	22.0
Niger	15.5	677	104.8	5.3	15.4	20.7
Burundi	8.4	403	68.7	4.0	9.0	13.0
Liberia	4.0	400	86.2	3.0	4.8	7.8
Congo-Kinshasa	66.0	327	95.9	3.5	9.0	12.5
Zimbabwe	12.6	187	75.5	3.0	3.0	6.0

Note: *Government pays the total cost of old age, disability and survivors programme.
**Employers pay the total costs of work injury benefits.
Source: ISSA: Africa 2011 (2011).

bottom 10 countries. Also contributions from insurers are much lower than those from employers in both the top 10 and bottom 10 countries – although contributions from both parties are generally lower than in Europe and Asia-Pacific. The total percentage contributions by insurers and employers in all social security programmes in the bottom 10 countries in Africa are lowest among the four regions examined here. But in the top 10 African countries, they are the second highest.

INTERNATIONAL AGENCIES AND EMPLOYMENT RELATIONS

Employment relationships are typically organised within the boundaries of nation states, where, with the possible exception of some TNCs, most employment relations decisions and rules are made. But there are also some international agencies that are players in employment relations internationally or globally. Typical examples on the employee side are presented in chapter 6, such as the global union federations and ITUC. Agencies representing the interests of employers globally include the International Organisation of Employers (IOE) (2013); those representing employers regionally include BUSINESSEUROPE, formerly the Union of Industrial and Employers' Confederations of Europe (UNICE); and those representing public enterprises include the *Centre européen des enterprises à participation publique* (CEEP), which speaks on behalf of public enterprises in the EU. In most cases the direct employment relations functions of such organisations are limited. But their industrial and commercial policies impact indirectly on employment relationships.

The IOE is the largest network of private-sector employers in the world, with a membership of some 150 business and employer federations in 143 countries. It is the recognised voice of business in social and labour policy debates taking place in the ILO, the UN, multi-lateral trading discussions, and the G20 group of leading economies. The G20 comprises the world's larger economies, made up of 19 countries plus the EU, led by national finance ministers and central bank governors. The role of the G20 in global economic co-ordination and co-operation has expanded significantly in recent times, prompted by the latest global economic crises and their impact on jobs. Within its remits, the IOE seeks to influence the contexts for 'doing business'. Its roles include advocacy of regulatory frameworks at international level to promote entrepreneurship, support for private-sector development, and encouraging sustainable job creation. The

IOE helps national business organisations by providing general guidance to its members in international labour standards, business and human rights, corporate social responsibility, occupational health and safety, and international employment relations (International Organisation of Employers 2013).

Another influential employer body is the International Chamber of Commerce (ICC). Established in 1919, the ICC is a strong advocate of neo-liberalism. The ICC claims to provide a forum for businesses and other organisations for reviewing and discussing the nature and significance of the major shifts taking place in the world economy. It also offers a channel for providing business leadership to governments managing change. Policy advocacy is a major part of ICC's work and everything it does aims to promote international trade and business investment. Much of its work is very practical and focused on making it easier for businesses to operate internationally. ICC has a well-known commercial arbitration and alternative dispute resolution service, which provides impartial and dependable private justice to clients. This gives more security to commercial partners doing business across national frontiers. The ICC also attempts to fight commercial crime, provides model contracts and clauses, and gives authoritative advice for financing trade and cross-national business transactions (International Chamber of Commerce 2013).

Formerly known as UNICE, and renamed in 2007, BUSINESSEUROPE has 45 members in 35 countries. It claims a crucial role in Europe as the main *horizontal* business organisation at EU level, acting as the Confederation of European Business. Through its member federations, BUSINESSEUROPE represents more than 20 million companies across the region. Its principal aim is to preserve and strengthen competitiveness in the European business community. A second aim is to ensure that the interests of the corporate sector are represented and defended within European institutions. A third aim is to be active in European social dialogue and promote the smooth functioning of European labour markets. Economically, the confederation wants to double Europe's growth rate from 1.25 per cent to 2.5 per cent. It also seeks to put public finances on a sustainable path, promote private investment, unleash the economic potential of the single European market, and expand EU external trade by building strong presences in global markets. BUSINESSEUROPE (2013) is a very market-oriented, entrepreneurial employer organisation.

CEEP members are providers of 'services of general interest' across Europe. CEEP is recognised at EU level as the general cross-industry social partner for public employers, whatever their legal ownership or status. Its members are enterprises and associations in public and private organisations at national, regional and local levels. In its role as a European social partner, CEEP participates in high-level meetings including the European social summit, macro-economic policy development, the European Economic and Social Committee, and the Dublin Foundation for the Improvement of Living and Working Conditions. CEEP seeks to influence all European-level decisions affecting public infrastructures such as transport, energy, water supply, waste management, and telecommunications. It also promotes the principle of 'subsidiarity' and the responsibilities of public authorities at regional and local levels, where services of general interest are increasingly being provided. Subsidiarity is the policy that EU decisions are taken as closely as possible to its citizens. This means the EU does not take actions where these can be done more effectively at national, regional or local levels, except on matters for which it alone is responsible (CEEP 2013).

A common critique of cross-national employers' bodies is their relatively low profiles internationally. A main reason for this is that individual employers, especially TNCs, are important international players in their own right. Thus TNCs are judged to have more power and autonomy at international level than many national governments. Indeed, Hertz (2001) argues that about half of the world's largest economic agencies in the world are TNCs, not national governments. Further, TNCs are not embedded in the institutions of most countries where they operate. As Gumbrell-McCormick (2008: 330) writes, TNCs 'have the capacity to pursue international strategies while most trade unions and employee representative institutions are nationally bounded'. This both underpins the dominance of TNCs internationally and undermines the efficacy of employment relations systems nationally (Katz and Darbishire 2000). Using their ability to shift production to low-cost, weakly regulated, union-free domains, TNCs can impose downward pressure on national employment regulations (Gray 2002).

A truly trans-global body is the ILO. Established in 1919, as an autonomous agency of the League of Nations, the ILO became the UN's first specialist agency in 1945 and has 185 member states out of 193 countries in the world. Using 'Conventions', the ILO's seeks to establish basic workers' rights internationally, with the purpose of setting international labour standards and improving workers' rights globally (Hughes 2011). In trying to establish international labour standards, the ILO is backed up by a unique system to supervise their application. The ILO's most significant institutional feature is its tri-partite structure, made up of government, employer and worker representatives. This special form of tripartism gives equal voices to all three players, ensuring the views of the social partners are closely reflected in establishing labour standards and shaping ILO's policies.

The mission of the ILO is to promote social justice, support internationally recognised human and labour rights, and sustain its founding principle that labour peace is essential to national economic prosperity. Today, the ILO helps advance the causes of decent work and working conditions to give working people and business people a stake in lasting peace, prosperity and progress. The ILO's main aims are to promote workers' rights, encourage decent employment opportunities, enhance social protection and strengthen dialogue on work-related issues. The organisation has four strategic objectives: to promote and realise standards and fundamental principles and rights at work; to create greater opportunities for women and men to decent employment and income; to enhance the coverage and effectiveness of social protection for all; and to strengthen tripartism and social dialogue (ILO 2014).

The ILO has eight 'core' Conventions, covering four areas of employment relations, which have won international recognition and acclaim as essential for protecting the social and legal rights of workers and their representatives. Formally adopted within the ILO's (2002) fundamental conventions, these core conventions form the basis of most voluntary codes of conduct adopted by companies, industries and governments throughout the world. They have the force of international law and are adopted through legislation by member states ratifying them. The first pair of conventions covers *the elimination of all forms of forced and compulsory labour*. The principles embodied in ILO Conventions No. 29 (1930) and No. 105 (1957) on forced labour are practically universally accepted and endorsed and are part of the fundamental rights of humankind. They are incorporated in various international instruments, both universally and regionally, so that prohibition of forced or compulsory labour in all its forms is now considered an unconditional norm of modern international law on human rights. These two fundamental ILO Conventions are the most widely ratified of all ILO instruments (ILO 2007).

Second, *freedom of association and the effective recognition of the right to collective bargain* are covered by Convention No. 87 (1948) and Convention No. 98 (1949). These assert that all workers and employers have the right to freely form and join groups to support and advance their occupational interests. These basic human rights go together with freedom of expression and provide the basis of democratic representation and governance. If people want to exercise their right to influence work-related matters of direct concern them, their voice needs to be heard and taken into account. Freedom of association means that workers and employers can set up, join and run their own organisations without interference from the state or one another, with the law respecting this principle. Realising the principle of freedom of association and the right to collective bargaining in practice requires a number of conditions. These include: a legal basis guaranteeing that these rights are enforced; an enabling institutional framework, which can be tripartite or between employers' and workers' organisations; absence of discrimination against individuals who wish to exercise their rights to have their voice heard; and acceptance by employers' and workers' organisations of their roles as partners to solve problems jointly and deal with mutual challenges together (ILO 2002).

Third, Conventions No. 100 (1951) and No. 111 (1958) are concerned with *eliminating discrimination in employment* and occupation on any grounds. These include gender, ethnic origin, nationality, religion, political opinion, age, status or disability, although sexual orientation is not included. For the ILO, eliminating discrimination starts with dismantling barriers and ensuring equality of access to training and education and ability to own and use resources such as land and credit. It also means creating the conditions for setting up and running enterprises of all types and sizes, and having policies and practices on hiring, assignment of tasks, working conditions, pay, benefits, promotions, lay-offs and termination of employment to do this. Merit and the ability to do a job, not irrelevant characteristics, are the guides to good practice.

Fourth, Conventions No. 138 (1973) and No. 182 (1999) support the principle of *the effective abolition of child labour*. This means that every girl and boy has the opportunity to develop physically and mentally to her or his full potential. It seeks to stop all work by children that jeopardises their education and development. This does not mean stopping all work performed by children. International labour standards allow the distinction to be made between acceptable and unacceptable forms of work for children at different ages and stages of development. To achieve the effective abolition of child labour, governments have to fix and enforce a minimum age or ages at which children can enter into different types of work. This Convention explicitly opposes slavery, trafficking, debt bondage and other forms of forced labour such as prostitution and pornography, forced recruitment of children for military purposes, and use of children for illicit activities such as drugs trafficking (ILO 2002).

CONCLUSION AND IMPLICATIONS

The role of the state and government in employment relations is a critical one. Government intervention or lack of it in national labour markets and national economic policy, as well as its role as an employer of public servants, has major impacts on organisations and those working in them in the private or public sectors. As Polanyi (1944) argues the creation of free markets in nineteenth-century Britain took place because of a massive deployment of state power to displace existing, customary economic and market relationships. For Polayni, the modern market economy and contemporary nation state are not separate entities but jointly constitute the 'market society'. Indeed, following Polanyi, variations in state policy provide a convincing historical explanation of the changing conditions under which labour power is bought and sold in capitalist market economies over time. His analysis is as appropriate now as it is historically, with neo-liberalism today being a product of market ideology and political power (Gall *et al.* 2011).

Further, the tradition of state abstention incorporated within the pluralistic industrialism of the Anglo-phone world is not the norm in employment relations today. Under contemporary globalisation, the liberalisation of cross-national trade, cross-national arrangements for production in TNCs, the loosening of cross-national investment and financial flows, and advances in ICTs mean that national boundaries and the nation state have become cumulatively less relevant in protecting domestic business interests. To accommodate the new global economic hegemony, governments have fostered national competitiveness by promoting labour market flexibility, reducing corporate taxes, weakening trade unions, as well as permitting increased economic inequalities of both income and wealth within nation states between those controlling capital and those selling their labour (Iversen and Wren 1998, Stiglitz 2013). The role of the state has also changed from one of steering the economy to the piecemeal correction of market failures through agencies of the regulatory state (Majone 1997, Moran 2003). As Hyman (2008: 279) argues, conflicts underlying the priorities of state action continue, with tensions remaining among the state's accumulation, pacification and legitimation functions (Offe 1984). There is never a single 'best-way' for the state to influence employment relations but many.

The state's role as an employer is important one. On the one hand, the state needs quality and committed public servants to provide efficient and effective public services to its citizens. But, on the other hand, it also needs to contain the costs of public employment by maintaining a public sector whose size is commensurate with the state's ability to fund and support it. Further, whether public employment is a career-based, department-based or position-based system, the state's role as a 'model' employer or one incorporating 'good' employment relations practices should not be underestimated. A moral but self-interested government commonly tries to act as a model good practice employer to ensure its employees are treated fairly. This covers appointment, terms and conditions of employment, promotion, and when employment is terminated. The concept of good state governance is only authenticated when civil servants or public employees know they are being treated justly by their employer and that trust in that employer is not being eroded or undermined by unethical employment practices (Pinnington *et al.* 2007).

In modern welfare states, the concept of being a model or good practice employer historically included union recognition, secure employment, fair terms and conditions, career development opportunities, and safe and healthy working environments. In some cases, another objective was to promote 'soft' forms of industrial democracy in public services, such as collective bargaining, joint consultation or works councils. The aim was to incentivise public servants, engage them in the workplace, and legitimise the personnel management decisions affecting them. Today the focus has shifted in many cases to a culture promoting continuous improved performance, quality services and customer care, especially in position-based systems. If performance and customers matter, four things follow: public services become target-driven; organisational power is delegated to line managers including HR issues; public servants are increasingly managed individually, appraised regularly and rewarded in line with personal performance; and public servants are expected to work flexibly. Working in public services today is distinctly different from what it was historically, with subtleties of distinction among career-based, department-based and position-based systems.

There is also now considerable overlap and synergy between the managerial and HR vocabularies being used in both the private and public sectors. In some leading-edge private corporations, for example, the role of HR departments is increasingly focused on developing organisational 'vision' and 'direction', monitoring the external environment, anticipating the need for cultural and organisational change, and supporting line managers in their HR roles. Working as partners, senior managers and HR specialists in private businesses commonly look to new orthodoxies associated with good HR practice and managing organisational change rather than demonstrating bureaucratic competence (Marchington *et al.* 2012). Some of these ideas are being transferred to public services, especially in position-based systems, with the goal of creating 'public businesses'. This involves new management systems, customer-focus and quality services, in line with broader vision, mission and organisational values. To achieve competence and value for money, public services are exhorted to recruit, retain and develop staff with knowledge and skills to improve these services; some of whom 'cross-over' from the private sector to do this. The situations are similar in non-position-based systems, which shift with a lighter touch (OECD 2004b).

Delegation of HR activities in public employment is more common than in the past. When delegation takes place in public services, the issues delegated to lower levels within OECD countries include, first, flexible working time, mobility, deployment, simplified and more open recruitment, more sophisticated selection methods, flexible terms of employment and easier termination of employment procedures. Second, classification and grading of posts are determined locally but made more flexible and less complex. Third, decisions about flexible pay arrangements are taken at decentralised levels. Fourth, staff numbers are decided locally too. With local delegation, central HR bodies take on more strategic roles and wider HR concerns. Delegation of discretion over operating costs appears to be a good indicator of the extent of devolution. Devolved budgetary frameworks provide single running cost appropriations for salary costs and other administrative expenditures; these are essential underpinnings for relaxing central controls over staff numbers, classifications, grading and pay. Such frameworks generally contain provisions for carrying over funds, which provide flexibility in managing staffing levels. Position-based systems, as in Canada, Denmark, Finland, the Netherlands, Sweden and the United Kingdom, are where most extensive delegation of HR practices has taken place. Here bulk funding of operating costs is used to initiate HR delegation and devolution.

Economic policies are redistributive in their effects. They impact heavily on employment relationships, the actors or players in employment relations, and families, households and communities. Although it is premature to argue that national economic policies are converging in all economic sectors in all countries in the capitalist world, the direction of travel is nevertheless towards economic liberalisation and the marketisation of goods and services (Sandel 2012). These are being implemented, however, in a variety of ways in different countries, depending on the institutions and historical-path dependencies in each case. Economic and social policies focusing on reducing inflation effectively prioritise the owners of financial assets and private property, whose incomes are commonly protected by indexation or asset inflation, over those of workers and the poor. Further, greater reliance on private pensions rather than public ones has resulted in regulatory decisions about financial markets having a disproportionate impact on large sectors of national populations. This happens because a larger percentage of household wealth has shifted from being in secure assets, such as bank deposits and savings, to riskier investments such as bonds and equity markets. Indeed, as Perez and Westrup (2010: 1180) observe, between 1980 and 2000, 'the total proportion of risk assets rose from 53 to 74 per cent of household savings in Britain, from 33 to 60 per cent in Germany, 30 to 61 per cent in France [and] 24 to 75 per cent in Italy'. In other words, increasing proportions of national populations are being exposed to the vicissitudes of risky financial products, as well as to the uncertainties of deregulated labour markets.

National social protection schemes are complex and diverse. But they underpin employment relationships and employee security, by providing protections against loss of wage incomes in periods of unemployment, sickness and retirement. There are wide variations by country and geographic region of GDP per head, dependency ratios, and arrangements for state provision of benefits for old age, disability and survivors, sickness and maternity, injury at work and unemployment. There are also variations how these programmes are funded and organised. Europe has the longest established systems and provides the best benefits to workers and their families, generally supported by high levels of contributions by both employees and employers. This is social-democratic and Christian-democratic social policy in action. The major exceptions in Europe are small jurisdictions such as Ireland, Cyprus and Guernsey (ISSA 2012a). Despite its GDPs per head being generally lower than in Asia-Pacific, Europe generally has not only generous social protection schemes but also the most structured employment relations systems.

Employment relations players operate largely within national institutional frameworks. But international organisations representing workers and employers exist at supra-national level. These international players have mostly indirect influences on employment relations rather than direct ones. The norms of employment relations that exist internationally derive largely out of ILO Conventions, which are accepted by wide sectors of public opinion. But international institutions have neither the legitimacy nor the accountability of democratic states. The processes used to monitor their cross-national compliance are limited; other than the moral authority exerted by international labour standards. This is because their powers to impose sanctions on governments and employers resisting them are largely absent.

part 3

PROCESSES AND OUTCOMES IN EMPLOYMENT RELATIONS

8

LEGAL REGULATION

The purpose of this chapter is to identify and review the changing faces of the law in work and employment relationships, focusing on the contract of employment, employment protection law and collective labour law. These are analysed comparatively, using a social science perspective. Work is any organised economic activity, which takes place in specific organisational, social and legal settings. Those doing work provide either something tangible or a service to another party. As a process, work involves some degree of co-operation between workers, and with those for whom they work, and occurs in all types of societies in the contemporary world and historically. In early modern times, workers, who were not independent producers of goods or services, were governed by a variety of legal regimes. These usually resulted in lack of personal freedom for the workers and their subordination to a dominant authority, whether monarch, religious institution or master. These regimes included slavery, serfdom, apprenticeships, voluntary or involuntary servitude, or master-and-servant relationships. Different forms of un-free labour, including child labour, continued in Europe and North America into the modern period and they persist in some parts of the world today. The ILO (2013) estimates that in 2013 about 10.5 million children worldwide – most of them under age – were working as domestic workers in people's homes, in often hazardous and sometimes slave-like conditions. Whatever the legal regime, laws around the world today attempt to regulate who works, how work is done and the obligations of the parties in work relationships. Here the debate returns to the legal tradition of employment relations.

LABOUR LAW AND TYPES OF LEGAL SYSTEM

During the early modern period in European history, and before the era of modern labour law, 'guilds' regulated the activities of craft apprentices and 'free' journeymen [sic] who were supervised by 'master' or established craft workers. The guilds were associations of artisans or merchants that controlled the practices and customs of their crafts or trades in a particular town. Gaining entry into the guilds was often difficult and their underpinning objective was to regulate almost every aspect of the lives of their members. These systems of work regulation persisted well into the nineteenth century (Weyrauch 1999). It was the laws governing these multifarious institutions that provided the proto-historical conditions out of which modern labour law emerged. The principal concern of labour law today is how labour markets and managerial decisions about work are regulated, largely within national domains. The origins of national labour laws are deep-seated and wide-ranging. In the United Kingdom, for example, labour law is rooted in the English Ordinance of Labourers 1349, Statute of Labourers 1350–1351, and all subsequent legislation regulating duration of employment, wages, methods of wage payments, mobility of labour, occupational choice and so on. Involvement of the law with worker protest, labour unrest and collective demands for better wages and conditions is also traced to a variety of sources. These include the *Ordonnances* of Charles VI in France during the fourteenth century, the *Reichpolizeiordnung* 1530, 1548 and 1577 in the Holy Roman Empire, and other statutes prohibiting combinations of workers in Britain, Ireland and mainland Europe in the early years of the industrial revolution.

Labour law and legal families

Labour law as a modern academic discipline, and area of professional practice, was created out of the social consequences of industrialisation and the widespread adoption of economic liberalism, which emerged in Britain, other parts of the English-speaking world and Europe in the nineteenth century. Economic liberalism freed labour markets from both governmental controls and the restrictions imposed on them by guilds. It also freed the worker, since it broke the bonds of even voluntary servitude of workers with their masters. It was the Master and Servant Act 1875 in Britain, Thirteenth Amendment to the US Constitution 1865 abolishing slavery and involuntary servitude, and Industrial Code of the North German Confederation 1867, which effectively put an end to the imprisonment of employees or servants for breaching the terms of their employment, when leaving their work prematurely. The dominant economic ideology of the late nineteenth and early twentieth centuries was laissez-faire, with its catchphrase 'freedom of contract'. With the growth of trade union power, collective bargaining and organised industrial conflict during the first three-quarters of the twentieth century in Western industrialised countries, bolstered in the 1940s, 1950s, 1960s and 1970s by Keynesian economic policies and welfare state regimes, labour law had to take account of more than the individual employment relationship. It also had to intervene in collective power relations between employers and organised labour (Kahn-Freund 1977).

More recently, with the emergence of the post-industrial economy, weakening of the Fordist model of production in western countries and promotion of neo-liberal economic policies cross-nationally, labour law now incorporates new issues in its field. These include flexibility, the individualisation of work and employment, the re-regulation of work, and demographic changes in the workplace (Iwagami 1999). The re-regulation of work, for example, towards very much heightened managerial control in the workplace, and managerial determination of labour markets, is evidenced by the growth of zero hours contracts in the United Kingdom and by the operations of Walmart and Amazon in countries such as the United States, as well as increasing use of bogus types of self-employment (Fishman 2006, O'Connor 2013).

This outcome is that labour law is now part of most modern legal systems, which are commonly classified into legal families or legal traditions. The subject matter, processes and impacts of labour law on employers, employees and trade unions thus vary widely internationally across nation states. One basic classificatory approach is to divide the legal systems of the world into four distinct families: civil law, common law, socialist law and other law, each with its own legal traditions. For Merryman (1985), a legal tradition is defined as a set of deeply rooted and historically conditioned attitudes about the nature of law, the role of law in society and the political ideology, organisation and operation of a legal system. Zweigert and Kotz (1998) also adopt the language of legal families, while emphasising the problem in achieving a consensus on the criteria to be used in classifying them. One weakness of the legal families approach is its narrow cultural focus, because these families are based largely on Western legalistic prototypes; the Roman, Germanic and common law models. Further, the 'Europeanisation' process within the EU today is claimed by some observers as possibly leading to a convergence of legal systems within its geographical and political boundaries (Twining 1999). Indeed, de Groot (1991) believes it likely that the legal systems of Europe will eventually form one great legal family, with uniform or strongly similar rules in many fields, such as labour law and business law. Another criticism of the legal families approach is its focus on private law at the expense of constitutional, administrative and criminal law. Another is the existence of hybrid or 'mixed' jurisdictions, such as in Scotland, South Africa, Quebec and Israel, which have more than one legal tradition co-existing with another (Palmer 2012).

Despite its weaknesses, the legal families approach seems to provide a reasoned and manageable framework for examining legal systems comparatively. However, as indicated in Figure 8.1, no single classificatory methodology is unanimously agreed by scholars. Hence although each approach 'can undoubtedly be justified from the point of view of the person proposing it...none can, in the end, be recognized as [being] exclusive' (David and Brierley 1985: 20). These writers note two main criteria for classifying legal systems into respective families. One is to base classification on the law's conceptual structure or the theory of sources of the law. The second approach is to recognise that these technical differences are of secondary importance. This classification emphasises the social objectives being sought through the legal system or the place of the law within the social order. For writers in this tradition, these two considerations seem equally decisive for the purposes of creating a classificatory structure.

Zweigert and Kotz (1998), in turn, suggest that juristic style is the crucial test that determines the classification of a legal system. For them, classification is the product of five factors: the historical background and development of the system; its characteristic and typical mode of thought; its distinctive institutions; the types of legal sources it acknowledges and its treatment of these; and the ideology of the economic or political doctrines underpinning it. Of these criteria, the historical development and ideology behind legal systems are particularly important in determining the construction of legal families and traditions.

Source	Classification of legal systems
Esmein (1905)	Roman, Germanic, Anglo-Saxon, Slavic, Islamic
Zweigert and Kotz (1977)	Roman, Germanic, Nordic, Common Law, Socialist, Far-Eastern, Islamic, Hindu
David and Brierley (1978)	Romano-Germanic, Common Law, Socialist, philosophical or religious (including Muslim, Jewish, Far East, Black Africa, Malagasy Republic)
van Hoecke and Warrington (1998)	African, Asian, Islamic, Western
Orucu (2004)	Legal systems as family trees resulting in 'mixed legal systems', according to parentage and constituent elements

Figure 8.1 Some classifications of legal systems

Civil law systems, for example, have the most variegated histories. This has resulted in writers such as David and Brierley (1985) labelling civil law regimes as 'Romano-Germanic'. This reflects the strong Roman law origins of civil law, the influence of the French civil code and the subsequent influence of the German civil code on it. Further, it is Roman law, with its codification, systematisation of concepts into categories, principles and divisions of laws, which has left a lasting imprint on the French and German legal codes. Countries that are normally designated civil law systems include Austria, France, Germany, Italy, Spain and Switzerland in Europe, Arab states in the Middle East, North Africa, Latin America, Japan in the Far East (which is modelled on the German system), and Madagascar (Anderson 2009).

Development of common law regimes, in contrast, is incorporated in a large body of rules founded on unwritten customary laws that have evolved and developed over centuries through pragmatism, strong monarchies, unwritten constitutions, and centralised courts. Common law systems also adopted substantive law principles embodied in statutory or written law. They developed in ad hoc fashions in response to resolving disputes between parties and depended largely on the disputants bringing their cases to the courts. As de Cruz (2007: 38) argues, there was no common law legislative tradition 'that sought to reform or redress the law by means of the legislature, unlike the civil law'. In other words, the common law was developed in and by the courts, giving judge-made law considerable weight in this type of legal regime. Civil law in contrast was formulated, compiled and refined in the universities and only codified later. It was then given statutory force by legislatures (David and Brierley 1985). Typical common law jurisdictions include England and Wales (not Scotland), Australia, Canada (not Quebec), Kenya, New Zealand, Nigeria, the United States, and parts of the Far East such as Hong Kong, Malaysia and Singapore (Ingman 2008). In the case of the United States, however, although its legal system is based on common law, it adopted a written constitution which has played a pivotal part in the development of citizen rights and responsibilities; similar to what happened in France and Germany.

In East Europe, including the former Soviet Union, legal systems were traditionally described as 'socialist' regimes, reflecting their Marxist-Leninist origins. This incorporates Marx's methodology of historical materialism, based on a theory of socio-economic development where changes in material conditions, such as technology and productive capacity, are the primary influences on how society and the economy are organised (McLellan 1971). With the fall of Communism in this region, and disintegration of the Soviet Union in 1991, the notion of 'socialist' law is now called into question (Sypnowich 1990).

Outside Europe, in contrast, the historical explanation of jurisdictions in the Far East, Antipodes and America is often found in British, French and Dutch colonialism. Thus British, French and Dutch control of Malaysia, India, Africa and Indonesia meant that either common law or civil law was imported into these geographic areas, depending on the colonial legal system at the time. However, because of the diversity and uncertainty of local customary laws, codifications of laws were introduced in India and the Far East. This was to clarify, modernise and adapt foreign law to local conditions. Hence the significant historical imperative in these regions was colonialism. This ultimately brought about a plurality of laws in these areas (Benton 2001). As a result, there are hybrid or mixed legal jurisdictions in South Africa, the Seychelles, Louisiana, Greece, Quebec and Puerto Rico. This makes it difficult to classify the precise legal family to which each belongs.

The ideology of a legal system reflects its underpinning political, economic or religious values. Thus it is widely recognised that the legal ideologies of the Anglo-Saxon, Germanic, Roman and Nordic families are in many respects similar to one another; this is reflected in their labour laws. Similarly, in China, North Vietnam and North Korea, a communist theory of law exists based on Marxist-Leninism, which justifies putting them in a separate category or legal family. This used to be the case, until recently, in the former Soviet Union and other East European states. But because of the dramatic political and economic changes that took place in this region during the last decades of the twentieth century, it is difficult to assess exactly what legal ideologies these states are likely to adopt in the future. One possibility is that a variant of social democracy will emerge, albeit one steeped in civil law rather than common law. Another is that a more autocratic, less democratic legal system could emerge. Whichever pathways are taken, these legal settlements will be heavily dependent upon state policy and legal enactment in each case (Reimann and Zimmerman 2006).

Religious legal regimes, in turn, such as Hindu and Muslim systems, also justify separate categorisation, because of their unique philosophical and ideological characteristics. Sources of law not only are a distinguishing feature of Hindu and Muslim law (Davis 2013, Hallaq 2009) but also help separate mainland Europe from Anglo-Saxon legal systems. Yet it is not easy to classify the legal families of Western states definitively, since their underpinning ideologies can be considered to be similar to one another. In cases of mixed jurisdictions or hybrid legal systems, where civil law and common law co-exist, with or without customary law, it is also difficult to apply any distinguishing criteria of these legal regimes (Reid and Palmer 2009). The basic features of different legal regimes are summarised in Figure 8.2.

	Civil law	Common law	Socialist law	Religious law
Sources of law	Statutes Legislation	Case law Statutes Legislation	Statutes Legislation	Religious texts Case law
Roles of lawyers	Judges dominant Judges careerists Judges independent	Lawyers control courtrooms Judges senior lawyers Judges independent	Judges dominant Judges party members Judges independence low	Lawyer roles secondary Judges legally and religiously trained Judges independence varies
Policy making	Courts have equal power with legislature	Courts power share with legislature	Courts subordinate to legislature	Courts subordinate to executive

Figure 8.2   The basic features of different legal regimes

Some features of national labour law

The development of labour law and its scope vary by country, history and the legal regime within which it operates. Here again the major distinction is between civil law and common law systems. As indicated earlier, France, Germany and Japan, for example, have civil law regimes; the United Kingdom, Australia, New Zealand and United States have common law regimes. In the case of pre-revolutionary France, the absolute authority of *le patron* or master dominated relations with workers, servants and apprentices. This paternalism derived from the concept of the patriarchal head of the household and the absolute right of parents over their children, linked with the divine right of monarchy and political absolutism (Wiesner 2000). Following the French revolution 1789–1799, however, freedom of contract became the means for adjusting individual interests in post-aristocratic, post-monarchic France, which was now increasingly oriented towards more market freedoms and new democratic principles (Rudé 1988). Equality of bargaining power or status became the new mantra for social relationships within the economic and political spheres. The new Civil Code in France regarded workers and employees as legal equals in their contractual relationships with the employer or *le patronat*. This emergence of economic laissez-faire was a reaction against the massive economic regulation that had swamped France under the *Ancien Régime*. By the early nineteenth century, French labour law had been effectively assimilated into the general body of national law and was part of the civil law (*droit civil*). Indeed, present-day labour law in France can for all intents and purposes be traced back to 1791, when the National Assembly of the revolutionary period enacted statutes abolishing the guilds, as well as outlawing workers' organisations (Goubert 1991).

In Germany, industrialisation started later than in Britain but by the middle of the nineteenth century, freedom of contract was also the governing legal principle in economic relations. But German law developed differently from France and England, since the working class began adopting political means to advance their economic interests with the state, government and employers. For example, the General German Workers' Association (GWA), founded in 1863, aimed to promote workers' interests through a universal right to vote. This was followed, in 1869, by the creation of the Social Democratic Worker's Party (SDWP). The merger of the GWA and SDWP in 1875 created the Socialist Workers' Party of Germany, which became the German Social Democratic Party (SDP) in 1890. So with organised unions in the labour market and the SDP in politics, by the last part of the nineteenth century German labour was well placed strategically to influence the political and economic agendas in the new German *Reich*. Thus when the unified *Deutsches Kaiserreich* was formed in 1871, Labour had not only a political party to promote workers' interests but also competing socialist and non-socialist trade unions (Blackbourn and Eley 1984). These historical circumstances, according to Kronstein (1952), show collective bargaining to have a long tradition in Germany, interrupted only by National Socialism from 1933 till 1945. He also demonstrates that German employers bargained collectively on a regional basis with organised labour, preferring to negotiate with closed craft unions of workers having similar skills and occupations, rather than open general unions.

Weiss and Schmidt (2008) highlight three fundamental developments in German labour law during the Weimar Republic (1919–1933), which are crucially important in the evolution of German employment relations and labour law. These are the Works Council Act 1920, creation of labour courts in 1926 and enactment of unemployment insurance and a placement service in 1927. Influenced by a politically and industrially active labour movement, the Weimar Republic guaranteed freedom of association in Article 159 of its Constitution. This was complemented by legislation introducing equal employee representation on various economic and political bodies under Article 165 (Berghahn and Karsten 1987). Thus a nascent concept of industrial democracy supported by the law was emerging in Germany, with the aim of giving workers a greater say in organisational decision-making. This only collapsed in the wake of the global economic crisis of 1929 and the rise of Nazism at this time.

In early nineteenth-century Britain, in contrast, labour law was primarily concerned with the individual relationship between employer and employee, underpinned by the law of master and servant, which continued effectively until the outbreak of the Second World War. The next phase in English labour law was a result of the dramatic changes that took place in employment relations between employers, unions and the state during the War. With collectivism slowly superseding individualism in the employment relationship, the law relating to trade unions, collective bargaining and industrial action now became important, being commonly described by Wedderburn (1986) and others as 'industrial law'. Prior to this, and well into the 1960s, English labour law had mainly created a set of legal rules dealing with termination of the employment relationship, founded on contract law. The practical consequence of this was that individual labour law in England developed in typical common law fashion, through specific cases coming to court. This usually happened when a dismissal had taken place but it was very difficult for employees to win such cases at this time (Kahn-Freund 1979).

In contemporary France, labour law now focuses on the status of employees in the employment relationship. This largely supplants contract, with mandatory legal rules replacing contractual arrangements. In French labour law, administrative regulation and adjudication have important functions (Dadomo and Farran 1996). French labour law also includes matters not connected directly with the employer–employee relationship such as social security legislation, administrative regulations, family allowances and old-age pensions (Dutton 2002, Smith 2003). Further, collective bargaining in France takes place at different levels. This involves a hierarchical legal structure, where national agreements constitute an industrial code, supplemented by regional agreements and local agreements. The national Labour Code enumerates a list of different collective agreements arranged by hierarchy: national agreements, local agreements, agreements limited to single or several enterprises, and agreements involving one of several workshops. According to de Cruz (2007: 486), French labour law 'has steadily become more systematised' and has 'been increasingly subjected to specialised interpretation by doctrinal writers'. It has thus acquired 'a unique substantive content, approach and methodology, which merits specialist treatment'.

Following re-unification of West and East Germany in 1990, contemporary German labour law has a number of distinctive features. First, a multiplicity of statutes exists, covering individual employment law, collective bargaining law and business constitution law. Second, as in France, German labour law operates at different hierarchical levels within a pyramidal structure. It is underpinned by the contract of employment which can be modified by collective bargaining but must comply with statutory law. Labour laws also operate in order of priority: binding statutory laws and regulations; collective agreements; factory agreements; internal collective agreements; and the individual contract. Third, there are specialist courts dealing with labour law cases in labour courts, labour appeal courts and the Federal Labour Court. Fourth, unions are organised by industry, not by occupation. Fifth, the law defines whether strikes are lawful or not, where the cardinal rule is that strikes can only be called and conducted by trade unions. Sixth, the law regulates the works council system. This enables all employees whether union members or not to participate in decision-making at plant level on economic, social and personal matters (Lingemann *et al.* 2012). Modern Germany, in short, has a highly regulated system of employment relations based on established civil law legal principles.

In the United Kingdom, the early development of English labour law was based on contract and this remains a feature of the present system. Even now, it is the individual contract of employment and its termination that are its focus, not collective bargaining. Thus the basis of English labour law is the case-derived law of contract. This is despite legislation since the 1970s that has significantly influenced the law of dismissal, non-discrimination in employment, and the whole field of labour market regulation. Basically, English labour law is now divided into contract-based rights, statutory employment protection and collective labour law (Deakin and Morris 2012). But, as Wedderburn (1995) points out, since the 1980s, successive UK governments have sought to disestablish collectivism in employment relations by weakening the trade union function and to de-regulate the individual employment relationship and labour market. Changes in the law therefore have been used to re-balance the employment relationship from employees to the advantage of employers.

THE EMPLOYMENT RELATIONSHIP

The employment relationship, in contrast to self-employment, is the legal term used in modern states to define the market relations agreed between an employer and an employee, where the employee works under a contract of employment for pay with that employer. An employment relationship exists in law wherever a worker performs certain work or job tasks for an employer in return for remuneration. Further, the employment relationship, whatever the legal regime, is a hierarchic one under the direction and control of the employer. It is the employer, through the agency of management, which has organisational power and discretionary authority over the individual worker, legitimised through either statute or case law. Managers assign job tasks to employees, monitor their performance and exert disciplinary sanctions on workers, if they demonstrate poor performance, disobey managerial orders or ignore corporate policies (Bronstein 2009).

The employment relationship continues to be the predominant means of arranging work around the world today, despite the developments currently taking place in the global labour market (Marsden 1999). These include changing patterns of employment, work becoming more complex, the range of work configurations growing, and the modernising of the occupational structure in response to technological and market factors. As a result, increasing numbers of workers have an employment status which is uncertain or not definitive. These include atypical workers, agency workers, workers with undeclared work, casual work, and work in the informal economy. Compared with employment in western post-war social democratic states, where employment status was generally unambiguous, secure and associated with direct, full-time, unionised employment, employment today is often less clear-cut, less certain and less unionised.

The subordination of labour

The concept of the 'subordination' of labour within the employment contract is central to understanding the employer–employee nexus. Indeed, subordination is explicit in both civil law and common law but more explicit in the former than the latter. However, subordination in common law systems draws upon different terminological distinctions from civil law, such as the tests or criteria used to determine employee status. These are the 'control', 'integration' and 'economic reality' tests. According to Deakin and Njoya (2008), civil law systems indicate that the modern contract of employment was a creation of the late nineteenth and early twentieth centuries. The implication is that the employment contract is associated with the rise of the integrated business enterprise and beginnings of the social or welfare state. The legal concept of the contract of employment, therefore, is a relatively new one in labour law in both civil and common law regimes. The term *contrat du travail*, for example, became common in France during the 1880s, underpinned by the argument of large employers that the duty of obedience should be required by all those hired as workers. Its adoption was promoted by commissions of jurists charged with developing a legal framework for collective bargaining and legal protections for workers. For Deakin and Njoya (2008: 290), the core of the relationship was the notion of subordination. Within this framework, 'the open-ended duty of obedience was traded off in return for the acceptance and absorption by the enterprise of a range of social risks' (Cottereau 2000, Petit and Sauze 2006).

In Germany too, a similar legal process took place, where emerging forms of wage labour in the legal codes of post-revolutionary, early nineteenth-century Europe were grafted onto the Roman law concept of *locatio conductio*. 'Location condition' is any consensual or consenting contract, by which a person becomes bound to deliver to another the use of a thing for a certain period of time or to do work for a person at a certain price. In adapting the *locatio* model to legal codes, jurists began grouping labour contracts with other types of contracts which were based on mutual exchanges between the parties. Thus labour became a commodity linked to price through the employment contract. Although the notion of worker subordination was absent from civil law codes, practice was different. This was because the law acknowledged the power of the employer to give orders and retain the worker in employment without a testimonial, until the work contracted for was completed. In Germany, this process culminated in the German Civil Code 1896. This led to the modern employment relationship becoming incorporated in the legislation of the Weimar Republic, following the legal recognition of collective bargaining and social legislation within the Constitution at this time.

In the common law states of Britain and the United States, legal events took different pathways. In Britain, the manual labourers associated with the factory system of the industrial revolution were not employed under contract of employments, which is a relatively recent innovation in English and UK law, but under the Master and Servant Acts. This meant that until these laws were repealed in the 1870s, any breach of their contract of service by workers with masters was a criminal offence and thousands of workers were imprisoned every year until 1875 (Deakin and Wilkinson 2005, Wedderburn 1986). Further, the disciplinary power of British employers was the result of parliamentary action from the mid-eighteenth century to the early-nineteenth century, which aimed to promote the prerogatives of employers. In England, the legal form of the employment relationship during early industrialism was statutory and hierarchic, not common law and contractual. The command relationship and duty of open-ended obedience by the worker, as well as the far reaching disciplinary powers of the employer, only flowed into the common law long after the repeal of the Master and Servant Acts. Thus many old assumptions of unmediated employer control at work were still applied by the courts, even as they developed English common law rules of the employment relationship.

It was the persistence of the master and servant model in Britain, and the influence of 'less eligibility' in the transition from the poor law to social security, that delayed the advent of the modern contract of employment in the British state. The National Insurance Act 1946 marks a turning point, where the distinction was made between those employed under a 'contract of service', which later became interchangeable with the phrase 'contract of employment', and independent workers working under 'contracts for services' (Deakin and Njoya 2008). This distinction was carried over into the United Kingdom's early employment protection statutes in the 1960s and 1970s (Wedderburn 1986).

By the early twentieth-century in the United States, a general model of the employment relationship based on contract had emerged. Almost all states in the United States had adopted an 'employment-at-will' rule. This meant that the contract of employment could be terminated by either party at a moment's notice, and without reason. Where the American and British common law systems diverged in the last years of the nineteenth century was whether all employment relationships should be presumed to be at-will, unless stated to the contrary. In the United States, the extension of the at-will model was largely the result of a constitutional debate about the legitimacy of social legislation. No such presumption was developed in Britain, largely because there was no equivalent to the constitutional dimension in the United States (Goldberg 1996).

It is through the employment relationship that reciprocal rights and obligations are created between employer and worker (Jansen *et al.* 2011). In common law systems, for example, both employers and employees have implied duties or 'common law' duties to each other under the contract of employment, although these are generally superseded by statutory rules today. Those duties are summarised in Figure 8.3. Breach of such a duty by either party to the contract are deemed to be as much a breach of contract as a breach of an 'express' or written term of employment. Hence a breach can form the basis of disciplinary action by the employer or, in some circumstances, a claim for damages being made against an employee. Similarly, breach of contract or a claim for constructive dismissal (where an employee resigns because of an employer's behaviour) may be bought by an employee against an employer. Importantly, because implied duties are created by judges, and new ones are established by test cases, this field of English labour law is continuously developing through the courts (Deakin and Morris 2012).

As the social contexts of work and organisations change, so does the nature of the employment relationship. This means that national labour law constantly faces the challenges of adapting its conceptual and theoretical frameworks to these changes. The individual employment relationship, for

The common law duties of employees to employers
> To co-operate with the employer
>
> To obey reasonable and lawful instructions with the employer
>
> To exercise reasonable care and skills as an employee
>
> To act in good faith and fidelity in relation to the employer

The common law duties of employers to employees
> To provide a general duty of care for the employee
>
> To pay agreed wages to the employee
>
> To provide work to the employee
>
> Not to treat an employee in an arbitrary or vindictive manner
>
> To provide support to an employee such as proper training in duties
>
> To provide safe systems of work
>
> To inform employees of important decisions
>
> To indemnify the employee against any expenses incurred
>
> To take account of an employee's legitimate grievances
>
> To provide a suitable working environment for the employee
>
> To provide references to an employee
>
> Not to conduct a corrupt or dishonest business

Figure 8.3 Common law duties in the contract of employment

example, is shaped by both the private law of 'contract' and the public law of 'social protection'; the balance of which varies widely by country. But reliance on the notion of 'contract' raises difficulties in regulating the termination of employment. Also, under globalisation, there is the question of balancing the employer's need for flexibility, profitability and economic competitiveness with the employee's need for job security, which is an important factor in determining the scope of employment protection legislation.

It is dismissal of workers for an economic or a commercial reason that is one of the more contested areas of legal intervention in the employment relationship. Nonetheless, internationally the law generally upholds the right of managers to dismiss workers for business reasons. In the EU, the Acquired Rights Directive supports dismissal for economic, technical or organisational reasons; in the United Kingdom, the common law requires labour law to balance the interests of employers and employees, with regard to the individual dignity and worth of employees and the general economic interest (Johnson v Unisys Ltd [2003]); in the United States, economic dismissals are justifiable on the ground of business necessity; and the ILO (2007b) acknowledges that the operational requirements of the undertaking may justify termination of employment by the employer. Thus national differences in levels of job protection reflect variations in the economic, political, institutional and historical contexts of nation states.

The changing nature of employment relationships

As indicated above, an employment relationship provides the mechanism through which an employer and worker establish their respective legal rights and obligations in an enterprise. Determination of the existence of such a relationship is normally guided by the facts relating to the performance of work and remuneration of the worker. The general rules determining whether an employment relationship exists or not derive from either statutory provisions or case law. These legal rules include, first, there must be a hierarchic power relationship between the parties. This legal feature of the employment relationship corresponds to its socio-economic function of providing employers with the capacity for flexible working in the enterprise. Second, workers are expected to perform their working activities on a continuous, loyal and diligent basis. Third, the employer's disciplinary power provides an important means to invoke sanctions against any employee deviating from the orders and directives of management. This allows the employer to enforce the internal or works rules of the organisation on existing employees, without entering into a new employment relationship with someone else and having to bear the transaction costs of doing this (Finkin 2006). The employment relationship, in short, provides employers with great flexibility and managerial discretion in the workplace and the employee with paid work and legal rights in the enterprise.

In post-Fordist workplaces, however, firms look for even more flexible systems of production. Compared with the traditional Fordist model, the number of outsourced work activities has increased in recent decades (Davies and Freedland 2007). From a legal perspective, the hierarchic, co-ordinating power of management is at the centre of the economic relationship. Indeed, the regulatory protection of employees has normally focused on this hierarchic power and attempts to reduce it. These protections have provided means for reducing working hours, regulating overtime, limiting the employer's power of control, restricting job demotion, and promoting union organisation and collective bargaining. Also collectivism in employment relations reduces competition among workers to gain better terms and conditions of employment. It also reduces the hierarchic power of managers, because collectivism seeks to limit this power and extend the countervailing power of organised workers against the employer, when the parties bargain collectively. Similarly, legal regulation of the individual employment relationship provides for disciplinary procedures, arrangements for transferring workers, protections against 'unfair' dismissal, and some restrictions on flexible working (Mitchell and Arup 2006).

Under such regulatory regimes, however, employers see attempts at employment or job protection as limiting their power and reducing scope for flexibility in the workplace. Reductions in flexibility also involve organisational costs to the employer, which can offset any transaction costs incurred. Accordingly, when deciding whether to organise work *internally* or outsource it *externally*, firms take account of the trade-offs between organisational costs and transaction costs. Two other factors are important. First, the contract of employment is not the only device by which firms get flexibility through a hierarchic relationship. Second, there are different types of employment contract other than 'transactional' ones. These are 'relational' contracts; the main features of which are their incompleteness and extension in time. Thus given the difficulty employers and employees have taking all circumstances into account in the duration of an employment relationship, they can choose to leave parts of the terms and conditions of work unspecified and determine these *during* the period of the relationship. This is due to the bounded rationality of the parties and the prohibitive transaction costs involved (Williamson 1973). This allows for adapting the performance of the parties to contingent business conditions, thereby affording great flexibility in the contractual relationship.

Where legal policy seeks to determine if an employment relationship exists or not, statutory regulation provides, first, definitions of the employment contract including indicators of what it covers. Second, the law determines specific types of contractual arrangements in which workers are regarded either as employees or self-employed. Third, the burden of proof of employment for workers is eased. Fourth, incentives to disguise the employment relationship are removed. Thus statutory regulation of the employment relationship, other legal provisions facilitate the existence of an employment relationship and they prescribe the administrative and judicial mechanisms for monitoring compliance with these laws and enforcing them. For example, changes in employment relations and the organisation of the economy in Poland have proved conducive to the development of new forms of employment. The contract of employment remains the most widespread form of employment in Poland but other more flexible forms of employment also attract considerable interest. So in recent years, civil law contracts have been increasingly used, largely because of the lower level of obligations placed on employers (Wiewiórski Law Firm 2013).

In case law, the mutual rights and obligations of the parties traditionally provided a focus for defining the nature of the employment relationship. The fundamental term of an employment contract was performance of work done under the employer's supervision and control in exchange for wages – the so-called wage–work bargain. Case law indicators of subordination and control became the fundamental characteristics of the employment relationship (Freedland 1976). However, with market, technological and organisational changes arising out of globalisation and ICTs, many employers no longer supervise their specialist workers directly. Subordination and control indicators were supplemented by others indicators such as the business indicator and integration indicator. The first concerns whether the worker is in business on her or his own account; the second whether the worker performs her or his duties as an integral part of the business of the user-enterprise (Deakin and Wilkinson 2005).

Further developments in work organisation, increased division of labour, and growing diversity in employment contracts have produced other indicators of an employment relationship. The complexity involved is demonstrated by the 10 indicators used in the United Kingdom, as indicated in Figure 8.4. In practice, no single indicator is decisive; it is a combination of two or more of them which determines whether or not an employment relationship

---

- the extent to which the user or commissioning enterprise determines when and how work should be performed, including instructions on where and when to do the work
- the extent to which there is supervisory authority and control of the user-enterprise over the work performed, including disciplinary authority
- whether the work is performed on a regular, continuous basis and the worker does the same work normally performed by regular employees of the user-enterprise
- whether the work performed is contractually stipulated as an activity or as a result or final product
- the extent to which the work performed is integrated into the normal activities of the user-enterprise
- whether the user-enterprise pays the amounts due to the worker periodically according to pre-established criteria
- the extent to which the user-enterprise invests and provides tools, materials and machinery for workers to perform the work
- whether the worker undertakes any risk in the business or has expectations of profits associated with the delivery of her or his services, as distinct from a fixed commission
- who is responsible for paying tax and social security contributions; the user-enterprise or the worker
- whether the user-enterprise trains the worker to develop her or his job skills

Figure 8.4 Indicators of an employment relationship under English law
Source: Kingston Smith (2013).

exists. In practice, these indicators demonstrate a continuum of dependency, subordination and control. This means that the distinction between an 'employment relationship' and an 'independent contracting relationship' lies in facts, not in the law. Where a work relationship involves one or more third parties, or a 'triangular' relationship is established, identification of the employer is a crucial factor. A triangular relationship occurs when an employee of an enterprise is made available by the employer to another enterprise to perform certain work or provide certain services. An example is when a professional footballer is sent 'on loan' from one football club to another. In this case, judges determine whether it is the user-enterprise that exercises the requisite control and economic domination over the individual worker or the originating one that does; such decisions are normally grounded in labour law.

EMPLOYMENT PROTECTION LEGISLATION

When someone is dismissed from a job or made redundant, the result is loss of income, other benefits and unemployment for the worker. The worker has to find another job and, where social protection exists, society bears the costs associated with unemployment payments, re-training and assistance with job searches. Accordingly, many countries, such as member states of the OECD for example, have enacted employment protection laws governing the dismissal of workers and use of temporary or non-permanent contracts of employment. One justification for this legislation is balance. Workers are protected from arbitrary decisions by management, while firms are required to bear some of the socio-economic costs of labour turnover. Second, there are some positive benefits for firms too. They are encouraged to establish longer-term work relationships with their workers and build up firm-specific human capital resources within their workforce (Piore 1986, Belot *et al.* 2007). Some observers argue, however, that employment protection legislation also prevents firms responding speedily to rapid changes in technology, consumer demand and new market opportunities. Indeed, Bassanini *et al.* (2009) demonstrate that over-strict employment protection legislation results in reduced job flows, hinders productivity, holds back economic growth, and is detrimental to the employment of some groups of workers such as young people. Thus finding an acceptable balance of interests between protecting workers by law from changes to product market pressures and promoting the business prospects of firms, which have to allocate labour to its most productive economic use, is a difficult task for national policy-makers to achieve.

The scope of employment protection legislation

Employment protection legislation provides three main types of protection for workers: protection for permanent workers against individual dismissal; regulations covering temporary forms of employment; and specific legal requirements for collective dismissals. Figures 8.5 and 8.6 show the strictness (or severity) of employment protection legislation in 30 OECD countries and 10 emerging economies in 2008 (Venn 2009a).

Figure 8.5 demonstrates that OECD countries with the strictest employment protection laws are the civil law states of Turkey, Luxembourg, Mexico, Spain and Greece; the least strict countries are the liberal market economies of United States, Canada, United Kingdom, New Zealand, Australia and Ireland. In most cases, strict regulation of permanent contracts is accompanied by

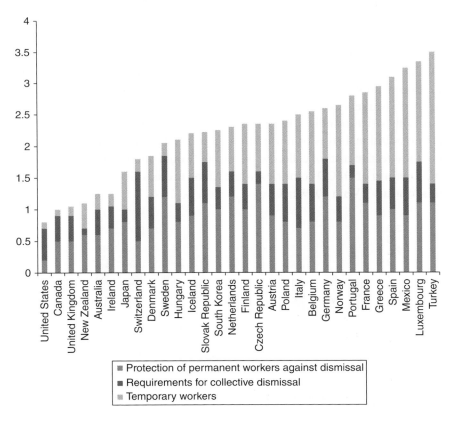

Figure 8.5 Strictness of employment protection legislation in OECD countries and
Norway 2008
Source: Venn (2009a).

strict regulation of temporary contracts but cross-country variations reflect differences in levels of regulation of temporary contracts. Based on this research, there are few or no restrictions on the use of temporary contracts in the Anglo-Saxon countries, whereas in Turkey and Mexico, temporary agency work is illegal and fixed-term contracts are only used in limited circumstances. Luxembourg, Spain, Greece and France also have strict rules covering temporary contracts of employment. These countries place limits too on the number of successive contracts of this type and their maximum duration. Notably, there is relative little cross-country variation in the level of additional regulation of collective dismissals (Boeri and Jimeno 2005).

Figure 8.6 shows the overall strictness of employment protection legislation varies widely across the 10 non-OECD emerging economies. Thus legislation in Indonesia, China, Slovenia and India is well in excess of the average in OECD countries. On the other hand, employment protection legislation in South Africa, Russia, Chile and Israel is relatively weak. However, despite these variations, and with the major exception of Brazil, the cost of individual dismissal in the emerging economies is almost universally higher than the OECD average. 'This is typically due to complicated or time-consuming notification requirements and regulations that make it difficult if not impossible to lay off workers for economic reasons.' Regulation of individual dismissal is especially strict in India, China and Indonesia. In India and Indonesia, there are no additional costs or notification requirements for collective dismissals, but the effective costs of collective dismissals 'would put both countries among the top third of OECD countries, while China exceeds all OECD countries on this measure' (Venn 2009a: 10).

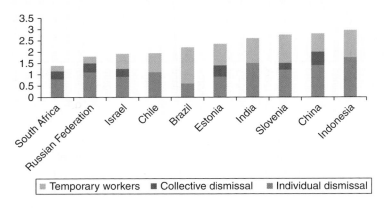

Figure 8.6 Strictness of employment protection legislation in 10 non-OECD countries 2008
Source: Venn (2009a).

Legislation is not the only source of employment protection rules. In many OECD countries, labour law establishes a minimum standard of legal protection but collective agreements or individual contracts sometimes include provisions that are more generous than those in legislation. The coverage of collective bargaining ranges from less than 20 per cent of the workforces in Japan, South Korea and the United States but is well over 80 per cent in Austria, Belgium, Finland, France, Slovenia and Sweden (see Chapter 11). It is countries with de-centralised bargaining that are more likely to have more generous employment protection provisions incorporated in collective agreement than those provided in legislation. These enhanced conditions are normally determined in negotiations between firms and unions in return for productivity improvements from the workforce (Lawrence and Ishikawa 2005).

Exemptions from legal coverage

Employment protection legislation commonly excludes some groups of workers from its scope. In many countries, excluded categories of workers include the self-employed, diplomats, domestic staff, entertainers, seafarers, those working in family businesses, political office-holders, sportspersons, the police and civil servants. These categories of workers are typically subject to different legal rules relating to selection and dismissal from those of the general workforce. In other countries, there are legal exemptions or alternative regulations covering particular sectors or industries. For example, construction work is exempt from most legislative provisions on employment protection in some Canadian provinces, while most agricultural workers are exempt in Greece, Turkey and the United States (Statistics Canada 2005, Haltiwanger *et al.* 2008, Blanpain 2008). Exemptions are also made for some groups of workers or firms to promote employment growth (Garibaldi *et al.* 2003). In most cases, however, the workers or groups covered, although exempt from employment protection legislation, remain covered by anti-discrimination legislation preventing dismissal on the grounds of gender, age, ethnicity, disability or union membership.

One category of exemption is small firms. Most commonly, small firms are exempt from additional notification or procedural requirements when carrying out collective dismissals. In addition, several countries reduce or remove severance payments, periods of notice or unfair dismissal provisions for small firms. In this context, dismissal is unfair if it is either without good reason or contrary to a country's national legislation. Thus blanket exemptions from dismissal apply to firms with less than five employees in South Korea, 10 or less in Germany, and 30 or less in Turkey. The scope of small firm exemptions is much greater than for other exemptions in most OECD countries where the data are available. These range from around 20 per cent of employees in South Korea to over 50 per cent in Australia, Spain, Italy and Turkey (Burgert 2005, Cho and Lee 2007, Australian Bureau of Statistics 2008). But legal protections against discriminatory dismissals continue to apply to these exempted categories.

The rationale for exempting small firms from some aspects of employment protection legislation is that regulation is likely to impose higher relative costs on them than larger firms. Further, small firms are less likely to have specialist HR departments to deal effectively with sometimes complex legislation. Small firms also have less scope for the internal re-deployment of workers than larger firms. However, evidence from firm-level surveys suggests that small firms, certainly in OECD countries, are actually less likely than larger firms to report employment protection legislation as being an obstacle to running a business, even after controlling for the age of the firm and the strictness of employment protection rules (Pierre and Scarpetta 2004, 2006). Part of this is explained by exemptions. It is reported in countries with small firm exemptions from employment protection legislation that differences in perception on the impact of this legislation between small and larger firms are much smaller than expected (Venn 2009b). And, regardless whether they are officially exempted from regulations, small firms are able to evade detection more easily than larger ones. They are also less likely to be subject to labour inspection or may simply be unaware of the legal regulations affecting them.

Disadvantaged groups of workers

A second category of workers exempt from employment protection legislations is disadvantaged groups. All OECD countries have legislation preventing dismissal of workers on grounds of discrimination, such as gender, age, ethnicity, disability or union membership (OECD 2008b). In some countries, however, exemptions to employment protection legislation, other than discriminatory dismissal, are made for particular groups of workers to encourage their employment. The most common type of exemption is for apprentices or workers undertaking training, as in Australia, Canada, Italy, Norway, Poland and Spain. Participants in active labour market programmes, disabled or older workers may also be exempt from regulations relating to dismissal or use of fixed-term employment contracts, although these typically affect less than 2 per cent of the workforce (Bassanini *et al.* 2009).

Policy-makers assume that targeting employment protection exemptions at groups with less attachment to the labour market is likely to improve their employment or job prospects. However, the impact of targeted exemptions is difficult to assess, because exemptions are commonly accompanied by other employment initiatives. These include wage, training or social contribution subsidies or discounts. But empirical evidence suggests that exemptions aimed at targeted groups have positive employment impacts for them, such as young people about to enter the labour market. Thus Kugler *et al.* (2002) conclude that a Spanish reform of the 1990s increased the recruitment of young workers, but had little impact on dismissal rates, while leading to a net increase in the probability of their being employed. In contrast, both recruitment and dismissal rates increased for older men but with no net change in their employment prospects; there was no impact in the case of women. In Italy, a later study by Berton *et al.* (2008) shows that Italian workers who enter the labour market on training or apprentice contracts are significantly more likely to move into regular, permanent contracts than those coming from non-work situations. After two years, 70 per cent of those who began working on a training contract and 29 per cent of apprentices had moved into open-ended employment contracts; the majority of them within the same firm.

A third category of exemptions are those on non-standard or atypical contracts of employment. Some sorts of employment, such as self-employment, casual, daily or seasonal contracts, are typically not covered by employment protection legislation. Where employment protection legislation on permanent contracts is very strict, employers try to find ways to circumvent it, by recruiting workers on atypical, non-standard contracts to avoid regulation. For example, temporary contracts are sometimes used to bypass the law, so that differences between the strictness of full-time and temporary contracts lead to labour market segmentation (Kahn 2007). Also self-employed workers are commonly not subject to employment protection legislation. This sometimes encourages employers to engage workers as self-employed contractors rather than as employees, purely to get around legislation and reduce their labour costs. But high taxes on wage income compared with capital income and high social security contributions also have similar impacts on employers and workers. Atypical workers may also miss out on other forms of protection such as minimum wages and social security benefits.

Pedersini (2002) reports that self-employed workers, getting most of their income from a single employer, varies from 4 per cent of self-employment in Greece, 5 per cent in Portugal, 12 per cent in Denmark, 14 per cent in Austria, 15 per cent in the Netherlands, and 28 per cent in Italy. Hála

(2007), in turn, estimates that between a quarter and a third of all self-employed workers in the Czech Republic could be falsely self-employed. However, there is little empirical evidence showing a positive relationship between the share of self-employment in national economies and the strictness of employment protection legislation. For example, Torrini (2005) finds few links between employment protection legislation and self-employment using pooled cross-sectional data for a sample of 25 OECD countries.

In addition to the self-employed, some disadvantaged workers are employed on casual, daily or seasonal contracts. Most of are covered only to a limited degree, or not at all, by employment protection legislation. Thus in Australia, one-in-four employees is reported as having a casual contract, a proportion that has remained relatively unchanged since the mid-1990s. The low cost of dismissal is one reason for this, even though casual employees generally receive a higher hourly rate than full-time employees to compensate them for lack of job protection and other entitlements. Use of casual contracts is highest in arts and recreational services (38 per cent), retail services (42 per cent) and accommodation and food services (65 per cent) (Australian Bureau of Statistics 2008). These are sectors where employers need flexibility to adjust to changes in customer demand.

Enforcing employment protection legislation

Where an employer fails to comply with employment protection legislation, the law is enforced by either courts or a pre-trial conflict-resolving process. For employers, this involves complex or time-consuming legal processes that can add significantly to the costs of recruiting workers and dismissing them. For employees, it can be difficult to pursue cases of unfair dismissal against employers, especially where the case is complicated or there is no union to represent them. So basically, it is in the interests of all parties for the process which enforces dismissal laws to be as quick, transparent and effective as possible. Many of the processes for enforcing unfair dismissal rules apply equally to disputes about other aspects of employment protection regulation, such as temporary contracts. These include workplace-based disputes procedures, mediation and specialist labour courts. The focus here is on unfair dismissal legislation, as this is one the key areas where interpretation of the law can lead to protracted legal proceedings to establish whether the dismissal was fair or not.

The problem of enforcement is most acute in low-income countries with ad hoc employment systems. In Brazil, for example, Almeida and Carneiro (2006) show that the distance of firms from the local Ministry of Labour office, where workplace inspectors are based, directly influences the likelihood of a firm being inspected. An increase in one hour from a firm to a local labour office reduces the likelihood of inspection by about 10 per cent. Further, firms in areas with lower enforcement capacity are more likely to employ informal workers. In geographic regions where Brazil's strict labour laws are enforced more robustly, the labour market is less dynamic and the productivity of firms can be impeded.

According to Gimpelson *et al.* (2008), a survey of judges, employment centres, employer associations and trade unions in Russia shows that labour law enforcement is seriously lacking. Almost 85 per cent of respondents considered that non-observance of labour law is a serious or very acute problem. The areas where labour law appears most frequently violated include recruitment and selection, determination and administration of employment contracts, dismissal and working time arrangements.

In India, factories with more than 100 employees are required to get permission from the Ministry of Labour before making dismissals. But evidence from the Ministry of Labour over many years indicates that very small numbers of firms and workers are actually involved in recorded dismissals annually. Moreover, job flows in Indian manufacturing are comparable to those in the United States, where labour regulation is very lax. While strict dismissal requirements appear to reduce job creation for full-time workers in large manufacturing companies, job destruction rates in large firms are relatively high (Dougherty 2008). This suggests there is widespread evasion of the requirement that large firms gain permission before making dismissals. Alternatively, the costly system for resolving disputes through the labour courts may discourage dismissed employees from seeking re-instatement or compensation from the employer. This leaves them with little recourse other than acceptance of the situation with unscrupulous employers.

In individual dismissals, employees make complaints that their dismissal either was unfair or, following the dismissal, that the employer did not follow the correct procedures in carrying it out. Many countries with sophisticated employment systems have pre-court disputes resolution procedures set out in legislation. Others have collective agreements designed to help the parties resolve disputes before an official complaint is made by an employee or group of employees against the employer. In several countries, such as Italy, New Zealand, Sweden and the United Kingdom, pre-court dispute resolution is an official prerequisite before a complaint is lodged with a court or tribunal. Indeed, the court or tribunal takes any pre-court negotiations into consideration when making a decision on unfair dismissal (Department of Labour 2008, European Presidents and Judges of Labour Courts 2005).

If the parties cannot resolve the dispute themselves, the employee can normally make a complaint of unfair dismissal to a court or tribunal. Just over a half of OECD countries have special courts or tribunals to hear labour disputes while in the remainder, disputes are held in civil courts. And in Italy, Poland and Portugal, there are special branches of the civil courts to hear first-instance labour disputes. Use of lay judges is also widespread in labour-related cases. Many courts and tribunals waive court costs such as administrative, witness and sitting fees for the parties in dispute. However, in around half of all OECD countries, the losing party pays the other's legal and court costs to discourage frivolous legal actions. Legal aid is commonly available in most countries, typically to those with little financial resources. Employers and unions sometimes provide legal advice and support to their members (Blanpain 2008).

In most OECD countries, the first stage of court or tribunal proceedings involves conciliation or mediation. This is to encourage the parties to resolve their dispute out of court. Where participation by the parties is nearly always mandatory, they generally opt for conciliation as in Australia, Germany, Hungary, Italy, New Zealand and Spain (European Presidents and Judges of Labour Courts 2005, Zack 2006). In some countries, an agreement reached in the conciliation stage of the legal process is legally binding or after verification by the court. The final decision of the court or tribunal can go to appeal in every country except Iceland and Sweden (ILO 2009). In Canada, grounds for appeal are very limited (Statistics Canada 2005). Most appeals are heard by higher courts; although some countries have higher-level labour courts for hearing appeals from lower-level ones, such as in the United Kingdom (Hammersley *et al.* 2007).

UNIONS, COLLECTIVE BARGAINING AND THE LAW

The role of collective labour law in the regulation of employment relations is a controversial, complex and sensitive one. If effective collective bargaining rests on achieving a balance of bargaining power between employers and unions, or the collective forces of management and organised labour, then the role of the law in supporting or resisting this process requires a delicate touch. As Kahn-Freund (1979) argues the part played by the law in the regulation of relations between employers and their organisations on the one hand and trade unions on the other is problematical everywhere. The central issue is that law is a technique for the regulation of social power within societies and understanding the law requires an examination of its close relationship to the social, economic and political contexts in which it is created and implemented, especially its dominant power relations (Harris 2007).

Kahn-Freund (1972: 4–5) also argues there is no society without a subordination of some of its members to others, 'without command and obedience, without rule makers and decision makers'. For him, the power to make policy and ensure that society's legal rules are obeyed is 'a social power'. For Kahn-Freund the principal purpose of collective labour law 'is to regulate, to support, and to restrain the power of management and the power of organised labour'. Marxists, such as Hyman (1975: 27), challenge this claimed neutrality of the law, by arguing that historically 'judges and legislators have regularly combined to impose the most rigorous restrictions on employee combination and union action'. Building on Kahn-Freund's analysis, contemporary labour lawyers claim that representation of workers through independent trade unions, which negotiated the terms and conditions of their members with employers or groups of employers, 'became the predominant model around the world around which the collective labor law of the twentieth century developed' (Deakin and Njoya 2008: 295). National systems of labour law differed, however, and they continue to do so, in the nature and 'extent of state encouragement for collective bargaining'. This varies widely cross-nationally as do 'the mechanisms for determining the representativeness of unions'.

Freedom of association and union recognition

There are five necessary conditions for effective collective bargaining to take place between employers and unions. First, the two parties must have a sufficient degree of organisation, especially on the part of workers, and a willingness to bargain with each other. Second, freedom of association is essential, so that workers as well as employers have the freedom to combine together and form their own independent organisations – trade unions and employers' associations – to protect and defend their employment interests in enterprises and workplaces. Third, there must be mutual recognition between the parties, since collective bargaining cannot take place, if employers are unwilling to recognise trade unions for this purpose. Fourth, the parties must negotiate in 'good faith', which requires employers and unions to make serious and sincere attempts to arrive at mutually agreeable settlements together. Fifth, the collective agreements arrived at must be adhered to and implemented by both employers and unions (Flanders 1970). However, if these five factors are necessary conditions for collective bargaining to take place, they are not sufficient. There must also be a supportive political and legal climate. Where government encourages and supports collective bargaining as a method of regulating relations between employers and unions, collective bargaining can be practised, as in North European social states. Where government restricts union organisation and activities, as in liberal market economies and most of the developing world, it cannot.

The debate at this point shifts to arguments about human rights. A major difference between open or democratic societies and closed non-democratic ones is that open societies incorporate certain fundamental human rights or civil liberties within them, which reflect the moral and civic aspirations of humankind. Emerging out of the ideas of the Enlightenment and post-revolutionary Europe at the beginning of the nineteenth century, these rights today include freedom of speech, freedom of thought, freedom of conscience and religion, freedom of personal assembly, and freedom from arbitrary arrest and seizure (Ales and Novitz 2010). Another is freedom of association. In a general sense, this is the claim by citizens of a state to assemble in public or private for the purpose of joining together in a common cause to achieve their collective objectives. In the context of employment relations, freedom of association is expressed in the ideas associated with freedom to organise in trade unions and employers' associations and bargain collectively over terms and conditions of employment. Organisations of workers cannot exist, for example, if workers are not free to join them, participate in them, work for them, or remain in them. Hence freedom of association is the foundation upon which the collective bargaining function is built.

In states with written constitutions, freedom of association often appears in the lists of fundamental rights upheld in some countries. These include the preamble to the French constitution of 1946, which was subsequently incorporated in the present constitution of 1958; article 9 of the basic law of the German Federal Republic; article 39 of the Italian constitution; and in the constitution of Brazil. Further, the constitutions of Austria, Belgium, the Netherlands and Switzerland guarantee the general freedom to form occupational and professional associations, without specifically referring to those operating in employment relations. As a basic human right, freedom of association is also encompassed in the declarations of some international bodies and covenants (Kiiver 2010). These include the UN's Universal Declaration of Human Rights 1946 (UN 2012), the International Covenant on Civil and Political Rights 1966 (UN 1966), article 11 of the European Convention for the Protection of Human Rights and Fundamental Freedoms 1950, as amended (Council of Europe 1950), and article 5 of the European Social Charter made under the auspices of the Council of Europe, adopted in 1961 (Council of Europe 1961), revised in 1996 (Ovey *et al.* 2010).

Of special importance are two ILO conventions created in 1948 and 1949. Convention 87 concerns freedom of association and protection of the right to organise; Convention 98 concerns application of the principles of the right to organise and bargain collectively. The ILO has built up an important organisation for the international protection of trade union freedoms (Jenks 1957). Its Committee on Freedom of Association investigates and reports on the many cases in which a complaint is made against any states infringing the principles embodied in these two Conventions. In one of the Director-General's reports on freedom of association, the ILO (2008: ix) reiterates the rights of workers not only to establish and join organisations of their choice to promote and defend their interests at work but also to negotiate collective agreements, without interference by employers and the state. For the ILO, 'The rights to organize and to bargain collectively are enabling rights that make it possible to promote democracy, sound labour market governance and decent conditions at work.' In this report, the ILO records those of its 181 member states which have ratified Conventions 87 and 98. Figure 8.7 shows by 2008 up to 35 states or about a quarter of them had not ratified either or both these Conventions. No European states are in this list but other countries with sophisticated employment systems, such as Canada, New Zealand, the United States, Malaysia and Singapore, are. The remainder of the countries listed are mainly in the Middle East and parts of Asia; these are developing or ad hoc employment systems, with some not ratifying either Convention, others only one of them.

Freedom of association is the floor upon which the ability of independent unions to enter into collective bargaining arrangements with managements is built. The next stage in this process is the act of trade union recognition by an employer. This is acceptance by an employer or group of employers of a trade union for the purposes of representing workers on matters dealing with their terms and conditions of employment. Two types of recognition are identified analytically. One is *procedural* recognition. This is acceptance by the employer that members of the union may have individual grievances handled on their behalf by a union representative. The other is *negotiating* recognition, which is further acceptance by the employer that, in addition to recognition for procedural purposes, the union may also negotiate collectively with the employer on terms and conditions of employment. The act of union recognition may be either on a *voluntary* basis, as is typically the cases in the United Kingdom and Ireland, or on *legal* basis as in the cases of United States, Canada and the United Kingdom (Strecker 2011).

It is impossible in practice to separate problems of freedom of association from those of union recognition, because unless employees join a union, there

Member states	Convention 87 on freedom of association and right to organise (ratified?)	Convention 98 on the right to organise and bargain collectively (ratified?)
Afghanistan	No	No
Bahrain	No	No
Brazil	No	*Yes*
Canada	*Yes*	No
China	No	No
Guinea-Bissau	No	*Yes*
India	No	No
Iran	No	No
Iraq	No	*Yes*
Jordan	No	*Yes*
Kenya	No	*Yes*
South Korea	No	No
Laos	No	No
Lebanon	No	*Yes*
Malaysia	No	*Yes*
Marshall Islands (new member)	No	No
Mexico	*Yes*	No
Morocco	No	*Yes*
Myanmar	*Yes*	No
Nepal	No	*Yes*
New Zealand	No	*Yes*
Oman	No	No
Qatar	No	No
Samoa	No	No
Saudi Arabia	No	No
Singapore	No	*Yes*
Solomon Islands	No	No
Somalia	No	No
Sudan	No	*Yes*
Thailand	No	No
Timor-Leste	No	No
United Arab Emirates	No	No
United States	No	No
Uzbekistan	No	*Yes*
Viet Nam	No	No

Figure 8.7 Nation states not ratifying both ILO Conventions 87 and 98, or one of them
Source: ILO (2008).

is no union for the employer to negotiate with. Further, where an employer is known to have an 'anti-union' stance, employees may be reluctant to join one for fear of being discriminated against by the firm's managers. Consequently, the union may fail to recruit enough members, thus justifying the employer's decision not to recognise it. Within a voluntary system of union recognition, any further debate about union recognition ends at this juncture. On the other side, where an employer recognises a union voluntarily, it is much easier for the union to persuade employees who are non-members that it is worthwhile to join. The attitudes of employers and senior managers to unions are thus a key factor in union recognition.

The longest standing systems of legally enforceable union recognition are found in North America. This is where an employer unwilling to recognise a union voluntarily is required to go through a complex legal process, through which union recognition rights and collective bargaining rights are determined. In the United States, the Wagner Act was passed in 1935. First, this gave employees the right to engage in concerted activities and prohibited employers from interfering with employees through 'unfair labor practices'. Second, the Act created procedures for employees to select and de-select union representation in their workplaces. Third, the law set up the National Labor Relations Board to enforce the law. Because of the consequences of the Wagner Act, the Taft-Hartley Act 1947 sought to redress the claimed imbalances of the legislation. This Act added 'union' unfair labor practices to the legislation, gave employees the explicit right to refrain from engaging in concerted activities, and assigned to states the legal right to pass so-called Right to Work laws. Following Wagner and Taft-Hartley, the Landrum-Griffin Act 1957 subsequently enacted how unions could treat their members. These included placing limitations on union authority to discipline members and creating legal rules on union finances and union dues. Collectively, these three Acts are known as the National Labor Relations Act (NLRA), which provides a legally supported system of union recognition in the United States (Strecker 2011).

Enactment of the NLRA in the United States prompted union pressure for similar legislation in Canada. Starting in 1948, the Canadian federal government used the NLRA as a model for labour legislation in airlines, railroads and telecommunications. Unlike in the United Sates where legislation is national, each province in Canada adopts its own laws covering industries that are not inter-provincial. All provinces except Quebec and Prince Edward Island use the NLRA model. The basic North American legal model of union recognition incorporates seven common legal features: employee choice; the majority decision of workers in the bargaining unit; de-centralised bargaining; exclusive union representation; acceptance of bargaining power and conflicts of interests between the players in the negotiation process; legally enforceable collective agreements; and administration of the law by a specialist agency (Lamare *et al.* 2009b). A statutory union recognition procedure was later introduced into the United Kingdom through the Employment Relations Act 1999, where absence of voluntary union recognition agreements was perceived to be a recurring issue in the post-industrial employment structure (Gall 2006).

Collective agreements

Collective agreements are the outcome of the process of collective bargaining between employers and trade unions: *substantive* agreements cover wages, terms, conditions, access to jobs and distribution of work among workers and *procedural* agreements cover relations between the bargaining partners and determine the substantive norms of employment relations. Collective bargaining can be either a voluntary (or 'free') process or regulated wholly or partially by law. In the cases of the United States and Canada, for example, as outlined above, collective bargaining is legally regulated and collective agreements are legally enforceable. Another example where collective bargaining is directly regulated by law is Slovenia. In this instance, a law on pay in the public sector came into force in July 2005. Several provisions of the law required implementation through collective agreements, thus having the effect of making collective agreements compulsory in the public sector (Eurofound 2013a).

In Europe, explicit legal rights to collective bargaining are found in the constitutions in a number of countries and member states of the EU. For example, a general definition of a collective agreement is specifically laid down in the laws of Belgium France, Germany, Luxembourg and the Netherlands (Perone and Vallebona 1984). This is not the case in Denmark, Ireland, Italy and the United Kingdom, where no general definition of a collective agreement exists. Otherwise rights of collective bargaining are said to derive from the broad right of association. Under article 28 of the Charter of Fundamental Rights of the European Union 2000 (European Communities 2000), workers, employers and their respective organisations have the right to negotiate and conclude collective agreements at appropriate levels. Further, where there are conflicts of interest with employers, workers and organisations of workers have the right to take collective action to defend their rights, including strike action. This right to collective bargaining stems from article 6 of the European Social Charter 1961 (Council of Europe 1961), as amended, and article 12 of the Community Charter of the Fundamental Social Rights of Workers 1989

(European Union 1989). The latter was signed by all members of the EU at the time, except the United Kingdom, which only did so in 1997. The European Social Charter established the major principles on which the European labour law model is based and it helped shape development of the European social model in the following decade. As Article 12 states: 'Employers or employers' organisations, on the one hand, and workers' organisations, on the other, shall have the right to negotiate and conclude collective agreements under the conditions laid down by national legislation and practice'.

Article 28 of the Charter of Fundamental Rights of the European Union 2000 (European Communities 2000) identifies the process of collective bargaining, collective agreements, the actors involved (workers, employers, and their organisations) and appropriate levels of bargaining. The right of collective bargaining involves all the steps taken from initiating negotiations to concluding the collective agreement, including actual negotiations. Article 6 of the European Social Charter 1961 (Council of Europe 1961, revised 1996) supports the 'right to bargain collectively'. This is 'with a view to the regulation of terms and conditions of employment by means of collective agreements'. All these rights are indicative of the minimum requirements expected of EU Member States. In providing a right to bargain collectively, the European Social Charter 1961 can influence various constitutional instruments and have an impact on national legal systems, without providing such rights at constitutional level. This means, whatever the constitutional position, collective bargaining in EU member states is affected by these legal rules. The phrase 'in accordance with Community law and national laws and practices' in Article 12 of the Community Charter of the Fundamental Social Rights of Workers 1989 leaves some scope for national rules, subject to review by the European Court of Justice.

In Romania, the practice of collective bargaining dates back to 1991 and was regulated by the Collective Agreement Act 13/1991, as amended by Act 130/1996. Apart from a few minor amendments, it remained in force until May 2011. For two decades, collective agreements could be made at four levels: company or unit; groups of companies or units; sector; and national level. The national collective agreement was very important, because it stipulated minimum rights and obligations applicable to all employees in Romania, irrespective of whether or not lower levels were covered by collective agreements. This national collective agreement was both unique and mandatory. It established the national minimum wage, length of working time and working conditions. In 2011, legislation abolished the national collective agreement as a reference point for collective bargaining at other levels. The outcome was that collective bargaining in Romania effectively came to a standstill, partly reflecting the difficulties that the social partners had in getting organised at sector level and obtaining representative status (Eurofound 2013b).

Sweden also provides an interesting case study on the role of the law in relation to collective bargaining, collective agreements and freedom of association. It was legislation in 1936, 1937 and 1940 on rights of association and collective bargaining that laid the foundation of its modern system of employment relations, covering wage earners, salaried workers and public servants. But no attempt was made in Sweden to develop a comprehensive set of legal principles guaranteeing the positive and negative rights to join trade unions. There is no protection in law against compulsion to organise, where the major defence is provided by the central Swedish Employers' Confederation. The main objective of this legislation is to promote collective bargaining, not freedom of association. The legal right of association is purely functional and auxiliary to the right to bargain collectively. While this necessitates some provision allowing workers to organise, the right to bargain collectively is given a higher priority than the right of association. As Johnston (1962: 137) comments, this 'approach emphasizes the willingness of the Swedish system to accept collectivization and to apportion to the collective contract a central place in the system of labour relations'.

This earlier legislation in Sweden is complemented by the Co-determination Act (*Medbestämmandelagen*, MBL, 1976). The MBL underpins the primacy of collectivism in Swedish employment relations and regulates employee consultation and participation in working life. The MBL is the main legislation for collective regulation in Sweden. It provides a framework law that must be implemented through collective agreements. It gives trade unions, as collective agents for their members, the right to elect their representatives, receive information or be consulted about management decisions (European Foundation for the Improvement of Living and Working Conditions 2013c).

In the case of Germany, the law also plays an important role supporting collective bargaining, as well as extending its coverage. Under the Collective Agreements Act 1969, collective agreements are binding on the bargaining parties. This includes members of unions and employers' associations, unless the latter have opted for membership without a binding commitment to collective agreements. Further, German legislation provides two mechanisms for extending collective agreements. First, Article 5 of the Collective Agreements Act 1969 stipulates that the ministries of labour at *Land* (regional) or national level can broaden the coverage of collective agreements by an 'order of extension'. To do this, unions and employer organisations must apply initially for such an extension. The ministry of labour and a committee consisting of trade union representatives and employer organisation representatives then vote on the extension. A collective agreement can only be extended if it is approved by a majority vote of the committee, where it is in the 'public interest' and the employers bound by the agreement employ a minimum of 50 per cent of the employees within the scope of the agreement. Second, the Federal Ministry of Labour and Social Affairs has a committee on collective agreements. This can declare collective agreements on minimum wages generally binding; the legislative basis for this is the Posted Workers Act (Weiss and Schmidt 2008).

The antithesis of the legal regulation of collective bargaining is 'free collective bargaining'; a position traditionally supported by some left-wing union leaders in the United Kingdom and right-wing union leaders in North America (Scargill and Kahn 1980, Sloane 1991). This is defined as collective bargaining that takes place between employers and independent 'free' trade unions, where the state's role is to abstain from intervening in the negotiation process; a concept generally described as 'legal abstention'. This model of trade unionism is based on the assumption that 'the essential characteristic of free trade unions' is that they alone 'are responsible to the workpeople themselves who comprise their membership and cannot be directed by any outside agency'. The theory underpinning legal abstention is no state, however benevolent, is able to perform the trade union function to defend working people. It is up to workpeople themselves to decide how best to further their employment interests. It is only where trade unions are not competent to perform their basic function that trade unionists 'welcome the state', and by derivation the law, to play 'a role in at least enforcing minimum standards'. Thus unions are only likely to seek state intervention where 'free collective bargaining is absent' (Trades Union Congress 1966: 69). Such a position is possibly sustainable in conditions of full employment in relatively closed economies with steady economic growth; it is generally unsustainable in conditions of flexible labour markets, even moderate levels of unemployment, slower growth, and aggressive employers seeking competitive advantage in global product markets.

The right to strike

The ILO has consistently supported respect for freedom of association as a fundamental social right, on the grounds that it is a necessary (but insufficient) condition for the promotion of collective bargaining. But the ILO did not traditionally set out explicit support for the right to strike in its conventions and recommendations. This could be regarded as an omission, since, with few exceptions, strikes were generally considered to be an unlawful criminal activity until late in the nineteenth century. Indeed, strikes were unlawful in many nation states until beyond the mid-twentieth century (Haimson and Tilly 2002). Even in some states today, strikes remain unlawful. Strikes are important economically, since they have economic implications for employers and national economies. They also have political implications for governments and the civil authorities, where they arise from social discontent.

However, absence of overt ILO standards on the right to strike for many years is not sufficient evidence to conclude that the ILO has typically opposed it. Nor is it the case that the ILO has abstained from providing some guidance and protective frameworks within which the right to strike might be exercised. It was only in the last decades of the twentieth century that the ILO began setting out some agreed guiding principles regarding strike action. This was done partly through the work carried out within its committees and partly by the evidence provided in its published reports. The major barrier to not doing so earlier had been the contrary opinions about the right to strike among the three interest groups represented within the Organisation: the employer, worker and government delegates. The two internal bodies most concerned with the right to strike issue were the Committee on Freedom of Association and the Committee of Experts on the Application of Conventions and Recommendations. Building on work that had evolved in the 1980s and 1990s, the ILO set out some governing principles on the issue.

By 1994, the ILO's Committee of Experts had concluded that 'restrictions of strikes and workplace occupations should be limited to cases where the action ceases to be peaceful' (ILO 1994: para 174). The Committee of Experts later reported that 48 of the ILO's 122 member states (39 per cent), while ratifying Convention 87 on freedom of association and the right to organise, had placed legal restrictions on the exercise of the right to strike by national legislation. Seven of these countries had sophisticated employment systems: Australia, Canada, Germany, Japan, Norway, Switzerland and the United Kingdom. The remaining 41 states were drawn from Africa, South America, the Middle-East, and other parts of Asia. They were mainly medium-size and small nation states with developing or ad hoc employment systems, The six most common restrictions on the right to strike in these countries were: the imposition of compulsory arbitration during a strike, often on the initiative of one party in dispute,; the imposition of penal sanctions for organising or participating in strikes; requiring an excessively large majority to support a legal strike; bans on strikes by public servants; the power to requisition workers during strikes; and banning strikes in essential services (Gernignon *et al.* 1998).

By the end of the twentieth century, events culminated in the ILO presenting a detailed review on its body of principles concerning the right to strike. These were the product of the series of studies undertaken by its Committee of Experts and the Committee on Freedom of Association. The principles provided account of the diversity of national labour law systems. They also sought to establish sufficient levels of protection for the exercise of the right to strike, while balancing the rights of those affected by strikes such as unions, employers, users of essential services and the state. The ILO's body of 13 principles on the right to strike are listed in Figure 8.8.

A cross-national study of the impact of national laws on right to strike in six EU states shows wide a wide variety of legal practices among them (Stewart and Bell 2009). The six countries examined were Belgium, France, Germany, Italy, the Netherlands and the United Kingdom. Only France and Italy guarantee the right to strike in their written constitutions, provided the act of striking does not impact on the freedoms of other parties affected by strikes. The right to strike is only supported as a fundamental right in France and Italy through the case-law of their highest courts. In France, this right is protected by both

---

1. The right to strike is a fundamental right for workers and their organisations
2. There is recognition of a general right to strike for workers in the private and public sectors, with only some exceptions such as essential services
3. The principles of freedom of association do not cover political strikes
4. A blanket ban on sympathy strikes could lead to abuse
5. A minimum safety service should be established in all cases of strike action
6. A minimum operational service may be established in the case of public utility strikes
7. There is an obligation to use strike ballots, give prior notice, engage in conciliation and have recourse to voluntary arbitration
8. Restrictions on picketing should be confined to cases where strike action ceases to be peaceful; picketing should not interfere with the freedom to work of non-strikers
9. Requisitioning of workers is only admissible in strikes involving essential services or acute national crises
10. Replacing striking workers seriously impairs the right to strike
11. Legal deductions of wages for those involved in strikes are admissible
12. Appropriate protections should be given to trade union officials and workers against dismissal for organising or participating in legitimate strikes
13. The protection of freedom of association does not cover abuses in the exercise of the right to strike such as criminal acts

Figure 8.8   The ILO's body of principles on the right to strike
Source: Gernignon *et al.* (1998).

the Constitution and the three highest courts in the land (Carta *et al.* 2009), whereas in Italy, the right to strike is an absolute individual right (Colli *et al.* 2009). The right to strike in relation to other fundamental freedoms and rights is broadly supported by the law in Belgium, France and Italy and, in practice, in the Netherlands. But this is not in the case in Germany or the United Kingdom. In Germany, there is no legislation governing industrial conflict and the right to strike is mainly regulated by the Federal Labour Court. Here only trade unions and employers' association can participate in lawful industrial action. In the United Kingdom, it is the common-law courts that determine the legitimacy of strikes (Barrett *et al.* 2009).

There is no legal definition of what constitutes a strike in Germany, France, Italy, the Netherlands and the United Kingdom, and, in Belgium, the term strike is only used when collective action involves labour issues (Abelshausen *et al.* 2009, Rook *et al.* 2009). The laws are more explicit, however, when they identify the types of industrial actions that are legal in each country. In Belgium, these include strikes, plant occupations and lock-outs; in France, economic strikes, solidarity strikes and sit-ins; in Germany, solidarity strikes in some cases; in Italy, 'articulate', sympathy, political and political-economic strikes; and in the Netherlands, there is no legal definition of strikes, since case-law determines what strike action is. In the United Kingdom, industrial action is normally unlawful as a tort (civil wrong) and the courts are especially hostile to solidarity action. Secondary action is not lawful but results in breaches of contract with employers not party to the dispute. In all six countries, named groups of workers are specifically excluded from taking strike action, such as some civil servants in civil law regimes, including the riot police, judges and those in essential services, and the armed services and the police in the United Kingdom. There is only a requirement in Belgium and Germany for the negotiating parties to uphold the 'social peace' or 'industrial peace' between them.

Finally, the role of the judiciary in the regulation of strike action varies widely in these countries. For example, there is a preference in Belgium for resolving industrial conflict by mediation or conciliation rather than by the courts. In France, the Labour Code organises the settlement of collective disputes, mainly through extra-judicial proceedings. In the Netherlands, the 'polder model' seeks to promote consensus and compromise in industrial disputes. But failing this, 'the judiciary has great influence and an important role to play as to the assessment of the legality of strikes' (Rook *et al.* 2009: 92). In the United Kingdom, the judiciary have no official role in managing of industrial conflict but can issue injunctions for workers and unions to refrain from taking industrial action.

CONCLUSION AND IMPLICATIONS

Modern labour law is the product of the industrial revolution of the late eighteenth and early nineteenth centuries in West Europe and North America. It has evolved in a variety of ways in these geographic areas since then and now well beyond them. As other countries industrialise and modernise, the political authorities within nation states attempt to legally regulate the employment relationship and employment relations, with a view either to getting some balance of power in the relationship between employers and workers or to subordinate the power of workers and their organisations to the state. In seeking a balanced approach, governments normally try to satisfy not only the employer's need for economic efficiency but also the employee's demands for employment protection, procedural justice within organisations and union recognition. Labour law thus continues to evolve in response to changes in the economic, political, social and technological environments that impact on nation states and firms around the world in an age of globalisation. Although there are some common features in different labour law regimes, each system is a product of its history, heritage, politics, institutions, culture and other distinctive social characteristics. Legal rights for employees within the employment relationship exist in many states but within well-defined legal parameters. In some countries, such as English-speaking liberal market economies, labour market de-regulation has increased and the employment protection rights of workers been weakened by successive governments during the past 30 years.

With collective bargaining, there are different means of administering collective agreements between civil law and common law regimes. As Schmidt and Neal (1984) argue, the major distinction arises when entering into a collective bargaining relationship. This is an action which in some countries represents the statement of a particular status quo between the bargaining parties. But in others, the collective agreement is viewed as a part of the continuing process of bargaining. In civil law systems, the collective bargaining relationship is maintained within a formalised system of administration, including recourse to the law. In common law systems, negotiations are ongoing at any time for the duration of the agreement. This may give rise to 'conflicts of rights' between the parties, which are expected not to force the issue, until the relevant procedure to avoid disputes has been exhausted. Further, despite differences in national labour law regimes, one common aspect of many systems is the consensus now existing on having a legally enforceable national minimum wage, based on an hourly wage rate. First introduced in France in 1950 and in 1999 in the United Kingdom, minimum wage legislation now operates in not only member states of the EU but also Australia, Canada, China, Japan, the United States and some developing economies (Cunningham 2007).

Comparative labour law research, especially studies carried out by the ILO (2008, 2013), recognises that regulation of the employment relationship remains one of the most challenging issues in labour market analysis and practice. Whether an employment relationship exists between the two parties is of crucial importance, not the least because most jurisdictions now link the legal protection of workers and their access to social security to this relationship. From a comparative perspective, the trend towards more flexible working arrangements, generated largely by globalisation and economic liberalism, has affected cross-national debate about the nature and extent of the employment relationship and how it is regulated.

Thus under globalisation and with increased labour market flexibility, there are growing numbers of workers whose employment status around the world is uncertain. Consequently, they are outside the scope of the legal protections normally associated with the employment relationship. These protections include agreed terms and conditions of employment, job security, decent work, health and safety, and issues such as non-discrimination in employment and social security systems. Further, developments associated with globalisation challenge the traditional legal categories of working relationships. These were based predominantly on a model of blue-collar employees working in stable jobs on assembly lines in large, bureaucratic and vertically integrated firms that recognised trade unions. Labour lawyers are aware that some new working practices do not fit easily into either employment status or self-employment status. These practices embody new forms of integration of work in business organisations, where the co-ordination exerted by firms on workers does not always match the hierarchic power structures developed by legal specialists and case law.

One reason given to explain different degrees of strictness in the application of national employment protection legislation is the origins of their legal regimes. The basic argument is that common law systems, with their emphasis on judicial precedent, are more market friendly, adapt quicker to changing economic conditions, and are less prone to inefficient rent-seeking activities than are civil law systems, with their detailed statutory codes. La Porta *et al.* (2000), for example, summarise the literature covering financial regulation, business registration, media ownership and labour markets. They find that common law countries have a lighter regulatory burden, with some positive economic outcomes. Hefeker and Neugart (2007) suggest, in turn, that legal origin might also explain the pace of regulatory reform. They argue that governments in common law states reform labour markets more during economic downturns than those in civil law states. They conclude that higher levels of uncertainty about judicial interpretation of the law in common law countries provide incentives for governments to undertake legislative reforms.

Critics argue, on the other hand, that legal origin is too simplistic an explanation for the strictness of employment protection legislation. It ignores regulatory convergence and fails to explain regulatory changes over time. Deakin *et al.* (2007) conclude that legal origin, which by definition is not time-bound, cannot explain changes in labour market regulation over time and thus has only a weak influence on levels of employment regulation. Using measures of labour regulation in five countries for the period 1970–2005, they indicate that many of the regulatory changes in the United Kingdom, France, Germany, the United States and India at this time were driven by political rather than legal factors.

Freedom of association, the right to bargain collectively and the right to strike have always been and remain key issues in national labour law. But nation states deal with these issues differently, depending on their national cultural traditions, institutions and the way in which the legal system and labour laws have developed historically. For unions to bargain effectively with employers, collective bargaining assumes freedom for workers to organise into independent trade unions and, where necessary, to participate in strikes and other forms of industrial action. 'Many modern systems of law positively establish rights to do these things', while others restrict them (Wedderburn 1986: 7). Hence any system of labour law has to define, operationalise and apply legal rules to a range of collective labour law issues. But each system responds to its particular and specific needs individually; collective bargaining

- the nature of the collective agreement
- legal regulation of collective agreements
- the formation of collective agreements
- the form and publication of collective agreements
- the contents of collective agreements
- restrictions imposed on collective agreements
- effects of collective agreements
- the application of collective agreements and co-ordination of bargaining levels
- the period of validity of a collective agreement
- the obligation to refrain from industrial action by unions and their member
- extending the effects of a collective agreement
- protection of workers' rights under collective agreements

Figure 8.9 Areas of common concern in national collective labour laws

does not lend itself to being harmonised and regulated by a uniform system of law. Areas of common concern in collective labour laws cross-nationally are generally agreed and are summarised in Figure 8.9. However, the practical worlds of employment relations and labour law are more complex. They are characterised by widely differing systems of legal regulation and national laws, as well as the ways in which labour laws are created and adjusted to changing circumstances.

9

EMPLOYER REGULATION

The purpose of this chapter is to review the changing faces of employer regulation in employment relationships on a comparative and theoretical basis, by building and expanding on some of the concepts and observations explored in Chapter 5. Developments in managing the employment relationship have come about in response to changes in forms of contemporary work and organisations, public policy and the global economy. Employer regulation is that part of the employment relationship managed by managers alone. Unilateral regulation is management's preferred method of managing the employment relationship around the world. But it is a stronger tradition in some countries than others, such as in liberal market Anglophone states and in nation states in Asia, compared with West Europe where co-ordinated market economies are generally common. However, in the relatively open societies of the developed world, employer regulation is rarely absolute; after all, and at a minimum, disaffected employees often have the choice to leave or quit overbearing, autocratic or unpleasant employers. In some cases, employees also have legal rights and trade unions to protect them in the workplace. Indeed, how employers behave towards their employees takes account of the constraints imposed on them by the regulatory framework of the employment relationship and public policy in all countries.

CONTINUITY AND CHANGE IN WORK AND ORGANISATIONS

In the contemporary world, work is paid for through employment or self-employment and is the means by which individuals earn a living to support themselves and their dependants. In pre-industrial societies, the relationship between work and basic necessities such as food, clothing and shelter is a direct one for individuals or small groups of humans, where individuals consume only what they produce. The evolution of societies through various forms of social production and property ownership progressively breaks down direct links between individual or small group productive effort and consumption. In advanced capitalist market economies, hard manual labour is less required, as machines, technology, and capital investment take over the more arduous tasks of production (Bell 1973, Castells 2010). The most common form of paid work in modern societies is employment, where an employer hires workers for set periods of working time, which involves an employment relationship. But paid employment has a wide variety of forms and management devises a range of strategies to use and control it (Salaman 1979, Seddon 2005).

Employment regulation

Typically, large, complex organisations with distinctive patterns of owner-ship, powerful super-structures, internal hierarchies, and advanced forms of technology, directed and controlled by management, are a major form of enterprise in the private and public sectors and parts of the third sector today. Organisations are co-ordinating systems where paid work is done. Those leading contemporary organisations attempt to integrate these systems and counteract any variances within them, including the internal and external socio-organisational links created by their members. Organisations adjust to changes in either their input or output requirements through the agency of management. The 'management function' is exercised in terms of planning, organising, co-ordinating, controlling and learning within the organisational superstructure by managers; the programmable 'transformation tasks' of daily working life are carried out by their internal workforces or external outsourced providers (Thompson and McHugh 2009).

It is recognised over the past 20–30 years that employment regula-tion has generally shifted from a predominantly institutional setting to an organisational one. This process is better described as one of *re-regulation* of the employment relationship rather than a deregulation, and it brings the roles of HR and the firm into closer public and intellectual scrutiny (Block *et al.* 2004). Thus the management of the employment relationship now involves key organisational players such as supervisors, HR managers and employees in the processes, rather than institutions such as trade unions, worker repre-sentatives and employers' associations. Within present regulatory frameworks, the basis of labour market regulation is to promote productivity and efficiency in the allocation and utilisation of labour resources to achieve desired lev-els of economic activity in nation states (Vaydia 2011). Evidence for this is provided by the employment relations reforms in many structured employment relations systems, which have strengthened individual employee rights and weakened their collective rights (Mitchell and Arup 2006). Consequently, the law now provides a strong reassertion of the right to manage, where employers are encouraged to hire labour within the framework of statutory measures limiting the ability of employees to obtain remedies for unlawful actions by employers. The fundamental aim of labour market regulation today is that many of the things that matter to managers and workers are left to employer and state regulation rather than to joint regulation as in the past (Ackers and Wilkinson 2008).

Work

In the world of work today, if some things have changed, 'much has stayed the same' (Bolton and Houlihan 2009: 3). Nevertheless, inequalities in access to well-paid quality work and safe working conditions persist globally. Thus Ghose and Majid (2008) claim that some three-quarters of the world's workers live in developing or transition economies, where there is large-scale underemployment and shortage of paid work. With the global labour force growing rapidly, especially in developing countries, and the volume of high-skill work rising, there is still a deficit in decent work in terms of pay, equity and security globally (ILO 2007).

A series of common themes of contemporary work is found within both advanced and transitional market economies. People repeatedly report feeling under increasing pressure in today's working environment. Work appears to have grown more stressful for all categories of employees from manual workers to senior managers, with employees working more intensely and clocking in more hours of work compared with the recent past (Green 2006, OECD 2007). In contrast, those focusing on the 'high road' of management respond by arguing that the development and utilisation of new skills and the increasing availability of 'good' or 'quality' work, which draw on high levels of technical skill and 'tacit knowledge' (or knowledge acquired by experience), counteract these developments (Zappavigna 2013). However, in an international economy, there is continual pressure on managements to push costs down an ever-lengthening global supply chain. Thus larger companies squeeze smaller organisations into agreeing lower-cost contractual terms, which is reflected in the pay, conditions and managing of workers. In the case of Apple iPhones, for example, these consist of parts produced in countries outside the United States, where each supplier adds value to the product in line with the significance of the part it produces. In public-sector organisations where market reforms have been introduced, similar conditions pertain (World Bank 2008, Lane 1997).

Noon and Blyton (2007: 382) contend that an abiding theme in the contemporary study of work is the extent to which there have been changes as well as continuities. 'Indeed there is now a growing body of empirical evidence to suggest that continuity is as an important a descriptor of contemporary work as is change.' Figure 9.1 summarises this debate. Also as Williams (2007: 287) concludes: 'there are multiple changes taking place that vary across space, sectors, occupations and populations'. The outcome is rather than convergence 'a divergence of trajectories is revealed'. Thus a picture of the future is painted 'that is much more variable, diverse and open than is usually considered in one-dimensional portraits'.

Five important arise from this analysis. First, recent developments in the structure of work have changed the composition of the workforce. These include size and location of workforces; distribution of employment between manufacturing and service sectors; proportions of male and female workers; those in full-time and part-time employment; and those who are employees or self-employed. Also unemployment, redundancy and an extension of non-permanent contracts have created a heightened sense of insecurity or precarious work among many workers (OECD 2011a). Second, there is a tension between a managerial rationality of 'time and work' and a counter-rationality of employees. The former is based on notions defining the working period

Continuity in work	Change in work
Persistence of the work ethic	New patterns of production and consumption
Routine boring jobs	Rise of the service sector
New types of low-skill, low-discretion jobs	Technological change and growth of some high-skill jobs
Management techniques for appropriating knowledge	Increasing importance of knowledge workers
Gendered division of labour	Feminisation of the labour force, with increased participation rate of women in the labour market
Undervaluing of social abilities as skill	Increase in emotional labour
Unfair treatment of women and minority groups	Recognition of institutional and less overt forms of discrimination
Work life issues concerned with campaigns for shorter working hours	Prominence of work-life issues, reflecting increased participation of women in the labour market

Figure 9.1 Continuity and change in work
Source: Noon and Blyton (2007).

and requiring workers to use the whole of that time in productive activity. The latter emphasises breaking up the monotony of work or reducing work pressures by occasional absences or lateness. The resulting tension between them is relevant for assessing recent efforts by management to impose controls over opportunities for employees to operate alternative time-schedules. It is also relevant for considering ways in which workers to resist their efforts to maintain their own counter-rationality to managerial expectations (Thompson 1967, Green and McIntosh 2001).

Third, 'time' is a critical component of work and organisation, so employee experience of work is heavily influenced by attitudes to working time. This means that arrangements and utilisation of time, as well as its duration, combine to shape employee experiences of time. Developments in time-consciousness and time-discipline are core issues. Working time remains a contested 'frontier of control' between managements and workers, where each player seeks ways to exert greater control and influence over it (Whipp *et al.* 2002). Fourth, the concept of the 'knowledge worker' is an important one, with two meanings. For writers such as Frenkel *et al.* (1999), it denotes work requiring theoretical knowledge, high creativity and intellectual skill. But for others, it denotes a specific type of expertise and professional influence (Newell *et al.* 2009). Whatever the form of 'knowledge work', managers seek to control 'knowledge creation' and 'knowledge capture'. Knowledge creation involves nurturing and developing new ideas, while knowledge capture is the process of transforming the tacit knowledge of individuals into explicit knowledge that can be disseminated throughout the organisation. In effect, this is a managerial strategy of expropriation, seeking to acquire and control knowledge from within the workforce to the benefit of organisations.

Fifth, 'emotional labour' is a relatively new concept (Fineman 2003). Its principal focus is where service employees are required, as part of their job descriptions, to display specific sets of emotions by verbal or non-verbal means to induce particular feelings and responses among those they serve. For Hochschild (2012), emotional labour is the management of feeling aimed at creating a publicly observable facial or body 'display'. In placing different emphases on the performer or recipient of emotional labour, writers underline the essentially interactive nature of this form of work. In essence, it is work performed by employees in direct contact with customers, patients, clients and others, where their responses have a direct bearing on the experiences of those doing this work. As Noon and Blyton (2007: 184) note: 'Emotional labour entails the performance of certain emotions in line with display rules established by management.' These display rules are monitored and backed by managerial sanctions or rewards in an attempt to gain compliance. In certain cases, emotional labour is associated with stress, emotional exhaustion and lower levels of general well-being. This is commonly associated with those who identify least with their job or the organisation for which they work. Those with restricted degrees of control how they perform their jobs often find emotional labour stressful and associate it with negative feelings, compared with those having higher levels of job autonomy (Wharton and Erickson 1995).

Motivation to work

Motivation to work by employees within the parameters of the wage–work bargain is a contested social and psychological terrain. It is an important concept to help understand how workers respond to the imperatives of work and how to retain employment with their employers. The early works of Mayo (1933) and Roethlisberger and Dickson (1939) in the United States, for example, were associated with the development of human relations theory in the Western Electric Company, especially the effects of supervisory style on work satisfaction and productivity. Later studies of relations at work by neo-human relations writers and theorists, again in the United States, such as Maslow (1954), McGregor (1960) and Herzberg *et al.* (1959), were concerned with the use of sophisticated behavioural science techniques by managers in the workplace. Thus Maslow (1954: 83), a 'need' theorist, whose work was at one time very influential, but has subsequently been largely discredited, puts forward a hierarchical pattern of motivation. His basic point is that humans have a hierarchy of needs, which, when one need is satisfied, ceases to motivate people until it is again unsatisfied. For him, 'basic human needs are organized into a hierarchy of relative prepotency'. In ascending order, these needs are: physiological; safety and security; belongingness and love; self-esteem; and self-actualisation or the need to become what any human being is capable of becoming.

By the mid-twentieth century, the meaning of work had changed, compared with these earlier studies. Early single-industry community studies in the United Kingdom, for example, demonstrated that the cash nexus of the employment relationship could be linked at that time, under specific historical circumstances, with orientations of collectivism and occupational identity. These permeated not only work but also community and social life to the extent that work often became a central life interest for workers (Goldthorpe *et al.* 1968a, 1968b and 1969). These classic studies of the interaction between workplace and household were carried out in the era of Fordist industrialism, characterised by large workplaces, male manual employment, high union density, extensive coverage of collective bargaining, and employment security.

The significance of these and other writers after the Second World War is they undertook their investigations in Western nation states in conditions of full employment and steady economic growth, where Keynesian demand management economic policies and union recognition were the norm. However, such theories contribute little to understanding the motivation to work in a period of re-regulated labour markets, national neo-liberal economic policies, and a competitive global economy. For workers in the early twenty-first century, fear of not having work, being underemployed or being made redundant are more pressing issues (Procoli 2004). The widespread decline of the standard employment relationship associated with well-paid, full-time, secure employment is well documented (Finkin 2006, van Wanrooy *et al.* 2013, Teicher *et al.* 2013).

Not surprisingly, theorising on motivation to work has moved on since these earlier studies, where it is now recognised that there are many ways of defining motivation, depending on how the human condition is perceived. Work motivation today is now commonly seen as the processes by which employee behaviour is energised, directed, and sustained in work settings – which are important to workers and managers alike. From this perspective, motivation to work is rooted in willingness to work and built on the assumption that it is partly personal drive that affects individual behaviour in employment. Moreover, many different factors and contrasting theories of work motivation have been discussed in the literature over the years. Some factors, such as payment, goal setting, work environment, leadership, and perceived risks, are *extrinsic* to individuals. But others relate to *intrinsic* motivation, where work interest, creativity, and perceived control are factors more related to internal individual psychological factors than outside ones (Vroom 1995, Steers and Porter 1991, Erez *et al.* 2001).

Today, economic value is found more in intangibles, such as new ideas, services and relationships, and less in tangibles like physical products, raw materials or land (Newell *et al.* 2009). Economic activity is also now more likely to be characterised by different organisational forms, more geographically dispersed and smaller workplaces, and a more feminised workforce. There is also 'a far wider range of contractual employment arrangements, flexibility of work organisation ... and the almost universal use of information technologies' (Baldry *et al.* 2007: 14). A main implication of recent studies is that worker autonomy in the workplace is becoming increasingly limited; it is bounded by complex managerial rules, stylised organisational processes, and forms of organisation aimed at increased management control.

Organisations

For more than 30 years, there has been a debate about how production systems have changed, the forms of organisation and management systems supporting them, and the implications for employment relations and human resources management within them. This debate has been dominated by two main sets of arguments: first, that production has shifted from a 'Fordist' to 'Post-Fordist' one and, second, that contemporary organisations have moved from bureaucratic to post-bureaucratic modes of operation (Bolton and Houlihan 2009). The main features of Fordism and Post-Fordism are summarised in Figure 9.2.

Fordism describes an epoch in time and form of production that dominated that epoch – the early and mid-years of the twentieth century. Fordism, so called because of its archetypal presence in the Ford Motor Company in the United States and later in Europe and elsewhere, consisted of a series of innovations in manufacturing that led to large-scale mass production of commodities, using highly specialised machinery, extensive division of labour, and assembly-line processes. Labour was highly fragmented, generally semi-skilled or unskilled, and employed in large factories. These factories produced long runs of standardised products at relatively low unit costs (Rubery *et al.* 2005). Fordism was associated with scientific management and the emergence of an expert managerial cadre, who claimed the right to manage within the workplace where there was a strong union presence (Rose 1988). Full-time male

Fordism	Post-Fordism
• Rational work systems • Mechanisation • Standardised products • Cost reduction	• Optimal productivity of all factor inputs • ICT applications • High-quality differentiated products • Continuous improvement
• Mass production • Centralised decision-making • Vertical integration and networks of subcontractors	• Niche production • Decentralised decision-making • Networks, partnerships and long-term subcontracting relationships
• Specialist division of labour • Minimal training for workforce • Hierarchical control • Adversarial employment relations, with strong unions	• Quality control, flexible working practices • Training to maximise competences • HRM strategy to develop employee loyalty • Employee competency and loyalty in exchange for stable employment

Figure 9.2 Main features of Fordist and Post-Fordist production systems

employment was the norm, with many families being dependent on a single earned income determined by collective bargaining, supported by a 'social wage' provided by the state in the forms of 'free' education, 'free' health care and family cash benefits distributed according to need. Fordism and mass production were linked to mass consumption.

Post-Fordist analyses argue, in contrast, that a qualitative shift has been taking place in the global economy over many years, where there is a transformation of mass production and mass consumption into a system of flexible specialisation and fragmented consumption. Murray (1989) argues that across industrial sectors there have been changes in product life and product innovation, with shorter flexible production runs and a wider range of products in niche markets. There are also claimed to be changes in stock control, such as 'just-in-time' management and in design and marketing in response to increasingly diverse patterns of consumer demand. Post-Fordist analyses also highlight the importance of re-skilling and multi-skilling in the labour force, less hierarchical work, and attempts to extend employee involvement and control over work, where unions are either absent or weakened. In Post-Fordist systems, flexible manufacturing provides speedy responses to market demand to ensure high-quality products in the market place (Beynon and Nicols 2006a, b).

The problem with this ideal typology is *all* forms of production are conflated into a dichotomy or dualism, namely Fordism and Post-Fordism. It then designates Fordism as the 'old' and Post-Fordism as the 'new' system. In more optimistic Post-Fordist accounts, the 'new' Post-Fordism is seen to have positive attributes, while the 'old' Fordist modes of production and consumption are deemed to have negative ones. But in practice, this shift from Fordism to Post-Fordism is not as clear-cut as sometimes intimated by its exponents. First, Fordism in the past was less universal than was commonly claimed. Second, Post-Fordism is less all-embracing in the present than is frequently argued. Third, what is being described are existing forms of production that are neatly divided into two typologies, one of which is privileged over the other. It seems more likely 'that many organisations include elements of both Fordist and Post-Fordist practices, and the boundaries between the two are much fuzzier than often suggested' (Williams 2007: 150).

The term 'Neo-Fordism' is sometimes used to describe an adaptive form of Fordism, which incorporates elements of both Fordist and Post-Fordist characteristics. Supporters of Neo-Fordism see it as a response by firms within capitalist market economies to the effects of overproduction, saturated domestic markets and squeezed profits. Although Neo-Fordist production systems might attempt to exploit new product and labour markets opportunities by a

Old bureaucratic forms of organisation	New post-bureaucratic forms of organisation
Stability	Dis-organisation
Rationality	Charisma, values
Planning	Spontaneity
Control	Empowerment
Command	Participation
Centralisation	Decentralisation
Hierarchy	Network
Formal	Informal/flexible
Large	Downsized/delayered

Figure 9.3   Ideal forms of bureaucratic and post-bureaucratic organisations
Source: Thompson and McHugh (2002).

process of renewal, the classical characteristics of Fordism remain in evidence and result in a reformed model of Fordism (Amin 1994).

The main features of bureaucratic and post-bureaucratic organisations are summarised in Figure 9.3, which contrasts and compares the features of 'old' bureaucratic organisations and 'new' post-bureaucratic ones. Bureaucratic organisations were large, formal, centralised and hierarchical, based on planning, rationality, control and command. Post-bureaucracies are seen as informal, decentralised, networked and based on spontaneity, empowerment and employee participation (Hardy and Clegg 1999). As Champy and Nohria (1996: 2) note: 'If the old model of organization was the large hierarchical firm, the model of organization that is considered characteristic of the New Competition is a network, of lateral and horizontal inter-linkages within and among firms'. Further, as indicated in Figure 9.4, bureaucratic organisations focus on direct control or compliance through close supervision, tight rules, prescribed procedures and centralised structures within a context of a low commitment, low trust and adversarial culture. Post-bureaucratic organisations emphasise indirect methods of control through loose rules, flexible procedures and de-centralised structures in a high-commitment, high-trust organisational culture of mutual interest. Bureaucracy is characterised by a hard industrial relations approach and post-bureaucracy by a soft HRM one. As Malone (2004: 5) states, the post-bureaucratic organisation is 'self-organizing, self-managed, empowered, emergent, democratic, participative, people-centred, swarming and peer-to-peer', where de-centralisation is 'the participation of people in making decisions that matter to them'.

Direct control approaches	Indirect control approaches
Close supervision	Empowerment and discretion in activities
Tight rules	Loose rules
Prescribed procedures	Flexible procedures
Centralised structures	Decentralised structures
Low commitment culture	High commitment culture
Low trust culture	High trust culture
Adversarial culture	Culture of mutual interest
Tight bureaucratic structure and culture	Loose bureaucratic structure and culture
Hard industrial relations approach	Soft HRM approach

Figure 9.4 Direct and indirect approaches to management control
Source: Watson (2003).

Continuity in organisations	Change in organisations
Taylorist/Fordist organisations remain	Emergence of post-Fordist organisations
Traditional methods of working and forms of control	New, flexible forms of work and patterns of working time
Traditional methods of control and reliance on employee consent	New management initiatives for work intensification
Desire for collective representation	Decline in trade union density
Traditional personnel administration	New forms of HRM

Figure 9.5 Continuity and change in organisations: A summary

Recent studies, however, reject the bureaucracy versus post-bureaucracy dichotomy, as others have the duality of Fordism and Post-Fordism. These observers suggest that the shift from bureaucratic management to post-bureaucratic management does not capture the complexity of the changes taking place in contemporary organisations (Grey 2009). Indeed, it has become commonplace for some observers to discuss the emergence of hybrid enterprises, indicating both continuity and change in organisations, as summarised in Figure 9.5. These hybrids may well have always existed and were not incorporated into these simplistic dichotomies discussed above (Parker 2002, Du Gay 2005).

MANAGING PSYCHOLOGICAL CONTRACTS

With more flexible employment, less employment security and decreased unionisation in workplaces in the last 30 years, increasing interest has been shown by managers in the concept of managing 'psychological contracts' between workers and employers when trying to understand worker behaviour in organisations in some Western countries. In the industrial relations paradigm, the managerial task was concerned primarily with managing employment contracts between the organisation and its employees, drawing typically upon legally enforceable collective agreements. With the weakening of collective bargaining and trade unionism, and creation of new types of more flexible working around the world, the managerial task is increasingly concerned with managing other forms of contract between employers and employees, in addition to the employment contract and, where it exists, the collective agreement between employer and union. A central concept is the 'psychological contract', as examined in depth by Rousseau (1995) in the United States, Guest and Conway (2005) and Cullinane and Dundon (2006) in Europe, and Witte *et al.* (2010) internationally.

The nature of psychological contracts

Where organisations are re-structured and organised labour is weak, the efficacy of employment contracts as a tool of managerial control and internal order is challenged, while worker influence on how the wage–work bargain is managed is also weakened. Employment contracts between employees and employers remain an essential element in this system of control but in 'new' enterprises, new forms of contracting between employees and employers have developed. All 'contracts' between employee and employer consist of promises, trust and acceptance between the players. Contracts are also based on some degree of mutuality between the parties, which provides the basis of flexibility within organisations given the indeterminacy of the contract of employment. Psychological contracts help shape relations at work, so that people 'who make and keep their commitments can anticipate and plan because their actions are more readily specified and predictable both to others as well as to themselves' (Rousseau 1985: 9).

For Guest and Conway (2005: 2), the psychological contract is 'the perceptions of the two parties, employee and employer, of what their mutual obligations are towards each other'. For these writers, attention focuses primarily on what 'obligations' the employer owes its employees. These may be inferred either from managerial behaviour or from what has happened in the past; they may also be inferred from statements made during recruitment or in performance appraisals. Some obligations are seen as 'promises'; others simply as 'expectations'. 'The common factor is that failure to meet employee expectations is seen as some kind of breach of

Inputs	Content	Outputs
Employee characteristics	Fairness	Employee behaviour
Organisation characteristics	⇨	⇨ Performance
HR practices	Trust	Delivery

Figure 9.6 A simplified model of the psychological contract
Source: Guest and Conway (2005).

faith.' Guest and Conway (2005: 1) claim that maintaining a positive psychological contract is essential to organisational performance and change can have a negative impact on individual perceptions of the psychological contract and damage performance. They also argue what constitutes a positive psychological contract changes as employees' expectations change. Their simplified model of the psychological contract is summarised in Figure 9.6.

Phases in psychological contracts

Rousseau argues that employment relations in modern organisations have been transformed in the course of three major historical phases: the 'emergent, bureaucratic and adhocratic' periods, with each phase giving rise to diverse forms of relations and employment contracts between employers and workers (Rousseau 1995: 93). Figure 9.7 identifies four main types of psychological contract between employees and employers, categorised by Rousseau in terms of their performance and duration: transactional, transitional, balanced and relational.

The emergent phase

In the emergent phase of employment relations, Rousseau views psychological contracts as *transactional*. Transactional psychological contracts are of limited duration, with well-specified terms of performance. She also identifies two other types of psychological contract: *transitional* and *balanced*. Transitional contracts result essentially from a breakdown in psychological contracts, reflecting absence of commitments by the employer for future employment, where there are little or no explicit performance demands or

Performance terms

	Specified	Not specified
Duration	Transactional	Transitional
Short term	• Low certainty in employment • Easy exit/high labour turnover • Low employee commitment • Freedom to enter new contracts	• Uncertainty in employment • High labour turnover • Instability
	Balanced	Relational
Long term	• High employee commitment • High identification with firm • Ongoing employee development • Mutual support • Dynamic	• High employee commitment • High affective commitment • High integration • Stability

Figure 9.7 Types of psychological contracts by performance and duration
Source: Rousseau (1995).

contingent incentives for employees. Balanced contracts deal with open-ended and relationship-oriented employment, with well-specified terms of performance subject to change over time. Each type of psychological contract is compatible with the others, when, for example, the organisation is able to specify different performance demands to different groups of workers as conditions of their employment.

In this phase, many industries change from being home-based crafts to factory systems (Chapman 1967, Robbins 2008). Efficiency results from the concentration of production in one or more workplaces, coupled with new technologies and increased investment opportunities for those providing financial capital to firms. In addition to the development of transactional psychological contracts between employers and employees, other features of the emergent era include centralised workplaces, functional distinctions between managers and subordinates, managerial control over working time and rate of production, and hierarchical controls over workers. This is done through enforcing regular hours of work and institutionalising supervisor–subordinate relations in the workplace.

The bureaucratic phase

The bureaucratic era results in the development of *relational* psychological contracts with employees including managers, and some identification of employees with the goals and values of the organisations employing them. This co-operation contributes to the achievement of the firm's or organisation's business objectives. On the one hand, employees have to make personal sacrifices to fulfil these objectives; on the other hand, employers are likely to invest in individuals to promote organisational commitment from them. Features of employment relations in the bureaucratic era include the development of internal labour markets (Hirsch 2004) and bureaucratic forms of organisation (Baron and Pfeffer 1988).

Internal labour markets have a number of implications. These include: employees enter organisations early-on in their careers; long-term retention of employees is facilitated; development of skills specific to the organisation is encouraged; employees are assimilated into the organisation's culture to promote efficiency; and organisations have seniority systems that provide delayed rewards for employee contributions to the business (Kanter 1996). Organisational hierarchies, in turn, facilitate managerial control over employee behaviour, as well as providing long-term career opportunities for workers. Moreover, slack resources in organisations are seen as a source of competitive advantage. As a result, workers are paid more than the market-clearing wage rate to foster labour retention, employee commitment is promoted, and hierarchical levels of organisation are expanded to reward and retain managers.

The adhocratic phase

In the adhocratic era of the contemporary world, employment relationships derive from shifts in the nature of work and forms of organisation, as outlined above. ICTs, globalisation, increased product market competition, and interdependence within and between organisations promote different types of enterprise and organisation. In the post-bureaucratic or 'adhocratic' era, psychological contracts are claimed to vary with the type of relationship between employees and employers, which may consist of both transactional and relational elements. Bureaucracies persist but adhocracies, 'post-bureaucracies' or 'networked' organisations emerge, where flexibility in terms of looser organisational structures and more individual autonomy in workplaces are major drivers of change.

The key features of contemporary employment relations identified by observers such as Handy (1984) and Hall (1993) include a proliferation of forms of psychological contract, with varying degrees of commitment between organisations and the people working in them. In some cases, boundary-less employment relationships are created, where work is performed in several organisations at the same time (Marchington *et al.* 2012). There is emphasis on continual skill development for workers and changed career structures, with less upward mobility but more alternative career-pathways. These include mid-career shifts, phased retirement, and options of 'high-involvement' or 'low-involvement' work roles. Most importantly, differentiated employment relations can emerge within the same firm. These consist of separate employment arrangements for *core* employees and *peripheral* employees, who may be outsourced workers. Core employees, who have long-term relationships with their employer, are essential to promote 'organisational memory' and continuity within organisations. Peripheral workers, in contrast, provide employment and cost flexibilities to the organisation, as product-market demand fluctuates or new work opportunities emerge. These workers have limited relationships with the organisation and insecure employment. Further, many adhocracies have union-free employment relations.

Mutuality and violations of psychological contracts

The concept of the psychological contract, then, is concerned with perceptions of both parties about the employment relationship. It focuses especially on their mutual obligations and expected behaviours towards each other in the workplace (Guest and Conway 2002). These obligations are commonly informal and imprecise. They may be inferred from what has happened in the past or from statements made by the employer. Some obligations are 'promises', others are 'expectations'. Guest and Conway (2002) argue for example, first, that the extent to which employers adopt appropriate HR practices influences the 'state' or balance of the psychological contract. Second, the contract is based on the employee's sense of 'fairness' and 'trust' and belief that the employer is honouring the 'deal' made between them. Third, where the psychological contract is positive, increased employee commitment and job satisfaction are likely to have positive effects on business performance. The kinds of promises or commitments employers and employees might typically make to each other, reflecting an 'employment proposition' between them, are indicated in Figure 9.8.

In contemporary workplaces, a series of factors influences employee and management behaviour. These include: the proportion of employees on part-time or flexible working arrangements; organisational downsizing and de-layering; market, technological and product changes; people or 'human resources' as sources of competitive advantage; and fluid or rigid organisational structures. In all cases, the effect of these changes on organisations is employees are increasingly recognised as key drivers of business performance. The ability of organisations to add-value to their businesses depends on good relations between the organisation and its front-line workers or its

The employer promises to	Employees promise to
Pay in line with performance	Work hard
Provide opportunities for learning and development	Develop skills and update new ones
Provide opportunities for promotion	Maintain high levels of attendance and punctuality
Give recognition for innovation	Suggest new ideas
Give feedback on job performance	Work extra hours when required
Provide interesting job tasks	Demonstrate loyalty to the employer
Have an attractive benefits package	Be honest
Demonstrate respectful treatment	Be courteous to clients and colleagues
Provide reasonable job security	Work flexibly
Provide a pleasant and safe working environment	Uphold corporate reputation

Figure 9.8 Employer and employee promises in the psychological contract

'human capital' (Boudreau and Ramstad 2007, Caplan 2011). Employers need to know what employees expect from their work and employees need to satisfy the employer's expectations about their contribution to organisational performance. From an employer's perspective, the psychological contract provides a framework for monitoring employee attitudes and their priorities in ways most likely to influence organisational performance. But from the employee's perspective, it can be seen as weakening collective voice and influence. The 'new deal' between employer and employee in the changing employment relationship, centred around flexibility and organisational change, is said to rest on an offer of fair wages and just treatment by the employer and opportunities for learning and development for employees (Wellin 2007).

Violation of psychological contracts is not uncommon. This results from a failure by either party to comply with the terms of the contract. Violated contracts promote mistrust, anger, attrition and change the way people behave in subsequent interactions together (Robinson and Rousseau 1994). Contract violation also results in reduced corporate loyalty by employees who, in turn, and in retaliation, withdraw their commitment to the organisation. With contract violation, at least one party has failed to keep its side of the psychological bargain (Hirsch 1987). Responses to such violations include: exit (voluntary termination of the relationship); actions to remedy the situation (filing a grievance or a disciplinary case); silence or non-response (waiting for things to improve); passive neglect (slowing down work or speeding it up); and active destruction (vandalism or theft). As Rousseau (1995: 140) concludes, contract violation erodes trust between the parties and undermines the symbiotic nature of the employment relationship. This yields lower employee contribution to the business (such as performance and attendance) and lower investments by employers in employees (such as retention and promotion). 'How people are treated following violation can repair the relationship or exacerbate its problems'.

CROSS-NATIONAL COMPARISONS IN HUMAN RESOURCES MANAGEMENT

The universalist model of HRM (HRM mark 2) is a special case rooted in North American HR practices and does not and cannot apply everywhere; it is a product of specific historical, institutional and cultural circumstances that are not valid universally. What happens in HR in the United States is normally atypical of the world as a whole and is more easily transferred to Anglophone countries and liberal market economies than to co-ordinated market economies or transitional economies. There are therefore varieties of management and human resources management practices around the world. The human resources management activities of managers deal with a range of policy and practical issues. These include the management of recruitment and selection, jobs and work activities, flexibility, performance, rewards and benefits, learning and development, employment relations and communications, but each within specific institutional and cultural contexts.

Regional clusters of human resources management

One method of analysing human resources management comparatively is by identifying possible regional or geographic clusters of HR, as in Figure 9.9. These clusters are predicated, first, on the assumption that there is no universal model of HR and no universal set of HR practices; a position supported by empirical evidence which is contextually specific (Brewster and Mayrhofer 2012). Second, regional clusters of HR practices are not completely homogeneous; nor wholly applied in every country within these geographic boundaries, and not practised in all organisations within each of them. But all are strongly influenced by the specific historical and spatial settings within which they have developed. These factors include the geography, languages, religions and ethnicities of each region. Thus in the English-speaking world, which is not strictly a region but an historical-political grouping of nation states, the development of HR practices has been strongly influenced by each country's

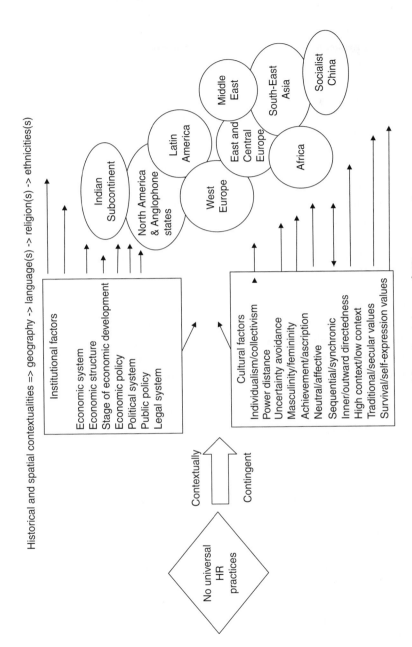

Historical and spatial contextualities => geography -> language(s) -> religion(s) -> ethnicities(s)

Institutional factors

Economic system
Economic structure
Stage of economic development
Economic policy
Political system
Public policy
Legal system

Cultural factors
Individualism/collectivism
Power distance
Uncertainty avoidance
Masculinity/femininity
Achievement/ascription
Neutral/affective
Sequential/synchronic
Inner/outward directedness
High context/low context
Traditional/secular values
Survival/self-expression values

Indian Subcontinent

North America & Anglophone states

Latin America

West Europe

East and Central Europe

Middle East

South-East Asia

Africa

Socialist China

Contextually

Contingent

No universal HR practices

Figure 9.9 Possible regional clusters of HR management

political and colonial histories, the spatial development, size and topography of these countries, their dominant language(s), the protestant religion, and white male ascendancies within them. In contrast to the English-speaking world, the pathways to human resources management practices in mainland West Europe are different. They are products of the region's interacting histories, its complex politico-spatial changes, its multiplicity of languages, the tensions between Catholicism and Protestantism (and Islam in Spain), and its multi-ethnic legacies between, say, Flemings and Walloons in modern Belgium and German speakers and Hungarian speakers in Central Europe (Davies 1996).

Third, each HR cluster is classified according to its socio-managerial heritage and their ideological antecedents. In addition to the North American and Anglophone cluster, clusters are found in the Indian subcontinent, West Europe, Latin America, Central and East Europe, the Middle East, Africa, South-East Asia, and Socialist China. The significant point is that within each regional grouping, particular forms of HR are practised arising from complex sets of institutional and cultural factors, as outlined in Figure 9.10. These factors impinge on each geographical region, resulting in preferred but distinctive HR solutions to specific problems and issues within them. In West Europe, for example, there is stronger legal regulation of HR and employment relationships than in Anglophone countries (Bamber *et al.* 2011). There are also overlapping HR practices among employers in the South-East Asia region and Socialist China, arising from their strong common cultural identities (Cooke 2005). Within the Indian subcontinent, in turn, the British imperial legacy provides a legal framework for the registration of trade unions under the Trade Unions Act 1926, which persists today (Hill 2009). In parts of Africa, the legacies of former French, Portuguese and German colonisers continue to affect HR practices and the legal systems within which businesses operate (Wood and Brewster 2007).

Fourth, as shown in Figure 9.10, the factors affecting HR policy and selected HR practices are specific to each regional cluster, with clear differences among them. What this analysis highlights is the different types of market capitalism in each cluster and their social origins, each with its implications for human resources management. For example, shareholder capitalism is dominant in Anglophone countries, stakeholder capitalism in West Europe, post-Communist capitalism in Central and East Europe, and market socialism in mainland China. Each type of capitalism results in different types of HR policies and HR practices within these geographic clusters. Legislation on the contract of employment exists everywhere, for example, but the specifics and details of this legislation vary by cluster and country (Casale 2011).

Regional clusters of HR	Some factors affecting HR policy in this cluster and selected HR practices
North America and Anglophone states (includes United States, Canada, United Kingdom, Ireland, Australia, New Zealand, with structured employment relations systems)	Individualist approach to HR, including performance-based rewards Strong right to manage linked with shareholder forms of capitalism Strong concern for diversity management Learning and development for human capital accumulation Weak trade unionism Growing importance of HR strategy to gain competitive advantage
West Europe (includes Anglo-Saxon, Romance, Germanic, Nordic versions, with structured employment relations systems)	Stakeholder forms of capitalism Important role of the state economically and socially Workers have human rights in the workplace Trade union power varies Importance of information and consultation within organisations Governance structures include worker representation systems HR function commonly administrative
Indian sub-continent (includes India, Pakistan, Bangladesh, Sri Lanka, Nepal, Bhutan, with developmental employment relations systems)	Influence of the British imperial legacy and different religious traditions Highly stratified societies and organisations, comprising hi-tech, commercial and informal sectors Wide variety of HR practices, especially where economic growth is strong as in India Range of informal, unstructured, indigenous work systems Relatively low status and underdeveloped role of the HR function Some recognition of HR's contribution to economic development
Latin America (includes Argentina, Brazil, Chile, Mexico, with developmental employment relations systems)	Importance of the individual in these societies Legacy of Catholicism in society, organisations and the workplace Enterprises as social institutions Organisations as constituencies of stakeholders Firms as providers of social benefits, as well as of employment and wages to their workers Importance of social inclusion to cover diverse Latin-American groups
East and Central Europe (includes post-Communist states and Russia, developmental or ad hoc employment relations systems)	Attitudinal and structural legacies of Communist period; also strong nationalist identities HR is conceptualised in different ways around this region Very weak trade unionism Flexible forms of employment not commonplace Reinforcement of the right to manage in post-Communist period Labour regulations still important in parts of this geographic region

Figure 9.10 Regional clusters of HRM and some factors affecting HR policy and HR practices

Sources: Scholz and Boehm (2008), Brewster (2007), Budhwar and Debrah (2001), Chen (1995), Cooke (2005), Dickmann *et al.* (2008), Domsch and Lidokhover (2006), Edwards and Rees (2011), Harzing *et al.* (2011), Gunnigle *et al.* (2011), Jackson (2004), Jackson and Tomioka (2004), Sharma and Khandekar (2006).

Regional clusters of HR	Some factors affecting HR policy in this cluster and selected HR practices
Africa (includes all parts of the continent, with *ad hoc* employment relations systems)	Wide variety of ethnic groups, with important informal networks of family and personal ties
	Influence of different colonial and historical legacies – British, French, German, Portuguese, Dutch
	Wide range of economic performance, with often low wages and poor working conditions
	Large informal economic sector, with strong communitarian cultures
	HR tends to be authoritarian, paternalist and 'personal' management
	South African exceptionalism, with strong trade unionism and pockets of good HR practice
Middle East (includes Turkey, Arabic kingdoms and autocracies, and Israel, with developmental or *ad hoc* employment relations systems)	Region of wars, conflict and authoritarian regimes, where Europe, Africa and Asia meet
	Importance of British, French and Ottoman imperial legacies
	Over-dependent on oil sector, with other sectors being underdeveloped
	influence of Arabic culture and Islamic values on management systems and HR principles (such as loyalty to family and to social networks)
	Wide variety of HR practices across the region but generally underdeveloped; trade unions weak
	Israeli exceptionalism, but political priorities override economic issues
South-East Asia (includes Japan, South Korea and Taiwan, with structured employment relations systems)	Embraced market capitalism in the second half of the twentieth century, with strong growth
	Important influence of Confucian and Buddhist values in these societies and organisations
	Preference for conflict avoidance in the enterprise
	Adopted systems of welfare-corporatism in organisations, promoting co-operation with workers
	Development of multi-pronged HR practices aimed at harmonious work relations
	Firms and workforces facing new economic challenges since the 1990s
Socialist China (includes Hong Kong, with developmental employment relations systems)	An economic superpower, adapting to rapid economic change and market reforms
	Traditional values of Confucianism, harmony and collectivism interacting with a new individualism
	Correlation between HR practices, ownership type and enterprise location
	No homogeneous model of HR in Chinese enterprises but a process of hybridisation
	Important role of the All-Chinese Confederation of Trade Unions, but no right to strike
	Economic reform and HR reforms a function of government interest in supporting new HR
	practices for both political purposes and the economic demands of business organisations

Figure 9.10 (Continued)

HR specialists and delivering HR

HR specialists can play an important role in contributing to HR strategy determination and delivery of HR in partnership with line managers. Some indication of the importance of HR professionals in managing and delivering the HR function, and the rising professional standing of HR specialists globally, are provided by the growth of independent international and national bodies representing HR professionals around the world. For example, the World Federation of People Management Associations (WFPMA) is the professional body, founded in 1976, which seeks to 'improve the quality and effectiveness of professional people management, and to demonstrate the importance of the HR role in all employing organisations, both public and private'. It claims to represent a membership of more than 600,000 HR professionals in over 90 national HR associations. As a federal organisation, the WFPMA is made up of five regional bodies: the African Human Resource Confederation (with 26 national organisations); the Asia-Pacific Federation of Human Resource Management (with 14 national organisations); the European Association for People Management (with 25 national organisations); the Inter-American Federation of People Management Associations (with 15 national organisations); and the North American Human Resource Management Association (with three national organisations). The most active regions within the World Federation are Asia-Pacific, Europe, Inter-America and North America (WFPMA 2013).

The structures, activities and memberships of national HR associations vary widely. Thus the Society of Human Resource Management in the United States is a long-established body with a large membership, as is the CIPD in the United Kingdom, whereas the professional bodies representing HR specialists in parts of Africa and Central and East Europe are generally newer, smaller and emergent organisations. In West Europe, Sweden has a well-resourced central organisation, Spain strong regional organisations, France's *L'Association Nationale des Directeurs des Ressources Humaines* is an elite body of senior HR practitioners, and Germany's *Deutche Gesellschaft fuer Personalfuehrung* represents over 2000 companies (Farndale and Brewster 2005). In Latin America, Brazil has the largest numbers of active HR professionals followed by Columbia, with much smaller membership bases in Argentina, Uraguay and Venezuela (American Federation of People Management Associations 2013).

Much of the literature in the universalist paradigm of HRM makes the case for HR departments being more strategic, with the aim of creating added-value and promoting organisational capability in enterprises (Beatty and Schneider 1997, Pfeffer 1994). Organisational capability means using the firm's internal processes, systems and management practices to meet customer needs by directing the skills and efforts of employees towards achieving the strategic goals of the organisation (Lake *et al.* 1997). This is commonly done by reducing the clerk of works roles of HR specialists, enabling HR departments to concentrate on their strategic partnership and HR leadership roles. More than 20 years ago in Sweden, for example, studies showed that there was a trend away from HR administrative roles to more strategic ones, thus providing space for HR professionals to take on more strategic activities. This was facilitated by routine HR work becoming more integrated into line or operational management (Doz *et al.* 1990). Decentralising HR processes and competencies helped promote this process in Sweden (Söderström 1997), OECD 2013). Further evidence suggests in Denmark, HR departments contribute to strategy formulation using opinion surveys, work environment surveys, and negotiations with top-level management committees (Brewster *et al.* 1994). In the United Kingdom, the Workplace Employee Relations Surveys show some HR departments are becoming more strategic (Sisson 2001, van Wanrooy *et al.* 2013).

Having senior HR specialists on company boards also enables HR to contribute to strategic decisions but this varies by country. About 50 per cent of German organisations had an HR specialist on their corporate boards in 2010, according to the Cranet Survey (Parry *et al.* 2011). But the legal requirement for employees to be represented on top-tier supervisory boards in larger German companies enables employees to influence HR strategy, even where managerial leadership is weak. In France and Sweden, the same survey shows about 90 per cent of organisations had HR professionals on company boards, whereas in the United Kingdom, the United States and Japan the proportion was nearer 60 per cent. In the United Kingdom, the proportion had fallen to around 56 per cent, according to WERS 2011 (van Wanrooy *et al.* 2013). Where there was no specialist presence at this level, responsibility for HR rested frequently with managing directors or administrative managers.

The Cranet studies (2005) show involvement of the HR function in corporate strategy varies by country. These studies indicate that between a half and two-thirds of senior HR specialists are involved in the development of corporate strategy in their organisations from the outset (Parry *et al.* 2013). The German data also show that HR issues are taken into account from the outset in the development of corporate strategy, even where there is no board-level HR representation, because board members consult with non-board HR specialists at an early stage of strategy formulation. In the United Kingdom,

HR influence on corporate strategy sometimes takes place from the outset, mirroring board-level involvement. In Sweden, however, the considerable numbers of HR specialists who sit on company boards are not involved in developing corporate strategy until a later stage.

The presence or not of trade unions in workplaces affects the nature, effectiveness and size of HR departments. Thus internationally, in countries where works councils exist and trade unions are strong, there is greater strategic integration of HR than in other countries. Organisations with works councils and well-organised unions, such as in Austria and Germany, are more likely to have HR representation on boards than companies without them. As a result, these boards become involved in strategic decision-making and develop formalised HR strategies. The Netherlands and France, with strong protective labour laws and generous welfare states, also promote the strategic integration of the HR department, whereas in the United States limited social regulation inhibits it (Parry *et al.* 2013). If employees have fewer resources to draw upon 'organisational commitment to the strategic integration of the specialist people management function is less than where employees are well-protected and independently represented' (Brewster *et al.* 2011: 283). Stronger unions are also generally associated with relatively smaller HR departments, although generally size of the function has changed very little over the past two decades (Brewster and Mayrhofer 2012).

Line managers and human resources management

The conventional wisdom is allocation of some HR responsibilities to line managers, and taking HR work away from centralised HR departments, plays a key part in promoting good HR practices. As Guest (1987: 51) writes: 'If HRM is to be taken seriously, personnel managers [*sic*] must give it away.' However, there are many reasons why delegation of HR responsibilities to line managers does not work. For example, line managers sometimes do not want to take ownership of HR in their areas of responsibility. Alternatively, they give HR low priority because they are too busy, do not understand the laws relating to HR and employment relations, or lack professional knowledge in the field. Further, they are often not trained to undertake HR duties and not particularly interested in HR anyway. And devolving HR to line managers is often a means of cost-cutting. However, devolved responsibility for HR also needs to be co-ordinated at some level, thus retaining a role for HR specialists (Paauwe 2004).

Many senior managers want HR professionals to adopt a strategic role but many line managers simply want HR departments to deal with the routine administration and record-keeping associated with managing the employ-ment contract. In other words, the administrative roles of human resources management still need to be done. The balance of responsibilities for HR between specialists and line managers also varies cross-nationally and is con-tinually shifting (Gennard and Kelly 1997). The ultimate challenge for HR specialists and line managers is how to integrate the specialist HR department and line managers to promote organisational performance.

There is plenty of case-study evidence indicating that devolution of HR activities is taking place internationally (Brewster and Larsen 1992, Mayrhofer and Brewster 2006, Brewster and Mayrhofer 2012). Data from early studies show activities most likely to be devolved to line managers are recruitment and selection, increases or decreases in the size of the workforce, and health and safety in the workplace. Activities less likely to be devolved are learning and development and employment relations. More recent data show con-trary trends, indicating that what is fashionable in HR at one time is not at others (Brewster and Mayrhofer 2012). However, the effects of country differences are clear within West Europe, for example, where Denmark and Switzerland consistently assign most responsibility for HR activities to line managers. Countries such as the United Kingdom, Ireland, France and Italy, on the other hand, commonly retain 'most responsibility for the [specialist] HRM function' (Brewster *et al.* 2011: 275). Thus within each country, there are variations among organisations but country of origin is an important determi-nant whether HR is devolved or not; managers can choose which HR activities to devolve and how to do this.

Sourcing and electronic HR

In addition to delivering HR through traditional in-house methods, some HR activities are located and delivered in different ways. Chakrabarty (2006) cat-egorises four 'core strategies' for delivering HR: *in-country in-sourcing* where the activities are performed 'in-house' by one of the organisation's own sub-sidiaries or a service centre; *global in-sourcing* which allows some geographical flexibility over the location of the activity; *outsourcing* where a third-party provider is used to carry out the activity, but still within the same country; and *off-shoring* where a broad range of tasks is executed by a firm in another coun-try. This results in transfer of responsibility for HR operations and provision guaranteeing services by the vendor for a period of time.

Many organisations remain hostile to this notion and there is a country-effect, with some outsourcers finding it difficult to make profits in certain countries. Thus Sparrow and Braun (2008) draw attention to the persistence of wide international differences in the pursuit of HR outsourcing. The practice of outsourcing is more common among US firms than those in West Europe, which mainly prefer in-sourcing. European HR directors see in-sourced shared services as a stepping stone to future outsourcing. Cooke and Budhwar (2009), in turn, argue that Asian firms are not adopting outsourcing as much as US and European organisations. This is a function of the size of businesses, sophistication of HR activities, extent to which there is a local HR outsourcing market, and cultural norms and institutional factors. Unlike IT outsourcing and off-shoring, HR decisions are tied to the internationalisation strategy of the firm, driven by motivations to reduce levels of uncertainty and gain insights into local market conditions.

Development of 'shared services' in HR, where organisations put administrative clerk of works activities into a back office function, using associated technologies to enhance delivery, represents a potential re-alignment of the HR function. In other words, the administration of certain HR activities is kept separate from the main HR group in organisations (Cooke 2006). According to Reilly and Williams (2003), the separation of strategy from service delivery and creation of shared services is in that league of change with the switch from welfare to personnel in the 1930s and from personnel to human resources in the 1980s. Further, outsourcing or developing shared services can be combined with ICTs to transform internal HR operations through e-enabled HRM (e-HRM) (Kettley and Reilly 2003, Gueutal and Stone 2005). This changes HR delivery from face-to-face relationships to an increasingly virtual one, which has implications for e-learning, knowledge management, deep-web mining for talent, interactive self-selection, career management, and other HR activities. Dissemination of e-HRM technologies is also uneven, 'reflecting the complex nature of inter- and intra-organisational relationships at regional and sectoral levels and between countries' (Brewster *et al.* 2011: 280).

MANAGING WITH OR WITHOUT UNIONS

The most fundamental employment policy decision made by senior managers is whether to manage its workforce unilaterally or bi-laterally with trade unions. Managing without a union protects management's right to manage and its ability to make uncontested decisions in the workplace on HR and other issues, subject only to laws protecting workers from unlawful workplace practices. Legal protections include not dismissing employees unfairly or discriminating against them unlawfully in employment matters (ILO 2010).

Where an employer recognises a union for the purposes of collective bargaining, a new player – the union – is introduced into the employment relationship. Employment is no longer based on an *individual agreement* and relationship between an organisation and its employees but on a *collective agreement* and a relationship between the employer and union. The terms of the collective agreement become incorporated into individual contracts of employment, but the balance of power between employer and employee changes by the act of recognition. The union provides a new, external challenge for management and to management's unilateral decision-making authority. How management reacts and adjusts to this situation determines the nature of the employer–union relationship and its impact on the efficiency and effectiveness of the organisation (Anthony 1986).

Unionised employment relations

In many countries, unionised employment relations used to be the norm; but today many employers globally do not recognise unions for collective bargaining purposes (OECD 2012). Employer rationale for union recognition rests in the business case. In deciding to recognise a union and enter into collective bargaining arrangements with it, an employer has to consider the benefits to the enterprise of collective bargaining, as well as its employees. First, recognising and working closely with a union, and having a single body for negotiating terms and conditions of employment for all workers, is simpler and more cost-effective for the employer than dealing with each worker individually, especially in large organisations. Second, collective bargaining provides a system of worker involvement. Where an employer negotiates terms and conditions and consults with a recognised union on workplace issues, workers are more likely to feel involved in the way the business is run. This can encourage trust and commitment among the workforce and help the business improve retention rates and reduce labour turnover. Third, union representatives commonly have wide experience of employment relations beyond the immediate workplace, because they represent workers in other businesses. Their representatives bring this knowledge and experience with them to every workplace where the union is involved. The union also has the organisational resources to service its members' employment needs and is likely to have a broad perspective on many issues which affect similar businesses (Chamberlain and Kuhn 1965). Indeed, experienced union representatives are a useful source of legal and HR advice, especially in SMEs.

Fourth, where an employer demonstrates to union representatives it is interested in hearing workers' concerns, the union may help the employer get its message across to union members more effectively than management doing it alone. Even unpopular decisions may be more acceptable to workers, if the union can persuade them that changes are necessary for the continued health of the business and future employment prospects. Further, where the union is involved in a consultative relationship with management, its role in communicating with members and managers enables a genuine two-way process of communication and information to take place. Fifth, all joint decisions made between employer and union are legitimised by involving both players – employer and union – in the bargaining and consultative processes (Gall *et al.* 2011).

Overall, it is in the interests of unions and their members to see the businesses in which they work doing well. A thriving well-run business is good for not only for management but also for the workers. Where relations between management and union are good, the union plays a positive role in building up this relationship. But the union does less obvious things too. For example, its representatives help with health and safety issues in the workplace. Reducing accidents and ill-health at work saves money for companies and keeps a workforce healthy, vigilant and motivated. Many employers cannot do without effective union safety representatives.

Non-union employment relations

Many employers around the world, whatever their cultural traditions and institutional arrangements, commonly prefer non-union employment relationships to unionised ones. Indeed, a non-union environment is the most common form of employment relationship globally. Non-union organisations include all kinds of employers such as SMEs, large companies in the private sector, family-owned businesses, public companies with shareholders, TNCs, and public-sector employers. Some helpful insight into the factors explaining this are provided in a study based on a questionnaire and follow-up interviews with a range of Irish managers. It reveals that out of 98 firms known to oppose union recognition 43.9 per cent were small firms, 39.8 per cent medium size firms and 16.3 per cent large firms. Seventy-six were Irish companies, 10 American, eight European and four United Kingdom or other. The major sectors resisting trade unionism in this study were manufacturing, the wholesale and retail trade, followed by transport, storage and communication. Adapting Purcell's and Ahlstrand's (1994) typology of managerial styles in employment relations cross-nationally (see Figure 9.11 below), the researchers conclude that some three-quarters of the managerial respondents supported the traditional cost-minimisation and no union recognition (or unitary) position

Employees as resources

Individualism		No union recognition	Adversarial	Co-operative
	Employee development focus	Sophisticated human relations (e.g. some large TNCs and large Anglo-Saxon firms)	Sophisticated human resources development (e.g. firms providing specialist professional services in US and Europe)	Sophisticated modern (consultative) (e.g. large firms in North Europe and German Mittelstand)
	Paternalism	Paternalist (e.g Asian, South American, European family firms and SMEs)	Sophisticated modern (constitutionalist) (e.g. large Anglo-Saxon firms)	Modern paternalist (e.g. Large Japanese and other Asian firms)
	Cost minimisation	Traditionalist (e.g.non-sophisticated SMEs and some large firms at national level)	Standard modern (e.g. large Anglo-Saxon and Irish firms, some firms in Asia)	Modern partnerships (e.g. worker co-operatives in UK and mainland Europe)

Employees as commodities

Collectivism

Figure 9.11 Management styles in employment relations
Source: Purcell and Ahlstrand (1994).

in employment relations. Relatively few were supportive of the paternalist, sophisticated human relations, standard modern, or sophisticated modern positions.

The interviews in the above study were very revealing. One director stated: 'The really important decisions are the preserve of management. And to be honest, [they] are never challenged by employees, because they don't know about them.' Another respondent took the view that 'Employers should be left alone to fix our own rates of pay, according to our own individual circumstances. Whether it's from unions or from the state, I'm opposed to blanket rates being imposed.' The unitary hostility evidenced by managers 'was based upon resistance to interference in an assumed "right to manage" '. The authors conclude that employer 'insistence on prerogatives and freedom from "outside" interference' appeared to represent 'points of principle' to the managers in the study (Cullinane and Dundon 2012: 12–15). Similar managerial views are common in non-union firms internationally (Dundon and Rollinson 2004, Flanagan 1999).

An earlier study of employment relations in non-union 'high-tech' firms in South England, where union membership is traditionally low, reviews the nature of management style and attitudes of non-union employees to employment issues (McLoughlin and Gourlay (1994: 147, 151). The first was conceptualised in terms of the degree of 'strategic integration' between HR policy and business strategy in each organisation and its relationship to the extent of individualism and collectivism in these firms. Four styles of management were identified. First, 'traditional HRM' combines high levels of strategic integration with an individualistic approach to managing the employment relationship. Second, 'strategic HRM' combines high levels of strategic integration with a contingent mix of individual and collective regulation. Third, where HR and business strategies are reactive and pragmatic, combined with individual employment relationships, management style is one of 'benevolent autocracy'. Fourth, where a pragmatic and reactive approach to HR and business strategy is combined with an opportunistic mix of individual and collective regulation, this is an 'opportunist' management style. The researchers note the importance of contingent factors in shaping management style, especially product market pressures. Both competitive pressures and customer pressures are important factors too. The study reports that the greater the product market pressures, the less room managers have for manoeuvre in managing employees, thus strengthening managerial prerogative. The 'weaker such pressures, the more management can exercise discretion and choice . . . the more able they may be to develop an HRM-type approach'.

The second issue in this study was reasons why employees did not join unions in these firms. Lack of an available union in the workplace for employees to join only explained non-union membership in one out of the four workforces surveyed. Union presence would apparently have largely made no difference. Neither did propensity to unionise appear to be an attitudinal outcome related to management styles. Rather, 'propensity to join a union appeared to have more to do with instrumental and ideological beliefs about unions than with attitudinal outcomes that might be anticipated as the consequence of HRM-type approaches' by management. In this study, most employees had 'little inclination towards making such demands in the first place'.

Managerial attitudes towards unions can be important too. In the United Kingdom's fifth workplace employment relations survey, for example, it is reported that in the absence of union recognition only 12 per cent of managers 'agreed that unions helped to find ways to improve work performance'. Even among managers who were in favour of union membership, 'there was a degree of scepticism as to whether collaboration with unions was the most effective means of managing the workforce' (Kersley *et al.* 2006: 115). In WERS 2011, 13 per cent of all employees judged managers in their workplace in favour of union membership. This was 'a statistically significant decline from the 15 per cent observed in 2004' (van Wanrooy *et al.* 2013: 57).

Another issue in non-union employment relations is the part played by union avoidance strategies by anti-union managements around the world. Certainly, some TNCs try to avoid unions for strategic and business reasons. Union avoidance is most ardently practised in the United States. Three main factors appear to drive senior American managers to oppose union organisation. First, the philosophy of top corporate executives generally leads them to oppose labour unions on grounds of economic costs and benefits of avoiding unions. Second, the personal views of top executives are normally unsupportive of the union function in principle, because of its claimed adverse impact on the operation of 'free' market forces and its association with 'collectivist' values in economic relations. Third, shifts in social climate and the political power of trade unions leads to rises and falls in the willingness of top managers to take them on aggressively.

In the United States, two different employer strategies have been developed to avoid unions. One is the *direct* 'union-suppression' approach which has gained ground in recent years. The other is the *indirect* 'union substitution' effect. Logan (2006: 1) notes in the last three decades of the twentieth century that US employers waged one of their most successful 'anti-union wars' in the history of the country, with some spectacular outcomes. These anti-union campaigns resulted in private-sector union membership falling to its lowest levels since the 1920s. Instrumental in this campaign were high-powered employment relations consultants, law firms, industrial psychologists and strike management firms, operating in a business worth several hundred million dollars per year. This 'union busting' industry enabled employers not only to resist unionisation but also 'to undermine union strength, or unload the existing union'. Logan notes that large US firms promoting union avoidance policies are increasingly seeking export markets for their services.

The second union avoidance approach of larger US companies is adopting proactive HR policies and practices which reduce incentives for workers to unionise. Foulkes (1980) and Jacoby (1991) identify the HR policies and practices most likely to avoid unions and motivate, incentivise and satisfy employees as individual members of a workforce. These include: paying above the market wage rate; using selective employment policies; rewarding merit; investing in training and career development; having pro-active communication and information systems; promoting an individualised employment relationship; and establishing new businesses on 'greenfield' non-union sites.

In contrast, although Canada's national system of employment relations has some similarities with that of the United States in terms of union organisation (where some American unions recruit cross-nationally), de-centralised collective bargaining, and some labour law issues (such as union recognition procedures), the Canadian system is a distinctive one. As Thompson and Taras (2011: 88, 113) argue: a large proportion of the workforce is covered directly or indirectly by collective bargaining; there is strong legal protection for collective bargaining; and its system incorporates 'traditions of adversarialism and moderate levels of strike activity'. However, employer attitudes and government policy towards trade union organisation and collective bargaining are softer and more measured than in the United States. The labour movement has legitimacy in Canada, governments rarely initiate 'anti-union' campaigns and the labour movement 'has close ties with the women's movement and consumer groups'. And, unlike in the United States, employer militancy towards trade unions is not a popular public position to take and unions have legal protections which 'make de-unionisation very difficult' to achieve.

MANAGEMENT'S ROLE IN EMPLOYMENT RELATIONS

How managers have managed the employment relationship historically and do so today remains to a large extent an elusive and inconclusive area of knowledge and research. Knowledge is elusive, because managerial sources discussing how employers unilaterally regulate the wage–work bargain, relations with employees, and how work is organised and managed in firms are more limited and closed, compared with those of other players in the field, such as trade unions and the state. But knowledge is also inconclusive, because the literature shows no consistency in managerial approaches to managing the employment relationship. Further, access to managerial data is often restricted in terms of written sources, availability to outsiders, and reliability. Nevertheless, some research has been published, commonly in the form of case studies. Examples include the strategic contexts to the Fawley productivity agreements in the United Kingdom (Flanders 1964), Purcell and Ahlstrand's (1994) study of HR practices in the multi-divisional company, and research by Kochan *et al.* (1986) into the transformation of American industrial relations in the 1980s, especially the importance of management's 'strategic choice' in employment reforms. But gaining definitive and conclusive insights into management's role in employment relations decision-making are constrained by the nature of the evidence available and wide diversity in management practices (Bacon 2008).

Managing the employment relationship

Early studies in the United Kingdom, for example, claimed that management interest or presence in managing the employment relationship was either absent or deficient – which may be equally true today in 'anti-union' cultures cross-nationally. For example, the report of the Royal Commission on Trade Unions and Employers' Associations (1968: 25) in the United Kingdom notes: 'If companies have their own personnel specialists, why have they not introduced effective personnel policies to control methods of negotiation and pay structures within their firms?' It adds: 'Many firms have no such policy, and perhaps no conception of it.' Other research by Winkler (1974: 193, 201) concludes: 'where the directors' role in [employment] relations was concerned ... What was found was purposive inaction, influential non-participation, a very active form of unconcern ... and instrumental inconsistency'. In short, 'directors literally do not want to know about industrial relations'.

An influential study by the Commission on Industrial Relations (1973) around this time reports that a dominant impression gained from many companies was employment relations did not receive the attention they need along with commercial and operational matters. The reasons were, and these may apposite in many instances today, first, many managers especially in the private sector continued to view the prospect of power-sharing with unions as threatening their decision-making authority and organisational legitimacy.

Second, responsibility for employment relationships was only part of the management function and employment relations were not readily quantifiable, as were finance and operations (Marsh 1982). Third, where industry-wide collective agreements operated at this time, there was reluctance by line managers or HR specialists to get involved in employment relations issues locally: the higher the level collective bargaining takes place, the more generic and external to the firm is employment relations policy.

Further, Clegg's (1970: 166, 167) standard textbook on British industrial relations during this period contains only a relative short chapter on 'Management' and it says virtually nothing about management's role in employment relations. His most pertinent observation is: 'Even now it is relatively rare to find a firm with a clear and accepted personnel policy in the sense of a coherent set of principles governing the employment and performance of staff.' Such a policy would be expected to be 'based where possible on tested evidence and with checks to see if it is applied'. For Clegg, there were also 'other obstacles to the development of a personnel policy' which he did not explore.

At the time of the WERS survey 2011, it was reported that only one in seven workplaces had senior managers in Britain with a job title indicating that they specialised in employment relations, HR or personnel work. This is not surprising, given that most workplaces were relatively small. Instead, in a large majority of workplaces (78 per cent), employment relations issues were the responsibility of the owner or general manager; in another 8 per cent, it was the responsibility of someone with another functional specialisation such as finance manager. Nevertheless, some of these managers were spending substantial amounts of time on employment relations issues. Indeed, over a fifth (22 per cent) of managers in all workplaces in this study spent more than half their time on employment relations or HR issues. This was not significantly different from the 20 per cent observed in 2004. But it suggests that 'the increasing specialisation in personnel that was seen at workplace level in the late 1990s and early 2000s has not continued' (van Wanrooy et al. 2013: 51).

From a policy perspective, the situation in the United States was similarly indeterminate. As Kochan (1980) points out, the vast majority of US firms have always vigorously opposed the organisation of employees into unions on ideological grounds and have refused, where they can, to recognise unions for the purposes of collective bargaining. For Kochan (1980: 181), 'management is generally a reluctant participant in collective bargaining'. Indeed, according to Witte (1954: 4), the prime employment relations objective of most American employers in the late nineteenth and early twentieth centuries was, if 'there was any management policy toward labor' at all, to 'treat them rough'. Witte argues that two distinct management strategies in employment relations emerged during this period. One was hard-line opposition to unionism through the 'blacklisting' of union members and organisers and using strike-breakers, industrial spies, armed guards, court injunctions, and other forms of discrimination against union supporters to suppress union organisation. A second strategy drew on the ideas emerging in the field of personnel management. Embodied in the literature of the human relations school, these advocated union avoidance techniques. Indeed, Brown and Myers (1957: 92) describe the sentiments of the majority of US business executives at this time by suggesting that, if by the next morning, 'the unions with which they dealt would have disappeared overnight, more management people than not would experience the happiest sleep of their lives'.

Major American textbooks at this time treated the labour relations function of management and its policy direction cursorily. Thus Pigor and Myers (1969: 32, 320) use 'the term "personnel administration" to describe the function that, in many firms, is called "industrial relations"'. However, their single chapter on 'Employees and Labor Organizations' makes a simple unsubstantiated point that only the personnel administrator can help 'influence the company's policy in dealing with the union'. They identify four possible alternatives for this: fighting the union, armed truce, working in harmony, and union-management co-operation. Further, Yoder's (1963: 156) text on personnel management and industrial relations was highly prescriptive, lacking any obvious evidence base. He states, for example: 'Policy on manpower [sic] management in a firm must integrate and combine the ideas and influence of individual managers and employees, and perhaps incorporate the viewpoint of unions, all within a framework of public policy on the management of people and in the setting of a particular firm.' However, public policy was probably more influential in the United States and Canada than corporate policy, as exemplified in the legal union recognition procedures embodied in the Taft-Hartley Act 1936 in the United States and the Canadian Labour Code (Godard 2004b).

A further difficulty in trying to understand the evolving role of management in employment relations is the sometimes inconsistent use made of terms by practitioners and researchers. Thus words such as 'practice', 'procedures', 'policy' and 'strategy' in employment relations are commonly used differently, interchangeably and inconsistently. Logically, *practice* is best used to describe 'what' line managers and HR specialists do in day-to-day employment relations, while *procedures* are 'how' they do it. As part of a total business strategy, *policy* is commonly led by HR specialists and senior management. It defines a company's guidelines for action or courses 'of action with regard to particular [employment] relations issues' (Commission on

Industrial Relations 1973: 4). Thus *policy* justifies what managements do in employment relations; *strategy* is the 'long-term policies which are developed by the management of an organization in order to preserve or change the procedures' or results of employment relations activities 'over time' (Thurley and Wood 1983: 198). Using this nomenclature, management's involvement in managing the employment relationship is multi-tiered: the *strategic* (or planning) level, the *policy* (or functional) level, and the *procedural and practical* (or operational) level. Management involvement may be at all these levels; it can be at both functional and operational levels; and it may be at largely operational level only.

Management styles in employment relations

Another issue in management's role in employment relations is the part played by managerial 'styles' in the field. A lot has been written about management styles in regulating work and employment relationships, mostly from an Anglo-Saxon perspective. These include: Fox's (1966, 1974) unitary and pluralist frames of reference; his typology of labour management styles; Purcell and Sissons (1983) 'traditional', 'sophisticated paternalists', 'constitutionalists', 'consulters' and 'standard modern' classifications; and Purcell's (1987: 534, 547) range of management styles measured on the dimensions of 'individualism' and 'collectivism'. Individualism is the extent to which HR policies are focused on the rights and capabilities of individual workers; collectivism is the extent to which management policy is directed towards 'inhibiting or encouraging the development of collective representation by employees and allowing [them] a collective voice in management decision making'. Purcell claims that 'once it is recognised that modern companies are capable of making strategic business choices we must allow for preferences to exist in the way employees are managed'. Where managers do this, style is closely related to business policy. In the context of competitive product markets, the corporate search for distinctive management styles appropriate to their circumstances gives rise to innovations and fresh initiatives in employment relations. These include the 'new industrial relations', HRM, the shift to emphasise the role of line management in these processes and 'new approaches to personnel management'. All are 'indicative of this search for a management style linked to business policy'.

Building on these concepts and adapting the work of Purcell and Ahlstrand (1994), nine management styles of employment relations, mapped on degrees of individualism and collectivism, are shown in Figure 9.11. Along the individualism dimension, employees are treated as resources by employers or commodities. Here firms adopt a cost-minimisation, paternalist or employee development focus. The collectivism dimension reflects the extent to which employees are jointly involved in decisions affecting them. Here the firm's approach towards unionisation is: no union recognition, an adversarial or a co-operative approach. These nine management styles are a function of these dimensions. The importance of Purcell's and Ahlstrand's indicative framework is it suggests managements develop policies and strategies in employment relations for the roles employees are expected to play in achieving a firm's business objectives. For them, it is business objectives that are more likely to determine management style in employment relations, not managerial ideology and managerial values as implied by writers such as Fox (1966, 1974).

Using this framework for the purposes of developing some international comparisons, three tentative groupings of employment relations management styles in firms can be inferred. First, companies with an 'employee development focus' are likely to draw on: a 'sophisticated human relations' management style in the cases of some large TNCs and large Anglo-Saxon firms; a 'sophisticated human resources development' style in firms providing specialist professional services in the United States and Europe; and a 'sophisticated modern (consultative)' style in large firms in North Europe and the German *Mittelstand*. Second, paternal firms are likely to draw on: a 'paternalist' style in Asian, South American and European family firms and some SMEs; a 'sophisticated modern (constitutionalist)' style in some large Anglo-Saxon firms; and a 'modern paternalist' style in large Japanese and other Asian firms. Third, where cost minimisation is the driver, firms are likely to draw on: a 'traditionalist' style in non-sophisticated SMEs and some large firms at national level; a 'standard modern' style in some large Anglo-Saxon and Irish firms and some Asia firms; and 'modern partnerships' in European worker co-operatives. Management style is an elusive concept, however, and the categories provided above are indicative ones only.

EMPLOYERS' ASSOCIATIONS

In unionised employment relations, employees are often organised into national and central labour organisations to protect their interests as workers. Employers, in turn, organise themselves into national and central associations to represent employers in relations with unions. Central employers' associations also deal with the state and, in Europe, employers' bodies are involved with supra-national institutions of the EU. There are three main types of employers' association: *specialist* associations representing employer interests in employment relations and labour market issues; *trade* associations representing the product market interests of their members; and *dual* associations that represent employers in both labour market and product market interests. In practice, many employers' associations today are dualistic or mixed bodies, resulting from economies of scale, de-centralised collective bargaining, and lessening importance of collective employment relations generally.

Making comparisons

In North America, the role of employers' associations in promoting employer interests collectively is largely negligible, because of anti-trust laws there. These are aimed at promoting fair business competition for the benefit of consumers and inhibiting employer co-operation and combination in business and employment relations issues (Taft *et al.* 2003). In the United States and Canada, an individualistic approach by employers to employment relations and HR predominates. Large domestic companies and TNCs are able to decide for themselves what their labour market interests are, so they pursue them individually without reference to other firms. Employers' associations are also very 'patchy' in 'much of the Third World' (Poole 1986: 55).

This contrasts with Europe, where both national and central associations normally have much stronger roles in employment relations and social policy issues. National associations arose historically in response to militant craft unions trying to impose their rule books on employers reluctant to accept them (Brown 1959, 1983). Thus historically, the formation of strong national trade unions preceded the establishment of employers' association, which incentivised employers to create their own countervailing national bodies. Similarly, powerful states with an interventionist or corporatist role in employment relations have encouraged employers to establish their own central employer's organisations or 'peak' associations.

Because of wide diversities in employment relations systems and different institutional traditions with dissimilar historical-path dependencies, the structure, membership and activities of employer associations cross-nationally differ widely by country. Commonly, there is more than one central body of employers within each state. Italy is an extreme case, where it is estimated there are 16 central organisations of employers alone. This compares with eight in Hungary, seven in Portugal, five in Sweden, two each in Spain and Ireland, and only one each in the United Kingdom and Germany (Behrens and Traxler 2004). However, distinctive patterns of organisation among employers' associations cross-nationally are hard to discern, since there is such a wide range of models.

Cross-national differences in the forms and roles of employers' associations impact significantly on national and local employment relations practices. For example, multi-employer bargaining only takes place when employers' associations participate in the negotiating process. Similarly, where statutory provisions extend collective agreements to employers not directly bound by them, this is only when employers have an association. Multi-employer bargaining and collective bargaining coverage depend strongly on the presence of employers' associations and the kinds of activities they perform (Traxler 2000). Further, employers' associations may contribute to national economic performance by providing 'public' goods. An example is where bargaining co-ordination promotes employment, price stability or participation in vocational training. Indeed, there is evidence to show that employers' associations, as well as unions, enjoy significantly greater rights to participate in public policy-making, where multi-employer bargaining rather than single-employer bargaining prevails (Behrens and Traxler 2004, Traxler *et al.* 2001). The reason is that multi-employer bargaining impacts on government's macro-economic policy goals; single-employer bargaining does not. In this way, the state has a strong incentive to seek the co-operation of the bargaining parties, by incorporating them into the policy-making process.

For these and other reasons, employers' associations and trade unions are also key players in employment relations at EU level, where they participate in EU social policy formation and employment relations initiatives in the European Community framework. Here the role of the social partners – organisations of employers and unions – is a key feature of the European social model, where the aim is to combine the values of responsibility, solidarity and participation in policy-making.

Central and lower-level associations

Employers' associations may be classified principally as 'central' or 'peak' associations and 'national', 'sector' or 'lower-level' associations. Peak associations are more inclusive bodies, because membership is national and cross-sector. Their role is to aggregate the interests of all employers nationally, despite their divergent concerns. Traxler (2008) examines the 22 largest peak employer organisations in Europe, North America, Asia and Australasia during the 1990s. He shows multi-employer bargaining predominantly took place at this level in 15 cases. In seven cases, the peak association carried out the bargaining function – Austria, Australia, Belgium, Finland, Ireland, Norway and Slovenia. Further, extension of collective agreements took place in eight countries – Austria, Belgium, Spain, France, Finland, the Netherlands, Portugal and Slovenia.

The appeal of employers' associations to firms turns on the power of multi-employer bargaining. The positive incentives to firms of multi-employer bargaining include, first, the transaction costs of the employment relationship to employers are reduced, since employment regulation is externalised to the signatory parties – the employers' association and union. Second, multi-employer bargaining takes wages out of inter-firm competition, through cartelising wages settlements among employers in a sector. Third, multi-employer bargaining neutralises workplaces from trade union activity by setting minimum employment standards using collective agreements. These restrict the right to manage less than single-employer agreements do. Fourth, employer access to corporate benefits not covered by collective bargaining is tied to membership of an employers' association (Clegg 1970, Sisson 1987, Traxler *et al.* 2001).

The negative incentives causing firms to join multi-employer bargaining are, first, membership reduces an employers' risk of strike action, because without multi-employer bargaining unions can exert pressure on individual employers through 'pattern bargaining' or 'whipsawing' tactics. Funds for collective disputes provide 'strike insurance' for firms. Second, where legally-binding extension mechanisms exist, this is a strong incentive to join the employers' association, because multi-employer agreements are applied to all companies not affiliated to the association within the sector. Third, in some countries such as Belgium, France and the Netherlands, employers' associations and unions use the extension mechanism as a means of performing public functions by supporting health and safety, vocational training and unemployment payouts (Traxler 2008).

In most countries, employers' association, which are either affiliated to the central body or unaffiliated to it, operate below peak level. In Austria, for example, most associations *not* affiliated to the central body, the *Wirtschaftskammer Österreich*, bargain collectively in particular sectors. These include printing, newspapers, electricity, and parts of agriculture. These associations tend to represent groups outside the core business areas covered by peak associations. Where lower-level affiliates exist, they make up an integrated multi-level system of employer representation. The number of levels across countries and across peak association varies. Thus within the largest peak association in each country, there are typically three levels of employer organisation, with as many as four or five levels in some countries (Traxler *et al.* 2001). In the case of the *Bundesvereinung der deutchen Arbeitgeberverbände* (BDA) in Germany, for example, there are branches in the regions (*Länder*). These are affiliated to cross-sectional *Länder* associations and to national sector associations. There are almost 700 associations under the umbrella of the BDA.

In 40 national employer confederations drawn from 15 countries listed in Europe by Behrens and Traxler (2004), first, many lower-level associations are multiple members of higher-level associations, because of the complex structure of confederations. This makes it difficult for these confederations, with large numbers of affiliated members, to know exactly how many associations are under their umbrella. Further, differences among confederations in numbers of hierarchic levels translates into differences of what 'affiliates' mean. Second, associations affiliated to peak associations are not always employers' organisations dealing with labour market issues. In many confederations, trade associations are included, particularly in the case of dual bodies. Third, employers' confederations often have mixed compositions of lower-level bodies and firms registered as direct members. Fourth, the number of affiliated associations varies among employers' confederations within and across countries but does not appear to correlate with country size. Thus some confederations in smaller countries, such as Austria and the Netherlands, have large numbers of affiliates, while some confederations in larger countries, such as France and Italy, have small numbers of affiliates (Behrens and Traxler 2004). Fifth, the number of affiliated associations in Nordic countries is generally low, due to mergers during the 1980s and 1990s. Also, confederations of SMEs, such as in Finland and the Netherlands, often have a relatively large number of affiliates. This is because either SMEs need more services provided them than their larger counterparts do or 'such firms may stick to traditional, narrowly-defined demarcations of craft-related business activities', resulting in corresponding patterns of association (Behrens and Traxler 2004: 11).

What has undermined the role of employers' associations in employment relations are two factors. One is the pressures that employers have put on unions to de-centralise collective bargaining since the 1980s, making employers' associations unnecessary. The other is the changing structures of national economies, where manufacturing is shrinking, services growing and SMEs expanding, thus making it harder for unions to organise workers and employers to organise firms.

BUSINESS PERFORMANCE AND EMPLOYMENT STRATEGY

In liberal market economies especially, business and HR strategy in the private sector under globalisation are driven by the imperatives of reducing costs and increasing returns to shareholders. In the public sector, the pressures are fiscal and reflected in continuous attempts at PMR (Farnham *et al.* 2005). In mainland Europe, by contrast, the 'Rhineland' model of the stakeholder co-ordinated market economy enables government, employers' associations and labour unions to consult each other about common economic goals, with a view to achieving some harmony of interests among them. Competition and confrontation are generally avoided in the belief they undermine sustainable and stable economic growth. Such a process constrains choices of corporate strategy, where the state patrols the economy as a referee, guarantor and employer in its own right (Bot 2004).

Employment relations strategy

Taking an historical perspective, Thomason (1991) argues that managements have always had HR and employment relations policies, even if they were not always explicit. He claims in the history of human resources management some relationship always exists between business strategy and HR responses to external labour market conditions, even if HR strategy is not fully integrated with business strategy. He argues that the acquisition and utilisation of human resources by firms have been approached in different ways at different times. Private firms are likely to express business strategies in terms of how they can compete with competitors, while public services do so in terms of how they can secure revenues in the face of competing calls on the public purse. In all organisations, strategic responses in the marketplace have to take account of the opportunities and threats posed by product markets and the strengths and weaknesses of their combination of resource inputs, not just labour.

Decisions relating to opportunities and threats in product markets indicate that firms select one of four possible business strategies. Building on Porter's (1998) classification of generic business strategies for competitive advantage, Thomason identifies them as low-cost leadership (mass production), differentiation (superior products commanding a premium price), focus (supply of a product or service to a niche market), and asset parsimony (with either high entry costs as a protection or flexible use of limited assets to generate high-output performance). Other decisions take account of whether the suppliers of an organisation's resources, including its human resources, are capable of meeting the firm's market demands. As Porter (1998) argues, competitive advantage depends on not only conditions in product markets but also availability of all factors of production.

Thomason (1991) identifies at least three historical shifts in business strategy since the industrial revolution, with businesses following any one of these to promote competitive advantage. The strategy of *asset parsimony* is losing ground, however, because low-cost modern technologies allow freer entry by competitor firms into many markets. The first period identified by Thomason was the industrial revolution, where the typical business strategy was one of *differentiation* or producing premium price products. The second period is associated with industrial rationalisation, starting in the late nineteenth century. Here the typical business strategy was *low-cost leadership*. The third period is associated with the 'new wave rationalisations' from the 1960s, where the typical business strategy was *focus* or supplying niche products. Here competitive advantage was secured by satisfying customer needs in the marketplace, emphasising quality, reliability and teamwork within organisations.

Thomason concludes there are four possible HR strategies used by firms in different market circumstances, with each serving different business strategies. First, 'Pre-Personnel Management' still exists in the SME sector and depends on the ability of firms to recruit skilled labour in external labour markets in response to their business needs. Here a *selection strategy* is used as a main mechanism for labour control. Second, 'Traditional Personnel Management' is associated with mass production industries and unionisation, where firms depend on their ability to draw upon the external labour market to supply the workers they need. Here a *supervision strategy* for labour control is adopted and company rules are policed to secure targeted levels of performance. Third, 'Human Resource Development' involves a *development strategy* for employee flexibility, typically adopted in modern niche markets, where businesses rely on low-cost leadership, and labour supply is obtained by developing internal labour markets. Fourth, 'Human Resource Management' involves a *partnership strategy* for employee commitment, where business strategy relies on differentiation, which requires problem-solving, creative skills.

The problem of developing explicit employment relations strategies is noted by Sisson and Marginson (2003). They demonstrate that diversified firms operating in different product markets are unlikely to make central employment relations policy decisions, as the needs of different business units vary. Highly divisionalised companies are also likely to exercise financial control from the centre, thus limiting discretionary HR expenditure at divisional level. Sisson and Storey (2000: 17) identify three 'significant changes' inside organisations affecting employment relations. First, divisionalisation breaks up large hierarchical organisations into semi-autonomous or quasi-business units 'responsible for most, if not all, activities within their jurisdiction'. Second, budgetary devolution sets specified financial targets and financial resources. Third, organisations with 'internal markets' trade 'services' between 'purchasers' and 'providers' within the business, leading to increasing 'diversity in employment relations practices'. Managers are left 'to cope in a contingent fashion' with employment relations 'in the best way they can'.

Further, employment relations strategy in some UK companies is described as a 'third order' strategy, involving decisions made *after* firms have developed and are starting to implement corporate and business unit strategies (Purcell and Ahlstrand 1994). Thus the HR function is more likely to be involved at the implementation stage of strategy decisions rather than the formulation stage. It follows that corporate-level business decisions restrict the HR strategic choices available and that corporate structure continues to exert an important downward influence on employment practices (Bacon 2008). However, involvement of managers responsible for employment relations and HR issues in the United Kingdom in preparing strategic plans has declined in recent years (Kersley *et al.* 2006). Indeed, by 2011, it is estimated in the United Kingdom that 'the recession appeared to have hindered the extension of strategic planning to some extent' (van Wanrooy *et al.* 2013: 55).

Strategic HRM (SHRM)

Increasing individualisation of the employment contract and global pressures on organisational performance, especially in Anglophone liberal market economies, means the drive in sophisticated organisations has been to create new types of HR strategies to promote competitive advantage. As Wilkinson *et al.* (2010: 4) put it: 'At its root, HRM focuses on managing the employment relationships and the implicit, as well as explicit agreements that are established between *individuals* and organizations' (emphasis added). They add that in many instances HR plays the role of employee advocate or employee 'champion' to obtain equitable treatment of employees 'to ensure that the interests of employees as well as the organisation are protected'. Such observations reflect the shift within firms from employment relations strategies dealing with unions to HRM strategies dealing with individuals.

Vertical and horizontal integration are key concepts in developing and implementing an effective HR strategy. Marchington *et al.* (2012) argue that both vertical and horizontal integration are at the heart of HRM. Vertical integration refers to links between HR and wider business strategies and the external political, economic, social, legal and institutional forces shaping them. Its concern is with degree of 'external fit' between HR strategies and activities, the management of an organisation as a whole, and the competitive contexts within which it operates. Horizontal integration is the fit between different HR strategies and practices and the degrees to which they support or contradict one another. Its concern is with the degree of 'internal fit' between core HR activities in an organisation. These include job and organisation design, organisation development, employee resourcing and talent planning, learning and talent development, performance and reward, employee engagement, employment relations, and service delivery and information. Marchington and Wilkinson (2008: 28) conclude that 'both vertical and horizontal integration need to be strengthened in order to maximise the HR contribution, as well as minimise the likelihood of conflicting messages'.

In the search within organisations for effective HRM strategies and practices which motivate employees, impact on their knowledge, skills and behaviours, and lead to improved employee, organisational and financial outcomes, there is no agreement within the literature on a definitive model of 'good' organisational practice. This literature, much of it from the United States, is within the universalist tradition of human resources management and it seeks to understand the ways in which HR practices contribute to improved performance and employee commitment. In the literature on contextual HRM, by contrast, the strategy process is different, involving different objectives and processes than in universalist HR. In Austria and Germany, for example, HR issues are taken into account from the outset in the development of corporate strategy, while the strategic implications of management decisions in companies are subject to the involvement or scrutiny of powerful works council representatives on supervisory boards. Indeed, in most German companies, knowledge that such decisions are subject to scrutiny, and can be reversed or varied, means managers tend to operate continually with HR issues in mind (Brandl and Pohler 2010, Wachter and Muller-Camen 2002).

MODELS OF STRATEGIC HUMAN RESOURCES MANAGEMENT

There is a vast amount of 'new' Anglo-American literature on models of SHRM. Colakoglu *et al.* (2010) for example, drawing upon Delery and Doty (1996), classify and categorise HR strategies into three alternative perspectives: the universal, contingency and configurational. They also identify two main theoretical frameworks influential in the field of strategic HR research, the resource-based view of the firm and the behavioural perspective, as well as some emerging perspectives. An alternative classification is provided in Figure 9.12. With its multiplicity of SHRM models, Figure 9.12 shows how far HR strategy has moved along a pathway from modest beginnings starting with low-level supervisors in the industrial revolution, barely recognised on

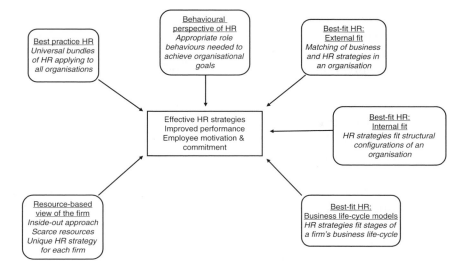

Figure 9.12 Main approaches to strategic HRM

the shop floor, to a widely debated topic discussed by top management teams in board rooms around the world today, in response to increasing global complexity. According to Morris and Snell (2008), the key objective of HR strategy in the universalistic paradigm today is to guide 'the process by which firms develop and deploy people, relationships, and capabilities to enhance their competitiveness'. In this approach, people are seen as valuable resources and sources of strategic capability for firms.

Morris and Snell (2009: 95–96) identify three evolutionary stages in HR strategy from the industrial revolution till today, similar to the Thomason model: the period of industrialisation, the global diversifications of the 1970s and 1980s, and the differentiated work systems and hyper-competition of today. Each stage has had to deal with 'the environmental factors of the time, particular assumptions, parallel strategy literature, and perspectives about managing people for firm advantage'. In their view, 'the co-evolution of HR and strategy [today] will benefit both fields by providing greater understanding of the vital intersection between people and firms as they try to co-exist'.

Best-practice HR

There is much debate about the notion of 'best-practice HR', sometimes called 'high-performance work systems' (HPWS) (Appelbaum *et al.* 2000), 'high-commitment HR' (Guest 1997) or 'high-involvement HR' (Wood 1999). The central idea of best-practice models is the claim that bundles of specific HR strategies and practices can bring about improved organisational performance in *all* organisations, irrespective of product markets, technology and other contingent factors. These HR bundles help organisations achieve competitive advantage, as well as improving employee attitudes and behaviours, decreasing absenteeism and labour turnover, raising productivity, improving quality and customer service, and increasing profitability. A well-known best-practice model is provided by Pfeffer (1994). His underpinning analysis is based on the importance of the 'human equation' in organisations, enabling profits to be built by prioritising people management issues. His seven components of best-practice are: employment security and internal labour markets; selective hiring and sophisticated selection; extensive training, learning and development; employee involvement, information sharing and worker voice; self-managed teams and team-working; high compensation base upon performance; and reduction of status differentials in organisations.

Another best-practice model is HPWS. First coined by Appelbaum and Batt (1994) and Appelbaum *et al.* (2000), it was followed by some UK studies (West *et al.* 2002). The terminology used by its researchers differs, but their key theme is that HPWS increase employee involvement in decision-making and improve employee motivation and commitment. These, in turn, result in improved business performance and enhanced employee outcomes. A key part of HR in this model is the conditions under which people perform well and is a function of three key factors: employee ability, employee motivation, and employee opportunity to perform well. Thus performance is likely to improve, where employees have the knowledge and skills to do this. Employees have the motivation to do so, because they want to perform well and are rewarded for it. And employees have a supportive working environment that gives them the support and opportunity for achieving good performance.

The term HPWS is nevertheless a contested one. As Lloyd and Payne (2004: 13) claim, 'there is no clear definition of this model'. There is also fundamental lack of agreement about the specific characteristics it incorporates. As noted above, a range of terms is used in relation to HPWS, including high involvement systems and high commitment management, where the significance of these is more than just semantic. But, according to Bélanger *et al.* (2002: 42), high performance management may be viewed as combining three elements. First, there is production management element, concerned with aspects of productive flexibility and process standardisation, where hard quality management typically involves the use of statistical tools of analysis. Second, there is a work organisation element, concerned with production activities based on knowledge, cognition and abstract labour, where the centrepiece is team working. Third, an employment relations element underpins the coherence of the other two components, given the requirement for a committed rather than a compliant workforce. There is a desire to align and support task flexibility through terms and conditions of employment, by typically making pay contingent on group performance (Appelbaum 2002). Further, adopting this approach, and by promoting a universal organisational culture and social system supporting the technical system, HR professionals are tasked with obtaining social cohesion and commitment to the production system and wider organisational goals by employees.

The matching model

This is a best-fit model of HR strategy, which seeks to match HR strategies to different business strategies. Best-fit models, sometimes described as 'outside–in' theories, are based on the proposition that different types of HR strategy are suitable for different types of business conditions and organisational contexts. The best-fit approach claims a link between HR strategy and competitive advantage but HR strategy is contingent upon the particular circumstances of each enterprise. Organisations have to identify those HR strategies which best 'fit' their enterprises in terms of product markets, labour markets, size, structures, strategies and other factors. What is right for one organisation is not appropriate for others. In other words, best-fit HR strategy is based on the idea that HR practices vary among organisations, depending on business strategy or product-market circumstances. Miles and Snow (1984), for example, identify three types of strategic behaviour – defenders, prospectors and analysers, linking these with different competitive, staffing and development, performance appraisal and pay strategies.

Other matching models draw on Porter's distinctions between innovation, quality enhancement, and cost reduction strategies (Porter 2004). Typical of these is the work of Schuler and Jackson (2007) which attempts to link the competitive strategies of firms with specific HR strategies and practices. They do this by conceiving HR strategy in terms of generating desired employee role behaviours required to fulfil given business strategies. They then identify three sets of HR strategies and practices likely to achieve and reinforce such behaviours.

First, where innovation is the strategic goal, this sets up predictable patterns of role behaviour such as creativity, longer-term goals, and moderate concern for quality. The HR strategies to match these include rewards based on internal equity, low pay rates, and broad career paths. Second, where the strategic goal is quality enhancement, Schuler and Jackson (2007) argue a long and medium-term focus and high concern for quality by employees can be generated by relatively egalitarian treatment of staff, with some guarantees of employment security. Quality enhancement also requires a moderate amount of co-operative, interdependent employee behaviour. The sorts of HR strategies encouraging this combine mixes of individual and group criteria for performance appraisal, which is mainly short-term and results oriented. Third, where the strategic goal is cost reduction, desired employee behaviour demands moderate concern for quality of output but high concern for quantity. The HR strategies supporting these behaviours are close monitoring of market pay levels and minimal levels of training and development. While agreeing that the success or failure of firms does not turn entirely on their HR strategies, Schuler and Jackson (2007) conclude that HRM practices are likely to be critical.

The structural-configuration model

These are sometimes called 'internal fit' models and relate HR strategic choices to the different strategic and structural configurations of organisations, as exemplified by Fombrun *et al.* (1984). For Fombrun and his colleagues (1984: 37), 'the critical managerial task is to align the formal structure and human resource systems so that they drive the strategic objectives of the organisation'. Known as the Michigan model, this best-fit approach identifies a range of HR strategic choices, in terms of selection, appraisal, rewards and development that are dependent upon an organisation's strategic-structural configurations.

These configurations range from single-product strategies with functional structures, through diversified-product strategies linked to multidivisional structures, and multiple-product strategies operating globally. Thus a business depending on a single-product strategy and a functional structure is likely to pursue basic HR strategies which are largely functional, subjective and unsystematic. Businesses following a diversification strategy within a multidivisional structure, in contrast, are characterised by an HR strategy driven by impersonal, systematic HR processes, adaptable to different parts of the organisation. Selection, for example, is likely to be functionally and generalist in orientation, with systematic criteria being used. Appraisal is impersonal, based on returns on investment and productivity, with subjective assessments being made of contribution to the business. Rewards, in turn, can incorporate large pay bonuses based on profitability, linked with subjective assessments of contribution to business performance. Finally, learning and development would be cross-functional, cross-divisional and cross-business.

Once management has articulated a philosophy about managing people, the Michigan model focuses on designing the HR system. Four generic functions performed by HR managers are identified in the model. These are the 'human resource cycle', where performance is a function of all HR components. The Michigan School argues that success in implementing strategic objectives depends on how well organisations carry out the human resource cycle. This requires four things: selecting the people best able to perform the jobs defined by the structure; appraising their performance to ensure equitable distribution of rewards; motivating employees by linking rewards to high-level performance; and developing employees to enhance their performance at work. The strength of this model is it provides a framework showing how selection, appraisal, rewards and development can be mutually linked to encourage appropriate employee behaviours.

The business life-cycle model

This tries to link HR strategy choices with the varying needs of firms at different stages in their life-cycles from start-up, through growth, maturity and decline. At each stage, it is claimed firm have different business priorities which demand different HR strategies. A number of these models have been proposed (Kochan and Barocci 1985, Baird and Meshoulam 1988, Lengnick-Hall and Lengnick Hall 1988). Kochan and Barocci's (1985) business life-cycle model identifies four critical HR activities: recruitment, selection and staffing; compensation and benefits; training and development; and employee relations. Each stage requires different HR responses at different phases of the business life-cycle – that is at the start-up, growth, maturity, and decline stages of a business.

During a firm's start-up stage, for example, the compensation and benefits function needs to meet or exceed labour market rates. During periods of growth, the compensation and benefits function concentrates on meeting external market rates, while considering the internal equity effects and establishing formal compensation structures. In the maturity stage, it concentrates on controlling compensation. In the decline stage, it focuses on tighter cost control. In employment relations, in the start-up stage, the firm sets out its basic employment relations philosophy and organisation. During the growth stage, the firm sets out to achieve labour peace and employee motivation and morale. In the maturity stage, the firm's focus is on controlling labour costs, maintaining labour peace and improving productivity. In the decline stage, most of the firm's efforts are directed at maintaining labour peace.

The resource-based view of the firm (RBVF)

The origins of this model emerged out of the new business strategy literature. Linking the resource-based model of strategy with HRM has been influential in initiating developments in pay systems, learning and development, and other HR issues. The significance of resource-based theory is that it led to a change in strategic management thinking, by shifting from an emphasis on an 'outside-in' approach, focusing on external industry-based competitive forces, to an 'inside-out' approach focusing on the firm. The inside-out approach views the firm's internal resources as the starting point for understanding successful organisational performance (Paauwe and Boselie 2003). The RBVF provides a critique of the dominant strategic models of the 1980s associated with Porter (1998, 2004). The outside-in approach of Porter analyses the external contexts of firms in terms of opportunities and threats, whereas the inside-out approach of Barney (1991) and others analyses their internal contexts in terms of strengths and weaknesses.

The essence of the RBVF is that organisations comprise unique bundles of assets, including 'human assets', and access to these and the firm's ability to make effective use of them provide its source of competitive advantage. The RBVF is generally accepted as the main theoretical foundation explaining the linkages between HRM and organisational performance at the present time. The assumption underpinning the RBVF is that sustained competitive advantage derives from astute use of a firm's internal resources, where the contribution of a firm's human resources is to promote the development of its human capital rather than just aligning human resources to the firm's strategic goals. The focus is on not only the behaviour of human resources but also the skills, knowledge, attitudes and competencies which people bring into an organisation, to promote sustained competitive advantage and business growth. An example is professional football clubs. In Europe for example, clubs compete for a scarce pool of international players to play for them to win football competitions, paying premium wages and transfer fees to attract and retain them. As Sisson and Storey (2000: 34) argue: 'such an approach to understanding strategy places managers' role in identifying, utilizing and renewing such assets centre-stage'.

RBVF theory is rooted in the business economics literature, where theories of profit and competition have identified the internal resources of the firm as the major determinants of competitive success (Penrose 2009). Proponents of this model, such as Barney (1991), define 'resources' as all the assets, capabilities, organisational processes, firm attributes, information, knowledge and other assets controlled by a firm that enable it to conceive and implement strategies to improve its efficiency and effectiveness. He classifies them into three categories: physical capital, organisational capital and human capital, where human capital resources include the experience, judgement and intelligence of individual managers and workers in the firm. In the RBVF, competitive advantage occurs when a firm implements a value-creating strategy that is not being simultaneously implemented by its competitors. This occurs in situations of 'resource heterogeneity' (i.e. where resources vary across firms) and 'resource immobility' (i.e. where competing firms are unable to obtain resources from other firms). The main assumptions underpinning the RBVF are, first, firms are heterogeneous regarding the strategic resources they control. Second, these resources are imperfectly mobile within factor markets. Third, firms controlling valuable, rare, imperfectly imitable and non-substitutable resources are able to generate sustained competitive advantage for themselves (Barney 1991).

CONCLUSION AND IMPLICATIONS

A strong theme running throughout this chapter is that no universal model of human resources management or personnel management exists which applies cross-internationally. HRM, the dominant orthodoxy in the field today, is a universalist approach based on research and experience originating in the United States; but it is not practised in co-ordinated market economies or transition market economies with different employment relations systems. The central argument is that the ways in which human resources are managed are culturally, institutionally and contextually determined. From the perspective of institutional theory, managerial decision-making is not just the outcome of strategic choices; it is also the product of powerful social choices within and outside enterprises. These include 'pulls' from external institutions, such as the law, culture and the role of the state (coercive pulls), from organisations modelling themselves on other organisations in response to uncertainty (mimetic or imitative pulls), and from practices disseminated by professional networks (normative pulls) (DiMaggio and Powell 1991).

This chapter also argues that within structured employment relations systems organisational bureaucracies continue to exist but new organisational forms in creative and service-oriented enterprises are emerging. These are replacing routinised manufacturing organisations, with their traditional job structures, rational management systems and compliant workforces. Post-bureaucratic organisational forms are defined as having moved on from a rational, positivist, technocratic knowledge base, seeking efficiency through standardisation, order and control, to networked, less-hierarchic, flexible, organisations, where learning plays a central role in organisational development. Such organisations are sometimes 'celebrated' as 'offering cleaner, safer and more supportive, even liberating working environments' (Bolton and Houlihan 2009: 6). It is also suggested that post-bureaucracy results in new, progressive managerial practices, including high-commitment HRM, sophisticated EI mechanisms, and opportunities for employee training and development within a continuous learning environment (Dyer and Reeves 1995). In post-bureaucratic organisations, employees are viewed as being treated as valuable resources and human capital rather than mere commodities, as illustrated by so-called exemplary organisations – like Google and Microsoft – in 'Best Places to Work' lists (Great Places to Work 2012). This new model of organisation also claims to incorporate flexible production systems, where both cost reduction and quality improvements are reconciled (Durrand and Boyer 1997). Employment relationships within such organisations are typically non-unionised.

Increasing interest has been shown recently in some advanced nation states how employers motivate employees and manage psychological contracts and what the key determinants of 'good' employment relations are. Breaching the psychological contract, seriously damages the employment relationship, with managers playing a key role in preventing or responding to this. Even if it is not possible to avoid a breach of the psychological contract, managers can choose to be open with employees about any employment issues needing to be addressed. The psychological contract does not provide a detailed model for managing employment relations; it only offers clues how employers can attempt to maintain employee commitment. With the decline in collective bargaining in many countries, and with more managerial attention being focused on maintaining 'good' relations between the organisation and individual employees, supporting a 'healthy' psychological contract between the parties is seen as vital. The psychological contract reinforces the need for managers to become more effective in communication and consultation, which helps to adjust expectations where the 'deal' between the parties needs re-negotiating. For some managers, the psychological contract provides a convincing rationale for promoting 'soft HRM' practices and enabling organisations to behave as 'good' employers. For some workers, however, the psychological contract is seen as further promoting managerial control of work and the employment relationship.

In the traditional industrial relations paradigm, the managerial task was primarily managing employment contracts between the organisation and its employees, drawing upon collective agreements between employer and union representatives. With the weakening of collective bargaining and trade unionism, and the creation of new types of more flexible organisations, the managerial task increasingly involves managing other forms of 'contract' between employers and employees. This is why managing the psychological contract becomes more important for those managers (Rousseau 1995, Guest and Conway 2005, Cullinane and Dundon 2006).

In reviewing the impact of issues affecting human resources management in 13 transitional political economies, Debrah and Budhwar (2004) identify three major influences: religious (such as Islam, Hinduism, Buddhism and traditional beliefs in spirits, fetishes and gods); traditional cultural beliefs (Confuscianism, African traditional practices and institutions); and western colonial and modern ones. Mellahi and Budhwar (2006) suggest, for example, that people in the Middle-East have retained their work-related cultural values over time and, as a result, have different attitudes towards work and employment from people in other geographic regions. Thus countries such as Kuwait, Egypt, Iran, Saudi Arabia, Turkey and Morocco show a high degree of homogeneity around high power distance, collectivism, Islamic values and Arab traditions. In India and Nepal, in turn, there is a strong influence of British colonial traditions in legislation and bureaucracy (Adhikari and Muller 2004). These states have *ad hoc* employment systems, where collective bargaining is weak. However, as countries and regions modernise, economically, politically and technologically, traditional impacts diminish and more professionalised and rational approaches to human resources management are more likely to emerge.

Controlling the employment relationship is central to the employer and management functions in contemporary organisations; employees are a cost to their employer and a resource to be used in combination with finance capital, physical capital and technology to produce goods and services for market-oriented customers. Management creates processes to organise, direct and control these human resources. This is summed up by Anthony and Govindarajan (2004: 4) who write: 'management control is the process by which managers of all levels ensure that the people they supervise implement their intended strategies'. Managing employee performance is thus a key management function and a central feature of control in today's complex worlds of work and organisation, with planned HRM policies and activities being used in the control process. The objective in selection, for example, is to match individuals to job requirements, thereby improving organisational performance; staff appraisals provide the basis for employee rewards and development and training; rewards help motivate employees and raise their performance; and employee development also contributes to better performance (Fombrun *et al.*

1984). Dedicated HR policies and procedures, in short, help recruit, manage, reward and develop people, thereby helping to control employee behaviour and performance at work. Also as 'non-union' employment relations policies or de-centralised collective bargaining become normalised, the roles of employers' associations in employment policy-making diminish.

What top managers look for in sophisticated organisations in the global economy, such as TNCs and large national companies, is sustained competitive advantage through appropriate SHRM initiatives without union involvement. Becker and Huselid (2010: 352) argue that SHRM differs from HRM in two important respects. 'First, SHRM focuses on organizational performance rather than individual performance. Second, it also emphasizes the role of HR management *systems* as solutions to business problems.' These include positive and negative complementarities rather than HR management practices in isolation, while the word 'strategic' means focusing on more than systems or financial performance. 'Strategy is about building sustainable competitive advantage that in turn creates above average financial performance. The simplest depiction of the SHRM model is a relationship between a firm's HR Architecture and firm performance.' HR architecture is the systems, practices, competences and employee behaviours that reflect the development and management of its strategic capital in firms. Above average performance by firms is associated with their HR architecture, reflects earnings in excess of the cost of the alternatives foregone (or quasi rents), and is 'associated with that strategic resource'.

Huws and Podro (2012: 2, 6) argue, however, that in many sectors global value chains have become more complex and volatile, 'with activities being shifted both contractually and spatially as they are subjected to outsourcing to or from companies that may themselves be undergoing restructuring through mergers or acquisitions or changes in global sourcing strategies'. They claim that outsourcing and off-shoring have deleterious impacts on a number of HR issues. These include: job security, terms and condition, equality in the workplace, autonomy and experience of work, new skill requirements, managing HR practices across organisational boundaries, employee voice, and the role of trade unions. For them, 'HR and trade unions, once the key players in the management of the employment relationship, are increasingly finding themselves detached from a relationship with the key decision makers.' They recommend creation of coherent systems of employment relations 'futures', with greater legal regulation, voluntary codes of practice, employee voice, and use of social media and virtual communication to offset the above difficulties.

10

WORKER RESISTANCE AND UNION REGULATION

The purpose of this chapter is to examine the changing faces of worker resistance and union regulation affecting management in organisations, through either informal or formal means, building on the frameworks provided in Chapter 6. To be competitive, enterprises need to be efficient and deliver quality goods or services to their customers, especially under conditions of 'turbo-capitalism'. To achieve this, work has to be suitably organised and co-ordinated by management. In modern workplaces, managers recruit, organise, allocate, reward, train and evaluate their workforces. Workers as employees, in turn, supply their knowledge, skills and experience to their employers and do their jobs within the frameworks of organisational policies, procedures and rules. Subsidiary parties in employment relations are HR specialists or HR professionals and, where recognised, trade unions. HR specialists are the organisational agents of employee efficiency and effectiveness and, ideally, they promote ethical HR practices; unions are collective bargaining agencies, which negotiate terms and conditions with management on behalf of their members as employees. In this complex set of work relationships, management typically seeks to employ co-operative, compliant workers able to contribute to the achievement of the goals and objectives of the organisation, especially its financial ones. In the contemporary world, however, many 'individuals live the contradiction between employers' need to exercise control over workers while at the same time securing their cooperation in the performance of their work' (Edwards and Wajcman 2005: 41, 32). So in practice, although some employees want to be active participants or 'citizens' in their organisations, 'the way that management power is organised can leave them little scope to demonstrate their commitment'.

RESISTANCE AND MISBEHAVIOUR AT WORK

As outlined in Chapter 6, workers are not always compliant with management decisions and managerial control. Consequently, they commonly try to find countervailing means of protecting and promoting their employment interests both in the workplace and beyond it. The matters of most concern to them include their terms and conditions of their employment, especially wages, hours of work, job security, and health and safety. But they are also interested in how work is organised, their workloads, the effort bargain, and the discretion they have in performing their job tasks. To protect their job interests, workers adopt either *informal* or *formal* methods of job regulation. Informal methods are autonomous and unorganised. They are primarily used to promote worker resistance to managerial controls or attempts at counter-control, which may be individually or workgroup-based. Formal methods of job regulation in contrast are institutionalised and based on worker solidarity, commonly through union organisation. These include collective bargaining, worker representation and two-way communications with management. Even where institutional arrangements exist, workers may also adopt unorganised individual and workgroup strategies that resist and dissent from management control and how it is exercised. These informal and formal methods of job regulation by workers and their representatives reflect those inevitable conflicts of interest arising between managers and subordinate employees over authority relations in the modern workplace, which at times undermine co-operation and goodwill between them.

Concepts of worker resistance

Worker resistance, misbehaviour and dissent are important components of everyday working life. The differences between them are difficult to define with precision. Basically, resistance in the workplace is willingness by workers to challenge or refuse to comply with certain managerial decisions or behaviour (such as working arrangements or bullying by managers); misbehaviour is acting in ways not in accordance with organisational norms and expectations about what are appropriate or inappropriate actions by workers and managers (such as theft); and dissent is expressing strong disagreement about any management policies or practices that are controversial or contentious for workers (such as unethical or 'unfair' employment practices). There is a continuum of protesting behaviours, ranging 'from rebellion, insurrections and riots, shading through strikes and other types of formally organized resistance in workplaces through sabotage, theft to destructiveness, work limitation, absenteeism, and time-wasting' to 'the cynical debunking of management pretensions and the satirical mockery of managers and authority figures' (Collinson and Ackroyd 2005: 306). With some exceptions, most literature in the field is Anglo-American in its origins. This tends to focus on *both* covert, unorganised oppositional worker practices (including absenteeism and labour turnover) *and* overt, organised oppositional practices by typically male, manual workers in unionised, especially manufacturing settings, including industrial action by union members.

The study of worker resistance in enterprises focuses either on the organisational attributes that affect the capacity of workplace actors to resist management behaviour or on shop-floor social relations affecting resistance. This dichotomy, driven by analytical and methodological preferences, also reflects different theoretical traditions in the field. Thus Roscigno and Hodson (2004) suggest that organisational attributes and interpersonal relations in the workplace, combined with union presence and the history of collective action, may be both meaningful for workers and how they structure their resistance strategies against management. Notably, the impact of workplace organisation and union presence on worker resistance varies widely, depending on social relations on the shop floor. Thus where there is union presence and significant interpersonal conflict with supervisors, the likelihood of collective resistance in the form of strike action is heightened. These patterns of behaviour coincide with certain individual forms of worker resistance such as non-physical or social sabotage, work avoidance, and absenteeism. Central to individual resistance, however, are workplace contexts characterised by poor organisational systems, insensitive or autocratic management, and lack of a tradition of collective action.

The study of organisations as places of resistance to managerial authority and dissenting worker behaviours started in the early twentieth century, when scientific management and human relations writers were well aware that not all worker behaviour was compliant and obedient (Taylor 1947, Mayo 1933). They sought to counter these tendencies through pay incentives and good human relations practices. Evidence-based knowledge and understanding in the field emerged out of a number of academic areas, each with its own perspective and analytical framework, such as organisation theory, industrial relations, industrial anthropology, industrial psychology, and industrial sociology. Even today, observers draw upon a variety of terms to describe employee practices whose purposes are to oppose and resist some managerial decisions or 'bad' managerial behaviours towards workers. The situation is further confused by the variety of concepts adopted in the field. Thus Jermier *et al.* (1994) use the term 'resistance', Ackroyd and Thompson

(1999) 'misbehaviour' – including managerial misbehaviour – and Tilly *et al.* (1975) 'dissent', while Goffman (1959) refers to 'secondary adjustments' and Greenberg and Giacalone (1997) to 'antisocial behavior'.

Whatever descriptors are used, resistance, struggle and effort bargaining are important components of everyday life in the workplace. Yet the topic of worker resistance has a limited place in theoretical models of the workplace. As a result, the study of worker resistance is commonly conceptually confused. However, Roscigno and Hodson (2004: 17) provide a useful framework for analysing it. They identify four theoretical models of resistance. The first is a *workplace organisation model*, which argues that workplaces with formal organisational structures and procedures exhibit less worker resistance than other workplaces. This may be due to formal capacity to deal with grievances, greater workplace bureaucratic control, and clear specification and constraints on job responsibilities and duties. The *social relations model* focuses on interpersonal relations in the workplace. Here abuse by managers, such as bullying and intermittent conflict between managers and workers, provokes resistance from workers by violating their 'normative expectations' and 'helping legitimate or justify resistance-oriented action'. The *conditional model* posits that the impact of workplace organisation on worker resistance is conditional on the quality of worker–manager relations and vice versa. Well-organised bureaucracies are likely to foster lower levels of worker resistance than others, while workplaces characterised by poor and informal organisation 'experience heightened resistance at both collective and individual levels, although this might be buffered by good shop floor social relations'. Under the *union and legacy model* of worker resistance, workplaces characterised 'by historical class identity and union presence will be more amenable' to labour organisation 'and activity'. In this case, direct and 'aggressive forms of individual resistance may be more notable'.

A variety of types of resistant behaviours by workers is identified by writers. These include: collective resistance such as striking; individual resistance such as 'social' sabotage which seeks to undermine and ridicule superiors; work avoidance by not doing allocated job tasks; 'playing dumb' by pretending not to understand job tasks or work procedures; absenteeism in response to workplace problems; and theft on the job. Whatever forms worker resistance and misbehaviour take, they are costly to the employer, reduce organisational performance and impact negatively on the business. But 'misbehaviour' at work is not limited to subordinate employees alone. Senior managers also 'misbehave' through insider trading, corporate fraud, tax avoidance and manipulating share prices. Clearly, senior managers have other opportunities for misbehaviour not available to non-managerial employees (Holcomb and Sethi

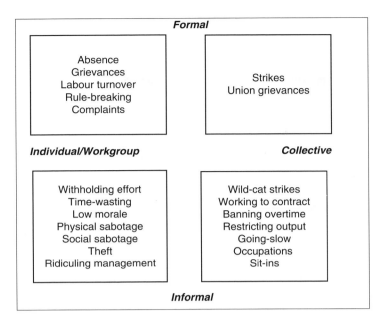

Figure 10.1 Manifestations of worker resistance

1992, Punch 1996). The main manifestations of worker resistance are provided in Figure 10.1.

Frameworks for understanding resistance

There is no single perspective or theoretical framework for analysing employee resistance in the workplace. However, a two-dimensional model of workplace and civic resistance in political democracies is presented in Figure 10.2, so the framework is less appropriate to one-party states such as China or North Korea. The first dimension is 'politics'; the second 'location'. Macro-politics is any large-scale, institutionalised political activity by people that takes place in the workplace and civil society; 'infra-politics' is the small-scale politics of protest that takes place within the workplace and civil society by individuals and groups (Böhm *et al.* 2008). Infra-politics, in other words, involves daily confrontations, evasive actions and thoughts of protest by individuals and groups at micro- and macro-levels. It is the workplace that provides the 'space' for conflicts about control of the labour process, since civil society has relatively little 'room' for it. Civil society's concern is conflict over legitimacy. Using this framework, resistance in the workplace takes two forms: either through organised worker resistance, normally involving trade unions,

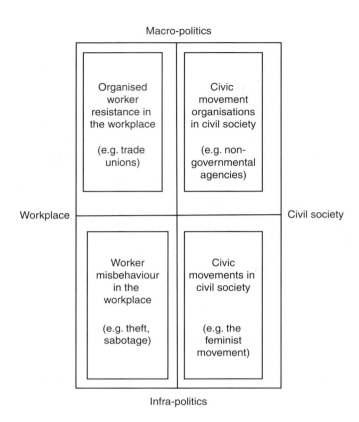

Macro-politics

| Organised worker resistance in the workplace (e.g. trade unions) | Civic movement organisations in civil society (e.g. non-governmental agencies) |

Workplace ─────────────────────────── Civil society

| Worker misbehaviour in the workplace (e.g. theft, sabotage) | Civic movements in civil society (e.g. the feminist movement) |

Infra-politics

Figure 10.2 A model of workplace and civic resistance
Source: Böhm *et al.* (2008).

or through autonomous misbehaviour by workers. The two remaining categories of resistance by people are *either* civic movement organisations (such as non-governmental organisations), which are politicised in the wider civil society, *or* civic movements (such as the feminist movement) which also take place in the wider civil society.

A number of theoretical perspectives can be identified in the literature on worker resistance and misbehaviour in organisations. First, in the North American literature on organisational behaviour, US scholars have tended to adopt a unitary ideology of worker compliance and obedience in organisations, based on the assumption that the interests of managers and employees are always identical. Conflict is deemed as being absent or largely frictional in organisations, provided managers treat employees with dignity, consideration and effective leadership. This perspective of business corporations views them as 'teams' united by shared interests and values, where senior management is the sole source of authority and single focus of loyalty (Fox 1966). The managerial approach to organisational behaviour in US text books coincides with the value systems of the managers running firms and businesses. Both writers and managers in the United States assume if employees are treated reasonably, then responsible worker behaviour follows. In recent years, however, such views have come under scrutiny, shaped by concerns that worker resistance is unprincipled, dangerous and has to be controlled by management. By this view, worker resistance and misbehaviour are harmful, need to be recognised, and have to be responded to. Management has to decide, therefore, whether or not to impose sanctions on these workers (Bennett and Robinson 2000). As Ackroyd and Thompson (1999) argue, the objective of these studies is to construct the idea of the obedient and compliant employee within organisations, based on the assumption that anything other than basic frictional conflict within organisations is dysfunctional, counterproductive and arises from malcontents in the workforce.

Second, labour process theory takes a contrary position, by claiming there is an inevitable and structured antagonism or conflict between management and labour within all capitalist business enterprises (Burawoy 1979, Edwards 1976, Edwards 1979). By this view, worker resistance is seen to result from the intrusive and rigid control imposed by managers on employees in the workplace, in response to the continuous search for profits and performance in competitive product markets. Indeed, market competition is seen as leading to constantly changing working conditions, so firms continually have to extract greater value from their labour resources to survive and grow (Braverman 1974). However, writers such as Beynon (1975) assert that managerial control is never complete and workers always find ways of resisting managerial power and authority in the workplace. This group of writers argues that managerial control is inherently contradictory in its attempts to treat employees as labour which is both dependable and disposable. Typically, managers try to harness employee commitment, while limiting employee discretion, because this might be applied in ways unacceptable to management. By seeking both commitment and control of employees, the contradictory nature of these managerial practices results in managers trying to manufacture consent, while at the same time exercising coercion on the workforce (Burawoy 1979).

Hodson (1995: 80) defines employee opposition as 'any individual or small group act intended to mitigate claims by management on workers or to advance workers' claims against management'. He proposes a model of worker resistance that conceptualises four basic agendas: *deflecting abuse, regulating the amount and intensity of work, defending autonomy,* and *expanding worker control* through worker participation schemes. He argues that each of the four agendas of worker resistance parallels modes of the labour process, characterised by Edwards (1979), Thompson (1989) and others. Deflecting abuse is typical of direct control; regulating the amount and intensity of work is typical of technical control; defending autonomy is typical of bureaucratic control; and manipulating participation opportunities is typical of worker resistance under participative forms of work. But agendas of worker resistance are not reducible to forms of control at the workplace, since each agenda emerges to differing degrees under any form of labour control. The parallel agendas of resistance and modes of control allow theories of labour control and worker resistance to be developed. To understand resistance, these arguments suggest an examination has to be made of 'such practices in relation to workplace discipline and managerial control' (Collinson and Ackroyd 2005: 314). Further, although resistance (actions taken by workers against management) and misbehaviour (behaviour by workers or managers that violates organisational or ethical norms) are distinct concepts, many studies equate the two, because both share similar behavioural domains.

Third, feminist studies of the workplace reveal the gendered nature of workplace power relations and the various identities constructed within organisations. Managerial control, it is argued, is commonly sustained through gendered job segregation and de-sexualisation of the workplace (Collinson and Hearn 2003, Burrell 1984). Such studies argue that gender and sexuality contribute to shaping worker resistance and misbehaviour. For example, male-dominated shop-floor cultures are typically characterised by masculine 'breadwinner' mentalities, sexualised forms of humour, elevation of manual skills as confirmation of working-class manhood, and hostility towards management (Cockburn 1991). Female dominated workplaces also engage in joking and sexualised counter-cultures, which seek to resist managerial control. However, there are differences between masculine and feminine dominated workplace cultures, with heterosexual and homosexual men and women also finding ways of resisting desexualisation of the workplace by management (Burrell 1993). Other feminist studies show that male dominated forms of worker resistance at work may even reproduce gender divisions and reinforce women's subordination in the workplace (Walby 2011). For example, male defence of 'breadwinner' wages can be a form of gendered control of jobs and work, through excluding women from protesting behaviours. Women's experience of workplace bullying is another area examined by students of feminism (Lewis and Orford 2004).

Kondo's (1990) case study of a small confectionery factory in the *shitamachi* or downtown area of Tokyo is about gender relations, power and discourses of identity in the workplace. She demonstrates that the Japanese ideology of the workplace as a family does not go uncontested by workers, who are quick to resist it and use it to criticise their managers. Kondo explores the discourse of the household, which survives extra-legally in Japan as a powerful normative force in family life and the workplace. Companies are seen as families, even though they are much less like families than in the past. But even as managers attempt to frame the workplace with a family ideology, workers are able to deploy and take advantage of that same family discourse to resist this. Kondo goes on to explore the myth and discourse of the independent artisan, which still survives at a certain level in Japanese society, as modern capitalism increasingly leaves it as a hollow set of ideals. Similarly, female employees, who are all part-timers, play a crucial part in maintaining the family discourse at the workplace, even though they are systematically disadvantaged and under-paid compared with their male counterparts. Significantly, female workers co-operate at times in maintaining their disadvantaged position, because of the benefits it provides outside the workplace, such as having more time with their families. These women were highly effective in asserting their gender identities, as surrogate mothers to younger male artisans, but were excluded from the central masculine discourses of artisan work, thus reinforcing their own exclusion. Paradoxically, these women workers asserted and marginalised themselves at the same time.

In another case study in the non-English-speaking world, Ong (2010) examines the responses of women factory workers in Malaysia to the discipline imposed upon them by Western industrialism. She offers a model and sophisticated analysis of culturally based resistance to the ideology, surveillance, and institutional authority of globalised corporate capitalism. Ong explores the disruptions, conflicts, and ambivalences in the lives of Malay women factory workers and their families, as they make the transition from peasant society to industrial production. This classic ethnographic study in anthropology, labour studies, gender and globalisation studies is based on field work in an agricultural district in Selangor, Peninsular Malaysia. In this work, Ong captures a time of transformation in the lives of Malay women during the rapid industrialisation associated with Malaysia's rise as a tiger economy. Her approach to the experiences of Malay women factory workers, and the contradictions of modern globalised capitalism, have inspired other feminist ethnographers to explore key questions of power, resistance, femininities, religious community, and social change.

A fourth perspective for analysing worker resistance derives from post-structural theory, where issues of surveillance and subjectivity are examined in organisations. Drawing upon Foucault's (1991) ideas of discipline, post-structural commentators try to show how 'contemporary management control is often exercised by new forms of workplace surveillance', such as CCTV, computer technology, performance targets and performance appraisal, and how disciplinary processes impact on workers (Collinson and Ackroyd 2005: 315, 316). Writers such as Willmott (1993) try to demonstrate the disciplinary effectiveness of surveillance regimes, while others argue that resistance reinforces power and discipline. For Burrell (1988: 228), 'discipline can grow stronger knowing where its next efforts must be directed'. Earlier writers were inclined to celebrate all forms of workplace resistance, but post-structural theorists do not. They suggest any examination of resistance needs to explore the conditions giving 'rise to misbehaviour', the 'meanings, motives, and diverse practices' and consequences or 'impact on selves and organizations'. Resisting and oppositional selves, in short, are open, negotiable, shifting, ambiguous, and potentially contradictory (Collinson 2003).

Fifth, worker cynicism towards management and work is another stream in the literature on worker resistance and misbehaviour. Deal and Kennedy (2000) claim that managerial innovations have intensified work, created more job insecurity and resulted in distrust of management. These include 'soft' management practices, such as culture management, quality circles and employee commitment, and 'hard' ones such as business process re-engineering, lean production, just-in-time management, powerful information management systems, outsourcing and downsizing. Thus for Wright and Smye (1998), lean production and performance management lead to intimidating management styles involving abuse, systematic bullying, scapegoating, and blame cultures. Fleming (2007), who examines worker cynicism in an Australian call centre, finds that its corporate culture treats staff as children. By constructing new opposing identities as dignified adults, staff exhibited cynicism enabling them to resist becoming corporate clones, thus constituting an effective form of resistance to management preferences. Other studies show that pressures for profits and growth lead some top executives to lie and cheat to maintain corporate success. This creates tensions and cynicism among workforces, compelling some senior executives to disclose this information outside the company through whistle-blowing (Miceli et al. 2008). For many employees, detached cynicism is their preferred response to the contradictory managerial responses they experience in many contemporary workplaces.

THE EXTERNAL CONTEXTS OF TRADE UNIONS

Trade unions exist in capitalist market economies around the world, but with varying degrees of density, power and influence. Their explicit aim is to protect, promote and regulate the employment and job interests of their members. As voluntary democratic bodies, unions are inverted hierarchies. They consist of their subscribing members and their professional secretariats, which are accountable to the membership. The explicit function of unions as regulators of employment relationships is to advance and maintain the interests of individual workers against discrimination and unfair employment practices by employers, using their collective power to do this. In most cases, unions are predominantly national organisations, except in the case of company or enterprise unions, such as in Japan and South Korea, where they are local bodies. Unions exist within evolving external contexts at any one time. It is these *external* contexts, such as employers, the economy and national political systems, which have major impacts on the *internal* dynamics of trade unions.

Like businesses and governments, trade unions do not operate in contextual vacuums. As national organisations of workers seeking to influence and regulate employer decision-making, and in some cases as players in politics, unions are embedded in a network of employer, economic, technological, political, legal and societal contexts, as illustrated in Figure 10.3. Further, as Poole (1981: 148) argues, there is little doubt 'that early structural and subjective influences, together with past struggles against employers and government, have made a lasting imprint upon the fabric of modern unionism', wherever they are located.

The employer context

The employer context is an important influence on the internal dynamics of unions. Key factors are the sectors or industries where employers are located, their product markets and employment policies in these sectors. The evidence indicates that large firms in private manufacturing industries, operating in competitive product markets and employing male workers in large employing units, tend to be unionised. Many public sector organisations also accept and even encourage union recognition and collective bargaining. SMEs in the service sector or 'greenfield' high-tech firms, in contrast, are less likely to recognise and deal with trade unions over terms and conditions of employment. Here individual bargaining, employer paternalism and the right to manage predominate. Another issue is the ideology of top managers and whether or not they accept the legitimacy of unions in the workplace and

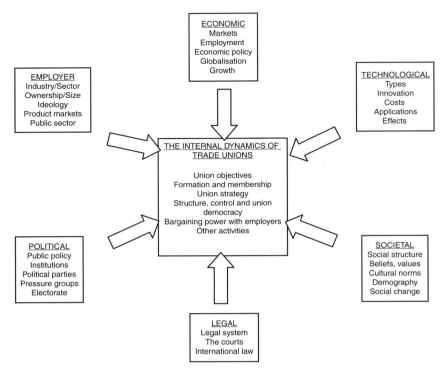

Figure 10.3   The external contexts and internal dynamics of trade unions

company. When senior managers hold unitary and paternalist values, these are commonly hostile to trade unionism, collective bargaining and employee representation. This is particularly the cases in North America, other English-speaking countries and some transition economies, where the right to manage is vigorously defended (Kaufman 2004a).

The economic context

The economic context of trade unions affects their internal dynamics through the interplay of public policy and market forces in the national economy, at both macro- and micro-levels. Employment or unemployment rates, for example, are critical determinants of membership density, membership retention, collective bargaining power and union policy-making. In general, where employment levels are high and near full employment, union membership rises, collective bargaining power increases, and industrial action such as strikes is more likely. The share of wages in national income also tends to rise. With increasing unemployment, union power is weakened, resulting in loss of members, less collective bargaining effectiveness, decreases in industrial action, and a falling share of wages as a proportion of national income. Similarly, where economic growth is incrementally upwards, unions normally benefit through membership growth and increased bargaining power. Where economic growth slows, union power and influence decreases (Gamble *et al.* 2007).

Because of its impact on employment levels, national economic policy is a crucial factor affecting unions and their members. For example, unions are generally strengthened when national governments stimulate aggregate demand using Keynesian counter-cyclical policy instruments. Finance ministers typically promote demand through appropriate monetary and/or fiscal policies. These aim to raise demand for labour and increase employment, thus enabling unions to use their bargaining power in negotiations with employers. Unions do this by threatening to withdraw the labour of their members through strike action. In these conditions, employers are likely to concede the wage claims of union leaders, thereby raising the pay of union members, enabling employers to retain scarce labour and helping them avoid costly industrial conflict. In contrast, where governments pursue neo-classical economic policies, union power is normally diminished. Neo-classical economic policy focuses on the determination of prices, outputs and income distribution through market supply and demand. With government policy instruments promoting price stability or lowering inflation at the cost of higher employment, unions are weakened. This makes them less attractive to workers who quit them, while other workers lose their jobs.

Globalisation and the growth of international trade impact on unions too. Globalisation weakens union bargaining power by lengthening the global supply chain. However in the EU, a cross-national tier of management–labour interaction has been promoted by the EU's requirement that TNCs operating in more than one country establish European-wide works councils, often with union members on them. In contrast, cross-national differences in culture, law and institutions under pressures of globalisation create employment relations and co-ordination problems for managers within TNCs, with knock-on effects for unions. Historically, senior managers in TNCs found there were substantial benefits from de-centralising employment relations, including the benefits of flexibility. Thus with managers in each country fashioning their own local employment relations policies, firms were able to create policies fitting local conditions (Kujawa 1980). However, there is accumulating evidence that there have been shifts in TNC strategy and structure due to globalisation (McGovern 1998).

To avoid boosting local employment conditions, more extensive co-ordination of employment relations policies emerged in some TNCs.

Centres of excellence, for example, give TNCs the capability to take advantage of economies of scale and continuous operation of advanced technological processes. In these circumstances, trade disputes that in the past would have only affected one country can now affect the regional or global supply chain of TNCs, giving some unions more bargaining power with management. (Katz *et al.* 2001).

The technological context

The impact of new technology and technological change on the internal dynamics of trade unions is an ambiguous one, since the introduction of new technology has positive and negative consequences for trade unions. Using the case of professional 'photography' as an occupational example, old technologies associated with film photography and classical cinematography are no longer used, because these have been replaced by radical technological developments. The outcomes have been job and union membership losses in work where union membership was often high. Introduction of digital photography, digital cinematography, digital video and videography has resulted in the creation of new jobs, new skills and new professional opportunities in this field of work (Galer 2008). The issue for unions, as in other occupational changes driven by technological developments, is whether or not they are able to organise the present generation of workers into the union. Such dramatic changes in technology over the past 20 years are associated with a general shift from traditional jobs, work and organisations towards new ones, many of which are fundamentally different from those preceding them. These reflect both the changing technologies involved and the changing values of the societies in which they are located (McLoughlin and Badham 2005).

The political and legal contexts

Political and legal contexts are inter-connected and are very important for unions in capitalist market economies. Unions try to influence public policy, political decision-making and the enactment of new but favourable labour laws promoting union interests, while resisting unfavourable ones. Thus in some countries, such as the Scandinavian states, Germany and the United Kingdom, unions have often had close links with Labour Parties or Social Democratic Parties and have tried to influence or participate in their policy-making processes (Boix and Stokes 2008). In other European countries, such France, Italy and Greece, a variety of trade unions groups try to influence the political and legal policies of governments, by acting as external pressure groups on their parliamentary systems. This includes lobbying, national campaigning, and taking 'direct action' on the streets to influence or to try and change major policy decisions. The areas that unions most commonly seek to influence are laws governing union organisation and union activities. These include the rights to organise, strike, take other forms of industrial action against employers, and collectively negotiate wage agreements with employers. Successful campaigns in these areas demonstrate union effectiveness in employment regulation and where union political power is used to best effect.

But the corollary is that laws can be enacted by governments hostile to trade unionism seeking to weaken union organisation, collective bargaining, and the right to strike. In the United States, Canada and the United Kingdom, for example, the pre-entry closed shop, where workers have to be union members *before* being selected by an employer, are unlawful. Ultimately, of course, within democratic states, trade union members exercise the right to vote in national and local elections and their influence as individual citizens can be important in determining the outcomes of these elections (Daniels and McIlroy 2009, Hayward 1980).

The societal context

Unions are also affected by the societal context in which they work. Factors such as changing patterns of demography, the evolving social structure, people's beliefs and values, cultural norms, and social change are all important. These can affect, to varying degrees, propensity to unionise, labour supply in relation to demand, willingness to strike, and the internal dynamics of unions in terms of their policies, programmes and activities. Thus Lichtenstein (2002) argues that the relationship between organised labour's power and 'national consciousness' is an important one. He claims that union power is high when people in society believe that the labour movement's ideals are central to national problems, such as when strong collective bargaining supported the Keynesian goals of Roosevelt's 'New Deal' in the United States in the 1930s and 1940s. But it is low when they are not. The latter has been the case from the 1970s till the present time, when strong collective bargaining was viewed by its opponents as undermining individual freedoms, economic competitiveness and the right to manage (Clements 2008).

THE INTERNAL DYNAMICS OF TRADE UNIONS

Union objectives

Generically trade unions are formed as agencies of job regulation and exist to achieve a series of job-related objectives on behalf of their members.

The union's underpinning objective is to engage in negotiations or collective bargaining with employers over terms and conditions of employment and authority relations at work. It is in this sense that the union performs its role as a loyal opposition to management. Properly conducted, collective bargaining enables union representatives to discuss a range of employment issues with management affecting the job interests of members. These include decisions over pay, working hours, holidays and changes to working practices. Unions also deal with grievances, disciplinary cases and disputes with management using relevant negotiating machinery.

Whatever model of trade unionism is adopted, trade unions also represent workers as individuals, when they have a problem at work. For example, where an employee feels she is being unfairly treated in the workplace, she can ask a union representative to help resolve the difficulty with her manager. Unions offer members legal representation too, such as helping workers get financial compensation for work-related injuries or assist members wishing to take their employer to court in legal disputes between them. However, the economic security of employees is determined not only by the level of wages and duration of their employment but also by management's HR policies including selection of employees for redundancy, promotion and transfer. All these policies directly affect workers. Sometimes the managerial criteria for such decisions are not seen as fair, so union intervention is a means through which workers have a say in matters affecting their employment interests at work (Income Data Services 2013).

In recent years, unions have increased the range of other services they offer members. These include education and training, such as training courses on employment rights, health and safety, and other issues. Some unions help members who have left school with little education by offering courses on basic skills or leading to professional qualifications. Legal advice and legal assistance is provided to members on employment issues, while some unions give help with housing, wills and personal debt.

Formation and membership

The literature on how unions are formed, such as through union recognition ballots or elections for bargaining units, is wide-ranging but largely indeterminate. Some observers stress the individual factors involved such as dissatisfaction about one's job, general beliefs about unions and the perceived benefits relative to costs of union formation or union 'instrumentalities'. These studies are based mainly on US, Canadian and UK data-sets (Kochan 1979, Gomez *et al.* 2001, Wood and Machin 2005). Alternative explanations include distrust in the employment relationship, desire for voice and representation, perceived injustice at work, fear of employer reprisal, fear of conflict, work orientation, and political beliefs and affiliations.

Godard (2008: 382, 386, 391) concludes: 'there has been little research into the importance of alternative and more specific possible explanations', including institutional determinants. The external factors influencing workers to join unions, based on voting propensities in union election ballots, have also been examined. These include: employer practices, job characteristics, pay, working conditions, social influences, and individual and demographic characteristics. But again, research in the external propensities for unionisation 'appear to yield surprisingly slim pickings'. Other research on organising union recognition reveals the importance of contextual factors such as union policy, organiser characteristics and size of bargaining unit. Also, research on union and employer tactics in union recognition campaigns 'would appear to suffer from potentially significant methodological and interpretive problems'.

Whatever the complex causes of union formation and recognition, a union's membership size provides its power-base. Union membership is based on the premise that the status of an employed person in a capitalist market economy is one of dependence on employment, earnings and representation. Equality before the law is only relevant to observance of the contract of employment, 'not to its terms or to the procedure by which it is made' (Trades Union Congress 1966: 29, 30). Combinations of working people realise that to exercise their individual rights they need to assert their collective will against employers. This enables them to redress any imbalances in strength or power in relations with their employers. Individual employees who join unions recognise that it is through combining together that they can best develop the essential means to harness their collective strength. 'The feeling of collective identity enhances the economic freedom of the individual, a freedom which rests on the knowledge that unity is strength.' Thus unions with large memberships, sound finances, and well-organised internal democracies are, in the majority of cases, more powerful and effective than those lacking these essential characteristics.

Union strategy

The literature on trade union strategy is a relatively new one, where 'life cycle' models and 'union portfolio' analyses are the dominant approaches (Boxall 2008, Boxall and Haynes 1997, Willman 2001). The modern concept of strategy has a long history and, as applied to unions, is developed and borrows from the business and managerial literature in the field. For business organisations, the case is made that with businesses operating in increasingly complex external contexts, those leading them – in the private, public and third sectors – are using techniques of strategic management in response to uncertainty, change and market competition, resulting in written, formal corporate strategies. There are, however, conflicting views of the strategic process (Whittington 2001) but two main perspectives are noted in the literature. First, the *deterministic* view is rationalist and assesses where an organisation is at the moment, how it got there, analyses the directions in which it might go to survive and prosper, determines how it can get there, and subsequently evaluates whether it has achieved its objectives (De Wit and Meyer 2010). Second, the *emergent* view is where strategy is 'shaped', without predetermined objectives, and 'emerges' over time in response to changing organisational needs. In this case, the final objectives of strategy are unclear and its elements are developed as strategy unfolds (Mintzberg 1987, Mintzberg 1994).

Life-cycle phases of union development

Drawing upon Mueller (1997) and others, Boxall and Purcell (2011) argue that industries evolve through a three-phase life-cycle of establishment, maturity, and a renewal crisis and potential decline. The *establishment phase* involves high levels of business start-ups, experimentation, and a range of business models. This leads to a *mature phase*, where organisations develop strategies that create 'dominant designs' or systems which are economically and socially sustainable. But, when mature organisations are challenged by external economic, political, social or technological changes, their dominant designs are reformed and renewed or these organisations decline and fail; this is the *renewal crisis* phase. This life-cycle model of industrial development provides a helpful framework for analysing union growth, evolution and possible decline (Lester and Harbison 2011, Kearney 2003).

Hannan (1995) argues that unions emerged as social movement organisations in the English-speaking world from the mid-nineteenth century onwards in North America, Britain and Australia. The driving motivation of the founding members and leaders of these unions was to protect workers collectively against harsh employers and bad working conditions, in response to low wages, unsafe working arrangements and dictatorial managerial regimes. The essential purpose of these early unions was to ensure that organised labour could play a key role in regulating the wage–work and effort bargains with managements on behalf of their members. These unions were often militant, with high membership participation, tense internal factionalism and strong opposition from employers. Further, concentrated networks of 'social capital' were created mainly by men and some women, who worked and lived in close proximity together in large cities (Jarley 2005). Union strategy at this time was organic. It derived out of working people's needs for economic and social change, power to influence their futures and organisational ability to promote their occupational interests at work.

As unions move into the mature phase, they no longer rely for organisational survival and growth on the spontaneity of their founders and early members (Farnham 1974). They now require bureaucratic organisation and solid internal structures to undertake their job regulation function effectively on behalf of their members. This means having permanent paid officials, management committees and policy-making bodies of elected members. This shift towards bureaucracy and the search for systems of internal union control generates potential conflict between administrative efficiency in the union, on the one hand, and democratic accountability on the other. Thus by recruiting paid officials, unions create tensions between hierarchical control by the administrative elite and democratic control by union members, since the goals of union leaders may differ from those of rank-and-file members (Fiorito *et al.* 2001). After all, unions are voluntary associations, whose members pay subscriptions to join the union, but they themselves are not union employees; this is one of their distinctive features.

In terms of strategic choices, some mature unions are officer-led organisations based on the servicing model, providing members with a range of services in exchange for their subscriptions. In other cases, unions adopt the organising model, which empowers members to lead the union and its policy making processes (Boxall and Haynes 1997). Top-down strategies may emerge by the actions of the full-time leaderships or bottom-up strategies by union members, although Turnbull (1988: 113) writes that 'trade union structure involves a *two-way* process of internal control'. This means that at various times full-time officials and/or lay officials may pull in one direction, while groups of members pull in another. Both groups, however, have to maintain long-term interdependence with each other or the union becomes dysfunctional (Heery 2005). In mature unions, in short, there is a 'politics of leadership' which needs analysing if strategic decision-making is to be explained and understood (Boxall and Haynes 1997: 571).

At workplace level, mature unions demonstrate a range of strategies, depending on how their relationships with workers and employers are structured. Boxall and Haynes (1997) argue that the dichotomy between the servicing and organising models of unions is questionable, since all unions provide some services to members. The strategic issue is the extent to which the union builds its organising capabilities to complement its servicing functions. Powerful forms of organisation can be built by union activists rather than by paid officials. Activists may also organise membership around certain solidarity issues, thereby generating 'surges of participation' in the union (Fosh 1993; 580). Depending how unions encompass or complement their servicing roles with these powerful forms of member participation, 'they are a threat to employer control in the workplace' (Boxall 2008: 215).

Boxall and Haynes (1997) also argue that employer determinants of union strategy do not indicate a simple dichotomy of *either* co-operative *or* adversarial relations between the players; unions depend on a blend between them. Five main choices are possible. First, the union can seek the best bargain in the circumstances, without identifying with the employer's agenda. Second, it can adopt a classical adversarial bargaining position, while exploring possibilities of 'concertation' or closer integration with the employer (Crouch 1982). Third, union officials can offer ideological support with rank-and-file members through 'attitudinal structuring' and accepting their policy objectives (Walton and McKersie 1991). Fourth, union officials can set up joint working parties with management, where union activists are involved rather than full-time paid officials (Frost 2001). Fifth, union leaders can raise levels of participation within firms by getting involved in their 'strategic activities', such as in portfolio choices or decisions on plant locations (Kochan *et al.* 1986: 15).

The renewal crisis phase in the life-cycle of trade unions has arisen in many unions around the world over the past 20 years, because of changing economic, political, social, technological and global factors. Indicators of this crisis include falling membership density, decreased collective bargaining coverage, and marginalisation of unions in workplaces and politics. As Boxall (2008: 219) argues, studies of union revitalisation 'need to consider not only the employer face of strategy but *simultaneously* examine the impacts on workers'. For him, union renewal is determined by analysing worker needs, how these evolve and how they might be addressed. One response is social movement unionism. This has emerged where low wages, bad working conditions and social exclusion persist. In the case of the US labour movement, Voss and Sherman (2000: 311) believe a blend of old and new union tactics are involved. These include: 'dignity and fairness'; 'material concerns'; 'corporate campaigns'; 'frequent direct actions'; alliances with 'community and religious groups'; and use of the media, including social media, 'to disseminate the union's message'. The fundamental point is resuscitating organic unionism is not the answer. The challenge for unions in a renewal crisis is to try rebalancing the roles of officials, activists and members and finding new ways of integrating centralised union decision-making with local democracy and membership involvement.

Union portfolios

Willman (2001: 114) provides a bargaining unit analysis of trade union strategy based on union portfolios, as illustrated in Figure 10.4. In his view, unions can be analysed as 'portfolios of viable and inviable bargaining units'. His framework identifies four broad types of bargaining unit: type A, where the employer is co-operative and union membership active; type B, where the employer is co-operative and membership passive; type C, where the employer is recalcitrant and membership active; and type D, where the employer is recalcitrant and membership passive. The optimum condition for the union is case A. Here union costs per member for the bargaining unit are reduced, thus enabling it to cross-subsidise or export funds to other bargaining units. In case B, union members pay their union dues but are not willing to participate in union bargaining activities, enabling some cross-subsidisation of other bargaining units to take place. In both cases C and D, bargaining units are net importers of union funds, which can undermine the union's financial viability, and are risky for the union. In case C, the costs involved in potential industrial action are high, while in case D union de-recognition is possible.

The main implication of union portfolio analysis is that some unions can increase membership but be heavily loaded towards risky bargaining units, whereas others with smaller memberships cluster around highly viable bargaining units. For Willman (2001: 105), this framework helps explain 'the size distribution of unions in the UK, with the persistence of viable small unions during a long period of increasing union concentration'.

	Employer	
	Co-operative	Recalcitrant
	A Lay representation Facilities agreements Union check-off Politically powerful in the union Exporter of funds	C Few facilities High official involvement High potential for conflict Importer of funds
Membership Passive	B Full facilities Low lay representation High official involvement Exporter of funds	D Potential de-recognition Politically low profile Importer of funds

Active applies to the top row and *Passive* to the bottom row of **Membership**.

Figure 10.4 Union type and union representation
Source: Willman (2001).

Structure, control and union democracy

A union's internal structure is a function of union purpose. Here two models of trade unionism are commonly presented. One is the 'servicing model'. This type of trade unionism is 'top-down' and discourages activism and self-representation by members in favour of provision of services by full-time paid officers. The services include collective bargaining or advice, representation and benefits to individual union members. The servicing model is often counter-posed to the 'organising model' of trade unions. The organising model is a 'bottom-up' approach and was adopted by American unions in the 1980s to recruit new members and develop union organisation, when neo-liberal economic policy was emerging as the dominant paradigm (Hurd 2004). It subsequently influenced union practices in Australia, Canada, Germany, New Zealand and the United Kingdom. At the heart of the organising model is the notion that unions should be based upon the 'self-activity' or activism of their members. Recruitment of workers into unions is not undertaken by providing membership services, but through mobilising workers in campaigns that create effective and self-reliant workplace organisations. The active organising model is contrasted with the passive servicing model, because it is informed by the concept of 'social movement unionism', as illustrated in Figure 10.5, which tries to link with external campaigns and other organisations. But in practice, as Banks and Metzgar (2005) acknowledge, the contrast between the two models is sometimes overstated.

Figure 10.5 illustrates the relationships between types of trade unionism and union representation. Thus job control unions and European social partnerships are passive *servicing models* of unionism, where members are represented by union officials. Worker empowerment unions and social movement unions, in contrast, are active *organising models*, where members are represented by union members. Job control unions and worker empowerment unions, in turn, are types of business unionism in the workplace, whereas

	Type of trade unionism	
Union representation	**Business unionism in the workplace**	**Social unionism in the wider social arena**
Union officials (passive servicing model)	Job control unions	European social partnerships
Union members (active organising model)	Worker empowerment unions	Social movement unions

Figure 10.5 Willman's portfolio analysis
Source: Budd (2004).

European social partnerships and social movement unions are types of social unionism in the wider political arena.

Internal union democracy is one of the dominant themes in debates about union government. A common denominator in discussions about union democracy is control and how power is distributed in unions. If a trade union is viewed typically as an inverted hierarchy where power is ultimately vested in its membership, each individual's ultimate power is quitting the union. But the collective power of a union is vested in its membership and this is delegated *upwards* through its branches and regions to the national executive and the union president or general secretary. At national level, the union's national leader is then accountable for implementing union policy decisions, established by lay members within its policy-making conference or convention. In this stylised model of union democracy, control is nominally exercised by a system of checks and balances within the union structure, as determined by the union rule book.

In early unions in the United States and Britain, small craft-based organisations of workers exerted membership or 'rank-and-file' control over union decision-making through 'primitive democracy', unlike modern large-scale unions today. Now representative systems of internal democracy predominate and expert cadres of full-time officials are employed to carry out their duties as professional negotiators, advocates, researchers and administrators, with ultimate accountability to the union. However, measures and definitions of internal union democracy are necessarily inexact or contested and the institutional and procedural mechanisms through which control in unions is exercised in practice vary widely. The factors influencing internal union control include: arrangements for elections to office; appointments of full-time officials; union rule books and internal procedures; access to communication networks; the activities of union factions and internal oppositions; attendance and participation at meetings; union conferences and conventions; the structural features and inter-relationships of the union's executive, legislative and judicial functions; and national laws on trade unions (Phelan 2007).

The most useful criterion for assessing democracy in unions, at both local and national levels, is the extent to which union leaders are responsive to the general will of their members. Of course, the larger the union or its unit of administration the more difficult it is to judge this. Intuitively it can be argued that most union leaders have a fairly good idea of what their members want or what members find acceptable from the union. It is also argued that most leaders normally manage to provide this to a reasonable degree. Indeed, failures by a union leadership to fulfil its membership's expectations are normally met in most unions by some form of opposition and ultimate rejection. Some observers argue that this happened, because of intra-union divisions, in the year-long national coal strike in the United Kingdom in 1984–1985. The result was the eventual demise of the National Union of Mineworkers and its collapse as an effective organisation, where the political and market contexts of this dispute were major factors in the miners' defeat (Richards 1998).

At least four factors affect control in trade unions. First, membership participation rates in union decision-making are generally low. The manifest apathy of most union members arises partly because the majority of members appear satisfied with what their full-time officials are doing. In other words, most union members regard their union strictly in instrumental terms, not as a social or community club. The main union function is as a bargaining agent with management and the extent to which it does this effectively is sufficient for most members as an indicator of union effectiveness. There is good reason to assume that strong oligarchic leadership in unions is all members want (Michels 1962). With busy working lives, families to care for, and their social life, most union members are not motivated to pursue union democracy for its own sake. It is not a burning issue for most members.

Second, Michels (1962) argues there is an inevitable tendency towards oligarchy in democratic organisations. He calls this 'iron law of oligarchy' and attributes it partly to membership attitudes and partly to union leaders. Members contribute to oligarchy by their disinterest, apathy and desire for strong leadership. Leaders, in turn, play a role in creating and maintaining oligarchy by controlling the main instruments of communication and information in the union, as well as their inside knowledge of the organisation. Union leaders, where they are elected, are insecure in their roles and removal from office results in substantial losses for them, financially and politically. They are likely, therefore, to devise means to protect their positions, which commonly means finding ways of restricting opposition to the official leadership in the union (Fairbrother 1984).

Third, most members accept centralised control in their unions on the implicit assumption that their employment interests are best realised in this way. It is the effective prosecution of a union's collective bargaining function that is the main instrument leading towards bureaucratic union organisations and oligarchic control. As John L. Lewis the US mineworkers' leader is reported to have said to his members: 'What do you want? Do you want an efficient organization or do you want merely a political instrumentality?' (Wechsler 1944: 80). Thus growing centralisation of business, government and the employment function of firms, as well as the need for union experts to service their memberships, have contributed to creating bureaucratic and centralised trade union organisations.

Fourth, in structured employment relations systems, unions have generally matured (Lester and Harbison 2011). This means that the missionary spirit of these unions and their disaffection towards management has been generally dissipated. Unions have become more business-like in the ways in which they are run and, in the process, have become centralised. Where unions are recognised by employers, their legitimacy with management and the formalisation of the employment relationship have moved them in the direction of greater centralisation and bureaucracy.

Bargaining power with employers

Collective bargaining power is the rationale underpinning the trade union function. Prime indicators of this power include: size of union membership; union density; employer recognition; legal support for collective bargaining; the financial stability of the union; the strategic importance of their members' jobs; the coherence of union membership boundaries; willingness of union members to withdraw their labour if necessary; unity and solidarity in the union; and effective leadership (Mishel and Matthew 2003). External economic and political factors either support or weaken this bargaining power. But in essence the greater the perceived bargaining power of the union with employers, the greater the appeal and utility of the union to its members and potential new members. Where a union's bargaining power with employers is weak, its appeal to its members is less persuasive.

Other union activities

Other activities of trade unions include: a union's relations with other unions; its participation within any central union organisation; the political networks within which its leaders are connected; its relations with overseas unions in the same or similar industrial/occupational sectors; and its relationship with regional or international trade union organisations. All these facets of union organisation extend the scope and potential effectiveness of trade unions as organisations representing the employment and job interests of working people (Addison and Schnabel 2003).

TRADE UNIONS: SOME REGIONAL COMPARISONS

Because of their institutional roots, unions are typically national organisations of workers. They can, however, be clustered in geographical regions. This does not mean that unions within any given geographical region, such as the United States, Europe or Asia, are identical with one another in terms of employer attitudes to them, collective bargaining, membership densities, and internal structures. But in practice, there are similarities and differences among unions in each of these regions, as well as similarities and differences between them across geographical boundaries. The underlying reasons are the specific institutional, cultural and historical origins of the unions in each case. Thus it is possible to discuss the general characteristics of unions in Asia, Europe and the United States, assess their similarities and differences, and draw some conclusions about similarities and differences between unions in different geographical regions.

Unions in Asia

There are large contrasts in the character and size of unions across Asia. This is due to different rates of economic development, the variety of their political systems, and their indigenous multi-ethnic social cultures. Some countries, such as Japan, are economically developed with stable political systems, while others, such as China or India, are economically diversified with either single-party or dysfunctional political regimes. In some Asian states, certain sectors are advanced technologically, but others are dominated by pre-industrial modes of production. Similarly, the ruling political parties in some countries are anti-union in their policies, whereas in others, the political elites accept trade unions as part of pluralistic democratic societies. In two cases, Taiwan and South Korea, the processes of economic modernisation and political democratisation have taken place in the shadows of adjacent Communist regimes which oppose them – Mainland China and North Korea (Kuruvilla *et al.* 2002).

Kuruvilla and Erickson (2002: 172) argue there are six types of employment relations systems in Asia: the flexible workplace model of Japan; the tripartite Singaporean model; the state employer-dominated model in Malaysia and Indonesia; the pluralist de-centralised and fragmented model in the Philippines; the politicised multi-union model in India and the rest of South Asia; and 'the transitory model' or residual category including South Korea, Taiwan, China and Vietnam. Such systems have little in common institutionally or ideologically with one another, compared with those in West Europe. What categorises them is that most systems were established in the period immediately after the Second World War, with the rise of anti-colonial sentiments. Thus in many Asian countries, the establishment of national systems of employment relations is connected with the post-colonial creation of Asian countries as independent states.

Kuruvilla and Erickson (2002) also explain the creation of these national systems of employment relations has been strongly associated with governments in this region wanting low levels of industrial conflict in labour markets. Thus a prime motive for Asian governments has been to enact laws covering the right to form unions and to strike, and legalisation on dismissal, in the expectation these would lead to low levels of industrial conflict. Cooney *et al.* (2003) and Singh (2009) show that Indian labour laws were formulated with the explicit purpose of containing industrial conflict and making it difficult for union members to go on strike or employers to lock-out. This was done, in both colonial and postcolonial regimes, by setting up third-party dispute resolution schemes and attempting to foster responsible trade unionism rather than militant unionism. Nevertheless, a key feature in Asia is that most labour forces are not organised in unions. Apart from China, union density in Asia is below 20 per cent of the workforce and very often less than 10 per cent, because large parts of the labour force work in the informal or agricultural sectors, although union density is generally higher in the industrialised sector.

Asian unions have a number of characteristics. First, they are de-centralised operating at company level, as in Japanese enterprise unions and South Korea (Jeong 2006), where density tends to be high. In both these countries, unions have also played important roles helping to democratise these states. Further, in a number of Asian countries, unions have been under pressure during the last two decades, as in Japan, from product market competition in the global economy. This has led companies to adopt flexible employment practices and PRP. National compromises, where trade unions have been accepted, or where some employee protection is embodied in labour law, are also under pressure. Other companies are questioning the principle of mutual loyalty between employer and employees and the principle of lifelong employment. All these factors have led to reduced union density in recent years.

Second, cultural factors are sometimes used to explain why unions are generally weaker in Asia compared with Europe. For example, Confusianism is claimed to account for the low levels of conflict between employers and employees in some Asian countries. As Chan and Snape (2000: 124) argue in the case of Chinese workers: 'This is reflected in the "Neo-Confusian" hypothesis, which suggests that workers in Chinese society will accept authoritarian management and avoid confrontation with the employer.' Such cultural arguments imply that demand for collective representation is largely absent in these circumstances. Cultural factors are also taken into account when relations between management and labour in Japan are examined.

Third, in many Asian countries, it is possible to distinguish between 'official' and 'unofficial' trade union movements. Thus in South Korea and Taiwan, unofficial trade unions sometimes have more influence than official ones. In some Asian countries too, unions were established during the liberation of these states from western colonial powers. In these cases, unions have sometimes been used by governments as part of a nation-building project. For this reason, independent trade unions have been unusual in a number of Asian countries, where their main purpose has been to hinder conflicts between employers and employees in the interests of national identity and national unity; especially where different ethnic groups co-exist as in Malaysia (Benson and Zhu 2008). It is only when economic growth has taken place in some Asian countries that unions have become freed from these nationalistic purposes.

Unions in Europe

In Europe, four main clusters of employment relations systems are commonly identified; each with its particular forms of trade unionism (Jensen *et al.* 1995). First, the Nordic or North European model includes Denmark, Finland, Germany, Norway and Sweden. In these states, there are strong employer and union institutions that work collaboratively to regulate employment relations. Employer attitudes to organised labour are generally supportive and organisations of workers and employers are important influences in these labour markets. As a result, union density tends to be relatively high and collective bargaining remains well rooted (Ebbinghaus and Visser 2000).

Second, employment relations in the United Kingdom and Ireland are different. Compared with mainland Europe, there is now generally weaker institutional and legal support for collective employment relationships in these two countries. Historically, unions in the United Kingdom played key roles in regulating relations with employers, largely through national-level collective bargaining. But, during the last 30 years, the major development in the regulation of employment relationships in the United Kingdom is the dramatic decline in multi-employer bargaining, together with union membership leakage. National bargaining has been substituted by either single-employer bargaining or individualised relations between management and labour. There has also been some de-recognition of trade unions (van Wanrooy *et al.* 2013).

Third, employment relations in South Europe include France, Portugal and Spain. In these countries, unions are generally weaker than in other parts of mainland Europe in terms of membership density and bargaining coverage. In France, for example, less than 10 per cent of the labour force is organised into unions. With weak labour market organisations, the state plays an active role in regulating labour market conditions and employment relationships in these countries (Ebbinghaus 2002). Thus although union membership is low, collective agreements are extended to non-union workers and unions are represented at workplace level through institutional mechanisms underwritten by the state. These give union delegates legal representational rights in the workplace, enabling them to protect workers in their dealings with management such as in works councils.

A fourth system of employment relations is in the former Communist states of central and eastern Europe. There are large differences and a variety of employment relations arrangements among these states. What they have in common is that unions do not have the power, authority and influence which is a main feature of employment relations in much of the rest of Europe, and collective bargaining coverage is much lower (Kohl and Platzer 2004).

During the last 30 years, then, some European trade unions have experienced serious declines in membership support, union density and collective bargaining coverage, as in Germany, Netherlands and United Kingdom. In other countries, union density has stabilised or even grown over the same period, such as in Belgium, Finland and Sweden. There is also a close link in some countries between trade unions and the payment of unemployment benefits – the so-called Ghent system.

There are wide structural differences in European trade unionism too. First, employment relations in Europe, despite its different national systems, is characterised by the integration of labour representatives in employment relationships, whether by collective bargaining or the law; the so-called European social model. Indeed, there is a relatively high degree of labour inclusiveness in different European countries, even in states such as France, where union membership is low. Organised labour's influence in Europe is typically strengthened through legal and institutional arrangements that extend collective agreements to whole labour markets in parts of Northern and West Europe (Hyman and Ferner 1998). In these countries, according to the principle of *erga omnes*, the terms of collective agreements are applied to all employees in a given sector or bargaining unit, whether or not they are union members.

Second, social class is the major structural determinant of why trade unions were formed and how they are organised in West Europe. Union formation was closely related to the establishment of class societies in Europe at the end of the nineteenth and beginning of the twentieth centuries. This resulted in European trade unions being concerned with not only wages but also public policies affecting the interests of workers and their families generally. European trade unions fought for both better pay and conditions for their members in a *narrow* sense and worked to establish political, civil and social rights in European societies for workers in a *broader* sense; this included the development of welfare states, social states or the *Wohlfahrstaat*. Nonetheless, decreases in union density in some European countries are partly related to European trade unions being formed through the class structures in industrial societies. With changes to the occupational structure in Europe from traditional male working-class jobs in large-scale manufacturing to more stratified, diverse types of labour in services, some unions have lost their traditional membership bases. These include the female workers, ethnic minorities, professional workers, part-time workers and flexible labour that service industries employ (Hyman 2001).

However, in European states where unions have responded to the challenges of changing employment structures, such as in northern Europe, unions remain more secure in terms of membership density and their regulatory functions than elsewhere. With European employers looking for flexible employment practices, they also want more flexible collective agreements. This has been a major issue facing unions in the last 20 years. With the exception of the United Kingdom, European employers and employers' organisations do not generally marginalise the unions. Indeed, in many European countries, especially in northern Europe, unions are looked upon as partners by employers, not as adversaries.

Third, the fundamental organisational principles in European trade unionism are that workers are organised either *vertically* according to the sector they work in or *horizontally* according to their skill or education. Company unions as in parts of Asia are uncommon. Horizontal and/or vertical ties between organised employees at different workplaces and in different organisations are generally strong, enabling European unions to apply their collective power against employers where necessary.

Unions in the United States

An enduring feature of trade unions in the United States is employer hostility to them. This has always been the case but has become more so in recent years, as the North American economy has shifted from an industrial economic base to a post-industrial one. Moreover, unlike many European businesses, employers in North America have never been interested in establishing industry-wide collective bargaining with unions. This is partly because of the size of the country with its wide regional differences and economic disparities. It is also because many US managers view trade unions as price-fixing labour cartels that damage the competitive advantage of firms in their product markets. This makes managers reluctant to engage in collective bargaining with them. But most American managers also object to labour unions on ideological grounds. This managerial antipathy to collective employment relationships leads US managers preferring to manage the employment relationship with individual employees, rather than collectively. Where unions are recognised, apart from important sectors such as the automobile industry, it is common for employers to de-centralise collective bargaining to enterprise or workplace levels (Cutcher- Gershenfeld *et al.* 1996).

Worryingly from the union perspective is the even greater hostility towards organised labour in United States since the 1980s. This is one reason why union density has declined so much in recent years. Further, although these changes are worldwide, levels of employer hostility to labour organisations are unique to the United States. This hostility is shown by the de-certification of unions, concession bargaining involving reductions in benefits to safeguard jobs, and employer lock-outs. But it is most marked in resisting union organising campaigns. Indeed, since the 1970s, there has been a series of systematic attempts by employers to maintain 'union free' workplaces, 'through delays, "information campaigns" and outright intimidation' (Clawson and Clawson 1999: 102). Other factors explaining union membership decline include the downsizing of traditional industrial sectors and emergence of new sectors, without a tradition of unionisation (Troy 1990, 1999, 2000). It is observed from 1945 to 1980 that union wage settlements almost always involved wage increases. Since then, Clawson and Clawson (1999: 97) note that unions have 'frequently made concessions on both wages and benefits'.

Three concluding observations can be made about trade unionism in the United States. First, American unions are predominantly market-centred organisations, oriented towards securing the best sectional wage deals for their members rather than developing a broad welfare state or social wage approach to work, as in West Europe (Perlman 1922). Second, US employment relations is characterised as one directed towards the exclusion of labour representation, with a preference for dealing with employees individually and integrating them in their employing organisations. This has resulted in a steadily growing employer opposition towards organised labour across the country (Becker and Huselid 2010). Third, US unions are not class-based in the same way as European unions. They are based on the characteristics of work and employment relations in traditional industrial societies. But with changes to the US economy, contemporary trade unionism is weakly organised in terms of the post-industrial workforce. It is these structural changes in the labour force that largely explain most of the decline in US union membership density and bargaining coverage during the last 30 years.

Cross-regional comparisons

Within regional trade union clusters, wide differences of density, structure and collective bargaining coverage persist. There is evidence, first, of declining union densities in Asia, Europe and the United States. There are several reasons for this but changes in the economic structure, from industrialism to post-industrialism, seem to have played an important role (Esping-Andersen 2002). Increasing unemployment in all three regions since the 1980s is also an important factor, with many employees quitting unions because of unemployment. Declining union density is not uniform, however, since density in some European countries has been stable or even increasing. In these countries, unions have been able to organise those parts of the labour force outside traditionally male-dominated industries. But although density has fallen in some Asian countries, union influence has increased. This is because unions in Taiwan and South Korea, for example, still act as autonomous agents in relations with governments.

Second, unions in the Asia, Europe and the United States differ in terms of their organisational structures. Both horizontal and vertical relations among unions are generally strongest in Europe, because European unions tend to have strong ties with other unions. These links are commonly at national level, as in Denmark, Germany and Sweden, and some other countries. Strong links among unions also exist at central level in some European countries, where unions try to influence government policy on a range of subjects. Unions in the United States and Asia, in contrast, tend to operate at single company level, with very little single sector coverage in the United States. Company unions, in turn, are common in Japan, Taiwan and South Korea, where inter-union relations are generally weaker than in Europe.

Third, European unions are generally class-based, because they deal with the traditional interests of workers in employment, by negotiating terms and conditions of employment. But they also get involved in broader political and social issues related to the working people. This social base has given unions a pivotal role in European societies (Hyman 2001). In the United States, unions also have a social base in the American working class but, from their early days, American unions focused mostly on the narrow wage interests of their members. Broader political initiatives have only played a secondary role in American trade unionism, making American unionism market-based and job-centred. In Asia, unions are also involved in both class and market-based issues but, in some Asian countries, they have also played an important role in post-colonial nation-building. Some Asian trade unions, therefore, can be described as nation-based unions. In South Korea, however, unions have tried to define themselves not only as nation-based trade unions but also as class and market-based unions, dealing with the interests of workers independently of general national interests.

UNION INDUSTRIAL ACTION

As indicated in Figure 10.1 above, there is a variety of collective actions adopted by workers as strategies of resistance against employers with whom they are in dispute. Conflicts or disputes between management and unions arise over issues such as union recognition, wages, conditions of employment, how work is organised, and job losses and redundancies. In all cases, workers seek to use their collective power through the union to protect their employment interests. This power is rooted in the dictum 'unity is strength' or worker solidarity against the employer. In addition to strikes, actions taken by union members against employers are generically called 'industrial action', which includes: working to contract, banning overtime, restricting output, going slow, and occupations and sit-ins.

Strikes

Taking strike action is one of the ultimate sanctions that union members use in disputes with their employer. It is overt, direct and power-based. Basically, a strike takes place wherever a stoppage of work occurs in a workplace, enterprise or industry. Sometimes a distinction is made between 'official' strikes and 'unofficial' strikes. An official strike is a stoppage of work by union members endorsed by the union and follows the legal requirements for striking, such as being voted for by a majority of members in the bargaining unit. During official strikes, the union sometimes provides strike pay or strike benefits to the strikers. Workers engaged in official strikes normally have better legal protections against being dismissed than those involved in unofficial strikes. An unofficial strike is a stoppage of work commonly led by local union leaders who, in upholding the principle of 'direct democracy', do not necessarily have official union support. An unofficial strike may, however, be an 'official' strike in the view of the union. 'Unconstitutional' strikes are normally in breach of agreed procedures for the avoidance of disputes between employers and unions. Where a group of workers or trade unionists are stopped working by an employer or a group of employers, this is an employer 'lock-out'.

A strike is a temporary stoppage of work or withdrawal of labour by one or more groups of trade unionists or workers against an employer or group of employers. Its objective is to enforce or resist demands, or express grievances, or support other workers in their demands or grievances against the employer(s) involved. Analytically, there are basically two main types of strike activity – economic strikes and political strikes. But Brenner *et al.* (2009) identify and analyse a much wider diversity of strikes in North American experience. These include: economic, unfair labour practices, grievances, recognition, wildcat, sympathy, secondary boycott, 'hot cargo', jurisdictional, employer lock-out, political, general, 'blow-off-steam' and sit-down strikes.

Sometimes these analytical distinctions are blurred, such as strikes involving civil servants or public employees and the employer is the state; are these economic or political strikes? But basically, an economic strike is any attempts by trade unionists to assert leverage on an employer (or a group of employers) to improve their terms and conditions of employment or to resist imposed changes by employers to their contracts of employment. Economic strikes normally take place within the workplace or an organisation and are the most common type of strike in English-speaking countries. Political strikes are more common in South Europe, parts of Asia, and parts of Latin America. These are attempts by trade unionists and workers to apply leverage on government or the political authorities, which usually take place outside the workplace. Political strikes are common in France, Greece, Italy and Spain. They include general strikes, public demonstrations, or direct action causing economic dislocations in the country involved.

Some historical comparisons of strike activity

There are various measures of strike activity within a country for a given period of time. One records the number of working days lost; a second is the number of stoppages; and a third is the numbers of workers involved, where the workers may be *directly* involved or *indirectly* involved by being prevented from working. For comparative purposes, such indicators sometimes specify the number of working days lost per 1,000 workers. In practice, these data are indicative rather than definitive, since national classifications of strikes vary depending on the sources of the statistics, their reliability and accessibility. In general, strike data are drawn from the administrative records of national conciliation services or labour relations institutions. In other cases, international bodies such as the ILO and OECD collect strike data. Data may also come from other sources, including strike notices, trade unions, newspaper reports, and direct enquiries addressed to employers' associations or trade unions. The data commonly cover both strikes and lock-outs, as most countries do not distinguish between them in their statistics. Care has to be taken,

Table 10.1 Strikes in selected OECD countries: Working days lost per 1,000 workers 1982–1995

Country	Averages 1982–1986	Averages 1987–1995
Denmark	250	43
France	80	102
Germany	50	12
Greece	560	3,641
Ireland	450	172
Italy	700	249
The Netherlands	20	24
Portugal	150	57
Spain	520	534
UK	420	81
Japan	10	4
US	120	62
Canada	490	292
Australia	280	176
New Zealand	550	242
Austria	–	4
Finland	530	321
Norway	170	102
Sweden	60	94

Source: Labour Market Trends for these years.

however, when examining and interpreting these national and international data-sets, as some sources are discontinued over time or the content of an established data-set can be changed.

For purely illustrative purposes, Table 10.1 shows the number of working days lost per 1,000 workers in all industries and services in selected OECD countries for the period 1982–1995, drawing on historical data-sets. Table 10.1 indicates that there were wide differences in working days lost among these countries within each of these time periods and between them. First, during the period 1982–1986, for example, six countries – Italy, Greece, New Zealand, Finland, Spain and Canada – had consistently higher numbers of working days lost than the remaining countries. Other countries such as Japan, the Netherlands, Germany, Sweden and France had consistently fewer numbers of working days lost during the same period. Second, in the period 1987–1995, the rank orders had changed, with Greece, Spain, Finland, Italy and Canada losing the most working days and Austria, Japan, Germany, the Netherlands and Denmark the least. In the case of Greece, there were general strikes in both

1987 and 1990 and these account for the relatively large number of working days lost per 1,000 Greek workers for the period 1987–1995. Third, there was a distinct downward trend in the incidence of working days lost during the whole period 1982–1995, with the number of working days lost for the period 1982–1986 being generally greater than for 1987–1995.

There is no general theory explaining why strikes occur. Economic, institutional and political explanations are provided. The economic factors cited include inter-industry comparisons, unemployment levels, and the business cycle (Kerr and Siegel 1954, Hibbs 1976, Smith 1978). The institutional factors include how conflict is resolved, the structure of collective bargaining, and the contexts of employment relations (Ross and Hartman 1960, Clegg 1976). For other scholars, political power is a major variable shaping long-term patterns of strikes and industrial action (Korpi and Shalev 1979, Shorter and Tilly 1974, Kelly 1998).

One consistent explanation of strike activity is its variation among different industries and sectors, where historically some industries have been identified as being particularly strike-prone such as mining and quarrying, manufacturing, seafaring, and construction. Although later critically challenged by others, such as Edwards (1977), the early comparative study by Kerr and Siegel (1954), based on inter-industry comparisons, tried to show why industrial conflict is prevalent in some sectors and absent in others. Previous studies had concentrated on labour market and product market factors, management and union policies, procedures for adjusting disputes, and the influence of dominant personalities on industrial conflict. Kerr and Siegel showed that these factors did not explain why some industries are strike-prone in many parts of the world and others are not. Their central explanation of strike propensities was the location of workers in society, with the nature of their jobs acting as secondary influences. Thus isolated masses of workers insulated from society-at-large were identified as being most likely to take strike action, especially when employed in unpleasant jobs. However, individuals and groups who were integrated into their general communities, through a multiplicity of associations, were identified as being less likely to strike. This classification of patterns of strike propensities is summarised in Figure 10.6.

Variation in strike activities in strike-prone industries and the contrasting economic structures of different countries explain *in part* why some countries have relatively high or low rates of strike activity compared with others. This is illustrated in Table 10.2, which compares working days lost per 1,000 workers in industries known to be particularly strike-prone in selected OECD

Propensity to strike	Industry
High	Mining and quarrying
	Seafaring and docks
Medium-high	Lumber
	Textiles
Medium	Chemicals
	Printing
	Leather
	Manufacturing
	Construction
	Food
Medium-low	Clothing
	Gas, water, electricity
	Services
Low	Railways
	Trade
	Agriculture

Figure 10.6 Patterns of strike propensity
Source: Kerr and Siegel (1954).

Table 10.2 Strikes in selected OECD countries: Working days lost per 1,000 workers in strike-prone industries 1982–1991

Country	Averages 1982–1986	Averages 1987–1991	Averages 1982–1991
Denmark	560	90	330
France	150	80	120
Germany	100	10	50
Greece	920	5,360	4,470
Ireland	510	350	430
Italy	280	440	360
The Netherlands	40	40	40
Portugal	270	110	200
Spain	520	770	650
UK	980	240	610
Japan	20	10	10
US	310	210	260
Canada	940	760	850
Australia	610	530	570
New Zealand	2,740	520	890
Finland	760	180	470
Norway	300	30	170
Sweden	10	170	90

Source: Labour Market Trends for these years.

Table 10.3 Annual average working days lost per 1,000 employees in EU member states and Norway 1998–2001

Annual average number of working days lost per 1,000 workers	Countries
More than 70	Denmark, Ireland, Norway, Spain
Between 20 and 69	Belgium, Finland, France, Greece, Hungary, Italy, Luxembourg
Less than 20	Austria, Germany, the Netherlands, Poland, Portugal, Slovakia, Sweden, UK

Source: European Industrial Relations Observatory (2012).

countries during the 1980s – mining and quarrying, manufacturing, construction, and transport and communication. For the period 1982–1991, compared with the data in Table 10.2, the incidence of working days lost per 1,000 workers in these strike-prone industries was between one-and-a-half times to twice as high for all industries and services and three times as high in the United States. However, like all industries and services, these strike-prone sectors also experienced general decreases in strike rates over this same period; a more general trend anticipated in earlier research by Ross and Hartman (1960).

Table 10.3 provides further evidence of the decline in strike activity in terms of working days lost per 1,000 workers within the EU and Norway for the years 1998 to 2001. Indeed Monger (2004) points to an overall decline in strike activity in this set of countries of some 25 per cent between 1993 and 1997 and between 1998 and 2002. Only four out of the 19 countries listed lost in excess of 70 annual average working days per 1,000 workers in this period: Denmark, Ireland, Norway and Spain.

Recent comparative data

Table 10.4 provides some crude descriptive data on strike activity in selected countries in Africa, the Americas, Asia and Israel, Europe, and Australasia for 2008, 2000, 1990 and 1980; these are indicative data only, which do *not* take account of the relative sizes of the workforces in these countries. The data are abstracted from the ILO's long-established labour statistics collection. The sources of these data widely vary by country and include government labour relations records, records of organisations of employers and workers, administrative records, special data collections, and various surveys. Further, this data-set is not complete and some of the countries in

Table 10.4 Number of workers involved in strikes, days lost and sector with most days lost for selected countries 2008, 2000, 1990, 1980

Region/Country	Workers involved 2008	Days lost 2008	Most days lost 2008	Workers involved 2000	Days lost 2000	Most days lost 2000	Workers involved 1990	Days lost 1990	Most days lost 1990	Workers involved 1980	Days lost 1980	Most days lost 1980
AFRICA												
Nigeria	n/a	n/a	n/a	344,722	6,287,733	Manu'frg	275,895	1,373,540	Services	141,676	1,353,893	Services
S Africa	118,979	497,436	Transport	1,142,428	1,669,966	Services	341,097	2,792,844	Manu'frg	58,213	n/a	n/a
AMERICAS												
Argentina	1,931,561	8,623,982	Pub admin	6,760,850	12,392,241	n/a	n/a	n/a	n/a	n/a	n/a	n/a
Brazil	2,043,124	143,432,937	n/a	3,834,116	238,921,522	n/a	14,243,000	17,000	Manu'frg	n/a	n/a	n/a
Canada	41,291	875,640	Manu'frg	113,888	1,644,100	Manu'frg	270,471	5,079,190	Manu'frg	441,025	8,975,390	Manu'frg
Chile	17,473	202,178	Manu'frg	13,227	114,306	Services	25,010	245,192	Manu'frg	29,730	428,300	Manu'frg
Mexico	13,242	286,430	Education	60,015	847,201	Manu'frg	49,315	1,598,700	Manu'frg	42,774	n/a	n/a
US	82,700	1,954,100	Manu'frg	393,700	20,419,400	Manu'frg	184,900	5,925,500	Transport	1,366,300	33,288,500	Manu'frg
ASIA/MID-EAST												
India	1,483,593	16,683,942	Manu'frg	1,418,299	16,720,762	Manu'frg	1,307,863	24,086,170	Manu'frg	n/a	n/a	n/a
Israel	19,275	87,151	Education	297,882	2,011,263	Health-care	571,200	1,071,300	Services	91,451	216,516	Manu'frg
Japan	8,284	11,205	Transport	15,322	35,050	Transport	84,303	144,511	Transport	562,921	1,001,224	Manu'frg
S Korea	114,290	809,402	n/a	177,969	1,893,563	Manu'frg	133,900	4,487,200	Manu'frg	48,970	61,269	Mining
EUROPE												
Austria	0	0	n/a	19,439	2,947	n/a	5,274	8,870	Manu'frg	24,181	16,960	Manu'frg
Denmark	91,409	1,869,100	Manu'frg	75,656	124,000	Manu'frg	37,386	97,600	Manu'frg	62,063	186,700	Manu'frg
Finland	15,992	16,352	Mining	84,092	253,838	Manu'frg	244,759	935,159	Finance	407,260	1,605,600	Manu'frg
France	n/a	1,418,500	Transport	18,520	807,758	Manu'frg	18,500	528,000	Manu'frg	500,800	1,522,900	Manu'frg

447

Table 10.4 (Continued)

Region/Country	Workers involved 2008	Days lost 2008	Most days lost 2008	Workers involved 2000	Days lost 2000	Most days lost 2000	Workers involved 1990	Days lost 1990	Most days lost 1990	Workers involved 1980	Days lost 1980	Most days lost 1980
Germany	154,052	131,679	n/a	7,428	10,776	Manu'frg	257,160	363,547	Health-care	45,159	128,386	Transport
Italy	669,153	722,714	Manu'frg	687,000	884,100	Manu'frg	1,633,996	5,181,300	Manu'frg	13,824,641	16,457,286	Manu'frg
Netherlands	51,900	120,600	Transport	10,300	9,400	Manu'frg	24,978	206,717	Construction	25,647	56,832	Manu'frg
Norway	12,963	62,568	Education	93,889	496,568	Manu'frg	60,674	139,047	Services	18,752	103,807	Construction
Poland	209,039	275,819	Services	7,858	74,266	Manu'frg	115,700	159,000	Transport	n/a	n/a	n/a
Romania	16,730	138,453	Mining	24,964	565,433	Manu'frg	n/a	579,600	Transport	n/a	n/a	n/a
Russia	1,920	29,081	Mining	31,000	236,400	Education	1,988,000*	117,609,000*	Transport	n/a*	n/a*	n/a*
Spain	543,008	1,510,219	Transport	2,067,287	3,616,907	Construction	977,000	2,612,900	Manu'frg	2,287,000	6,177,500	Manu'frg
Sweden	12,766	106,801	Transport	163	272	Construction	73,159	770,356	Finance	746,677	4,478,511	Manu'frg
Turkey	5,040	145,725	Manu'frg	18,705	368,475	Manu'frg	166,306	3,466,550	Manu'frg	84,832	1,303,253	n/a
UK	511,200	758,861	Pub admin	183,200	498,800	Health-care	298,200	1,903,000	Manu'frg	833,700	11,964,000	Manu'frg
ASIA PACIFIC												
Australia	172,900	196,500	Education	325,400	469,100	Manu'frg	729,900	1,376,500	Manu'frg	1,172,600	3,319,700	Manu'frg
N Zealand	n/a	n/a	n/a	2,632	11,495	Manu'frg	50,007	330,923	Manu'frg	127,651	373,496	Manu'frg

n/a = not available

* = USSR

Source: Laborstat.ilo.org/accessed 28-03-2013.

earlier collections, such as the Union of Soviet Socialist Republics, no longer exist. What were some former Communist states, as in East Europe, are now emerging market economies and aspiring democratic states, with new and evolving institutions of employment relations. Thus it is difficult to explain the differences between the relatively low rates of strike activity recorded within the post-Communist Russian Federation, compared with the higher rates noted during the Soviet regime, except perhaps by under-recording. The data in Table 10.3 identify selected countries only, omitting smaller Latin American and Asian states, the Baltic states, and Ireland. So the data must be treated critically and with caution and no definitive conclusions can be drawn from them.

First, in Africa, the data-sets are relatively limited and cover only a narrow range of countries, Botswana, Egypt and South Africa in 2008, where employment relations institutions are not deeply embedded or institutionally rooted. Nigeria and South Africa are two large major states in this diverse continent, whose employment relations institutions emerged out of their British colonial pasts (Damachi et al. 1979). Both countries are transitional market economies and trade unions and collective bargaining exist in some sectors, such as manufacturing, mining and the public sector. But difficulties in trade union organisation remain because of economic, geographic, ethnic, linguistic and religious differences. However, there have always been industrial conflicts in both countries, especially during the 1980s and 1990s, largely in manufacturing, transport and communication, and community services. On the other hand, the numbers of workers involved in strikes and days lost in these two states appear to have diminished in the 2000s, provided the data are accurate (Brewster and Wood 2007). However, the situation regarding industrial action can be potentially volatile in countries such as Nigeria and South Africa. This was demonstrated by the unofficial strike by mineworkers at the Lonmin mine in Marikana, in the north-west province of South Africa, in August 2012. During the four week strike, the police opened fire on striking miners and 44 people died, more than 70 persons were injured, and some 250 people arrested (Marikana Commission of Inquiry 2014).

Second, in North, Central and South America, the dominant union movement was traditionally located in the United States and the most intense strikes took place in this country and continent during the late nineteenth and early twentieth centuries. Since the 1980s, union membership, union recognition and strike activity in the United States have declined, as they have in Canada, as both economies have restructured and shifted towards a service-sector economic model. Earlier strikes in the United States were principally in manufacturing but in recent years other sectors such as transport and communication have been involved (Brenner *et al.* 2009). In Argentina, unions traditionally have been strongly organised, where the *Confederación General del Trabajo* has been an important political force since the 1930s. In Brazil, the *Central Única dos Trabalhadores* is the largest trade union centre in Latin America with long experience of employment relations. For economic and political reasons, both Argentina and Brazil have experienced relatively high and bitter levels of strike activity, in state employment, manufacturing and public administration over the years. In Chile and Mexico, in contrast, strikes have not been so large scale (Cardoso 2004). In Mexico, unions have lost power over the last two decades, despite some limited strike activity (Fairiss 2006).

Third, in Asia and the Middle-East, patterns of strike activity have varied over time. In recent years, both India and South Korea have had more strike activity than Israel and Japan, with the latter having a relatively low incidence of strikes for structural and cultural reasons, such as enterprise unions and a cultural tradition of conflict-avoidance. But there was greater convergence among all four countries in the 1980s and 1990s, when they generally experienced higher levels of strike action than now. Previously, most strikes were mainly in manufacturing but recent strikes have taken place in manufacturing, education, and transport and communication. In India, there has always been a multiplicity of unions with different political affiliations, which partly explains its patterns of strikes (Patil 1992, European Foundation for the Improvement of Living and Working Conditions 2006). In Israel, *Histadrut* or the General Federation of Labour in Israel is the main union organisation, whereas South Korea has two national trade union centres (Traub-Merz and Zhang 2010).

Fourth, in Europe, wide differences in strike activity are demonstrated across countries over time. One group appears to have a high propensity to strike; another group a low propensity; and a third group lies in the middle ranges. The first group includes Finland, France, Italy, Spain and to a lesser degree Poland. The second includes Austria, Germany, the Netherlands, Norway and Sweden. The third includes the remaining countries in Table 10.3. In all these European countries, with their diverse employment relations traditions and institutions, the sectors with most days lost used to be largely in manufacturing, whereas in recent years the sectors include not only manufacturing but also mining and quarrying, transport and communication, education, administrative services, and public administration. However, explaining the different strike propensities among these three groups is problematic. If a single generic observation can be made, it is that the first group includes France, Italy and Spain, where large-scale general strikes are fairly common and are part of the social fabrics of these states. The second group, in contrast, consists of relatively small cohesive states (apart from Germany which is a large federal state), with long-established employment relations institutions, strong labour movements and consensus-seeking political systems (European Commission 2013).

Fifth, in Australasia, the numbers of workers involved and days lost in strikes have reduced dramatically since 1980. Manufacturing has always been the most strike-prone sector in Australia and New Zealand. But in both countries, a series of labour market reforms, economic re-structuring and neo-liberal economic policies over the past 30 years have severely reduced the power of the unions and ability of their members to take effective strike action (Bamber *et al.* 2011).

A final overall observation is that these strike data provide some support for the Kerr and Siegel (1954) thesis of strike-prone sectors. For example, in most countries included in this data-set, manufacturing had the highest number of days lost in 1980. Since then, in addition to manufacturing, other sectors such as transport and communication, mining and quarrying, construction, community services, public administration, education, administrative services, health and social work, and financial services, have all recorded the most days lost at some time and country over this period. Indeed, manufacturing made up 80 per cent of most days lost in all the countries listed in 1980, 57 per cent in 1990, 69 per cent in 2000, but only 30 per cent in 2008. By 2008, strike activity also appears to have been more widely distributed in terms of sectors with the most days lost. In 2008, manufacturing accounted for 30.4 per cent of all strikes in these five regions, transport and communication 26.1 per cent, education 17.4 per cent, mining and quarrying 13.0 per cent, public administration 8.8 per cent and administrative services 4.3 per cent.

CONCLUSION AND IMPLICATIONS

The study of worker resistance in the workplace is a complex field of academic inquiry. Definitions of its subject matter, and the defensive strategies used by workers against management, vary according to the organisational contexts within which these behaviours take place. The scope and incidence of worker resistance have widened and increased, as employers press for more effort, constrain job discretion, and seek higher levels of job performance in workplaces cross-nationally (Black and Lynch 2001). However, most of the literature is Western in origin and it draws largely on Anglo-American sources in structured employment relations systems. With a few exceptions, such as

Ong (2010), this is the result of hostility to research in this field in developing and ad hoc employment relations systems. Dysfunctional workplace conflict is also either ignored or suppressed by management in some developing countries, as their governments do not want to draw attention to worker resistance and misbehaviour. Nevertheless, at a time where societies and organisations are increasingly characterised by surveillance and attempts at organisational and civic control (Lyon 2001), workers continue find ways to protest and resist contested managerial policies and unacceptable managerial behaviours within increasingly insecure and stressful workplaces. Some studies, such as those of Hebdon and Sung (2013: 44), warn that organisational behaviour scholars 'may have to go beyond studies of individual expressions if they want to fully understand conflict within organizations'.

The prime function of unions is acting as agents of job regulation with employers on behalf of their members, where collective bargaining is their main method for doing this. Although collective bargaining is the major influence on union behaviour, it is not the only one. However, if collective bargaining is the main method of job regulation 'its dimensions account for union behaviour more adequately than any other set of explanatory variables can do' (Clegg 1976: 11). Thus when the institutions of collective bargaining are weakened, as has happened over the past 30 years and the external contexts change, unions are weakened too.

Centralisation in unions underscores their basically functional purpose and normally pragmatic character. In practice, unions are not striving towards centralisation and internal bureaucracy or de-centralisation and anti-bureaucracy for their own sakes. Principally, they pursue economic and institutional survival goals to promote union regulation of the employment relationship by doing 'what works'. Trends towards centralisation and bureaucracy in union government and administration are the results of everyday working life and the political arena with which unions and management interact. These include growth in union size and complexity, the employers they deal with, the roles of government in the contemporary world, union concern with economic ends, and the practical means unions use for survival. These factors have also contributed to more centralisation in businesses in response to union presence and tactics. But, where recognised, unions contribute to the diffusion of control and counter-control in organisations. Where they are able to influence important employment relations decisions, union power tends to reflect, on balance, the interests of their members, despite what critics say about unions being 'undemocratic' and 'unrepresentative'.

Unions like businesses have strategic choices to ensure their survival. This means having the capability to develop and pursue alternative union strategies, according to the circumstances facing them. This is particularly important when unions are losing members, coming to terms with declining collective bargaining power, and becoming less appealing to employers and employees. As Fairbrother and Yates (2003: 1) write: 'Union memberships are stagnant or declining and new workers slow to join unions.' Taking the United States, Australia, New Zealand and the United Kingdom as examples, they explain these trends 'as part of a consequence of structural factors, in particular major changes in the labour market, involving the increased flexibility of labour, deregulation and a shift from manufacturing to services'. They also link these trends with 'growing ethnic, racial and cultural diversity of working populations and the failure of unions to adapt to these developments'. Further, there is 'the declining legitimacy of social democratic ideas'. The implications are that union leaders and active members have to choose appropriate strategic directions for their unions to remain major players in employment relations. Unless they do so, unions are unable to be effective bodies protecting the job and employment interests of their members in workplaces, enterprises and society. These choices may be either deterministic or shaped by events and unions have to take account of the internal constraints and external contexts confronting them to do this.

Ultimately, however, union leaders like business leaders have some discretion in determining their strategic choices when challenged by neo-liberal economic policies, as outlined in Figure 10.7. The possible strategic choices available are the stronger patterns of classical and paper-tiger unionism (which requires strong state support), contrasted with weaker forms of partnership and consultancy unionism (where there is greater co-operation with employers). Large unions of course may adopt one or more of these strategic choices.

Classic trade unionism	Partnership unionism
Servicing and solid organising relations with members	Servicing and solid organising relations with members
Adversarial relations with employers	Adversarial and co-operative relations with employers
Paper-tiger unionism	**Consultancy unionism**
Servicing relations with members	Servicing and limited organising relations with members
Adversarial relations with employers	Adversarial and some co-operative relations with employers

Figure 10.7 Union strategic choices under neo-liberals
Source: Boxall and Haynes (1997).

Unions in Asia, Europe and the United States have all been challenged by globalisation and the search for job flexibility by employers. Employers in all three regions claim that global competition has intensified and there is a need for more individualised, market-based pay and flexible working arrangements. For example, de-centralised collective bargaining has increased in all three regions although, in Germany, this trend is viewed with scepticism by the unions. On the other hand, pressures of globalisation are felt more strongly in Europe and Asia than in the United States, because the American economy is still a large internal, national economic market, linked into the NAFTA with Canada and Mexico. European states, the EU notwithstanding, and Asian states, in contrast, are subject to fierce multi-lateral trading competition by lean businesses around the world. The underlying problem for unions everywhere is they are fundamentally national bodies. And, although attempts have been made to internationalise the union movement in response to globalisation of companies, business practices, and finance capital, these attempts have never been really convincing.

The incidence of industrial action by unions and their members has declined in recent years too, in reaction to creative managerial employment relations tactics and HR strategies, weakened state support for trade unions, deregulated or re-regulated labour markets, and the de-centralisation of collective bargaining around the world. But there is no definitive or general theory of industrial conflict or why trade unionists participate in strikes. Different disciplinary perspectives and the variety of methodological approaches used for analysing industrial conflict provide no universalistic answer to this issue. As Jackson (1987: 149) comments, strikes are enormously complex phenomena. They 'are themselves a classification of different kinds of activity under one head'. Each strike is undertaken 'for different reasons at different times and has different meanings for different participants'.

11

COLLECTIVE BARGAINING, WORKER PARTICIPATION AND MEDIATION

The purpose of this chapter is to examine and critically review the collective faces of employment relations and how they contribute to the regulation of the employment relationship. Collective employment relations are institution-alised and contrast with the individual employment relationship, between an employer and an employee, incorporated into the contract of employment, which is commonly viewed as a 'personal' one. Employment relationships are institutionalised when they are jointly regulated between employer and union representatives to determine terms and conditions of employment. The most common form of joint regulation is called 'collective bargaining', which was a term first coined by Beatrice Webb (1987) in her study of the Co-operative movement in Britain, originally published in 1891. Early usage by writers such as Crompton (1876) had described meetings between employer and worker representatives to bargain over wages and conditions as 'boards of conciliation'. Today, conciliation has a different meaning and the term collective bargaining is normally used to describe the process of negotiating collective agreements between employers and groups of employees to regulate terms and conditions of employment. Collective agreements set out wages structures, working hours, overtime, training, health and safety, grievance and disciplinary procedures, and rights to participate in workplace or company affairs. Worker participation is traditionally a broader concept than collective bargaining. Its concern is how workers participate in managerial decision-making, including terms and conditions within undertakings, corporate ownership and corporate governance. In its broadest sense, mediation incorporates a number of employment relations processes. This is where a neutral third party tries to resolve any conflicts or 'rights' or 'interests' between an employer and a union or an employer and a worker, or where relations between them have broken down, with the objective of reaching an agreement between them.

CONCEPTS AND THEORY IN COLLECTIVE BARGAINING

There are some basic concepts in collective bargaining and a variety of theories, which are sometimes contested. But basically, collective bargaining is a power relationship between autonomous, self-governing employers, operating in the market, public and third sectors of nation states, and independent trade unions. Its purposes are to regulate employment relationships between an employer and its employees using collective processes. Collective bargaining covers terms and conditions of employment for particular groups of employees, as well as the ways in which issues such as individual grievances, collective disputes and disciplinary matters are resolved at workplace and corporate levels. The outcomes of collective bargaining are collective agreements, which cover both *substantive* and *procedural* issues. The former deal with pay and conditions and involve direct financial costs to employers; the latter with the responsibilities and duties of the parties, the stages or steps how the parties deal with each other and what happens when they fail to agree. Direct financial employer costs, however, are usually recouped or even exceeded, through longer term productivity gains and natural wastage from the workforce.

In most countries, collective agreements are legally enforceable contracts between employers and the unions with which they negotiate, where Ireland, New Zealand and the United Kingdom are exceptions. In these cases, collective agreements are not legally enforceable but are voluntary agreements between the parties, which are binding in honour between them, unless they sign them as collective contracts. Any breaches of agreed collective contracts can result in the aggrieved party taking legal action against the other. But in all instances, the contents or subject matter of collective agreements, such as terms and conditions of employment and procedural arrangements, become incorporated into the individual contracts of employment of the workers covered by the agreement, whether they are union members or not. Where there is a breach of a voluntary collective agreement by an employer, this can only be pursued by the employee as a breach of individual contract, although this rarely happens in practice. Wherever collective bargaining takes place, the goal is to agree joint rules to promote compromises between the parties over their conflicting interests over terms and conditions of employment. Figure 11.1 shows some examples of substantive and procedural collective agreements.

Substantive pay rewards	Substantive conditions of employment	Procedural agreements
Hourly wage rates	Hours of work	General principles
Annual salaries	Length of working week	Union recognition
Shift work payments	Shift work hours	Union facilities
Unsocial hours payments	Shift work systems	Rights of the parties
Pay structures	Clocking-in arrangements	Duties of the parties
Payments for performance	Signing-off arrangements	Avoidance of disputes
Pay bonuses	Refreshment facilities	Grievances
Overtime payments	Parental leave	Discipline/ dismissal
Holiday pay	Time-off work	Lay-offs/ redeployment
Sick pay	Short-time working	Promotion/ seniority
Parental pay	Holiday periods	Health and safety
Pensions	Pension arrangements	Harassment at work

Figure 11.1 Some examples of substantive and procedural collective agreements

Relative advantage in the negotiating process is determined by the balance of bargaining power between the two sides in the bargaining relationship. Where the power balance favours the employer side, such as when unemployment is high and the economy in recession, this is a relative disadvantage to the union and its members. Where the power balance favours the union side, such as in conditions of tight labour markets or labour shortages and the economy is growing, this is to the relative disadvantage of the employer and management. The essence of an effective and balanced collective bargaining relationship between an employer and union is to reach negotiated and agreed settlements together. This is done by concessions, exchanges and compromises on both sides, where each side feels satisfied with and committed to their joint bargaining outcomes (Clegg 1975).

There are many theories of collective bargaining and a range of critiques of it. It was Webb and Webb (1920b) who first provided a heterodox analysis of collective bargaining, by challenging the economic orthodoxy of the neo-classical economists in relation to the union role in wage determination. For neo-classical economists, wages are determined by 'free', competitive market forces and supply and demand in the labour market. For them, union intervention in wage determination inhibits and distorts the unfettered interplay of market forces. But the Webbs argue that workers are disadvantaged in the labour market, because the employer has greater bargaining power than the individual worker. The role of the union is to offset the inequalities of bargaining power in wage negotiations between individual workers and employers by enforcing the 'common rules' of the trade. For the Webbs, unions are primarily economic wage bargaining agents on behalf of workers. However, Flanders (1968) takes the debate further by arguing that collective bargaining is a political or power process rather than an economic one. For him, unions use their collective bargaining power, through union organisation and threat of industrial action, to penetrate the management function and act as institutions of 'job regulation' on any matters affecting the employment interests of their members. Ross, Kornhauser and Dubin (1954) see collective bargaining as the industrial counterpart to political democracy, which provides a source of social stability, social order and social change in modern industry and society.

Kahn-Freund (1954), a labour lawyer, provides a penetrating analysis of collective bargaining from a socio-legal perspective by arguing it is linked with the evolution of social norms for regulating industrial conflict. For him, the emergence of collective bargaining depends on the extent and forms of legal intervention by the state to promote and support it. For some Marxists, on the other hand, collective bargaining is the process by which the working class becomes politicised, through the experiences of union membership, union militancy, industrial action and employer exploitation. For them, unions are the means for not only protecting the employment interests of their members but also furthering the class struggle between the wage-earning class and the profit-seeking capitalist class (Hyman 1975). Radical Marxists argue that collective bargaining weakens the need for worker revolution to overthrow the capitalist system. By achieving marginal improvements in employment conditions, workers become satisfied with these minor gains, allowing capitalists to continue their profit-seeking exploitation of them.

The North American scholars Chamberlain and Kuhn (1965) provide one of the most comprehensive and persuasive analyses of collective bargaining. They identify three views of the process: 'the marketing concept', 'the governmental concept' and the 'industrial relations concept'. Within the marketing concept, collective agreements act as a 'contract' between employers and unions; in the governmental concept, collective agreements are a system of 'law-making' adjudicated through collective bargaining; and in the 'industrial relations concept', collective agreements provide a method of 'industrial governance'.

The marketing concept of collective bargaining views it as an exchange relationship and a means of contracting for the sale of labour between employer and employee through the agency of the union. In determining the wage–work bargain, the collective agreement acts as a contract for the buying and selling of labour for a specified period of time. This view of collective bargaining is similar to that of the Webbs and is based on the assumption that bargaining inequality in the labour market between employer and employee oppresses individual workers and needs to be redressed. Whether or not substantive agreements establish a balance of bargaining power is irrelevant; what is important is the strict interpretation and application of the collective agreement thus determined. Its terms represent the bargain struck, with its clauses being honoured for the period it runs. Disputes over contractual terms are referred to the relevant procedural arrangements between the parties.

The governmental concept of collective bargaining views it as a constitutional process in industry, where bargaining is a system of industrial jurisprudence. In this analysis, it is a political relationship, where the union shares industrial sovereignty with management and the union uses its collective power to further the interests of its members. The industrial constitution, written by management and union representatives, has legislative, executive and judicial elements. The legislative branch is made up of management-union committees, which determine and interpret joint agreements. Executive authority and the right to initiate decisions are vested in management, within the framework of industrial 'legislation' jointly determined by the parties. Management has the right to manage, plan product development, change working methods, and establish personnel or HR policies, but only within the boundaries of established 'rules'. Where differences between the players cannot be resolved by negotiation, the judicial element of the industrial constitution comes into play. This draws upon agreed procedures to settle differences between the parties, with the intervention of third parties only being used where these procedures are exhausted.

Importantly for Chamberlain and Kuhn (1965: 124), there is an ethical principle underlying the governmental concept of collective bargaining. This concerns the 'sharing of industrial sovereignty', which has two sides. The first 'involves a sharing by management with the union of power over those who are governed, the employees'. The second involves 'a joint defense of the autonomy of the government established to exercise such power, a defense primarily against interference by the state'. The sharing of power between management and union means that only employment rules that are mutually acceptable, and have the consent of the governed, can be legitimised and enforced. Sovereignty is held jointly by management and union in the bargaining process, resulting in participation by the union in job control on behalf of its members. But sovereignty also limits the control of those outside the industrial relations constitution, such as the state, who might want to interfere in the autonomy of collective bargaining.

Chamberlain and Kuhn (1965: 128) go on to distinguish between the 'constitutional law of industry' and its 'common law'. The former is incorporated in collective agreements and establishes the terms of the employer–employee relationship and individual cases are governed by these terms. The firm's 'common law' is developed through joint procedures for settling grievances and differences of interpretation of collective agreements. There are no written standards of control. 'It is the mutual recognition of the requirements of morality and the needs of the operation which provides the basis of decision and ultimately the norms of action.' These are commonly incorporated in the social customs and unwritten conventions of the enterprise.

The industrial relations concept of collective bargaining is a functional relationship, where the union joins with managers in reaching decisions in which both players have vital interests. This involves a system of industrial governance, following out of collective bargaining as a system of industrial jurisprudence. Thus the presence of the union allows workers, through their representatives, to participate in the determination of policies guiding and ruling their working lives. Indeed, 'collective bargaining by its very nature involves unions in decision-making roles' (Chamberlain and Kuhn 1965: 130). Thus collective bargaining uses industrial relations procedures for making joint decisions on all matters affecting labour; its scope is almost limitless. The ethical principle underlying the concept of industrial governance is that those who are integral to the conduct of an enterprise – its workers – should have a voice in making those decisions most affecting their daily working lives. This is the principle of 'mutuality' and is a correlate of political democracy. Subscribing to this ethical principle is a matter of choice. Some employers similarly believe, as agents of shareholders, maximisation of returns on shareholder investment is ethical and a matter of principle.

For Chamberlain and Kuhn (1965), Brandeis (1934), Poole (1986), McCarthy (1988), and other analysts of democracy in the workplace, collective bargaining is ultimately the means for establishing industrial democracy in organisations or the means for providing workers in industry the sense of worth, freedom and participation that democratic government promises them as citizens. 'And as the area of joint concern expands, so does the participation of the union in the management of the enterprise' (Chamberlain and Kuhn 1965: 135). Ultimately, collective bargaining becomes a system of management. It is for this underpinning reason that many employers have rejected and continue to reject joint regulation of terms and conditions of employment for the workforces they employ; collective bargaining weakens and challenges their right to manage. Some governments have introduced legislation which promotes democracy at work, while others have sought to weaken the power of unions and strengthen the right to manage.

THE STRUCTURE OF COLLECTIVE BARGAINING

Collective bargaining between employers and trade unions takes place within dedicated bargaining structures or institutional frameworks. The main elements within any collective bargaining structure are the *bargaining unit* and *bargaining level*, although some commentators also refer to *bargaining forms* (how decisions are recorded, whether in writing or informally) and *bargaining scope* (whether bargaining is narrow or wide in its subject matter) (Flanagan 1999). Basically, the bargaining unit specifies the parties or bargaining agents representing the employers (management) and employees (the union) in each case. Normally, the employer side is represented by senior managers, which may or may not include HR specialists, and the employee side by union officers (either full-time and/or lay officials) who negotiate on behalf of their members. In some types of collective bargaining, such as multi-employer or sector-wide bargaining, the employer side is represented by officers of an employers' association, which speaks for all the organised employers in a given sector of work. But both sides are bound by the terms and decisions incorporated in the relevant collective agreements, whether they are a collective contract or non-legally enforceable agreement.

Bargaining levels

Flanagan (2008: 407) argues that collective bargaining 'occurs in an impressive variety of negotiating units around the world'. But three concepts summarise the distinctions in bargaining level that have proved to be important for analysing how bargaining structure may influence bargaining processes and bargaining outcomes. These are: *centralised bargaining* between national organisations or national federations of employers and unions, common at times in Scandinavian countries and in Ireland; *multi-employer bargaining* at sector level between industry-wide or regional employers' organisations and national unions, common in parts of West Europe; and *de-centralised bargaining* at either single-employer or enterprise level. Single-employer bargaining takes place at company level between an employer and the union(s) recognised for collective bargaining purposes and enterprise bargaining takes place at workplace level between local management and local unions. De-centralised bargaining is common in North America, the United Kingdom and parts of East Europe. Some advantages and disadvantages of bargaining levels for employers and union are summarised in Figure 11.2.

	Advantages	Disadvantages
Centralised collective bargaining	Greater wage equality is promoted For the union, its bargaining power is concentrated All employers and employees are covered by the collective agreement Negotiation costs are rationalised for both employers and union	For employers, union bargaining power is concentrated For employers, the needs of local firms are not taken into account The scope of collective bargaining is narrow Wage inflation can be stimulated Wage drift occurs Variations in productivity are not taken into account in the bargaining process
Multi-employer collective bargaining	Employer and union resources are concentrated Local management can concentrate on business and domestic HR issues All employees are treated equitably Employers cannot play each other off in the bargaining process	The ability of employers to negotiate according to local circumstances is reduced Employers have to pay 'something for nothing' locally Some employers will want to pay less than the agreed wage increases Local labour markets, productivity and worker performance are ignored in bargaining
De-centralised single-employer collective bargaining	Standardised terms and conditions are negotiated for similar jobs across the firm Stable pay differentials are provided between occupational groups Labour costs for employers are predictable Management avoids wage parity claims across the company	For the union, its bargaining power is weakened It can be expensive for management to maintain a professional HR system It is inflexible and does not take into account differences in operations, product markets and labour markets across the company
De-centralised enterprise collective bargaining	For management, the authority of local management is increased and terms and conditions customised For management, union power is dissociated For management, employee commitment is increased Management can respond flexibly and quickly to local employment relations issues Communication between the parties is speeded up	For the union, its bargaining power is weakened For management, the danger of wage parity claims increase For management, labour cost control is complicated For management, total pay decentralisation is required, otherwise it is difficult to maintain wage differentials

Figure 11.2 Some advantages and disadvantages of bargaining levels for employers and unions

462

Centralised collective bargaining

Centralised bargaining, sometimes called economy-wide bargaining, establishes nationwide working conditions in firms and is particularly well suited for pursuing greater wage equality among workgroups. Indeed, empirical analyses identify negative cross-country correlations between bargaining level and wage distribution (OECD 2004a). Greater wage equality arises from central negotiations, because these restrain the collective bargaining power of the most powerful union, which normally represents high-wage workers, while providing extra wage payments to low-wage workers. The post-Second World War wages solidarity policy in Sweden, for example, clearly demonstrates how centralised collective bargaining not only increases wage equality but also creates internal tensions within this policy. Such policies address fewer issues than de-centralised single-employer or enterprise bargaining. This is because nationwide collective bargaining must limit itself to issues shared by most workplaces, which largely limits bargaining to changes in pay or working hours. In short, centralised negotiations cannot address specific workplace issues that may be of greater concern to managers and workers, whereas localised bargaining (at company or workplace levels) can address a wide range of pay, conditions, health and safety, and works rules issues unique to an organisation or workplace.

In practice, centralised bargaining often requires additional bargaining at supplementary levels, so that typically multi-tiers of bargaining emerge in centralised bargaining systems. These are the cases in Belgium (a small continental market regime) and Ireland (a small liberal market regime). Thus centralised bargaining provides a less reliable indicator of actual earnings than de-centralised bargaining, because 'wage drift' occurs, where actual earnings to increase more rapidly than negotiated wage rates. The reason is either the employers agree to pay more to improve their recruitment and retention needs or the unions supplement centralised negotiations with local bargaining to raise actual wages for their members at firm or workplace levels. Wage drift adds uncertainty to earnings growth and tends to reverse the greater wage equality these systems seek to establish (Hibbs and Locking 1995). Centralised negotiations can also adversely affect macro-economic policy, by stimulating wage inflation and, under fixed exchange rates, contribute to balance of payments disequilibria. In the Second World War and post-war period, there were many attempts at incomes policies aimed at restraining wage, but with varying degrees of effectiveness (Willman 1982, Wootton 1974, Levy and Temin 2010).

Multi-employer collective bargaining

Multi-employer bargaining, sometimes called industry-wide, sector or national bargaining, is where terms and conditions of employment are negotiated for all the employers that are party to the national collective agreement or, in the case of Germany, to the regional agreement. Multi-employer bargaining requires constituent employers to belong to appropriate employers' association and union(s) to be well organised nationally. These are also the cases in Austria (a small social democratic regime) and Greece (an ex-dictatorship). Multi-employer bargaining provides advantages to both employers and unions. With all employers in the same bargaining unit, the elasticity of demand for labour is reduced by effectively limiting the opportunity for consumers to shift to less costly producers when wages or prices rise. Faced with member companies that vary in their efficiency and labour market needs, multi-employer agreements result in collective agreements enabling the least efficient firms to survive. Increases in pay also result in smaller job losses for union members in multi-employer bargaining than in single-employer bargaining. Having a common front throughout an industry further 'accords with the unionist's desire for solidarity, and his [sic] sense that it is only fair to have one and the same rate for the job wherever it is done' (Brown 1962: 170).

Employers have generally supported multi-employer bargaining in mainland West Europe. In these cases, wages are taken out of competition among employers and all key competitors are shut down in the event of a dispute. Studies indicate that wages tend to be higher in multi-employer bargaining than single-employer bargaining (Hendricks and Kahn 1984). Also where employers decide not to resist union bargaining power by conceding inflationary wage increases, firms are likely to pass on higher product prices to their consumers.

Historically, there have been some limited multi-employer agreements in North America but a variant called 'pattern bargaining' (or 'follow-the-leader' bargaining) existed in oligopolistic industries for many years, such as in the motor assembly sector in Canada. Using this tactic, the union targets the 'softest' employer in the industry or the one most likely and most able to agree to the terms of a new collective contract. It then repeats the 'pattern' sequentially with other employers and is willing to take industrial action against them if they fail to agree similar wage increases. In this way, a series of collective agreements are made, the terms of which follow the pattern set in the industry by the initial wage deal.

De-centralised collective bargaining (at single-employer and/or enterprise levels)

De-centralised collective bargaining is either single-employer (sometimes called company bargaining) or enterprise bargaining. In single-employer bargaining all terms and conditions of employment are negotiated at employer level, in either multi-site organisations or single-site ones. Enterprise bargaining operates at establishment, workplace or plant level. Single-employer bargaining and enterprise bargaining characterise de-centralised bargaining. The appeal of company bargaining varies with the market conditions facing the firm. In competitive industries, companies are in a weak position during strikes. Demand for the firm's products is highly elastic, because consumers can easily switch to buying the products of other companies with the same or similar products. But for unions, loss of business to other firms is less threatening, since members who lose their jobs can find jobs elsewhere. In oligopolistic industries, in contrast, there is less scope for product substitution by consumers. Hence single-employer bargaining is more attractive to these types of businesses. In buoyant labour market conditions, the bargaining power of the union is increased but, with unemployment, union bargaining power is seriously weakened (Hendricks and Kahn 1984). Examples include Japan (a large liberal market regime) and Denmark (a small social democratic regime).

Enterprise bargaining is where terms and conditions of employment are negotiated between management and union representatives locally or at plant level, not corporate level. Enterprise bargaining is either *autonomous* or *co-ordinated*. Autonomous enterprise bargaining is where each plant has the authority to settle all terms and conditions locally. Co-ordinated enterprise bargaining is where negotiations are conducted at plant level, within limits set by corporate centre. The conditions promoting enterprise or plant bargaining are not dissimilar to those promoting single-employer bargaining. Both are stimulated by the needs of the employer to de-centralise bargaining decision-making as closely as possible to where labour is directly employed, managed and financially accountable. In this way, the employer attempts to match its employment relations strategies and HR practices to the requirements of the business.

Influences on bargaining levels

Many factors influence the level where collective bargaining takes place. First, Hartog and Teulings (1998) show how indices of 'corporatism' or tripartite arrangements, involving social partnerships between government, business and labour interest groups, vary with measures of national culture developed by Hofstede *et al.* (2010). They conclude that centralised collective bargaining structures are more common in societies where high values are placed on equality and quality of life (Grant 1985, Cox and O'Sullivan and Cox 1988). Second, economic influences supplement cultural factors. Thus where business competition is largely domestic, and tariff barriers impede international trade, collective bargaining structures are likely to be centralised or at multi-employer level, which take wages out of competition, as in West Europe in the post-Second World War period. This benefits both employers and unions. Where competition is global, collective bargaining levels become more de-centralised, as has happened in many countries since the 1980s. As Flanagan (2008: 408) argues: 'The spread of international competition in product markets appears to be an important element in this development.' Third, legal influences are important too. Where statutory union recognition is determined in elections at places of work, as in the United States and Canada, de-centralised collective bargaining is dominant. On the other hand, pricing policies enabling all producers in an industry to pass on costs to their customers facilitate multi-employer bargaining.

Bargaining power also influences collective bargaining levels. Here union organisation is a major factor, since unions typically want to raise the real wages of their members without losing members' jobs. The basic argument is that unions are attracted by collective bargaining structures that result in an *inelastic* demand for their members' services. The elasticity of demand for labour is the percentage change in the employment of union members divided by the percentage change in the union wage, which is typically negative. This indicates that a positive increase in the union wage causes a reduction in the number of workers employed but by a lesser proportion. Hicks (1963) identifies four factors leading to the demand for labour services of unionised workers being inelastic. First, union labour is a small percentage of total costs. Second, it is easy to substitute other resource inputs, such as capital, for union workers. Third, efforts to use substitutes for union labour do not provoke large increases in the price of substitute inputs. Fourth, the price elasticity of the product made by labour is low, meaning that most consumers lack acceptable substitutes for the product or service produced by union labour. In these conditions, union bargaining power is relatively high. 'As a rough rule of thumb, the demand for union labor becomes less elastic as the level of bargaining increases' (Flanagan 2008: 409).

BARGAINING COVERAGE, EXTENSION MECHANISMS AND CO-ORDINATION

An important indicator of the extent to which the terms and conditions of employment for workers are influenced by collective bargaining or collective agreements is the *coverage rate*; this is the number of employees covered by a collective agreement divided by the total number of wage and salary earners expressed as a percentage. This is not identical with *union membership density* within each country, which is the percentage of workers in the labour force who are union members (see Chapter 6). In other words, collective agreements cover all employees in a bargaining unit, whether or not they are union members. But the coverage of collective bargaining is wider than just the bargaining unit, because some collective agreements are expanded by legal *extension mechanisms* which make a collective agreement generally binding in a particular sector or region. Collective agreements of this sort cover both employers and employees not affiliated with the bargaining parties. A third issue is where there is more than one bargaining level, with some degree of co-ordination between them. This is called *bargaining co-ordination*. This covers a variety of arrangements described as covert or indirect co-ordination, as in Austria, Germany and Japan, or overt or direct co-ordination in institutionalised multi-tiers of collective bargaining, as in Belgium, France, Ireland, Spain and Norway.

Collective bargaining coverage

Table 11.1 shows the percentage collective bargaining coverage in OECD countries for selected years between 1980 and 2012. The first observation is that collective bargaining coverage varies widely among countries. In 2012, coverage varied greatly from 99 per cent in Austria, 96 per cent in Belgium, 95 per cent in France and 92 per cent in Sweden to 13 per cent in the United States and 12 per cent in South Korea. Slovenia with a claimed 100 per cent coverage is a special case, since it has gone the furthest among Central and East European countries in institutionalising co-ordinated collective bargaining, employee representation, social pacts and collective bargaining coverage (European Commission 2012). Among relatively new member states of the OECD, such as Chile, the Czech Republic, Hungary, Poland, the Slovak Republic, and Turkey, collective bargaining coverage was relatively low, varying between 24 per cent (Chile and Turkey) and 44 per cent (the Czech Republic). Four of these countries (the Czech Republic, Hungary, Poland, and the Slovak Republic) were East European post-communist states, where collective bargaining free from state intervention is a new phenomenon.

Table 11.1 Percentage coverage of collective bargaining in OECD countries for selected years 1980–2012

Country	1980	1990	2000	2012
Australia	80	80	80	60
Austria	95	95	95	99
Belgium	90	90	90	96
Canada	37	38	32	32
Chile	..	..	..	24
Czech Republic	..		25	44
Denmark	70	70	80	82
Estonia	..	..	..	22
Finland	90	90	90	90
France	80	90	90	95
Germany	80	80	68	63
Greece	..	..	..	85
Hungary	..	..	30	35
Iceland	..	..	..	88
Ireland	..	..	..	..
Italy	80	80	80	80
Japan	25	20	15	16
Korea	15	20	10	12
Luxembourg	..	..	60	60
Mexico	..	..	..	..
Netherlands	70	70	80	82
New Zealand	60	60	25	30
Norway	70	70	70	72
Poland	..	..	40	35
Portugal	70	70	80	62
Slovak Republic	..	..	50	35
Slovenia	..	..	..	100
Spain	60	70	80	80
Sweden	80	80	90	92
Switzerland	50	50	40	48
Turkey	..	..	..	24
UK	70	40	30	35
US	26	18	14	13
Unweighted average	64.9	64.1	57.8	57.8

Source: OECD, *Economic Outlook*, for these years.

Second, in 11 out of 31 countries in 2012, collective bargaining coverage was more than 80 per cent. This contrasted with nine countries – Canada, Chile, Japan, South Korea, New Zealand, Poland, the Slovak Republic, the United Kingdom and the United States – where collective bargaining was 35 per cent or less in each case. In the first group of high-coverage countries, cen-tralised and/or multi-employer bargaining is common, whereas in the second group of low-coverage countries, such as Canada, Japan, New Zealand, the United Kingdom and the United States, single-employer or enterprise bar-gaining is the norm. The polar cases of Austria and the United States show the importance of the institutional and organisational contexts of employ-ment relations for understanding national differences in coverage rates. Thus US labour law encourages single-employer bargaining through union election ballots, while Austrian labour law allows only bargaining units that operate at multi-employer level to sign collective agreements. Further, while employer associations play virtually no role in the United States, Austria's Federal Cham-ber of Business and Commerce (*Bundeswirtschaftskammer* – BWK) is among the best-equipped and most influential national associations in the world (Traxler 2000). Further, in Austria, collective agreements negotiated at multi-employer level are normally extended to unaffiliated employers within BWK's sphere of influence (Klein 1992). In the United States, extension mechanisms are unknown.

Third, there has been an overall decline in collective bargaining coverage between 1980 and 2012 from an average of almost two-thirds (64.9 per cent) among all OECD countries to under three-fifths (57.8 per cent). Of the 20 countries providing data over this 32-year period, 10 had increased their cov-erage or had stayed constant (Austria, Belgium, Denmark, Finland, France, Italy, the Netherlands, Norway, Spain, and Sweden), while 10 had decreased coverage (Australia, Canada, Germany, Japan, South Korea, New Zealand, Portugal, Switzerland, the United Kingdom and the United States). The coun-tries where collective bargaining coverage had increased over these years were all mainland West European states. Apart from Italy and Spain, these had relatively small working populations, variable union membership densi-ties, with only five of these 10 countries having union densities more than 50 per cent (Belgium, Denmark, France, Norway and Sweden), and centralised or multi-employer bargaining. Countries where collective bargaining cover-age had decreased over the 32-year period included the major Anglophone states, Germany, and Japan. These had large working populations, generally low union membership density and predominantly de-centralised collective bargaining structures, with Germany the main exception to this (OECD 2012).

Fourth, in mainland Europe, most countries are characterised by stable or increasing coverage rates and generally about two-out-of-three workers tend to be covered by collective bargaining wage-setting arrangements. The excep-tions are Switzerland, Central and East European countries, where collective bargaining lacks strong historical roots. But importantly, countries where significant declines in collective bargaining coverage have taken place since the 1980s are normally those with predominantly single-employer or enterprise bargaining, where coverage was low to begin with.

Fifth, it is apparent taking a longer-term view that collective bargaining coverage has fallen dramatically in the period 1980–2012 in three OECD countries: Australia, New Zealand, and the United Kingdom. In all these cases, coverage has fallen from over 70 per cent or more to 60 per cent in Australia, 35 per cent in the United Kingdom and 30 per cent in New Zealand. All three countries experienced radical employment relations and labour law reforms during these years, resulting in the weakening of collective bargaining structures and trade union organisation and a deregulation (or re-regulation) of labour markets (OECD 2004).

Bargaining extension mechanisms

Governments influence collective bargaining coverage in at least three ways. They define the rights and duties of the parties, such as union recognition and union security provisions, regulate the legal right to strike and lockout, and provide bargaining extension mechanisms. Bargaining extension rules or practices have two functions. First, they make collective agreements generally binding within a sector or a region, by covering employers and employees not affiliated to the bargaining parties. This is normally done by the Ministry of Labour at the request of the parties. In Germany and Finland, for example, labour law enables collective agreements to be declared generally binding where the bargaining parties cover more than a certain percentage of employees within the agreement's sphere of influence. Second, collective bargaining enlargement, as in France, is designed to make collective agreements binding on employers and employees in certain geographical or sectors outside the agreement's immediate coverage. This is provided that they are economically similar to those covered by the collective agreement and where the new parties have the capability of conducting collective bargaining. Such provisions may encourage membership in, or discourage defection from, employer federations. Under administrative extensions of this sort, an individual employer must observe minimum wages and/or working conditions agreed by the employers' association in the economic sector. Rather than having terms dictated by outside bodies, employers thus have an incentive to join the employers' associations to influence agreements (OECD 2010).

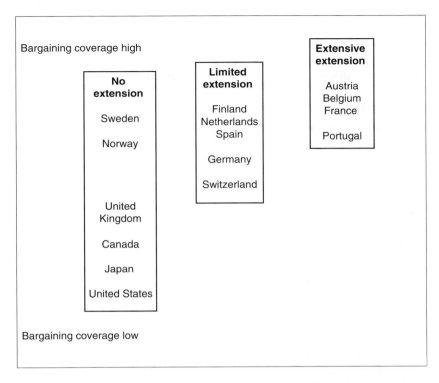

Figure 11.3   Examples of collective bargaining coverage and bargaining extension
mechanisms

Figure 11.3 classifies OECD countries in terms of their collective bargaining coverage and bargaining extension mechanisms. There are three partly overlapping groups: countries with no extension mechanisms, those with limited extension mechanisms, and those with significant extension mechanisms. The first group with extensive extension mechanisms includes Austria, Belgium, France and Portugal. In these countries, a significant number of collective agreements are regularly extended. In France and Portugal, for example, despite having very low union membership densities, ministerial decrees commonly extend collective agreements to non-affiliated employers and workers (Ferner and Hyman 1992).

A second group of countries with limited extension mechanisms includes Finland, the Netherlands and Switzerland. The share of employees covered by extension mechanisms among all employees in these states has been variously estimated at about 19, 14 and 13 per cent respectively (Kerckhofs 2011, Kauppinen 1992, Korver 1991, Bauer and Baumann 1993). Germany, where non-affiliated employers largely follow the outcomes of multi-employer bargaining, and Spain, are characterised by more moderate use of extension mechanisms.

The third group of countries without extension mechanisms includes the United States, Canada and the United Kingdom, which indicates the normal incompatibility of single-employer bargaining and extension mechanisms. In the United Kingdom, decline in multi-employer bargaining was accompanied by the dismantling of extension mechanisms. In Japan also, extension mechanisms are rarely used, although provided for in labour law. Further, Sweden and Norway demonstrate that extension mechanisms can be absent in not only de-centralised bargaining systems but also highly centralised ones. But where employers' associations are strong, collective agreements tend to determine terms and working conditions outside their immediate constituencies. Swedish unions, for example, normally conclude subsidiary agreements with un-affiliated employers' associations (European Trade Union Institute 2012).

What these data indicate is, first, collective bargaining coverage rates are high in most countries having extensive extension mechanisms. However, high coverage rates are not just associated with such mechanisms, as in Sweden and Norway. Second, where extension is common, union density is not necessarily low, as in Austria, Belgium and Portugal, although France stands out as having the lowest union density apart from Turkey. Third, countries where differences between extension mechanisms and union density are greatest, as in Belgium and France, are often those where extension possibilities are the strongest. This means that these differences are not necessarily indicative of the importance of extension procedures in explaining the rate of collective bargaining coverage. Fourth, interest in the application of extension mechanisms is not limited to employers and trade unions. Governments use extension provisions to develop regulation where direct prescription is not possible or not desired. For example, in France, governments have frequently encouraged the conclusion of collective agreements to achieve a consensus on legislative reforms, which would have been more difficult to do so in the political arena. In Finland and the Netherlands, governments have encouraged collective agreements as a basis for establishing supplementary pension funds and other social insurance provisions (Kohli and Arza 2011).

Bargaining co-ordination

Within certain limits set by each country's national labour laws, the parties to collective bargaining are, as a rule, generally free to choose the level of negotiation or a specific mixture of levels appropriate to their needs. But collective bargaining is also characterised by degrees of co-ordination between these levels – central, multi-employer, and de-centralised bargaining at single-employer or enterprise levels. Basically, centralised bargaining between central government, central employers' organisations and union confederations aims to provide a floor for lower-level bargaining on the terms of employment, taking account of macro-economic policy goals. Centralised bargaining is sometimes called 'concertation', or 'social dialogue', or 'co-decision-making', and has been common at one time or another in Australia, Belgium, Finland, the Netherlands, Portugal, Spain and Sweden. However, there has been a move away from centralised bargaining in some of these countries, such as Finland, the Netherlands and Sweden in recent years. Multi-employer bargaining, which has been common in Austria, Germany and Switzerland, aims at standardising terms of employment in a single industry. The bargaining may be broadly or narrowly defined, split into geographical subunits or conducted nationally. De-centralised bargaining at company or enterprise levels is predominant in Canada, the United States, New Zealand (since the 1990s) and the United Kingdom. As a supplementary type of negotiation, de-centralised bargaining also occurs in a number of mainland European states, emphasising that bargaining levels need not be mutually exclusive (Wilkinson and Townsend 2011). A summary of bargaining levels and co-ordination for 23 selected OECD countries in the second half of the 2000s before the financial crisis is presented in Figure 11.4.

Non-co-ordinated bargaining tends to be where single-employer and enterprise bargaining predominate. This type of bargaining is characteristic of North America, New Zealand, the United Kingdom and Switzerland, where there is little co-ordination of bargaining. Comparing the United States with France, for example, the United States has no centralised or sector agreements that establish a framework for supplementary agreements at lower levels. Single-employer bargaining is by far the dominant model of bargaining in the United States. Multi-employer bargaining used to be important in steel, coal and transport but has been disbanded (Kochan *et al.* 1986). Where co-ordination of bargaining occurs, it is through pattern bargaining. Both single-employer and pattern bargaining usually result in precise wage rates rather than minima. They also determine other employment conditions in detail, including work rules, job classifications and fringe benefits. To some extent, pattern bargaining has declined along with multi-employer bargaining, as continual labour market deregulation has fostered the entry of non-union firms in many sectors of employment.

In France, by contrast, collective bargaining has expanded, partly as a result of government initiatives into a fully fledged three-tier negotiation system,

Dominant Level	Country	Central (1)	Sector (2)	Local (3)	Change since 1990	Co-ordination¹	Type
Centralised	Belgium	xxx	xx	x		xxx state imposed	Overt
	Ireland	xxx	x	xx		xxx tri-partite	Overt
Multi-employer	Austria		xxx	x		xxx pattern bargaining	Covert
	Germany		xxx			xxx pattern bargaining	Covert
	Spain	x	xxx	xx		xxx inter-associational	Overt
	Finland		xxx	x	1 -> 2, 3	xx intra-associational	Overt
	Greece		xxx	x		xx inter-associational	Overt
	Italy		xxx	x		xx inter-associational	Overt
	Netherlands		xxx	x		xxx pattern bargaining	Overt
	Norway	x	xxx	x		xxx pattern bargaining	Overt
	Portugal		xxx	x		xx intra-associational	Overt
De-centralised	Australia		x	xxx	2 -> 3	..	..
	Canada		x	xxx		..	..
	Czech Rep		xx	xxx		x inter-associational	Overt
	Denmark		xx	xxx	2 -> 3	xx pattern bargaining	Overt
	France	x	xx	xxx	2 -> 3	x intra-associational	Overt
	Hungary	x	x	xxx		x tri-partite	Overt
	Japan			xxx		x intra-associational	Covert
	Poland	x	x	xxx		..	..
	Slovak Rep		x	xxx	1, 2 -> 3	x intra-associational	Covert
	Sweden		xx	xxx	2 -> 3	xx pattern bargaining	Overt
	United Kingdom		xx	xxx		..	..
	United States		x	xxx		..	..

Figure 11.4 Bargaining levels and co-ordination in 23 selected OECD countries in the mid-2000s, before the financial crisis

.. = not applicable.

xxx very important, xx important, x quite important.

Source: OECD (2012).

despite union membership density only being around 7 per cent – the lowest in West Europe (OECD 2012). Collective bargaining in France was generalised by law in 1950, which established the industry as the main bargaining level. In 1971, collective bargaining at the 'inter-professional' or cross-industry level was also established. Finally, the 'Auroux laws' 1982 imposed an annual obligation to bargain about wages and working time at the workplace or company level, with an annual obligation to bargain about wages, as well as a five-year obligation to bargain on job classifications at industry level. One of the paradoxes of French employment relations is that despite its low rate of unionisation, it has a very high rate of collective bargaining coverage, close to 98 per cent. Two major reasons for this are, first, the extension of collective agreements by the Ministry of Labour and, second, the legal form of union recognition. According to this, since 1966, each of its five union confederations has been recognised by government as 'representative' at national level. They are, therefore, entitled to sign collective agreements at any level (Rehfeldt 2010).

Covert co-ordination

Austria, Germany and Japan rely on covert co-ordination. Austria, for example, had a long tradition of central-level concertation but this has decayed recently. This is because co-operation between the central parties has declined due to globalisation and the national economy's growing internationalisation. The key area of collective bargaining has shifted to multi-employer or sector level. Further, although labour law excludes bargaining at company or enterprise levels, in practice works councils often negotiate supplementary wage increases. As in Germany, there has been some de-centralisation to local levels on flexible working hours. Clauses in sector agreements allow works councils to accept wage cuts when working hours are reduced to prevent redundancies (Fulton 2011).

In Germany, most collective agreements are determined at multi-employer level, differentiated by region. Single-employer bargaining involves only small firms whose separate agreements closely follow sector-wide agreements. Co-ordination takes place, because of the strength of industry-wide employers' organisations and powerful unions, which control and co-ordinate bargaining rounds at regional level. Further, pilot agreements in key regions and branches of the metalworkers' union serve as a benchmark for bargaining in the rest of the sector and its branches. Multi-employer bargaining is supported by labour law, which makes supplementary bargaining over wages in works councils illegal. Yet in practice, works councils have always been able to make some amendments to sector-wide wage agreements by negotiating piece rates and wage premia related to performance and effort (Jacobi *et al.* 1992). Strains appeared in the eastern *Länder* or regions, however, following re-unification, where firms were opposed to the speedy adjustment of wages to those in the western regions.

In Japan, most collective bargaining takes place at single-employer level. But the annual bargaining round is launched through the *Shuntō* or the national 'spring offensive' of the unions. This is based on general guidelines for wages, set jointly by national trade union centres. These guidelines are specified by each sector-based union, which decides on the average wage increase to be sought in the sector and guides the particular demands of each enterprise union. Parallel efforts are made by employers' associations and the major companies. This means that company responses to union wage demands largely converge. Company agreements in Japan, however, provide opportunities to modify individual collective agreements, because several wage components are linked with managerial assessment of worker performance (Rebick 2005).

Overt co-ordination

This is institutionalised in three-tier systems of collective bargaining as in Belgium, France, Norway and Spain, and at times in Ireland. In Belgium, there is a long-established three-tier system of collective bargaining laid down in law, so that collective bargaining in Belgium is highly structured. Central level covers the whole of the private sector and the industrial level covers specific industrial sectors, with company-level negotiations at the base of this hierarchy, although wage negotiations only take place in some companies. In each case, the lower level can only agree improvements on what has been negotiated at the level above, where collective agreements are legally binding. The state plays a major role in collective bargaining, with the law allowing it to link wage increases to pay trends to Belgium's neighbours, Germany, France and the Netherlands. This is to maintain the country's competitiveness. In central-level negotiations, the government has power to intervene if the two sides cannot agree. This structure means that the proportion of employees covered by collective bargaining is relatively high.

Bargaining at central level in Belgium normally sets a two-year binding framework for wages and other issues and takes place between employer and union groups. At sector level, negotiations are carried out by unions and employers' federations meeting in joint committees. These cover the whole of the private sector, with sub-committees for smaller industrial groupings. In 2011, there were 102 joint committees and 70 sub-committees. The agreements reached in these joint committees and sub-committees are binding on all employers in the industries they cover. At company level, trade union delegations, together with local union organisations, negotiate with individual employers. However, these agreements are only valid when signed by a trade union official outside the workplace. The normal cycle of negotiations is biennially, with national negotiations being followed by industry-level and company-level negotiations (Fulton 2011).

Collective bargaining in Spain takes place at central, multi-employer and company levels and, since 2001, annual negotiations provide a framework agreement for lower-level bargaining. The overall coverage is high at around 70 per cent of the total workforce. Central-level agreements cover both non-wage issues and, since 2002, guidelines on wage increases for lower-level negotiators. In recent years, major non-wage agreements between government, employer and union representatives have covered a range of topics. These include: attempts to increase the number of workers on permanent contracts and reduce the number of temporary workers, improvements in training, changes in social security, equality of treatment and opportunities for women and men, and health and safety. Since 2001, central agreements have made recommendations to negotiators at sector and company levels for wage bargaining in the coming year. In each case, the agreed formula was that negotiators should settle for a wage increase in line with inflation, with an amount taking account of higher productivity. There was also to be a clause guaranteeing a catch-up payment, if inflation turned out to be higher than forecast.

Below central level in Spain, the structure is complex and overlapping and several attempts have been made to create more coherent structural arrangements. An agreement on reform reached in 1997 by employers and unions has not yet been implemented. However, in 2011, government introduced legislation giving a greater role to company bargaining. Company agreements are able to set wages, hours, grading and other issues, which can be either worse or better than those in sector-level agreements. Currently, most employers and employees are covered by provincial-level agreements for their industries. But in future, company agreements will have precedence, even if the provincial agreement is still in force.

Overall coverage of collective bargaining is high in Spain but the situation is complex. There are some multi-employer agreements for the whole of Spain, such as construction, banking and chemicals. But this is not typical. Large and medium size firms normally have their own collective agreements, sometimes at enterprise or plant level, while smaller employers are covered by provincial agreements for their industry, which can cover the same issues. Figures compiled by the tri-partite Economic and Social Council indicate this complexity. In 2009, for example, three-quarters of all collective agreements were company agreements but these only determined the terms and conditions of about 10 per cent of all employees covered by collective bargaining. At the other end of the scale, multi-employer agreements made up 2 per cent of all agreements but covered about a quarter of all employees. Provincial agreements accounting for 20 per cent of all collective agreements covered over 50 per cent of employees. The remaining 10 per cent of workers were covered by agreements at regional level. These proportions have remained more or less constant in recent years (Fulton 2011).

WORKER REPRESENTATION AT WORKPLACE AND COMPANY LEVELS

There are many types of worker participation and worker representation at workplace and firm levels. Works councils, for example, are typically an institutional means of worker participation in some West European countries. They deal with issues typically covered by domestic procedural agreements in firms within liberal market economies. In co-ordinated market economies, such as Austria, Germany and Sweden, workers also sit on company boards established by legislation. The underpinning objective of worker participation is to integrate the interests of managers and workers in the workplace and enterprise on matters of common interest between them. It seeks to substitute adversarial relations between the managerial agents of capital and the people working in enterprises with co-operative relationships. In this way, it helps promote 'industrial democracy'; another term coined by Webb and Webb (1920b). The aim of industrial democracy is to create more democratic decision-making in organisations through power-sharing between managements and workers. However, while collective bargaining is defined as a 'rule making' process with no counterpart in individual bargaining (Flanders 1970), it is difficult in practice to draw a clear dividing line between the concepts of collective bargaining and worker participation; both are systems of joint regulation. Third-party intervention in relations between employers and unions, and managers and workers, enables differences between them to be resolved constitutionally and peacefully, where they are unable to do so themselves.

Workplace representation

Institutionalised relations between employer and employee representatives are, therefore, not limited to formalised collective bargaining arrangements or, in the case of employees, representation through trade unions. Even in centralised and multi-employer bargaining systems, representatives of management and employees meet together at enterprise (workplace) and sometimes single-employer (company) levels to discuss non-bargaining issues of common interest to them, especially in larger enterprises and public-sector organisations. But largely for historical reasons, and the dominant political economy in each case, such representative systems, often based on some form of consultation or communication between the parties, are particularly found in mainland Europe. So most of the discussion here focuses on institutions and practices commonly found in mainland Europe; this has the most penetrating examples of worker representation. Moreover, Europe has some reliable data-sets.

As Jenkins and Blyton (2008: 354) argue: 'Workplace committees, involving either elected or nominated worker representatives are a widespread form of management-workforce interaction.' They add, however, that outside mainland Europe and, particularly in countries such as Australia, the United States and the United Kingdom, 'where adversarial relations have been more evident in past industrial relations, the likelihood of any thoroughgoing development of [collective] employee participation looks a distant prospect'.

A framework for analysing worker representation beyond collective bargaining is provided in Figure 11.5. This contrasts with individual *direct* participation techniques or processes, initiated by managements (see Chapter 9). Figure 11.5 identifies five methods of collective *indirect* participation for employees, involving representative systems where employees and management have joint interests at workplace and company levels. Two are workplace issues (workplace representation and health and safety committees), one is a company issue (employee representation at board level), and two are European-level issues (employee membership of EWCs and European companies). Financial participation (or involvement) is matter of individual choice at company level and is more appropriately considered to be a form of direct participation rather than a representative one.

Figure 11.5 shows that the predominant form of workplace representation for employees in these 25 countries is through local trade union representatives (52 per cent), followed by a combination of works councils and/or trade union representation (28 per cent) and works councils alone (20 per cent). In other words, all these countries have, to varying degrees of effectiveness, some types of workplace representation. Local union representatives are commonly from union delegations and have differing degrees of power and influence, depending on the strength and resources of the national unions to which they belong, as well as the support of their local memberships. Such strength

Country	Workplace representation	Employee representation at board level	Company structure	Employee members of European works councils	Employee members of European company	Health and safety committees (HSCs)	Financial participation
Austria	Works councils	One-third of some supervisory boards in state-owned and private companies, chosen by works council	Dualistic	Appointed through works council structure	Appointed through works council structure	Safety officers, chosen by works council HSCs	Limited
Belgium	Union delegations Works councils	None (except in some state enterprises)	Monistic	Appointed by employee reps on works council	Appointed by employee reps on works council	HSCs	Limited
Bulgaria	No universal system Mainly union reps	None	Monistic/ dualistic	Elected by general meeting of employees or employee delegates	Elected by general meeting of employees or employee delegates	None	Employee ownership Co-operatives

Figure 11.5 A summary of worker representation within companies in 25 selected European states 2012

Sources: European Trade Union Institute (2012).

480

Czech Republic	Local union reps Works councils	One-third of supervisory boards of medium to large public companies	Dualistic	Chosen by meeting of employee reps	Chosen by meeting of employee reps	No precise legal provisions, but HS is central to collective agreements	Very limited due to the privatisation process
Denmark	Local union reps Union members on co-operation committees	One-third of supervisory boards of some state and private companies	Dualistic	Appointed by co-operation committee, union reps or employee ballot	Appointed by co-operation committee, union reps or employee ballot	Safety reps HSCs	High *relative* share ownership & profit sharing
Estonia	Union reps or none	None	Dualistic	Elected at general meeting of employees	Elected at general meeting of employees	Where there is no union, employees may elect an agent	Profit sharing
Finland	Local union bodies	Right to board representation, subject to local negotiations with unions in large companies	Monistic/dualistic	Chosen by employees	Chosen by employees	Safety reps HSCs	Schemes widespread

Figure 11.5 (Continued)

Country	Workplace representation	Employee representation at board level	Company structure	Employee members of European works councils	Employee members of European company	Health and safety committees (HSCs)	Financial participation
France	Complex structure, with union delegates and elected employees, includes works councils and employee delegates at workplace and company levels	Complex structure, including employee reps on boards of state enterprises and some private organisations	Monistic/dualistic	Appointed by the unions	Chosen by union from works council members or union delegates	Statutory health, safety and working conditions committees	Strong state support for financial participation
Germany	Works councils, with substantial powers	Employee reps on supervisory boards of large companies	Dualistic	Chosen through works council structure	Chosen through works council structure	Safety officers HSCs	Limited
Hungary	Local trade unions Works councils	One-third of supervisory boards in large companies	Monistic/dualistic	Appointed by works council or elected by workforce	Appointed by works council or elected by employees	Safety reps HSCs	Very limited
Ireland	Union reps or none	Employee reps in the state sector	Monistic	Elected by employees, appointed by employees or by management	Elected by employees	Safety reps Safety committees	Limited

Figure 11.5 (Continued)

			Monistic/dualistic	Appointed by unions and local union bodies	Elected or appointed by the union body in the company		Very limited
Italy	Union bodies elected by all employees	None				Elected employee reps Some HSCs	Very limited
Latvia	Union reps or none	None	Dualistic	Chosen at meeting of employee reps	Chosen at meeting of employee reps	Governed by the Labour Code	Employee ownership Profit sharing Co-operatives but limited
Luxembourg	Elected employee delegates Joint employer-employee bodies in larger firms	One-third of supervisory boards in large companies	Monistic	Appointed by main employee delegation	Appointed by central employee delegation	Mixed works councils Staff delegations that appoint safety reps	Not required by law
Malta	Union reps or none	None	Monistic	Elected by employees	Not applicable	Some union safety reps but largely through collective bargaining	Very limited

Figure 11.5 (Continued)

483

Country	Workplace representation	Employee representation at board level	Company structure	Employee members of European works councils	Employee members of European company	Health and safety committees (HSCs)	Financial participation
Netherlands	Works councils (employees only)	One-third of supervisory boards in large companies	Dualistic	Appointed by central works council or elected by employees, with unions having nomination rights	Appointed by central works council or elected by employees, with unions having nomination rights	Safety reps Elected works councils, with responsibility for H&S	Main one is a 'save-as-you' earn scheme to purchase shares
Norway	Union reps Works councils, with limited functions	One-third of boards in large companies	Monistic	Elected by employees	Chosen by the union or elected by employees	Safety reps Joint work environment committees of employer and workforce reps	None
Poland	Union reps or none	Employee reps on supervisory boards of state enterprises	Dualistic	Appointed by the union	Appointed by the union	Social enterprise inspectors Employee reps in the state sector	Largely employee owned companies and co-operatives
Portugal	Union reps Works councils (rare)	No effective legislation for employee reps	Dualistic	Agreement between the unions and works council or by the works council	Agreement between the unions and works council or by the works council	Safety, hygiene and health reps	Mainly profit sharing but limited

Figure 11.5 (Continued)

Romania	Union reps including consultation rights	None	Monistic	Appointed by union reps or elected by workforce	Appointed by union reps or elected by employees	HSCs in enterprises with more than 50 employees	Privatisation shares now sold off
Slovak Republic	Works councils Union reps (weak)	50 per cent of supervisory boards in state sector One third in large private sector	Dualistic	Appointed by employee reps	Appointed by employee reps	None	Limited
Spain	Employee/ union repre- sentation Works councils	No legal right to employee reps on boards but reps found in certain sectors	Monistic	Appointed by unions, works council or employee delegates	Appointed by unions, works councils or employee delegates	Safety reps HS delegates HSCs	Largely through employee share ownership

Figure 11.5 (Continued)

485

Country	Workplace representation	Employee representation at board level	Company structure	Employee members of European works councils	Employee members of European company	Health and safety committees (HSCs)	Financial participation
Sweden	Union reps	About one-third of boards chosen by the union	Monistic	Appointed by local unions	Appointed by local unions	Safety reps Safety committees	None
Switzerland	Limited rights to information, consultation and representation, normally through the union	None	Monistic	No legal obligations	No legal obligations	Employers must give information on HS and consult employees	Share ownership, limited to managers
United Kingdom	Union reps or none	None	Monistic	Elected by employees	Elected by employees	Union safety reps Non-union reps HSCs	Profit sharing Share ownership

Figure 11.5 (Continued)

486

is derived from union density levels nationally, the procedures within which these representatives operate and the responsiveness of their constituents to current issues. In countries such as Denmark, Finland, Malta, Norway and Sweden, where union density is relatively high and the union tradition is strong, local union influence is likely to be high. But in transition economies, such as Bulgaria, the Czech Republic, Estonia, Hungary, Latvia, Poland, Portugal, Romania and the Slovak Republic, where union density is low and the union tradition much weaker, local union influence is likely to be low too. Indeed, the presence of both channels of workplace representation, in the Czech Republic, Hungary, Poland and Slovak Republic, probably reflect the comparative weaknesses of both types of worker representation in these countries. Union influence locally is also likely to be low, where union representation is the only viable means of workplace representation, as in Ireland and the United Kingdom. Union power is further weakened where, as in the United Kingdom, collective bargaining takes place at company or workplace level.

Mainland Europe is where works councils have a long history of acceptance, legitimacy and success. For example, in Germany, works councils were originally a product of the factory council movement during the 1918 revolution and became a core element in the institutional structure of the Weimar Republic (1919–1933). They were revived and given a new statutory basis in post-war Germany in 1952, with subsequent amendments, as in 2011, which permits works councils to be set up in any private workplaces with at least five employees (Incomes Data Services 1991, Fulton 2011). In the early twenty-first century, works councils in Europe are found in a wide variety of forms and levels in 13 of the 25 countries examined in Figure 11.5.

A definitive definition of works councils is problematic, because their terms of reference, nomenclatures, legal basis, membership, structures, traditions, levels of operation, and the cultural and institutional contexts in which they operate, differ widely among the countries where they exist. Thus Rogers and Streeck (1995: 6–10) in their detailed analysis of works councils define them as '*institutionalized bodies for representative communication between a single employer ('management') and the employees ('workforce') of a single plant or enterprise ('workplace')* (original emphasis). They provide eight distinctive features of works councils, as indicated in Figure 11.6.

Rogers and Streeck (1995: 10) go on to distinguish between three ideal types of works councils. They identify, first, 'paternalistic' councils are formed by employers or governments to oppose trade unions. Second, 'consultative' councils are set up to improve communications between management and workers through information exchanges and consultation. Their overall purpose is to facilitate co-operation in production arrangements and enhance

(1) They represent all the workers in a workplace, whether or not they are union members
(2) They represent the workforce in a plant or enterprise, not an industry or sector
(3) They are not company unions
(4) They differ from managerial employee involvement strategies, which are directed at individuals and small workgroups, whereas works councils are representative institutions
(5) They are concerned with representative communications that may originate from either the workforce or management in the forms of information exchanges (normally from management), consultation between the parties or co-determination between them
(6) They normally have a defined legal status, although some may not
(7) They vary widely amongst and within countries
(8) They are not the same as worker representation on company boards

Figure 11.6 Distinctive features of works councils in Europe
Source: Rogers and Streeck (1995).

the competitive performance of the enterprise or plant. They provide a parallel channel of employment relations, supplementing collective bargaining. Third, 'representative' councils are typically set up by collective agreement or legislation, giving the entire workforce of a plant or enterprise (whether unionised or not) some form of institutionalised voice in relation to management. Representative councils enable workers to assert distributional or general interests the employer would not be willing to accommodate for paternalistic or economic reasons alone. 'As a second-channel institution existing alongside unions and collective bargaining', these institutions assume workers have work-based interests, requiring 'some form of worker participation in management'.

As demonstrated in Figure 11.5, there are safety representatives and different kinds of health and safety committees (HSCs) in at least 18 of the listed states. In two states, the Czech Republic and Malta, health and safety is covered by collective agreements between the parties. Only Bulgaria, the Slovak Republic and Switzerland have no local institutions for health and safety; in Latvia health and safety is governed by a Labour Code; and in Poland, health and safety is dealt with by social enterprise inspectors. This demonstrates that health and safety is a very important issue at workplace level but is managed differently in different countries. HSCs play an important part in this process, as do employee safety representatives within workplaces. Improving health and safety at work is crucial to the prevention of industrial accidents, diseases and absenteeism. It begins at company level but also requires a significant amount of government involvement, as well as support from employee and employer organisations. The high safety standards currently in force in most European countries are the result of long-term policies promoting tri-partite social dialogue in the area, collective bargaining between unions and employers, and effective health and safety legislation backed up by an efficient labour inspectorate. But the process begins with worker representation in health and safety at workplace level through elected safety representatives and HSCs (Gazzane 2006).

Board-level representation

Employee representatives on company boards are common in some parts of mainland Europe. Figure 11.5 shows that 14 of the 25 states listed have some form of elected employee representation at board level. Ten have two-tier board structures – a top-tier 'supervisory' board that oversees the activities of a lower-tier 'executive' board. In Austria, the Czech Republic, Denmark, Germany, Hungary, Luxembourg, the Netherlands, Norway, Poland and Slovak Republic, employee representatives sit on supervisory boards, where the typical proportion of employee representatives is one-third of board members. Four countries have other forms of employee representation on company boards. In Finland employees have a right to board representation subject to local negotiations with trade unions in large organisations; France has a complex structure enabling employee representatives to sit on the boards of state enterprises and some private organisations; Ireland has some employee representatives on boards in the state sector; and in Sweden, board members are chosen by the union and make up about one-third of board members in most companies in a single board structure.

Austria provides a typical example of employee representation at board level. The works council has the right to choose one-third of representatives of the supervisory board of all stock-owned corporations and most limited companies with at least 300 employees. Supervisory boards oversee the actions of the executive board which runs the business on a day-to-day basis. There are estimated to be 1,500 companies with employee representatives on supervisory boards, employing 400,000 people, or around 12 per cent of all employees. Employee board representatives are chosen by the works council and must be works council members and employees of the business. They have the same rights and duties as other supervisory board members, although they are not paid for this work. In Sweden, employee representation on boards is very extensive. Employees are represented on the boards of all companies with more than 25 employees in single-tier board system. There are two or three employee members per board and they account for around one-third of board members in most companies. They are chosen by the union and are generally key figures in a whole range of employer-union relations (Fulton 2011).

European Works Councils

European-wide Works Councils (EWCs) are standing bodies providing for the information and consultation of employees in European-wide undertakings and European-wide groups of undertakings, as required by the European Works Council Directive (EWC Directive 1994, Article 2). Employers are required to consult with employee representatives over a range of cross-national issues including restructuring and employment developments. EWCs are thus quite significant in terms of European employment relations, since they represent the first genuinely European institution of interest-group representation at enterprise level. Indeed, they reflect a growing recognition of the need to respond to the Europeanisation of business, emerging from the single European market as a result of the Single European Act 1986. EWCs supplement existing national channels of information and consultation, a goal expressed in the Community Charter of the Fundamental Social Rights of Workers (European Union 1989) and the accompanying Social Action Programme. Negotiations to establish EWCs require a special negotiating body (SNB) to be set up. Crucially, it is up to the undertaking's central management and the SNB to agree on the precise form and function of their EWC. Thus how employee representatives are chosen varies by country.

Three examples demonstrate this. German members of the SNB for the EWC are chosen from the group works council, where such a body exists. If there are only central or ordinary works councils, and they do not cover all workplaces, they are extended to cover workplaces not otherwise represented. Employees representing senior management can be members of the SNB too, if they are chosen under this procedure. There is also a requirement for members to reflect the gender make-up of the workforce. Finnish members of the SNB, in contrast, are chosen by employees, with health and safety delegates representing the largest groups of workers organising the procedure if it cannot be agreed in any other way. Legislation does not specifically exclude external union representatives from being members but does not specifically include them. The situation is the same where a EWC is set up under the fallback procedure in the annex to the Directive, although in this case only employees may be members. French members of the SNB are appointed by the unions, on the basis of their support in works council elections. This is done from among either works council members or trade union delegates in the company. If there is no union presence, employees make the choice. However, as Jenkins and Blyton (2008) argue, weak regulation governing the nature, scope and function of EWCs, coupled with the ambivalent views of the parties to these arrangements, has resulted in EWCs operating in ways at variance with the objectives of the original legislation.

European companies

The European Company Statute enables companies to operate their businesses on a trans-national basis within the EU under the same corporate regime. A particular feature of this legal form consists of obligatory negotiations on the right to worker involvement in European companies, including employee representation at board level. A European company (*Societas Europaea* or SE) operates on a Europe-wide basis and is governed by European Community law directly applicable in member states rather than by national law. It was established by the European Company Statute (ECS) Regulation 2001. The Directive supplementing the ECS establishes a legal right to employee involvement in SEs for informing and consulting employees and, in some cases, board-level participation. EU-based companies may become SEs in four ways: merger; creation of a joint holding company; creation of a subsidiary; or when a single EU-based company is transformed into an SE, provided it has had a subsidiary governed by the law of another member state for at least two years.

Three examples show how this is done in different countries. In Denmark, members of the SNB are appointed by the co-operation committee of the company or, if that does not exist, by union representatives, or by a ballot of all employees. Only employees may be members. The process is the same for members of the SE representative body or works council set up under the Directive. However, Danish employee representatives at board level in European companies based in Denmark are elected by all employees, in accordance with the rules on board-level representation covered by Danish company law. The election is organised by an electoral committee consisting of employee and management representatives. Latvian employees in an SE can decide that their interests should be represented in the SNB by their existing employee representatives. If not, SNB members from Latvia are elected by the employees. Latvian members of the SE representative body, set up under the fallback procedures in the annex to the Directive, are elected by employee representatives, whether union representatives or authorised workplace representatives where they exist. Where they do not, members of the SE representative body are elected by the whole workforce.

Third, Portuguese members of the SNB of a European Company are appointed by agreement between the works council and unions, provided the unions represent at least 5 per cent of employees. If there are no unions, the works council chooses the Portuguese members. The unions can choose the members, as long as they represent in total at least two-thirds of the employees or, where this cannot be shown, each union represents at least 5 per cent of the employees involved. Yet progress is slow in developing European companies. By 2013, it was reported there were 1,601 registered SEs in the ETUI's European Company Database (Carlson *et al.* 2013). By far the most companies registered were in the Czech Republic, with others in Germany, Slovak Republic, France, Denmark and Cyprus.

CONFLICT RESOLUTION IN EMPLOYMENT RELATIONS

The employment relationship is a contested phenomenon. It is not surprising that differences and difficulties arise out of issues of economic distribution and managerial authority in the regulation of the wage–work bargain, whether at sector, organisational or workplace levels. This sometimes gives rise to conflicts between the parties which are resolved by negotiation. These include disputes over terms and conditions of employment, job losses, issues about managerial discretion, union recognition (or de-recognition) and union jurisdictions. In collective employment relations, breakdowns in relations between an employer and union can result in strikes, lock-outs, working-to-contract and other forms of industrial action. The consequences are lost output and reduced corporate image to the employers and lost wages and weakened job security to workers, resulting in economic costs for all involved. In individual employment issues, breakdowns take place between managers and subordinates, or between managerial or workplace colleagues and can result in tensions between individuals. This can have adverse effects on relationships in the workplace, output, efficiency, and general morale at work. All these situations provide opportunities for third parties to intervene or 'mediate' where the parties are in dispute and, with their consent, help resolve these issues. The most common interventions are conciliation, arbitration and workplace mediation.

Conciliation

Historically, Webb and Webb (1920b: 223) note that 'there has been, until recently, no clear distinction between Collective Bargaining, Conciliation and Arbitration'. Today, conciliation is sometimes synonymous with 'mediation' but it differs substantively from arbitration. Both conciliation and collective mediation are commonly processes for the voluntary settlement of employment relations disputes through some form of third-party intervention or facilitation. On a strict interpretation of the terms conciliation and mediation, conciliation is limited to encouraging the parties to discuss their differences and helping them develop their own proposed solutions to them. Mediation, in contrast, implies a stronger form and more directive style of intervention, where a mediator offers the parties proposals for a settlement. The role of the conciliator is to assist the parties reach their own negotiated settlement, making 'suggestions as appropriate'. The mediator proceeds by way of conciliation 'but in addition is prepared and expected to make [his/her] formal proposals or recommendations which may be accepted as they stand or provide the basis for further negotiation leading to a settlement' (Advisory Conciliation and Arbitration Service 1982: 20). However, the distinction between the two terms has tended to disappear in practice and there is no consistency in usage among countries. In some cases either conciliation or mediation is used; in other cases both terms are used inter-changeably to denote the same process of third-party intervention; and, in other countries, the two terms are employed to designate different forms of third-party intervention (ILO 2006).

The most common usage of conciliation is a procedure whereby a neutral third party attempts to persuade the players to settle their dispute without seeking to impose its own terms of settlement upon them. Conciliation involves, therefore, a process where the third party, a public conciliation officer or a private conciliator, is invited to help the two sides in dispute – employer and union – resolve their differences. The ideal method for settling a dispute is where both sides, by making concessions and compromises, are willing to come together and negotiate a satisfactory outcome, using agreed negotiating procedures or the procedure to avoid disputes to do so. Solutions arrived at by mutual decision between the parties, without involving an outsider, are more likely to result in smooth implementation, without further damaging their relationship. It is normally only with the agreement of both sides, and agreed procedures have been fully used, that a conciliator is invited to help bring matters to a positive conclusion. Being privy to both sets of views and feelings between the parties puts the conciliator in a privileged position. From an awareness of the attitudes of both sides and their respective positions, the conciliator tries to bring about some movement between them to obtain a mutually acceptable solution.

Viewed in these terms, conciliation is a process of peace-making. It is a method of dispute resolution by which the services of the neutral third party are used to help the parties in dispute reduce the extent of their differences and arrive at an amicable settlement or agreed solution. It involves orderly discussion of differences between the parties under guidance of the conciliator. The steps a conciliator takes to bring about an amicable settlement vary from country to country but the purpose is always to assist the parties towards a mutually acceptable compromise or solution. 'A unique and essential characteristic of the conciliation process is its flexibility, which sets it apart from other methods of settling disputes' (International Labour Office 1973: 4).

In practice, conciliation has developed mainly in connection with disputes arising from the failure of collective bargaining. It is therefore described as an extension of collective bargaining or assisted collective bargaining. Representatives of the parties in collective bargaining are normally also their representatives at conciliation meetings. At negotiating meetings, these representatives make up each party's negotiating committee. At the conciliation stage, the parties continue to have their negotiating committees, whose views are taken into account in the conciliation process. It is usual to speak of joint discussions between the parties in conciliation proceedings as negotiations. The aim of the conciliation process is to reach a settlement between the parties, which means them agreeing jointly together, as they do from unaided collective bargaining. The same process is used in conciliation as in collective bargaining, except the conciliator participates in the process, but the joint decision aimed for is one made by the parties themselves. The view of collective bargaining as a joint decision-making process makes it easier to understand the dynamics and complexity of conciliation. This is especially the case in face-to-face relationships between the negotiators, as well as within each party's negotiating committee (ILO 1983).

Arbitration

The distinction between conciliation and arbitration in the settlement of disputes between employers and unions is generally established in national laws and regulations (Shen 2007). Arbitration is used sometimes where conciliation has failed or, in a separate dispute, where the employer and union cannot find a mutual solution themselves. It is the process where an impartial third party – an individual arbitrator or a board of arbitration – is authorised to settle the dispute by collecting information from both sides and making a judgement. With a single arbitrator, an individual hears the evidence on their own and has sole responsibility for the outcome. In a board of arbitration, this commonly consists of three persons, one of whom chairs the panel in its discussions with the parties, as well as taking account of the written evidence provided by them. A consensus is normally sought in panel arbitration, but sometimes a majority view has to prevail (Guillebaud 1969).

Arbitration produces a settlement between the parties, whereas conciliation or collective mediation cannot guarantee a settlement. Thus in seeking arbitration, the parties give authority to the third party to impose a settlement on them. The essential difference between the arbitrator's function and a conciliator and mediator is the arbitrator determines the issue. Moreover, having reached a stage which might be described as a post-collective bargaining one, the parties find themselves in a new situation. Arbitrators have to follow a different process from that of conciliators. While the conciliator stands on the sidelines by giving advice and guidance to both sides, the arbitrator is solely responsible for the outcome. No purpose is served in arbitration by separate meetings or joint negotiating conferences. Arbitration hearings follow different patterns of behaviour, where the main objective of each side is to provide the arbitrator with the facts of the case from its perspective. The parties put their cases to the arbitrator in turn, who probes the facts by detailed questioning.

Arbitrators also require written statements from each side, setting out the facts of the case and the contentions of both parties. Normally, oral submissions made to the arbitrator are amplifications of what is set out in their written submissions (Metcalf and Milner 1993). The arbitration process thus incorporates various methods of informing the arbitrator. It incorporates both the 'adversary' and 'inquisitorial' concepts. The first is where each side presents its case to the third party and attempts to counter the other side; the second is where the arbitrator takes the initiative and obtains relevant facts from the parties. In many cases, arbitrators visit the organisations and workplaces where the dispute is taking place. After the hearing, the arbitrators reflect on the evidence, determine the case and prepare the award, which is binding on both sides (Sen 2012).

The main characteristic which sets arbitration apart from other methods of third-party intervention in employment disputes is it imposes a settlement upon the parties, by mutual consent. This determines the procedures to be followed so that all the relevant facts are provided to the arbitrator and the parties feel their cases have been considered properly and fairly. The logic of the post-bargaining period implies that the exercise of further industrial pressure by either side is irrelevant. Because the parties have accepted the arbitrator, and have agreed to accept the decision whatever the outcome, there is no point in the union continuing any threat of industrial action. The same is true in the event of a possible employer lock-out.

As far as the participants are concerned, arbitration is a complicated and exacting process. When going to arbitration, the parties have to make a number of important decisions. These include agreeing the terms of reference, the form of arbitration, and who shall arbitrate. They also play a positive part in the actual process. Both employers and unions take account of these processes before going to arbitration, in the context of the dominant social culture within which arbitration is offered (Shen 2007).

Workplace mediation

Work and workplaces continually change locally, nationally and globally and conflicts of interest are endemic within any workplace. Traditional methods used to resolve workplace conflict were through formal employment relations procedures and trade unionism. These procedures typically covered grievances, disputes, harassment, equality and diversity, and discrimination at work. However, in those countries where collective employment relationships are being superseded by individual relationships, different methods are being used to resolve such issues. The underpinning reasons for this new frontier in conflict resolution derive out of the changing worlds of work and human resources management. The factors involved are complex but include the shift from collectivism to individualism, the effects of globalisation on work and workplace relations, employment flexibility, performance management, issues of trust and leadership within organisations, and uncertainty and insecurity in the world of work (Greenspan 2007).

Research funded by the Advisory Conciliation and Arbitration Service in the United Kingdom, where individual employment relations are increasingly the norm, reports the issues giving rise to individual and interpersonal conflicts within organisations. These typically include discrimination on the grounds of gender, ethnicity and age, dismissal, bullying or harassment, pay and conditions, discipline, and breakdowns in relationships. The most effective methods for resolving these types of individual workplace conflict include informal discussions between those affected, grievance procedures, compromise agreements, and workplace mediation. Of these processes, workplace mediation is proving to be of growing importance in the regulation of relations between managers and workers, workers and workers, and within groups in the workplace (Latrielle 2010). There are various definitions and expositions of workplace mediation (Bevan *et al.* 2004, Doherty and Guyler 2008, Brown and Marriott 2011). Lewis (2009: 75), for example, defines mediation as 'a process used for resolving disputes in which a third person helps the parties negotiate a settlement. It is future focused and less concerned with who is right or wrong, and concentrates on solving problems so that they don't occur again'. In other words, mediation is a 'facilitative' process and the parties in conflict retain responsibility themselves for achieving a solution. The role of the mediator is to bring the parties together, so they arrive at a point where they can reach a settlement. The mediator does not normally impose a settlement, except in 'directive' mediation, which is rarely used in workplace issues.

Workplace mediation is a confidential and informal way to resolve disagreements or disputes between people who work together. The process is assisted by the mediator who encourages the parties to speak to each other and reach a mutually acceptable solution to resolve their problems. It gives the parties a chance to talk about the situation, express their concerns to each other, and come up with practical ideas about how things can change for the better. Such disputes can be between two or more people. Typical issues dealt with in workplace mediation include: communication, personality clashes, on-going but unresolved grievances, perceived harassment, discrimination and bullying, differences of work style, and inappropriate use of power, status or position. The mediator's role is to act as an independent and impartial facilitator. The individual does not take sides, or judge what is right or wrong, but co-ordinates the process by making sure that each party has an equal voice, is heard and able to respond (Doherty and Guyler 2008).

Workplace mediation has five main characteristics. First, it is voluntary. This means that it cannot work unless all parties agree to it. It is essential the parties are not put under pressure to attend mediation, or feel it acts against them if they decide not to take part in it. Second, workplace mediation is a means for reaching an agreement. The parties are asked to identify their issues and concerns and, from this, an agenda is set to help them work jointly together towards an acceptable agreement. The mediator encourages open communications and helps the parties generate options and ideas to improve the situation. It is often said the aim of mediation is to achieve a 'win/win' outcome, with the parties taking responsibility for making changes and agreeing a more positive way of working for the future. Third, mediation is confidential. The process is carried out on the basis of agreed confidentiality between the parties and the mediator. The exception is where a party raises issues of harm to self or others or issues of serious misconduct. The content of mediation is not fed back to HR staff or managers, nor is it recorded on the employee's personnel file. Fourth, mediation is quick, with the aim of resolving issues at the earliest opportunity. Finally, mediation is impartial and effective. As Lewis (2009: 76) concludes, the mediator 'provides a clear head, impartiality, process management, encouragement, optimism, and above all, brings hope to situations that may seem hopeless'.

CONCLUSION AND IMPLICATIONS

Collective bargaining remains an important feature of contemporary employment relations internationally, but its incidence and coverage is considerably less than it was 40 years ago. The reasons for the shrinkage of collective bargaining are varied. This is despite the potential value of collective bargaining to employers in terms of mitigating employer–employee conflict within organisations, its legitimising of jointly agreed employment decisions and as a means of communication between managers and workers. One reason for its decline includes the expansion of the international economy, which lengthens the global supply chain and makes it more difficult for unions to organise workers nationally and cross-nationally. It is also more difficult to get union recognition from large national companies, TNCs and SMEs, and to negotiate effectively with powerful employers which oppose unions. Many employers are also adopting non-union HRM strategies and practices, seen as promoting competitive advantage in product markets. Further, finance capital and physical capital are mobile internationally, whereas labour is less mobile and organising labour internationally has always proved to be a difficult task for trade unions. This results in falling union memberships, loss of bargaining power and decreased union influence at workplace and firm levels.

Other factors include changing economic structures within capitalist market economies, such as large and expanding service sectors, the contracting out of public services, and the sub-contracting and outsourcing of labour resources. All these changes inhibit unionisation among workforces. Other influences are: neo-liberal and austerity economic policies by governments that do not take account of unions in the policy making process; employment insecurity and unemployment within national labour forces; and the rise of consumerism globally, which emphasises the importance of individuals and households as consumers rather than as producers and workers.

The historical progress of collective bargaining characterised by steady expansion and coverage for the first three-quarters of the twentieth century has halted and even regressed. However, the threes view of collective bargaining espoused by Chamberlain and Kuhn (1965) are helpful in demonstrating how collective bargaining and its coverage ebb and flow. They can be seen as stages in the development and regression of the bargaining process and the bargaining relationship between employers and unions. As the scope or coverage of collective bargaining expands or contracts, there is a shift forwards and backwards along the spectrum from the marketing, to the jurisprudential, to the industrial governance concepts and back. These three approaches represent different conceptions of what collective bargaining is about and they express normative judgements about it. Each concept or stage stresses a different guiding principle and each influences the actions taken by the parties. For example, under the marketing concept, withholding data or distorting facts may be a legitimate tactic by the players. Under the governmental concept, it may be difficult to determine whether specific data should be accessible to both parties or confidential to one. But under the industrial relations concept, all relevant data become necessary to make informed joint decisions between the parties to negotiation.

Distinctions between these three approaches are not just academic but practical. The marketing concept, for example, emphasises the existence of alternative choices in employer–employee relationships, whereas the governmental and industrial relations approaches emphasise the continuity of employment relationships and regard collective bargaining as a continuous process. Which approach is stressed is determined by three endogenous factors and two exogenous ones. Internally, these are the views adopted by the players regarding the nature of the collective bargaining process; the importance they place on the nature of bargaining outcomes; and the balance of bargaining power between them. Externally, the two major forces are the institutional and cultural contexts in which collective bargaining takes place.

The structure of collective bargaining varies widely cross-nationally and sub-nationally. But while the incidence of single-employer bargaining and enterprise bargaining has increased in recent years, in response to globalisation and changing product markets, examples of centralised and multi-employer bargaining remain. For Clegg (1976), the shaping of the structure of collective bargaining is determined largely by the structures of management and employers' associations and, where it has intervened in the early stages of industrialism, by the law. Most observers argue it is employer attitudes towards unions that are the major determinant of both structure and behaviour in collective bargaining. Employers, in short, initiate collective bargaining policy; unions react to it. Thus Adams (1995) points out that the behaviour of West European employers towards unions differs fundamentally from those in North America. In Europe, firms have been typically organised into powerful employers' associations, whereas in North America employers have not formed strong associations. He attributes this to the specific political, economic and organisational strategies of the early unions, which resulted in differing employer and state responses to union organisation.

Sisson (1987), in turn, compares the role of employers' associations in the development of collective bargaining in seven countries – the United Kingdom, the United States, Japan, France, Sweden, Italy, and (West) Germany. He concludes that differences among these countries are rooted in their historical experiences flowing from industrialisation. Thus in West Europe, multi-employer bargaining was the predominant model, because employers in metal-working industries were confronted by national unions organised by occupation or sector. In contrast, single-employer bargaining developed in the United States and Japan because, in the early stages of industrialisation, relatively large-scale employers were able to assert collective pressure on unions to bargain at enterprise level.

Irrespective of level of collective bargaining, a central goal of the bargaining process is to reach compromises between management and union representatives and agree rules to facilitate conflict resolution. Importantly too, collective bargaining over terms and conditions of employment has the function of providing 'collective goods', the nature of which depends on the central features of the bargaining system. Thus multi-employer bargaining facilitates certain kinds of economic re-structuring such as through provisions on training and skill formation (Soskice 1991). It may also standardise employment conditions, by taking wages out of competition. But nothing guarantees that such collective goods will be produced, if the parties do not attach the same value to them. In the case of single-employer bargaining, companies may develop HR strategies as an alternative to union recognition (Jacoby 1990). Incentives to opt out of collective bargaining may also rise if inter-enterprise wage differentials reach a critical level and are not offset by productivity differences (Blanchflower and Freeman 1992).

There are wide differences in collective bargaining rates across OECD countries, with coverage being lower in countries with single-employer and/or enterprise bargaining than with multi-employer or centralised systems. Evaluating the impact of legal extension mechanisms is not easy. Extension is absent in some countries with high coverage rates. Also single-employer bargaining tends to set actual wage rates, thus restricting the employer's room for wages flexibility. Since multi-employer bargaining is more removed from management prerogatives than single-employer bargaining, it restricts managerial prerogatives less. Multi-employer bargaining moderates inter-firm competition in the labour market; single-employer agreements discriminate between the company and its competitors, unless wage differences are offset by increases in productivity. This is a strong incentive for employers to avoid collective bargaining in company-centred HR systems.

Coverage of collective bargaining cross-nationally appears to reveal three features. First, workers in manufacturing, transport and public administration are more likely to be union members and be covered by collective bargaining than workers in agriculture, trade and financial services. But there remain clear differences between countries (OECD 1991). Second, data on coverage by firm size indicate bargaining coverage in all countries increases with size of firm (Lawrence and Ishikawa 2005). Third, government policy is important too, since it can legislate to support collective bargaining, such as in the United States under the National Labor Relations Act 1935, or resist it. The NLRA 1935 mandates ballots for union certification and the National Labor Relations Board is the gateway to gaining union bargaining rights from employers, where they refuse to do so voluntarily. In Canada, there are similar arrangements for statutory union recognition (Strecker 2011, Adams 2006).

To measure the extent of collective bargaining and worker participation in European countries, researchers have developed an index, called the European Participation Index (EPI). It is a composite index that measures the formal rights and extent of worker participation within the 27 member states of the EU at three levels. The current version, EPI 2.0, consists of three equally weighted components: collective bargaining participation, establishment level or workplace participation, and board level participation (Vitols 2010). The EPIs in the top quartile of countries range from 0.83 to 0.63. The countries in descending order are: Denmark, Sweden, Finland, Slovenia, Luxembourg, the Netherlands and Austria. The indices in the second quartile range from 0.61 to 0.43, with Germany, Slovak Republic, Czech Republic, Spain, France, Hungary and Belgium in this group. The third quartile ranges from an index of 0.41 to 0.31 and covers Malta, Ireland, Greece, Poland, Cyprus, Portugal and Italy. The bottom quartile consists of Romania, Estonia, Bulgaria, Latvia, the United Kingdom and Lithuania, with the EPI ranging from 0.27 to 0.11. Once again, it is countries practising the Nordic model of market capitalism and the Rhineland model of employment relations which score highest. Countries with the lowest scores are drawn from the transition economies of North and East Europe and the liberal market economies of Malta, Ireland and the United Kingdom, where labour market deregulation and neo-liberal economic policies have penetrated deepest in the past 30 years. Vitols (2010: 1) concludes 'that countries with stronger worker participation rights perform better in terms of [the Europe 2020] strategy than countries with weaker participation rights'.

Given that overt and covert forms of conflict are inherent and endemic in work organisations and employment relationships, the parties commonly seek ways to resolve immediate conflicts of interest between them. The main processes used are collective bargaining, conciliation, arbitration and, in some cases, workplace mediation. With the increasing individualisation of employment relations, traditional processes of conflict resolution and conflict management are weakened and are less helpful for resolving conflict at work.

As Lewin (2008: 461) points out, there are changes in the nature of industrial conflict and in patterns of conflict resolution. He notes the significant shift away from collective towards more individual expressions of conflict and the resulting expansion of conflict resolution methods, outside of collectively-agreed procedures or processes. He concludes use of grievance procedures 'is negatively associated with organizational performance'; for him more effective means of conflict resolution such as workplace mediation need to be developed in times of change.

part **4**

CONCLUSION

12

EMPLOYMENT RELATIONS
IN A GLOBAL AGE

The purpose of this chapter is to reflect on some of the arguments presented in this text and to examine the changing faces of employment relations, as well as continuities in the field, in a global and neo-liberal age, as presented in Figure 12.1. In capitalist market economies, the employment relationship begins as an individual one between employer and employee, regulated by the contract of employment and management. Rooted in market and unitary theories of employment relations, this model of employment regulation and its associated HR practices is the one preferred by most employers in many employment relations systems. Collective employment relationships, rooted in pluralist theory, are an alternative way of determining the wage–work bargain, through systems of employee representation and employment relations institutions, but residual power to manage remains with managers. In whatever ways employment relations are organised in modern societies, how this is done is nationally specific. There is no universal model of employment relations; any more than there are universal models of politics, law, social structures or management practices – contexts matter. Hence national differences can be observed between structured, developmental and ad hoc employment relations systems; liberal market, co-ordinated market and transition economies; and laissez-faire, social and developmental states – as well as variations within them.

For some observers, the third quarter of the twentieth century was 'a golden age' of labour in the United States, Europe and Japan. This was exemplified by relatively low levels of unemployment, rising real incomes negotiated through collective bargaining, job security and often generous social security provisions. But sometime 'in the fourth quarter of the [twentieth]

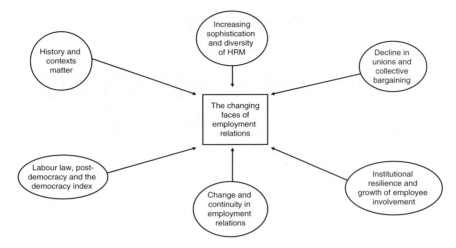

Figure 12.1 The changing faces of employment relations in a global and neo-liberal era

century, this situation began to change' (Brown *et al.* 2010: 1). In addition to profound technological changes affecting work and employment, four mega-explanations are given for this historic shift in the contexts of employment relations: global competition facing businesses and labour; deregulation of industry and more reliance on markets; weakening of employment legislation to protect workers and provide income security for them and their families; and increased migration of workers from developing to developed countries (Brown *et al.* 2010).

HISTORY AND CONTEXTS MATTER

As argued throughout this text, employment relationships are vitally important to all parties involved in them. They are nationally embedded but continually evolving, in response to the changing external environments or contexts within which employment relationships are structured. Further, employment relations take place within the frameworks of national economic policies, labour laws, politics, social structures, and management systems, bounded by what Hall and Soskice (2001) describe as state-wide institutional complementarities and hierarchies. It is a series of changing contexts of employment relations and the influence of history upon them, which is the *first* major change in the field over the past 30 years.

Neo-liberalism and economic freedoms

The period since the late 1970s is characterised by globalisation cross-nationally and by the neo-liberal settlement nationally. This is tied, in turn, to many of the changes prompted by globalisation. Much of the new global economy has been shaped by the policies of supra-national agencies such as the World Bank, IMF and OECD, predicated on neo-liberal prescriptions emanating from Washington DC or the so-called Washington consensus. This has witnessed rising unemployment, falling relative incomes for many workers, less egalitarian wages structures, less job security throughout countries in different regions of the world and stronger management control in organisations. In the United States, for example, diversity 'in employment relations is growing as a product of the growth of non-union employment and the variety of non-union employment practices' (Katz and Colvin 2011: 84). And in the United Kingdom, 'employers have been relatively free to set or negotiate terms and conditions at levels they deem to be appropriate for their own competitive circumstances' (Marchington *et al.* 2011: 58). Growing self-employment has witnessed the phenomenon of a working-class 'white van man' in the United Kingdom, who is classed as an independent trader, such as by installing double-glazing or security systems, and running a small enterprise (Internet Movie Database 2014).

Economic policy is major context affecting a country's employment relations and the behaviour of the parties within it. The dominant national policy orthodoxy today is the neo-liberal settlement. This has been further embedded in contemporary economic thinking and policy-making by the drive for economic austerity in many western states after the financial crisis 2007–2008. Neo-liberalism began replacing the Keynesian consensus from the mid-1970s, first in the English-speaking world and subsequently elsewhere. It has five basic economic tenets, as indicated in Figure 12.2 (Hurd *et al.* 2011, Huffschmid 2006).

Economic freedoms underpin the neo-liberal settlement. The Heritage Foundation, a free market think-tank in the United States, provides a global Index of economic freedoms (IEFs) annually. The IEF measures 10 'economic freedoms' organised into four broad categories: the rule of law, limited government, regulatory efficiency, and open markets. These freedoms are: property rights, freedom from corruption, fiscal freedom, government spending, business freedom, monetary freedom, trade freedom, investment freedom, financial freedom and labour freedom. The Foundation reflects market thinking and the market theory of employment relations, where it defines labour freedom as the ability of individuals to work as much as they want, wherever

> (1) the rule of the market by opening up trade, freedom of movement for capital, goods and services, reducing wages by de-unionisation, and limiting workers' rights
> (2) cutting public expenditure, especially social expenditure on education, health care and low-cost housing
> (3) de-regulation by reducing regulation on safety at work, the eco-environment and business 'red tape'
> (4) privatisation by selling state enterprises and assets, including utilities, telecommunications, transport, schools, universities and transferring ownership to private individuals or shareholders for profit
> (5) eliminating the concept of the 'public good', replacing it with individual responsibility and private provision

Figure 12.2   The five basic economic tenets of neo-liberalism

they want. Equally, the ability of businesses to contract freely for labour, and dismiss redundant workers when they are no longer needed, 'is a vital mechanism for enhancing productivity and sustaining overall economic growth. The core principle of any market is free, voluntary exchange. That is as true in the labor market as it is in the market for goods' (Heritage Foundation 2013) Table 12.1 lists the 15 countries with the highest global IEFs. It is dominated by high-income per head liberal market economies, located predominantly in Asia-Pacific and North America. In these countries, freedom to contract is high, individual employment relationships the norm, managerial control in workplaces strong, and employment protection legislation weak.

Labour law

All the contexts of employment relations are affected by the cultural norms and histories within which each has developed and matured. For example, there are differences in how labour law has grown and been operationalised in civil law regimes, compared with common law ones. The law is historically path dependent and the way it has evolved impacts on the trajectory of national labour law over time. Castel (1977: xii) shows how wage earners were affected by the shift from tutelage in the pre-modern period to the precarious nature of 'free' labour in the industrial revolution on mainland Europe during the nineteenth century. 'To be or fall to the level of wage labourer was to be put into a condition of dependency, to be condemned to live "from day to day," to find one's self subject to the empire of necessity.' As a result, the 'contract of individual employment came to be thought of as sui generis; it called for the creation of a body of law unto itself' (Finkin 2006: 1135). Britain as the most advanced industrialised country at this time took the lead in enacting legislation to deal with the harshness of economic and social life. It was the first

Table 12.1 Index of economic freedoms in 15 most-free
countries 2013

Country	IEF
Hong Kong	89.3
Singapore	88.0
Australia	82.6
New Zealand	81.4
Switzerland	81.0
Canada	79.4
Chile	79.0
Mauritius	76.9
Denmark	76.1
US	76.0
Ireland	75.7
Bahrain	75.5
Estonia	75.3
UK	74.8
Luxembourg	74.2

Source: The Heritage Foundation (2013).

to deal with child labour in 1819, for example, which was expanded and built upon later.

From around 1875 till 1925, national legislation established an agenda of issues, clustering around the labour question in the United States and Britain and the social question in mainland Europe. These issues covered: child and female labour; wage setting and wage payments; hours of work; accident, sickness and old age; unemployment; and the right to organise, bargain collectively and strike. Twentieth-century capitalism generated its own employment and social problems requiring solution, such as employment protection and health and safety, building on previous developments. Twenty-first-century capitalism, in turn, is generating its own employment and social problems such as flexible employment, unorganised workers and ageing workforces in some countries, which nation states are having to address (Pollert 2005). But the creation of effective national laws dealing with all these matters effectively is unlikely to be completed in the short term (Finkin 2006).

National politics

National political systems differ too; some are long-established, others newly created, and others still evolving. Some states are democracies, others autarchies and others dictatorships; some are democratically accountable states, others corrupt oligarchies or nepotisms. Constitutions may be written or unwritten, government may be unitary or federal; some states were formerly imperial powers, while others were formerly dependent colonies (Ball and Peters 2000). All these factors influence employment relations structures and behaviours within nation states. It is not surprising, for example, that the United States and Britain, which are long-established democratic states, were the first to develop institutions of employment relations and systems of labour law, as well as the study of the subject. Similarly, when states such as France, Germany, Japan and the Netherlands rebuilt their economies after the end of the Second World War, they also created or restructured their employment relations institutions, underpinned by supportive labour laws.

In Sweden, by contrast, which was nominally neutral during the Second World War, this had already been done in the 1930s, following a period of labour unrest in the country. A Basic Agreement between the central employers and LO was concluded in 1938, which remains essentially in force today. It was an institutional milestone, served as a model for the entire labour market, and stood for a particular type of employment relations, the so-called *Saltsjöbaden* spirit. This is marked by willingness to co-operate between the institutional players, mutual respect between them, arriving at peaceful solutions based on compromises, and a sense of responsibility for developments in the Swedish labour market. The Agreement came into force in response to a threat of legislation, because certain forms of industrial action were causing serious concerns at the time. The Agreement reflected the wishes of the social partners to safeguard their freedom to regulate their own affairs, without interference from government. The *Saltsjöbaden* spirit characterised the employment relations climate in Sweden during the post-war decades (Johnston 1962), demonstrating how structured employment relations systems are strongly embedded in democratic institutions. Despite more recent economic changes, the cross-class alliance between organised capital and labour agreed in the 1930s 'seems to have adapted to new economic and political pressures and emerged in a new modernized version in which Sweden still represents a typical coordinated market economy' (Svensson 2013: 241).

Social structures

National social structures have an important impact on employment relations. For example, union organisation tends to be class-based in Europe, market-based in the United States and normally market and state-based in Asia. In some Asian countries, unions have played an important role in nation building in the post-colonial period and are described as nation-based unions. In India, by contrast, there is a multiplicity of trade unions, with no common external structures. They are organised mainly along political lines but also by ethnicity, region and occupation (Mamoria *et al.* 2008). In Malaysia during the colonial period, the Communist Party of Malaya tried to develop the labour movement, by encouraging unskilled workers to join unions. In the post-War period before de-colonisation, the Party leadership attempted to create a revolutionary climate to enable them take over government from the colonial powers. Legislation was passed, which largely remains in force today, to limit Communist involvement in trade unions and control them by requiring unions to register with the Registrar of Trade Unions (Aminuddin 1990). In nearby Singapore, unions are strongly regulated by the state. They are incorporated in a form of tripartism with governmental and employer representatives. But many Singaporeans see this as a situation where ministers, employers and union leaders simply work together to advance their own interests at the expense of ordinary Singaporeans (Leggett 1993).

National management systems

National systems of management – commonly rooted in unitary employment relations theory and HRM or contextual approaches to human resources management – impact on employment relations in a variety of ways. Thus the structured employment relations systems of North America and Anglophone states are characterised by cultural-institutional contexts supporting free enterprise, shareholder capitalism and a limited role for the state in market transactions, including the labour market. In these countries today, the political power of unions tends to be weak and values such as individualism, personal freedom, equality of opportunity and direct communications in low-context cultures are deeply entrenched (Wells 2003, Panitch and Gindin 2004). Current neo-managerialist systems in these countries are dominated by organisational metrics, such as in planning, performance management, HR and ICTs, with strong pressures on getting good financial results. The HR policies developed tend to be individualist in orientation, supportive of the right to manage, and often hostile or resistant to trade unionism.

In mainland West Europe, in contrast, current management systems are more likely to reflect some elements of pluralist employment relations theory and consensus building in the workplace. Clearly, there is diversity of cultural-institutional contexts, incorporating the Anglo-Irish, Germanic, Greek, Latin, Low Countries, and Scandinavian versions. But collectively these contexts have common themes running through them. Within some of these countries, for example, there is a strong welfare-state tradition, a preference for social market rather than free market exchanges, support for government intervention in HR and employment relations, a solid tradition of political democracy, and a tradition of worker participation in works councils and company boards. Managers tend to be recruited from specialist professional groups (such as engineers) rather than being managerially qualified (through MBAs and management development programmes) and companies are stakeholder-oriented, rather than putting shareholders at the top of their priorities. Governance structures in companies include worker representation, information and communication systems, and workers' rights in the workplace. The HR role is often administrative and a collectivist tradition is embedded in these employment relations systems, even where union membership is low (Dickman *et al.* 2008). Further, government's role in HR and employment relations tends to be interventionist.

In Latin America, in contrast, the significant social-cultural contexts affecting management and HR issues in developmental employment relations systems are different. They include: strong linguistic and cultural links with Iberian Europe; their high-context cultures; the importance of personal relationships and connections in business and society; and markets for labour, physical and financial resources are constrained. Business leaders tend to be well educated, but with limited managerial mobility between firms and few female business leaders. Prominent businesses are family-controlled, formal corporate planning systems problematic, and stock markets weak instruments of organisational control.

In a region where job control unionism is weak, the main implications of these cultural-institutional contexts for HR and employment relations are, first, Latin-American enterprises are seen as social institutions, with constituencies made up of a range of stakeholders. Second, firms are providers of social benefits, as well as employment and wages to their workers. Third, there is a legacy of Catholicism in these countries associated with Catholic social teaching, whose impacts on workplaces, organisations and society, are significant. Fourth, the status and importance of the individual in these countries is respected. Fifth, social inclusion is an important issue and covers a diverse range of Latin-American groups (Davila and Elvira 2008). Sixth, corporate leadership tends to be authoritarian, personal and paternalistic, which is reflected in the HR practices of firms.

Following the collapse of the Soviet Union in 1991, the Russian Federation has an ad hoc employment relations system. The socio-cultural influences on Russian management include the widespread transfer of former state assets to private hands, the presence of owner-managers in many enterprises, and close links between business leaders and politicians, whose legitimacy is sometimes questioned. Autocratic paternalist management styles are commonplace, where senior managers have absolute power. But there are different types of managers, described variously as post-socialist, pragmatic, predatory and socially responsible. Networks are important in Russian management, with a strong desire to create monopolistic businesses. In the post-Communist period, the management of employment relations is epitomised by weak trade unions and reinforcement of the right to manage. But flexible forms of employment do not appear to be commonplace (Holden *et al.* 1998, Fey *et al.* 2009). Further, as Stiglitz (2002: 185) argues, China built the foundations of a new economy on existing institutions and enhanced social capital, 'while in Russia it eroded'. As Ashwin and Kozina (2013: 302) conclude: 'Contemplation of Russia's current predicament provides a salutary reminder of the crucial role that organized labour can play in democratization and embedding "civilised" modes of capitalism'.

Institutional complementarities and hierarchies in nation states

With firms continually searching for effective innovation and production, institutional analyses of modern economies draw upon the 'complementarity' and 'hierarchy' of national institutions to explain differences and similarities between them. Institutional arrangements, which are complementary to each other, define the coherence and potential for the evolution of various types of economy; the hierarchy of institutions indicates which element of an institution drives the others. This helps in understanding the historical evolution and development of national economic systems (Amble 2000). These are important contexts of business and employment relationships because, despite critiques of the varieties of capitalism literature, alternatives and challenges to market capitalism in the early twenty-first century are limited.

The different structures of present-day capitalism are central to this debate. It is *how* contemporary capitalism is organised within nation states by firms, and trans-nationally in TNCs, which are major factors determining how the wage–work bargain and employment relations are regulated. Much labour market regulation is devolved, so regulation now commonly takes place at enterprise level between organisational rather than institutional players. This underscores the importance of firm-specific HRM policies and practices in managing human resources and employment relations and, where it exists, de-centralised collective bargaining at enterprise level. But the capacity of the firm's actors to do this is conditioned by the history of the firm, its culture, style of management, sector and where it is located. It is the *national* context 'which defines the overarching regulatory system that gives expression to the capacity of HRM to play either an expansive or limited role in the regulation of the employment relationship' (Barry 2010: 82).

INCREASING SOPHISTICATION AND DIVERSITY OF HRM

The *second* and *third* major changes in employment relations in a global age are the increasing sophistication of HRM, on the one hand, and its increasing diversity on the other. The sophistication of HRM is reflected in the prime objective of HR strategy in cutting-edge companies in structured employment relations systems. This seeks to guide the processes by which firms recruit, deploy and develop people, and create relationships and capabilities to enhance competitive advantage. Diversity is illustrated by the varied spread of HR practices in developing countries and SMEs.

Sophisticated HRM

Two factors distinguish the role of HR in large organisations today from previously. First, the distinction between HR strategy and competitive strategy blurs. Where capability in firms rests increasingly on the knowledge and service activities of the people employed within them, strategy depends largely on what people know and how they behave in firms (Snell *et al.* 2002). Second, where a firm's human resources are identified as the prime source of market value and the key to strategic capability, how people are managed is a potentially unique source of strategic leverage for them (Chadwick and Dabu 2008). But defining the firm as a knowledge-based community means managing not only the collective knowledge of the individuals within it but also the relationships among them, across cultures and geographical boundaries (Kang *et al.* 2007).

In the industrial revolution, cost-cutting, speed of production and division of labour were emphasised within organisations and, to manage people strategically, standardised jobs were developed and people were 'fitted' to jobs (person-job fit). With the growth of global trade, international competition and TNCs from the 1970s through to the 1990s, issues of 'systematising' internal (horizontal) fit and external (vertical) fit, linked with bundling, HPWS and configurations, underpinned leading-edge HR thinking (systemic fit). But by the early twenty-first century, differentiated and globally dispersed workforces, hyper-efficiency, knowledge-based competition, and powerful ICTs are the major factors determining how human resources are managed. Here the strategic role of HR becomes one of 'value creation' (Morris and Snell 2010). What complicates things is the idea of the firm as a single entity with full-time employees and a recognisable hierarchy; this is challenged by the new orthodoxy of value creation. Emerging out of this are ever-shifting networks of suppliers, partners, outsourcers and contingent workers, who join together when necessary for business purposes (Lepak and Snell 1999).

Firms facing hyper-competition in the contexts of globalisation and the WWW put a premium on knowledge-based assets such as human capital, knowledge creation and transfer, organisational learning, and relationships underpinning learning and innovation within them (Leonard-Barton 1992). Knowledge, skills and abilities (KSAs) become the primary components of a firm's human capital and are judged to be among the most valuable and distinctive resources which a firm can draw upon for business success (Barney and Wright 1998). But with market competition increasing, differences within workforces widening, and spatial distances between workforces growing, the managing of individual knowledge becomes important, as does managing the co-ordination and integration of that knowledge. Such firms are often viewed as 'networks' of individual knowledge (its human capital) that need to be integrated and shared (its social capital) to deliver value (Grant 1996). Used in these senses, human capital is the individual's economic worth to the employer and social capital is the collective sum of human capital available to the employer at any one time.

In these conditions, two issues become of increasing importance to managing people in cutting-edge organisations. One is talent management. This means, first, underlying individual heterogeneity and a differentiated work environment, HR strategy focuses on an 'architectural' approach to managing talent. This takes account of people having different KSAs, implying they have to be managed differently (Lepak and Snell 1999). Second, Rousseau (1995), Tsui *et al.* 1995 and others point to the variety of employment relationships within organisations, ranging from long-term core employees to short-term contract labour. Third, according to Lepak and Snell (1999), differentiated workforces can be strategically managed by deciding how valuable and unique they are in terms of their KSAs. This means that HR strategies have to emphasise contingencies within the firm, based on differentiated workforces. Best practices exist but what is best for *one* strategic business process may not be good for *another* in the same firm. This results in HR becoming involved in 'improving decisions about key or "pivotal talent pools" throughout the firm' (Morris and Snell 2010: 91–92). To do this, HR applies tools of 'segmentation', as is done to improve decisions about customers and financial markets (Boudreau and Ramstad 2005). 'Such pools are linked, not around people' but around their KSAs and how these 'are vital to the firm's strategy at the moment'.

Another issue in the increasing sophistication of HRM is a focus on 'relationship management' within these firms. This emphasises identifying the characteristics of HR systems which create strong relationships and collective meaning among employees. These characteristics include visibility, understanding, legitimacy and relevance. Here HR strategy plays a significant role in getting people to work together as social capital, where knowledge is embedded or available in relationships (Leana and Van Buren 1999). Drawing upon knowledge-based views of the firm, Kang *et al.* (2007) argue it is important not only to focus on social capital and relationships within the firm but also to consider these relationships in the contexts of differentiated work groups or talent pools. Firms thus seek to understand both their differentiated human capital needs and differentiated social capital needs. A firm, in short, needs to manage its talent pools and facilitate appropriate relationships and interactions between these pools. Investments in different talent pools may either help or hinder knowledge-sharing across employee groups (Lepak *et al.* 2007). Thus the importance of relationships and learning has brought HR strategy firmly into the 'strategy mix', where knowledge in the firm is *the* source of competitive advantage (Kogut and Zander 1992). In short, differentiated pools of talent are managed strategically; but it is also necessary to manage the relationships within and between these talent pools.

Diversity of HRM

There has been varied spread of HR practices in developing countries in recent years. As Mendonca (2000) argues, this is not surprising since state-of-the-art management and HR practices are dictated by unique configurations of different cultural and institutional factors, which have evolved in the contexts of Western cultural values. These practices cannot be adopted uncritically in developing countries, which have their own cultural and institutional traditions. Thus Budhwar and Sparrow (1998, 2002) use a contextual model of HRM to help analyse the context-specific nature of people management practices in cross-national settings. They claim three levels of factors and variables influence HR policies and practices cross-nationally. These are: national factors (national culture, national institutions, business sectors and the business environment); contingency variables (including the age, size, nature, ownership, and life-cycle stage of organisations); and organisational strategies and policies relating to primary HR functions and internal labour markets (Miles and Snow 1984, Porter 1980).

A number of studies illustrate the diversity of HRM in developing economies cross-nationally. First, in the Middle-East, Egypt, Iran, Kuwait, Morocco, Saudi Arabia and Turkey show a degree of homogeneity around high power-distance, collectivism, Islamic values and Arab traditions (Mellahi and Budhwar 2006). Second, the influence of Islam is the dominant one in Algeria, Iran, Pakistan and Saudi Arabia, while in parts of Africa, such as Ghana, Kenya and Nigeria, people in organisations still place emphasis on traditional beliefs, such as spirits, witchcraft, fetishes and gods (Debrah and Budhwar 2004, Beugre and Offodile 2001). Third, HRM in India and Nepal is influenced by culture and institutions, where Hinduism is the dominant religion. Adhikari and Muller (2004) show these countries are governed by social contracts based on caste, religion, economic status and political affiliation, as well as the strong British colonial tradition. In China and Taiwan, in turn, Confusian values are found in management practices, where *guanxi*, *renqing* and face are means for regulating interpersonal relationships in organisations.

Fourth, in some developing countries, there are skills and competency shortages in local labour markets, such as in Kuwait, Oman, Qatar, Saudi Arabia and the United Arab Emirates. But strong efforts have been made to employ local workers, such as through state policies of 'Emiratisation' and 'Omanisation' (Rees *et al.* 2007). Fifth, as a result of economic liberalisation, de-regulation and privatisation feature prominently in many developing countries. These have initiated changes in HR policies and practices, as in sub-Saharan Africa. These include flexible employment, insecure workforces and ending open-ended employment contracts (Mbaku 1999). In short, all the above factors result in different approaches to HRM in different countries.

Another illustration of diversity in HRM is demonstrated by the range of HR policies and practices present in SMEs or lack of them (Goss 1988). These contrast with the major features of HRM in TNCs, large national firms and public services, which are formal and institutionalised. Compared with SMEs, large firms are more likely to recognise trade unions, have formal HR strategies, draw on structured employment relations practices, be affected by strikes and employ HR specialists. Large organisations are also strongly shaped by their national and local contexts. Hence large firms in Northern Europe are likely to have formal systems of employee representation, whereas managers in large North American firms find this difficult to understand and accept (Wever 1995).

Throughout industrialised economies around the world, over 95 per cent or more of firms are SMEs; most firms are small ones. Although a lot is written about SMEs, attention to human resources management within them

> - a typical feature is family ownership
> - SME workplaces tend to be relatively non-formalised
> - some SMEs have structured communication systems and basic employment relations procedures
> - internationally *collective* employment relationships are virtually absent in SMEs
> - union membership is low or absent
> - wage setting is at workplace level
> - wages structures in SMEs are implemented at workplace level, unlike in large firms where collective agreements sometimes exist
> - there are hardly any external rules influencing wage determination, rates of pay and human resources management procedures in SMEs, other than legal regulation

Figure 12.3   Characteristics of SMEs

is limited. As Curran (1990: 139) notes, there is lack of attention to 'real people in real enterprises' and the 'complex ways in which the small scale sector is integrated into the economy'. As a guide, small firms are often defined as organisations with up to 49 employees and medium-size firms up to 249. In the United States and the United Kingdom, SMEs account for the smallest proportions of total employment; SMEs in Greece and Spain, by contrast, make up about 80 per cent of the total (European Industrial Relations Observatory 2006). Some specific characteristics of SMEs compared with large firms are indicated in Figure 12.3.

Data on HRM practices in SMEs are generally patchy. But based on surveys in Europe, there are notable cross-national differences lacking a ready explanation. The general picture reported from several countries in Europe is of relatively low take-up of HR practices in SMEs such as teamwork, formal appraisal and career development. In Norway, for example, teamwork is reported in 50 per cent of small enterprises with 11–49 employees, compared with 90 per cent of large firms, with similar contrasts in the presence of an HR manager. However, PRP and training vary little by firm size. This contrasts with Finland, where clear size effects are present in both these cases. Why similar Nordic countries with similar training records differ from one another is not clear from the evidence (Eurofound 2013d).

THE DECLINE IN UNION MEMBERSHIP AND COLLECTIVE BARGAINING

Other than the rise of HRM, the decline in collectivism in employment relations, in terms of union membership and coverage of collective bargaining, is the *fourth* and probably the most distinctive change within the field over the past 30 years. Clearly, decreases in union membership density, the ability of unions to use the power of organised industrial action and the weakening of collective bargaining coverage cross-nationally are not evenly distributed. But the depth and intensity of these declines are more noticeable in liberal market economies and transition economies than in co-ordinated market economies or social democratic regimes. The impacts of globalisation cross-nationally and neo-liberal economic policies nationally on wages and conditions have taken their toll on the collectivist tradition in employment relations. With successive waves of product market competition and business and labour market de-regulation, the dominant model of employment relations today is employer regulation, supplemented by supportive legal regulation for employers; not for collective bargaining.

Union avoidance strategies by TNCs

An important factor is the common practice of TNCs to pursue union-avoidance HR strategies. First, TNCs are less likely to invest in countries where trade unions are organised or where collective bargaining exists (Lamare *et al.* 2009a). Second, where TNCs do invest, they pursue employment relations strategies in foreign locations aimed at minimising their chances of having to deal with unions and managing collective agreements. The outcomes of these union avoidance strategies increase the possibilities for TNCs to pit unions against one another across national borders. They do this by shifting or threatening to shift investment to 'soft' union or non-union operations. Through calculated coercive comparisons cross-internationally involving unionised and non-unionised operations, TNCs are better able to extract concessions from the unions or weaken their viability, as each centre competes for scarce capital investment or limited production opportunities (Streeck 1992, Marginson *et al.* 1995, Sisson and Marginson 2002). With the growth in TNC activity internationally, and generally declining or stagnating union membership globally, union avoidance and marginalisation strategies have shifted the balance of bargaining power in labour markets towards TNCs (Cooke 2003). Also as Ietto-Gilles (2005: 175) notes, the cross-national fragmentation of labour employed by the same TNCs in different countries makes it difficult for workers to organise effectively and negotiate with these companies. Such labour force fragmentation strategies are based on location (by nation state) or on an organisational basis. 'In both cases, they are likely to lead to the weakening of the power of labour towards capital'.

The decline of collectivism and its impact on income distribution

One consequence of the retrenchment of collective bargaining as a method of wage determination is a decline in the *functional* distribution of income or share of wages in the national incomes of nation states, compared with income on capital. Stockhammer (2013) shows that the share of wages within nation incomes has fallen in virtually all OECD countries in recent years, with the decreases being typically even more pronounced in mainland European countries and Japan than in the Anglo-Saxon countries of the United States, the United Kingdom, Ireland, Australia, New Zealand and Canada. But in all the advanced economies of high-income OECD countries, except South Korea, the adjusted share of wages as a proportion of national income fell, on average, from 73.4 per cent in 1980 to 64.0 per cent in 2007. In Germany, the fall was from 72.2 per cent to 61.8 per cent; in Japan, the decline was somewhat stronger from 77.2 per cent to 62.2 per cent; and in the United States, it was a little weaker from 70.0 per cent to 64.9 per cent. Overall, real wage growth has clearly lagged behind productivity growth in this group of countries since the late 1970s. This constitutes a major historical shift, as the share of wages in national income within these nation states had been relatively stable or increasing in the early post-war period (Stockhammer 2009).

Data on the functional distribution of income for developing economies are not readily available but, where these exist, they are commonly less reliable than those in developed countries and advanced political economies. However, among developing countries which have at least 10 years of adjusted wage-share data, 14 are identified with declining wage shares (Argentina, Botswana, Brazil, Bulgaria, China, Cote d'Ivoire, Mexico, Namibia, Oman, Panama, South Africa, South Korea, Thailand, Turkey); three with broadly stable wage shares (Mauritius, Russia, Sri Lanka); and seven with increasing wage shares (Belarus, Chile, Colombia, Costa Rica, Hong Kong, Kenya, Peru) (Stockhammer 2013, Soskice 2010, Daudey and García-Peñalosa 2007).

A second consequence of the de-institutionalisation of employment relations is changes in the *personal* distribution of incomes within nation states. This shift favours owners of capital and rentiers or those living on incomes from property or rent, high-status groups of employed workers such as those in banking and financial services, and senior managers in the large corporate sector – all at the expense of the incomes of low status, less skilled labour and those not working. This shift in personal income distribution has taken different forms in different countries. In Anglo-Saxon states, for example, a sharp polarisation of the personal distribution of income has occurred, combined with a modest decline in the wage share. In particular, top incomes – usually measured as the income share of the top 10 per cent, 5 per cent or 1 per cent of incomes – have increased their share of incomes dramatically since the 1980s (Piketty and Saez 2007, OECD 2008a, Atkinson *et al.* 2011, Piketty 2014). In the United States, for example, those in the top 1 per cent of income distribution increased their share of national income by more than 10 percentage points during this period. In mainland European countries, functional rather than personal income distribution has shifted dramatically, with the shares of wages in national income in the Eurozone having decreased by around 10 percentage points of GDP (Stockhammer 2009). But the distribution of personal income has remained comparably stable and often has not changed in the same way as in the United States and the United Kingdom (OECD 2008, 2011a).

In Germany, for example, personal income distribution was stable until the mid-1990s, but afterwards the bottom of the distribution lost ground. This is likely to be the result of the traditional German approach to corporate governance, based on multi-stakeholders, being 'gradually replaced by a more neo-liberal, market-driven orientation towards short-term maximisation of shareholder interests' (Keller and Kirsch 2011: 221). In France, personal income distribution among wage earners has become more equal. While at first sight these developments appear rather different, they share a common trend: the share of non-managerial wage earners in national income has decreased sharply. In France, in large companies, unions are able to exercise their rights in company-level bargaining but unions and representative institutions are rare in SMEs (Goetschy and Jobert 2011). The increase in income inequality in the United States is, in contrast, driven to a significant extent by changes in the remuneration of top managers, whose salaries and bonuses are counted as labour compensation (i.e. as wages) in the national accounts. If they were counted, in terms of nineteenth-century political economy as part of profits, trends in the United States and mainland Europe would look rather similar.

Growing income inequality in nation states

To review the debate so far, with collective bargaining in sharp decline, the functional distribution of income has changed substantially during the last three decades from wages to capital. In all OECD countries, this decline in the share of wages in national income is part of a broader trend towards greater income and social inequality within them. In developing and emerging economies, the situation is less uniform, although in most of these countries the share of wages in national income has also declined. Table 12.2 ranks income inequality in the 34 OECD member states of the OECD in the late 2000s, using the Gini co-efficient. The Gini co-efficient (or Index) ranges from 0 to 1, where, in this case, zero represents perfect income equality and one represents maximum income inequality. Table 12.2 indicates that liberal market economies (and laissez-faire states), with declining collective bargaining, tend towards greater income inequality than co-ordinated market economies (and social states), which have tended to retain collective bargaining and the extension of collective agreements.

For developing countries, decline in the share of wages in national income is part of a broader trend of changes in personal income distribution, where social inequalities have increased. Amsden and van der Hoeven (1996), for example, highlight a shift in manufacturing wage formation in the 1980s due to a change towards free-market public policies. Goldberg and Pavcnik (2007: 54) conclude, in turn, from a comprehensive survey of inequality in developing countries: 'In summary, the evolution of various measures of inequality suggests that most of the developing countries experienced an increase in inequality during the past two decades.' Similarly, the OECD (2011b) reports increasing income inequality in most but not all emerging economies.

One explanation given for this is the increased role of financial institutions in national economies and the global economy. This includes the rising indebtedness of households, more volatile exchange rates, asset price inflation, the short-termism of financial institutions, and the shareholder value orientation of non-financial businesses (Erturk *et al.* 2008, Stockhammer 2010). Other explanations include globalisation, retrenchment of the welfare state and technological change. However, drawing on a data-set covering 28 advanced economies and 43 developing and emerging economies from 1970 to 2007, Stockhammer (2013: 43) concludes that the increased role of financial institutions in national economies and the international economy 'has been the main cause of the decline in the wage share'. Further, globalisation has had negative effects on income distribution in developing as well as in advanced economies. There have also been substantial negative effects from welfare-state retrenchment in advanced economies; but technological and structural changes have had positive effects in developing countries.

Other data-sets in advanced economies confirm these findings for this group of countries. Financial institutions again emerge as the single most important cause for the decline of wages in the functional distribution of income. Welfare state retrenchment and globalisation have had negative effects too. There have also been some modest negative effects of technological

Table 12.2 Income inequality by rank order in OECD countries late 2000s

Country	Gini index
Slovenia	0.24
Denmark	0.25
Norway	0.25
Czech Republic	0.26
Slovak Republic	0.26
Belgium	0.26
Sweden	0.26
Finland	0.26
Austria	0.26
Hungary	0.27
Luxembourg	0.29
France	0.29
Ireland	0.29
Netherlands	0.29
Germany	0.30
Iceland	0.30
Switzerland	0.30
Greece	0.31
Poland	0.31
South Korea	0.32
Estonia	0.32
Spain	0.32
Canada	0.32
Japan	0.33
New Zealand	0.33
Australia	0.34
Italy	0.34
United Kingdom	0.34
Portugal	0.35
Israel	0.37
United States	0.38
Turkey	0.41
Mexico	0.48
Chile	0.49
(OECD average)	(0.31)

Source: OECD (2013).

change on the share of wages in national income in advanced economies. These studies refute two widely held views about patterns of income distribution. The first is that changes in income distribution in advanced economies have mainly been driven by technological change. This is patently not the case. Technological change has had a negative effect on the share of wages in the national incomes of developed economies but its effect is smaller than for other factors. Second, the prediction that globalisation benefits workers in both developing and emerging economies is not demonstrated. In both advanced and developing economies, globalisation results in an overall negative impact on the shares of wages in national incomes.

For Stockhammer (2013: 43), these findings have important implications for economic and social policy. They suggest that income distribution is not primarily determined by technological progress but depends rather on social institutions and the structure of the financial system. 'Strengthening the welfare state, in particular changing union legislation to foster collective bargaining and financial regulation could help increase the wage share with little if any costs in terms of economic efficiency'.

The exceptionalism of the United States

In a related debate, Soskice (2010) re-examines the conventional wisdom that the United States, as an advanced liberal market economy, consistently underperforms on a range of social indicators such as labour rights, redistribution of income, inequality of education, and crime and punishment. He shows that American outcomes are exceptional, given even this country's institutional arrangements. He argues that the socio-economic institutions of the United States are not dissimilar from those in other liberal market economies, which, the United Kingdom apart, were typically settler economies in which guild systems were absent and political decision-making was heavily de-centralised in the nineteenth century. He concludes that in the three decades since the collapse of Fordism, inequality has increased sharply in all Anglo-Saxon 'liberal countries (but especially in the United States) at the same time as the decline of industrial unionism, the move towards deregulation, and the end of the postwar consensus' (Soskice 2010: 54). Indeed, for Gross (2010: 34), the 'promotion of human rights at US workplaces pose challenges to some of the most fundamental principles upon which the US labor relations systems is based'.

Soskice (2010: 90) accepts the United States falls within the liberal market cluster of national economies but it 'is an odd and slightly uncomfortable member'. And 'even by the low standards of the other Anglo-Saxon countries, the United States performs exceptionally poorly in terms of inequality and poverty'. Drawing on a political systems perspective, Soskice supplements traditional economic analyses of the United States, which concentrate on the employment relations system, financial structures, and labour, capital and product market regulation. He argues that *majoritarian* political systems tend to produce centre-right governments that provide the business sector with an unusually influential role in economic legislation and regulation; these are where candidates win elections by having the largest number of votes, as in the United States and increasingly in the United Kingdom, This contrasts with *proportional representation* systems, commonly found in co-ordinated market economies in mainland Europe, where there is a greater tendency to elect centre-left governments, reflecting labour's and the labour movement's political leverage within this geographical region.

However, even within majoritarian political systems, such as in the United States, the United Kingdom, Australia and Canada, there are differences among countries. Of particular importance in the United States is its weak party discipline and de-centralised political decision-making, which enhance the political leverage of the business community. This enables businesses to move where the economic climate is most congenial to them; a situation further promoted by the United States's leadership within the NAFTA. The implication is that to take account of the broader contexts of business practices and their impacts on labour and employment outcomes, political institutional analyses need to supplement economic ones. Soskice's analysis also gives further weight to Crouch's (2004) post-democracy thesis (see below) which, he claims, underpins neo-liberal economic policies within nation states.

INSTITUTIONAL RESILIENCE AND THE GROWTH OF EMPLOYEE INVOLVEMENT

With the coverage and scope of collective bargaining shrinking over the past 30 years, the *fifth* major development in employment relations during this period is the remarkable resilience of other employment relations institutions, largely within the framework of the European social model of mainland Europe. As observed throughout this work, in addition to collective bargaining in EU member states, a variety of formal systems of *indirect, collective, representative participation* exists within these countries. These include works councils in the workplace, worker representation on company boards, employee members of European companies, and worker representation at European level in bodies such as EWCs (Cremers *et al.* 2013). This is paralleled by a *sixth* major change – the growth in employee involvement in some organisations and countries. This *direct, low-level participation through employee involvement* (EI) is based on individual or small group participative processes in workplaces. These continue to grow in companies particularly in liberal market economies, where collective bargaining has largely disappeared in much of the private sector (Storey 2005). EI takes a variety of forms including information provision, communication exchange, teamworking and continuous improvement groups. In developing economies, however, employer paternalism tends to be the dominant paradigm of managerial control, with often little either indirect or direct worker participation. Indeed, patterns of employment relations in these countries are disparate, but with some coherent features emerging within them (Da Silva 1995).

Institutional resilience

Each European country has different experiences and its own forms of employment relations institutions. Thus union density varies widely across the 28 EU member states plus Norway, from over 70 per cent in Finland, Sweden and Denmark to 8 per cent in France. However, membership density is not the sole indicator of union capacity to mobilise workers since, even in France, unions are not weak and are able to organise large-scale industrial action. In most of these countries, union membership has been falling recently, and, even where membership is increasing, it has not generally kept pace with rises in numbers employed. Most European states have several competing union confederations, often divided on political lines, although ideological differences may be less important now than in the past. Union mergers continue to remake the trade union landscape, although generally within rather than between confederations (Jacobs 1973, Ebbinghaus and Visser 2000).

Turning to workplace institutions, employee representation also varies widely across Europe, combining both representation through local union bodies and works councils or similar structures elected by all employees in the workplace. In the EU's 28 member states plus Norway, there are four states where the main form of representation is works councils, with no statutory provision for unions at workplace level; eight where representation is essentially through the unions; another 12 where it is a mixture of the two, although sometimes unions dominate; and a further five where unions have been the sole channel, but legislation now offers additional options. In many countries, national legislation implementing the EU's information and consultation directive has complicated the picture. A common feature of most of these states is unions play a central role in workplace representation, often supported by law (Syrpis 2007).

EU legislation means all EU states have structures providing employee representation in health and safety. However, there are differences how this representation is organised. A combination of employee health and safety representatives, with their own powers, and joint employer–employee committees is the structure most frequently used, but some states have only joint committees, some only employee representatives, and in others the works council plays the key role. The ways health and safety representatives are chosen also varies. In about a half these countries, they are elected directly by the workforce, while in the others existing bodies such as unions or works councils choose them. There are also variations in the thresholds for choosing representatives and setting up committees, as well as in their powers of action (Fulton 2013).

Arrangements for employee representation at board level in the 28 EU countries plus Norway can be divided into three groups. In 10 countries, there is no board-level representation and a further group of five has board-level representation limited to state-owned or privatised companies. However, the biggest group of 14 states provides for employees to be represented on the boards of private companies, once they have reached a certain size. These thresholds vary greatly, as do other elements of national arrangements (Kluge and Stollt 2006). National representatives on bodies linked to EWCs and the European Company (SE) are generally chosen in ways which reflect existing structures in the country concerned. This is done by either the union or the works council. However, in seven countries, they are elected by all employees.

Since the beginning of European integration, there has been a clear commitment within the EU to provide employees in Europe with the right to be involved in company decision-making. From the 1970s, this led to the adoption of a number of European directives supplementing and enhancing national worker participation rights. With the adoption of the European Works Council Directive, the European Company (SE) Directive and the Directive on Information and Consultation, the importance of European legislation has increased significantly. With more companies operating on a European-wide basis and globally, the trans-national level of employee representation is becoming more important. This means company managements, employee representatives and their unions have to deal increasingly with cross-border questions of worker participation at different levels.

All these systems of worker participation or representative participation in the EU are a Fundamental Right, laid down in Article 27 of the Charter of Fundamental Rights of the EU (European Communities 2000). Further, the

The case for worker participation in Europe
(1) It strengthens European democracy in practice and the economic competitiveness of European companies in particular
(2) It highlights that companies are defined not only by the interests of their share-holders and managers but also by their other stakeholders as a leading principle of corporate governance
(3) It enables social interests to be protected in corporate-level decision-making through law
(4) It is underpinned by European legislation enabling workers to defend their corporate interests to the same extent as shareholders defend theirs
(5) European legislation promoting worker participation rights at trans-national level is based on a broad political consensus of the European Parliament and European governments, although some national ministers, such as in the United Kingdom, who traditionally support market liberal economic policies, would personally dissent from this point of view

Figure 12.4 The five basic principles of worker participation in Europe
Source: Jepsen and Serrano Pascual (2006).

ideas and support for institutionalised forms of worker participation in EU member states form an essential feature of the European social model and are underpinned by five basic principles, which, in turn, have helped maintain the resilience of these European-wide institutions in both 'good' and 'bad' times, as indicated in Figure 12.4.

Growth of employee involvement

In parallel with the survival of various institutional mechanisms of employment relations in mainland Europe, EI in its wide variety of forms at firm level has expanded in recent years. This leads to an extensive debate about what the precise nature of EI is and how to define it (Dietz *et al.* 2010). But whatever *forms* EI takes, one of its main purposes is to enable decisions to be made within organisations where employees are invited to help solve organisational problems. At the same time, EI gives employees legitimacy to discuss organisational issues and problems, while providing a setting for this decision-making to happen (Tjosvold 1987). In practice, all EI schemes seek to push influence and/or responsibility for such decisions down the organisation to the employees or workgroups concerned, by 'empowering' them, in the expectation this contributes to organisational effectiveness (MaMahan *et al.* 1998).

Another distinguishing feature of EI is the claim that it improves organisational performance and enhances employee well-being. This is indicated, first, by the apparent necessity of including some form of EI in most models of SHRM, such as Pfeffer's (1998) best practice bundles in better performing firms. Many observers of human capital theory also argue that harnessing the knowledge and skills of employees adds economic value to the firm (Becker 1964), while Hodson (2001) claims EI enhances organisational decision-making by drawing on the knowledge of employees to provide possible solutions to organisational problems. This links with the RBVF, where the unique knowledge and skills of employees are seen as one source of sustainable competitive advantage for the business (Barney 1991).

Second, EI is a feature of Appelbaum's *et al.* (2000) 'AMO' model in their study of HPWS. 'A' stands for enhancing the ability of employees; 'M' for enhancing their motivation; and 'O' for providing opportunities for employees to participate or use their abilities and motivation at work. EI also arguably increases employee motivation and allows employees to use their abilities more than where EI is absent. It also expected to improve performance levels. Another performance-driven rationale for EI is employee participation provides opportunity for additional or discretionary effort by employees, resulting in them working 'beyond contract' (Fox 1974). Further, according to Cappelli and Rogovsky (1998), higher levels of 'organizational citizenship behaviors' are likely to improve organisational performance. Yet for others, such as Ramsay *et al.* (2000), such behaviours are seen as a form of work intensification, where EI becomes expected as a part of everyday work activity.

Third, EI is also used by managers to develop shared values in organisations (Sashkin 1976). Spreitzer and Mishra (1999) conclude, for example, that getting employees to comply with organisational goals results in firms both obtaining discretionary effort from employees and reducing managerial monitoring of employee behaviour. Critics of EI or direct participation, on the other hand, equate it with union substitution strategies, where employers seek to create organisational commitment among their employees to reduce commitment to their unions. EI can also undermine union militancy, maintain managerial prerogative and weaken trade unionism in the workplace (Parker and Slaughter 1988). But Hoell (2004) argues EI affects union commitment positively, with each additional experience increasing employee commitment to the union, while employee dissatisfaction with ineffective EI drives employees back to their union.

Fourth, empirical studies of the claimed links between improved organisational performance and firm HR practices commonly include EI practices within them. Thus in a meta-analysis of 104 studies between 1995 and 2004, Boselie *et al.* (2005) found 39 included variants of EI and 11 included indirect forms of participation. The latter contained the studies of Batt *et al.* (2002) on employee voice, HR practices and quit rates and Delery and Doty (1996) on theorising in SHRM in terms of universalistic, contingency and configurational performance predictions. There is also the 'democratic humanism' argument in favour of EI. This views EI and engaging employees in organisational decisions as a social 'good' in any case, regardless of the impact on organisational performance. In other words, managers may use EI 'as a counter-weight to otherwise dispiriting aspects of daily work' (Dietz *et al.* 2010: 248). Despite such studies and the positive case made for EI by its supporters, meta-analyses of its impacts on organisational performance are mixed. For example, Locke and Schweiger (1979) found some positive effects of EI on job satisfaction but less on performance levels.

In another meta-review of 47 studies of EI, Miller and Monge (1986) examine the effects of EI schemes on productivity and job satisfaction. They present three theoretical rationales for effectiveness. In the *cognitive* model, EI enhances information flow, leading to better decisions and employee understanding of these decisions, while increasing job satisfaction because of its positive outcomes for the firm. In the *affective* model, EI satisfies employee needs for self-expression, personal growth and independence but also contributes to improved productivity, because of enhanced employee motivation, resulting, in turn, in greater job satisfaction for workers. However, this could be interpreted as EI working in ways unrelated to the outcomes of the process. In the *contingent* model, EI is moderated by a number of factors. These include the personalities of the participants, job level, the decisions taken, organisational climate, and relations between managers and subordinates. Across these 47 studies, there was no support for the predictions of the contingent model; stronger support for the cognitive over the affective model; and stronger support for the effects of EI on job satisfaction than on productivity. Miller and Monge (1986) conclude that the cognitive model might be better for explaining the effects of EI on productivity and the affective model better for explaining its effects on job satisfaction.

Handel and Levine (2004: 38–40) examine the link between EI, wage levels and other employee outcomes in the United States. They conclude EI 'can improve organisational outcomes if the reforms are serious', adding that the evidence of the impact on worker welfare including wages is 'mixed', while the most positive effects are only modest. However, their findings do not support the most positive views of EI or that it is 'a "high-road" solution to the problem of poor wage growth and increased inequality'. But they do not suggest that management by stress is typical or 'that skill-biased organisational change is a significant cause of inequality growth'.

LABOUR LAW, POST-DEMOCRACY AND THE DEMOCRACY INDEX

The *seventh, eighth* and *ninth* changes acting on employment relations in the post-Keynesian world are the evolving role of labour law, debates about post-democracy, and attempts to measure comparatively the standing of democracy in nation states, such as by the 'democracy index'.

The evolving role of labour law

Labour law in the western world emerged in response to economic liberalism and industrialism, the factory system after the 1870s, and especially Henry Ford's creation of the factory assembly line in the early twentieth century. The latter incorporated full-time male employment, long-service in the same firm, standardised work systems, separation of working time from private time, relatively short life expectancy after retiring, and a predominantly industrial form of unionism, and industry-wide collective bargaining (Iwagami 1999). In what is loosely called a 'post-industrial' world of global capitalism, almost all these elements of working life have become unpacked. The legal challenges provoked by global capitalism include employment flexibility, the individualisation of employment relations, workforce heterogeneity, and questions about the capacity of the state to protect workers' rights in the early twentieth-first century (Finkin 2006). With the general decline of union membership around the world, there has been a growth of triangular employment relationships, unpaid internships, extended probationary periods, labour outsourcing, unemployment and the rise of citizen-initiated campaigns such as that for the 'living wage' (Unwin, 2013, Gertner 2006, Ivanova and Klein 2013).

Employment flexibility is where employers find ways to adjust and re-adjust wages, benefits, working time and job tasks in response to constantly changing product markets in pursuit of higher profits. These include temporary workers, part-time workers, just-in-time workers, fixed-term workers and independent contractors. All these forms of employment depart from the Fordist model of full-time, permanent employment and can be insecure. Some result, in effect, in a 'spot market' for the sale of labour by independent contractors, which is entirely a *sales* transaction, where each element of what is to be done and the price for it are agreed by buyers and sellers in advance. By contrast, under an employment contract, the employer knows the worker is available for work as required; workers have continuity of wages and employment; and both parties benefit 'by substituting a single transaction for what otherwise might have been many' (Marsden 1999: 11). Flexibility raises a series of questions about how to define the employment relationship, as distinct from what makes the sale or lease of labour separate from the general body of law dealing with such transactions. Labour law emerged to protect the weaker party – the worker – in the employment relationship with the employer. However, if there is no functional difference between a worker and a contractor, labour law has to either incorporate a wider set of relationships within its boundaries or become absorbed into commercial law. These new forms of work also shift the risks employment associated with job loss, sickness or death at work from employer to the seller of labour.

Individualisation of employment arises from the decline of trade unionism and collective bargaining throughout the world over the past 30 years. In workplaces without employee representation, employers are free to adopt unilaterally any employment arrangements, working conditions or human resources management policies believed to be economically beneficial to the firm; no matter how exploitative or invasive it is to employees, unless limited by law. Issues such as job security, employee benefits, pace of work, job scheduling, health and safety, and employee privacy are treated as solely employer decisions, where no employee or job applicant is able to bargain about them. Nation states with embedded labour law have three choices: allow employers freedom of action, constrained only by market forces; legislate a minimum floor of employment rights for all workers; or provide legal systems of worker representation requiring employers to negotiate and consult with employees. However, legal mandates are often enabling and are not always carried out in practice, as in the case of co-determination systems in some German firms (Streeck 2009). This means that employment flexibility, individualisation of employment and pressures of globalisation can combine together to induce atomised forms of employment based on the US model. This may reduce the capacities of nation states to fill the gaps with labour laws supporting workers' rights.

Many advanced political economies have shifted from predominantly manufacturing bases to business and professional services. Further, the ageing of their populations puts pressures on national social security systems, while absence of younger workers in the labour market creates pressures to find alternative sources of labour including women and migrant workers. The first can result in tensions between employer demands for labour productivity and the family lives of workers; the second can result in a volatile mix of different cultures and social traditions within nation states. Ageing

(1) negotiating international labour standards
(2) incorporating labour standards in international trade agreements
(3) engaging in multi-national collective bargaining
(4) introducing 'soft' laws with unilaterally adopted corporate codes of 'good practice' or international framework agreements with international trade union confederations
(5) ensuring corporate governance and its relationship to worker protection and representation are brought into the public domain

Figure 12.5   How national governments try to protect citizen-worker rights internationally
Source: Makhija and Kose (2011).

workforces are particularly characteristic of Germany, Japan and the United Kingdom. In Germany, this has been partly met by immigration, since there is a tradition of mothers withdrawing from the labour market to bring up young children. But Japanese culture is particularly resistant to the assimilation of non-indigenous populations and their traditions, making the ageing of the population especially difficult to resolve. In the United Kingdom, the response has been migration from not only mainland Europe but also internationally. Special claims have also been made by disabled people in national economies for integration within labour markets, resulting in divergent legal responses to this (European Commission 2009). With the relatively free flow of financial capital and jobs across national borders, the capability of nation states to protect the rights of their citizen-workers is weakened. National governments have four ways of responding to this, as indicated in Figure 12.5 (Makhija and Kose 2011).

The immense economic and social problems associated with nineteenth- and twentieth-century forms of capitalism proved, in retrospect, to be responsive to ameliorative legal responses over time. Comparative labour law provided not only legal options for doing this but also legitimised various forms of legal redress (Bronstein 2009). In the early twenty-first century, however, global capitalism is generating new sets of economic and social problems. These include: insecure work; alternative forms of work through outsourcing and sub-contracting; systematic invasion of the privacy of workers (made possible through ICTs); demands to integrate women, ethnic minorities, older workers, religious groups, and the disabled into workplaces; improving systems of employee representation; and the need for socially responsible labour policies internationally (Bronstein 2009). Dynamic forms of 'new' capitalism, in short, create new tensions and issues to be resolved in the labour process; new labour laws can have a vital role to play in this.

Post-democracy

Turning to the political contexts of nation states, it was increasingly being argued throughout the industrialised world by the late 1990s that: 'there was steady, consistent pressure for state policy to favour the interests of the wealthy – those who benefited from the unrestricted operation of the capitalist economy rather than those who needed some protection from it' (Crouch 2004: vii, 2–4). Observing this development, Crouch provides definitions of 'maximal' or ideal 'democracy', 'liberal democracy' and 'post-democracy', all of which impact on national economic policies, work and employment relations in different ways. He argues that ideal democracy thrives where there are major opportunities for the mass of ordinary people to participate in politics actively, through discussion and autonomous organisations, 'in shaping the agenda of public life, and when they are actively using these opportunities'. He claims, however, that democracy is increasingly being defined as 'liberal democracy', under influence from the United States. This form of democracy stresses citizen participation in elections, extensive freedom for lobbying activities which 'mainly means business lobbies, and a form of polity that avoids interfering with a capitalist economy'. This model has 'little interest in widespread citizen involvement or the role of organizations outside the business sector'.

Crouch suggests satisfaction with 'the unambitious democratic expectations of liberal democracy produces complacency about the rise of [what he calls] post-democracy'. For him under this model of democracy, elections exist which can change governments but 'public electoral debate is a tightly controlled spectacle, managed by rival teams of professionals expert in the techniques of persuasion, and considering a small range of issues selected by those teams'. In the post-democracy model, the mass of citizens plays a passive quiescent role, responding only to the 'signals given them'. He further argues that this model is effectively shaped in private by interaction between elected governments and elites overwhelmingly representing business interests. Within post-democracy, power is also increasingly ceded to business lobbies, with little hope of producing an agenda for redistributive egalitarian policies, re-distributing power and wealth, or restraining powerful vested interests.

For Crouch, four main factors lead to post-democracy. First, if global firms, as key institutions in the post-democratic world, fail to find congenial fiscal and labour policy regimes locally, they threaten governments they will relocate elsewhere to get them. Also with growing dependence of governments on the knowledge and expertise of corporate executives, and the dependence of political parties on funds from this powerful group, a new dominant economic class emerges. Second, with the decline of the manual working class in national politics, the vacuum is filled by senior managerial and professional workers who associate with the interests of capital. Third, the structure of political parties changes, with groups of advisors and lobbyists surrounding party leaderships; not their traditional membership bases. This results in professionalised politics and the emergence of a specialised occupation of professional politicians, recruited from increasingly narrow social groups and backgrounds. Fourth, throughout the advanced capitalist world a generation ago, the model of a citizenship state existed alongside a robust market sector. But today, these assumptions are being challenged. The outcome is that increasingly 'powerful lobbies of business interests ask why public services and welfare policies should not be available to them for profit-making purposes just like everything else' (Crouch 2004: 79).

Post-democracy in western political systems has clear policy implications for employment relations. First, it results in the public realm of employment relations shrinking under pressures of privatisation, outsourcing and contracting out, thus increasing the size and scope of the non-union sector of employment. Second, public-sector employers import individualist HR practices, such as PRP, performance management and low-level forms of employee voice, from the private sector into public organisations (Farnham *et al.* 2005). Third, collective bargaining and trade unionism are generally weakened throughout the post-democratic state. Fourth, labour markets are de-regulated and worker protections loosened or removed. Fifth, governments elected to office are commonly detached from their traditional supporters, such as social democratic parties, trade unions and working people. There are also divided oppositions to governments especially in majoritarian political systems, which fail to protect or advance workers' interests (Caramani 2011).

The democracy index

Another concept, the 'democracy index', compiled by the Economist Intelligence Unit (EIU) since 2006, attempts to measure the status of democracy in 167 countries, including the 165 member states of the UN. This index is based on 60 indicators grouped into five different categories: electoral processes and pluralism; civil liberties; the functioning of government; political participation; and political culture. In addition to a numerical score, as

Table 12.3 Types of political regime and democratic indices for selected years

Type of regime	Region	2006	2008	2010	2011	2012
Full democracies	North America	8.64	8.64	8.63	8.59	8.59
	West Europe	8.60	8.61	8.45	8.40	8.44
Flawed democracies	Latin America, Caribbean	6.37	6.43	6.37	6.35	6.36
Hybrid regimes	Asia-Pacific	5.44	5.58	5.53	5.51	5.56
	Central and East Europe	5.76	5.67	5.55	5.50	5.51
	Sub-Saharan Africa	4.24	4.28	4.23	4.32	4.32
Authoritarian regimes	Middle-East and North Africa	3.54	3.48	3.52	3.68	3.73
World		**5.52**	**5.55**	**5.46**	**5.49**	**5.52**

Source: Economist Intelligence Unit (2013).

shown in Table 12.3, the democracy index categorises countries into four types of political regime: (1) *full democracies*, with scores of 8–10; (2) *flawed democracies*, with scores of 6–7.9; (3) *hybrid regimes*, with scores of 4–5.9; and (4) *authoritarian regimes*, with scores of 0–3.9 (Economic Intelligence Unit 2013).

The EIU shows that full democracies are located in North America and West Europe. It is these 25 countries, making up some 11 per cent of the world's population, that have the most structured employment relations systems. Flawed democracies are located in Latin America and the Caribbean and consist of countries with developmental employment relations systems. Hybrid political regimes are located in Asia-Pacific, Central and East Europe, and Sub-Saharan Africa. Countries in these regions have either developmental or ad hoc employment relations systems. And countries with authoritarian political regimes, located in the Middle-East and North Africa, typically have ad hoc employment relations systems. Thus there appears to be a strong correlation between full democracy and structured, orderly, national employment relations systems, where there is some degree of worker participation and/or employee involvement within them. The top 10 'full' democracies in the EIU's list in rank order in 2012 were: Norway, Sweden, Iceland, Denmark, New Zealand, Australia, Switzerland, Canada, Finland, and the Netherlands. These are mainly co-ordinated market economies, with only New Zealand, Australia and Canada liberal market economies. These strongly democratic states, in short, are associated with established, structured employment relations systems.

CHANGE AND CONTINUITY IN EMPLOYMENT RELATIONS

The study of employment relations began over 100 years ago. Many changes have taken place in scholars' knowledge and understanding of employment relationships, its practices and its theories over this time. But there is some continuity too. The study of contemporary employment relations is the domain of the specialist chronicler; commentary on the *longue durée* is the domain of the cultural or social historian. The short-term examines what is happening now and tries to explain and evaluate it; the long-term exposes the changing structures, processes and contexts of employment relationships over time. The importance of the *longue durée* is that it prioritises the slowly evolving structures of employment relations over time, while recognising that beyond the long-term cycles and structural changes of the subject lie 'old attitudes of thought and action, resistant frameworks dying hard, at times defying logic' (Braudel 1958: 773). In other words, understanding contemporary employment relations systems and practices, using global, comparative and theoretical perspectives, requires taking a broad view of the subject, including different disciplinary perspectives and drawing on what has happened in the past to illuminate the present. The importance of these inter-disciplinary and historical dimensions should not be underestimated, since they provide a 'bigger picture' or overview of employment relationships and reveal their complexities at any one time (the short term) and over time (the long term). They also help identify significant lasting changes, incremental evolving changes, and recognised continuities in the field.

As argued throughout this text, employment relationships are an essential feature of market capitalism, since labour is commodified within it. However, capitalism is not a homogenous static system but a constantly evolving and changing one. Effectively, it emerges and progresses through three broad sequential stages of historical development in different countries and geographical regions. These are: pre-capitalism (or proto-capitalism), classical industrial capitalism and new global capitalism, each with its own work systems and methods of regulating work. Some 'ideal' stylised features of pre-capitalism, industrial capitalism and global capitalism are shown in Figure 12.6. However, as ideal typologies of capitalist development, they do not acknowledge that *more than one* variant of capitalism, such as industrial *and* global capitalism, can co-exist together in a single country – or the world

	Pre-capitalism	Classical industrial capitalism	New global capitalism
Economic system	Driven by law, custom, tradition Local Agriculture dominant Hand-based technology	Market-driven Local, national Industrial, manufacturing, extractive dominant Advanced technology	Market and innovation driven Local, national, global Hi-tech manufacturing, services dominant Robotics, ICTs, bio-technology
Political system	Monarchical, aristocratic Absolute, oligarchic Interests of a social elite protected, based on land wealth and a merchant class	Democratic Representative Demand-led economic policy (Keynesianism)	Post-democratic New elite groups dominant Supply-led economic policy (neo-liberalism)
Social system	Status-based Change slow Social structure stable Feudal, tribes	Class-based Change continuous Social structure mobile Mono-cultural	Network-based Change exponential Social structure post-industrial Multi-cultural
Work system	Small organisations, work often informal Labour un-free Patronage, nepotism Traders, craftwork, priesthoods Young traditional workforces Production for consumption or use Regulated by guilds, princedoms, custom	Large organisations Local, national labour markets Management and ownership separate Specialist division of labour Ageing traditional workforces Fordist production Regulated by institutions, collective labour law	Global firms, networks of organisations Local, national, global labour-markets Management through leadership Flexible and segmented work Young educated workforces Post-Fordist or neo-Fordist production Regulated by HRM, individual labour law
Value system	Spiritual Survival Traditional	Secular Collectivist Instrumental	Secular Individualist Self-fulfilment
Dominant context	Religion and tradition	Social and technological progress	TNCs and global capital

Figure 12.6 Some stylised features of pre-capitalism, industrial capitalism and global capitalism

order – at any one time to greater or lesser degrees, although today global capitalism is more likely to be the dominant one. This means that both change and continuity can be observed simultaneously in national and sub-national systems of employment relations, because different variants of capitalism subsist together in national political economies. The result is the creation of hybrid forms of capitalism cross-nationally.

Some developing traditional countries, such as parts of Africa, are still at the stage of pre-capitalism or proto-capitalism; other developing countries, such as parts of Latin America and parts of Asia, are largely at the stage of industrial capitalism; and advanced national economies, such as in North America, Europe and other parts of Asia, typically combine elements of *both* industrial capitalism *and* new global capitalism. Probably, no advanced economy can be described *solely* as a new global capitalist system; each incorporates some features of global capitalism with elements of industrial capitalism subsumed within it, resulting in 'mixed' or hybrid forms of contemporary capitalism around the world. These, as argued above, incorporate elements of both change and continuity in the economic, political, social, legal, work, and employment relations spheres of nation states.

Under late industrial capitalism, work tends to be structured in large organisations, management and ownership are commonly separated, there is a specialist division of labour, labour markets are largely local and national, and the workforce is ageing. Production is Fordist and employment relations are regulated by collective institutions, such as trade unions, employers' associations and collective bargaining, within a framework of collective labour law. Under global capitalism, work tends to be structured in global firms and networks of organisations, 'management' becomes synonymous with 'leadership', work is flexible and segmented, labour markets are local, national and global, and the workforce is young and well-educated. Production is post-Fordist or neo-Fordist and employment relationships are regulated primarily through sophisticated HRM strategies and individual labour law, aimed at preventing discrimination and promoting equality and diversity in employment practices.

Within hybrid forms of contemporary capitalism, in addition to the nine mega-changes or trends in employment relations observed since the mid-1970s – explored both in this chapter and picked up throughout the text – there are also some changes in the structure of work and employment relationships at enterprise and workplace levels nationally and cross-nationally, as summarised in Figure 12.7. Two particular trends in the world of work that could be destabilising, if not properly addressed, are: the polarisation of the workforce and decline of the standard employment contract.

- work and employment are becoming generally more insecure
- legal definitions of employment relationships are more problematic, with more workers in some countries not employees but with self-employed status
- employment relations decision-making is increasingly de-centralised to firm and workplace levels
- some types of labour such as professional and unskilled workers are becoming more mobile geographically
- wage differentials between the high-paid (such as senior managers) and low-paid (such as less skilled workers) are widening
- systems of management, supported by ICTs and advanced technologies, are becoming more sophisticated, complicated and intrusive in places of work
- people's expectations about what they want from work are typically varied, often specific and sometimes contradictory
- workers in sophisticated employment relations systems are better educated and trained than those in developing and *ad hoc* employment relations systems and are therefore more employable
- incremental change is a continual challenge facing managers and workers within workplaces
- technologies are constantly changing and being renewed, with impacts on management systems, working conditions, employment relationships and especially future opportunities for working

Figure 12.7 Some changes in the structure of work and employment relationships at enterprise and workplace levels nationally and cross-nationally

Polarisation of the workforce, or 'hollowing of the middle', is a phenomenon observed mainly in advanced economies, where there is a decline in the proportion of middle-skilled, middle-income jobs, compared with 'high-end' and 'low-end jobs'. This is of concern because as the number of middle-skilled jobs decreases, workers in those jobs will have to either qualify for the far fewer high-end jobs or move to lower-end jobs, receiving less pay and working below their potential. The standard open-ended employment contract, which became the norm in the middle of the last century, provided stability to workers and improved people's living standards in many countries. But the number of workers with open-ended contracts is declining, while other kinds of work arrangements are becoming increasingly common. This is indicated by the growth of triangular employment relationships, unpaid internships, extended trial or probationary periods, zero-hours contracts, and high unemployment globally. There has also been the rise of citizen-based campaigns such as that of the 'living wage' (Stabile 2008).

These trends are linked to growing inequalities in workplaces, with economic recovery being slow to translate into real wage growth for workers. Weil (2014) claims that an important factor here is what he describes in the United States as 'The Fissured Workplace'. This is the process whereby large 'branded' firms devolve responsibility for managing their workforces to complex external networks of suppliers and franchises in extended supply chains.

This results in downward pressures on pay, working conditions and health and safety. Moreover, these trends affect not only those doing low-paid less skilled work but also higher-paid skilled jobs in sectors such as public services, the media and other professions. In a race to the bottom, this increases the incentive to achieve firm competitive advantage by breaking minimum wage and health and safety legislation. Or, as Friedman (2013: 151) comments, 'the American workplace today is filled with scared workers grateful for temporary work and willing to accept low wages and bad treatment for fear of losing their jobs to China'.

However, some long-term continuities can also be observed in the structure of work and employment relationships, as illustrated in Figure 12.8. It is within nationally embedded employment relations systems that the basic principles of work and employment relationships in capitalist market economies are embodied and resolved. These principles include: how the economic, social and legal interests of managers, workers and the state in the employment relationship are structured and regularised; how co-operation, resistance and conflict between managers and workers manifest themselves in work organisations; the critical role of unions in employment relationships; and the central and indeterminate nature of the contract of employment.

- national cultures and institutions affecting work and employment relationships vary widely by region and country
- employment relations systems are nationally embedded
- work and organisations in capital market economies are largely profit-driven
- organisations vary in size, structure and complexity
- managers play key roles in organising, managing and controlling labour inputs in the workplace
- employees and workers are subordinate to the organisational purposes and interests defined for them, especially to those who own and control capital resources
- labour costs and labour productivity are constantly under scrutiny by managements in organisations
- wage differentials between female and male workers remain
- managerial styles of employment relations and human resources management differ widely
- internal labour markets, not just external ones, are important sources of employer investment in human capital
- some work continues to be exploitative, poorly rewarded and dangerous
- what is deemed to be ethical behaviour by employers, managers and workers in workplaces and enterprises is problematic
- the state and politics play key roles in mediating between the interests of capital and labour
- national labour laws are important sources of employment rules affecting managers, workers and unions
- international organisations in employment relations are generally weak

Figure 12.8   Some continuities in the structure of work and employment relationships at enterprise and workplace levels nationally and cross-nationally

It is also arguable that the most sophisticated and structured employment relations systems are found within civilised and democratic societies. Similarly, structured employment relations systems are unlikely to be present in non-democratic states, where informal work is often the dominant mode of employment.

There are three main implications arising from the observations of employment relations systems made in this chapter. First, there is no single pattern of employment relations in the world of comparative work today – and there never was one; just plural and diverse pathways. Second, at any one time, a number of elements within any employment relations system pull in different directions, not cohesively or in an integrated way together. This means there are often contradictory shifts in employment relations structures, processes and outcomes at cross-national, national and sub-national levels. Third, change occurs in employment relationships but continuity persists too; but neither change nor continuity is rooted in any single-dimensional configuration. Instead, multiple changes take place in employment relationships horizontally across regions and countries and vertically by sector, firm and location, but within the boundaries of social continuity and national institutional inertia.

The outcome is that rather than a convergence of employment relations trajectories, the pressures of divergence and variation appear stronger; they reveal variable and different patterns of employment relationships and processes, not unidirectional ones nationally or cross-nationally. In short, there is no linear trajectory of change in employment relations over time, only heterogeneous pathways, with some elements pushing simultaneously in the same and opposite directions. These varied, inconsistent, ambiguous trajectories are the reality of employment relations in the short and long terms.

The many faces of contemporary employment relations examined in this book are inherently complex. They embody a breadth of perspectives, different national cultures, specific institutional arrangements and distinctive historical-path dependencies. The study of employment relations also draws upon a deepening knowledge base. And to repeat, the wide variations in employment relationships explored in this text demonstrate there is no single trajectory of contemporary employment relations globally, nationally or comparatively; only multiple, contradictory ones. Further, although the underlying principles of work and employment relationships are universal under global capitalism, how they are operationalised in practice varies enormously between and within nation states. At one level, employment relations systems are nationally embedded, with elements of change and continuity observable within them. At another level, employment relationships between managers and workers have immediacy for both parties and are typically organisation-specific. The ultimate efficacy of any balanced employment relations system, however, is not just its effects on creating a fair wage–work bargain and improving economic performance. It also has to be judged by its contribution in promoting the values of a civilised society.

REFERENCES

Abelshausen, K., Claessens, S., Francken, S. and Mondelaers, Y. (2009) 'Belgium' in Stewart, A. and Bell, M. (eds) *The Right to Strike: A Comparative Perspective. A Study of National Law in Six EU States*. London: Institute of Employment Studies.

Abel-Smith, B. (1960) *A History of the Nursing Profession*. London: Heinemann.

Ackers, P. and Wilkinson, A. (2003) *Understanding Work and Employment: Industrial Relations in Transition*. Oxford: Oxford University Press.

Ackers, P. and Wilkinson, A. (2008) 'Industrial relations and the social sciences' in Blyton, P., Bacon, N., Fiorito, J. and Heery, E. (eds) *The SAGE Handbook of Industrial Relations*. London: Sage.

Ackhoff, R. and Rivett, P. (1963) *A Manager's Guide to Operations Research*. New York: Wiley.

Ackroyd, S., Batt, R., Thompson, P. and Tolbert, P. (eds) (2005) *The Oxford Handbook of Work and Organisation*. Oxford: Oxford University Press.

Ackroyd, S. and Procter, S. (1998) 'Against Japanisation: Understanding the re-organisation of British manufacturing'. *Employee Relations* 20 (3): 237–247.

Ackroyd, S. and Thompson, P. (1999) *Organisational Misbehaviour*. London: Sage.

Adams, R. (1988) 'Desperately seeking industrial relations theory'. *International Journal of Comparative Labor Law and Industrial Relations* 4 (1): 1–10.

Adams, R. (ed.) (1991) *Comparative Industrial Relations: Contemporary Research and Theory*. London: Harper Collins.

Adams, R. (1995) *Industrial Relations under Liberal Democracy: North America in Comparative Perspective*. Columbia, SC: University of South Carolina Press.

Adams, R. (2006) *Labour Left Out: Canada's Failure to Protect and Promote Collective Bargaining as a Human Right*. Ottawa: Canadian Centre for Policy Alternatives.

Adams, R. and Meltz, N. (eds) (1993) *Industrial Relations Theory: Its Nature, Scope, and Pedagogy*. Metuchen, NJ: IMLR Press/Rutgers University.

Addison, J. and Schnabel, C. (2003) *International Handbook of Trade Unions*. Cheltenham: Edward Elgar.

Adhikari, D. and Muller, M. (2004) 'Human resource management in Nepal' in Budhwar, P. and Debrah, Y. (eds) *Human Resource Management in Developing Countries*. London: Routledge.

Adler, P. and Cole, R. (1993) 'Designed for learning: A tale of two auto plants'. *Sloan Management Review* 34 (3): 85–94.

Adler, P., Kochan, T., MacDuffie, J., Pil, F. and Rubenstein, S. (1997) 'United States: Variation on a theme' in Kochan, T., Lansbury, R. and MacDuffie, J. (eds) *After Lean Production: Evolving Employment Practices in the World Auto Industry*. Ithaca, New York: ILR Press.

Advisory Conciliation and Arbitration Service (ACAS) (1982) *The ACAS Role in Conciliation, Arbitration and Mediation*. London: Her Majesty' Stationery Office.

Advisory Conciliation and Arbitration Service (2009) *Trade Union Representation in the Workplace*. London: ACAS.

Advisory Conciliation and Arbitration Service (2010) *Building Employee Engagement*. London: ACAS.

Ahiauzu, A. (1982) 'Cross-cultural study of job regulation at the workplace: A framework for analysis', Working Paper No. 234, University of Aston Management Centre.

Alber, J. (1981) 'Government responses to the challenges of unemployment: The development of unemployment insurance in Western Europe' in Flora, P. and Heidenheimer, A. (eds) *The Development of Welfare States in Europe and America*. London: Transaction Books.

Ales, E. and Novitz, T. (2010) *Collective Action and Fundamental Freedoms in Europe: Striking the Balance*. Antwerp: Intersentia.

Alfes, K., Truss, C., Soane, E., Rees, C. and Gatenby, M. (2010) *Creating an Engaged Workforce: Findings from the Kingston Employee Engagement Consortium Project*. London: Chartered Institute of Personnel and Development.

All-China Federation of Trade Unions (2013) About the ACFTU. Retrieved from http://www.acftu. 21 March.

Allen, V. (1966) *Militant Trade Unionism*. London: Merlin Press.

Allen, V. (1971) *The Sociology of Industrial Relations*. London: Longmans.

Almeida, R. and Carneiro, P. (2006) 'Enforcement of regulation, informal labour, firm size and firm performance'. Working Paper No. 5976, Centre for Economic Policy Research. London.

Alston, J. (1989) '*Wa, guanxi* and *inhwa*: Managerial principles in Japan, China and Korea'. *Business Horizons* March–April: 26–31.

Altmann, N., Kohler, C. and Meil, P. (eds.) (1992) *Technology and Work in German Industry*. London: Routledge.

Alvesson, M. and Thompson, P. (2005) 'Post-bureaucracy?' in Ackroyd, S., Batt, R., Thompson, P. and Tolbert, P. (eds) *A Handbook of Work and Organisation*. Oxford: Oxford University Press.

Alvesson, M. and Willmott, H. (eds) (2003) *Studying Management Critically*. London: Sage.

Amabile, T. and Kramer, S. (2011) 'The power of small wins'. *Harvard Business Review* 89 (5): 71–80.

Amable, B. (2000) 'Institutional complementarity and the diversity of social systems of innovation and production'. *Review of International Political Economy* 7 (4): 645–687.

Amable, B. (2003) *The Diversity of Modern Capitalism*. Oxford: Oxford University Press.

American Federation of Labor-Congress of Industrial Organisations (2013) About the AFL- CIO. Retrieved from http://www.afl-cio.org, 14 May.

American Federation of People Management Associations (2013) National Association Members. Retrieved from http://www.fidagh.com, 6 March.

Amin, A. (1994) *Post-Fordism: A Reader*. Oxford: Blackwell.

Aminuddin, M. (1990) *Malaysian Employment Law and Industrial Relations*. 7th ed. Kuala Lumpur: McGraw-Hill.

Amsden, A. and van der Hoeven, B. (1996) 'Manufacturing output, employment and real wages in the 1980s: Labour's loss until the century's end'. *Journal of Development Studies* 32 (4): 506–30.

Andersen, S. (1988) *British and Norwegian Offshore Industrial Relations*. Avebury: Gower.

Anderson, C. (2009) *Roman Law*. Dundee: Dundee University Press.

Andriesse, E. and Van Westen, G. (2012) 'Varieties of embedded mercantilism in regional development in the Thailand-Malaysia borderlands'. *Journal of Development Alternatives and Area Studies* 31: Online.

Anner, M. and Veiga, J. (2013) 'Brazil' in Frege, C. and Kelly, J. (eds) *Comparative Employment Relations in the Global Economy*. Abingdon: Routledge.

Anthony, P. (1986) *The Foundation of Management*. London: Tavistock Publications.

Anthony, A. and Govindarajan, V. (2004) *Management Control Systems*. 6th ed. Singapore: Irwin.

Appelbaum, E. (2002) 'The impact of new forms of work organisations on workers' in Murray, G., Bélanger, J., Giles, A. and Lapointe, P. (eds) *Work Employment Relations in the High Performance Workplace*. London: Continuum.

Appelbaum, E. and Batt, R. (1994) *The New American Workplace: Transforming Work Systems in the United States*. Ithaca: Cornell University Press.

Appelbaum, E., Berg, P., Kalleberg, A. and Bailey, T. (2000) *Manufacturing Advantage: Why High Performance Work Systems Pay Off*. Ithaca: Cornell University Press.

Appelbaum, E. and Leana, C. (2011) *Improving Job Quality: Direct Care Workers in the US*. Washington, DC: Center for Economic Policy and Research.

Appelbaum, E. and Schmitt, J. (2013) 'Employment relations and economic performance' in Frege, C. and Kelly, J. (eds) *Comparative Employment Relations in the Global Economy*. Abingdon: Routledge.

Argyris, C. (1970) *Personality and Organisation: The Conflict Between System and the Individual.* London: Harper and Row.

Ariga, K., Brunello, G. and Ohkusa, Y. (2000) *Internal Labour Markets in Japan.* Cambridge: Cambridge University Press.

Armstrong, P. (1989) 'Limits and possibilities of HRM in the age of accountancy' in Storey, J. (ed.) *New Perspectives on Human Resource Management.* London: Routledge.

Armstrong, M. (2009) *Armstrong's Handbook of Human Resource Management Practice.* London: Kogan Page.

Arun, T. and Turner, J. (2009) *Corporate Governance and Development: Reform, Financial Systems and Legal Frameworks.* Cheltenham: Edward Elgar.

Ashwin, S. and Clarke, S. (2002) *Russian Trade Unions and Industrial Relations in Russia.* Basingstoke: Palgrave Macmillan.

Ashwin, S. and Kozina, I. (2013) 'Russia' in Frege, C. and Kelly, J. (eds) *Comparative Employment Relations in the Global Economy.* Abingdon: Routledge.

Atkinson, A., Piketty, T. and Saez, E. (2011) 'Top incomes in the long run of history'. *Journal of Economic Literature* 49 (1): 3–71.

Attridge, M. (2009) 'Measuring and managing employee work engagement: A review of the research and business literature'. *Journal of Workplace Behavioral Health* 24 (4): 383–398.

Auer, P. (1996) 'Codetermination in Germany: Institutional stability in a changing environment' in Davis, E. and Lansbury, R. (eds) *Managing Together: Consultation and Participation in the Workplace.* Melbourne: Addison-Wesley Longman.

Austin, R., Nolan, R. and O'Donnell, S. (2012) *Harder than I Thought: Adventures of a Twenty-First Century Leader.* Cambridge, MA: Harvard Business Review Press.

Australian Bureau of Statistics (2008) *Forms of Employment, Australia, November 2007.* Catalogue No. 6359.0. Canberra: Australian Bureau of Statistics.

Bach, S. and Kessler, I. (2012) *The Modernisation of the Public Services and Employee Relations: Targeted Change.* Basingstoke: Palgrave Macmillan.

Bacon, N. (2008) 'Management strategy and industrial relations' in Blyton, P., Bacon, N., Fiorito, J. and Heery, E. (eds) *The SAGE Handbook of Industrial Relations.* London: Sage.

Badigannavar, V. (2013) 'India' in Frege, C. and Kelly, J. (eds) *Comparative Employment Relations in Global Economy.* Abingdon: Routledge.

Bain, G. and Elsheikh, F. (1976) *Union Growth and the Business Cycle: An Economic Analysis.* Oxford: Basil Blackwell.

Baird, L. and Meshoulham, L. (1988) 'Managing two fits of strategic human resource management'. *Academy of Management Review* 13 (1): 116–128.

Bakke, E., Kerr, C. and Anrod, C. (1960) *Unions, Management, and the Public.* San Diego: Harcourt, Brace.

Balderston, C. (1935) *Executive Guidance of Industrial Relations*. Philadelphia: University of Pennsylvania Press.

Baldry, C., Bain, P., Taylor, P., Hyman, J., Scholarios, D., Marks, A., Watson, A., Gilbert, K., Gall, G. and Bunzel, D. (2007) *The Meaning of Work in the New Economy*. Basingstoke: Palgrave Macmillan.

Ball, A. and Peters, G. (2000) *Modern Politics and Government*. Basingstoke: Macmillan.

Bamber, G., Lansbury, R. and Wailes, N. (2011) *International and Comparative Employment Relations: Globalisation and Change*. 5th ed. London: Sage.

Banks, J. (2009) *Risk and Financial Catastrophe*. London: Palgrave Macmillan.

Banks, A. and Metzgar, J. (2005) 'Response to "Unions as Social Capital" '. *Labor Studies Journal* 29 (4): 27–35.

Bannock, G. (2005) *The Economics and Management of Small Business: An International Perspective*. London: Routledge.

Barbash, J. (1984) *The Elements of Industrial Relations*. Madison: University of Wisconsin Press.

Barber, B. (1995) *Jihad vs McWorld*. New York: Times Books.

Barker, J. (1993) 'The concept and practice of discipline in contemporary organisational life'. *Communication Monographs* 61 March: 19–43.

Barney, J. (1991) 'Firm resources and sustainable competitive advantage'. *Journal of Management* 17: 99–112.

Barney, J. and Wright, P. (1998) 'On becoming a strategic partner: The role of human resources in gaining competitive advantage'. *Human Resource Management* 37 (1): 31–47.

Baron, J. and Pfeffer, J. (1994) 'The social psychology of organisations and inequality'. *Social Psychology Quarterly* 57 (3): 190–209.

Barrett, R. (1999) 'Industrial relations in small firms: The case of the Australian information industry'. *Employee Relations* 21 (3): 311–325.

Barrett, D., Earl, K. and Lynch, K. (2009) 'The United Kingdom' in Stewart, A. and Bell, M. (eds) *The Right to Strike: A Comparative Perspective. A Study of National Law in Six EU States*. London: Institute of Employment Studies.

Barron, R. and Norris, G. (1976) 'Sexual divisions and the dual labour market' in Barker, D. and Allen, S. (eds) *Dependence and Exploitation in Work and Marriage*. London: Longman.

Barry, M. (2010) 'The regulative framework for HRM' in Wilkinson, A., Bacon, N., Redman, T. and Snell, S. (eds) *The SAGE Handbook of Human Resource Management*. London: Sage.

Barry, M. and Wilkinson, A. (eds) (2011) *Research Handbook of Comparative Employment Relations*. Cheltenham: Edward Elgar.

Bassanini, A., Nunziata, L. and Venn, D. (2009) 'Job protection legislation and productivity growth in OECD Countries'. *Economic Policy* 58: 349–402.

Batt, R., Colvin, A. and Keefe, J. (2002) 'Employee voice, human resource practices, and quit rates: Evidence from the telecommunications industry'. *Industrial and Labor Relations Review* 55 (4): 573–594.

Bauer, T. and Baumann, B. (1993) 'Les Conventions Collectives de Travail en Suisse en 1992'. *La vie économique* 5: 54–60.

Bauman, Z. (1998) *Work, Consumerism and the New Poor*. Milton Keynes: Open University Press.

Bean, C. (1994) *Comparative Industrial Relations: An Introduction to Cross-National Perspectives*. 2nd ed. London: International Thomson Business.

Beatty, R. and Schneider, C. (1997) 'New human resources role to impact organisational performance: From "partners" to "players" ' in Urlich, D., Losey, M. and Lake, G. (eds) *Tomorrow's HR Management*. New York: Wiley.

Beaumont, P. (2013) 'Global protest grows as citizens lose faith in politics and the state'. *The Observer* 22 June.

Becker, B. and Gerhart, B. (1996) 'The impact of human resource management on organisational performance: Progress and prospects'. *Academy of Management Journal* 39 (4): 779–803.

Becker, B. and Huselid, M. (2010) 'SHRM and job design: Narrowing the divide'. *Journal of Organizational Behavior* 31: 379–388.

Becker, G. (1964) *Human Capital*. New York: Columbia University Press.

Behrens, M. (2013) 'Germany' in Frege, C. and Kelly, J. (eds) *Comparative Employment Relations in the Global Economy*. Abingdon: Routledge.

Behrens, M. and Traxler, F. (2004) Employers' organisations in Europe. Retrieved from http://www.eiro.eurofound.eu.int, 4 August.

Bélanger, P., Giles, A. and Murray, G. (2002) 'Workplace innovation and the role of institutions' in Murray, G., Bélanger, J., Giles, A. and Lapointe, P. (eds) *Work and Employment Relations in the High-Performance Workplace*. London: Continuum.

Bell, D. (1973) *The Coming of Post-Industrial Society: A Venture in Social Forecasting*. New York: Basic Books.

Belot, M., Boone, J. and van Ours, J. (2007) 'Welfare effects of employment protection'. *Economica* 74: 381–96.

Bendix, R. (1956) *Work and Authority in Industry: Ideologies of Management in the Course of Industrialisation*. New York: Wiley.

Bendix, R. (1974) *Work and Authority in Industry: Ideologies of Management in the Course of Industrialisation*. New edition. Berkeley, CA: University of California Press.

Bennett, R. and Robinson, S. (2000) 'Development of a measure of workplace deviance'. *Journal of Applied Psychology* 85 (3): 349–360.

Bennis, W. (1969) *Organisation Development: Its Nature, Origins, and Prospects*. London: Addison-Wesley.

Benson, J. and Debroux, P. (2004) 'The changing nature of Japanese HRM: The impact of the recession and the Asian financial crisis'. *International Studies of Management and Organization* 34 (1): 32–51.

Benson, J. and Zhu, Y. (2008) *Trade Unions in Asia: An Economic and Sociological Analysis*. New York: Routledge.

Benton, L. (2001) *Law and Colonial Cultures: Legal Regimes in World History 1400–1900*. Cambridge: Cambridge University Press.

Bercusson, B. (2009) *European Labour Law*. 2nd ed. Cambridge: Cambridge University Press.

Berghahn, V. and Karsten, D. (1987) *Industrial Relations in West Germany*. Oxford: Berg.

Berkeley-Thomas, A. (1993) *Controversies in Management*. London: Routledge.

Bernstein, I. (1960) *The Lean Years*. Boston: Houghton Mifflin.

Berton, F., Devicienti, F. and Pacelli, L. (2008) 'Temporary jobs: Port of entry, trap, or just unobserved heterogeneity?' Labor Working Paper No. 79. Laboratorio Riccardo Revelli, Collegio Carlo Alberto, Moncalieri.

Beugre, D. and Offodile, F. (2001) 'Managing for organisational effectiveness in sub-Saharan Africa: A culture fit model'. *International Journal of Human Resource Management* 12 (4): 535–550.

Bevan, A., Hollebon, G. and Passow, S. (2004) *Mediation in the Workplace*. Kingston upon Thames: Wolters Kluwer.

Beynon, H. (1975) *Working for Ford*. Wakefield: E.P. Publishing.

Beynon, H., Grimshaw, D., Rubery, J. and Ward, K. (2002) *Managing Employment Change: the New Realities of Work*. Oxford: Oxford University Press.

Beynon, H. and Nicols, T. (2006a) *The Fordism of Ford and Modern Management: Fordism and post-Fordism; Vol. 1*. Cheltenham: Edward Elgar.

Beynon, H. and Nicols, T. (2006b) *The Fordism of Ford and Modern Management: Fordism and post-Fordism; Vol. 2*. Cheltenham: Edward Elgar.

Black, S. and Lynch, M. (2001) 'The impact of workplace practices and information technology on productivity'. *Review of Economics and Statistics* 83 (3): 434–445.

Blackbourn, D. and Eley, G. (1984) *The Peculiarities of German History: Bourgeois Society and Politics in Nineteenth-Century Germany*. Oxford: Oxford University Press.

Blain, A. and Gennard, J. (1970) 'Industrial relations theory'. *British Journal of Industrial Relations* 8 (3): 389–407.

Blanchflower, D. and Freeman, R (1992) 'Unionism in the United States and other advanced OECD countries'. *Industrial Relations* 3: 56–77.

Blanpain, R. (ed.) (2008) *International Encyclopaedia for Labour Law and Industrial Relations*. London: Kluwer Law International.

Blanplan, R. and Engels, C. (1995) *European Labour Law*. Alphen aan den Rijn: Kluwer Law and Taxation.

Blauner, R. (1964) *Alienation and Freedom: The Factory Worker and His Industry.* London: Chicago University Press.

Block, R., Berg, P. and Belman, D. (2004) 'The economic dimension of the employment relationship' in Coyle-Shapiro, J., Shore, L., Taylor, S. and Tetrick, L. (eds) *The Employment Relationship: Examining Psychological and Contextual Perspectives.* Oxford: Oxford University Press.

Bloom, G. and Northrup, H. (1973) *Economics of Labor Relations.* 7th ed. Homewood, IL: Irwin.

Blyth, M. (2013) *Austerity: The History of a Dangerous Idea.* New York: Oxford University Press.

Blyton, P., Bacon, N., Fiorito, J. and Heery, E. (eds) (2008) *The SAGE Handbook of Industrial Relations.* London: Sage.

Boeri, T. and Jimeno, J. (2005) 'The effects of employment protection: Learning from variable enforcement'. *European Economic Review* 49: 2057–2077.

Böhm, S., Spicer, A. and Fleming, P. (2008) 'Infra-political dimensions of resistance to international business: A neo-Gramscian approach'. *Scandinavian Journal of Management* 24 (3): 169–182.

Boileau, D. (1998) *Principles of Catholic Social Teaching.* Milwaukee, WI: Marquette University Press.

Boix, C. and Stokes, S. (eds) (2008) *The Oxford Handbook of Comparative Politics.* Oxford: Oxford University Press.

Boltanski, L. and Chiapello, È. (2005) *The New Spirit of Capitalism.* London-New York: Verso.

Bolton, S. and Houlihan, M. (2009) *Work Matters: Critical Reflections on Contemporary Work.* Basingstoke: Palgrave Macmillan.

Booth, A. (1995) *The Economics of the Trade Union.* Cambridge: Cambridge University Press.

Booth, P. (2007) *Catholic Social Teaching and the Market Economy.* London: Institute of Economic Affairs.

Bordogna, L. and Cella, G. (1999) 'Admission, exclusion, correction: The changing role of the state in industrial relations'. *Transfer* 1 (2): 14–33.

Borjas, G. (2013) *Labor Economics.* 6th ed. New York: McGraw-Hill/Irwin.

Boselie, P., Dietz, G. and Boon, C. (2005) 'Commonalities and contradictions in research on human resource management and performance'. *Human Resource Management Journal* 15 (3): 67–94.

Bot, B. (2004) 'Towards a European social contract'. *Speech at Humboldt University Berlin* 2 June.

Boudreau, J. and Ramstad, P. (2005) 'Talentship, talent segmentation, and sustainability: A new HR decision science paradigm for a new strategy definition' in Losey, M., Meisinger, S. and Ulrich, D. (eds) *The Future of Human Resources Management.* Washington, DC: Society for Human Resource Management.

Boudreau, J. and Ramstad, P. (2007) *Beyond HR: The New Science of Human Capital.* Boston, MA: Harvard Business School Press.

Bowles, S. and Gintis, H. (1990) 'Contested exchange: New microfoundations for the political economy of capitalism'. *Politics and Society* 18(2): 165–222.

Boxall, P. (1992) 'Strategic human resource management: Beginnings of a new theoretical sophistication?' *Human Resource Management Journal* 2 (3): 60–79.

Boxall, P. (2008) 'Trade union strategy' in Blyton, P., Bacon, N., Fiorito, J. and Heery, E. (eds) *The SAGE Handbook of Industrial Relations.* London: Sage.

Boxall, P. and Haynes, P. (1997) 'Strategy and trade union effectiveness in a neo-liberal environment'. *British Journal of Industrial Relations* 35 (4): 567–591.

Boxall, P. and Purcell, J. (2000) 'Strategic human resource management: Where have we come from and where are we going?' *International Journal of Management Reviews* 2 (2): 183–203.

Boxall, P. and Purcell, J. (2011) *Strategy and Human Resource Management.* 3rd ed. Basingstoke: Palgrave Macmillan.

Boydell, T., Pedler, M. and Burgoyne, J. (2007) *A Manager's Guide to Self-Development.* Maidenhead: McGraw-Hill Education.

Bradley, H. (1999) *Gender and Power in the Workplace: Analysing the Impact of Economic Change.* Basingstoke: Macmillan.

Bramble, T. (2008) *Trade Unionism in Australia: A History from Flood to Ebb Tide.* Cambridge: Cambridge University Press.

Brandeis, L. (1934) *The Curse of Bigness.* New York: Viking Press.

Brandl, J. and Pohler, D. (2010) 'The role of the human resource department and conditions that affect its development: Explanations from Austrian CEOs'. *Human Resource Management Journal* 49 (6): 1027–1049.

Braudel, F. (1958) 'Histoire et Science Sociale: La Longue Durée'. *Annales ESC* 13 (4): 725–753.

Braudel, F. (1995) *A History of Civilisations.* London: Penguin Books.

Braverman, H. (1974) *Labor and Monopoly Capital: The Degradation of Work in the Twentieth Century.* New York: Monthly Review Press.

Braybrooke, D. (1987) *Philosophy of Social Science.* London: Prentice-Hall.

Brenner, A., Day, B. and Ness, I. (eds) (2009) *Encyclopaedia of Strikes in America.* Armonk, New York: Sharpe.

Brewster, C. (2007) 'A European perspective on HRM'. *European Journal of International Management* 1 (3): 239–259.

Brewster, C., Hegewisch, A. and Mayne, L. (1994) 'Trends in European HRM' in Kirkbride, P. (ed.) *Human Resource Management in Europe: Perspectives for the 1990s.* London: Routledge.

Brewster, C. and Larsen, H. (1992) 'Human resource management in Europe: Evidence from ten countries'. *International Journal of Human Resource Management* 3 (3): 409–434.

Brewster, C. and Mayrhofer, W. (eds) (2012) *Handbook of Research on Comparative Human Resource Management*. Cheltenham: Edward Elgar.

Brewster, C., Sparrow, P. and Harris, H. (2005) 'Towards a new model of globalising HRM'. *International Journal of Human Resource Management* 16 (6): 949–970.

Brewster, C., Sparrow, P., Vernon. G. and Houldsworth, L. (2011) *International Human Resource Management*. 3rd ed. London: Chartered Institute of Personnel and Development.

Brewster, C. and Wood, G. (eds) (2007) *Industrial Relations in Africa*. Basingstoke: Palgrave Macmillan.

Bronstein, A. (2009) *International and Comparative Labour Law: Current Challenges*. Basingstoke: Palgrave Macmillan.

Brookings Institution (2014) 'The Arab awakening and middle east unrest'. Retrieved from http://www.brookings.edu/research/topics/middle-east-and-arab-awakening, 15 May.

Brown, H. (1959) *The Growth of British Industrial Relations: A Study from the Standpoint of 1906–14*. London: Macmillan.

Brown, H. (1962) *The Economics of Labor*. New Haven: Yale University Press.

Brown, W. (1973) *Piecework Bargaining*. London: Heinemann.

Brown, H. (1983) *The Origins of Trade Union Power*. Oxford: Clarendon.

Brown, W. (2008) 'The influence of product markets on industrial relations' in Blyton, P., Bacon, N., Fiorito, J. and Heery, E. (eds) *The SAGE Handbook of Industrial Relations*. London: Sage.

Brown, W., Bryson, A., Forth, J. and Whitfield, K. (2009) *The Evolution of the Modern Workplace*. Cambridge: Cambridge University Press.

Brown, C., Eichergreen, B. and Reich, M. (eds) (2010) *Labor in an Era of Globalisation*. Cambridge: Cambridge University Press.

Brown, H. and Marriott, A. (2011) *ADR Principles and Practice*. London: Sweet and Maxwell.

Brown, D. and Myers, C. (1957) 'The changing industrial relations philosophy of American Management' *Proceedings of the Ninth Annual Winter Meetings of the Industrial Relations Research Association*. Madison, WI: IRRA.

Bryman, A. and Bell, E. (2011) *Business Research Methods*. 3rd ed. Oxford: Oxford University.

Buckland, W. (2010) *The Roman Law of Slavery: The Condition of the Slave in Private Law from Augustus to Justinian*. Cambridge: Cambridge University Press.

Budd, J. (2004) *Employment with a Human Face: Balancing Efficiency, Equity and Voice*. Ithaca, New York: Cornell University Press.

Budd, J. (2005) *Labor Relations: Striking a Balance*. Boston: McGraw-Hill/Urwin.

Budd, J. and Bhave, D. (2008) 'Values, ideologies, and frames of reference in industrial relations' in Blyton, P., Bacon, N., Fiorito, J. and Heery, E. (eds) *The SAGE Handbook of Industrial Relations*. London: Sage.

Budd, J. and Bhave, D. (2010) 'The employment relationship' in Wilkinson, A., Bacon, N., Redman, T. and Snell, S. (eds) *The SAGE Handbook of Human Resource Management*. London: Sage.

Budhwar, P. (ed.) (2004) *Managing Human Resources in Asia-Pacific*. London: Routledge.

Budhwar, P. and Sparrow, P. (1998) 'National factors determining Indian and British HRM practices: An empirical study'. *Management International Review* 38 (2): 105–121.

Budhwar, P. and Sparrow, P. (2002) 'An integrative framework for determining cross national Human resource management practices'. *Human Resource Management Review* 12 (3): 377–403.

Burawoy, M. (1979) *Manufacturing Consent: Changes in the Labor Process under Monopoly Capitalism*. Chicago: University of Chicago Press.

Burawoy, M. (1983) 'Between the labour process and the state: The changing face of factory regimes under advanced capitalism'. *American Sociological Review* 48: 587–605.

Burchholder, N. (2007) *Ultimate Performance: Measuring Human Resources at Work*. Hoboken, NJ: Wiley.

Burgert, D. (2005) 'The impact of German job protection legislation on job creation in small establishments: An application of the regression discontinuity design'. MPRA Paper 5971. University of Munich.

Burnett, J. (1994) *Idle Hands: The Experience of Unemployment 1790–1990*. London: Routledge.

Burns, T. and Stalker, G. (1961) *The Management of Innovation*. London: Tavistock Publications.

Burrell, G. (1984) 'Sex and organisational analysis'. *Organisation Studies* 5 (2): 97–118.

Burrell, G. (1998) 'Modernism, post modernism and organisational analysis 2: The contribution of Michel Foucault'. *Organisation Studies* 9 (2): 221–235.

Burrell, G. and Morgan, G. (1998) *Sociological Paradigms and Organisational Analysis: Elements of the Sociology of Corporate Life*. Aldershot: Ashgate.

Burroughs, A., Palmer, L. and Hunter, I. (2008) *HR Transformation Technology: Delivering Systems to Support the New HR Model*. Aldershot: Gower.

Business Europe (2013) Home Page. Retrieved from http://www.businesseurope.eu/, 10 November.

Buxton, L.-A. (1995) *Employment Law in Europe: A Country by Country Guide for Employers*. 2nd ed. Aldershot: Gower.

Byung-Sun, O. (1997) 'Cultural values and human rights: The Korean perspective' in Jefferson, R. and Sebasti, R. (eds) *Human Rights in Asian Cultures: Continuity and Change*. Osaka/Delhi: Asia-Pacific Human Rights Information Center.

Cable, V. (2009) *The Storm: The World Economic Crisis and What It Means*. London: Atlantic Books.

Calmfors, L., Brugiavini, A. and Boeri, T. (2001) *The Role of Unions in the Twenty-First Century: A Report for the Fondazione Rodolfo Debenedetti.* Oxford: Oxford University Press.

Caplin, J. (2011) *The Value of Talent: Promoting Talent Management across the Organisation.* London: Kogan Page.

Cappelli, P. (1999) *Employment Practices and Business Strategy.* New York: Oxford University Press.

Cappelli, P. and Rogovsky, N. (1998) 'Employee involvement and organisational citizenship: Implications for labour law reform and "lean production" '. *Industrial and Labor Relations Review* 51 (4): 633–653.

Caramani, D. (2011) *Comparative Politics.* Oxford: Oxford University Press.

Cardoso, A. (2004) *Industrial Relations, Social Dialogue and Employment in Argentina, Brazil and Mexico.* Geneva: International Labour Organisation.

Carew, A., Dreyfus, M., Van Goethem, G., Gumbrell-McCormick, R. and Van Der Linden, M. (2000) *The International Confederation of Free Trade Unions.* Bern: Peter Lang.

Carlson, A., Kelemen, C. and Stolt, M. (2013) *Overview of Current State of SE Foundations in Europe.* Brussels: European Trade Union Institute.

Carnall, C. (1995) *Managing Change in Organisations.* Harlow: Prentice Hall.

Carney, M. (2008) *Asian Business Groups: Context, Governance and Performance.* Oxford: Chandos.

Carrter, A. and Marshall, F. (1972) *Labor Economics: Wages, Employment, and Trade Unionism.* Homewood, IL: Irwin.

Carta, L., Deschamps, M., Jannin, A. and Le Luduec, A-L (2009) 'France' in Stewart, A. and Bell, M. (eds) *The Right to Strike: A Comparative Perspective. A Study of National Law in Six EU States.* London: Institute of Employment Studies.

Casale, G. (ed.) (2011) *The Employment Relationship: A Comparative Overview.* Oxford: Hart.

Cassidy, J. (2010) *How Markets Fail: The Logic of Economic Calamities.* London: Penguin.

Casson, M. (1983) *Economics of Unemployment: An Historical Perspective.* Oxford: Robertson.

Castel, R. (1977) *Les métamorphoses de la question sociale. Une chronique du salariat.* Paris: Fayard.

Castells, M. (2010) *The Rise of the Network Society.* 2nd ed. Oxford: Blackwell.

Central Intelligence Agency (2012) *The CIA Factbook.* Washington, DC: CIA.

Centre européen des enterprises à participation publique (2013) About CEEP. Retrieved from http://www.ceep.eu/, 5 September.

Chadwick, C. and Dabu, A. (2008) 'Human resources, human resource management and the competitive advantage of firms: Toward a more comprehensive model of causal linkages'. *Organisation Science* 20 (1): 273–277.

Chakrabarty, S. (2006) 'Making sense of the sourcing and shoring maze: Various outsourcing and offshoring alternatives' in Kehal, H. and Singh, P. (eds) *Outsourcing and Offshoring in the 21st Century: A Socio Economic Perspective.* Hershey: IGI.

Chamberlain, N. and Kuhn, J. (1965) *Collective Bargaining.* 2nd ed. New York: McGraw-Hill.

Champy, J. and Nohria, N. (1996) *Fast Forward: The Best Ideas on Managing Business Change.* Boston, MA: Harvard Business School Press.

Chan, A. and Snape, E. (2000) 'Union weakness in Hong Kong: Workplace industrial relations and the federation of trade unions'. *Economic and Industrial Democracy* 21 (2): 117–146.

Chandler, A. and Hikino, T. (1990) *Scale and Scope: The Dynamics of Industrial Capitalism.* London: Belknap Press.

Chang, H-J. (2010) *23 Things They Don't Tell You About Capitalism.* London: Penguin.

Chanock, M. (2001) *The Making of South African Legal Culture 1902–1936: Fear, Favour and Prejudice.* Cambridge: Cambridge University Press.

Chapman, S. (1967) *The Early Factory Masters: The Transition to the Factory System in the Midlands Textile Industry.* Newton Abbott: David and Charles.

Chartered Institute of Personnel and Development (2013) 'One million workers on zero hours contracts'. Retrieved from http://www.cipd.co.uk/pm/peoplemanagement, 6 August 2013.

Chen, M. (1995) *Asian Management Systems: Chinese, Japanese and Korean Styles of Business.* London: Routledge.

Cherif, R. (2013) *Public Debt Dynamics: The Effects of Austerity, Inflation and Growth Shocks.* Washington, DC: International Monetary Fund.

Child, J. (1981) 'Culture, contingency and capitalism in the cross-national study of organizations'. *Research in Organizational Behavior* 3: 303–356.

Child, J. (2005) *Organization: Contemporary Principles and Practice.* Oxford: Blackwell.

Child, J. and Tayeb, M. (1983) 'Theoretical perspectives in cross-national organizational research'. *International Studies of Management and Organization* 10 (1): 23–70.

China Briefing (2012) 'Minimum wage levels across China'. *Magazine and Daily News Service* 22 February: 1.

Chinese Government (2013) The Chinese Government's Official Web Portal. Retrieved from http://www.gov.cn/english, 14 May.

Chinn, C. (1998) *The Cadbury Story: A Short History.* Birmingham: Brewer Books.

Cho, J. and Lee, K. (2007) 'Deregulation of dismissal law and unjust dismissal in Korea'. *International Review of Law and Economics* 27: 409–422.

Clark, J. (1995) *Managing Innovation and Change: People, Technology and Strategy.* London: Sage.

Clark, T., Gospel, H. and Montgomery, J. (1999) 'Running on the spot? A review of twenty years of research on the management of human resources in comparative and international perspective'. *International Journal of Human Resource Management* 10 (3): 520–544.

Clarke, L., Donnelly, E., Hyman, R., Kelly, J., McKay, S. and Moore, S. (2011) 'What's the point of industrial relations?' *International Journal of Comparative Labour Law and Industrial Relations* 27 (3): 239–253.

Clarke, R. (1957) 'The dispute in the British Engineering Industry 1897–98: An evaluation'. *Economica* 24 (94): 128–137.

Clawson, D. and Clawson, M. (1999) 'What has happened to the US labor movement? Union decline and renewal'. *Annual Review of Sociology* 25: 95–119.

Clay, H. (1929) *The Problem of Industrial Relations and Other Lectures.* London: Macmillan.

Clegg, H. (1960) *A New Approach to Industrial Democracy.* Oxford: Blackwell.

Clegg, H. (1970) *The System of Industrial Relations in Great Britain.* Oxford: Blackwell.

Clegg, H. (1975) 'Pluralism in industrial relations'. *British Journal of Industrial Relations* 13 (3): 309–316.

Clegg, H. (1976) *Trade Unionism Under Collective Bargaining.* Oxford: Blackwell.

Clegg, H. (1985) *A History of British Trade Unions Since 1889. Vol.2, 1911–1933.* Oxford: Clarendon Press.

Clegg, H. (1994) *A History of British Trade Unions Since 1889. Vol.3, 1934–1951.* Oxford: Clarendon Press.

Clegg, H., Fox, A. and Thompson, A. (1964) *A History of British Trade Unions Since 1889. Vol.1, 1889–1910.* Oxford: Clarendon Press.

Clegg, S. and Dunkerley, D. (1980) *Organisation, Class and Control.* Routledge: Kegan Paul.

Clegg, S., Pitsis, T. and Kornberger, M. (eds) (2011) *Managing and Organisations: An Introduction to Theory and Practice.* London: Sage.

Clements, P. (2008) *Prosperity, Depression and the New Deal.* London: Hodder Education.

Coase, R. (1937) 'The nature of the firm'. *Economica* 4: 386–405.

Coates, D. (2000) *Models of Capitalism: Growth and Stagnation in the Modern Era.* Cambridge: Polity Press.

Coates, D. (ed.) (2005) *Varieties of Capitalism, Varieties of Approaches.* Basingstoke: Palgrave Macmillan.

Coates, K. and Topham, T. (1980) *Trade Unions in Britain.* Nottingham: Spokesman.

Coch, L. and French, J. (1948) 'Overcoming resistance to change'. *Human Relations* 11: 512–532.

Cockburn, C. (1991) *In the Way of Women: Men's Resistance to Sex Equality in Organisations.* Basingstoke: Macmillan.

Colakoglu, S., Hong, Y. and Lepak, D. (2010) 'Models of strategic Human Resource Management' in Wilkinson, A., Bacon, N., Redman, T. and Snell, S. (eds) *The SAGE Handbook of Human Resource Management.* London: Sage.

Cole, G. (1913) *The World of Labour: A Discussion of the Present and Future of Trade Unionism*. London: Bell.

Cole, G. (1972) *Self-Government in Industry*. 1st ed. Reprinted. London: Hutchinson.

Colli, N., Di Toro, E., Fabrizi, A. and ForteIn, L. (2009) 'Italy' in Stewart, A. and Bell, M. (eds) *The Right to Strike: A Comparative Perspective. A Study of National Law in Six EU States*. London: Institute of Employment Studies.

Collinson, D. (2003) 'Identities and insecurities: Selves at work'. *Organisation* 10 (3): 527–547.

Collinson, D. and Ackroyd, S. (2005) 'Resistance, misbehaviour and dissent' in Ackroyd, S., Batt, R., Thompson, P. and Tolbert, P. (eds) *The Oxford Handbook of Work and Organisation*. Oxford: Oxford University Press.

Collinson, D. and Hearn, J. (2003) 'Naming men as men: Implications for work, organisation and management' in Ely, R., Scully, M. and Foldy, E. (eds) *Reader in Gender, Work and Organisation*. Oxford: Blackwell.

Commission of the European Communities (1994) *European Social Policy: A Way Forward for the Union*. Luxembourg: Office for Official Publications of the European Communities.

Commission of the European Communities (1997a) *Finland*. Luxembourg: Office for Official Publications of the European Communities.

Commission of the European Communities (1997b) *Sweden*. Luxembourg: Office for Official Publications of the European Communities.

Commission of the European Communities (2000) *Charter of Fundamental Rights of the European Union*. Luxembourg: Office for Official Publications of the European Communities.

Commission of Industrial Relations (1973) *Report No. 34: The Role of Management in Industrial Relations*. London: Her Majesty's Stationery Office.

Commons, J. (1909) 'American shoemakers 1648–1895: A sketch of industrial evolution'. *Quarterly Journal of Economics* 24: 39–83.

Commons, J. (1919) *Industrial Goodwill*. New York: McGraw-Hill.

Commons, J. (1921a) *Trade Unionism and Labor Problems*. New York: Augustus Kelley.

Commons, J. (1921b) *Industrial Government*. New York: Macmillan.

Commons, J. (1926) 'Introduction' in Commons, J., Saposs, D., Sumner, H., Mittelman, E., Hoagland, H. and Andrews, J. (eds) *History of Labor in the United States. Vol II*. New York: Macmillan and Co.

Commons, J. (1950) *The Economics of Collective Action*. Madison, WI: University of Wisconsin Press.

Commons, J. (1959) *The Legal Foundations of Capitalism*. Madison, WI: University of Wisconsin Press.

Commons, J. and Andrews, J. (1916) *Principles of Labor Legislation*. 4th ed. New York: Harper and Brothers.

Commons, J. and Andrews, J. (1936) *Principles of Labor Legislation.* Revised ed. New York: Harper and Brothers.

Conway, D. and Heynen, N. (eds) (2006) *Globalisation's Contradictions: Geographies of Discipline, Destruction and Transformation.* Abingdon: Routledge.

Cook, L. (1998) 'Toward a flexible industrial relations? Neo-liberalism, democracy and labor reform in Latin America'. *Industrial Relations* 37 (3): 311–336.

Cooke, F. (2003) *Multinational Companies and Global Human Resource Strategies.* Westport, CT: Quorum Books.

Cooke, F. (2005) *HRM, Work and Employment in China.* London: Routledge.

Cooke, F. (2006) 'Modelling an HR shared services centre: Experience of an MNC in the UK'. *Human Resource Management Journal* 45 (2): 211–227.

Cooke, F. (2011a) 'Unions in China in a period of marketisation' in Gall, G., Wilkinson, A. and Hurd, R. (eds) *International Handbook on Labour Unions: Responses to Neo-Liberalism.* Cheltenham: Edward Elgar.

Cooke, F. (2011b) 'Employment relations in China' in Bamber, G., Lansbury, R. and Wailes, N. (eds) *International and Comparative Employment Relations.* 5th ed. London: Sage.

Cooke, F. and Budhwar, P. (2009) 'HR offshoring and outsourcing: Research issues for IHRM' in Sparrow, P. (ed.) *Handbook of International Human Resource Management.* Chichester: John Wiley.

Cooney, S., Lindsey, T., Mitchell, R. and Zhu, Y. (eds) (2003) *Law and Labour Market Regulation in East Asia.* London: Routledge.

Cornfield, D. (2006) 'Immigration, economic restructuring, and labor ruptures: From the amalgamated to change to win'. *Working USA* 9 (2): 215–223.

Coser, L. (1956) *The Functions of Social Conflict.* London: Routledge and Kegan Paul.

Costas, J. (2012) ' "We are all friends here": Reinforcing paradoxes of normative control in a culture of friendship'. *Journal of Management Inquiry* 21 (4): 377–395.

Cottereau, A. (2000) 'Industrial relations and the establishment of a kind of common law of labour in nineteenth century France' in Steinmetz, W. (ed.) *Private Law and Social Inequality in the Industrial Age. Comparing Legal Cultures in Britain, France, Germany and the United States.* Oxford: Oxford University Press.

Council of Europe (1950) *Convention for the Protection of Human Rights and Fundamental Freedoms as amended by Protocols No. 11 and No. 14.* Strasbourg: Council of Europe.

Council of Europe (1961) *The European Social Charter.* Strasbourg: Council of Europe.

Craig, A. and Solomon, N. (1992) *The System of Industrial Relations in Canada.* Ottowa: Prentice Hall.

Cramford, A., Harbridge, R. and Hince, K. (1996) Unions and Union Membership in New Zealand. Annual review for 1995. Working Paper 2/96: Victoria University.

Cranet Survey on International Human Resource Management (2005) *International Executive Report.* Retrieved from http://www.cranet, 20 February 2012.

Cremers, J., Stollt, M. and Vitols, S. (eds) *A Decade of Experience with the European Company*. Brussels: European Trade Union Institute.

Crompton, H. (1876) *Industrial Conciliation*. London: Henry King.

Crompton, R. (1998) *Class and Stratification: An Introduction to Current Debates*. Cambridge: Polity Press.

Crouch, C. (1979) *The Politics of Industrial Relations*. London: Fontana.

Crouch, C. (1982) *Trade Unions: The Logic of Collective Action*. Glasgow: Fontana.

Crouch, C. (1993) *Industrial Relations and European State Traditions*. Oxford: Clarendon Press.

Crouch, C. (2004) *Post-democracy*. Cambridge: Polity.

Crouch, C. (2005) *Capitalist Diversity and Change: Recombinant Governance and Institutional Entrepreneurs*. Oxford: Oxford University Press.

Crouch, C. (2011) *The Strange Non-Death of Neoliberalism*. Cambridge: Polity.

Crouch, C. and Streeck, W. (1997) 'Introduction: The future of capitalist diversity' in Barbash, J., Barbash, K., Crouch, C. and Streeck, W. (eds) *The Political Economy of Modern Capitalism: Mapping Convergence and Diversity*. London: Sage.

Croucher, R. and Cotton, E. (2009) *Global Unions, Global Business: Global Union Federations and International Business*. London: Middlesex University.

Crozier, M. (1964) *The Bureaucratic Phenomenon*. Chicago: University of Chicago Press.

Cullinane, N. and Dundon, T. (2006) 'The psychological contract: A critical review'. *International Journal of Management Reviews* 8 (2): 113–129.

Cullinane, N. and Dundon, T. (2012) 'Unitarism and employer resistance to trade unionism'. *International Journal of Human Resource Management*. iFirst/doi:10.1080/09585192.2012.667428.

Cunningham, W. (2007) *Minimum Wages and Social policy: Lessons from Developing Countries*. Washington, DC: World Bank.

Curran, J. (1990) 'Rethinking economic structure: exploring the role of the small firm in the British economy'. *Work, Employment and Society* 4: 125–146.

Cutcher-Gershenfeld, J., Power, D. and McCabe-Power, M. (1996) 'Global implications of recent innovations in US collective bargaining'. *Relations Industrielles/Industrial Relations* 51 (2): 281–301.

Czarniawska, B. and Joerges, B. (1996) 'Travel of ideas' in Sevón, G., Czarniawska, B. and Joerges, B. (eds) *Translating Organizational Change*. New York: Walter de Gruyter.

Dabashi, H. (2012) 'Iran: The next war'. *New Statesman* 141 (5112): 38.

Dabscheck, B. (1989) *Australian Industrial Relations in the 1980s*. Melbourne: Oxford University Press.

Dabscheck, B. (1995) *The Struggle for Australian Industrial Relations*. Oxford: Oxford University Press.

Dadomo, C. and Farran, S. (1996) *The French Legal System*. 2nd ed. London: Sweet and Maxwell.

Daft, R., Kendrick, M. and Vershinina, N. (2010) *Management*. Australia: South-Western Cengage Learning.

Dahl, R. and Lindblom, C. (1976) *Politics, Economics and Welfare: Planning and Politico- Economic Systems Resolved into Basic Social Processes*. Chicago, IL: University of Chicago Press.

Dahrendorf, R. (1959) *Class and Class Conflict in Industrial Society*. London: Routledge and Kegan Paul.

Dale, B. (2003) *Managing Quality*. 4th ed. Oxford: Blackwell.

Daley, A. (1999) 'The hollowing out of French unions: Politics and industrial relations after 1981' in Martin, A. and Ross, G. (eds) *The Brave New World of European Labor: European Trade Unions at the Millenium*. New York: Berghahn Books.

Daly, M. (1997) 'Welfare states under pressure: Cash benefits in European welfare states over the last ten years'. *Journal of European Social Policy* 7 (2): 129–146.

Damachi, U. (1992) 'Industrial relations and African development' in Fashoyin, T. (ed.) *Industrial Relations and African Development*. New Delhi: South Asian Publishers.

Damachi, U., Seibel, H. and Trachtman, L. (eds) (1979) *Industrial Relations in Africa*. Basingstoke: Macmillan Press.

Daniels, G. and McIlroy, J. (eds) (2009) *Trade Unions in a Neoliberal World: British Trade Unions Under New Labour*. London: Routledge.

Danna, K. and Griffin, R. (1999) 'Health and well-being in the workplace: A review and synthesis of the literature'. *Journal of Management* 25 (3): 357–384.

Darlington, R. (2008) *Syndicalism and the Transition to Communism: An International Comparative Analysis*. Aldershot: Ashgate.

Das, S. (2007) *Microeconomics for Business*. London: Sage.

Da Silva, S. (1995) *Elements in the Shaping of Asian Industrial Relations*. Geneva: ILO.

Daudey, E. and García-Peñalosa, C. (2007) 'The personal and the factor distributions of income in a cross-section of countries'. *Journal of Development Studies* 43 (5): 812–829.

David, R. and Brierley, J. (1985) *Major Legal Systems in the World Today: An Introduction to the Comparative Study of Law*. 3rd ed. London: Stevens.

Davidson, P. (2009) *John Maynard Keynes*. Basingstoke: Palgrave Macmillan.

Davies, N. (1996) *Europe: A History*. Oxford: Oxford University Press.

Davies, P. and Freedland, M. (2007) *Towards a Flexible Labour Market: Labour Legislation and Regulation Since the 1990s*. Oxford: Oxford University Press.

Davila, A. and Elvira, M. (2007) *Best Human Resource Management Practices in Latin America*. Bradford: Emerald Group Publishing.

Davila, A. and Elvira, M. (2008) 'Theoretical approaches to best HRM practices in Latin America' in Davila, A. and Elvira, M. (eds) *Best Human Resource Management Practices in Latin America*. Oxford: Routledge.

Davis, D. (2013) *The Spirit of Hindu Law*. Cambridge: Cambridge University Press.

Davis, S. (2001) *Trade Unions in Russia and Ukraine 1985–95*. Basingstoke: Palgrave Macmillan.

Day, B., Brenner, A. and Ness, I. (2010) *The Encyclopedia of Strikes in American History*. New York: M.E. Sharpe.

Deacon, A. (2008) 'Employment' in Alcock, P., May, M., Rowlingson, K. (eds) *The Student's Companion to Social Policy*. Oxford: Blackwell.

Deakin, S., Lele, P. and Siems, M. (2007) 'The evolution of labour law: Calibrating and comparing regulatory regimes'. *International Labour Review* 146: 133–162.

Deakin, S. and Morris, G. (2012) *Labour Law*. 6th ed. Oxford: Hart.

Deakin, S. and Njoya, W. (2008) 'The legal framework of employment relations' in Blyton, P., Bacon, N., Fiorito, J. and Heery, E. (eds) *The SAGE Handbook of Industrial Relations*. London: Sage.

Deakin, S. and Wilkinson, F. (1991) 'Labour law, social security and economic inequality'. *Cambridge Journal of Economics* 15: 125–148.

Deakin, S. and Wilkinson, F. (2005) *The Law of the Labour Market: Industrialisation, Employment and Legal Evolution*. Oxford: Oxford University Press.

Deal, T. and Kennedy, A. (2000) *Corporate Cultures: The Rites and Rituals of Corporate Life*. Cambridge, MA: Perseus.

Debra, Y. and Budhwar, P. (2004) 'Conclusion: International competitive pressures and the challenges for HRM in developing countries' in Budhwar, P. and Debrah, Y. (eds) *Human Resource Management in Developing Countries*. London: Routledge.

De Cruz, P. (2007) *Comparative Law in a Changing World*. 3rd ed. London: Routledge-Cavendish.

Dedoussis, V. (1995) 'Simply a case of cultural barriers? The search for new perspectives in the transfer of Japanese management practices'. *Journal of Management Studies* 32 (6): 731–745.

Deeks, J. (1978) *Industrial Relations in New Zealand*. Victoria: Paul Longman.

De Groot, G-R. (1991) European education in the 21st century. Research Paper, Maastricht University.

Delbridge, R. (1998) *Life on the Line in Contemporary Manufacturing: The Workplace Experience of Lean Production and the 'Japanese' Model*. Oxford: Oxford University Press.

Delery, J. and Doty, D. (1996) 'Modes of theorising in strategic management: Tests of universalistic, contingency, and configurational performance predictions'. *Academy of Management Journal* 39 (4): 802–835.

Deming, W. (1986) *Out of the Crisis*. Cambridge, MA: MIT Press.

Deming, W. (2000) *The New Economics for Industry, Government, Education.* 2nd ed. Cambridge, MA: MIT Press.

Department of Industrial Relations (1997) *The 1995 Australian Workplace Industrial Relations Survey. Technical Report and Data Release.* Canberra: Australian Bureau of Statistics.

Department of Labour (2008) Review of the Employment Relationship Problem Resolution System. Report prepared for the Cabinet Economic Development Committee. Wellington.

Derber, M. (1980) 'Collective bargaining: The American approach to industrial democracy' in Lansbury, R. (ed.) *Democracy in the Workplace.* Melbourne: Longman Cheshire.

Derlien, H-U. and Peters, B. (2008) *The State at Work Vol. 1: Public Sector Employment in Ten Western Countries.* Cheltenham: Edward Elgar.

Devereaux, R. (2012) 'Occupy May Day protests across US as activists and unions link up'. *The Guardian* 2 May.

De Wit, B. and Meyer, R. (2010) *Strategy: Process, Content, Context: An International Perspective.* 4th ed. Australia: South-Western Cengage Learning.

Diallo, Y., Etienne, A. and Mehran, F. (2013) *Global Child Labour Trends.* Geneva: International Labour Organisation.

Dickman, M., Sparrow, P. and Brewster, C. (2008) *International HRM: Contemporary Issues in Europe.* 2nd ed. London: Routledge.

Diehl, P. (2001) *The Politics of Global Governance: International Organisations in an Interdependent World.* London: Lynne Rienner.

Dietz, G. (2004) 'Partnership and the development of trust in British workplaces'. *Human Resource Management Journal* 14 (1): 5–24.

Dietz, G., Wilkinson, G. and Redman, T. (2010) 'Involvement and participation' in Wilkinson, A., Bacon, N., Redman, T. and Snell, S. (eds) *The SAGE Handbook of Human Resource Management.* London: Sage.

DiMaggio, P. and Powell, W. (1991) *The New Institutionalism in Organizational Analysis.* London: University of Chicago Press.

Di Vittorio, A. (2006) *An Economic History of Europe: From Expansion to Development.* London: Routledge.

Dodds, A. (2011) 'Logics, thresholds, strategic power, and the promotion of liberalisation by governments: A case study from British higher education'. *Public Policy and Administration.* I First/doi:10.1177/0952076711407954.

Dodds, A. (2012) *Comparative Public Policy.* Basingstoke: Palgrave Macmillan.

Dodgson, M. (2009) Asia's national innovation systems: Institutional adaptability and rigidity in the face of global innovation challenges. Conference on Varieties of Asian Capitalism. Brisbane, Queensland, Australia. December.

Doeringer, P. and Piore, M. (1971) *Internal Labor Markets and Manpower Analysis.* Lexington, MA: D.C. Heath.

Doherty, N. and Guyler, M. (2008) *The Essential Guide to Workplace Mediation and Conflict Resolution: Rebuilding Working Relationships*. London: Kogan Page.

Dolan, R. and Worden, R. (eds.) (1994) *Japan: A Country Study – Labor Unions, Employment and Labor Relations*. Washington: Library of Congress.

Domsch, M. and Lidokhover, T. (2006) *Human Resource Management in Russia*. Aldershot: Ashgate.

Donnellon, A., Heckscher, C. and Donnellon, A. (1984) *The Post-Bureaucratic Organisation: New Perspectives on Organisational Change*. London: Sage.

Doogan, K. (2009) *New Capitalism?* Cambridge: Polity.

Doray, B. (1988) *From Taylorism to Fordism: A Rational Madness*. London: Free Association.

Dore, R. (1973) *British Factory, Japanese Factory: the Origins of National Diversity in Industrial Relations*. London: Allen and Unwin.

Dore, R., Lazonick, W. and O'Sullivan, M. (1999) 'Varieties of capitalism in the twentieth century'. *Oxford Review of Economic Policy* 15 (4): 102–120.

Dougherty, S. (2008) 'Labour regulation and employment dynamics at the state level in India'. Economics Department, Working Paper No. 624. Paris: OECD.

Douglas, L., Roberts, A. and Thompson, R. (1988) *Oral History: A Handbook*. Sydney: Allen and Unwin.

Doz, Y., Bartlett, C. and Hedlund, G. (1990) *Managing the Global Firm*. London: Routledge.

Dray, P. (2010) *There Is Power in a Union: The Epic Story of Labor in America*. New York: Doubleday.

Drobny, A. (1988) *Real Wages and Employment: Keynes, Monetarism and the Labour Market*. London: Routledge.

Drucker, P. (1968) *The Practice of Management*. London: Pan.

Duclos, J. (1974) *Bakounine et Marx: ombre et lumière*. Paris: Plon.

Du Gay, P. (2005) *The Values of Bureaucracy*. Oxford: Oxford University Press.

Dundon, T. and Gall, G. (2013) *Global Anti-Unionism: Nature, Dynamics, Trajectories and Outcomes*. Basingstoke: Palgrave Macmillan.

Dundon, T. and Rollinson, D. (2004) *Employment Relations in Non-Union Firms*. London: Routledge.

Dundon, T. and Rollinson, D. (2011) *Understanding Employment Relations*. 2nd ed. London: McGraw-Hill.

Dundon, T., Wilkinson, A., Marchington, M. and Ackers, P. (2004) 'The meanings and purpose of employee voice'. *International Journal of Human Resource Management* 15 (6): 1149–1170.

Dunkerley, J. (1984) *Rebellion in the Veins: Political Struggle in Bolivia 1952–82*. London: Verso.

Dunlop, J. (1958) *Industrial Relations Systems*. New York: Holt.

Dunlop. J. (1993) *Industrial Relations Systems*. Revised ed. Boston: Harvard Business School Press.

Dunlop, J. and Galenson, W. (1978) *Labor in the Twentieth Century*. London: Academic Press.

Dunning, J. and Lundan, S. (2008) *Multinational Enterprises and the Global Economy*. 2nd ed. Cheltenham: Edward Elgar.

Durrand, R. and Boyer, J-P. (1997) *After Fordism*. Basingstoke: Palgrave Macmillan.

Dutton, P. (2002) *Origins of the French Welfare State: The Struggle for Social Reform in France 1914–1947*. Cambridge: Cambridge University Press.

Dyer, L. and Reeves, T. (1995) 'HR strategies and firm performance: What do we know and where do we need to go'. *International Journal of Human Resource Management* 6: 656–670.

Eagleton, T. (1994) *Ideology*. New York: Longman.

Eaton, J. (2000) *Comparative Industrial Relations: An Introduction*. Cambridge: Polity Press.

Ebbinghaus, B. (2002) 'Trade unions' changing role: Membership erosion, organisational reform, and social partnership in Europe'. *Industrial Relations Journal* 33 (5): 465–483.

Ebbinghaus, B. and Manow, P. (eds) (2001) *Comparing Welfare Capitalism, Social Policy and Political Economy in Europe, Japan and the USA*. London: Routledge.

Ebbinghaus, B. and Visser, J. (1999) 'When institutions matter: Union growth and decline in Western Europe 1950–1995'. *European Sociological Review* 15 (2): 135–158.

Ebbinghaus, B. and Visser, J. (2000) *Trade Unions in Western Europe since 1945*. London: Macmillan Reference.

Ebell, M. and Haefke, C. (2006) Product market regulation and endogenous union formation. Discussion Paper No. 2222, Institute for the Study of Labor, Bonn.

Economic Intelligence Unit (2013) *Democracy Index 2013*. London: EIU.

Edfelt, R. (2009) *Global Comparative Management: A Functional Approach*. Los Angeles: Sage.

Edwards, P. (1976) *Conflict at Work: A Materialist Analysis of Workplace Relations*. Oxford: Blackwell.

Edwards, P. (1977) 'The Kerr-Siegel hypothesis of strikes and the isolated mass: A study of the falsification of sociological knowledge'. *Sociological Review* 25: 551–574.

Edwards, P. and Wajcman, J. (2005) *The Politics of Working Life*. Oxford: Oxford University Press.

Edwards, P. and Whitston, C. (1993) *Attending to Work: The Management of Attendance and Shopfloor Order*. Cambridge, MA: Blackwell Business.

Edwards, R. (1979) *Contested Terrain: The Transformation of the Workplace in the Twentieth Century*. London: Heinemann.

Edwards, T. and Rees, C. (eds) (2011) *International Human Resource Management: Globalization, National Systems and Multinational Companies.* 2nd ed. Harlow: Financial Times Prentice Hall.

Edwards, T., Edwards, P., Ferner, A., Marginson, P. and Tregaskis, O. (2007) 'The changing contours of multinationals in Britain'. Project report, University of Warwick Conference Papers.

Edwards, V. and Lawrence, P. (2000) *Management in Eastern Europe.* Basingstoke: Palgrave Macmillan.

Ehrenberg, R. and Smith, R. (2006) *Modern Labor Economics: Theory and Public Policy.* 9th ed. Boston: Pearson/Addison Wesley.

Eisner, M. and Meier, K. (1990) 'Presidential control versus bureaucratic power: Explaining the Reagan revolution in antitrust'. *American Journal of Political Science* 34 (1): 269–287.

Emery, F. and Thorsrud, E. (1976) *Form and Content in Industrial Democracy: Some Experiences from Norway and Other European Countries.* London: Tavistock Publications.

Erez, M., Kleinbeck, U. and Thierry, H. (2001) *Work Motivation in the Context of a Globalising Economy.* New Jersey: Erlbaum Associates.

Ertürk, I., Froud, J., Johal, S., Leaver, A. and Williams, K. (eds) (2008) *Financialisation at Work: Key Texts and Commentary.* London: Routledge.

Esping-Andersen, G. (1990) *The Three Worlds of Welfare Capitalism.* Cambridge: Polity.

Esping-Andersen, G. (2002) *Why We Need a New Welfare State.* New York: Oxford University Press.

Eurofound (2005) *European Industrial Relations Dictionary.* Luxembourg: Office for Official Publications of the European Communities.

Eurofound (2013a) Slovenia. Retrieved from http://www.search.eurofound.europa.eu, 2 April.

Eurofound (2013b) Romania. Retrieved from http://www.search.eurofound.europa. eu, 2 April.

Eurofound (2013c). Sweden. Retrieved from http://www.search.eurofound.europa.eu, 4 April.

Eurofound (2013d) Country Studies. Retrieved from http://www.Eurofoundation. europa.eu.eiro/2006/02/study, 13 September.

European Commission (2008) *Consolidated Version of the Treaty on the Functioning of the European Union.* Brussels: Official Journal of the European Union.

European Commission (2009) *European Disability Strategy 2010–2020.* Brussels: European Commission.

European Commission (2010) *New Skills for New Jobs.* Brussels: Education, Audiovisual and Culture Executive Agency.

European Commission (2012) *Industrial Relations in Europe*. Brussels: European Commission.

European Commission (2013) *Key Figures on Europe: Eurostat Yearbook*. Brussels: European Commission.

European Communities (2000) *Charter of Fundamental Rights of the European Union 2000*. Brussels: Official Journal of the European Communities.

European Foundation for the Improvement of Living and Working Conditions (2006) *Industrial Relations in the EU, Japan, US and other Global Economies, 2005–2006*. Dublin: Eurofound.

European Industrial Relations Observatory (2006) Employment relations in SMEs. Retrieved from http://www.eiro.eurofoundation.eu.int, 19 May.

European Presidents and Judges of Labour Courts (2005) The Use of Mediation/ Conciliation by Labour Courts. Thirteenth Meeting of European Labour Court Judges. September. Bologna.

European Trade Union Confederation (2013) News. Retrieved from http://www.etuc. org/, 20 February.

European Trade Union Institute (2010) Sweden. Retrieved from http://www.worker-participation.eu/Sweden, 4 December.

European Trade Union Institute (2012) Worker-Participation. Retrieved from http:// www.worker-participation.eu/National-Industrial-Relations/Countries/Germany/ Trade-Unions, 18 April.

European Union (1989) *Community Charter of the Fundamental Social Rights of Workers*. Brussels: European Communities.

Eurostat (2013) News Release: Euro-area unemployment rate at 12.1%, 30 April.

Ewing, K. (1998) 'The state and industrial relations: "collective laissez faire" revisited'. *Historical Studies in Industrial Relations* 5: 1–31.

Fairbrother, P. (1984) *All Those in Favour: The Politics of Union Democracy*. London: Pluto.

Fairbrother, P. and Yates, C. (eds) (2003) *Trade Unions in Renewal: A Comparative Study*. London: Continuum.

Fairiss, D. (2006) 'What do Unions do in Mexico?' Department of Economics, University of California Riverside, 27pp.

Faria, A., Ibarra-Colado, E. and Guedes, A. (2010) 'Internationalisation of management, neoliberalism and the Latin America challenge'. *Critical Perspectives on International Business* 6 (2/3): 97–115.

Farndale, E. and Brewster, C. (2005) 'In search of legitimacy: National professional associations and the professionalism of HR practitioners'. *Human Resource Management Journal* 15 (3): 33–48.

Farnham, D. (1974) 'The Association of Teachers in Technical Institutions: A case study of a white-collar organisation'. *International Review of Social History* XIX (3): 377–395.

Farnham, D. (1978) 'Sixty years of Whitleyism'. *Personnel Management* 10 (7) July: 29–32.

Farnham, D. (1993) *Employee Relations.* London: Institute of Personnel Management.

Farnham, D. (2008) 'Beatrice and Sidney Webb and the intellectual origins of British industrial relations'. *Employee Relations* 30 (5): 534–552.

Farnham, D. (2010a) *Human Resource Management in Context: Strategy, Insights and Solutions.* London: Chartered Institute of Personnel and Development.

Farnham, D. (2010b) 'Working life in the public organisation' in Fenwick, J. and McMillan, J. (eds) *Public Management in the Postmodern Era.* Cheltenham: Edward Elgar.

Farnham, D., Hondeghem, A. and Horton, S. (eds) (2005) *Staff Participation and Public Management Reform: Some International Comparisons.* Basingstoke: Palgrave Macmillan.

Farnham, D. and Horton, S. (eds) (2000) *Human Resources Flexibilities in the Public Services: International Perspectives.* London: Macmillan.

Farnham, D., Horton, S., Hondeghem, A. and Barlow, J. (eds) (1996) *New Public Managers in Europe: Public Servants in Transition.* London: Macmillan.

Farnham, D. and Pimlott, J. (1979) *Understanding Industrial Relations.* London: Cassell.

Farnham, D. and Pimlott, J. (1995) *Understanding Industrial Relations.* 5th ed. London: Cassell.

Farnham, D. and White, G. (2011) 'Rewarding leaders in the UK public services: What's happening to executive pay?' *International Journal of Employment Studies* 19 (1): 26–49.

Ferguson, N. (2009) *The Ascent of Money: A Financial History of the World.* London: Penguin Books.

Ferner, A. (2009) 'HRM in multinational companies' in Wilkinson, A., Bacon, N., Redman, T. and Snell, S. (eds) *The SAGE Handbook of Human Resource Management.* London: Sage.

Ferner, A. and Hyman, R. (eds) (1992) *Industrial Relations in the New Europe.* Oxford: Blackwell.

Ferner, A. and Hyman, R. (eds) (1994) *New Frontiers in European Industrial Relations.* Oxford: Blackwell.

Fernie, S. and Metcalf, D. (eds) (2005) *Trade Unions: Resurgence or Demise?* London: Routledge.

Fey, C., Morgulis-Yakushev, S., Park, J. and Björkman, I. (2009) 'Opening the black box of the relationship between HRM practices and firm performance: A comparison of MNE subsidiaries in the USA, Finland, and Russia'. *Journal of International Business Studies* 40: 690–712.

Fineman, S. (2003) *Understanding Emotion at Work.* London: Sage.

Fink, A. (1995) *The Survey Handbook*. Thousand Oaks, CA: Sage.

Finkin, M. (2006) 'Comparative labour law' in Reimann, M. and Zimmermann, R. (eds) *The Oxford Handbook of Comparative Law*. Oxford: Oxford University Press.

Fiorito, J. (2004) 'Union renewal and the organising model in the United Kingdom'. *Labor Studies Journal* 29 (2): 21–53.

Fiorito, J., Gramm, L. and Hendricks, W. (1991) 'Union structural choices' in Strauss, G., Gallager, D. and Fiorito, J. (eds) *The State of Unions*. Madison, WI: Industrial Relations Research Association.

Fiorito, J. and Jarley, P. (2008) 'Trade union morphology' in Blyton, P., Bacon, N., Fiorito, J. and Heery, E. (eds) *The SAGE Handbook of Industrial Relations*. London: Sage.

Fiorito, J., Jarley, P. and Delaney, J. (2001) 'National unions as organisations'. *Research in Personnel and Human Resource Management* 20: 231–268.

Fishman, C. (2006) *The Walmart Effect: How the World's Most Powerful Company Really Works – And How It's Transforming the American Economy*. New York: Penguin Press.

Flanagan, R. (1999) 'Macroeconomic performance and collective bargaining'. *Journal of Economic Literature* 37 (3): 1150–1175.

Flanagan, R. (2008) 'The changing structure of collective bargaining' in Blyton, P., Bacon, N., Fiorito, J. and Heery, E. (eds) *The SAGE Handbook of Industrial Relations*. London: Sage.

Flanders, A. (1964) *The Fawley Productivity Agreements: A Case Study of Management and Collective Bargaining*. London: Faber.

Flanders, A. (1968) 'Collective bargaining: A theoretical analysis'. *British Journal of Industrial Relations* 6 (1): 1–26.

Flanders, A. (1970) *Management and Unions: The Theory and Reform of Industrial Relations*. London: Faber.

Flecha, R. and Santa Cruz, I. (2011) 'Cooperation for economic success: The Mondragon case'. *Analyse and Kritik* 33 (1): 157–170.

Fleming, P. (2007) 'Sexuality, power and resistance in the workplace'. *Organisation Studies* 28 (2): 239–256.

Fletcher, B. and Gaspasin, F. (2008) *Solidarity Divided: The Crisis in Organised Labor and a New Path toward Social Justice*. Berkeley, CA: University of California Press.

Flyvbjerg, B. (2001) *Making Social Science Matter: Why Social Inquiry Fails and How It Can Succeed Again*. Cambridge: Cambridge University Press.

Foerster, A. (2001) 'Confronting the dilemmas of organising: Obstacles and innovations at the AFL-CIO's Organising Institute' in Turner, L., Katz, H. and Hurd, R. (eds) *Rekindling the Movement: Labor's Quest for Relevance in the 21st Century*. Ithaca: ILR Press.

Fombrun, C., Tichy, N. and Devanna, M. (1984) *Strategic Human Resource Management*. New York: Wiley.

Foner, P. (1997) *History of the Labor Movement in the United States Vol. 4. The Industrial Workers of the World 1905–1917*. New York: International Publishers.

Fosh, P. (1993) 'Membership participation in workplace unionism: The possibility of union renewal'. *British Journal of Industrial Relations* 31 (4): 577–592.

Fosh, P., Morris, H., Martin, R., Smith, P. and Undy, R. (1993) 'Union autonomy, a terminal case in the UK? A comparison with the approach in other Western European countries and the USA'. *Employee Relations* 15 (3): 3–21.

Foucault, M. (1991) *Discipline and Punish: The Birth of the Prison*. London: Penguin.

Foulkes, F. (1980) *Personnel Policies in Large Non-Union Companies*. Englewood Cliffs, NJ: Prentice Hall.

Fox, A. (1966) *Industrial Sociology and Industrial Relations: An Assessment of the Contribution Which Industrial Sociology Can Make Towards Understanding and Resolving Some of the Problems Now Being Considered by the Royal Commission*. London: HMSO.

Fox, A. (1974) *Beyond Contract: Work, Trust and Power Relations*. London: Faber and Faber.

Fox, A. (1985) *History and Heritage: The Social Origins of the British Industrial Relations System*. London: Allen and Unwin.

Franklin, A. and Gale, D. (2007) *Understanding Financial Crises*. Oxford: Oxford University Press.

Freedland, M. (1976) *The Contract of Employment*. Oxford: Oxford University Press.

Freeman, R. (2002) *Institutional Differences and Economic Performance Among OECD Countries*. London: Centre for the Economics of Education.

Freeman, R. (2012) 'The workplace employment relations surveys in Britain'. Retrieved from http://www.natcen.ac.uk, 6 July 2012.

Freeman, R. and Medoff, J. (1984) *What Do Unions Do?* New York: Basic Books.

Frege, C. (1999a) *Social Partnership at Work: Workplace Relations in Post-unification Germany*. London: Routledge.

Frege, C. (1999b) 'Transferring labor institutions to emerging economies: The case of East Germany'. *Industrial Relations* 38 (4): 459–481.

Frege, C. (2005) 'Varieties of industrial relations research: Take-over, convergence or divergence?' *British Journal of Industrial Relations* 43 (2): 179–207.

Frege, C. (2007) *Employment Research and State Traditions: A Comparative History of Britain, Germany and the United States*. Oxford: Oxford University Press.

Frege, C. and Kelly, J. (eds) (2013) *Comparative Employment Relations in the Global Economy*. Abingdon: Routledge.

French, W. and Bell, C. (1990) *Organisation Development: Behavioral Science Interventions for Organisation Improvement*. 4th ed. Englewood Cliffs, NJ: Prentice Hall.

Frenkel, S., Korczynski, M., Shire, K. and Tam, M. (eds) (1999) *On the Front Line: Organisation of Work in the Information Economy*. Ithaca: Cornell University Press.

Frenkel, S. and Peetz, D. (1998) 'Globalisation and industrial relations in East Asia'. *Industrial Relations* 37 (3): 282–310.

Friedman, G. (2013) 'The United States' in Frege, C. and Kelly, J. (eds) *Comparative Employment Relations in the Global Economy*. Abingdon: Routledge.

Friedman, M. (1962) *Capitalism and Freedom*. Chicago: Chicago University Press.

Friedman, M. (1968) 'The role of monetary policy'. *American Economic Review* 58: 1–17.

Frost, A. (2001) 'Reconceptualising local union responses to workplace restructuring in North America'. *British Journal of Industrial Relations* 39 (4): 539–564.

Fulcher, J. (2004) *Capitalism: A Very Short Introduction*. Oxford: Oxford University Press.

Fulton, L. (2011) *Worker Representation in Europe*. London: Labour Research Department.

Fulton, L. (2013) *Health and Safety Representation in Europe*. London: Labour Research Department.

Furnham, A. (2011) *Managing People in a Downturn*. Basingstoke: Palgrave Macmillan.

Galbraith, J. (1975) *The Great Crash 1929*. 3rd ed. Harmondsworth: Penguin.

Galenson, W. (1994) *Trade Union Growth and Decline: An International Study*. New York: Praeger.

Galer, M. (2008) *Digital Photography*. London: Elsevier.

Gall, G. (2003a) 'Marxism and industrial relations' in Ackers, P. and Wilkinson, A. *Understanding Work and Employment: Industrial Relations in Transition*. Oxford: Oxford University Press.

Gall, G. (ed.) (2003b) *Union Organising: Campaigning for Trade Union Recognition*. London: Routledge.

Gall, G. (2006) *Union Recognition: Organising and Bargaining Outcomes*. London: Routledge.

Gall, G., Wilkinson, A. and Hurd, R. (eds) (2011) *The International Handbook of Labour Unions: Responses to Neo-Liberalism*. Edward Elgar.

Gallie, D. (ed.) (2007) *Employment Regimes and the Quality of Work*. Oxford: Oxford University Press.

Gamble, A. (1988) *The Free Economy and the Strong State*. Basingstoke: Macmillan Education.

Gamble, A., Ludlam, S., Taylor, A. and Wood, S. (eds) (2007) *Labour, the State, Social Movements and the Challenge of Neo-Liberal Globalisation*. Manchester: Manchester University Press.

Garibaldi, P. (2006) *Personnel Economics in Imperfect Labour Markets*. Oxford: Oxford University Press.

Garibaldi, P., Pacelli, L. and Borgarello, A. (2003) Employment protection legislation and the size of firms. Innocenzo Gasparini Institute for Economic Research. Working Paper 247.

Gatenby, M., Rees, C., Soane, E. and Truss, C. (2010) *Employee Engagement in Context: An Interim Report*. London: Chartered Institute of Personnel and Development.

Gazzane, S. (2006) *Health and Safety Representation of Employees in EU Countries*. Brussels: European Trade Union Institute.

Gennard, J. (1990) *A History of the National Graphical Association*. London: Unwin Hyman.

Gennard, J. and Bain, P. (1995) *A History of the Society of Graphical and Allied Trades*. London: Psychology Press.

Gennard, J. and Hayward. J. (2008) *A History of the Graphical, Paper and Media Union*. London: GPMU.

Gennard, J. and Kelly, J. (1997) 'The unimportance of labels: The diffusion of the personnel/HRM function'. *Industrial Relations Journal* 28 (4): 27–42.

Gernignon, B., Odero, A. and Guido, H. (1998) *ILO Principles Regarding the Right to Strike*. Geneva: International Labour Office.

Gertner, J. (2006) 'What is a living wage?' *New York Times* 15 January.

Ghere, R. and Frederickson, H. (2005) *Ethics in Public Management*. Armonk, New York: M.E. Sharpe.

Ghose, A. and Majid, N. (2008) *The Global Employment Challenge*. Geneva: International Labour Office.

Gill, C. (1985) *Work, Unemployment and the New Technology*. Cambridge: Polity.

Gill, C. and Krieger, H. (1999) 'Direct and representative participation in Europe: Recent survey evidence'. *International Journal of Human Resource Management* 10 (4): 572–591.

Gimpelson, V., Kapeliushnikov, R. and Lukiyanova, A. (2008) Regional variation in employment protection enforcement and labour market performance. Presentation to OECD. Paris.

Godard, J. (2004a) 'The new institutionalism, capitalist diversity, and industrial relations' in Kaufman, B. (ed.) *Theoretical Perspectives on Work and the Employment Relationship* Urbana-Champaign: IL: Industrial Relations Research Association.

Godard, J. (2004b) *Trade Union Recognition: Statutory Unfair Labour Practices Regimes in the USA and Canada*. London: Department of Trade and Industry.

Godard, J. (2008) 'An institutional environments approach to IR?' in Whalen, C. (ed.) *Industrial Relations as an Academic Enterprise: Roads to Revitalisation?* Northampton, MA: Edward Elgar.

Godard, J. (2011) *Industrial Relations, the Economy, and Society*. 4th ed. Toronto: Captus Press.

Goetschy, J. (1998) 'France: The limits of reform' in Ferner, A. and Hyman, R. (eds) *Changing Industrial Relations in Europe*. Oxford: Blackwell.

Goetschy, J. and Jobert, A. (2011) 'Employment relations in France' in Bamber, G., Lansbury, R. and Wailes, N. *International and Comparative Employment Relations: Globalisation and Change*. 5th ed. London: Sage.

Goffman, E. (1959). *The Presentation of Self in Everyday Life*. Garden City, New York: Doubleday.

Gold, M. (2009) *Employment Policy in the European Union: Origins, Themes and Prospects*. Basingstoke: Palgrave Macmillan.

Gold, J. (ed.) (2010) *Human Resource Development: Theory and Practice*. Basingstoke: Palgrave Macmillan.

Goldberg, A. (1996) *New Deal Liberal*. New York: Oxford University Press.

Goldberg, P. and Pavcnik, N. (2007) 'Distributional effects of globalisation in developing countries'. *Journal of Economic Literature* 45 (1): 39–82.

Goldfield, M. (1987) *The Decline of Organized Labor in the United States*. Chicago: University of Chicago Press.

Goldthorpe, J. (1974) 'Industrial relations in Britain: A critique of reformism'. *Politics and Society* 4 (4): 419–452.

Goldthorpe, J. and McKnight, A. (2004) The economic basis of social class. Centre for Analysis of Social Exclusion, Paper 80. London School of Economics and Political Science. London.

Goldthorpe, J., Lockwood, D., Bechhofer, F. and Platt, J. (1968a) *The Affluent Worker: Industrial Attitudes and Behaviour*. London: Cambridge University Press.

Goldthorpe, J., Lockwood, D., Bechhofer, F. and Platt, J. (1968b) *The Affluent Worker: Political Attitudes and Behaviour*. London: Cambridge University Press.

Goldthorpe, J., Lockwood, D., Bechhofer, F. and Platt, J. (1969) *The Affluent Worker in the Class Structure*. London: Cambridge University Press.

Gollan, P. (2003) Faces of non-union representation in the UK: Management strategies, processes and practice. Paper presented to Industrial Relations Association World Congress. Berlin.

Gomez, R., Lipset, S-M. and Meltz, N. (2001) Frustrated demand for unionisation: The case of the United States and Canada. *Proceedings of the 53rd Annual Meeting*. Champaign, IL: Industrial Relations Research Association.

Goodrich, C. (1920) *The Frontier of Control*. New York: Harcourt, Brace and Howe.

Gospel, H. (2009) 'Human resources management' in Wilkinson, A., Bacon, N., Redman, T. and Snell, S. (eds) *The SAGE Handbook of Human Resource Management*. London: Sage.

Gospel, H. (2011) *Markets, Firms and the Management of Labour in Modern Britain*. Cambridge: Cambridge University Press.

Goss, D. (1988) 'Social harmony and the small firm'. *Sociological Review* 36 (1): 114–132.

Goss, D. (1997) *Human Resource Management: The Basics*. London: International Thomson Business Press.

Goubert, P. (1991) *The Course of French History*. London: Routledge.

Gramsci, A. (1957) *The Modern Prince and other Writings*. New York: International Publishers.

Grant, R. (1996) 'Toward a knowledge-based view of the firm'. *Strategic Management Journal* 17 (2): 109–122.

Grant, W. (1985) *The Political Economy of Corporatism*. London: Macmillan.

Grant, W. (2002) *Economic Policy in Britain*. Basingstoke: Palgrave Macmillan.

Graverson, G. and Lansbury, R. (1988) *New Technology and Industrial Relations in Scandinavia*. Avebury: Avebury Press.

Gray, J. (1996) *After Social Democracy: Politics, Capitalism and the Common Life*. London: Demos.

Gray, J. (2002) *False Dawn: The Delusions of Global Capitalism*. London: Granta.

Great Places to Work (2012) Retrieved from http://www.greatplacetowork.com/, 15 July.

Greeley, J. (1856) *The Social Problem*. Boston: Shepherd, Clark.

Green, F. (2006) *Demanding Work: The Paradox of Job Quality in the Affluent Economy*. Princeton, NJ: Princeton University Press.

Green, F. and McIntosh, S. (2001) 'The intensification of work in Europe'. *Labour Economics* 8 (2): 291–308.

Greenberg, J. and Giacalone, R. (1997) *Antisocial Behavior in Organisations*. London: Sage.

Greene, A. (2003) 'Women and industrial relations' in Ackers, P. and Wilkinson, A. (eds) *Understanding Work and Employment*. Oxford: Oxford University Press.

Greenspan, A. (2007) *The Age of Turbulence*. New York: Penguin.

Greenwald, B. (1986) 'Adverse selection in the labour market'. *Review of Economic Studies* 53 (3): 325–347.

Grey, C. (2009) *A Very Short, Fairly Interesting and Reasonably Cheap Book About Studying Organisations*. 2nd ed. London: Sage.

Grey, C. and Willmott, H. (2005) *Critical Management Studies: A Reader*. Oxford: Oxford University Press.

Grimshaw, D. and Rubbery, J. (2003) 'Economics and industrial relations' in Ackers, P. and Wilkinson, A. (eds) *Understanding Work and Employment: Industrial Relations in Transition*. Oxford: Oxford University Press.

Grimshaw, D., Ward, G., Rubery, J. and Beynon, H. (1999) 'Organisations and the transformation of the internal labour market'. Paper presented at the 21st Conference of the International Working Party on Labour Market Segmentation. Bremen, Germany.

Groom, B. (2012) 'Qinetiq to derecognise unions'. *Financial Times* 21 February.

Gross, J. (2010) *A Shameful Business: The Case for Human Rights in the American Workplace*. Ithaca: Cornell University.

Grübler, A. (1998) *Technology and Global Change*. Cambridge: Cambridge University Press.

Guest, D. (1987) 'Human resource management and industrial relations'. *Journal of Management Studies* 24 (5): 503–521.

Guest, D. (1997) 'Human resource management and performance: A review and research agenda'. *International Journal of Human Resource Management* 8 (3): 263–276.

Guest, D. and Conway, N. (2002) *Pressure at Work and the Psychological Contract.* London: Chartered Institute of Personnel and Development.

Guest, D. and Conway, N. (2005) *Managing Change: The Role of the Psychological Contract.* London: Chartered Institute of Personnel and Development.

Gueutal, H. and Stone, D. (2005) *Brave New World of eHR: Human Resources Management in the Digital Age.* San Francisco: Jossey-Bass.

Guglielmo, M. (2011) 'Understanding trade union cultures'. *Industrielle Beziehungen* 18 (4): 336–345.

Guillebaud, C. (1969) *The Role of the Arbitrator in Industrial Wage Disputes.* London: James Nesbet and Co. Ltd.

Gumbrell-McCormick, R. (2008) 'International actors and international regulation' in Blyton, P., Bacon, N., Fiorito, J. and Heery, E. (eds) *The SAGE Handbook of Industrial Relations.* London: Sage.

Gunnigle, P., McMahon, G. and Fitzgerald, G. (1999) *Industrial Relations in Ireland: Theory and Practice.* Revised ed. Dublin: Gill and Macmillan.

Gwatney, J., Lawson, R. and Holcombe, R. (1998) *The Size and Functions of Government and Economic Growth.* Washington, DC: Congress of the United States.

Haak, R. and Pudelko, M. (eds) (2005) *Japanese Management: The Search for a New Balance Between Continuity and Change.* Basingstoke: Palgrave Macmillan.

Haimson, L. and Tilly, C. (2002) *Strikes, Wars, and Revolutions in an International Perspective: Strike Waves in the Late Nineteenth and Early Twentieth Centuries.* Cambridge: Cambridge University Press.

Hakim, C (1992) *Research Design: Strategies and Choices in the Design of Social Research.* London: Routledge.

Hakim, C. (1996) *Key Issues in Women's Work: Female Heterogeneity and the Polarisation of Women's Employment.* London: Athlone Press.

Hála, J. (2007) Economically Dependent Workers in the Czech Republic. European Industrial Relations Observatory. Retrieved from http://www.eurofound.europa.eu/eiro/2007/02, 15 December 2012.

Hales, C. (2001) *Managing through Organisation: The Management Process, Forms of Organisation and the Work of Managers.* 2nd ed. London: Thomson.

Hall, E. (1959) *How Cultures Collide.* Garden City, New York: Doubleday.

Hall, E. (1976) 'How cultures collide'. *Psychology Today* 10 (2) 66–74.

Hall, P. (1986) *Governing the Economy.* Oxford: Oxford University Press.

Hall, P. (1993) 'Policy paradigms, social learning, and the state: The case of economic policymaking in Britain'. *Comparative Politics* 25 (3): 275–296.

Hall, P. and Soskice, D. (eds) (2001) *Varieties of Capitalism: The Institutional Foundations of Comparative Advantage*. Oxford: Oxford University Press.

Hall, R. and Wailes, N. (2009) 'International and comparative Human Resource Management' in Wilkinson, A., Bacon, N., Redman, T. and Snell, S. (eds) *The SAGE Handbook of Human Resource Management*. London: Sage.

Hallaq, W. (2009) *An Introduction to Islamic Law*. Cambridge: Cambridge University Press.

Haltiwanger, J., Scarpetta, S. and Schweiger, H. (2008) Assessing Job flows across-countries: The role of industry, firm size and regulations. NBER Working Paper 13920. Washington.

Hamann, K. and Kelly, J. (2008) 'Varieties of capitalism and industrial relations' in Blyton, P., Bacon, N., Fiorito, J. and Heery, E. (eds) *The Sage Handbook of Industrial Relations*. London: Sage.

Hammersley, G., Johnson, J. and Morris, D. (2007) *The Influence of Legal Representation at Employment Tribunals on Case Outcomes. Employment Relations Research Series No. 84.*

Hammersley, M. and Atkinson, R. (1995) *Ethnography: Principles in Practice*. London: Routledge.

Hancké, B. (ed.) (2009) *Debating Varieties of Capitalism: A Reader*. Oxford: Oxford University Press.

Handel, M. and Levine, D. (2004) 'Editor's introduction: The effects of new work practices on workers'. *Industrial Relations* 43 (10): 1–43.

Handy, C. (1984) *The Future of Work: A Guide to a Changing Society*. Oxford: Blackwell.

Hannan, M. (1995) 'Labor unions' in Carroll, G. and Hannan, M. (eds) *Organisations in Industry: Strategy, Structure, and Selection*. Oxford: Oxford University Press.

Harbison, F. and Myers, C. (1959) *Management in the Industrial World: An International Analysis*. New York: McGraw Hill.

Hardy, C. and Clegg, S. (1999) *Studying Organisation: Theory and Method*. London: Sage.

Harley, B. (1999) 'The myth of empowerment: Work organisation, hierarchy and autonomy in contemporary Australian workplaces'. *Work, Employment and Society* 13 (1): 41–66.

Harris, P. (2007) *An Introduction to Law*. Cambridge: Cambridge University Press.

Hartog, J. and Teulings, C. (1998) *Corporatism or Competition? Labour Contracts, Institutions and Wage Structures in International Comparison*. Cambridge: Cambridge University Press.

Harzing, A-W. and Pinnington, A. (eds) (2011) *International Human Resource Management*. London: Sage.

Hatch, A. and Cunliffe, A. (2012) *Organization Theory: Modern, Symbolic and Postmodern Perspectives*. 3rd ed. Oxford: Oxford University Press.

Hathaway, O. (2001) 'Path dependence in the law: The course and pattern of legal change in a common law system'. *Iowa Law Review* 86: 601–664.

Hawkins, K. (1972) *Conflict and Change: Aspects of Industrial Relations.* London: Holt, Rinehart and Winston.

Hayek, F. (1944) *The Road to Serfdom.* London: Routledge and Kegan Paul.

Hayek, F. (1960) *The Constitution of Liberty.* Chicago: Chicago University Press.

Hayward, J. (1980) *Trade Unions and Politics in Western Europe.* London: Cass.

Hazama, H. (1997) *History of Labour Management in Japan.* London: Macmillan.

Hebdon, R. and Sung, C. (2013) 'A theory of workplace conflict development: From grievances to strikes' in Gall, G. (ed.) (2013) *New Forms and Expressions of Conflict at Work.* Basingstoke: Palgrave Macmillan.

Hecht, G. (2009) *The Radiance of France: Nuclear Power and National Identity after World War II.* New ed. Cambridge, MA: MIT Press.

Heery, E. (2003) 'Trade unions and industrial relations' in Ackers, P. and Wilkinson, A. (eds) *Understanding Work and Employment: Industrial Relations in Transition.* Oxford: Oxford University Press.

Heery, E. (2005) 'Sources of change in trade unions'. *Work, Employment and Society* 19 (1): 91–106.

Heery, E. (2008) 'System and change in industrial relations analysis' in Blyton, P., Bacon, N., Fiorito, J. and Heery, E. (eds) *The SAGE Handbook of Industrial Relations.* London: Sage.

Heery, E., Delbridge, R., Salmon, J. Simms, M. and Stewart, P. (2002) 'Global labour? The transfer of the organising model to the United Kingdom' in Debrah, Y. and Smith, I. (eds) *Globalisation, Employment and the Workplace.* Basingstoke: Palgrave Macmillan.

Hefeker, C. and Neugart, M. (2007) Labor market regulation and the legal system. CESifo Working Paper No. 2041. July.

Heidenheimer, A., Heclo, H. and Adams, T. (1990) *Comparative Public Policy: The Politics of Social Change in America, Europe and Japan.* New York: St Martin's Press.

Heilbroner, R. and Milberg, W. (2012) *The Making of Economic Society.* 13th ed. New Jersey: Pearson Education.

Held, D. (1983) 'Introduction: Central perspectives on the modern state' in Held, D. (ed.) *States and Societies.* Oxford: Blackwell.

Helm, D. and Tindall, T. (2009) 'The evolution of infrastructure and utility ownership and its implications'. *Oxford Review of Economic Policy* 25 (3): 411–434.

Hendricks, W. and Kahn, L. (1984) 'The demand for labor market structure'. *Journal of Labor Economics* 2 (3): 412–438.

Hensman, R. (2011) *Workers, Unions, and Global Capitalism: Lessons from India.* New York: Columbia University Press.

Herbst, J. (1965) *The German Historical School in American Scholarship: A Study in the Transfer of Culture.* Ithaca: Cornell University Press.

Heritage Foundation (2013) Country Rankings. Retrieved from http://www.heritage .org/index, 1 September.

Hertz, N. (2001) *The Silent Takeover: Global Capitalism and the Death of Democracy.* London: Heinemann.

Herzberg, F., Snyderman, B. and Mausner, B. (1959) *The Motivation to Work.* New York: Wiley.

Hessels, J. and Terjesen, S. (2010) 'Resource dependency and institutional theory perspectives on direct and indirect export choices'. *Small Business Economics* 34 (2): 203–220.

Hibbs, D. (1976) 'Industrial conflict in advanced industrial societies'. *The American Political Science Review* 70 (4): 1033–1058.

Hibbs, D. and Locking, H. (1995) 'Solidarity wage policies and industrial productivity in Sweden'. *Nordic Journal of Political Economy* 22: 95–108.

Hicks, J. (1932) *The Theory of Wages.* London: Macmillan.

Hicks, J. (1963) *The Theory of Wages.* 2nd ed. London: Macmillan.

Hickson, D., Hinings, C., Macmillan, C. and Schwitter, J. (1974) 'The culture-free context of organisational structure: A tri-national comparison'. *Sociology* 8: 59–80.

Hill, E. (2009) 'The Indian industrial relations system: Struggling to address the dynamics of a global economy'. *The Journal of Industrial Relations* 51 (3): 395–410.

Hirata, J. (2011) *Happiness, Ethics and Economics.* New York: Routledge.

Hirsch, P. (1987) *Pack Your Own Parachute: How to Survive Mergers, Takeovers, and Other Corporate Disasters.* Reading, MA: Addison-Wesley.

Hirsch, B. (2004) Match bias: When does it matter? When does it not? Labor Markets and Human Capital Session, Western Economic Association Meetings, Vancouver, 30 June–3 July.

Hirschman, A. (1991) *The Rhetoric of Reaction: Perversity, Futility, Jeopardy.* Cambridge, MA: Belknap Press.

Hirst, P., Thompson, G. and Bromley, S. (2009) *Globalisation in Question.* 3rd ed. Cambridge: Polity.

Hochschild, A. (2012) *The Managed Heart: Commercialisation of Human Feeling.* Updated ed. Berkeley, CA: University of California Press.

Hodson, R. (1995) 'Worker resistance: An underdeveloped concept in the sociology of work'. *Economic and Industrial Democracy* 16 (1): 79–110.

Hodson, R. (2001) 'Disorganised, unilateral, and participative organisations: New insights from the ethnographic literature'. *Industrial Relations* 40 (2): 204–230.

Hoell, R. (2004) 'How employee commitment affects union commitment'. *Journal of Labor Research* 25 (2): 267–277.

Hofstede, G. (1993) *Culture's Consequences: Comparing Values, Behaviors, Institutions, and Organisations across Nations.* London: Sage Publications.

Hofstede, G. H., Minkov, M. and Hofstede, G. J. (2010) *Cultures and Organisations: Software of the Mind: International Cooperation and its Importance for Survival.* 3rd ed. New York: McGraw-Hill.

Holcomb, J. and Sethi, S. (1992) 'Corporate and executive criminal liability: Appropriate standards, remedies and managerial responses'. *Business in the Contemporary World* IV (3): 81–105.

Holden, N., Carr, J. and Cooper, C. (1998) *Dealing with the New Russia: Management Cultures in Collision.* Chichester: Wiley.

Hollinshead, G. (2010) *International and Comparative Human Resource Management.* London: McGraw-Hill Higher Education.

Hollis, M. (1994) *The Philosophy of Social Science.* Cambridge: Cambridge University Press.

Hopper, K. and Hopper, W. (2007) *The Puritan Gift: Triumph, Collapse and Revival of an American Dream.* London: I. B. Tauris.

Hoque, K. and Noon, M. (2004) 'Equal opportunities policy and practice in Britain: Evaluating the "empty shell" hypothesis'. *Work, Employment and Society* 18 (3): 481–506.

Hosseini, S. (2009) 'Global complexities and the rise of the global justice movement: A new notion of justice'. *The Global Studies Journal* 2 (3): 15–36.

House, R., Hanges, P., Javidan, M., Dorfman, P., Gupta, V. (2004) *Leadership Culture and Organizations: The GLOBE Study of 62 Societies.* Thousand Oaks, CA: Sage.

House of Representatives Standing Committee on Employment, Education and Workplace Relations (2000) *Shared Endeavours: An Inquiry into Employee Share Ownership in Australia.* Canberra: Commonwealth of Australia Parliament.

Howell, C. (2003) 'Varieties of capitalism: And then there was one?' *Comparative Politics* 36 (1): 103–124.

Howell, C. (2005) *Trade Unions and the State: The Construction of Industrial Relations Institutions in Britain 1800–2000.* Princeton: Princeton University Press.

Howell, C. (2006) New democratic trends in China: Reforming the all-China Federation of Trade Unions. Incomes Data Services Working Paper 263. Brighton: Incomes Data Services.

Hoxie, R. (1917) *Trade Unionism in the United States.* New York: Appleton and Co.

Huber, E. and Stephens, J. (2001) *Development and Crisis of the Welfare State: Parties and Policies in Global Markets.* Chicago: Chicago University Press.

Hudson, K. (1970) *Working to Rule: Railway Workshop Rules – a Study of Industrial Discipline.* Bath: Adams and Dart.

Huffschmid, J. (2006) *Economic Policy for a Social Europe: A Critique of Neo-Liberalism and Proposals for Alternatives.* Basingstoke: Palgrave Macmillan.

Hughes, J. (1976) *Trade Union Structure and Government. Part 1, Structure and Development.* London: HMSO.

Hughes, S. (2011) *International Labour Organisation (ILO): Coming in from the Cold.* London: Routledge.

Hughes, J. and Pollins, H. (1973) *Trade Unions in Great Britain.* Newton Abbot: David and Charles.

Hurd, R. (2004) 'The rise and fall of the organising model in the US' in Harcourt, M. and. Wood, G. (eds) *Trade Unions and Democracy: Strategies and Perspectives.* Manchester: Manchester University Press.

Hurd, R., Wilkinson, A. and Gall, G. (2011) *The International Handbook of Labour Unions: Responses to Neo-Liberalism.* Cheltenham: Edward Elgar.

Huselid, M., Beatty, R. and Becker, B. (2005) *The Workforce Scorecard: Managing Human Capital to Execute Strategy.* London: McGraw-Hill.

Hutchinson, S. and Purcell, J. (2003) *Bringing Policies to Life: The Vital Role of Front Line Managers in People Management.* London: Chartered Institute of Personnel and Development.

Huws, U. and Podro, S. (2012) *Outsourcing and the Fragmentation of Employment Relations: The Challenges Ahead.* London: Advisory Conciliation and Arbitration Service.

Hyman, R. (1975) *Industrial Relations: A Marxist Introduction.* London: Macmillan.

Hyman, R. (1987) 'Strategy or structure: Capital, labour and control'. *Work, Employment and Society* 1 (1): 35–55.

Hyman, R. (2001) *Understanding European Trade Unionism: Between Market, Class and Society.* London: Sage.

Hyman, R. (2004) 'Is industrial relations theory always ethnocentric?' in Kaufman, B. (ed.) *Theoretical Perspectives on Work and the Employment Relationship.* Champagne, IL: Industrial Relations Research Association.

Hyman, R. (2005) 'Trade unions and the politics of European integration'. *Economic and Industrial Democracy* 26 (1): 9–40.

Hyman, R. (2008) 'The state in industrial relations' in Blyton, P., Bacon, N., Fiorito, J. and Heery, E. (eds) *The SAGE Handbook of Industrial Relations.* London: Sage.

Hyman, R. (2009) 'How can we study industrial relations comparatively?' in Blanpain, R. (ed.) *The Modernisation of Labour Law and Industrial Relations in a Comparative Perspective. Bulletin of Comparative Labour Relations.* New York: Wolters Kluwer.

Hyman, R. and Brough, I. (1975) *Social Values and Industrial Relations: A Study of Fairness and Equality.* Oxford: Blackwell.

Hyman, R. and Ferner, A. (1998) *Changing Industrial Relations in Europe.* 2nd ed. Oxford: Blackwell.

Hyman, J. and Mason, B. (1995) *Managing Employee Involvement and Participation.* London: Sage.

Ichniowski, C., Kochan, T., Levine, D., Olson, C. and Strauss, G. (1996) 'What works at work: Overview and assessment'. *Industrial Relations* 35 (3): 299–333.

Ietto-Gillies, G. (2005) *Transnational Corporations and International Production: Concepts, Theories and Effects*. Cheltenham: Edgar Elgar Publishing.

Incomes Data Services (1991) *Industrial Relations: European Management Guides*. London: Institute of Personnel Management.

Income Data Services (2013) *Trade Unions*. London: IDS.

Industrial Relations Observatory (2012) Strikes. Retrieved from http://www.eurofound.europa.eu/eiro, 24 June.

Ingelhart, R. and Welzel, C. (2005) *Modernisation, Cultural Change and Democracy*. New York: Cambridge University Press.

Ingman, T. (2008) *The English Legal Process*. 12th ed. Oxford: Oxford University Press.

Ingman, T. (2011) *The English Legal Process*. 13th ed. Oxford: Oxford University Press.

International Centre for Trade Union Rights (2005) *Trade Unions of the World*. London: John Harper Publishing.

International Centre for Trade Union Rights (2012) *Trade Unions of the World*. London: John Harper Publishing.

International Chamber of Commerce (2013) About ICCC. Retrieved from http://www.iccwbo.org/, 22 July.

International Labour Office (1973) *Conciliation in Industrial Disputes*. Geneva: International Labour Office.

International Labour Office (1983) *Conciliation Services: Structures, Functions and Techniques*. Geneva: International Labour Office.

International Labour Office (2011) *The Global Crisis: Causes, Responses and Challenges*. Geneva: ILO.

International Labour Office (2012) *Global Estimates and Trends of Child Labour 2000–2012*. Geneva: ILO.

International Labour Organisation (1994) *Freedom of Association and Collective Bargaining*. General Survey of the Reports on the Freedom of Association and Protection of the Right to Organise Convention 1948 (No. 87), and the Right to Organise and Collective Bargaining Convention 1949 (No. 98). International Labour Conference, 81st Session. Geneva.

International Labour Organisation (1996a) *Facts and Figures on Child Labour*. Geneva: ILO.

International Labour Organisation (1996b) *International Labour Conventions and Recommendations, 1919–1951*. Vol. I. Geneva: ILO.

International Labour Organisation (2002) *The International Labour Organisation's Fundamental Conventions*. Geneva: ILO.

International Labour Organisation (2006) *Manual Mediation, Conciliation, Arbitration*. Geneva: ILO.

International Labour Organisation (2007a) *Decent Work and the Transition to Formalisation: Recent Trends, Policy Debates and Good Practices*. Geneva: ILO.

International Labour Organisation (2007b) *Note on Convention No. 158 and Recommendation No. 166 Concerning Termination of Employment*. Geneva: ILO.

International Labour Organisation (2008) *Freedom of Association in Practice: Lessons Learned. Report of the Director-General*. Geneva: ILO.

International Labour Organisation (2009) Termination of Employment Legislation Digest. Retrieved from http://www.ilo.org/public/english/dialogue, 9 December.

International Labour Organisation (2010) *The International Labour Organisation and the Quest for Social Justice*. Geneva: ILO.

International Labour Organisation (2011) *Database of Conditions of Work and Employment Law*. Geneva: ILO [electronic resource].

International Labour Organisation (2012) *Key Indicators of the Labour Market*. Geneva: ILO.

International Labour Organisation (2013) *Ending Child Labour in Domestic Work and Protecting Young Workers from Abusive Working Conditions*. Geneva: ILO.

International Labour Organisation (2014) About the ILO. Retrieved from http://www .ilo.or/global/lang--en/index.htmg, 10 February.

International Monetary Fund (2013) *Balance of Payments Manual*. Washington, DC: IMF.

International Organisation of Employers (2013) Home Page. Retrieved from http:// www.ioe-emp.org/, 10 February.

International Social Security Association (2011) *Africa 2011*. Geneva: International Labour Office.

International Social Security Association (2012a) *Europe 2011*. Geneva: International Labour Office.

International Social Security Association (2012b) *The Americas 2011*. Geneva: International Labour Office.

International Social Security Association (2013) *Asia-Pacific 2012*. Geneva: International Labour Office.

International Trade Union Confederation (2006) *Programme Document*. Brussels: ITUC.

Internet Movie Database (2014) *White Van Man: BBC TV Comedy Series*. Retrieved from http://www.imdb.com/title/tt1711422/, 20 April.

Ivanova, I. and Klein, S. (2013) *Working for a Living Wage: Making Paid Work Meet Basic Family Needs in Metro-Vancouver*. Vancouver: Canadian Centre for Policy Alternatives.

Iversen, T. (2005) *Capitalism, Democracy and Welfare*. Cambridge: Cambridge University Press.

Iversen, T. and Wren, A. (1998) 'Equality, employment, and budgetary restraint: The trilemma of the service economy'. *World Politics* 50 (4): 507–546.

Iwagami, T. (1999) 'The end of classic model of labor law and post-Fordism'. *Comparative Labour Law and Policy Journal* 20: 691–692.

Jackson, K. and Tomioka, M. (2004) *The Changing Face of Japanese Management*. London: Routledge.

Jackson, M. (1987) *Strikes*. Brighton: Wheatsheaf.

Jackson, T. (2004) *International HRM: A Cross-Cultural Approach*. London: Sage.

Jacobi, O., Keller, B. and Müller-Jentsch, W. (1992) 'Germany: Continuity and structural change' in Ferner, A. and Hyman, R. (eds) *Industrial Relations in the New Europe*. Oxford: Blackwell.

Jacobs, E. (1973) *European Trade Unionism*. London: Croom Helm.

Jacoby, S. (1990) 'Norms and cycles: The dynamics of industrial relations in the United States, 1897–1987' in Abraham, K. and McKersie, R. (eds) *New Developments in the Labor Market: Toward a New Institutional Paradigm*. Cambridge, MA: MIT Press.

Jacoby, S. (1991) 'American exceptionalism revisited: The importance of management' in Jacoby, S. (ed.) *Masters to Managers: Historical and Comparative Perspectives on American Employers*. New York: Columbia University Press.

Jacoby, S. (1997) *Modern Manors: Welfare Capitalism since the New Deal*. Princeton, NJ: Princeton University Press.

James, H. (2003) *Europe Reborn: A History of Europe 1914–2000*. Harlow: Pearson Longman.

Jansen, M., Peters, R. and Salazar-Xirinachs, J. (eds) (2011) *Trade and Employment: From Myths to Facts*. International Labour Office: Geneva.

Japanese Institute for Labour Policy and Training (2013) *Japanese Working Life Profile: Labor Statistics*. Tokyo: Japanese Institute for Labour Policy and Training.

Jarley, P. (2005) 'Unions as social capital: Renewal through a return to the logic of mutual aid?' *Labor Studies Journal* 29 (4): 1–26.

Jenkins, J. and Blyton, P. (2008) 'Works councils' in Blyton, P., Bacon, N., Fiorito, J. and Heery, E. (eds) *The SAGE Handbook of Industrial Relations*. London: Sage.

Jenks, C. (1957) *The International Protection of Trade Union Freedom*. London: Stevens and Sons.

Jensen, C., Madsen, J. and Due, J. (1995) 'A role for a pan-European trade union movement? possibilities in European industrial relations regulation'. *Industrial Relations Journal* 26 (1): 4–18.

Jeong, J. (2006) *Industrial Relations in Korea: Diversity and Dynamism of Korean Enterprise Unions from a Comparative Perspective*. London: Taylor and Francis.

Jepsen, M. and Serrano Pascual, A. (eds) (2006) *Unwrapping the European Social Model*. Bristol: Policy Press.

Jermier, J., Nord, W. and Knights, D. (1994) *Resistance and Power in Organisations*. London: Routledge.

Johnson, C. (1982) *MITI and the Japanese Miracle: The Growth of Industry Policy 1925–1975*. Stanford: Stanford University Press.

Johnson v Unisys Ltd [2003] 1 AC 518.

Johnston, T. (1962) *Collective Bargaining in Sweden*. London: George Allen and Unwin.

Jones, D. and Kato, T. (1995) 'The productivity effects of employee stock ownership plans and bonuses: Evidence from Japanese data'. *American Economic Review* 85 (3): 39–414.

Judt, T. (2010) *Postwar: A History of Europe Since 1945*. London: Vintage Books.

Juss, S. (2006) *International Migration and Social Justice*. London: Ashgate Press.

Kahn, L. (2007) 'The impact of employment protection mandates on demographic temporary employment patterns: International microeconomic evidence'. *Economic Journal* 117 (521): 333–356.

Kahn-Freund, O. (1954) 'Legal framework' in Flanders, A. and Clegg, H. (eds) *The System of Industrial Relations in Great Britain*. Oxford: Blackwell.

Kahn-Freund, O. (1972) *Labour and the Law*. London: Stevens and Son.

Kahn-Freund, O. (1977) *Labour and the Law*. 2nd ed. London: Stevens and Son.

Kahn-Freund, O. (1979) *Labour Relations: Heritage and Adjustment*. Oxford: Oxford University Press.

Kaiser, W. and Gehler, M. (2004) *Christian Democracy in Europe Since 1945, Vol. 2*. London: Routledge.

Kang, S-C., Morris, S. and Snell, S. (2007) 'Relational arctypes, organisational learning, and value creation: Extending the human resource architecture'. *Academy of Management Review* 32 (1): 236–256.

Kanter, R. (1996) *The Change Masters: Corporate Entrepreneurs at Work*. London: International Thomson Business Press.

Kapila, S. and Mead, D. (2002) *Building Businesses with Small Producers: Successful Business Development Services in Africa, Asia and Latin America*. Ottawa: International Development Research Centre.

Katz, H. and Colvin, A. (2011) 'Employment relations in the United States' in Bamber, G., Lansbury, R. and Wailes, N. (eds) *International and Comparative Employment Relations: Globalisation and Change*. 5th ed. London: Sage.

Katz, H. and Darbishire, O. (2000) *Converging Divergences: Worldwide Changes in Employment Systems*. Ithaca, New York: ILR Press.

Katz, H., Kochan, T. and Colvin, A. (2007) *An Introduction to Collective Bargaining and Industrial Relations*. 4th ed. London: McGraw-Hill.

Katz, H., Turner, L. and Hurd, R. (eds) (2001) *Rekindling the Labor Movement*. Ithaca, New York: Cornell University Press.

Katzenstein, P. (1985) *Small States and World Markets: Industrial Policy in Europe*. Ithaca: Cornell University Press.

Kaufman, B. (1988) 'The postwar view of labor markets and wage determination' in Kaufman, B. (ed.) *How Labor Markets Work: Reflections on Theory and Practice by John Dunlop, Clark Kerr, Richard Lester, and Lloyd Reynolds*. Lexington: Lexington Books.

Kaufman, B. (2003) 'John R. Commons and the Wisconsin School of industrial relations strategy and policy'. *Industrial and Labor Relations Review* 57 (1): 3–30.

Kaufman, B. (2004a) *The Global Evolution of Industrial Relations: Events, Ideas and the IIRA*. Geneva: International Labour Office.

Kaufman, B. (ed.) (2004b) *Theoretical Perspectives on Work and the Employment Relationship*. Champagne, IL: Industrial Relations Research Association.

Kaufman, B. (2005) 'The social welfare objectives and ethical principles of industrial relations' in Budd, J. and Scoville, J. (eds) *The Ethics of Human Resources and Industrial Relations*. Champaign, IL: Labor and Employment Relations Association.

Kaufman, B. and Taras, D. (eds) (2000) *Nonunion Employee Representation: History, Contemporary Practice and Policy*. New York: ME Sharpe.

Kaufmann, C. (2007) *Globalisation and Labour Rights: The Conflict Between Core Labour Rights and International Economic Law*. Oxford: Hart.

Kauppinen, T. (1992) Note on collective bargaining in Finland. Unpublished paper for the OECD. Paris: OECD.

Kawasaki, S. and Hart, R. (1999) *Work and Pay in Japan*. Cambridge: Cambridge University Press.

Kearney, R. (2003) 'Patterns of union decline and growth: An organisational ecology perspective'. *Journal of Labor Research* 24 (4): 561–578.

Keech, W. (1980) 'Elections and macroeconomic policy optimisation'. *American Journal of Political Science* 24: 345–367.

Keller, B. and Kirsch, A. (2011) 'Employment relations in Germany' in Bamber, G., Lansbury, R. and Wailes, N. (eds) *International and Comparative Employment Relations: Globalisation and Change*. 5th ed. London: Sage.

Kelly, J. (1998) *Rethinking Industrial Relations: Mobilisation, Collectivism and Long Waves*. London: Routledge.

Kerckhofs, P. (2011) *Extension of Collective Bargaining in the EU*. Dublin: European Foundation for the Improvement of Living and Working Conditions.

Kerr, C. and Siegel, A (1954) 'The interindustry propensity to strike: An international comparison' in Ross, A., Kornhauser, A. and Dubin, R. (eds) *Industrial Conflict*. London: McGraw-Hill.

Kerr, C., Dunlop, J., Harbinson, F. and Myers, C. (1962) *Industrialism and Industrial Man: the Problems of Labor and Management in Economic Growth*. London: Heinemann.

Kersley, B., Alpin, C., Forth, J. and Bryson, A. (2006) *Inside the Workplace: Findings from the 2004 Workplace Employment Relations Survey*. London: Routledge.

Kettley, P. and Reilly, P. (2003) 'E-HR: An introduction' *Institute of Employment Studies Report* 398. Brighton: Institute of Employment Studies.

Kiiver, P. (2010) *Sources of Constitutional Law: Constitutions and Fundamental Legal Provisions from the United States, France, Germany, the Netherlands, the United Kingdom, the ECHR and the EU*. Groningen: Europa Law.

King, W. (1918) *Industry and Humanity*. Toronto: Toronto University Press.

Kingston Smith (2013) HR Insight: Human Resource and Employment Law Experts. Retrieved from http://www.kingstonsmith.co.uk, 3 July.

Klein, C. (1992) Note on collective bargaining in Austria. Unpublished report for OECD. Paris: OECD.

Kluge, N. and Stollt, M. (eds) *The European Company – Prospects for Worker Board-Level Participation in the Enlarged EU*. Brussels: European Trade Union Institute.

Kochan, T. (1979) 'How Americans view labor unions'. *Monthly Labor Review* 102: 23–31.

Kochan, T. (1980) *Collective Bargaining and Industrial Relations: From Theory to Policy and Practice*. Homewood, IL: Irwin-Dorsey.

Kochan, T. (2009) *Healing Together: The Labor-Management Partnership at Kaiser Permanente*. Ithaca: ILR Press/Cornell University Press.

Kochan, T. and Barocci, T. (1985) *Human Resource Management and Industrial Relations*. Boston, MA: Little Brown.

Kochan, T., Katz, H. and Colvin, A. (2007) *An Introduction to Collective Bargaining and Industrial Relations*. 4th ed. New York: McGraw Hill.

Kochan, T., McKersie, R. and Katz, H. (1986) *The Transformation of American Industrial Relations*. New York: Basic Books.

Kochan, T. and Osterman, P. (1994) *The Mutual Gains Enterprise*. Boston, MA: Harvard Business School Press.

Kochan, T. and Rubenstein, P. (2001) *Learning from Saturn*. Ithaca, New York: Cornell University Press.

Koen, C. (2005) *Comparative International Management*. London: McGraw-Hill.

Kogut, B. and Zander, U. (1992) 'Knowledge of the firm, combinative capabilities, and the replication of technology'. *Organization Science* 3 (3): 383–397.

Kohl, H. and Platzer, H-W. (2004) *Industrial Relations in Central and Eastern Europe*. Brussels: ETUI.

Kohli, M. and Arza, C. (2011) *Pension Reform in Europe: Politics, Policies and Outcomes*. London: Routledge.

Kohli, M. and Camila, A. (2011) *Pension Reform in Europe: Politics, Policies and Outcomes*. London: Routledge.

Kondo, D. (1990) *Crafting Selves: Power, Gender, and Discourses of Identity in a Japanese Workplace*. Chicago: University of Chicago Press.

Kondratiev, N. (1935) 'The long waves in economic life'. *Review of Economic Statistics* 17: 105–115.

Koot, G. (1987) *English Historical Economics*. Cambridge: Cambridge University Press.

Korpi, W. and Shalev, M. (1979) 'Strikes, industrial relations and class conflict in capitalist societies'. *British Journal of Sociology* 30: 164–187.

Korver, A. (1991) Database on collective bargaining: The Netherlands. Unpublished report for the OECD. Paris: OECD.

Kougut, B. and Zander, U. (1992) 'Knowledge of the firm, combinative capabilities, and the replication of technology'. *Organisation Science* 3: 383–397.

Kronstein, H. (1952) 'Collective bargaining in Germany: Before 1933 and after 1945'. *The American Journal of Comparative Law* 1 (3): 199–214.

Kugler, A., Jimeno, J. and Hernanz, V. (2002) Employment consequences of restrictive permanent contracts: Evidence from Spanish labour market reforms. IZA Discussion Paper No. 657. Bonn.

Kuhn, J. (1961) *Bargaining in Grievance Settlement: The Power of Industrial Work Groups.* New York: Columbia University Press.

Kujawa, D. (1980) *Employment Effects of Multinational Enterprises: The Case of the United States.* Geneva. International Labour Office.

Kuruvilla, S. (1995) 'Economic development strategies, industrial relations policies and workplace IR/HR practices in Southeast Asia' in Wever, K. and Turner, L. (eds) *The Comparative Political Economy of Industrial Relations.* Madison: Industrial Relations Research Association.

Kuruvilla, S., Das, S., Kwon, H. and Kwon, S. (2002) 'Trade union growth and decline in Asia'. *British Journal of Industrial Relations* 40 (3): 431–461.

Kuruvilla, S. and Erickson, C. (2002) 'Change and transformation in Asian industrial relations'. *Industrial Relations* 41: 171–228.

Kuznets, S. (1966) *Economic Growth and Structure: Selected Essays.* London: Heinemann.

Kwon, D-B. (2009) Human capital and its measurement. The 3rd OECD World Forum on Statistics, Knowledge and Policy. Korea, 27–30 October.

LABORSTA (2013) International Labour Statistics. Retrieved from http://www .laborstat.ilo.com, 10 January.

Labour Research Department (2012) *Social Media, Monitoring and Surveillance at Work: Practical Guide for Trade Unionists.* London: Labour Research Department.

Lake, G., Losey, M. and Ulrich, D. (1997) *Tomorrow's HR Management: 48 Thought Leaders Call for Change.* Chichester: Wiley.

Lamare, J., Gunnigle, P., Marginson, P. and Murray, G. (2009a) Multinationals' union avoidance practices at new sites: Transatlantic variations. Paper at MNCs Symposium: IIRA World Congress. Sydney, August.

Lamare, J., Gunnigle, P., Marginson, P. and Murray, G. (2009b) Employee representation, multinational companies and institutional context: Union recognition in Canada, Ireland, and the United Kingdom. Paper at MNCs Symposium: IIRA World Congress. Sydney, August.

Lanchester, J. (2010) *Whoops! Why Everyone Owes Everyone and No One Can Pay.* New ed. London: Penguin.

Landsorganisationen i Sverige (2013) Home Page. Retrieved from http://www.lo.se, 14 May.

Landström, H. (2010) *Pioneers in Entrepreneurship and Small Business Research.* New York: Springer.

Lane, C. (1989) *Management and Labour in Europe: The Industrial Enterprise in Germany, Britain and France.* Aldershot: Edward Elgar.

Lane, C. (1995) *Industry and Society in Europe. Stability and Change in Britain, Germany and France.* Aldershot: Edward Elgar.

Lane, C. and Bachmann, R. (1998) *Trust Within and Between Organizations: Conceptual Issues and Empirical Applications.* Oxford: Oxford University Press.

Lane, J-E. (1997) *Public Sector Reform: Rationale, Trends and Problems.* Thousand Oaks, CA: Sage.

Lange, P. and Garrett, G. (1987) 'The politics of growth reconsidered'. *Journal of Politics* 49: 257–274.

Lansbury, R. and Wailes, N. (2004) 'Employment relations in Australia' in Bamber, G., Lansbury, R. and Wailes, N. (eds) *International and Comparative Employment Relations: Globalisation and Change.* 5th ed. London: Sage.

Lansbury, R. and Wailes, N. (2008) 'Employee involvement and direct participation' in Blyton, P., Bacon, N., Fiorito, J. and Heery, E. (eds) *The SAGE Handbook of Industrial Relations.* London: Sage.

Lansbury, R. and Wailes, N. (2011) 'Employment relations in Australia' in Bamber, G., Lansbury, R. and Wailes, N. (eds) *International and Comparative Employment Relations: Globalisation and Change.* 5th ed. London: Sage.

La Porta, R., Lopez de Silanes, F., Shleifer, F. and Vishny, R. (2000) 'Investor protection and corporate governance'. *Journal of Financial Economics* 58: 3–27.

Laski, H. (1935) *The State in Theory and Practice.* New Brunswick, NJ: Transaction Publishers.

Latrielle, P. (2010) *Research Paper 06/10. Mediation at Work: Of Success, Failure and Fragility.* London: Advisory Conciliation and Arbitration Service.

Lawler, E., Ford, R. and Blegen, M. (1988) 'Coercive capability in conflict: A test of bilateral deterrence versus conflict spiral theory'. *Social Psychology Quarterly* 51: 93–107.

Lawrence, P. (1996) *Management in the USA.* London: Sage.

Lawrence, P. and Edwards, V. (2000) *Management in Western Europe.* Basingstoke: Macmillan.

Lawrence, P. and Elliott, K. (1985) *Introducing Management.* London: Penguin.

Lawrence, S. and Ishikawa, J. (2005) Social dialogue indicators: Trade union membership and collective bargaining coverage – statistical concepts, methods and findings. Working Paper No. 59. Geneva: International Labour Organisation.

Laws, Jerry (2011) 'Building unions in the Arab world'. Retrieved from http://online.com. Blog posted. 28 April.

Leana, C. and Van Buren, H. (1999) 'Organizational social capital and employment practices'. *Academy of Management Review* 24 (3): 538–555.

Lee, C. (1999) 'From organized dependence to disorganized despotism: Changing labour regimes in Chinese factories'. *The China Quarterly* 157: 44–71.

Lee, B-H. (2011) 'Employment relations in South Korea' in Bamber, G., Lansbury, R. and Wailes, N. (eds) *International and Comparative Employment Relations: Globalisation and Change.* 5th ed. London: Sage.

Legge, K. (1978) *Power, Innovation and Problem-Solving in Personnel Management.* London: McGraw-Hill.

Legge, K. (2005) *Human Resource Management: Rhetorics and Realities.* Anniversary ed. Basingstoke: Palgrave Macmillan.

Leggett, C. (1993) 'Corporatist trade unions in Singapore' in Frenkel, S. (ed.) *Organised Labor in the Asia-Pacific Region: A Comparative Study of Trade Unionism in nine Countries.* Cornell International Industrial and Labour Relations Report, 24. Ithaca, New York: ILR Press.

Lengnick-Hall, C. and Lengnick-Hall, M. (1988) 'Strategic human resource management: A review of the literature and a proposed typology'. *Academy of Management Review* 13 (3): 454–470.

Lenin, V. (1947) *What is to be Done? Burning Questions of our Movement.* Moscow: Progress Publishers.

Leonard-Barton, D. (1992) 'Core capabilities and core rigidities: A paradox in managing new product development'. *Strategic Management Journal* 13 (1): 111–125.

Lepak, D. and Snell, S. (1999) 'The human resource management architecture: Toward a theory human capital allocation and development'. *Academy of Management Review* 32 (1): 599–612.

Lepak, D. and Snell, S. (2007) 'Employment sub-systems and the HR architecture' in Boxall, P., Purcell, J. and Wright, P. (eds) *Oxford Handbook of Human Resource Management.* Oxford: Oxford University Press.

Lepak, D., Taylor, M., Tekleab, A., Marrone, J. and Cohen, D. (2007) 'Examining variability in High investment human resource system use across employee groups, establishments, and industries'. *Human Resource Management* 46: 223–246.

Lester, R. and Harbison, F. (2011) *As Unions Mature: An Analysis of American Unionism.* Princeton: Princeton University Press.

Levich, R. (2001) *International Financial Markets: Prices and Policies.* 2nd ed. London: Irwin McGraw-Hill.

Levy, F. and Temin, P. (2010) 'Institutions and wages in post-war II America' in Brown, C., Eichergreen, B. and Reich, M. (eds) *Labor in an Era of Globalisation.* Cambridge: Cambridge University Press.

Lewin, D. (2008) 'Resolving conflict' in Blyton, P., Bacon, N., Fiorito, J. and Heery, E. (eds) *The SAGE Handbook of Industrial Relations.* London: Sage.

Lewis, C. (2009) *The Definitive Guide to Workplace Mediation and Managing Conflict at Work.* Weybridge: Roperpenberthy Publishing.

Lewis, S. and Orford, J. (2004) 'Women's experiences of workplace bullying: Changes in social relationships'. *Journal of Community and Applied Social Psychology* 15 (1): 29–47.

Lewis, P., Thornhill, A. and Saunders, M. (2003) *Employee Relations: Understanding the Employment Relationship*. Harlow: Prentice-Hall.

Lichtenstein, N. (2002) *State of the Union: A Century of American Labor*. Princeton: Princeton University Press.

Lindblom, C. (1977) *Politics and Markets: The World's Political Economic Systems*. New York: Basic Books.

Lingemann, S., von Steinau-Steinrück, R. and Mengel, A. (2012) *Employment and Labor Law in Germany*. 3rd ed. Munich: Beck.

Liu, M. (2013) 'China' in Frege, C. and Kelly, J. (eds) *Comparative Employment Relations in the Global Economy*. Abingdon: Routledge.

Lloyd, C. and Payne, J. (2004) 'The political economy of skill: A theoretical approach to developing a high skills strategy in the UK' in Grugulis, I., Keep, E. and Warhurst, C. (eds) *The Skills That Matter*. Basingstoke: Palgrave Macmillan.

Locke, E. and Schweiger, D. (1979) 'Participation in decision-making: One more look' in Staw, B. (ed.) *Research in Organisational Behavior* 1: 265–339.

Locke, R. (1992) 'The demise of the national union in Italy: Lessons for comparative industrial relations theory'. *Industrial and Labor Relations Review* 45: 229–249.

Locke, R. (1995) *Remaking the Italian Economy*. Ithaca, New York: Cornell University Press.

Locke, R. (1996) *The Collapse of the American Management Mystique*. Oxford: Oxford University Press.

Lockwood, D. (1958) *The Blackcoated Worker: A Study in Class Consciousness*. London: Allen and Unwin.

Logan, J. (2006) 'The union avoidance industry in the United States'. *British Journal of Industrial Relations* 44 (4): 651–675.

Ludlam, S. and Taylor, A. (2003) 'The political representation of the labour interest in Britain'. *British Journal of Industrial Relations* 41 (4): 727–749.

Lundberg, U. and Cooper, C. (2011) *The Science of Occupational Health: Stress, Psychobiology, and the New World of Work*. Chichester: Wiley-Blackwell.

Luttwak, D. (1999) *Turbo-Capitalism: Winners and Losers in the Global Economy*. London: Orion Business.

Luxemburg, R. (1971) *The Mass Strike, the Political Party, and the Trade Unions and The Junius Pamphlet*. London: Harper and Row.

Lyddon, D. (2003) 'History and industrial relations' in Ackers, P. and Wilkinson, A. (eds) *Understanding Work and Employment: Industrial Relations in Transition*. Oxford: Oxford University Press.

Lyon, D. (2001) *Surveillance Society: Monitoring Everyday Life*. Buckingham: Open University Press.

Ma, Z. (2011) *The ACFTU and Chinese Industrial Relations*. Oxford: Peter Lang.

MacLeod, D. and Clarke, N. (2009) *Engaging for Success: Enhancing Performance Through Employee Engagement*. London: Department for Business, Information and Skills.

MacShane, D. (1981) *Solidarity: Poland's Independent Trade Union*. Nottingham: Spokesman.

Majone, G. (1997) 'From the positive to the regulatory state: Causes and consequences of changes in the mode of governance'. *Journal of Public Policy* 17 (2): 139–167.

Makhija, A. and Kose, K. (2011) *International Corporate Governance*. Bingley: Emerald.

Mallin, C. (2006) *Handbook on International Corporate Governance: Country Analyses*. Cheltenham: Edward Elgar.

Mallin, C. (2013) *Corporate Governance*. 4th ed. Oxford: Oxford University Press.

Malone, T. (2004) *The Future of Work: How the New Order of Business Will Shape Your Organization, Your Management Style, and Your Life*. Boston, MA: Harvard Business School.

Mamoria, C., Mamoria, S. and Gankar, S. (2008) *Dynamics of Industrial Relations*. Mumbai: Himalaya Publishing House.

Marchington, M., Marchington, L. and Wilkinson, A. (2012) *Human Resource Management at Work*. 5th ed. London: Chartered Institute of Personnel and Development.

Marchington, M., Waddington, J. and Timming, A. (2011) 'Employment relations in Britain' in Bamber, G., Lansbury, R. and Wailes, N. (eds) *International and Comparative Employment Relations: Globalisation and Change*. 5th ed. London: Sage.

Marchington, M. and Wilkinson, A. (2005) *Human Resource Management at Work: People Management and Development*. 3rd ed. London: Chartered Institute of Personnel and Development.

Marchington, M. and Wilkinson, A. (2008) *Human Resource Management at Work: People Management and Development*. 4th ed. London: Chartered Institute of Personnel and Development.

Marcia, J. (1966) 'Development and validation of ego identity status'. *Journal of Personality and Social Psychology* 3: 551–558.

Marginson, P., Armstrong, P., Edwards, P. and Purcell, J. (1995) 'Facing the multinational challenge' in Leisink, P., van Leempur, J. and Vilrokx, J. (eds) *Innovation or Adaption? Trade Unions and Industrial Relations in Changing Europe*. London: Edward Elgar.

Marikana Commission of Inquiry (2014) *About the Commission*. Retrieved from http://www.marikanacomm.org.za, 14 April.

Marsden, D. (1978) Industrial democracy and industrial control in West Germany, France and Great Britain. Research Paper 4. London: Department of Employment.

Marsden, D. (1999) *A Theory of Employment Systems: Micro-foundations of Societal Diversity*. Oxford: Oxford University Press.

Marsh, A. (1979) *The Dictionary of Industrial Relations*. Gower: London.

Marsh, A. (1982) *Employee Relations Policy and Decision Making*. Aldershot: Gower.

Marshall, D. (1949) *The English Domestic Servant in History*. London: George Philip and Son.

Marshall, T. and Bottomore, T. (1992) *Citizenship and Social Class*. London: Pluto Press.

Marshall, S., Mitchell, R. and Ramsey, I. (eds) (2008) *Varieties of Capitalism, Corporate Governance and Employment Systems*. Victoria: Melbourne University Press.

Martin, R. (1992) *Bargaining Power*. Oxford: Clarendon.

Marx, K. and Engels, F. (1970) *Capital: A Critique of Political Economy. Volume I: A Critical Analysis of the Process of Capitalist Production*. London: Lawrence and Wishart.

Marx, K. and Engels, F. (1973) *Manifesto of the Communist Party*. 2nd ed. Peking: Foreign Languages Press.

Marx, K. and Engels, F. (1974) *Capital: A Critique of Political Economy. Volume II: The Process of Circulation of Capital*. London: Lawrence and Wishart.

Maslow, A. (1954) *Motivation and Personality*. New York: Harper.

Masters, M. and Delaney, T. (2005) 'Organised labor's political scorecard'. *Journal of Labor Research* 26 (3): 365–392.

Matsumoto, K. (1991) *The Rise of the Japanese Corporate System* (translated by T. Elliot). New York: Kegan Paul International.

Mayo, E. (1933) *The Human Problems of an Industrial Civilisation*. New York: Macmillan.

Mayrhofer, W. and Brewster, C. (2006) 'European Human Resource Management: Researching developments over time' in Schuler, R. and Jackson, S. (eds) *Strategic Human Resource Management*. 2nd ed. Oxford: Blackwell.

Mbaku, J. (1999) 'A balance sheet of structural adjustment in Africa: Towards a sustainable development agenda' in Mkabu, J. (ed.) *Preparing Africa for the Twenty-First Century: Strategies for Peaceful Coexistence and Sustainable Development*. Aldershot: Ashgate.

McCarthy, W. (1988) *The Future of Industrial Democracy*. London: Fabian Society.

McDowell, L., Batnitzky, A. and Dyer, S. (2008) 'Internationalisation and the spaces of temporary labour: The global assembly of a local workforce'. *British Journal of Industrial Relations* 46 (4): 750–770.

McGovern, P. (1998) *HRM, Technical Workers and the Multinational Corporation*. London: Routledge.

McGregor, D. (1960) *The Human Side of Enterprise*. London: McGraw-Hill.

McGrew, A. and Held, D. (2000) *Globalisation Theory: Approaches and Controversies*. Polity: Cambridge.

McLellan, D. (1971) *The Thought of Karl Marx: An Introduction*. London: Macmillan.

McLoughlin, I. and Badham, R. (2005) 'Political process perspectives on organisation and technological change'. *Human Relations* 58 (7): 827–943.

McLoughlin, I. and Gourlay, S. (1994) *Enterprise Without Unions: Industrial Relations in the Non-Union Firm*. Buckingham: Open University Press.

McMahan, G., Bell, M. and Virick, M. (1998) 'Strategic human resource management: Employee involvement, diversity, and international issues'. *Human Resource Management Review* 8 (3): 193–214.

McMurtry, J. (1999) *The Cancer Stage of Capitalism*. London: Pluto Press.

Mellahi, K. and Budhwar, P. (2006) 'HRM challenges in the Middle-East: Agenda for future research and policy' in Budhwar, P. and Mellani, K. (eds) *Managing Human Resources in the Middle-East*. London: Routledge.

Meltz, N. (1991) 'Dunlop's industrial relations systems after three decades' in Adams, R. (ed.) *Comparative Industrial Relations: Contemporary Research and Theory*. London: Harper Collins Academic.

Mendonca, M. (2000) 'Human resource management in the emerging countries' in Warner, M. (ed.) *Regional Encylopaedia of Business and Management in the Emerging Countries*. London: Thomson Learning Business Press.

Merkle, J. (1980) *Management and Ideology: The Legacy of the International Scientific Management Movement*. Berkeley, CA: University of California Press.

Merryman, J. (1985) *The Civil Law Tradition*. Stanford: Stanford University Press.

Merton, R. (1968) *Social Theory and Social Structure*. 3rd ed. London: Collier-Macmillan.

Metcalf, D. (1999) The British Minimum National Wage. CEPDP 419. Centre for Economic Performance. London: London School of Economics and Political Science.

Metcalf, D. (2005) 'Trade unions: Resurgence or perdition? An economic analysis' in Fernie, S. and Metcalf, D. (eds) *Trade Unions: Resurgence or Decline? The Future of Trade Unions in Britain*. London: Routledge.

Metcalf, D. and Milner, S. (eds) (1993) *New Perspectives on Industrial Disputes*. London: Routledge.

Meyer, W. (1967) 'The study of foreign labour and industrial relations' in Barkin, S., Dymond, W., Kassolow, E., Meyers, F. and Myers, C. (eds) *International Labour*. New York: Harper and Row.

Miceli, M., Near, J. and Dworkin, T. (2008) *Whistle-Blowing in Organisations*. New York: Routledge.

Michalet, C. (1980) 'International sub-contracting: A state-of-the-art'. in Germidis, D. (ed.) *International Sub-Contracting: A Form of Investment*. Paris: OECD.

Michels, R. (1962) *Political Parties: A Sociological Study of the Oligarchical Tendencies of Modern Democracy*. Translated into English by Eden Paul and Cedar Paul. New York: The Free Press.

Miles, R. and Snow, C. (1984) *Organisational Strategy, Structure and Process*. New York: McGraw-Hill.

Miliband, R. (1973) *The State in Capitalist Society*. London: Quartet Books.

Miller, K. and Monge, P. (1986) 'Participation, productivity and satisfaction: A meta-analytic review'. *Academy of Management Journal* 29 (4): 727–753.

Millward, N., Bryson, A. and Forth, J. (2000) *All Change at Work? British Employment Relations 1980–1998, as Portrayed by the Workplace Industrial Relations Survey Series*. London: Routledge.

Milner, H. and Moravcsik, A. (2009) *Power, Interdependence, and Nonstate Actors in World Politics*. Princeton, NJ: Princeton University.

Ministry of Reconstruction (1918) *Committee on Relations Between Employers and Employed. Final Report*. Cmnd 9153. London: His Majesty's Stationery Office.

Mintzberg, H. (1980) *The Nature of Managerial Work*. London: Prentice-Hall.

Mintzberg, H. (1987) 'Crafting strategy'. *Harvard Business Review* 65 (4): 66–75.

Mintzberg, H, (1994) *The Rise and Fall of Strategic Planning*. London: Prentice-Hall.

Mirow, M. (2004) *Latin American Law: A History of Private Law and Institutions in Spanish America*. Austin, TX: University of Texas Press.

Mishel, L. and Matthew, W. (2003) How unions help all workers. Economic Policy Institute Briefing Paper No. 143.

Mishel, L. and Voos, P. (eds) (2006) *Unions and Economic Competitiveness*. Washington, DC: Economic Policy Institute.

Mishra, R. (1999) *Globalisation and He Welfare State*. Cheltenham: Edward Elgar.

Mitchell, R. and Arup, C. (2006) 'Labor law and labour market regulation' in Arup, C., Gahan, J., Howe, R., Johnstone, R., Mitchell, R. and O'Donnell, A. (eds) *Labor Law and Labor Market Regulation*. Sydney: Federation Press.

Mommsen, W. (1974) *The Age of Bureaucracy: Perspectives on the Political Sociology of Max Weber*. Oxford: Blackwell.

Mommsen, W. and Hirschfeld, G. (1982) *Social Protest, Violence and Terror in Nineteenth- and Twentieth-Century Europe*. London: Macmillan.

Monger, J. (2004) 'International comparisons of labour disputes in 2002'. *Labour Market Trends* 112 (4): 145–152.

Moran, M. (2003) *The British Regulatory State: High Modernism and Hyper-Innovation*. Oxford: Oxford University Press.

Morikawa, H. (2001) *A History of Top Management in Japan: Managerial Enterprises and Family Enterprises*. Oxford: Oxford University Press.

Morley, M., Gunnigle, P. and Collings, D. (eds) (2006) *Global Industrial Relations*. London: Routledge.

Morley, M., Herity, N. and, Michailova, S. (eds) (2009) *Managing Human Resources in Central and Eastern Europe* (Global HRM). London: Routledge.

Morris, T. (2003) 'Unionisation matters: An analysis of post–world war II strikes'. *Sociological Inquiry* 73 (2): 245–264.

Morris, S. and Snell, S. (2008) 'The evolution of HR strategy: Adaptations to increasing global complexity' in Wilkinson, A., Bacon, N., Redman, T. and Snell, S. (eds) *The SAGE Handbook of Human Resource Management*. London: Sage.

Morehead, A., Steel, M., Alexander, M., Stephen, K. and Duffin, L. (1997) *Change at Work: the 1994 Australian Industrial Relations Survey*. Melbourne: Addison-Wesley Longman.

Morrison, C. (1854) *An Essay on the Relations Between Capital and Labour*. New York: Arno Press.

Morton, A. (1962) *The Life and Ideas of Robert Owen*. London: Lawrence and Wishart.

Mowat, C. (1955) *Britain Between the Wars 1918–1940*. London: Methuen.

Moxon, G. (1946) *Functions of a Personnel Department*. London: Institute of Personnel Management.

Mueller, D. (1997) 'First-mover advantage and path dependence'. *International Journal of Industrial Organisation* 15 (6): 827–850.

Mueller-Jentsch, W. (2003) 'Re-assessing codetermination' in Mueller-Jentsch, W. and Weitbrecht, H. (eds) *The Changing Contours of German Industrial Relations*. Rainer Hampp: Munich.

Mulhearn, C. and Vane, H. (2012) *Economics for Business*. Basingstoke: Palgrave Macmillan.

Mulvey, C. (1986) 'Wage levels: Do unions make a difference?' in Niland, J. (ed.) *Wage Fixation in Australia*. Sydney: Allen and Unwin.

Murray, G. (2002) *Work and Employment Relations in the High Performance Workplace*. London: Continuum.

Murray, R. (1989) 'Fordism and post-Fordism' in Hall, S. and Jacques, M. (eds) *New Times: the Changing Face of Politics in the 1990s*. London: Lawrence and Wishart.

Nedopil, C., Steger, U. and Amann, W. (2011) *Managing Complexity in Organizations: Text and Cases*. Basingstoke: Palgrave Macmillan.

Newell, S., Robertson, M., Scarbrough, H. and Swan, J. (2009) *Managing Knowledge Work and Innovation*. 2nd ed. Basingstoke: Palgrave Macmillan.

Noiriel, G. (1990) *Workers in French Society in the 19th and 20th Centuries*. Oxford: Berg.

Noon, M. and Blyton, P. (2007) *The Realities of Work: Experiencing Work and Employment in Contemporary Society*. Basingstoke: Palgrave Macmillan.

Oatley, T. (2012) *International Political Economy*. 5th ed. Harlow: Pearson Education.

O'Brien, R. and Williams, M. (2010) *Global Political Economy: Evolution and Dynamics*. 3rd ed. Basingstoke: Palgrave Macmillan.

O'Connor, D. and Faille, E. (2000) *Basic Economic Principles: A Guide for Students*. London: Greenwood Press.

O'Connor, S. (2013) 'Amazon's human robots: They trek 15 miles a day around a warehouse, their every move dictated by computers checking their work. Is this the future of the British workplace?' *The Daily Mail* 28 February.

Offe, C. (1984) *Contradictions of the Welfare State*. London: Hutchinson.

Offe, C. and Keane, J. (1985) *Disorganised Capitalism: Contemporary Transformations of Work and Politics*. Cambridge: Polity.

Ohmae, K. (1996) *End of the Nation State: The Rise of Regional Economies*. London: HarperCollins.

Okun, A. (1975) *Equality and Efficiency: The Big Trade-Off*. Washington, DC: Brookings Institution.

Oliver, N. and Wilkinson, B. (1992) *The Japanisation of British industry: New Developments in the 1990s*. 2nd ed. Oxford: Blackwell.

Olson, M. (1982) *The Rise and Decline of Nations: Economic Growth, Stagflation and Social Rigidities*. New Haven: Yale University Press.

Ong, A. (2010) *Spirits of Resistance and Capitalist Discipline: Factory Women in Malaysia*. 2nd ed. Alba, New York: SUNY Press.

Öniş, Z. (1991) 'The logic of the developmental state'. *Comparative Politics* 24 (1): 109–126.

Organisation for Economic Co-operation and Development (1991) *Economic Outlook*. July. Paris: OECD.

Organisation for Economic Co-operation and Development (1999) *Financial Market Trends, No. 72* February. Paris: OECD.

Organisation for Economic Co-operation and Development (2003) *Managing Senior Management: Senior Civil Service Reform in OECD Member Countries*. Paris: OECD.

Organisation for Economic Co-operation and Development (2004a) *Economic Outlook*. June. Paris: OECD.

Organisation for Economic Co-operation and Development (2004b) *Trends in Human Resources Management Policies in OECD Countries: An Analysis of the Results of the OECD Survey on Strategic Human Resources Management*. Paris: OECD.

Organisation for Economic Co-operation and Development (2005) *HRM Working Party Report*. Paris: OECD.

Organisation for Economic Co-operation and Development (2007) *Policy Brief: Globalisation, Jobs and Wages*. June: 1–8. Paris: OECD.

Organisation for Economic Co-operation and Development (2008a) *Growing Unequal? Income Distribution and Poverty in OECD Countries*. Paris: OECD.

Organisation for Economic Co-operation and Development (2008b) *OECD Labour Force Statistics 1987–2007*. Paris: OECD.

Organisation for Economic Co-operation and Development (2009a) *Bridging State Capacity Gaps in Situations of Fragility*. Paris: OECD.

Organisation for Economic Co-operation and Development (2009b) 'Employment in general government and public corporations'. *Government at a Glance 2009*. Paris: OECD.

Organisation for Economic Co-operation and Development (2010) *Economic Outlook*. June. Paris: OECD.

Organisation for Economic Co-operation and Development (2011a) *Economic Policy Reforms: Going for Growth*. Paris: OECD.

Organisation for Economic Co-operation and Development (2011b) *Divided We Stand: Why Inequality Keeps Rising*. Paris: OECD.

Organisation for Economic Co-operation and Development (2012) *Economic Outlook*. June. Paris: OECD.

Organisation for Economic Co-operation and Development (2013) *Human Resources Management Country Profiles: Sweden*. Paris: OECD.

Osterman, P. (ed.) (1983) *Employment Policies of Large Firms*. Massachusetts: MIT Press.

Osterman, P. (1999) *Securing Prosperity: The American Labor Market: How It Has Changed and What to Do About It*. Princeton, NJ: Princeton University Press.

Osterman, P. (2004) 'Labor market intermediaries in the modern labor market' in Giloth, R. (ed.) *Workforce Intermediaries for the Twenty-First Century*. Philadelphia: Temple University Press.

Osterman, P., Kochan, T., Locke, R. and Piore, M. (2001) *Working in America: Labor Market Policies for the New Century*. Cambridge, MA: MIT Press.

O'Sullivan, N. and Cox, A. (1988) *The Corporate State: Corporatism and the State Tradition in Western Europe*. Aldershot: Elgar.

Ovey, C., White, R. and Jacobs, F. (2010) *The European Convention on Human Rights*. Oxford: Oxford University.

Owen, R. (1970) *The Book of the New Moral World*. New York: A.M. Kelly (first printed 1842).

Paauwe, J. (2004) *HRM and Performance: Achieving Long-Term Viability*. Oxford: Oxford University Press.

Paauwe, J. and Boselie, P. (2003) 'Challenging "Strategic HRM" and the relevance of the institutional setting'. *Human Resource Management Journal* 13 (3): 56–70.

Palmer, V. (ed.) (2012) *Mixed Jurisdictions Worldwide: The Third Legal Family*. Cambridge: Cambridge University Press.

Panitch, L. and Gindin, S. (2004) *Global Capitalism and American Empire*. London: Merlin.

Pankoke, E. (1970) *Soziale Bewegung, Soziale Frage, Soziale Politik*. Stuttgart: Jahrhundert.

Parker, M. (2002) *Against Management: Organisation in the Age of Managerialism*. Cambridge: Polity.

Parker, M. and Slaughter, J. (1988) *Choosing Sides: Unions and the Team Concept*. Boston, MA: South End Press.

Parry, E., Stavrou, E. and Lazarova, M. (2013) *Global Trends in Human Resource Management*. Basingstoke: Palgrave Macmillan.

Parry, E., Stavrou-Costea, E. and Morley, M. (2011) 'The Cranet international research network on Human Resource Management in retrospect and prospect'. *Human Resource Management Review* 21 (1): 1–4.

Parsons, N. (2013) 'France' in Frege, C. and Kelly, J. (eds) *Comparative Employment Relations in the Global Economy*. Abingdon: Routledge.

Pascale, R. and Athos, A. (1982) *The Art of Japanese Management*. London: Allen Lane.

Patil, B. (1992) Industrial Relations in India. Indian Institute of Management: IIM Bangalore Research Paper 30. 30 November.

Pedersini, R. (2002) *Economically Dependent Workers, Employment Law and Industrial Relations*. Dublin: European Foundation for the Improvement of Working and Living Conditions.

Pedler, M., Burgoyne, J. and Boydell, T. (2007) *A Manager's Guide to Self-Development*. Maidenhead: McGraw-Hill Education.

Penrose, E. (1959) *The Theory of the Growth of the Firm*. New York: Wiley and Son.

Penrose, E. (1980) *The Theory of the Growth of the Firm*. 2nd ed. Oxford: Blackwell.

Penrose, E. (2009) *The Theory of the Growth of the Firm*. 4th ed., rev. ed. Oxford: Oxford University Press.

Perez, S. A. and Westrup, J. (2010) 'Finance and the macroeconomy: The politics of regulatory reform in Europe'. *Journal of European Public Policy* 17 (8): 1171–1192.

Perkins, S. and White, G. (2008) *Employee Reward: Alternatives, Consequences and Contexts*. London: Chartered Institute of Personnel and Development.

Perkins, S. and White, G. (2011) *Reward Management: Alternatives, Consequences and Contexts*. 2nd ed. London: Chartered Institute of Personnel and Development.

Perlman, S. (1922) *A History of Trade Unionism in the United States*. New York: Macmillan.

Perlman, S. (1928) *A Theory of the Labor Movement*. New York: Macmillan.

Perone, G. and Vallebona, A. (1984) *The Law of Collective Agreements in the Countries of the European Community*. Luxembourg: Office for Official Publications of the European Communities.

Peters, B. and Pierre, J. (2008) *Handbook of Public Administration*. London: Sage.

Petit, H. and Sauze, D, (2006) 'Une lecture historique de la relation salariale comme structure de repartition des aléas. En partant du travail de Salais' in Eymard-Duvernay, F. (ed.) *L'économie des conventions: methods et resultants. Tome II: Développments*. Paris: La Découverte.

Petrella, R. (1996) 'Globalisation and internationalisation' in Boyer, R. and Drache, D. (eds) *States Against States*. London: Routledge.

Pfeffer, J. (1994) *Competitive Advantage Through People: Unleashing the Power of the Work Force*. Boston, MA: Harvard Business School Press.

Pfeffer, J. (1997) *New Directions for Organisation Theory*. New York: Oxford University Press.

Pfeffer, J. (1998) *The Human Equation: Building Profits by Putting People First*. Boston, MA: Harvard Business School.

Phelan, C. (ed.) (2007) *Trade Union Revitalisation: Trends and Prospects in 34 Countries*. New York: Peter Lang.

Pieper, R. (ed.) (1990) *Human Resource Management: An International Comparison*. Berlin: De Gruyter.

Pierre, G. and Scarpetta, S. (2004) Employment regulations through the eyes of employers: Do they matter and how do firms respond to them? IZA Discussion Paper No. 1424. Bonn.

Pierre, G. and Scarpetta, S. (2006) 'Employment protection: Do firms' perceptions match with legislation?' *Economics Letters* 90: 328–334.

Pigors, P. and Myers, C. (1969) *Personnel Administration: A Point of View and a Method*. 6th ed. New York: McGraw-Hill.

Piketty, T. (2014) *Capital in the Twenty-First Century*. Cambridge, MA: Harvard University Press.

Piketty, T. and Saez, E. (2007) 'Income inequality in the United States 1913–1998' in Atkinson, A. and Piketty, T. (eds.) *Top Incomes in a Global Perspective*. Oxford: Oxford University Press.

Pilbeam, P. (2013) *French Socialists Before Marx: Workers, Women and the Social Question in France*. Cambridge: Cambridge University Press.

Pinnington, A., Mackin, R. and Campbell, T. (2007) *Human Resource Management: Ethics and Employment*. Oxford: Oxford University Press.

Piore, M. (1986) 'Perspectives on labor market flexibility'. *Industrial Relations* 25: 146–166.

Piore, M. and Sabel, C. (1984) *The Second Industrial Divide: Possibilities for Prosperity*. New York: Basic Books.

Ploetner, O. (ed.) (2012) *Counter Strategies in Global Markets*. Basingstoke: Palgrave Macmillan.

Polachek, S. and Siebert, W. (1993) *Economics of Earnings*. Cambridge: Cambridge University Press.

Polanyi, K. (1944) *The Great Transformation*. Boston, MA: Beacon Press.

Pollert, A. (2005) 'The unorganised worker: The decline of collectivism and new hurdles to individual employment rights'. *Industrial Law Journal* 34: 533–667.

Pollitt, C. (1990) *Managerialism and the Public Services: The Anglo-American Experience*. Oxford: Basil Blackwell.

Pollitt, C. and Bouckaert, G. (2004) *Public Management Reform: A Comparative Analysis*. Oxford: Oxford University Press.

Poole, M. (1981) *Theories of Trade Unionism: A Sociology of Industrial Relations*. London: Routledge and Kegan Paul.

Poole, M. (1986) *Industrial Relations: Origins and Patterns of National Diversity*. London: Routledge and Kegan Paul.

Porrini, P., Hiris, L. and Poncini, G. (2009) *Above the Board: How Ethical CEOs Create Honest Corporations.* New York: McGraw-Hill Professional.

Porter, L. and Steers, R. (1991) *Motivation and Work Behavior.* London: McGraw-Hill.

Porter, M. (1980) *Competitive Strategy: Techniques for Analyzing Industries and Competitors.* New York: Free Press.

Porter, M. (1998) *Competitive Strategy: Techniques for Analyzing Industries and Competitors: With a New Introduction.* New York: Free Press.

Porter, M. (2004) *Competitive Advantage: Creating and Sustaining Superior Performance.* New York: Free Press.

Portmann, R. (2013) *Legal Personality in International Law.* Cambridge: Cambridge University Press.

Pringle, T. (2011) *Trade Unions in China: The Challenge of Labour Unrest.* London: Routledge.

Procoli, A. (2004) *Workers and Narratives of Survival in Europe: The Management of Precariousness at the End of the Twentieth Century.* Albany, New York: State University of New York Press.

Punch, K. (2005) *Introduction to Social Research: Quantitative and Qualitative Approaches.* 2nd ed. London: Sage.

Punch, M. (1996) *Dirty Business.* London: Sage.

Purcell, J. (1987) 'Mapping management styles in employee relations'. *Journal of Management Studies* 24 (5): 533–548.

Purcell, J. (2009) *People Management and Performance.* London: Routledge.

Purcell, J. and Ahlstrand, B. (1994) *Human Resource Management in the Multi-Divisional Company.* Oxford: Oxford University Press.

Purcell, J. and Gray, A. (1986) 'Corporate and personnel departments and the management of industrial relations: two case studies in ambiguity'. *Journal of Management Studies* 23 (2): 205–233.

Purcell, J. and Sisson, K. (1983) 'Strategies and practice in the management of industrial relations' in Bain, G. (ed.) *Industrial Relations in Britain.* Oxford: Basil Blackwell.

Pye, L. (1992) *Chinese Commercial Negotiating Style.* New York: Quorum Books.

Ramasamy, N. (2004) 'The future of the trade union movement in Malaysia'. Retrieved from http://www.mtuc.org.my, 1 May 2013.

Ramsay, H. (1977) 'Cycles of control: Workers' participation in sociological and historical perspective'. *Sociology* 11 (3): 481–506.

Ramsay, H., Scholarios, D. and Harley, B. (2000) 'Employees and high performance work systems: Testing inside the black box'. *British Journal of Industrial Relations* 38 (3): 501–531.

Ravenhill, M. (2011) *Global Political Economy.* 3rd ed. Oxford: Oxford University Press.

Rebick, M. (2005) *The Japanese Employment System: Adapting to a New Economic Environment*. New York: Oxford University Press.

Redman, T. and Snape, E. (2005) 'Unpacking commitment: Multiple loyalties and employee behaviour'. *Journal of Management Studies* 42 (2): 301–328.

Rees, C., Alfers, K., Gatenby, M., Soane, E. and Truss, K. (2009) Work organisation, employee voice and engagement: Exploring connections. Paper given at the British Universities Industrial Relations Association Annual Conference, Cardiff.

Rees, C., Mamman, A. and Braik, A. (2007) 'Emirisation as a strategic HRM change initiative: Case study evidence from a UAE petroleum company'. *The International of HRM* 18 (1): 33–53.

Regini, M. (1986) 'Political bargaining in Western Europe during the economic crisis of the 1980s' in Jacobi, O., Jessop, B., Kastendiek, H. and Regini, M. (eds) *Economic Crisis, Trade Unions and the State*. London: Croom Helm.

Rehfeldt, U. (2010) 'The French system of collective bargaining'. *Social Europe Journal* 29 August. Retrieved from http://www.social-europe.eu, 18 January 2013.

Reich, R. (1991) *The Work of Nations: Preparing Ourselves for 21st Century Capitalism*. New York: Knopf.

Reid, E. and Palmer, V. (eds) (2009) *Mixed Jurisdictions Compared*. Edinburgh: Edinburgh University Press.

Reilly, P. and Williams, T. (2003) *How to Get the Best Value from HR: The Shared Services Option*. Aldershot: Gower.

Reimann, M. and Zimmerman, R. (eds) (2006) *The Oxford Handbook of Comparative Law*. Oxford: Oxford University Press.

Renwick, D. (2003) 'HR managers: Guardians of employee well being?' *Personnel Review* 32 (3): 341–359.

Renwick, D., Redman, T. and Maguire, S. (2008) 'Green HRM: A review, process model, and research agenda'. Discussion Paper No 2008.01. University of Sheffield Management School. April.

Richards, A. (1998) *Miners on Strike: Class Solidarity and Division in Britain*. New York: Berg.

Ricardo, D. (1973) *The Principles of Political Economy and Taxation*. London: Dent.

Richardson, J. (1954) *An Introduction to the Study of Industrial Relations*. London: Allen and Unwin.

Ridley, F. (1970) *Revolutionary Syndicalism in France: The Direct Action of its Time*. London: Cambridge University Press.

Rifkin, J. (2004) *The End of Work: The Decline of the Global Labor Force and the Dawn of the Post-Market Era*. New York: Penguin.

Robbins, R. (2008) *Global Problems and the Culture of Capitalism*. Boston: Pearson.

Roberts, B. (ed.) (1968) *Industrial Relations: Contemporary Problems and Perspectives*. Revised ed. London: Methuen.

Robinson, S. and Rousseau, D. (1994) 'Violating the psychological contract: not the exception but the norm'. *Journal of Organizational Behavior* 15: 245–259.

Rockefeller, J. (1923) *The Personal Relation in Industry*. New York: Boni and Liverwright.

Roethlisberger, F. and Dickson, W. (1939) *Management and the Worker: An Account of a Research Program Conducted by the Western Electric Company, Hawthorne Works, Chicago*. Cambridge, MA: Harvard University Press.

Rogers, J. and Streeck, W. (1995) *Works Councils: Consultation, Representation and Cooperation in Industrial Relations*. Chicago: University of Chicago Press.

Rohlen, T. (1974) *For Harmony and Strength: Japanese White-Collar Organization in Anthropological Perspective*. Berkeley, CA: University of California Press.

Rook, S., Rodenhuis, G., Kortooms, W. and Blanke, A. (2009) 'The Netherlands' in Stewart, A. and Bell, M. (eds) *The Right to Strike: A Comparative Perspective. A Study of National Law in Six EU States*. London: Institute of Employment Studies.

Rose, M. (1985) 'Universalism, culturalism and the aix group: Promise and problems of a societal approach to economic institutions'. *European Sociological Review* 11 (1): 65–83.

Rose, M. (1988) *Industrial Behaviour: Research and Control*. London: Penguin.

Roscigno, V. and Hodson, R. (2004) 'The organisational and social foundations of worker resistance'. *American Sociological Review* 69 (1): 14–39.

Rosefielde, S. (2005) *Russia in the 21st Century: The Prodigal Superpower*. Cambridge: Cambridge University Press.

Rosenzweig, P. and Nohria, N. (1994) 'Influences of human resource management practices in multinational corporations'. *Journal of International Business Studies* 25 (2): 229–251.

Ross, A. and Hartman, P. (1960) *Changing Patterns of Industrial Conflict*. New York: Wiley.

Ross, A., Kornhauser, A. and Dubin, R. (1954) *Industrial Conflict*. New York: McGraw-Hill.

Rossi, P. and Freeman, H. (1982) *Evaluation: A Systematic Approach*. 2nd ed. Beverley Hill, CA: Sage.

Roth, S. (1997) 'Germany's perspective in lean production' in Kochan, T., Lansbury, R. and MacDuffie, J. (eds) *After Lean Production: Evolving Employment Practices in the World Auto Industry*. Ithaca, New York: ILR Press.

Rousseau, D. (1977) 'Technological differences in job characteristics, employee satisfaction, and motivation: A synthesis of job design research and sociotechnical systems theory'. *Organizational Behaviour and Human Performance* 9: 78–99.

Rousseau, D. (1995) *Psychological Contracts in Organisations: Understanding Written and Unwritten Agreements*. London: Sage.

Rowley, C. and Abdul-Rahman, S. (eds.) (2008) *The Changing Face of Management in South East Asia*. London: Routledge.

Rowley, C. and Benson, J. (2004) *The Management of Human Resources in the Asia Pacific Region: Convergence Reconsidered*. London: Frank Cass.

Rowley, C. and Cooke, F. (2010) *The Changing Face of Management in China*. London: Routledge.

Rowley, C. and Yongsun, P. (eds) (2009) *The Changing Face of Korean Management*. London and New York: Routledge.

Roy, D. (1954) 'Efficiency and "the fix": Informal intergroup relations in a piece-work machine shop'. *American Journal of Sociology* 60: 255–266.

Royal Commission of Labour, Great Britain (1894) *Final Report*. London: Her Majesty's Stationery Office.

Royal Commission on Trade Unions and Employers' Associations (1968) *Report*. London: Her Majesty's Stationery Office.

Rubenstein, S. and Kochan, T. (2000) *Learning From Saturn: Possibilities for Corporate Governance and Employee Relations*. New York: ILR Press.

Rubery, J. (1999) 'Fragmenting the internal labour market' in Leisink, P. (ed.) *Globalisation and Labour Relations*. Cheltenham: Edward Elgar.

Rubery, J., Grimshaw, D. and Ward, K. (2005) 'The changing employment relationship and the implications for quality part-time work'. *Labour and Industry* 15: 7–28.

Ruble, B. (1981) *Soviet Trade Unions: Their Development in the 1970s*. Cambridge: Cambridge University Press.

Rudé, G. (1988) *The French Revolution*. London: Weidenfeld and Nicolson.

Rugman, A. (ed.) (2009) *The Oxford Handbook of International Business*. 2nd ed. Oxford: Oxford University Press.

Salaman, G. (1979) *Work Organisations: Resistance and Control*. London: Longman.

Salt, J. (1997) International movements of the highly skilled. In Organisation for Economic Co-operation and Development: Directorate for Education, Employment, Labour and Social Affairs: International Migration Unit. Occasional Paper 3. Paris: OECD.

Sandel, M. (2013) *What Money Can't Buy: The Moral Limits of Markets*. London: Penguin.

Sashkin, M. (1976) 'Changing toward participative management approaches: A model and methods'. *Academy of Management Review* July: 75–86.

Sassen, S. (1988) *The Mobility of Capital and Labor: A Study in International Investment and Labor Flow*. Cambridge: Cambridge University Press.

Sauvant, K. (ed.) (2008) *The Rise of Tranational Corporations from Emerging Markets: Threat or Opportunity?* Cheltenham: Edward Elgar.

Sayles, L. (1958) *Behavior of Industrial Work Groups: Prediction and Control*. New York: John Wiley and Sons.

Scargill, A. and Kahn, P. (1980) *The Myth of Workers' Control*. Leeds: University of Leeds and University of Nottingham.

Scharf, K. (1997) Voting for taxes and tax incentives for giving. Warwick Economics Research Paper Series, 497. University of Warwick, Department of Economics.

Schmidt, V. (2003) 'French capitalism transformed, yet still a third variety of capitalism' *Economy and Society* 32 (4): 526–554.

Schmidt, F. and Neal, A. (1984) 'Collective agreements and collective bargaining' in Hepple, B. (ed.) *International Encyclopedia of Comparative Law: Labour Law.* 17 Vols. Tübingen: International Association of Legal Science.

Schmitter, P. (1974) 'Still the century of corporatism?' *Review of Politics* 36 (1): 85–131.

Scholz, C. and Boehm, H. (eds) (2008) *Human Resource Management in Europe: Comparative Analysis and Contextual Understanding.* London: Taylor and Francis.

Schuler, R. and Jackson, S. (eds) (2007) *Strategic Human Resource Management.* Oxford: Blackwell.

Schumpeter, J. (1976) *Capitalism, Socialism and Democracy.* 5th Ed. London: Allen and Unwin.

Scott, W. (2001) *Institutions and Organisations.* London: Sage.

Scullion, H. and Morley, M. (2004) *International Human Resource Management in Retrospect and Prospect.* Bradford: Emerald Group Publishing.

Scullion, H. and Sisson, K. (1985) 'Putting the corporate personnel department in its place'. *Personnel Management.* Offprint. London: Chartered Institute of Personnel and Development.

Seddon, J. (2005) *Freedom from Command and Control: Rethinking Management for Lean Service.* New York: Productivity Press.

Sen, A. (2012) 'The role of ACAS in dispute resolution'. Retrieved from http://www .acas.org, 23 January.

Senior Salaries Review Body (2009) *Thirty-First Report on Senior Salaries 2009: Report No. 68.* London: Cm. 7556.

Shah, M. (2007) *Analysis of Transaction Cost.* Jaipur, India: Sunrise Publishers.

Shen, J. (2007) *Labour Disputes and Their Resolution in China.* Oxford: Chandos Publishing.

Shenhav, V. (1999) *Manufacturing Rationality: The Engineering Foundations of the Managerial Revolution.* Oxford: Oxford University Press.

Shiva, V. (2000) *Stolen Harvest: The Hijacking of the Global Supply Chain.* London: Zed.

Shonfield, A. (1965) *Modern Capitalism: The Changing Balance of Public and Private Power.* London: Oxford University Press.

Shorter, E. and Tilly, C. (1974) *Strikes in France 1830–1968.* London: Cambridge University Press.

Simmel, G. (1964) *Conflict and the Web of Group Affiliations.* New York: Free Press.

Sinclair, A. (1992) 'The tyranny of a team ideology'. *Organisation Studies* 13 (4): 611–626.

Singh, B. (2009) *Industrial Relations and Labour Laws.* New Delhi: Excel Books India.

Sisson, K. (1987) *The Management of Collective Bargaining: An International Comparison*. Oxford: Basil Blackwell.

Sisson, K. (2001) 'Human resource management and the personnel function: A case of partial impact?' in Storey, J (ed.) *Human Resource Management, A Critical Text*. 2nd ed. London: Thomson Learning.

Sisson, K. and Marginson, P. (2002) 'Co-ordinated bargaining: A process for our times?' *British Journal of Industrial Relations* 40 (2): 197–220.

Sisson, K. and Marginson, P. (2003) 'Management systems, structures and strategy' in Edwards, P. (ed.) *Industrial Relations*. 2nd ed. Oxford: Blackwell.

Sisson, K. and Storey, J. (2000) *The Realities of Human Resource Management: Managing the Employment Relationship*. Milton Keynes: Open University Press.

Skidelsky, R. and Bogdanor, V. (1970) *The Age of Affluence 1951–1964*. London: Macmillan.

Skocpol, T. (1979) *States and Social Revolutions*. Cambridge: Cambridge University Press.

Skocpol, T. (1985) 'Bringing the state back in current research' in Evans, P., Rueschmeyer, D. and Skocpol, T. (eds) *Bringing the State Back In*. Cambridge: Cambridge University Press.

Slack, E. (1980) 'Plant-level bargaining in France'. *Industrial Relations Journal* 11 (4): 27–38.

Slichter, S. (1928) 'What is the labor problem?' in Hardman, J. (ed.) *American Labor Dynamics*. New York: Harcourt Brace.

Slichter, S. (1941) *Union Policies and Industrial Management*. Washington, DC: Brookings Institution.

Slichter, S. (1961) 'Are we becoming a "Laboristic" state?' in Dunlop, J. (ed.) *Potentials of the American Economy*. Cambridge, MA: Harvard University Press.

Sloane, A. (1991) *Hoffa*. Massachusetts: Massachusetts Institute of Technology Press.

Slomp, H. (1998) *Between Bargaining and Politics: An Introduction to European Labour Relations*. Westport-London: Praeger.

Smith, A. (1977) *An Inquiry into the Nature and Causes of the Wealth of Nations*. London: Dent.

Smith, C. (1978) *Strikes in Britain: A Research Study of Industrial Stoppages in the United Kingdom*. London: Her Majesty's Stationery Office.

Smith, S. (2003) *Labour Economics*. 2nd ed. London: Routledge.

Smith, T. (2003) *Creating the Welfare State in France 1880–1940*. Montreal, Ithaca: McGill-Queen's University Press.

Smith, C. and Meiksins, P. (1995) 'System, society and dominance effects in cross-national organisational analysis'. *Work, Employment and Society* 9 (2): 241–267.

Snell, S., Shadur, M. and Wright, P. (2002) 'Human resources strategy: The era of our ways' in Hitt, M., Freeman, R. and Harrison, J. (eds) *The Blackwell Handbook of Strategic Management*. Oxford: Blackwell.

Söderström, M. (1997) 'HRM in Sweden: A strategic challenge or a struggle for survival?' in Tyson, S. and Gilgeous, V. (eds) *The Practice of Human Resource Strategy*. London: Pitman.

Solomon, R. (1992) *Ethics and Excellence: Cooperation and Integrity in Business*. New York: Oxford University Press.

Solow, R. (1990) *The Labour Market as a Social Institution*. Oxford: Basil Blackwell.

Song, B-N. (1990) *The Rise of the Korean Economy*. New York: Oxford University Press.

Sorge, A. (2003) 'Cross-national differences in human resources and organization' in Harzing, A- W. and Van Ruisseveldt, J. (eds) *Human Resource Management*. 2nd ed. London: Sage.

Soros, G. (1995) *Soros on Soros*. New York: Wiley.

Soros, G. (1998). *The Crisis of Global Capitalism: Open Society Endangered*. New York: Public Affairs.

Soros, G. (2000) *Reforming Global Capitalism*. New York: Public Affairs.

Soskice, D. (1991) 'Skill mismatch, training systems and equilibrium unemployment: a comparative institutional analysis' in Padoa Schioppa. F. (ed.) *Mismatch and Labour Mobility*. Cambridge: Cambridge University Press.

Soskice, D. (1996) *German Technology Policy, Innovation, and National Institutional Frameworks*. Wissendschaft Zentrum Berlin: Discussion Paper FS1: 96–329.

Soskice, D. (2010) 'American exceptionalism and comparative political economy' in Brown, C., Eichengreen, B. and Reich, M. (eds) *Labor in the Era of Globalisation*. Cambridge: Cambridge University Press.

Sparrow, P. and Braun, W. (2008) 'HR sourcing and sharing: Strategies, drivers, success factors and implications for HR' in Dickmann, M., Brewster, C. and Sparrow, P. (eds) *International Human Resource Management*. London: Routledge.

Sparrow, P. and Hiltrop, J. (1994) *European Human Resource Management in Transition*. London: Prentice-Hall.

Spencer, H. (1969) *Social Statics: Or The Conditions Essential to Human Happiness Specified and the First of them Developed*. New York: Kelley.

Spreitzer, G. and Mishra, A. (1999) 'Giving up without losing control: Trust and its substitutes' effects on managers' involving employees in decision making'. *Group and Organisation Management* 24 (2): 155–187.

Stabile, D. (2008) *The Living Wage: Lessons from the History of Economic Thought*. Cheltenham: Edward Elgar.

Stanworth, P. and Giddens, A. (1974) *Elites and Power in British Society*. London: Cambridge University Press.

Statistics Canada (2005) *The Canadian Labour Market at a Glance*. Ottawa: Statistics Canada.

Steger, M. (2009) *Globalisation: A Very Short Introduction.* London: Oxford University Press.

Steger, M. (2010) *Globalisation: The Greatest Hits, a Global Studies Reader.* Boulder: Paradigm.

Stewart, A. and Bell, M. (2009) *The Right to Strike: A Comparative Perspective. A Study of National Law in Six EU States.* London: Institute of Employment Studies.

Stewart, P., Garrahan, P. and Crowther, S. (eds) (1990) *Restructuring for Economic Prosperity.* Aldershot: Avebury.

Steiner, E. (2010) *French Law: A Comparative Approach.* Oxford: Oxford University Press.

Stigler, G. (1962) 'Information in the labor market'. *Journal of Political Economy* 70 (5): 94–105.

Stiglitz, J. (2002) *Globalisation and Its Discontents.* London: Allen Lane.

Stiglitz, J. (2013) *The Price of Inequality.* London: Penguin.

Stockhammer, E. (2009) *Determinants of Functional Income Distribution in OECD Countries.* Düsseldorf: Hans Böckler Stifftung.

Stockhammer, E. (2010) Financialisation and the Global Economy. Political Economy Research Institute Working Paper 242.

Stockhammer, E. (2013) *Why have Wages Fallen? A Panel Analysis of the Determinants of Functional Income Distribution.* Geneva: International Labour Office.

Storey, J. (1983) *Managerial Prerogative and the Question of Control.* London: Routledge and Kegan Paul.

Storey, J. (ed.) (2002) *Human Resource Management: A Critical Text.* 2nd ed. London: Thomson Learning.

Storey, J. (2005) *Adding Value through Information and Consultation.* Basingstoke: Palgrave Macmillan.

Storey, J. (ed.) (2007) *Human Resource Management: A Critical Text.* 3rd ed. London: Thomson.

Strange, S. (1986) *Casino Capitalism.* Oxford: Basil Blackwell.

Strange, S. (1994) *States and Markets.* 2nd ed. London: Pinter.

Stråth, B. (1996) *The Organisation of Labour Markets.* London: Routledge.

Strauss, G. (1994) 'Issues in union structure' in Bacharach, S., Seeber, R. and Walsh, D. (eds) *Research in the Sociology of Organisations.* Greenwich, CT: JAI Press.

Strauss, G. (1996) 'Participation in the United States: Progress and barriers' in Davis, E. and Lansbury, R. (eds) *Managing Together: Consultation and Participation in the Workplace.* Melbourne: Addison-Wesley Longman.

Strauss, G. (1998) 'Comparative international industrial relations' in Whitfield, K. and Strauss, G. (eds) *Researching the World of Work: Strategies and Methods in Studying Industrial Relations.* Ithaca, New York: Cornell University Press.

Strauss, G. (2006) 'Worker participation: Some under-considered issues'. *Industrial Relations* 45 (4): 778–803.

Strauss, G. and Whitfield, K. (1998) 'Research methods in industrial relations' in Whitfield, K. and Strauss, G. (eds) *Researching the World of Work: Strategies and Methods in Studying Industrial Relations*. Ithaca, New York: Cornell University Press.

Strecker, D. (2011) *Labor Law: A Basic Guide to the National Labor Relations Act*. London: Taylor and Francis.

Streeck, W. (1992) *Societal Institutions and Economic Performance: Studies of Industrial Relations in Advanced Capitalist Economies*. London: Sage.

Streeck, W. (2009) *Re-Forming Capitalism: Institutional Change in the German Political Economy*. Oxford: Oxford University Press.

Sturmthal, A. (1958) 'The labor movement abroad' in Chamberlain, N. (ed.) *A Decade of Industrial Relations Research 1946–56*. New York: Harper.

Sturmthal, A. (1973) 'Industrial relations strategies' in Sturmthal, A. and Scoville, J. (eds) *The International Labor Movement in Transition*. Urbana: University of Illinois Press.

Suggs, G. (1991) *Colorado's War on Militant Unionism: James H. Peabody and the Western Federation of Miners*. Oklahoma: University of Oklahoma Press.

Suzuki, H. and Kubo, K. (2011) 'Employment relations in Japan' in Bamber, G., Lansbury, R. and Wailes, N. (eds) *International and Comparative Employment Relations: Globalisation and Change*. 5th ed. London: Sage.

Svensson, T. (2013) 'Sweden' in Frege, C. and Kelly, J. (eds) *Comparative Employment Relations in the Global Economy*. Abingdon: Routledge.

Sveriges Akademikers Central Organisation (2013) News from SACO. Retrieved from http://www.saco.se, 21 April.

Swedish Trade Union Confederation (2000) *The Swedish Trade Union Confederation*. Stockholm: Swedish Trade Union Confederation.

Sypnowich, C. (1990) *The Concept of Socialist Law*. Oxford: Clarendon.

Syrpis, P. (2007) *EU Intervention in Domestic Labour Law*. Oxford: Oxford University Press.

Tachibanaki, T. and Noda, T. (2000) *The Economic Effects of Trade Unions in Japan*. Basingstoke: Macmillan.

Taft, W., Potash, D. and Anderson, D. (2003) *Popular Government and the Anti-Trust Act and the Supreme Court*. Athens: Ohio University Press.

Taylor, F. (1947) *Scientific Management: Comprising Shop Management, The Principles of Scientific Management: Testimony Before the Special House Committee*. New York: Harper.

Taylor, S., Beechler, S. and Napier, N. (1996) 'Toward an integrative model of strategic international human resource management'. *Academy of Management Review* 21 (4): 959–985.

Teicher, J. and Bryan, D. (2013) 'Globalisation, economic policy and the labour market' in Teicher, J., Holland, P. and Gough, R. (eds) *Australian Workplace Relations*. Cambridge: Cambridge University Press.

Teicher, J., Holland, P. and Gough, R. (2013) 'Conclusion: The current state of Australian workplace relations' in Teicher, J., Holland, P. and Gough, R. (eds) *Australian Workplace Relations*. Cambridge: Cambridge University Press.

Terrick, L. and Baring, J. (1995) *Changing Employment Relations: Behavioral and Social Perspectives*. Washington, DC: American Psychological Association.

Thatcher, M., Rhodes, M. and Hancké, B. (2007) *Beyond Varieties of Capitalism: Conflict, Contradictions, and Complementarities in the European Economy*. Oxford: Oxford University Press.

Thatcher, M. and Stone Sweet, A. (2002) 'Theory and practice of delegation to non-majoritarian institutions'. *West European Politics* 25 (1): 1–22.

Thelen, H. (1949) 'Three frames of reference: The description of climate'. *Human Relations* 2 (2): 159–176.

Thelen, K. (2001) 'Varieties of politics in the developed democracies' in Hall, P. and Soskice, D. (eds) *Varieties of Capitalism: The Institutional Foundations of Comparative Advantage*. Oxford: Oxford University Press.

Thelen, K. and Steinmo, S. (1992) 'Historical institutionalism in comparative politics' in Steinmo, S., Thelen, K. and Longstreth, F. *Historical Institutionalism in Comparative Politics: State, Society, and Economy*. New York: Cambridge University Press.

Thompson, E. (1967) 'Time, work discipline and industrial capitalism'. *Past and Present* 38: 56–97.

Thompson, P. (1989) *The Nature of Work: An Introduction to Debates on the Labour Process*. 2nd ed. London: Macmillan.

Thomason, G. (1991) 'The management of personnel'. *Personnel Review* 20 (2): 3–10.

Thompson, D. (2011) 'Occupy the world: The "99 percent" movement goes global'. *The Atlantic* 15 October. Retrieved from http://www.theatlantic.com, 30 August 2013.

Thompson, P. and Alvesson, M. (2005) 'Bureaucracy at work: Misunderstandings and mixed blessings' in Du Gay, P. (ed.) *The Values of Bureaucracy*. Oxford: Oxford University Press.

Thompson, P. and McHugh, D. (2009) *Work Organisations: A Critical Approach*. 4th ed. Basingstoke: Palgrave Macmillan.

Thompson, M. and Taras, D. (2011) 'Employment relations in Canada' in Bamber, G., Lansbury, R. and Wailes, N. (eds) *International and Comparative Employment Relations: Globalisation and Change*. 5th ed. London: Sage.

Thompson, P., Warhurst, C. and Callaghan, G. (2000) 'Human capital or capitalising on humanity? Knowledge, skills and competencies in interactive service work' in Pritchard, C., Hull, R., Chumer, M. and Willmott, H. (eds) *Managing Knowledge: Critical Investigations of Work and Learning*. London: Macmillan.

Thomson-Reuters (2011) 'Quick guide to the greek crisis'. Retrieved from http://www.reuters.com/article/2011/06/20/greece-crisis-quickguide, 6 June 2013.

Thomson-Reuters (2012) 'From BBC to NYT: Mark Thompson named CEO of Times Co'. Retrieved from http://www.reuters.com/article, 17 August.

Thurley, K. and Wood, S. (1983) *Industrial Relations and Management Strategy*. Cambridge: Cambridge University Press.

Tillman, R. and Cummings, M. (eds) (1999) *The Transformation of US Unions: Voices, Visions, and Strategies from the Grassroots*. Boulder, CO: Lynne Rienner.

Tilly, C., Tilly, L. and Tilly, R. (1975) *Rebellious Century*. Cambridge, MA: Harvard University Press.

Tipton, F. (2009) 'Southeast Asian capitalism: History, institutions, states and firms'. *Asia Pacific Management Journal* 26: 401–434.

Tjänstemännens Centralorganisation (2013) This is TCO. Retrieved from http://www.tco.se, 14 September.

Tjosvold, D. (1987) 'Participation: A close look at its dynamics'. *Journal of Management* 13 (4): 739–50.

Tolliday, S. and Zeitlin, J. (eds) (1986) *The Automobile Industry and Its Workers: Between Fordism and Flexibility*. Cambridge: Polity Press.

Torrence, G. (1959) *Management's Right to Manage*. Washington, DC: Bureau of National Affairs.

Torrington, D. (1991) *Employee Resourcing*. London: Institute of Personnel Management.

Torrington, D., Hall, L., Taylor, S. and Atkinson, C. (2011) *Human Resource Management*. 8th ed. Harlow: Financial Times Prentice Hall.

Torrini, R. (2005) 'Cross-country differences in self-employment rates: The role of Institutions'. *Labour Economics* 12: 661–683.

Towers Perrin (2009) *Towers Perrin Global Engagement Workforce Study*. Stanford, CT: Towers Perrin.

Towers Perrin (2010) *Global Workforce Study 2010*. Stamford, CT: Towers Perrin.

Trades Union Congress (1966) *Trade Unionism: The Evidence of the Trades Union Congress to the Royal Commission on Trade Unions and Employers' Associations*. London: Trades Union Congress.

Traub-Merz, R. and Zhang, J. (eds) (2010) *Comparative Industrial Relations: China, South- Korea and Germany/Europe*. Beijing: China Social Press.

Traxler, F. (2000) 'Employers and employer organisations in Europe: Membership strength, density and representativeness'. *Industrial Relations Journal* 31: 308–316.

Traxler, F. (2008) 'Employers' organisations' in Blyton, P., Bacon, N., Fiorito, J. and Heery, E. (eds) *The SAGE Handbook of Industrial Relations*. London: Sage.

Traxler, F. Blaschke, S. and Kittel, B. (2001) *National Labour Relations in Internationalised Markets: A Comparative Study of Institutions, Change, and Performance*. Oxford: Oxford University Press.

Trompenaars, A. (1993) *Riding the Waves of Culture: Understanding Cultural Diversity in Business*. London: Brealey Publishing.

Troy, L. (1990) 'Is the US unique in the decline of private sector unionism?' *Journal of Labor Research* 11: 111–143.

Troy, L. (1999) *Beyond Unions and Collective Bargaining*. New York: M. E. Sharpe.

Troy, L. (2000) 'US and Canadian industrial relations: Convergent or divergent?' *Industrial Relations* 39 (4): 695–713.

Truss, C., Soane, E. and Edwards, C. (2006) *Working Life: Employee Attitudes and Engagement*. Research report. London: Chartered Institute of Personnel and Development.

Tsui, A., Pearce, J., Porter, L. and Hite, J. (1995) 'Choice of employee-organizational relationship: Influence of external and internal organization factors' in Ferris, G. (ed.) *Research in Personnel and Human Resource Management*. Greenwich, CT: JAI Press.

Tung, R. and Worm, V. (2001) 'Network capitalism: The role of human resources in penetrating the China market'. *International Journal of Human Resource Management* 12 (4): 517–534.

Turmann, A. (2004) *Obstacles to European Labour Mobility: A New European Agenda for Labour Mobility*. Brussels: The Centre for European Policy Studies.

Turnbull, P. (1988) 'An economic theory of trade union behaviour'. *British Journal of Industrial Relations* 26 (1): 85–188.

Turner, H. (1962) *Trade Union Growth, Structure and Policy: A Comparative Study of the Cotton Unions*. London: George Allen and Unwin.

Twining, W. (1999) 'Globalisation and comparative law'. *Maastricht Journal of European and Comparative Law* 6: 217.

Tyson, S. (1995) *Human Resource Strategy: Towards a General Theory of Human Resource Management*. London: Pitman.

Tyson, S. and Fell, A. (1992) *Evaluating the Personnel Function*. 2nd ed. Cheltenham: Stanley Thornes.

Ulrich, D. (1997) *Human Resource Champions: The Next Agenda for Adding Value and Delivering Results*. Boston, MA: Harvard Business School Press.

Ulrich, D. and Brockbank, W. (2005) *The HR Value Proposition*. Boston, MA: Harvard Business School Press.

United Nations (1966) *International Covenant on Civil and Political Rights (1966)*. New York: United Nations.

United Nations (2012) *The Universal Declaration of Human Rights*. New York: United Nations.

United Nations Conference on Trade and Development (2012) *World Investment Report 2012: Towards a New Generation of Investment Policies*. New York: United Nations.

University of Chicago (1914) *The Elementary School Teacher*. Vol. 14. Chicago: University of Chicago Press.

Unwin, J. (2013) 'New living wage for the UK'. Press release. Joseph Rowntree Foundation 5 November.

Upchurch, M., Mathers, A. and Taylor, G. (2009) *The Crisis of Social Democratic Trade Unionism in Western Europe: The Search for Alternatives*. Farnham: Ashgate.

Valdez, S. and Molyneux, P. (2010) *An Introduction to Global Financial Markets*. 6th ed. Basingstoke: Palgrave Macmillan.

Van Thiel, S., Homburg, V. and Pollitt, C. (2007) *New Public Management in Europe: Adaptation and Alternatives*. Basingstoke: Palgrave Macmillan.

Van Waarden, F. (1995) 'Government intervention in industrial relations' in Van Ruysseveldt, J., Huiskamp, R. and van Hoof, J. (eds) *Comparative Industrial and Employment Relations*. London: Sage.

Van Wanrooy, B., Bewley, H., Bryson, A., Forth, J., Freeth, S., Stokes, L. and Wood, S. (2013) *Employment Relations in the Shadow of Recession: Findings from the 2011 Workplace Employment Relations Study*. Basingstoke: Palgrave Macmillan.

Vaydia, A. (ed.) (2011) *Globalization: Encyclopedia of Trade, Labor, and Politics*. Santa Barbara: Credo Reference.

Venn, D. (2009a) *Legislation, Collective bargaining and Enforcement: Updating the OECD Employment Protection Indicators*. Paris: OECD.

Venn, D. (2009b) The impact of small-firm exemptions from employment protection. OECD Social, Employment and Migration Working Papers. Paris: OECD.

Venohr, B. and Meyer, K. (2007) The German miracle keeps running: How Germany's hidden champions stay ahead in the global economy. Working Paper 30. Berlin: Institute of Management, Berlin School of Management.

Visser, J. (2002) *Unions, Unionisation and Collective Bargaining Trends Around the World. Paper for the International Labour Office*. Geneva: ILO.

Visser, J. (2006) 'Union membership statistics in 24 countries'. *Monthly Labor Review* January: 38–49.

Visser, J. (2011a) *ICTWSS Database*. Retrieved from http://www.uva-aias.net/2008, 20 July.

Visser, J. (2011b) *The Age of Responsibility: CSR 2.0 and the New DNA of Business*. Chichester: John Wiley and Sons.

Visser, J. (2013) *Database on Institutional Characteristics of Trade Unions, Wage Setting, State Intervention and Social Pacts in 34 Countries Between 1960 and 2007. Version 4*. Amsterdam: University of Amsterdam.

Vitols, S. (2010) *The European Participation Index (EPI): A Tool for National Cross-National Comparison*. Brussels: The European Trade Union Institute.

Voos, P. (1993) 'Designing an industrial relations theory curriculum for graduate students' in Adams, R. and Meltz, N. (eds) *Industrial Relations Theory: Its Nature, Scope, and Pedagogy*. Metuchen, NJ: IMLR Press/Rutgers University.

Voss, K. and Sherman, R. (2000) 'Breaking the iron law of oligarchy: Union revitalisation in the American labor movement'. *American Journal of Sociology* 106 (2): 303–349.

Vroom, V. (1995) *Work and Motivation*. San Francisco: Jossey-Bass.

Wachter, H. and Muller-Camen, M. (2002) 'Co-determination and strategic Integration in German Firms'. *Human Resource Management Journal* 12 (3): 76–87.

Wajcman, J. (2000) 'Feminist facing industrial relations in Britain'. *British Journal of Industrial Relations* 38 (2): 183–201.

Walby, S. (2011) *The Future of Feminism*. Cambridge: Polity.

Walker, K. (1967) 'The comparative study of industrial relations'. *Bulletin of the International Institute for Labour Studies* 3: 105–132.

Walton, R. (1985) 'From control to commitment in the workplace'. *Harvard Business Review* 63 (92): 76–84.

Walton, R. and McKersie, R. (1991) *A Behavioral Theory of Labor Negotiations: An Analysis of a Social Interaction System*. 2nd ed. Ithaca, New York: ILR Press.

Watson, T. (2006) *Organising and Managing Work: Organisational, Managerial and Strategic Behaviour in Theory and Practice*. Harlow: Pearson Longman.

Webb, B. (1987) *The Co-operative Movement in Great Britain*. Aldershot: Gower.

Webb, S. and Webb, B. (1897) *Industrial Democracy*. London: Longmans.

Webb, S. and Webb, B. (1913) *Industrial Democracy*. New ed. London: Longmans.

Webb, S. and Webb, B. (1920a) *The History of Trade Unionism*. London: Longmans, Green and Co.

Webb, S. and Webb, B. (1920b) *Industrial Democracy*. Revised ed. London: Longmans.

Wedderburn, W. (1986) *The Worker and the Law*. 3rd ed. Harmondsworth: Penguin.

Wedderburn, W. (1995) *Labour Law and Freedom: Further Essays in Labour Law*. London: Lawrence and Wishart.

Wei, Q., Yan, D. and Ye, J. (2013) *Rethinking the Labour Contract Law of China*. Peking: Labour Law and Social Security Law Institute.

Weil, D. (2014) *The Fissured Workplace: Why Work Became So Bad for So Many and What Can Be Done to Improve It*. Cambridge, MA: Harvard University Press.

Weiss, L. (1998) *The Myth of the Powerless State*. Ithaca, New York: Cornell University Press.

Weiss, M. and Schmidt, M. (2008) *Labour Law and Industrial Relations in Germany*. 4th ed. Alphen aan den Rijn, Netherlands: Wolters Kluwer.

Wellin, M. (2007) *Managing the Psychological Contract: Using the Personal Deal to Increase Business Performance*. Aldershot: Gower.

Wells, W. (2003) *American Capitalism 1945–2000: Continuity and Change from Mass Production to the Information Society*. Oxford: Oxford Publicity Partnership.

Wechsler, J. (1944) *Labor Baron: A Portrait of John L. Lewis*. Michigan: Morrow and Company.

West, J., Borrill, C. and Dawson, J. (2002) 'The link between the management of employees and patient mortality in acute hospitals'. *International Journal of Human Resource Management* 13 (8): 1299–1310.

Wever, K. (1995) *Negotiating Competiveness.* Cambridge, MA: Harvard Business School Press.

Weyrauch, T. (1999) *Craftsmen and Their Associations in Asia, Africa and Europe.* Wettenberg: VVB Laufersweiler.

Wharton, A. and Erickson, R. (1995) 'The consequences of caring: Exploring the links between women's job and family emotion work'. *Sociological Quarterly* 36 (2): 273–296.

Whipp, R., Adam, B. and Sabelis, I. (2002) *Making Time: Time and Management in Modern Organisations.* Oxford: Oxford University Press.

Whitfield, K. (1998) 'Quantitative methods: It's not what you do' in Whitfield, K. and Strauss, G. (eds) *Researching the World of Work: Strategies and Methods in Studying Industrial Relations.* London: ILR Press.

Whitfield, K. and Strauss, G. (1998) *Researching the World of Work: Strategies and Methods in Studying Industrial Relations.* London: ILR Press.

Whitley, R. (1999) *Divergent Capitalisms: The Social Structuring and Change of Business Systems.* Oxford: Oxford University Press.

Whittaker, D. (2013) 'Japan' in Frege, C. and Kelly, J. (eds) (2013) *Comparative Employment Relations in the Global Economy.* Abingdon: Routledge.

Whittington, R. (2001) *What Is Strategy – and Does It Matter?* 2nd ed. London: Thomson Learning.

Whyte, W. (ed.) (1991) *Participatory Action Research.* Newbury Park, CA: Sage.

Wickens, P. (1987) *The Road to Nissan.* London: Macmillan.

Wickens, P. (1995) *The Ascendant Organisation: Combining Commitment and Control for Long-Term, Sustainable Business Success.* Basingstoke: Macmillan.

Wickham, C. (2005) *Framing the Early Middle Ages.* Oxford: Oxford University Press.

Wiesner, M. (2000) *Women and Gender in early Modern Europe.* 2nd ed. Cambridge: Cambridge University Press.

Wiewiórski Law Firm (2013) 'General information on polish labour law'. Retrieved from http://www.wiewiorski.eu/cms, 3 April.

Wigham, E. (1982) *Strikes and the Government 1893–1981.* London: Macmillan.

Wilcynski, J. (1983) *Comparative Industrial Relations: Ideologies, Institutions, Practices and Problems under Different Social Systems with Special Reference to Socialist Planned Economies.* London: Macmillan.

Wilensky, H. (1975) *The Welfare State and Equality: Structural and Ideological Roots of Public Expenditures.* Berkeley, CA: University of California Press.

Wilensky, H. and Turner, L. (1987) *Democratic Corporatism and Policy Linkages: The Interdependence of Industrial, Labor Market, Incomes and Social Policies in Eight Countries.* Berkeley, CA: University of California.

Wilkinson, A. (1998) 'Empowerment: Theory and practice'. *Personnel Review* 27 (1): 40–56.

Wilkinson, A., Bacon, N., Redman, T. and Snell, S. (eds) (2010) *The SAGE Handbook of Human Resource Management*. London: Sage.

Wilkinson, A., Dundon, T., Marchington, M. and Ackers, P. (2004) 'Changing patterns of employee voice: Case studies from the UK and Republic of Ireland'. *The Journal of Industrial Relations* 46 (3): 298–322.

Wilkinson, A. and Townsend, K. (2011) *Research Handbook on the Future of Work and Employment Relations*. Cheltenham: Edward Elgar.

Willey, B. (2012) *Employment Law in Context: An Introduction for HR Professionals*. 4th ed. Harlow: Pearson.

Williams, C. (2007) *Re-thinking the Future of Work: Directions and Visions*. Basingstoke: Palgrave Macmillan.

Williams, S. (2014) *Introducing Employment Relations: A Critical Approach*. Oxford: Oxford University Press.

Williams, S. and Adam-Smith, D. (2010) *Contemporary Employment Relations: A Critical Introduction*. 2nd ed. Oxford: Oxford University Press.

Williamson, O. (1973) 'Markets and hierarchies: Some elementary considerations'. *American Economic Review* 63 (2): 316–325.

Willman, P. (1982) *Fairness, Collective Bargaining, and Incomes Policy*. Oxford: Clarendon.

Willman, P. (2001) 'The viability of trade union organisation: A bargaining unit analysis'. *British Journal of Industrial Relations* 39 (1): 97–117.

Willmott, H. (1993) 'Strength is ignorance: Slavery is freedom: Managing culture in modern organisations'. *Journal of Management Studies* 30 (4): 515–552.

Winch, P. (1990) *The Idea of a Social Science and its Relation to Philosophy*. New York: Humanities Press.

Winkler, J. (1974) 'The ghost at the bargaining table: directors and industrial relations'. *British Journal of Industrial Relations* 12 (2): 191–212.

Witte, E. (1954) *The Evolution of Managerial Ideas in Industrial Relations*. Ithaca, New York: Cornell University.

Witte, H., Guest, D. and Isaksson, K. (2010) *Employment Contracts, Psychological Contracts, and Employee Well-being: An International Study*. Oxford: Oxford University Press.

Wood, S. (1999) 'Human resource management and performance'. *International Journal of Management Reviews* 1 (4): 368–413.

Wood, G. and Brewster, C. (eds) (2007) *Industrial Relations in Africa*. Basingstoke: Palgrave Macmillan.

Wood, S. and Machin, S. (2005) 'HRM as a substitute for trade unions in British workplaces'. *Industrial and Labor Relations Review* 58: 201–218.

Woodward, J. (1980) *Industrial Organisation: Theory and Practice*. 2nd ed. Oxford: Oxford University Press.

Woolf, L. (1949) 'Political thought and the Webbs' in Cole, M. (ed.) *The Webbs and Their Work*. London: Frederick Muller.

Wootton, B. (1974) *Fair Pay, Relativities and a Policy for Incomes*. Southampton: University of Southampton.

World Bank (1995) *World Development Report: Workers in an Integrating World*. New York: Oxford University Press.

World Bank (2008) *Public Sector Reform: What Works and Why: An Independent Evaluation Group Evaluation of World Bank Support*. Washington, DC: World Bank.

World Federation of People Management Associations (2013) Members. Retrieved from http://www.wfpma.com, 26 October.

World Trade Organisation (2012) *Press Release: World export of commercial services up by 3% in first quarter of 2012*. 13 July.

Wright, L. and Smye, M. (1998) *Corporate Abuse*. New York: Simon and Schuster.

Yang, S. (1957) 'The concept of *pao* as a basis for social relations in China' in Fairbank, J. (ed.) *Chinese Thought and Institutions*. Chicago: University of Chicago Press.

Yoder, D. (1963) *Personnel Management and Industrial Relations*. New York: Prentice Hall.

Youngs, R. (2007) *English, French and German Comparative Law*. 2nd ed. London: Routledge-Cavendish.

Zack, A. (2006) 'Conciliation of labor court disputes'. *Comparative Labor Law and Policy Journal* 26: 401–420.

Zappavigna, M. (2013) *Tacit Knowledge and Spoken Discourse*. New York: Bloomsbury Academic.

Zeitlin, J. (1987) 'From labour history to the history of industrial relations'. *Economic History Review* 11: 159–184.

Zweigert, K. and Kotz, H. (1998) *An Introduction to Comparative Law*. North Holland: Clarendon.

INDEX

employment protection legislation, 329, 331
employment relations, 2, 9
employment systems, 346
Fordist mass production techniques, 65
GGFCE in, 271–5
HRM practices, 43, 63, 148, 204–7, 376
income inequality, 523
Kieretsu groups, 187
labour laws, 510
labour markets, 65, 109, 154, 505
liberal market regimes, 97
life-long learning strategies, 283
management theory, 42, 151–2, 382, 390, 417
non-market mechanisms, 30
right to strike, 76, 443, 446, 447, 450
Saikō keiei sekinin-sha (professional managers), 177–8
skill structures, 88
'social question,' 51
social security expenditure, 291, 295, 297
taxation and social security expenditure, 291
Toyota Industries, 93
trade unions, 166, 221, 238–9, 242–3, 269, 419, 434–5, 440
wage legislation, 350
Jarley, P., 237, 427
Jenkins, J., 80, 479, 491
Jenks, C., 339
Jensen, C.,436
Jeong, J., 435
Jepsen, M., 528
Jermier, J., 411
Jimeno, J., 330
Jobert, A., 96, 521
Joerges, B., 213
Johnson, C., 268
Johnston, T., 344, 510
Jones, D., 234
Jordan
    ILO Conventions 87 and 98 (not ratified), 340
Judt, T., 115, 190, 267
Juss, S., 25

Kahn, L., 333, 464, 465
Kahn, P., 345
Kahn-Freund, O., 57, 58, 265, 266, 313, 319, 336, 337, 458
Kaiser, W., 289

kaizen (continuous improvement), 151, 232, 236
kanban (just-in-time production), 151
Kang, S-C., 514, 516
Kanter, R., 145, 367
Kapila, S., 63
Karsten, D., 318
Kato, T., 234
Katz, H., 12, 31, 302, 422, 507
Katzenstein, P., 286, 290
Kaufman, B., 2, 11, 12, 28, 37, 38, 39, 49, 51, 52, 79, 88, 93, 118, 122, 123, 139, 161, 226, 420
Kaufmann, C., 114
Kauppinen, T., 471
Kawasaki, S., 205
Keane, J., 8
Kearney, R., 426
Keech, W., 284
Keller, B., 521
Kelly, J., 26, 33, 69, 100, 123, 162, 378, 444
Kennedy, A., 418
Kenya
    common law jurisdictions, 315
    HRM, 517
    ILO Conventions 87 and 98 (not ratified), 340
    wage share, 520
Kerckhofs, P., 471
Kerr, C., 36, 37, 119, 154, 172, 264, 268, 444, 445, 451
Kersley, B., 167, 384, 397
Kessler, I., 111
Kettley, P., 379
Keynesian economic policies, 19
Kiiver, P., 338
King, W., 66
Kirsch, A., 521
Klein, C., 469, 531
Klein, S., 469, 531
Kluge, N., 527
Knowledge, skills and abilities (KSAs), 515
Kochan, T., 36, 37, 63, 73, 140, 164, 167, 171, 236, 245, 386, 387, 403, 424, 428, 473
Koen, C., 182, 183
Kogut, B., 516
Kohl, H., 437
Kohli, M., 472
Kondo, D., 417
Kondratiev, N., 153
Koot, G., 125
Kornhauser, A., 458

Williams, C., 356
Williams, M., 101
Williams, S., 12, 264
Williams, T., 379
Williamson, O., 326
Willman, P., 425, 429, 463
Willman's portfolio analysis, 430
Willmott, H., 182, 418
Winch, P., 157
Winkler, J., 386
Wirtschaftskammer Österreich (Austria), 393
Witte, E., 387
Witte, H., 364
Wobblies, *see* Industrial Workers of the World (IWW)
women
    as alternative sources of labour, 532–3
    Canadian, 385
    Collective bargaining (Spain), 477
    critical theory on, 162
    domestic service, 49
    employment relations, 3, 37
    gendered nature of work, 416–17
    ILO's mission, 303
    Italian, 333
    ITUC campaigns for, 259, 262
    role in workplace, 122
    service contract, 51
    socialism and, 81
    Swedish Confederation of Professional Associations (SACO), 256
    TCO members, 256
    technological revolution, 50
    unionism and, 83, 248, 426
Wood, G., 372, 449
Wood, S., 399, 424
Woodward, J., 119
Woolf, L., 139
Wootton, B., 463
Worden, R., 166
work
    change in, 356
    common theme, 355–8
    continuity in, 356
    motivation to, 358–60
    and workplace mediation, 492, 496
Work Choices Act 2006, 232
worker empowerment unionism, 73–4
worker resistance
    concept, 410–13
    manifestations, 413

model, 414
theoretical framework, 413–18
Workplace Employment Relations Surveys/Studies (WERS), 113, 167, 222, 235, 376, 387
Works Council Act 1920, 318
works councils
    definition, 487
    employee involvement, 231, 267, 478–85, 512, 525–7
    employee voice, 224
    in Europe, 79, 209, 421, 436, 487–8
    in Germany, 80, 233–4, 475
    non-union, 226, 377
    pluralist thinking, 141
    in welfare states, 306
    see also European-wide Work Councils (EWCs); *in individual nations*
World Bank, 3, 21–2, 258, 271, 290, 356, 507
World Confederation of Labour (WCL), 257–8
World Federation of People Management Associations (WFPMA), 375
World Federation of Trade Unions (WFTU), 257
World Trade Organisation (WTO), 21, 179, 271
Worm, V., 214
Wren, A., 305
Wright, L., 418

Yang, S., 189
Yates, C., 34, 453
Yoder, D., 388
Yongsun, P., 191
Youngs, R., 57

Zack, A., 336
Zander, U., 516
Zappavigna, M., 355
Zeitlin, J., 65, 166
zero-hours contracts, 150, 313, 540
Zhang, J., 450
Zhonghuá Zonggōng Huì (ACFTU)
    see also All-China Federation of Trade Unions (ACFTU)
Zhu, Y., 436
Zimmerman, R., 316
Zweigert, K., 313, 314